Food Processing

Food Processing

An Industrial Powerhouse in Transition

John M. Connor
Purdue University

Lexington Books
D.C. Heath and Company/Lexington, Massachusetts/Toronto

This book had its origins in a report commissioned by the Research Committee of the Institute of Food Technologists.

Library of Congress Cataloging-in-Publication Data

Connor, John M.
  Food processing: An Industrial powerhouse in transition / John M. Connor.
    p. cm.
  Bibliography: p.
  Includes index.
  ISBN 0–669–19511–1 (alk. paper)
  1. Food industry and trade—United States. 2. Food industry and trade. 3. Big business—United States. 4. Big business.
  I. Title.
HD9005.C59 1988
338.4'7664'00973—dc19   88–10053
                                                                      CIP

Published simultaneously in Canada
Printed in the United States of America
International Standard Book Number: 0–669–19511–1
Library of Congress Catalog Card Number 88–10053

The paper used in this publication meets the minimum requirements of American National Standard for Information Sciences—Permanence of Paper for Printed Library Materials, ANSI Z39.48–1984. ∞™

89 90 91 92 8 7 6 5 4 3 2

For Timo

Contents

Part III.   Importance of Food Processing to Individual States   149

Tables

Figures

Foreword

When our committee approached John Connor to write a comprehensive report to our members about the economic contributions of the food processing industries, he responded with an outline that was patently too ambitious. The resulting report, however, was more than we had expected.

This book is a meticulously researched examination of a wide range of historic and contemporary information, most of which is accessible only to specialists. In an admirably concise treatment mercifully free of economists' jargon, Connor identifies and documents a number of major features of the food processing industry. Industry trends are presented in scores of tables that display data in a remarkably consistent fashion. Readers will likely discover some new facts or fresh viewpoints about their industry, their state, or their special interests.

Most individuals are familiar with the fact that food processing and its associated industries account for about 20 percent of the nation's gross national product, but this book goes much further in documenting the economic contributions of the industry. The sometimes mysterious concepts of "value added" and "income multipliers" are lucidly explained with numerical estimates relevant to food processing. The often great differences in size and growth among the food processing industries are shown in some detail. Perhaps the most novel feature of the work is the detailed state-by-state information on the size and growth of the food processing industries. Would you like to know the number of ice cream plants in Massachusetts and their output and employment? Somewhere in this book lies the answer.

Connor takes the long view on economic trends, and he presents many suggestions on the future shape of the industry that may challenge many a reader's long-held views. There were a number that struck us. While getting slightly larger over time, most food processing plants are likely to remain quite small in terms of employment size. Food processing is one of the most heavily capitalized U.S. manufacturing industries; in contrast, labor and energy costs play a relatively small role in most food processing industries.

Many billions of dollars of new investment in food processing plants and equipment have brought rapid increases in industry productivity (more rapid than most other manufacturing lines) and falling relative costs of food to consumers. The rising need for more R&D resources in food processing may be met in part by increased transfers of scientific advances from other linked industries. The frenetic pace of merger activity during the last decade has contributed to a significant rise in business consolidation, a trend that Connor believes is likely to persist for some time. Many of the mergers involve takeovers by foreign corporations, and this is one of the forces internationalizing the food industries. The long-term relocation of food processing plants to the South and West has slowed and may even reverse itself in the near future.

The picture that emerges from these several trends is of an industry that is adaptive and in many respects dynamic. Together with the author's more technical companion volume (*The Food Manufacturing Industries*, Lexington Books, 1985), this book provides an excellent reference for strategic policy decisions by industry leaders and public officials alike.

Arnold E. Denton, Ph.D., D. Ag.
Senior Vice President, Campbell Soup Co.
and
Chairman, Committee on Research,
Institute of Food Technologists

Susan K. Harlander, Ph.D.
Assistant Professor, University of Minnesota
and
Secretary, Committee on Research,
Institute of Food Technologists

Acknowledgments

T his book had its origins in a report commissioned by the Research Committee of the Institute of Food Technologists (IFT), the principal professional organization of U.S. food scientists, engineers, and technologists. The author was charged with the task of providing a comprehensive economic portrait of the industries in which IFT members toil. In particular, the Research Committee was interested in quantifying two aspects of the U.S. food processing industries. First, information was to be provided on the economic size and growth of the industries, both for the nation as a whole and for each of the states. Second, the author was to identify the major contributions that food processing makes to economic development. A third objective, less quantitative and requiring more judgment, was to assess the economic performance and pinpoint likely future long-term performance trends of the food processing industries.

In attempting to meet these ambitious goals, the author was assisted by several individuals. First and foremost, the author must thank the members of the IFT Research Committee who read and criticized earlier drafts of the book's manuscript. Particularly detailed and constructive comments were received from the following committee members: Dr. Arnold E. Denton (committee chair and Campbell Soup Company), Mr. Donald Diltz (Escagen Corporation), Dr. Susan K. Harlander (University of Minnesota), Dr. Philip Nelson (Purdue University), Dr. William L. Brown (ABC Research), and Dr. Kent K. Stewart (Virginia Polytechnic). Similarly useful reviews were given by the author's colleagues at Purdue University: Professors Paul Farris and Charles Sargent. The author is grateful to all these individuals for helping make this book accessible to nonspecialists as well as meeting the high standards of scientific peer review.

Special thanks are due to Mr. Sei Kyun Choi, Ph.D. candidate in Agricultural Economics at Purdue University. Under the author's direction Mr. Choi performed the painstaking work required to put together the tabular data on food processing activity in the various states. He also prepared the first drafts of many of the state portraits. His assiduous cooperation and good judgment are much appreciated.

The author was assisted by several others in preparing the manuscript. Tana Taylor was inordinately successful in meeting formidable typing deadlines. Joyce Sichts and Cindy Helms were burdened with the necessarily dull task of proofreading text and tables. Finally, Bill Van Beek, Connie Schwartz, and Mike Francis were responsible for the scores of charts and maps that appear, plus many others set aside in the interest of concision.

Material support for the research upon which this book is based came from the Institute of Food Technologists and the School of Agriculture of Purdue University.

Introduction

The nation's food processing industries seem often to be taken for granted—a feature of the economic landscape so unremarkable as to be nearly invisible. Perhaps these industries are viewed as ordinary because the methods of production are in many cases quite ancient, because food factories appear to be organized on a small scale, because processed food products seem so familiar, or because processing is believed to be tied closely to agriculture, civilization's first "industry." Economists specializing in the analysis of industries are more likely to be drawn to industries other than food processing, industries that appear more dynamic or technologically progressive.

There is an element of truth in each of these views. Some of the processes employed by food processors, flour milling for example, are indeed prehistoric in their origins, but the methods and equipment in use today bear little resemblance to colonial grist mills. Most of the technologies in place today are the result of modern scientific discoveries and decades of technological refinement. It is also true that the majority of the country's 20,000 food processing plants are quite small (fewer than twenty employees). Yet there are at the same time some plants that rival the nation's largest in size. Moreover, small scale at the plant level belies a mode of business organization at the corporate level that is as modern as any in the manufacturing sector, if not more so. Many raw and semiprocessed materials must be assembled to finish a given processed food, and each commodity most likely has a unique procurement system. Once finished, the typical food or beverage is distributed through multiple channels, each of which has special business practices. Understanding the merchandising operations of food processors involves such complications as regional markets, intensive product differentiation efforts, and a variety of pricing practices.

And it must be conceded that food processing was traditionally closely linked to agriculture. Many processing industries were originally part of farm operations (such as butter or cheese making) or skills found only in domestic kitchens (pickling or baking). However, an oft-repeated theme of this book is the current similarity of food processing to the rest of manufacturing. The rupture between farming and processing is not yet complete, but it has gone far.

This book also addresses the question of whether the food processing industries have participated in the overall improvement in economic performance that has characterized the unregulated sectors of the U.S. economy during the last few decades. To assess the performance of the food processing industries is a complex task, partly because performance itself is a multifaceted phenomenon. The aspects of performance chosen for any analysis are necessarily fewer than all possible. Special attention was devoted to selecting long-term trends that are likely to persist for the rest of the century. Long-term growth is one aspect of performance, and this dimension is explored in detail using sales, employment, and value added as measures. Other performance-related factors are examined: market structures, techno-logical change, and the international linkages of the U.S. food processing industries. Every effort was made to obtain the most appropriate data series and to extend the series forward to the most recent year in the mid-1980s. However, if the choice had to be made, precision was favored over currency.

A major contribution of this book is its thorough and unprecedented attention to the economic geography of the U.S. food processing industries. Preparation for the summary information to be provided required developing estimates for shipments and employment in each of forty-one food processing industries in each of the fifty states for three terminal years. Data at this level of detail is simply not fully published, even for the largest states. It was a necessary step, however, in order to provide a complete picture for the vignettes, in Part III, about each state's food processing industries. The result is a meticulous portrait of the food processing industries that many analysts might admire, but few will emulate.

Scope and Definitions

The focus of this book is the growth and economic development of U.S. commercial food processing activity. By *U.S.* is meant the fifty states plus the District of Columbia. *Commercial food processing* is the branch of manufacturing that starts with raw animal, vegetable, or marine materials and transforms them into intermediate foodstuffs or edible products through the application of labor, machinery, energy, and scientific knowledge. Various processes are used to convert relatively bulky, perishable, and typically inedible food materials into ultimately more useful, concentrated, shelf-stable, and palatable foods or potable beverages. Heat, cold, drying, and other preservation techniques are applied to enhance storability. Containers and packaging materials confer portability as well as extend shelf life. Changes in product forms often reduce preparation time for consumers. Increasing palatability, storability, portability, and convenience are all aspects of "adding value." In other words, food processors utilize factory systems to add economic value by transforming products grown on farms or fished from the sea. Steers become meat; wheat, flour; corn, fructose; and tuna, canned.

Adding value to farm products and other material ingredients is the way in which the food processing industries contribute to state and national economies. The sum of the value added of each company is the value added of an industry; the sum of the value added of all industries approximates Gross National Product (GNP). There are two ways of thinking about the value-added activities of business. First, one can compare the value of food products shipped from a factory with the costs of all material inputs and services purchased from other industries. The difference between sales and these purchases is the size of value added; that is, value added is a kind of *gross margin* added on to all costs of purchased inputs. Second, value added may be considered the sum of all income received by factors of production internal to a food processing enterprise. Thus, the wages paid to workers, salaries paid to managers and professionals, the depreciation on plant and equipment, the dividends paid to owners, and certain taxes also sum up to value added. Conceptually, the gross-margin approach and the factor-payments approach should yield identical measures of value added. Both approaches are used to calculate GNP.

The principal and unique economic function of food processing is to convert various food materials into finished, consumer-ready products, but the economic contributions do not end there. Food processors perform a number of value-adding economic functions that are shared with other food marketing companies: farm product assemblers, grocery wholesalers, food transporters, food retailers, and food service operators. For example, food processors add value by transforming products through space and time. That is, most processors are willing to deliver or arrange for delivery of their finished products to grocery wholesalers. Moreover, the procurement operations of food manufacturers arrange for the orderly flow of the many material inputs and supplies required to manufacture foods. Often, food processors will maintain a significant inventory of material inputs and finished goods; in some food processing industries, such as canned vegetables, processors typically have a year's supply of canned goods on hand at the end of the canning season. Many food processors act as wholesalers by purchasing finished products from other processors for resale. In short, processors perform several storage and transportation functions that are essential for ensuring a steady food supply throughout the year and in all parts of the country.

Perhaps more important than physical storage and movement is the information function of food processing firms. Because of their central position in the U.S. food system, food processors have abundant and at times unique access to sources of information on the quality, quantities, and prices of processed foods. Food processors, especially those specialized in making semiprocessed food ingredients, spend significant corporate resources collecting, studying, and forecasting information on agricultural supplies in their region or possibly worldwide. The collective judgment of purchasing agents in a given food processing industry can quickly drive farm prices up or down. Other food processors, particularly those manufacturing consumer products, have teams of analysts that are experts on business practices in the food distribution industries and that follow consumer expenditure trends in minute detail. What is not generated internally within food processing companies can be purchased from specialized grocery information consulting firms.

The information collected about consumer demand and agricultural supply conditions comes together at the processing nexus. Tight supplies for a given food product at the retail level eventually get transmitted into higher processor prices, a greater willingness to pay for key inputs, and a price signal to farmers to expand production or sell off their stored crops. It works in the other direction, too, with an unexpectedly short crop impelling manufacturers to encourage consumers to reduce their purchases by raising prices on those food products that incorporate the crop. In short, processors are in a strategic position to use price increases to signal lower-than-expected supplies to farmers, consumers, and all the other middlemen in the food system; unexpected abundance is indicated by holding prices steady, price cuts, or more generous deals to retailers.

In addition to price-quantity information, processors are typically knowledgeable about food and agricultural product quality: fine gradations in the flavor of coffee beans, the moisture content of a shipment of corn, the shelf life of products under various handling conditions, and nutritional characteristics, to name a few. Thus, food processors are typically in the sole position to formulate and design foods, taking into account consumer preferences, distributors' demands, ingredient availability, scientific knowledge of biological properties, technological feasibility, and profitability—a complex but essential task. Processors share some of their food quality information through ingredient labeling, nutrition labeling, and other programs that assist consumer choices. Through quality control and product testing, food processors assume much of the responsibility of protecting the safety of the nation's food supply.

This study adopts the industry definition and concepts that underlie the U.S. government's Standard Industrial Classification (SIC) system. In the SIC system, food and beverage processing is a major industry group, one of twenty such groups that form the manufacturing sector, entitled "Food and

Kindred Products." A detailed, annotated list of the food processing industries is provided in Appendix D, but suffice it to say that roughly 95 percent of the retail value of the foods and beverages purchased by Americans is made by food processors. All other foods are considered unprocessed. The main unprocessed items consumed by Americans are fresh produce, never-frozen unpackaged fish, shell eggs, a few specialty foods made in retail shops (for example, "homemade" ice cream), tap water, and food from home gardens. These items are outside the scope of this study, as are products made from tobacco, cotton, wool, leather, and other farm fibers.

The book concentrates on the 1963–1985 period, with some older and more recent data employed where available and with projections several years into the future. More detailed data are provided for the Economic Census Years 1963, 1972, and 1982. The initial Census year 1963 was chosen because there was a substantial redefinition of the SIC codes prior to 1963, which would have affected the continuity of certain time series. The terminal Census year 1982 is the most recent one for which published results are complete, some publications having been released as late as 1986. The year 1985 is the most recent year for which the Census Bureau's Annual Survey of Manufacturers publications have been released (late 1987). The Annual Survey is based on a large sample of manufacturers, but it contains limited geographic breakdowns and omits other information available in the economic censuses.

Organization

The book is organized into three major parts, each of which may be read independently. The first two parts concentrate on national and international data. Part I treats the food processing industries as a whole, whereas Part II brings out comparisons and contrasts among the forty-one industries selected for analysis. Both Parts I and II have parallel organizations. Each first discusses the size and growth of the industries; this discussion is followed by analyses of input mixes, market organization, technological changes, future expected growth, and finally international linkages. However, the two parts are not exactly parallel. Part I does have a unique description of the role of processing in the vertically organized "food system," and Part II contains a somewhat more elaborate examination of the concept of value added. Short summaries are provided at the end of most chapters.

Part III examines the economic dimensions of food processing, separately in each of the fifty states. First, there is an extensive discussion of the economic geography of food processing for the nation as a whole. Relying extensively on national maps, several geographic topics are covered: the major producing states, changes in employment, output growth, and the sources of processed food exports. The rest of Part III is organized according to the nine geographic divisions long utilized by the Census Bureau (New England, Pacific, etc.). Each division is examined by way of introduction, followed by a vignette for each state that covers the size and growth of food processing.

Part I
National Size, Growth, and Contribution of the Food Processing Industries

1
Size Measures, 1963–1985

I t is conventional to divide the U.S. economy into ten sectors, including agriculture, manufacturing, wholesale trade, retail trade, and government. Of these ten sectors, manufacturing is the largest, accounting for about 25 percent of U.S. Gross National Product (GNP).

The food processing industries are among the largest of the twenty industry groups that form the manufacturing sector. Based on value of industry shipments, food processing is the largest of the industry groups in manufacturing (table 1–1). In 1985, the latest year for which these data are available, the food processing industries shipped products worth $302 billion, which was 13.2 percent of the shipments of all manufacturing industries.[1] Indeed, food processing shipments were over $85 billion higher than the next largest industry group, nonelectrical machinery (which includes engines, farm equipment, construction machinery, industrial machinery, and computers). Based on shipments, food processing is nearly double the size of petroleum refining and over five times the size of such industries as textiles, apparel, and iron and steel.

A second index of industry size is the number of employees. Food processing establishments employ over 1.5 million, the third largest manufacturing industry group after electrical (2.2 million) and nonelectrical (2.1 million) machinery. Food processing accounted for about 8 percent of the 18.8 million employees in the manufacturing sector in 1985. Thus, food processing is a relatively *labor-extensive* manufacturing activity; that is, food processing exhibits a relatively high ratio of sales to employment. In 1985, the average food processing employee accounted for nearly $200,000 worth of products. This is higher than all the other manufacturing industry groups, except for petroleum refining ($868,000). By contrast, the average furniture employee turns out only $65,000 of furniture products per year. The major factor that explains differences in labor/sales ratios is the amount of investment in plant and machinery employed in an industry. Food processing ranks among the leading manufacturing industries in the amount of physical assets available per employee.

The measure of size preferred by economists for comparing industries of differing technological characteristics is value added. Value added is the difference between the value of shipments and most costs of production purchased from other firms.[2] The great advantage of value added as a measure of economic activity is that it largely avoids the problem of

Table 1–1
The Size of Food Processing Relative to Other Manufacturing Industries, 1985

Industry Group[a]	Value of Shipments	Employment	Value Added
	Billion dollars	Thousands	Billion dollars
Food processing	301.6	1,545	104.1
Nonelectrical machinery	215.1	2,133	110.2
Chemicals	197.3	1,046	95.3
Electrical & electronic machinery	192.7	2,203	109.9
Motor vehicles	188.5	752	57.1
Petroleum refining	167.5	193	13.7
Fabricated metal products	139.6	1,523	69.2
Paper	93.4	637	40.4
Instruments	61.0	662	40.3
Iron and steel	58.7	414	22.2
Apparel	57.0	1,099	27.7
Textile mills	53.3	688	20.7
Furniture	31.3	484	16.5
All manufacturing	2,279.1	18,791	999.1

Source: *Annual Survey of Manufactures* (M85 (AS)-1).
[a]Omitted are tobacco, lumber, printing, rubber, leather, nonmetallic minerals, and a few other industries.

duplication inherent in shipments values. Duplication arises because the products of some industries are used as materials by others. Value added includes only the contribution of labor, capital, and management dedicated to production in a single plant or industry. Consequently, value added is a superior measure of the relative economic importance of diverse manufacturing industries and of the contribution of an industry to the nation's GNP.

In the food processing industries, value added in 1985 amounted to about one-third of the value of shipments (Table 1–1). That means that approximately two-thirds of the total value of food industry shipments was "double counted." For example, the shipments of the bread baking industry included the sales of oven makers and flour millers to the bread bakers (as well as the sales of wheat farmers to flour mills). The value added by bakers excludes the sales of all such input-supply firms.[3] The value added of the bakery industry includes the total compensation of employees, the rents or imputed rents (depreciation) of physical assets (plants, equipment, land), earnings from intangible assets (e.g., royalties or trademark license fees), and pretax profits.

In 1985, the food processing industries generated $104 billion in value added or 10.4 percent of the value added by the whole manufacturing sector. As was the case with employment, food processing ranks third among the twenty major manufacturing industry groups, falling slightly below the electrical and nonelectrical machinery industry groups. The value added by food processors is many times the value added of the petroleum refining and iron and steel industries and nearly double the size of the motor vehicle industries.

Value added represents the contribution an industry makes to a national or regional economy, but alternative measures of economic impact are income or employment *multipliers*. When a food industry purchases inputs from another industry, those purchases in turn generate indirect demands for additional inputs for the supplying industries. Moreover, a food industry can sell a product (like starch) that is an input for another industry (such as the paper industry). Multipliers are indexes that indicate the direct and indirect increases in all industries from a one-unit increase in economic activity in one industry. The greater an industry's economic linkages, the greater the multiplier. Industries that are relatively self-contained or isolated will have a multiplier value close to one. Investments in industries with high multipliers have greater benefits to the surrounding economy than the same investment in an industry with a low multiplier.

Blandford, et al. (1988) recently completed a study of the income and employment multipliers for the food processing industry using data from the year 1977. The *income multiplier* for food processing was 3.81. That is, if final demand for processed foods rises enough to create an additional $1 million in payments to workers in food processing, then in the whole U.S. economy incomes rise by $3.81 million. This is an impressively large multiplier. The average multiplier for all industries was 2.15 and for all manufacturing industries was 2.56. The *employment multiplier* for food processing was 3.74. So, if food processing industry activity increases such that employment in food processing rises by 1,000 jobs, then an additional 2,740 jobs will be generated in other U.S. industries. For all industries the employment multiplier was 2.18.

The total employment generated by the U.S. food processing industries can be broken down into three categories. First, there is the *direct* employment in the food processing industries due to final export and domestic demand. Direct employment in 1981 was about 1.1 million persons, or 71 percent of total food processing employment (Blandford, et al. 1988). Second, the remaining 0.4 million in direct employment is due to intermediate demand for food processing products by other industries (such as animal feeds, starch, inedible vegetable oils, and biologics used by the drug industry). Third, there is *indirect* employment created in many other industries that sell inputs to food processing, such as agriculture, food machinery manufacturing, and transportation. Indirect employment generated by food processing in 1981 amounted to 2.7 million jobs. Therefore, taking into account all three sources of employment, about 4.2 million jobs were created by the operations of the food processing industries, of which 65 percent was indirect employment.

In summary, the food processing industries rank first in value of shipments of manufactures but rank third in terms of employment and value added. The latter measures of size are somewhat preferred because they avoid problems of duplication inherent in shipments values. Not only are the food processing industries large, but they also have many close linkages with the rest of the economies. Whenever activity rises in food processing, almost triple the amount of income and employment is generated in the rest of the economy as is created in food processing.

2
Growth of the Food Processing Industries

The number of workers in the U.S. food processing industries has declined throughout the 1963–1985 period. Total full-time-equivalent employment[4] in 1963 was 1,725,000 and in 1985 was 1,545,000—a reduction of 10.4 percent in twenty-two years or a compounded rate of 0.5 percent per year (appendix table A1). Employment fell in every Economic Census year and continued to fall even during the 1982–1985 recovery phase. Of course, employment in the whole manufacturing sector also fell during the period, but food processing fell at a faster rate. Food processing accounted for about 2.7 percent of total 1963 U.S. employment as compared to 1.6 percent in 1985; as a proportion of total manufacturing employment, the corresponding percentages are 10.2 (1963) and 7.8 (1985).

The principal reason for the absolute and relative decline of employment is the impressive labor productivity change in the food processing industries. While this topic will be discussed in greater detail in chapter 6, it is clear that more capital equipment and other inputs have been substituted for labor in food processing plants. Thus, far fewer employees are needed today to produce the same amount of a given food product as twenty years ago. The decline in employment has affected production workers equally as strongly as nonproduction employees. Production workers (plant workers up to first-level supervisors) accounted for about 65 percent of total employment throughout the 1963–1985 period (appendix table A1). However, the workplaces of nonproduction workers did shift considerably. In 1963, only 11 percent of all nonproduction workers (salesmen, office workers, and the like) worked in *separate* headquarters' locations on in auxiliary establishments, but by 1985 twenty-three percent worked away from operating establishments.

All other growth indicators for the food processing industries are positive. The value of food product shipments (excluding nonfood byproducts) more than quadrupled from 1963 ($65 billion) to 1985 ($282 billion) (figure 1–1). In 1985, the output of the food processing industries consisted of $282 billion of food and beverage products plus $20 billion of nonfood products (e.g., hides, inedible starches, tallow, insulin, and so forth). During the relatively inflation-free period from 1963 to 1972, food product shipments rose at a compounded rate of 5.7 percent per year; during the highly inflationary period 1972–1982, the growth rate averaged 9.2 percent per

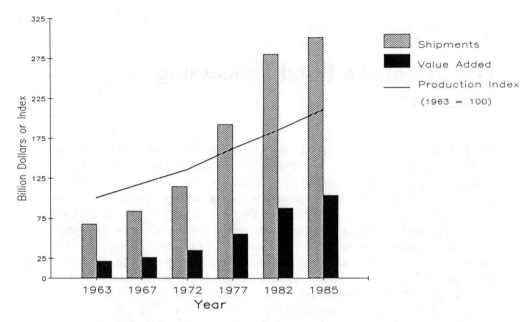

Figure 2–1. Growth of Food Processing Shipments and Value Added, 1963–1985

Source: Appendix Table A1

year; finally, during the low-inflation recovery period 1982–1985, growth was 2.9 percent per year (table 2–1).

Value added by the food processing industries rose slightly faster than value of shipments after 1972. From 1972 to 1982, the growth rate was a compounded 9.5 percent per year, and from 1982 to 1985, it was 5.6 per year. Assuming vertical integration did not increase during the period, this means that food processors were able to increase product prices faster than the prices of purchased inputs (e.g., farm products), especially after 1982 when farm product prices fell. The reasons for widening value added are further explored in Part II.

A final index of growth is the amount of new capital invested in plant and equipment. Food processors invested $1.3 billion in 1963, and this rose to $7.0 billion in 1985. New capital investment increased slightly faster than shipments. In 1963, food processors invested only 1.9 percent of receipts, but by 1982–1985, that ratio had risen to 2.3 percent.

All three growth measures (shipments, value added, and investment) are affected by price inflation. The three subperiods were characterized by moderate, high, and low inflation, respectively (table 1–2). Inflation indexes can be applied to reliable current-dollar shipments data to derive production

Table 2–1
Growth Rates of the Food Processing Industries, 1963–1985

Measure	1963-1972	1972-1982	1982-1985	1963-1985
	Percent per year			
Employment	-0.4	-0.4	-1.2	-0.5
Value of product shipments	5.7	9.2	2.9	6.9
Value added	5.6	9.5	5.6	7.4
New capital investment	7.1	10.8	1.5	8.0
Inflation (producer price index)[a]	3.2	7.9	1.5	5.1
Index of Production (deflated)	3.5	3.2	4.5	3.5

Source: Appendix Tables A1, A2, and A5.

[a]Normally inflation at the producer level is approximately the difference between growth in value of shipments and growth in (real) production. During 1963–1982, this relationship held up fairly well in the sense that the *implied* inflation rate (shipments growth less output growth) was 1.0–1.8 percent lower than the officially reported inflation rates shown in this row. That is, quality change led to an annual 1.0–1.8 percent overstatement in unit growth rates (or the same overstatement in inflation increases). However, in 1982–1985, the degree of overstatement widened considerably to 3.1 percent per year; that is, either production rose only 1.4 percent per year or fairly unusual *deflation* of 1.6 percent per year occurred or some combination of the two. The widening discrepancy between reported inflation and implied inflation is consistent with increasing new product introductions (see section 6.3). It is my judgment that both the producer price index and the production index were exaggerated during 1963–1985; probably actual unit production rose about 2.5 percent annually during this period.

indexes supposedly free of the inflation factor. Inflation factors are available only for fairly standardized products. A production index for the food processing industries prepared by the Federal Reserve Board is shown in figure 1–1. The index rose from a value of 100 in 1963 to 211 in 1985—an increase of 11 percent. The quantity of output of the food processing industries grew 3.5 percent per year during 1963–1985, with average growth highest in the 1982–1985 period (table 1–2). These growth rates may be slightly overstated because of the inability of price deflators to adjust for improved quality over time. However, these data are comparable to more precise production indexes developed by the Census Bureau (appendix table A18).

Historically, since the end of World War II, the food processing industries have maintained an average annual real growth rate (compounded) of almost 3 percent (Connor et al. 1985:35). Real growth (that is, inflation-adjusted production changes) of the food processing industries was about one-fifth lower than the manufacturing sector as a whole, although since the mid-1960s food processing growth was about one-third higher than the other manufacturing industries. The main factor explaining the superior growth record of food processing since the mid-1960s is that there have been four general recessions during the period (1969, 1974, 1980, and 1981–1982). Food processing is relatively insensitive to the peaks and troughs of production caused by the business cycle. In fact, industrial production of food products has dipped only twice since the end of World War II, by 1 percent in 1948 and 1975 (appendix table A2). These years were characterized by both severe recessions and hyperinflation. Production is considerably more variable in the manufacture of apparel, chemicals, automobiles, metals, and machinery.

It should also be mentioned that purchases of food and beverages in eating and drinking places are strongly procyclic, while purchases in food and grocery stores are countercyclic (tend to increase faster during mild recession and slow down during periods of rapid growth). As a result, the utilization of plant capacity in the food processing industries tends to be much steadier and more predictable than most other manufacturing industries. For example, according to one reliable source, capacity utilization for food processing averaged 77 percent of the "ideal" (maximum profit) level over 1974–1980 with an average year-to-year change of only 1 percentage point (Connor et al. 1985:39). By contrast, capacity utilization in the motor vehicle industry shifted from 97 percent in 1978 to 54 percent in 1980.

Although the food processing industries possess an enviable stability in annual growth rates, there is a pronounced seasonality of production patterns. Unlike nearly all the other manufacturing industries (except perhaps apparel), food processing displays a regular seasonal cycle of production. Peak output, in September, is 7 percent above normal annual production, and the January trough is 5 percent below normal output. Even greater peaks occur during harvest time for the canning, freezing, sugar, and vegetable oil industries. The dairy industries peak in May, but the meat and grain–based processing industries have only weak seasonal production patterns. In addition to seasonal fluctuations induced by farm product supplies, some food processing industries must contend with strong variations in seasonal demand (soft drinks, candy, liquor, and turkeys are examples).

In the long run, the domestic household demand for food drives most of the growth of the food processing industry. Of course, some individual food processing industries find demand for their products strongly influenced by other factors, for example, export demand (important for rice milling), imports (wine), nonfood industrial by-products (leather for the footwear industry), and the government sector (food for the military, prisons, PL 480 program, or storage). (For a fuller discussion, see chapter 7.) However, by and large, the U.S. consumer demand for food and beverages (of which 95 percent of the value of consumer purchases is processed) is responsible for 85 percent of the retail sales of the food processing industries.

The allocation of U.S. personal expenditures for several years is shown in tables 2–2 and 2–3. Values in the table are measured at retail, not producer levels. In 1985, U.S. households spent $469 billion on food and beverages, of which about $420 billion was on domestic processed products;

Table 2–2
U.S. Personal Consumption Expenditures, Selected Years 1947–1985

Expenditure Category	1947	1954	1963	1972	1982	1985
			Billion dollars			
Nondurable goods:						
Food and beverage	52	67	90	159	399	469
Clothing and shoes	19	22	30	56	124	155
Other nondurables	20	31	50	90	248	281
Durable goods:						
Motor vehicles	7	13	24	52	109	169
Furniture & household equipment	11	15	21	42	96	127
Other durables	3	4	7	17	48	63
Services:						
Housing services[a]	16	32	58	112	321	404
Household operation	8	13	24	45	143	175
Transportation services	5	8	13	30	70	89
Medical care	6	10	21	58	218	290
Other services	16	25	45	97	275	378
Total	162	240	382	758	2,051	2,601

Source: *Economic Report of the President 1987* (Table B14).
[a]Rents and the imputed rental value of owner-occupied housing.

Table 2–3
Allocation of U.S. Personal Consumption Expenditures, Selected Years, 1947–1985

Expenditure Category	1947	1954	1963	1972	1982	1985
			Percent			
Food and beverages	32.1	27.9	23.6	21.0	19.5	18.0
Clothing and shoes	11.3	9.2	7.9	7.4	6.1	6.0
Other nondurables	12.4	12.9	13.1	11.9	12.1	10.8
Total nondurables	56.1	49.9	44.4	40.3	37.6	34.8
Motor vehicles	4.3	5.4	6.3	6.9	5.3	6.5
Household furniture and equipment	6.8	6.3	5.5	5.5	4.7	4.9
Other durables	1.9	1.7	1.8	2.2	2.3	2.4
Total durables	12.6	13.4	13.6	14.7	12.3	13.8
Housing services[a]	9.9	13.3	15.2	14.8	15.7	15.5
Household operation	4.9	5.4	6.3	5.9	7.0	6.7
Transportation services	3.1	3.3	3.4	4.0	3.4	3.4
Medical care	3.7	4.2	5.5	7.7	10.6	11.2
Other services	9.9	10.4	11.8	12.8	13.4	14.5
Total services	31.2	36.7	42.1	49.2	50.1	51.4
Total expenditures	100.0	100.0	100.0	100.0	100.0	100.0

Source: *Economic Report of the President 1987* (Table B14).
[a]Rents and the imputed rental value of owner-occupied housing.

the corresponding value measured at processors' prices was $240 billion; the difference of $180 billion represents the cost to consumers of grocery wholesale-retail services. Consumer expenditures for food and beverages (including unprocessed) increased over fivefold between 1963 and 1985; however, expenditures on all other goods and services rose more than sevenfold. The proportion of total expenditures on food and beverages fell from 24 percent in 1963 to 18 percent in 1985. This trend mirrors that of clothing, personal care products, and other nondurables. The proportion of consumer expenditures on durable products mostly held steady, whereas the proportion spent on medical, travel, educational, and other services rose by 50 percent during the period.

Consumer demand for foods is met through two distinct distribution channels: food for use at home and food consumed on the premises. Beginning in the early 1970s, there has been a pronounced shift in food expenditures away from foods to be prepared at home and toward food service purchases. However, before 1972, there is no discernable trend.

As a proportion of all disposable income, food and beverages (including alcoholic) purchased for on-premise consumption show a remarkable constancy—about 5 percent throughout the 1963–1985 period. On the other hand, food purchased in food stores declined from 18 percent of personal expenditures in 1963 to only 13 percent in 1985 (figure 2–2). This trend is

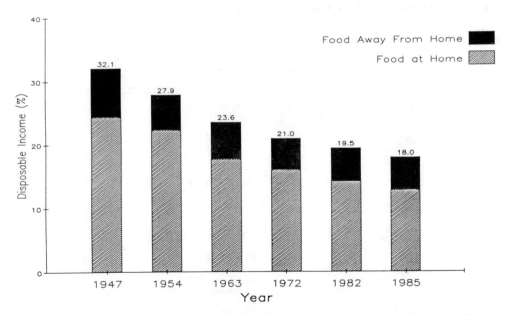

Figure 2–2. Food and Beverage Expenditures as a Proportion of Household Disposable Income, 1947–1985

Source: Tables 2–3 and 2–4.

in accord with economic research that shows that changes in food service expenditures almost keep pace with changes in personal disposable income (income elasticity close to 1.0), whereas for every $1 increase in disposable household income only about $0.20 is spent on additional at-home foods (Blaylock & Smallwood 1986). Just as with other services, U.S. consumers appear to be more willing to allocate additional income to food *service* than to food that needs to be prepared at home (table 2–4).

Measured in 1972 dollars, food expenditures increased from $99 billion in 1963 to $151 billion in 1985—an increase of 53 percent in twenty-three years. What accounted for this average increase of 1.9 percent per year?

The increase in the U.S. population can explain only about half of the increase in real food expenditures during 1963–1985. In recent years, rates of natural population increase have been slowing, and immigration has accounted for almost half of the total increase in population. The rest of the increase in real food expenditures can be attributed to the phenomenon often called *trading-up;* that is, shifts in the mix of foods purchased toward foods that have higher prices per pound. The substitution of away-from-home food

Table 2–4
Consumer Purchases of Foods and Beverages, 1947–1985

Category	1947	1954	1963	1972	1982	1985
			Billion dollars			
Food, at-home	38.3	55.6	68.1	121	291	331
Food, away-from-home	12.3	14.2	22.7	38	108	138
Total food	50.6	69.8	90.8	159	399	469
			Percent			
Food, at-home	76	80	75	74	73	71
Food, away-from-home	24	20	25	24	27	29
Total food	100	100	100	100	100	100

Source: Data from Connor et al. (1985:64) and Lee et al. (1987).

for at-home food is but one example of this trend, which also occurs among grocery products. This "enriching" of the demand mix is explained by a number of factors besides income: greater product variety, improved quality (more costly ingredients, more elaborate packaging, greater convenience of preparation, or improved preservation), changing national preferences, and several demographic changes. The appearance of a greater variety of foods is attested to by a number of sources charting the increase in new food product introductions. Most new products are introduced to markets accompanied by claims of product quality improvement. Quality and preference changes are notoriously difficult to measure satisfactorily within a conventional economic framework, but product novelty and variety necessarily come at a price. Product development costs, introductory promotion campaigns, and losses in economies of scale inevitably accompany rapid new product introductions. Some new products use more expensive ingredients or packaging. By substituting new products for old, consumers in effect pay higher overall prices for the foods in their market basket. Of course, in some cases there are offsetting quality improvements.

Advertising efforts play a key role in the attempts by food processors to get consumers to try new products, switch their allegiance to new brands, and maintain their loyalty to established brands in a market. In other words, advertising and other types of selling effort are directed at changing consumer tastes or at least at activating the latent preferences of consumers. An extension of this argument is that the brand advertising of all the brands in a market has the effect of increasing sales and consumption of foods in that market relative to consumption of foods in less-advertised markets. There is fairly solid evidence that real industry sales increase faster in the presence of intensive advertising (Gallo & Connor 1982). But whether advertising *causes* sales increases or simply becomes more intense as a *result of* sales growth is a much debated question. What is not debatable is the pervasiveness and tremendous growth of advertising of food and related products. In 1984 food company advertising expenditures exceeded $8.5 billion, nearly all of it on processed products; advertising by "tobacco" companies (most of which by this time had become large food processors) was $2.9 billion (table 2–5). Advertising by companies engaged in food processing amounted to over one-third of all advertising by manufacturers, and this share has risen over time. The rate of increase in advertising expenditures was 8.8 percent per year from 1963 to 1984.

The net effects of the crosscurrents of sociodemographic changes in the United States are more difficult to assess. Higher education levels, more dual-career married households, fewer children per household, more single-person households, and the aging of the population all appear to contribute to a greater willingness to pay higher unit prices for foods, to eat out, and to buy products tailored more precisely to the consumer's demand segment

Table 2–5
Reported Advertising Expenditures by Food Processors and Other Manufacturers, 1963, 1972, 1982, and 1984

Companies Primarily Classified:	1963	1972	1982	1984
	Million dollars			
Food processing	1,637	2,532	6,564	8,535
Tobacco manufacturing	317	398	1,478	2,941
All manufacturing	5,993	10,474	24,798	33,382
	Percent			
Food and tobacco as a proportion of all manufacturing	27	28	32	34

Source: Data from Connor et al. (1985) and Internal Revenue Service, *Source Book: Statistics of Income 1984: Corporation Income Tax Returns,* Publication 1053, Washington, DC: U.S. Department of the Treasury (Revised July 1987).

Note: Advertising expenditures as reported by companies on their corporate income tax return to the Internal Revenue Service. Appears to include the costs of media advertising and point-of-purchase displays but probably excludes free samples, costs of field sales forces, and most promotional activity. Some of the expenditures reported are on nonfood products made by food processing companies, and much of the advertising by tobacco companies is on food products.

(Kinsey & Heien 1988). Because smaller households are less "efficient" in their utilization of foods, greater per capita demand for food generally and foodservice in particular will be one result of aging. Increased food preparation by men and more part-time spousal employment will reinforce these positive impacts on food demand. Countervailing demographic changes include the increasing proportion of nonwhite households and the geographic shift of the population to the West and South (consumers in the Northeast spend significantly more on foods than consumers in other regions). On balance, population increases, trading-up, and demographic shifts will yield future increases in inflation-adjusted food expenditures of about 1 percent per year. However, incomes will likely increase faster, so the proportion spent on food will probably continue to decline.

In summary, several indicators of growth were reviewed for the food processing industries for the period 1963–1985. Only employment fell during that period, by about 0.5 percent per year. Value of processed food shipments rose on average at 6.9 percent per year (compounded), whereas value added and capital expenditures increased slightly faster. However, these three dollar values were seriously affected by rapid inflation during 1972–1982. Corrected for inflation, output in the food industries rose about 3.5 percent per year from 1963 to 1985, though the reader is cautioned that the inability to correct for food quality changes may lead to an overstatement of actual unit growth rates. Actual unit growth probably was in the range of 2 to 2.5 percent per year.

Because growth of the food processing industries is driven mainly by domestic consumer expenditures, except for some seasonal fluctuations, growth is quite steady for the industries. Steady growth has promoted relatively high capacity utilization in the industries' plants. Household demand for food away-from-home is more responsive to changes in household income, which will mean somewhat more cyclic output patterns in the future. Industry growth will increasingly come from persuading consumers to purchase more expensive foods that incorporate greater convenience or other valued attributes. Another potentially fast-growing segment of demand for processed foods is the export sector, though in this case much depends on economic growth rates of America's traditional trading partners.

3
Role of Processing in the Food System

U p to this point the food processing industries have been compared to other manufacturing industries. Another way of examining the role of food processing is as a stage in a vertically connected system stretching from farms and ranches to retail food stores. Each stage of this articulated *food system* performs a unique set of functions in the evolution of raw farm products into comestibles. Taken together, the stages of this food system compose the nation's largest single economic activity. And food processing, by several measures, plays an increasingly important role in this U.S. food system.

Value Added

The best overall indicator of the economic contribution of food processing to the U.S. food system is value added. Recall that value added is the contribution an industry makes to the GNP and that it avoids the problem of double counting inherent in sales measures. One way of defining value added is as the sum of all payments to all factors of production utilized by the industry.

The net value added by each major stage of the food system is shown in table 3–1. Of the six stages identified, the value added by wholesale and retail trade in foods and beverages is the greatest ($129 billion in 1982) and food processing is the second largest ($74 billion). Together, processing and distribution account for over three-fifths of the value added in the food system. Agriculture itself supplied only one-fifth of the system's value added in 1982. Foodservice and food transportation played rather minor roles. The entire food system, as defined in table 3–1 (agriculture, processing, and distribution), accounted for over 11 percent of the U.S. GNP in 1982.

What table 3–1 ignores is all of the industries that supply various inputs to agriculture (agricultural machinery, chemicals, energy, etc.), to processing (containers, chemicals, business services, etc.), and to food distribution (motor vehicles, refrigeration equipment, construction services, etc.). Calculations made by the USDA for 1982 indicate that about $140 billion in value added can be attributed to the many industries selling materials,

Table 3–1

The Contribution of Food Manufacturing to the U.S. Food System, 1947 and 1982

Stage of the Food System	Year 1947	1982
	Value added in $ billion	
Agriculture	19.5	71.1
Food processing	11.3	74.1
Tobacco manufacturing	0.6	8.1
Transportation	11.6	22.8
Wholesale-retail trade	22.7	128.6
Foodservice	6.0	42.6
Total food system	71.7	347.3
	Percent	
Agriculture	27.2	20.5
Food processing	15.8	21.3
Tobacco manufacturing	0.8	2.3
Transportation	16.2	6.6
Wholesale-retail trade	31.7	37.0
Foodservice	8.4	12.3
Total food system	100.0	100.0
System/U.S. GNP	30.8	11.2

Source: Data from Connor et al. (1985).

Note: Excludes contribution of input-supply industries and agricultural fibers except tobacco. Consumers spent $424 billion at retail for food, beverages, and tobacco products in 1982. In addition, government, business, and exports accounted for about $63 billion of food purchases. The difference between $487 billion and the $347 billion in value added shown in this table is mainly explained by the value added provided by industries that supply material imports to the stages of the food system listed above. That is, industries that supply imports to agriculture (fertilizer, farm machinery, etc.), food and tobacco processing (containers, chemicals, manufacturing equipment, etc.), and food distribution (transportation equipment, refrigerators, construction services, etc.) accounted for about $140 billion of the food system's value added.

equipment, and services to the industries shown in table 3–1 (Manchester 1983). In 1982, the food system, defined more broadly to include value added by the input-supply industries, contributed about $487 billion to U.S. GNP or almost 16 percent of total U.S. economic activity. (For an even broader definition that includes clothing, shoes, flowers, and the like, see Lee et al. 1987).

The value added by the U.S. food system has grown nearly fivefold since 1947. Nevertheless, the declining demand for food relative to other consumer purchases has meant that the food system has also diminished in relative importance. In 1947 the food system (narrowly defined) accounted for at least 30 percent of the U.S. GNP (Davis and Goldberg 1957). (Unfortunately, estimates of the broader concept of the food system are not available but probably would fall in the 40–50 percent range.) What is interesting is the shifting importance of the stages of the food system since the end of World War II. Food processing increased its share of food-system value added considerably (from 15.8 percent in 1947 to 21.3 percent in 1982), surpassing the contribution of agriculture itself around 1980. Agriculture and transportation fell in importance, partly because of significant improvements in efficiency in those industries. Wholesale-retail trade and foodservice also added proportionately more value to the U.S. food system.

Employment

Another way of showing the relative importance of food processing in the U.S. food system is by employment. Except for the inability to identify employment related to food transportation activities, employment figures are in many ways more revealing and, like value added, involve little or no double counting. Employment in the food system (ignoring the input-supply industries) rose modestly (about 12 percent) from 1950 to 1982 (table 3–2). As a proportion of all U.S. private-sector employment, food-system employment fell from 25 percent in 1950 to a smaller but still impressive 18 percent in 1982. The biggest changes in employment were the 50 percent decline in agricultural jobs and 290 percent increase in foodservice jobs between 1950 to 1982. All other types of food retail and wholesale jobs also increased. As previously mentioned, processing jobs declined slightly. The change in the mix of food-system jobs is shown in figure 3–1.

Channels of Distribution

An important distinction among processed food products is the type of distribution channels employed in marketing the products. This distinction is important for several reasons. First, different marketing channels serve different sets of customers (or demand segments). By implication, methods of informing, persuading, and servicing customers vary systematically by channel type. Second, although some industries utilize only one type of marketing channel, most industries face the possibility of distributing their product through alternative distribution channels. Otherwise identical products distributed via two channels interact in two different markets (where a "market" is the place where a group of sellers meet and exchange with a group of buyers). Finally, food processing companies (or the major

Table 3–2
Employment in the U.S. Food and Fiber System, 1950–1982

Stage of the Food System	1950	1963	1982	1984
		Millions		
Agriculture & agricultural services	7.3	5.5	3.7	3.4
Food processing	1.9	1.8	1.7	1.6
Wholesale trade, grocery products	0.2	0.4	0.8	0.8
Wholesale trade, farm products	0.2	0.3	0.4	0.4
Retail trade, food stores	1.5	1.9	2.4	2.7
Retail trade, foodservice	1.2	2.9	4.7	5.4
Total food system	12.2	12.8	13.7	14.3
		Percent		
Agriculture & agricultural services	60	43	27	24
Food processing	16	14	12	11
Wholesale trade, grocery products	2	3	6	6
Wholesale trade, farm products	2	2	3	3
Retail trade, food stores	12	15	18	19
Retail trade, foodservice	10	23	34	38
System/U.S. private total	24.7	23.7	17.7	18.2

Source: Data from Connor (1987).
Note: This is a count of paid employment. It ignores self-employed persons (except in agriculture) and makes no adjustment for part-time employment.

divisions of diversified companies) tend to specialize in only one marketing channel. Indeed, to be financially successful, a food processor must specialize in a channel, if only to become intimately familiar with the customers, selling methods, and strategies of major competitors.

Although the following breakdown of channel types represents an oversimplification, the five types delineated make a fine point of departure. Figure 3–2 shows the relative size of the five major marketing channels for processed foods, measured in 1977 producer value of shipments *at all levels* of the food system. (See also table 7–1.)

The smallest marketing channel available to food processors, accounting for only 5 percent of shipments, are the routes to and from the rest of the world—imports and exports. Selling in export markets requires a host of specialized marketing institutions unique to this channel: freight forwarders, customs forms, methods of avoiding foreign exchange risks, unfamiliar safety and labeling regulations, and so forth. Internationally traded food products

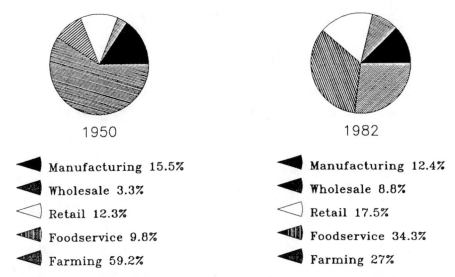

Figure 3–1. Employment Trends in the U.S. Food System, 1950 and 1982

Sources: Data from Bureau of the Census and Labor Statistics

involve a mixture of consumer and industrial products. The second largest of the five marketing channels for food processors involves domestic sales to other producers. The industrial or producer-goods channel accounts for over one-fourth of the value of shipments, and this proportion appears to be rising slowly over time. Semiprocessed foodstuffs and by-products are typically highly standardized (often graded) commodities shipped in large lots directly to the industrial users. Prices are continually renegotiated by well-informed purchasing agents; advertising is minimal.

The remaining three channels distribute consumer goods—finished, kitchen-ready foods. The foodservice channel (including "institutional" sales) takes only about 15 percent of the value of processed-food shipments and has many of the characteristics of the producer-goods channel (brands are relatively unimportant marketing tools and grading is common), but distribution for most nonperishable foodservice products occurs through specialized wholesalers. Foodservice products require special packaging and are often formulated for specific cooking methods. Shipments in this channel have increased a percentage point or two since 1977.

Products designed to be sold through retail grocery and food stores constitute nearly 60 percent of the manufacturers' value of processed-foods shipments. These consumer products divide into two distinct channels, those

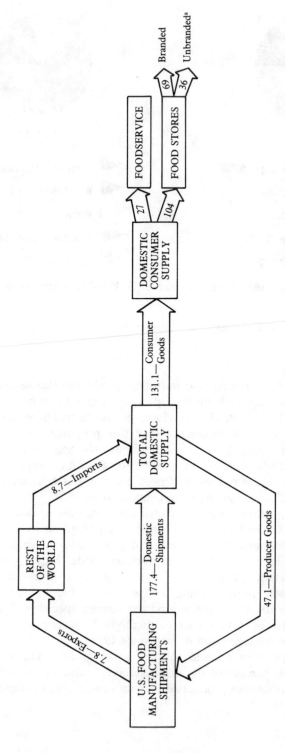

Figure 3–2. Major Marketing Channels for Processed Food Products (billion dollars of 1977 shipments)

[a]Store brands and generics.

carrying manufacturers' brands (40 percent) and those with store brands or no brands (20 percent). With the exception of bread, milk, soft drinks, and a few other foods delivered directly to stores by processors, grocery products are purchased first by a variety of wholesalers before being resold to grocery stores. Large grocery chains perform their own wholesaling functions.

Branded foods are shipped in consumer-sized packages; manufacturers use a variety of selling techniques, directed at both consumers and food-store operators, to maintain product distinctiveness and market share. Consumers hold the manufacturers of branded foods primarily responsible for the healthfulness and quality of the products. Manufacturers of branded foods generally use the "posted price" method (a set schedule of prices not open to negotiation), with prices occasionally discounted on a regional basis.

Unbranded (most fresh meat and produce) and private-label foods are marketed quite differently. Some are made in retailer-owned factories, while most of the rest are purchased in large lots after hard price negotiations and subject to rigorous quality specifications. Specification buying is done directly by grocery chains or by wholesalers for smaller food retailers. As is the case with foodservice, consumers hold the retailers primarily responsible for guaranteeing food product integrity and quality. Store brands (and generics) are rarely advertised and appear in product categories only if the retail price can be set significantly below leading brands in the category.

Smaller food processors and the divisions of large companies tend to specialize in selling products through only one marketing channel, though there is some overlap. This situation is illustrated schematically in figure 3–3. All food processors selling in the domestic market fall into one of the five circles in the figure, where the size of the circles is roughly proportional to sales in the channel. Most processors occupy only one circle; that is, they are completely specialized in one marketing strategy and serve only one category of buyer. Industrial food processors are particularly specialized. A soybean crusher, for example, will typically sell semirefined soybean oil to other vegetable-oil users but will refrain from selling branded margarine (or will have a separate division organized for that purpose). Branded-foods processors are also fairly specialized, particularly those with highly differentiated leading brands. The suggestion that the Kellogg company would consider selling its famous corn flakes under a Safeway brand is simply unthinkable, assuming identical product quality is sold at a lower-than-normal price. However, it is not unusual for food processors with low market shares or limited regional distribution to pack some private-label product, especially under conditions that would limit competition with its own flagship brand. Also, it is not unusual for brand manufacturers to sell foodservice versions, often under different packaging. Private-label and foodservice manufacturers are the most likely to be involved in two or even three channels simultaneously, though even in these cases that is the exception rather than the rule.

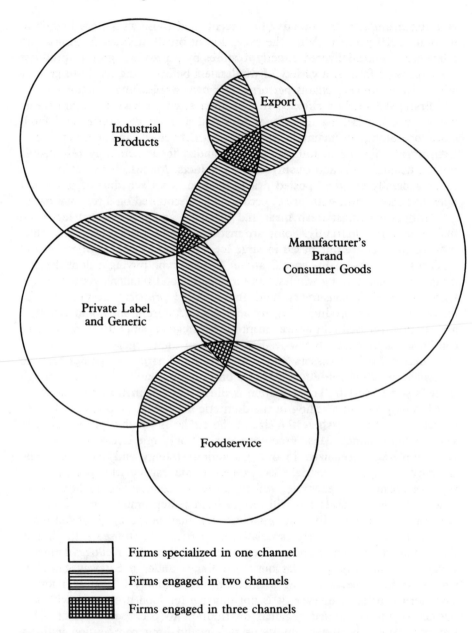

Industrial
Products

Export

Manufacturer's
Brand
Consumer Goods

Private Label
and Generic

Foodservice

Firms specialized in one channel

Firms engaged in two channels

Firms engaged in three channels

Figure 3–3. Five Strategic Groups In Food Processing

Summary

Processing occupies a key position in the food system—those vertically linked industries that stretch from agriculture to the food retailer. Food processors provide over one-fifth of the value added by the food system, a proportion that has increased from only one-seventh since 1947. Partly because of improved labor productivity, employment in the processing stage of the food system has declined slightly; the biggest increase in employment has come in the wholesale and retail distribution of food.

Sales by processors to domestic food retailers constitute by far the largest distribution channel, almost 60 percent of total sales. Over one-fourth of sales are in the form of "producer goods," semiprocessed ingredients sold to other manufacturers. The third-largest marketing channel, foodservice and institutional sales, accounts for a surprisingly small 15 percent of food processors' sales (evaluated at manufacturers' prices not at the consumer level). The remaining channel is by far the smallest; exports account for only about 4 percent of shipments value in recent years, and these consist primarily of semiprocessed food products.

4
Inputs Purchased by Food Processors

F
ood processing requires the application of a wide variety of production inputs to transform lower-valued food materials into higher-valued food products. Labor, machinery, energy, and knowledge are combined on factory floors to convert raw animal, vegetable, and marine materials into intermediate food-stuffs or finished edibles. In establishments employing one worker or thousands, farm and fishery products are slaughtered and sliced, milled and mixed, blended and bottled, fried and frozen, or subjected to any of dozens of other processes. The result is that relatively bulky, perishable, and often inedible farm products are converted into more refined, concentrated, shelf-stable, and palatable foods.

Table 4–1 shows the major categories of inputs purchased by all the U.S. food processing industries in 1947 (the first year for which such data are available) and 1977 (the most recent year). The dollar value (in producers' prices) of gross purchases by all operating food processing establishments sums up roughly to total output; the percentage distribution of those purchases provides a profile of input use by a typical or "representative" food processing establishment. (Note that the operations of separate company headquarters and R&D labs are not included.) Three entries in table 4–1 correspond to the value added of food processors: labor compensation of employees, government services and indirect taxes (mostly property taxes but not income or sales taxes), and capital utilization and profit (capital consumption allowances such as depreciation on plant and equipment, net interest earned, profits, dividends, compensation of self-employed business persons, and other property-type income). The remaining purchases appear as value added in other industries of the economy. Recall that the value added by all businesses sums up to GNP.[5]

Knowing that pretax profits are about 4 percent of sales, one can get a fairly precise picture of the distribution of costs. The procedure is to divide the percentages in table 4–1 by 0.96. By far the greatest category of costs (60 percent in 1977) is for material inputs. The four types of material costs are domestic and imported agricultural and fisheries products (30 percent of output or 32 percent of total costs), semiprocessed food ingredients (18 percent of costs), containers and packaging (9 percent), and chemicals including salt (0.6 percent). Of course, these proportions vary widely for

Table 4–1
Gross Purchases by the Food Manufacturing Industries from Other U.S. Industries, 1947 and 1977

Seller	1947		1977	
	$ Billion	Percent	$ Billion	Percent
Labor	8.6	20.4	25.4	13.4
Capital utilization and profit			19.1	10.1
Agriculture and fisheries:	16.9	40.3	53.0	28.1
Livestock	10.6	25.4	36.1	19.1
Crops	6.2	14.6	15.6	8.3
Marine products	0.1	0.3	1.5	0.7
Semifinished foodstuffs	8.5	20.3	33.2	17.6
Containers and packaging	1.7	4.0	17.2	9.1
Paper	0.7	1.7	5.7	3.0
Metal	0.5	1.2	6.4	3.4
Glass	0.3	0.6	3.0	1.6
Closures	0.1	0.3	0.4	0.2
Wooden	0.1	0.3	0.1	0.0
Plastic	0.0	0.0	1.8	1.0
Transportation services	1.2	2.8	4.8	2.6
Railroads	0.6	1.5	1.3	0.7
Trucks	0.3	0.8	2.5	1.3
Automobile	0.2	0.4	0.4	0.2
Air	0.0	0.0	0.4	0.2
Water and miscellaneous	0.1	0.1	0.4	0.2
Government services and taxes	1.3	3.0	11.0	3.6
Imports (mostly tropical commodities)	0.8	2.0	4.5	2.4
Advertising and other business services	1.0E	2.3E	6.6	3.5
Wholesale and retail trade	0.6	1.4	10.3	5.4
Chemicals, selected	0.4	0.9	1.1	0.6
Power and fuels	0.3	0.7	2.8	1.5
Real estate and rentals	0.1	0.2	0.5	0.3
Construction and maintenance	0.1	0.2	0.9	0.5
All other industries	0.6	1.3	2.5	1.3
Total inputs and profit	42.1	100.0	189.2	100.0

Source: Data from Davis and Goldberg (1957) and U.S. Department of Commerce, Bureau of Economic Analysis, 1977 U.S. Input/Output Table, published May 1984.
E = Estimated "other business services" for 1947 to be $0.4 billion.

individual food processing industries (see chapter 10). Butter making requires large purchases of farm milk and only very little packaging and salt. Frozen pizza manufacturers, on the other hand, use large proportions of semiprocessed ingredients (flour, cheese, sausage, etc.) and more expensive packaging but buy directly little or no farm output.

Labor is the next largest category of costs (14 percent in 1977), and capital-related expenditures (construction, maintenance, and equipment replacement) is the third largest category (about 7 percent of costs). The contribution of "knowledge" as an input to food processing activities is intermixed in the labor and capital input categories. Management science and food science appear primarily as a salary cost; innovations adopted from other industries appear as a capital cost; and much information is purchased as a business service. Wholesale services, including brokers and purchased warehousing, amounted to almost 6 percent of costs, whereas purchased transportation services added up to less than 3 percent of costs. (Processors that deliver directly to distributors incur these costs in the labor, energy, and capital utilization categories.) Taxes and business services each accounted for less than 4 percent of total costs. Energy costs (after the first oil price "shock" of 1973 but before the second shock in 1979) were quite modest, though again several food processes are quite energy-intensive. The "other industries" category includes such items as printing ($900 million), purchased machinery ($200 million), insurance and financial services ($800 million), and catering ($400 million).

There have been several changes in the composition of inputs used by food processors since 1947. The proportion of expenditures on containers and packaging rose by over 125 percent; much more plastic, metal containers, foil, glass, and paper are being utilized now but proportionately less wood. Transportation costs declined slightly relative to output, and air, water, and trucking modes have partially replaced expenditures on railroad services. Relatively more distribution and other business services are now being purchased by food processors. The costs of both agricultural products and food materials declined as a proportion of total costs, mainly because by 1977 the prices of finished processed foods had risen twice as fast as the prices of farm commodities (appendix table A5). Corrected for inflation since 1947, it appears that the (real) expenditures on agricultural inputs declined a couple of percentage points, while the (real) costs of industrial foodstuffs rose about 3 percentage points of total costs. In short, food processors in the late 1970s were using about the same total quantity of farm and food ingredients per unit of output but were buying *relatively* more of the latter.

Prices of finished processed foods have increased quite a bit more than the prices of farm goods (appendix tables A5, A6, and A7). For example, from 1963 to 1985, farm product prices rose 142 percent but processed food prices rose 198 percent (that is, the latter increase was 40 percent higher).

Processed food prices tend to change more slowly than farm products prices, and agricultural commodity prices are by far the most volatile of all input prices faced by food processors. For example, between 1972 and 1974, when farm prices exploded by over 50 percent, processed foods prices rose only 37 percent; however, processed prices rarely fall even when farm prices slump, as during the 1981–1982 and 1984–1986 periods. One reason why processed product prices are "sticky downward" is that the prices of other inputs typically do not fall when farm prices do. The prices for labor, containers, supplies, and energy each rose every year between 1953 and 1982 (and only energy prices have fallen since 1982). Moreover, some food processors try to widen their margins during periods when commodity prices are flat or falling, to "make up" for periods when profits were squeezed due to rapid rises in commodity input prices. In general, the long-term trends in producer prices of processed foods are roughly in line with movements of most other consumer-good manufacturers.

In summary, for the average food processing operation the principal category of input is purchased materials (62 percent of total costs). The major inputs are raw agricultural commodities (32 percent of costs), semiprocessed foodstuffs (18 percent), and packaging (9 percent). Labor and management is the second largest input utilized (14 percent), whereas capital-related costs (7 percent) are third. There is a vast array of other, smaller purchases made from the service sector, such as wholesale brokers, transportation, advertising, real estate, and financial services (10 percent of costs). Purchased fuels and energy averaged less than 2 percent of costs.

There have been many changes in the input mix of the food processing industries in the post-World War II era. Processors are using about the same proportion of agricultural and food ingredients as before, but the amount of semiprocessed foodstuffs has increased relative to the amount of agricultural inputs. The proportion of costs of containers and packaging more than doubled, with even greater increases observed for glass, metal, foil, and plastic materials. Transportation costs declined slightly relative to total costs, though proportionately more truck and air modes are now being utilized. Processors now buy relatively more distributional and other business services.

Overall, food processors have raised their prices faster than the increase in farm prices. However, when agricultural prices rise sharply, processors absorb part of the increase. Conversely, when farm prices decline or remain steady, food processors tend to raise prices and widen their margins.

5
Business Organization of Food Processing

T his chapter looks at what is commonly called the industrial structure of the food processing industries. In particular, the focus will be on the numbers and sizes of establishments and companies. The term *establishment* covers plants, warehouses, stores, R&D centers, and all other separate places of business. Companies are legal entities that own one or more establishments. Whereas each establishment usually pursues only one line of business, larger companies usually have a principal activity and several secondary ones. Most small food processing companies have only one place of business—a single plant with adjacent or attached offices and storage areas.

Number and Sizes of Plants

The number of food processing plants counted by the Census Bureau in each census year from 1963 to 1982 is shown in table 5–1. From 37,521 U.S. operating plants in 1963, foods were processed in only 22,130 plants in 1982—a decrease of 41 percent in nineteen years. During the most recent census period (1977–1982), there was a *net* decrease of almost 4 percent per year. This figure masks the fact that over 100 new plants are built each year for food processing, so during 1977–1982 about 1,000 plants were closed on average each year. Of course, such a high rate and number of plant closings cannot continue much longer, but it is likely that there will be only 12,000–14,000 plants by the year 2000.

In the rest of manufacturing, the number of plants has increased each year since 1963. As a result, the number of food processing plants represents a shrinking share of the manufacturing sector—from 12.3 percent in 1963 to 6.4 percent in 1982. The trend in processing plant numbers also runs counter to trends in the rest of the food system (except for agriculture). The number of food warehouses, eating and drinking places, and food stores has as a group remained fairly constant from 1963 to 1982 (table 5–1).

Most food processing plants are quite small (table 5–2). About half of all food processing plants had fewer than 20 employees in 1982. Many of the smallest plants are open for only a few weeks or months of the year,

Table 5–1
Number of U.S. Food Marketing Establishments, 1963–1982

Year	Food Processing	Grocery Wholesaling	Eating and Drinking Places[a]	Food Retailing	Total
			Number		
1963	37,521	41,890	334,481	319,433	733,325
1967	32,517	40,005	271,182	294,243	637,947
1972	28,193	38,531	359,524	267,352	693,420
1977	26,656	37,960	368,066	252,853	685,135
1982	22,130	38,516	379,444	241,737	684,084

Source: National Economics Division (1987:61).

[a]Excludes all "noncommercial" eating facilities and such commercial outlets as hotel restaurants, department store coffee shops, and food concessions in sports facilities. Noncommercial eating facilities numbered over 397,000 in 1982 and over 343,000 in 1977. Also excludes all plants and stores run entirely by family labor unless they were incorporated; this category amounted to about 7,000 processing plants and 75,000 food stores in 1982.

Table 5–2
Size Distribution of Food Processing Plants, 1963 and 1982

Size Category	1963		1982	
	Number of Plants	Proportion in Category	Number of Plants	Proportion in Category
	Number	Percent	Number	Percent
1 to 19 employees	23,412	62.4	11,449	51.7
20 to 49 employees	6,862	18.3	4,383	19.8
50 to 99 employees	3,365	9.0	2,609	11.8
100 to 249 employees	2,768	7.4	2,310	10.4
250 to 999 employees	1,024	2.7	1,270	5.7
1000 employees or more	96	0.3	109	0.5
Total	37,521	100.0	22,130	100.0

Source: U.S. Bureau of the Census, *1982 Census of Manufactures*, General Summary (Part 2) and previous years.

often with the assistance of unpaid family labor (family workers are not counted as employees unless paid salaries). At the other end of the spectrum, there were 3,689 plants in 1982 with an annual average employment of 100 persons or more; these large plants constituted about one-sixth of the total number. Food processing actually has a higher proportion of large-size plants (over 99 employees) than the rest of manufacturing where only 10 percent of the plants are large. Since 1963, the number of large plants in food processing has grown relative to the number of small plants with 250 or more employees.

Although there are relatively few of them, the largest food processing plants account for the lion's share of industry shipments and employment (table 5–3). In 1982 plants with 100 or more employees accounted for 73 percent of the value of shipments and 72 percent total employment. The fact that the large plants have about the same share of shipments and employment indicates that their average labor productivity is about the same

Table 5–3
Proportion of Output and Employment in Food Processing Plants, by Size Category, 1963 and 1982

Size Category	1963		1982	
	Shipments	Employment	Shipments	Employment
	Percent			
1 to 19 employees	7.3	9.2	4.3	5.2
20 to 49 employees	12.6	13.2	9.8	9.4
50 to 99 employees	15.4	14.3	13.9	12.3
100 to 249 employees	25.8	25.8	24.3	24.2
250 to 999 employees	27.2	26.8	34.5	37.2
1000 employees or more	11.8	10.8	13.2	11.7
Total	100.0	100.0	100.0	100.0
	Millions			
Total	$68,466[a]	1.64[b]	$280,529[a]	1.49[b]

Source: U.S. Bureau of the Census, *1982 Census of Manufactures*, General Summary (Part 2) and previous years.
[a]Measured in millions of dollars.
[b]Measured in millions.

as the smaller plants. (The plants with 1–19 employees have distinctly lower productivity whereas the plants with 50–99 employees have the highest.) These differences in labor productivity could be due to efficiency or to differences in product mix among plant size classes. The situation in 1963 was slightly different. Plants with 100 or more employees accounted for 65 percent of shipments and 63 percent of employment. All plant categories with 50 or more employees displayed average or above-average productivity (the highest was for plants with 1,000 employees or more).

Number and Size of Companies

The number of food processors has declined drastically in every census year since 1947. From over 42,000 companies in 1947, the net number of food processing companies had declined by over 25,000 companies by 1982 or by 60 percent (table 5–4). (The definition of food processing company used here is any corporation, cooperative, partnership, or proprietorship that manages at least one food processing plant.) Moreover, the rate of decline was faster after 1963 than before—a 3.6 percent annual loss between 1963 and 1982 as compared to a 1.7 percent annual decrease between 1947 and 1963. As will be shown later, the highest rates of disappearance occurred during periods of intense merger activity, especially 1965–1970 and 1979 to the present. Because of the very high numbers of mergers since 1982 involving two food processing companies, it is likely that only 13,000 to 14,000 food processors remain today (1987).

The decline in food processors has occurred at a time when the number of all other manufacturing firms was increasing. On average, in the rest of the manufacturing sector the net number of company formation increased by an average of 1.2 percent per year since 1947, though the rate was only 0.6 percent per year since 1963. It is noteworthy that company formations in manufacturing also faltered during the two peak periods of merger activity (1963–1967 and 1977–1982). However, the change in food processing company numbers does parallel the trends in the other segments of the food system—agriculture, food wholesaling, food retailing, and even foodservice (appendix table A8). Therefore, it is likely that increasing economies of firm operation combined with the relatively slower growth of foods purchased have contributed to the decline in company numbers throughout the food system.

One result of declining company numbers is increasing consolidation of sales and assets among fewer and fewer firms. As shown in figure 5–1, the top 50 food processors (ranked by asset size) owned an increasing share of the depreciated book assets of all food processors (that is, companies whose

Table 5–4
Number of U.S. Food Processing Companies, Census Years, 1947–1982

Year	Companies[a]		Average Compounded Annual Change from Previous Year	
	Food	Rest of Manufacturing	Food	Rest of Manufacturing
	- - Number - -		- - Percent - -	
1947	42,469E	183,482E	- -	- -
1954	38,557E	220,279E	-1.37	+2.65
1958	36,545	232,961	-1.33	+1.41[b]
1963	32,617	252,530	-2.25	+1.63
1967	26,549	242,722	-4.84	-0.99
1972	22,172	245,254	-3.68	+0.21
1977	20,616	279,777	-1.44	+2.67
1982	16,813	281,616	-4.16	+0.13
1987	13,600E	- -	-4.16	- -
Change:				
1947-63	-9,852	+69,048	-1.66	+2.02
1963-82	-15,804	+29,086	-3.55	+0.58
1947-82	-25,656	+98,134	-2.68	+1.23

Sources: Data from Connor (1982b:Table 8) and *1982 Census of Manufactures.*

E = Estimated from 1977–1982 rate of change.

— = Not available.

[a]From 1947 to 1963, the number of different legal entities (corporations, partnerships, proprietorships, cooperatives, trusts, and others) owning one or more plants in any one of the forty-seven SIC food industries; companies with plants in two food industries are counted twice. From 1967 on, the table shows the number of unduplicated companies. Duplication was 947, 1154, 1416, and 1072 in 1967, 1972, 1977, and 1982, respectively. The "rest of manufacturing" is adjusted upward to reflect the number of fluid milk companies formerly excluded from manufacturing and downward by the number of unrefined fats and oils companies.

[b]Part of this increase is due to the redefinition of logging camps from the forestry sector to the manufacturing sector in 1958.

principal business is food processing). In 1950 the top 50 firms owned only 36 percent of all such assets; by 1969 their share had risen to 53 percent and by 1987 to 75 percent. In 1987 the top 200 firms (which represented only 1 percent of all food processors) owned 88 percent of all food-processing assets.[6] The rate of increase in the concentration of asset ownership has been so high since 1950 that, should the rate be sustained, the top 50 will control at least 90 percent of industry assets by the year 2000.

Because the leading food processing firms are more heavily capitalized than smaller processors, asset concentration tends to be higher than sales concentration, though the same trends are evident. U.S. Census Bureau data show that the top 50 processors (ranked by sales in food processing)

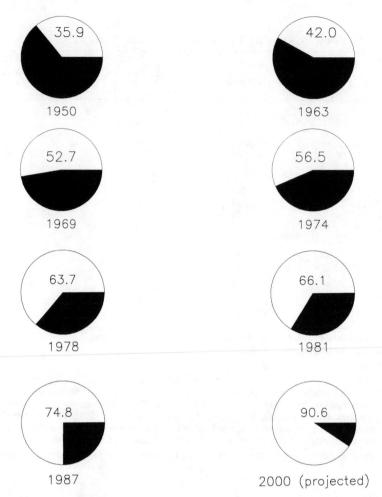

Figure 5–1. Percentage of Food Processing Assets Owned by the Fifty Largest Firms, 1950–1987

Sources: Data from Internal Revenue Service, *Source Book of Corporation Income Tax Returns* and special tabulations of the U.S. Bureau of the Census, *Quarterly Financial Report* (Second Quarter 1987 and previous reports).

Note: Data for years 1950 to 1974 were developed from published reports of the Internal Revenue Service using a method explained in Connor (1982b:38). Data for the years 1978, 1981, and 1987 were provided by a special tabulation by the Quarterly Financial Reports Program of the U.S. Bureau of the Census (formerly in the Federal Trade Commission). For 1987 only , new coding procedures required combining the assets of food and tobacco manufacturing firms. The projection for the year 2000 is an average of five linear regressions of asset concentration on time; five initial years (1950, 1963, 1974, 1978) were tested using from three to seven observations; the coefficient of determination ranged from 98.1 percent to 99.4 percent and the projected asset concentration ranged from 86.7 percent to 92.7 percent.

controlled 43 percent of all food processing sales in 1982 (table 5–5). That share increased about 11 percentage points or 34 percent from 1963. A list of the top 50 processors is shown in table 5–6.

U.S. sales concentration also increased in food wholesaling and foodservice in recent years, while it remained constant in food retailing. However, it is doubtful that such measures at the *national* level are very meaningful for food distributors. Most of the leading food processors sell most of their products nationally or across several regions, but leading food wholesalers and retailers operate at most in a few regions of the United States. Less than ten of the leading foodservice companies sell across all parts of the United States. Thus, sales concentration measured in approximately defined geographic and product *markets* is likely to show considerably higher levels.

Most data on market concentration derive from Census Bureau sales or shipments values. The most common measure is the four-firm concentration ratio; that is, the ratio of the market shares of the top four companies to total market sales. An analysis of four-firm seller concentration for about 150 food products in 1977 found that the average was about 48 percent (partially adjusted for subnational market areas and imports) (Connor 1982b:41–42). This was about equal to the average for the whole manufacturing sector, where the range ran from a high of 82 percent for tobacco manufacturing to a low of 27 percent for apparel manufacturing.

Table 5–5
Aggregate Sales Concentration in Food Marketing, Census Years, 1963–1982
(percentage share of market controlled by top firms)

Year	Share of Market Controlled by Top Firms			
	Top 50 Processing Firms	Top 50 Wholesaling Firms	Top 20 Retailing Firms	Top 50 Foodservice Firms
	Percent			
1963	32.0E	- -	34.0	- -
1967	35.0	- -	34.4	- -
1972	38.0	48.0	34.8	13.3
1977	40.0	57.0	34.5	17.8
1982	43.0	64.0	34.9	20.2

Source: National Economics Division (1987).
E = Estimated.
— = Not available.

Table 5–6
U.S. Sales of Top Fifty Food Processing Companies, 1984 and 1985

Company	1984	1985
	Million Dollars	
General Foods (Philip Morris)	8,600	9,020
Beatrice Foods	5,840	8,130
RJR-Nabisco	4,700	8,000
Kraft, Inc. (Dart & Kraft)	6,800	7,100
Coca-Cola Company	6,270	6,830
Anheuser-Busch	6,340	6,820
PepsiCo, Inc.	5,620	5,970
Sara Lee Corporation	5,060	5,950
Borden, Inc.	4,570	4,720
H.J. Heinz Company	3,950	4,040
Campbell Soup Company	3,650	3,980
Philip Morris Companies, Inc. (Philip Morris)	3,660	3,590
ConAgra	1,430	3,560
Ralston-Purina	1,880	3,550
Kellogg Company	2,600	2,930
Nestlé Enterprises, Inc. (Nestlé, SA)	2,700	2,880
Proctor & Gamble	2,460	2,810
General Mills	2,710	2,770
Quaker Oats Company	2,560	2,750
C.P.C. International, Inc.	2,550	2,520
Pillsbury Company	1,790	2,410
Hershey Foods Corporation	1,840	1,990
United Brands Company	1,920	1,900
Anderson Clayton	1,400	1,750
Wilson Foods Corporation	1,880	1,530
George A. Hormel and Company	1,450	1,500
Strohs Brewery Company	1,500	1,500
I.C. Industries	1,250	1,380
G. Heilman Brewing Company	1,340	1,330
Thomas J. Lipton, Inc. (Unilever, Ltd.)	1,140	1,270
Tyson Foods, Inc.	750	1,400
Adolph Coors Company	948	1,070
Dean Foods Company	923	1,030
American Home Products	996	1,020
Keebler Company	876	939
McCormick and Company, Inc.	747	826
The Southland Corporation	725	803
Interstate Bakeries Corporation	686	704
Smithfield Foods	542	669
Thorn Apple Valley, Inc.	664	659
Curtice-Burns, Inc.	612	636
Flowers Industries, Inc.	603	626
Ocean Spray Cranberries, Inc.	466	542
Cadbury Schweppes, Inc. (Cadbury Schweppes, Ltd.)	564	512
American Brands, Inc.	494	510
Winn Enterprises	411	502
Universal Foods Corporation	433	493
SCM Corporation	393	422
S.S. Pierce Company	377	404
Gerber Products	406	401

Source: National Economics Division (1987:64).

Concentration in food processing has trended slowly upward over time. Between 1963 and 1982, average market concentration in food processing rose about 10 percent, but the increase differed considerably by type of product. In general, markets for industrial foodstuffs or highly standardized consumer foods showed a slight decline in concentration, whereas industries that market highly advertised consumer products experienced twice the average increase in concentration (Marion & NC-117 Committee 1986:212–13). Other evidence suggests that brand loyalty created by advertising boosts the market shares of leading brands and acts as a barrier to new competition. The principle holds for all manufacturing as well as food processing (Mueller & Rogers 1984).

Market concentration data for other stages of the food marketing system are hard to come by, except for grocery retailing, but the little there is suggests that there is quite concentrated ownership among distributors of processed foods. For grocery retailing the appropriate level of market measurement is the metropolitan area, the territory within which decisions are made about pricing, advertising, and investments. The city concentration of sales among the four leading grocery retailers averaged 58 percent in 1982 (table 5–7). Metropolitan-area concentration rose 17 percent from 1963 to 1982, with most of the increase occurring since the mid 1970s when federal merger enforcement relaxed.

A USDA study of 1972 four-firm concentration among general-line grocery wholesalers in fourteen grocery-marketing areas found that average concentration was 73 percent (Marion & NC-117 Committee 1986:348). A grocery-marketing area was defined as an area of about 200 or more miles in radius with a large metropolitan center, such as the eastern third of Colorado. Specialty wholesalers (meat, produce, confectionery, etc.) ranged somewhat lower, generally between 35 and 60 percent. No comparable data

Table 5–7
Average Four-Firm Concentration in Food Retailing, All SMSAs and 173 Matched SMSAs, 1958–1982

Item	1958	1963	1967	1972	1977	1982
			Percent			
All SMSAs	49.3	49.7	50.0	52.4	56.3	58.3
173 SMSAs[a]	48.7	49.4	50.1	52.2	56.4	58.7

Source: National Economics Division (1987:29).
[a]Identity remains unchanged over 1958–1982.

are available for local foodservice markets, but procurement of foodservice operators generally occurs through local specialty wholesalers or, in the case of large chains, through direct contracts with processors by national representatives of the chain.

In sum, the degree of sales concentration in most segments of the food distribution industries is from moderate to high levels in appropriately defined markets. Food processors must sell their products to a decreasing number of relatively large distributors (except for the few processors that sell direct to consumer buying clubs or by mail-order catalogs). This simplifies contacting customers but can raise the bargaining power of distributors in their dealings with processors.

Mergers

The pace of merger activity in food processing quickened in the 1980s. Large "mega mergers" have become more common, as have a panopoly of novel merger methods. As will be seen, the recent merger wave represents a dramatic acceleration of a long-term trend. Mergers have had profound effects on the number and size differences among food processors, business practices in the industry, and the performance of the economy in general.

The best measure of the size of merger activity is the value of assets acquired, particularly the market value of those assets. However, purchase values are often very difficult to compute because of the complex terms of large transactions or because of secrecy. So figure 5–2 uses the somewhat more accessible book assets figures of firms in the year prior to being acquired, an asset value typically quite a bit lower than the exchange value of the assets. Moreover, data collection is restricted to only companies with at least $10 million in book assets, a cutoff that still captures over 90 percent of the value of all assets acquired. (The data for years 1980–1985 were book asset values or, where those were available, consideration paid; these data are probably somewhat less complete than the data up to 1979.)

The striking feature of the lines in figure 5–2 is the seemingly inexorable rise in acquisition activity in each of the five-year periods shown, except for the pause in the early 1970s. Less than $200 million per year in assets of large food processing companies were acquired up through the mid-1960s. During the "conglomerate merger wave" of the late 1960s, when such companies as ITT, LTV, and SCM were making large, unrelated acquisitions, mergers averaged nearly $900 million per year. Finally, after a brief hiatus in the early 1970s, merger activity exploded again. In the early 1980s, assets worth over $5 billion per year were being acquired, a figure that is probably underestimated. So far, merger activity in 1986 and 1987 appears to be running at levels higher than that of the early 1980s. Figure 5–2 also shows

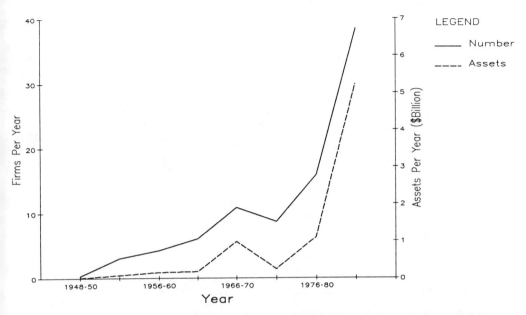

Figure 5–2. Large Food and Tobacco Processing Companies Acquired, Five-Year Averages, 1948–1985

Sources: Connor et al. (1985:Figure 4–4) and Connor and Geithman (1988).

Note: Companies with $10 million in book assets. For 1980–1985, total assets or consideration paid, which was available for 49 percent of the companies acquired.

that the number of large food processors acquired per year rose from an average of six in 1961–1965 to over 38 per year in 1981–1985.

One disadvantage of using book assets is that they are affected by inflation. Deflating assets is a daunting task, but one such analysis converted assets acquired to a 1981–1984 value base (Marion & NC-117 Committee 1986:238). This analysis found that about $1.2 billion of assets were acquired per year during 1961–1965 measured in 1981—1984 dollars. Thus, the 1981–1985 acquisition rate of $4.4 billion was nearly four times higher than the rate in the 1961–1965 period in real terms.

Another method of "deflating" assets of acquired companies is shown in figure 5–3. Here, the value of assets acquired is divided by the total book assets of all food processing companies. Thus, in 1961–1965 about 0.6 percent of all assets "available" for acquisition were actually acquired on average each year (or 3.0 percent for the whole period). Of course, a large portion of the assets of "available" food processors are assets of very large firms, family-owned companies, wholly owned foreign subsidiaries, or other companies that are unlikely merger targets. The graph shows that in relative

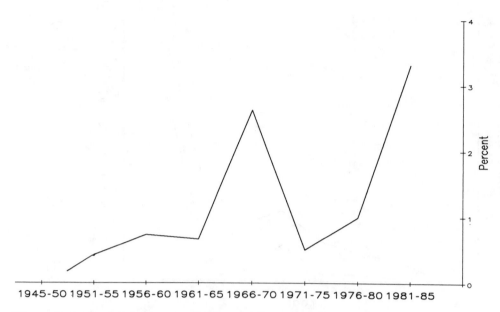

Figure 5–3. Acquired Assets of Large Food and Tobacco Processing Companies Relative to Total Food Manufacturers' Assets, Five-Year Averages, 1948–1985

Sources: Connor et al. (1985:Table C–11) and Connor and Geithman (1988).

terms 1966–1970 and 1981—1985 were extraordinary merger periods; in each merger wave at least 2.5 percent of all assets were acquired. The proportion of merged assets in 1981–1985 was six times the proportion in 1961–1965.

Why are food processing companies being acquired at such a rapid rate? There are many potential motives for merger, but three that seem best documented in the case of food processing are growth, diversification, and profits (Connor et al. 1981:185–95). Mergers are a fast route to broadening a firm's product line, and one that may appear to be cheaper than building new capacity. In addition, food processors tend to acquire other food processors that are growing relatively fast and are in the same marketing channels with the same sets of customers. They also tend to acquire more frequently if they have considerable marketing or technological expertise, as evidenced by relatively high advertising or R&D expenditures.

Profit expectations appear to play a subtle and hard-to-measure role in the acquisition process. High growth rates in target firms or industries may serve as close indicators of future profitability, so the two measures are difficult to disentangle empirically. There is weak evidence that high profits in the target industry (compared to the industry of the acquiring company) foster mergers. However, relatively steady profits in the target industry may have the same effect; in any case, the profits and sales of companies operating in two or more markets are inherently more stable than single-market firms. Managers and stockholders seem to prefer to invest in companies with less year-to-year movements in profits. Thus, both the prospect of profits that are higher and less risky appear to induce mergers.

The profit characteristics of food processing fit this description. Figure 5–4 shows the trend in after-tax profitability (relative to stockholders' equity) of food processors since 1971. Economists generally favor profits on equity as a measure of return to investors, and it is generally insensitive to the inflation rate. Since the late 1960s, the profit rate of food processors has been above that of the rest of manufacturing in most years. Indeed, the gap appears to widen in recent years; in the early 1980s, profit rates of food processors were 4 percentage points higher (38 percent higher) than the rates of all other manufacturers (appendix table A9). Moreover, food processors'

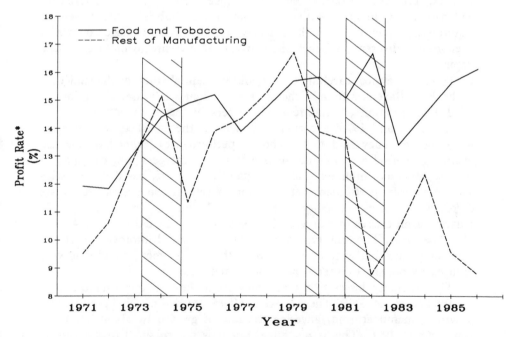

Figure 5–4. Profits of Food and Tobacco Processors, 1971–1986

Source: Data from Appendix Table A9.
Recession periods are shaded.
*After-tax profits over stockholders' equity.

profits are more stable, especially during recession periods. For example, from 1979 to 1982, during which the United States experienced two recessions, profits in the rest of manufacturing plunged from 16.7 percent of stockholders' equity to 8.7 percent—a drop of 52 percent in three years. However, food processors' profits actually rose slightly during the same period (even the drop in 1983 was only 15 percent below the 1979 level). The high level and enviable stability of profits certainly adds to the motives for mergers of food processors. As will be discussed later, the high rates of foreign investment into the United States, instigated in part by the low value of the dollar from 1972 to 1982, added fuel to merger fires.

It is important to emphasize that although high *expected* profits are a motive for merger, in the long run and on average these expectations are not realized (Connor & Geithman 1988). Prior to acquisition, companies acquired tend to be well managed with growth rates and profit rates above comparable firms, but after acquisition these units tend to become average or below-average performers. To put it plainly, the vaunted benefits of "synergy" do not appear on average. On the contrary, for most types of mergers, efficiency losses eventually accrue. The principal alternative explanation for merger motives is "managerial hubris"—the belief by acquirers that they can beat the markets and effectively manage companies of enormous diversity, a belief often driven by a desire to build corporate empires.

Perhaps the most carefully crafted and influential study of the subject is the book by Ravenscraft and Scherer (1987). Their study used exceptionally detailed information on hundreds of mergers in the manufacturing sector between 1962 and 1976, a period that includes the so-called conglomerate merger wave. They find that economic performance declined during the postmerger period for three out of five classes of mergers. For example, in the case of units purchased and subsequently spun off, based on the sales price and profit performance at the time of sell-off (on average ten years after merger), efficiency losses were $1.8–2.2 billion per year in 1975–1977 dollars; for all classes of mergers, the losses were estimated to be $2.4—3.3 billion per year. The only type of mergers that showed improved efficiency were companies that were of equal size at the time of merger and that were financed by pooling-of-interest accounting methods.

The efficiency losses to the economy from these mergers amounted to 0.6–0.8 percent of GNP. These losses in effect retarded national productivity growth in manufacturing, lowering the rate of growth by about one-tenth from 1968 to 1976. This is not huge, but it is not so small that it can be ignored either.

Perhaps of equal interest, Ravenscraft and Scherer (1987) found that mergers tended to reduce R&D outlays in the acquired units in the postmerger period. In their sample, manufacturing R&D expenditures fell by 5 percent by the end of the study period. From other research, it is known that R&D is positively related to U.S. productivity increases in all sectors. Therefore, in addition to the impact of efficiency losses due to mergers on productivity, reduced R&D due to mergers lowered U.S. productivity change by about 0.03 percentage points per year; that was about one-thirty-third of the productivity slowdown that occurred in the 1970s. Again, this impact is small, but hardly negligible.

To sum up, manufacturing mergers from 1962 to 1976 *were* profitable on average, but acquired units tended to drop from high to below-average rates of financial performance. Ravenscraft and Scherer calculate that the internal, after-tax return on investment from mergers was 6.05 percent of assets. This return on investment is about half the "hurdle rate" used by most larger corporations in the 1960s to decide whether to go ahead on a proposed investment; it is also substantially below the return investors earned from a portfolio of the Standard and Poor's 500 in the same period. Thus, acquiring managers, in the heat of the chase, ended up paying too much for their quarry and, after bagging it, eviscerated rather than preserved it. Unfortunately, it is the stockholders who end up paying for this sport.

Location of Company Headquarters

The location of production facilities will be discussed in Part III, but this section focuses on the headquarters of major food companies. Only a small portion of all food processing firms have separate administrative establishments. In 1982 only 989 administrative establishments were operated by the 16,800 food processing companies in the United States. (appendix table A10), so at most 6 percent of all processors have separate headquarters' buildings. However, the number of headquarters increased from about 600 in 1963, as has the number of office, clerical, and managerial employees working in headquarters.

Food processing has a somewhat rural image, but this image is at best outdated. In Indiana, not only are most food-processing shipments from plants in metropolitan areas, but a higher proportion of food plants are located there than are other manufacturing plants (Connor 1987). Moreover, as can be seen in table 5–8, the headquarters of the largest food processing companies and their major divisions are predominately located in the nation's major metropolitan areas. In 1986 nearly half of the largest food processing units (each of which had sales of $500 million or more) had their principal offices in the ten largest cities; about three-fourths are located in the fifty largest metropolitan areas. Although smaller food processors may well be located primarily in rural areas, the larger companies appear to be as urbanized as manufacturers generally.

Table 5–8
Location of Company or Subsidiary Headquarters, Largest Food Processing Units, 1986

1985 Rank	Metropolitan Statistical Area	Number of Headquarters	Companies or Divisions[a]
1	New York	23	United Brands, General Foods, Borden, Philip Morris, Kane Miller, Hanson Inds., Allied-Lyons, Norton Simon, Amstar, CPC Int'l., Continental Grain, Pepsico, Continental Baking, W.R. Grace, American Brands, W.M. Wrigley, Tate & Lyle, Seagram, National Distillers, Nestle Foods, T.J. Lipton, Unilever USA, Nabisco Brands.
2	Los Angeles	4	Golden State Foods, Carnation, Winn, Knudsen.
3	Chicago	9	Esmark, Beatrice, John Morell, Libby, Sara Lee, Kraft, Dean Foods, Quaker Oats, Keebler.
4	San Francisco-Oakland	4	Del Monte, Tri-Valley, C&H Sugar, Hills Bros.
5	Philadelphia	1	Campbell Soup.
6	Detroit	5	Thorn Apple Valley, Hygrade, Michigan Milk Producers, Stroh Brewery, Hiram Walker.
7	Boston	3	H.P. Hood, Ocean-Spray, General Cinema.
8	Houston	3	Coca-Cola Foods, Riviana Foods, Anderson-Clayton.
9	Dallas-Fort Worth	3	Swift, Campbell Taggert, Frito-Lay.
10	Washington, DC	3	Smithfield Foods, Mars, Allegheny Beverage.
11	Miami	0	
12	Cleveland	1	Stouffer.
13	Atlanta	2	Coca-Cola, Gold Kist.
14	St. Louis	4	Pet, Ralston Purina, Anheuser Busch, Conagra Frozen Foods.
15	Pittsburgh	1	H.J. Heinz.
16	Minneapolis	5	Cargill, Land O'lakes, Pillsbury, General Mills, Int'l. Multifoods.
17	Baltimore	1	McCormick & Co.
18	Seattle-Tacoma	1	Darigold.
19	San Diego	0	
20	Tampa-St. Petersburg	0	
21	Phoenix	0	
22	Denver	2	Adolph Coors, Litvac Meat.
23	Cincinatti	1	Procter & Gamble.
24	Milwaukee	2	Miller Brewing, Pabst Brewing.
25	Kansas City, MO	2	Farmland, Interstate Bakeries.

Table 5–8 continued

1985 Rank	Metropolitan Statistical Area	Number of Headquarters	Companies or Divisions[a]
26	Portland, OR	0	
27	New Orleans	0	
28	Norfolk, VA	0	
29	Columbus, OH	1	Big Bear Stores.
30	Sacramento, CA	0	
31	San Antonio	0	
32	Indianapolis	0	
33	Buffalo	1	Rich Foods.
34	Providence, RI	0	
35	Charlotte, NC	1	Imasco, USA.
36	Hartford, CN	0	
37	Salt Lake City	0	
38	Rochester, NY	1	Curtice-Burns.
39	Oklahoma City	1	Wilson Foods.
40	Louisville, KY	3	Armour Foods, Dairymen, Inc., Brown-Forman.
41	Memphis, TN	2	Federal, Valmac.
42	Dayton, OH	0	
43	Nashville, TN	0	
44	Birmingham, AL	0	
45	Greensboro, NC	1	RJR Nabisco.
46	Orlando, FL	0	
47	Albany, NY	0	
48	Jacksonville, FL	0	
49	Honolulu	0	
50	Richmond, VA	0	
	Other cities	34	
	Total	125	

Source: Data from *Ward's Directory of Private and Public Companies*, 1977.
[a]Each had 1986 sales of about $500 million or more.

Technical Research Facilities

The Census of Manufactures recorded 208 physically separate research and development (R&D) facilities in 1982, employing 7,000 workers primarily engaged in food processing work (appendix table A10). This source undercounts the number of R&D workers in industry. Many companies have quality control and testing laboratories located in production facilities whereas other companies assign their R&D activities to headquarters complexes, but employment in these facilities is not separately recorded. (In addition, researchers and technicians are employed in electronic data processing centers, of which food processors operated 288 in 1982.) In many small food processing companies, owners, plant managers, and engineers become involved in making improvements in plant and equipment, a form of R&D that goes completely unrecorded by the Census Bureau. More complete information on scientists and engineers involved in food-related R&D is given in the following chapter.

Summary

The food processing industries have undergone significant changes in their industrial organization. The number of food processing plants and companies has fallen sharply in recent decades. To cite one statistic, the number of food processing firms declined by almost 4 percent per year since 1963, down to an historic low of less than 14,000 companies in the late 1980s. Because smaller food processors have borne the brunt of this decline, industrial concentration has risen. In 1963 the fifty largest food processors owned 42 percent of all food processing assets, but by 1987 the figure had climbed to an enormous 75 percent share. Concentration in specific processed food markets also rose, particularly where the products are highly advertised consumer goods.

Perhaps the chief mechanism responsible for structural change in food processing since the early 1960s is mergers and acquisitions. The volume of acquisitions of food processing companies in the early 1980s was at least four times the amount in the early 1960s. In the early 1980s food processors with book values of more than $7 billion were being acquired each year. The relatively high profitability of the food processing companies appears to be a major motive for mergers. But recent research indicates that most types of mergers eventually turn out to be relatively poor investments, probably because of mismanagement by acquiring firms. Mergers are responsible for declining R&D outlays in the postmerger units and consequently, retarded national productivity growth.

6
Technological Change

Technological change is a complex, multistage, and typically lengthy process. The process begins with an individual's intuition that some human need could be satisfied by a new product or that an existing product could be made with longer storability, less waste, reduced quality variability, or in a more efficient manner. Often at this first stage there is a glimmer of understanding as to what technical approach will result in the new product or process. After this initial insight or discovery, the stage of invention begins. Through a process of basic research, a feasible method is developed to produce the new product or implement the new process. It is at this stage, paper plans, small-scale models, or laboratory experiments are developed from the application scientific knowledge that yield a patentable invention. At this point technological change evolves from inventive to innovative activity. During the innovation stage, the invention is "scaled up" to make the process faster and more efficient or alternative production methods are tried to find the best method of manufacturing the new product. The result, if successful (and many are not), is a commercially available new ingredient, component, machine, or finished product. The final stage is diffusion of the innovation, that is, commercial adoption of the new product or process as a replacement (sometimes partial) for an existing technology. For major technological improvements, historical case studies indicate that diffusion typically takes ten to twenty years.

How does technological change reveal itself? How is it measured? There are no systematic methods of measuring the amount of technological inspiration; only anecdotal evidence from biographies of inventors, company histories, or other historical case studies can illuminate such discoveries. Such evidence is of doubtful usefulness for developing generalizations about the discovery process.

Better proxies are available for the rate of technological innovation. The most common measures of innovative activity are various data series that total up resources committed to R&D activity. Such input-type measures include R&D expenditures and scientists and engineers employed in the industry. In addition, there are output-type measures such as patents issued or scientific publications assigned to companies in the industry. Often these data are expressed as intensities; that is, as percentages of total industry sales, industry employment, and so forth. This stage mainly establishes technical feasibility of an innovation.

The commercialization stage of technological change differs according to whether one considers product or process development. New product introductions are one rather ambiguous measure of technological change. More direct measures of quality improvement that can accurately predict consumer acceptance are elusive. As for new process introductions, only rather indirect measures are available such as rates of capital investment, improved labor quality, and productivity increases. Finally, there are studies available of diffusion rates for specific new products or processes that measure the speed of adoption in an industry from the time of first commercial availability.

Innovative Activity in Food Processing

The most widely used indicator of innovative activity is R&D expenditures, and the best source of such information is the annual National Science Foundation survey. The NSF data include both private R&D expenditures (those made from company funds) and government R&D grants and awards to private firms. Government grants are very important in the defense-related industries but are practically zero in food processing. In 1984 food processors spent $834 million on R&D, up from $259 million in 1972 and $130 million in 1963 (table 6–1). From 1963 to 1984 R&D expenditures by companies in all industries (almost all are manufacturing) grew by an impressive 463 percent, or by an average of 8.6 percent per year; during the same period R&D expenditures by food processing companies grew even faster—at 9.3 percent per year. Yet, the amount of R&D expended in the food industries is a tiny portion of total private-sector R&D; in 1963 food R&D was 1.0 percent of the total, rose to a peak of 1.4 percent in 1977, and fell to 1.2 percent by 1984.

According to the NSF, there were about 1,200 firms with an R&D program in the food processing industries in 1982. However, R&D activity is highly concentrated in a few large firms. Recall that only 208 companies maintain separate R&D labs. Almost 70 percent of R&D funds in industry were expended by the top 20 food R&D programs; alternatively, 65 percent of all R&D was accounted for by those food processors with $10 million or more in 1983 sales.

Over 95 percent of industrially sponsored R&D is of the applied or developmental type, geared toward product development, process engineering, and quality control (table 6–1). Basic research in the food processing industries has varied from about 5 percent to 9 percent of the total in recent years, a ratio slightly but consistently above that for all industries. There is also a modest amount of more basic research on food science and engineering supported by federal government agencies (like the Agricultural Research

Table 6–1
R&D Expenditures by Industry, 1958–1984

Category	Year						
	1958	1963	1967	1972	1977	1982	1984

Million dollars

R&D expenditures:

Food processing	83	130	183	259	415	762	834
All industries	8,389	12,630	16,385	19,552	29,825	57,996	71,137

Percent of net sales

Food processing	0.3	0.4	0.5	0.4	0.4	0.4	0.4
All industries	3.8	4.5	4.2	3.4	2.9	3.8	3.8

Percent

Food processing:

Basic research	6.0	9.2	9.3	5.0	4.8	5.5E	6.6
Applied research	--	--	--	--	--	--	31.6
Development	--	--	--	--	--	--	61.8

All industry:

Basic research	3.5	4.1	3.8	3.0	3.1	3.2	3.5
Applied research	22.8	19.5	17.8	18.0	18.9	20.1	20.0
Development	73.7	76.4	78.4	79.0	78.1	75.8	76.5

Source: Data from National Science Foundation (1987).
— = Not available.
E = Estimated.

Service) and by the states through their support of state universities. In 1985 government-supported food science research amounted to $177 million, up from $67 million in 1973 (ESCOP 1988).

Impressive as these total R&D expenditures may seem, they are small in relation to sales or scientists supported (table 6–2). R&D expenditures in food processing have only just kept pace with total sales, representing just 0.4 percent of sales in all recent years and among the lowest ratios of any of the industry groups in manufacturing. Why are R&D expenditures such a small portion of sales in the food processing industries? One factor that can be dismissed is company size. As can be seen in table 6–3, food processing companies spent less on R&D relative to sales in *all* size classes. Indeed the discrepancy between food and other industries is especially wide for the largest-size companies; non-food-processing companies with 25,000 or more employees had an R&D intensity in 1984 over sixteen times as great as food

Table 6–2
R&D Expenditures in U.S. Manufacturing Industries, 1975, 1980, and 1984

Industry	Total R&D funds[b]			R&D funds relative to net sales		
	1975	1980	1984	1975	1980	1984
	Million dollars			Percent[c]		
Aircraft and missiles	5,713	9,198	16,076	12.7	13.7	16.9
Electrical equipment	5,105	9,175	15,122	6.5	6.6	7.2
Scientific instruments	1,173	3,029	4,910	5.9	7.5	9.3
Nonelectrical machinery	3,196	5,901	9,671	4.8	5.0	6.0
Chemicals, drugs, etc.	2,727	4,636	8,024	3.7	3.6	4.5
Motor vehicles & equipment	2,430	5,117	6,245	3.5	4.9	3.6
Rubber products	467	656	841	2.5	2.2	2.2
Stone, clay and glass	233	406	508	1.2	1.4	1.4
Fabricated metals	324	558	756	1.2	1.4	1.7
Paper products	249	495	782	0.9	1.0	1.2
Other manufacturing[a]	205	364	569	0.8	0.4	0.9
Primary metals	433	728	1,093	0.8	0.7	1.2
Wood and furniture	88	148	181	0.7	0.8	0.7
Petroleum	693	1,552	2,177	0.7	0.6	0.7
Textiles and clothing	70	115	139	0.4	0.4	0.5
Food manufacturing	335	620	834	0.4	0.4	0.4
Total	24,187	44,505	71,137	3.1	3.0	3.8

Source: Data from U.S. National Science Foundation, *Research and Development in Industry, 1984* and previous issues.
[a]Tobacco, leather, printing and publishing, and miscellaneous.
[b]Company funds and federal government awards to companies.
[c]Net sales of R&D-performing companies only.

processors of the same size. Another factor that does not contribute to the low R&D intensity of food processing is the amount spent per scientist and engineer employed; indeed, food processors are slightly ahead of other industries on this score.

Table 6–3
Company R&D Funds by Size of Company's Total Employment, 1984

Industry	Companies with Total Employment of					
	1 to 999	1,000 to 5,000	5,000 to 9,999	10,000 to 24,999	25,000 or more	Total
Million dollars						
Food processing	29	82	130	195	399	834
All industries	2,905	3,716	2,416	8,137	30,891	48,065
Million dollars per company						
Food processing	--	1.7	5.1	11.5	39.9	--
All industries	--	4.8	13.1	42.6	243.2	--
Percent R&D of net sales						
Food processing	0.21	0.28	0.39	0.45	0.53	0.43
All industries	1.83	1.73	1.22	2.09	8.69	2.94
R&D per scientist or engineer (dollars)						
Food processing	70,700	96,800	108,900	--	--	--
All industries	66,900	95,000	101,600	123,200	144,900	127,600

Source: Data from National Science Foundation (1987).
— = Not available.

So it appears that one factor that explains low R&D intensity is the relatively few scientists and engineers employed by food processing companies. This is borne out by data presented in table 6–4. (These data are quite compatible with Census Bureau data for 1982 that showed about 7,000 employees of food processing companies working in R&D establishments.) In 1985 there were almost 8,000 scientists and engineers employed by food processors, up from about 5,000 in 1963. From 1963 to 1972, the proportion of scientists and engineers in food processing rose, but since 1972 R&D employment growth in food processing has not kept up with the vast increases in other industries. In 1972, 1.9 percent of all private-sector scientists and engineers were employed by food processors, but that ratio had slipped to 1.4 percent by 1985. Although such employment has grown relative to total employment in industry generally, the ratio has remained virtually constant in the food industries at 7 per 1,000. Food scientists themselves are convinced that the present and future need for more scientists is large (Liska & Marion 1986; ESCOP 1988). Tremendous optimism is expressed about the discovery and commercial adoption of many new

Table 6–4
Scientists and Engineers Employed in Industry R&D, 1958–1985

Industry	1958	1963	1967	1972	1977	1982	1985
				Thousands (FTE)			
Food processing	4.8	5.1	6.1	6.5	6.9	7.4	7.9
All industry	234.8	327.3	367.2	350.2	382.8	509.8	570.3
				per 1000 employees[a]			
Food processing	6	7	7	7	7	6	7
All industry	21	28	27	24	27	33	36

Source: Data from National Science Foundation (1987).
[a]Employees of R&D-performing firms only.

ingredients, packaging materials, processes, and products by the food processing industries (Sanderson and Schweigert 1988). However, the demand for biological scientists and industrial engineers is also strong in other industries. Thus, the rising need for technically trained employees in the food industries will not guarantee that increases will actually occur.

There is a large supply of scientists and engineers (S/E) in the United States. In 1986, 4.6 million S/E were employed in the United States (with B.S. or equivalent training), or 3.6 percent of the workforce (National Science Foundation 1986; 1987). About 36 percent of all S/E were directly involved in R&D activities. The S/E supply has been rising at 7 percent per year since the mid-1970s, which is about three times faster than general U.S. employment. Clearly, the 8,000 scientists and engineers employed by food processors in R&D represent only a minor portion of all technically trained individuals working on food and agricultural matters. This statement is confirmed by a special 1986 survey by the National Science Foundation (table 6–5). The survey covers all persons trained as and still primarily working in science- and engineering-related occupations. At least 80,000 S/E were directly employed in food-related R&D in 1986, counting industry, academic, government, and self-employed persons. Another 68,000 S/E were engaged in other food-related activities such as production, quality control, general business management, government regulation, sales, and the like. Thus, altogether there were 148,000 S/E involved in food-related activities— approximately 3.2 percent of all U.S. scientists and engineers.

Of the S/E engaged in food R&D, the greatest portion are agricultural (33 percent) and other life scientists (27 percent). Engineers accounted for 16 percent, followed by mathematics/computer specialists (7 percent),

Table 6–5
Scientists and Engineers in United States, by Field of Interest, 1986

| | | Primary Field of Interest | | | |
| | Number [a] | Food [b] | | R&D in Food [c] | |
Field of Training	Employed	Number	Proportion of Field	Number	Proportion of Field
			Percent		Percent
Chemists	184,700	6,185	3.4	4,333	2.4
Other physical scientists	103,700	415	0.4	348	0.3
Mathematicians & statisticians	131,000	1,400	1.1	1,056	0.8
Computer specialists	562,600	5,200	1.0	4,342	0.8
Environmental scientists	111,300	2,200	2.0	1,312	1.2
Chemical engineers	149,000	3,200	2.2	1,832	1.2
Civil engineers	346,300	2,800	0.8	1,153	0.3
Electrical engineers	574,500	1,500	0.3	994	0.2
Industrial engineers	137,700	2,700	2.0	1,075	0.8
Mechanical engineers	492,600	4,500	0.9	2,773	0.6
Other engineers	740,000	9,000	1.2	5,057	0.7
Biologists	245,600	27,719	11.3	19,491	7.9
Biochemists	27,700	2,489	9.0	1,750	6.3
Agricultural scientists	103,300	58,383	56.5	26,055	25.2
Medical researchers	35,200	2,109	6.0	388	1.1
Psychologists	253,500	3,900	1.5	1,249	0.5
Economists	163,600	9,666	5.9	4,910	3.0
Other social scientists	264,200	4,234	1.6	1,913	0.7
Total	4,626,500	147,700	3.2	80,031	1.7

Source: Data from National Science Foundation, *The 1982 Postcensal Survey of Scientists and Engineers* (NSF 84-330) and *U.S. Scientists and Engineers: 1986* (NSF 87-322).

[a]Includes trained scientists and engineers engaged in science- or engineering-related occupations.

[b]"Food" was one of thirteen fields of interest. The others were energy, health, environment, national defense, transportation, communication, space, technology development, teaching, minerals, housing, and community development. "Agriculture", "fibers", and "flavorings" were not options for field of interest. Also, 22 percent of the survey respondents did not choose a primary field of interest.

[c]In all primary fields of interest, 36 percent of the S/E were directly involved in R&D work or in the management of R&D. In addition, this column includes S/E whose primary activities were teaching (8 percent), consulting (5 percent), and statistical or reporting (10 percent) on the assumption that such activities are partially or indirectly related to R&D. The proportion of all S/E in R&D-related activities in each field of training was calculated; that percentage was multiplied by the number of R&D primarily interested in food to arrive at the number in food R&D. These estimates are based on a 1986 sample of 100,000 S/E and are subject to sampling errors.

physical scientists (6 percent), and social scientists (10 percent). Except for agricultural and life scientists, no other field of training dedicates as much as 5 percent of its members to research on food-related subjects.

An important qualification must be made when examining R&D data. Not all the scientific knowledge used by the food processing industries originated from work done in the R&D laboratories of food processors.

Likewise, not all the inventions resulting from R&D work in the food processing industries has applications solely to processed foods. In other words, food processors both "export" and "import" innovations to and from other industries in the economy. Sometimes interindustry flows of knowledge occur through normal channels of scientific communication or through the regular movement of scientists between companies. In addition to serendipity and technological spillovers, such transfers occur through interindustry sales of capital goods, intermediate materials, or components that embody technological advances.

The first empirical study of the input-output relationships for R&D was by F. M. Scherer (1984). His study is based on 1974–1977 data on hundreds of corporations and thousands of patents. He calculated that 25 percent of all R&D expenditures in the economy involved new processes; most process innovations are appropriated by the originating industry and will influence postively productivity change in that industry. Another 7 percent of R&D innovations yielded "consumer" products (including those for the foodservice industry). However, the remaining 67 percent of R&D resulted in innovative capital goods or industrial materials and components. In this case, the productivity benefits of R&D will accrue to the "consuming" (that is, buying) industry or industries.

Appendix table A11 shows in matrix form the interindustry flows of R&D for the industries composing the food system. For the food processing industries a simplified breakdown of R&D flows is shown in table 6–6; the percentage breakdowns are expected to persist for many years beyond 1977. The main lesson is that, of the total innovations used by ("consumed" by) food processors, only about 50 percent were "originated" or developed by food processors (and of that 50 percent, probably less than half was developed by the same company that utilized the invention). The remaining half of all innovations adopted by food processors came from a wide array of technologically linked industries—machinery, paper, plastics, and many others. In addition, food processors "exported" nearly 40 percent of the innovations that resulted from their R&D to other sectors, including consumers in the form of new products. As will be explained further in Part II, these technological flows also vary considerably by specific food industry.

In addition to R&D inputs, innovation may be measured by the *results* from R&D, such as patents assigned to or publications by scientists working for food processing companies. An analysis of several hundred (process-type) patents with specific applications in six broadly defined industries issued over an eight-year period found that most patents (almost 90 percent) originated outside food processing firms (table 6–7). Indeed, individuals and foreign corporations accounted for over half of these patents, and the share of patents originating abroad was rising over time. While patent analyses have many limitations,[7] the general lessons are clear—most innovations

Table 6–6
Sources and Uses of R&D Funds in the Food Processing Industries, 1974–1977

Category	Annual R&D funds	Proportion of R&D	
		Originating in food processing	Used by food processors
	Mil. dollars	Percent	
Originating in food processing:[a]	445	100	--
Used by food processors	278	62	--
Used by other industries (including consumers)	167	38	--
Used by food processors:	523	--	100
From food processors	278	--	53
From food machinery manufacturing	64	--	12
From paper products manufacturing	26	--	5
From fabricated metals manufacturing	19	--	4
From motor vehicles manufacturing	26	--	5
From rubber and plastic manufacturing	19	--	4
From computers manufacturing	17	--	3
From other manufacturing	64	--	12
From non-manufacturing	1	--	0

Source: Data from Appendix Table A11.
[a]R&D sponsored by companies primarily classified as food processors and carried out by their own employees.

affecting food industry efficiency originate from a wide variety of sources outside the food processing industries. These technologies can be transferred through licensing agreements or through the purchase of efficiency-enhancing inputs.

The heterogeneous sources of food industry innovations is confirmed by an analysis of Putnam Award recipients (table 6–8). These awards, sponsored by the publisher of *Food Processing* magazine, are given to innovations already available on the market (thus well past the technical feasibility or patentable stage of development) judged to make significant contributions to the efficiency of food processing production. Again, food processors were responsible for only a small proportion (13 percent) of these awards. Over two-thirds of the awards were made to manufacturers other than food processors. Moreover, most of the award recipients were small firms; 44 percent had annual sales of under $10 million (Connor et al. 1985:308). A follow-up survey determined that about 25 percent of recipients that were small firms were acquired between 1970 and 1982, a rate of merger that was eight times the U.S. average.

Table 6–7
Sources of Patents for Inventions with Applications to Six Food Manufacturing Industries,[a] 1969–1977

Sources of Patents	Proportion of Total
	Percent
1. U.S. firms in same food industry	10.2
2. Other U.S. food manufacturers	2.4
3. U.S. food machinery manufacturers	18.2
4. Other U.S. firms	16.3
5. Non-U.S. corporations	21.2
6. Individuals	30.5
7. U.S. governments	0.7
8. Non-U.S. governments	0.4

Source: Data from Mueller, Culbertson, and Peckham (1982).
[a]The industries were Brewing, Meat, Dairy, Sugar, Poultry, and Starch.

Table 6–8
Recipients of the Putnam Award,[a] 1971–1977

Type of Recipient[b]	Proportion of Awards
	Percent
1. U.S. food processors and ingredient manufacturers	13
2. U.S. food machinery manufacturers	35
3. Plant maintenance, sanitation, and design firms	11
4. Instrument and controls manufacturers	9
5. Packaging and paper manufacturers	6
6. Chemical manufacturers	5
7. Other firms	19
8. Governments	2

Source: Data from Mueller, Culbertson, and Peckham (1982).
[a]Given for commercialized innovations that improve the efficiency of food processing operations.
[b]There were 265 recipients.

Commercial Adoption of Innovations

Food processors currently spend $6–7 billion per year on purchases of new plants, machinery, and equipment. These investments typically substitute more efficient inputs for those that embody out-of-date technologies. In addition, processors hire scientists, engineers, and skilled workmen who have more advanced training and skills. Hiring consultants, in-service training, and the acquisition of technologically progressive firms may also help improve industry productivity.

The information available on the most conventional measure of productivity change (labor productivity) shows significant improvements in the food processing industries. Labor productivity measures the change in real output (that is, deflated changes in the value of shipments or value added) relative to the change in the amount of labor employed. Labor productivity in food processing increased between 3 percent and 4 percent per year from 1963 to 1977 (table 6–9). These rates were slightly higher than those for the rest of manufacturing, though before 1963 the opposite was the case.

An USDA productivity-change series provides data from 1972 to 1985 (table 6–10). Here productivity is measured by the 1982 value added per full-time-equivalent (FTE) employee. During 1977–1982 labor productivity growth in food processing slowed considerably to one-third the rates observed between 1963 and 1977. Yet, compared to other food marketing industries, that was quite a good performance record. During the 1982–1984 recovery phase of the economy, labor productivity growth in food processing was

Table 6–9
Productivity Change, Food Processing and All Manufacturing, 1947–1982

Industry	1947-1954	1954-1958	1958-1963	1963-1967	1967-1972	1972-1977	1977-1982
	Percent per year						
Labor productivity:							
Food processing	1.4	2.8	4.5	3.5	4.1	2.8	2.2
All manufacturing	2.4	3.0	5.2	3.4	3.7	2.1	0.8
Multifactor productivity:							
Food processing	--	--	0.6	-0.3	0.5	-0.1	0.7
All manufacturing	1.7	0.2	4.0	1.8	2.2	1.9	0.0

Source: Data from Connor (1982b:Appendix Table 8), adapted from U.S. Census Bureau reports, and Lee (1986).

Table 6–10
Value Added per Full-Time-Equivalent Employee, 1972–1985

Sector	1972	1977	1982	1983	1984	1985
			1982 dollars			
Food marketing:	25,636	27,660	27,767	28,902	29,540	29,560
Processing	36,184	41,009	43,928	45,781	47,416	47,427
Retailing and wholesaling	25,557	29,498	27,022	28,066	28,972	28,892
Transportation	39,105	42,068	41,940	43,546	44,634	44,660
Eating and drinking places	12,822	13,787	13,773	14,069	14,654	14,652
Other supporting sectors	30,065	32,798	32,284	34,497	35,472	35,888
			Percent per year[a]			
Food marketing:	--	1.5	0.1	4.1	2.2	0.1
Processing	--	2.6	1.4	4.1	3.6	0.0
Retailing and wholesaling	--	2.9	-1.7	3.9	3.2	-0.3
Transportation	--	1.5	-0.1	4.8	2.5	0.1
Eating and drinking places	--	1.5	-0.0	2.2	4.2	0.0
Other supporting sectors	--	1.8	-0.3	6.9	2.8	1.2

Source: Data from Lee, *et al.* (1987).
[a]From previous year.

quite high, around 4 percent per year, and better than most other food marketing industries. During 1984–1985, productivity growth throughout the food system apparently faltered.

There is a major defect in examining only *labor* productivity. It is that labor is only one input among many utilized by the food processing industries. In many cases, a process innovation requires substituting additional equipment, energy, or materials for the labor that is saved. Connor (1986: table 5) examined a large sample of commercially available innovations for food processors and found that most had labor-saving or plant-saving impacts. However, a large number of innovations required additional machinery or equipment. Thus, the proper measure of productivity change would compare output growth with changes in the quantities required of *all* inputs not just labor. This concept is called *multifactor productivity change* (see Bureau of Labor Statistics 1983). Generally, multifactor productivity change is smaller than single-factor productivity change. For manufacturing for the years 1948–1981, labor productivity increased by 2.6 percent per year, whereas multifactor productivity rose only 1.8 percent per year.

There is only one such study available for the food processing industry. Lee (1986) calculated multifactor productivity for food processing for the years 1958–1982 (see table 6–9). For the whole period productivity change averaged only 0.3 percent per year—about one-tenth the rate of simple labor productivity change. There was little variation in that rate in various subperiods. While subsequent research may find slightly different rates, it is very likely that multifactor productivity growth was quite low in food processing, certainly less than 1 percent per year. Except in the 1977–1982 period, the food processing annual multifactor productivity change was 2–4 percentage points lower than all manufacturing.

New Product Introductions

It is a well-known fact that hundreds or even thousands of new grocery products are introduced to the marketplace by manufacturers each year. The Nielsen Early Intelligence System recorded 5,000 to 7,000 new grocery items introduced per year in the 1970s (Connor 1980b). This system counts even the most minor changes as new products, even one-ounce changes in packaging size.

A more restrictive definition of what constitutes a new product is used by the Dancer-Fitzgerald-Sample (DFS) agency. This source counts the number of branded grocery products that have a new brand name or new generic designation (e.g., low-calorie cranberry cocktail is different from regular cranberry cocktail), but differences in flavor, color, packaging, size, and formulation are ignored (figure 6–1).

From 1964 to 1972, the DFS count of numbers of new processed foods introduced per year varied from about 500 to 600. After 1972 the number of new product introductions rose considerably, tripling during the next fourteen years, an increase of 7 percent per year. Of course, success rates are quite low. Because introductory promotion costs are so high, less than one-third of all new products become profitable within the first or second year. The physical limits of shelf space make new product introductions a contentious issue between processors and retailers. Meanwhile, the size of grocery stores continues to expand to handle a cornucopia of grocery items. According to Selling-Area Markets, Inc., there were over 250,000 warehoused grocery items in national distribution in 1980.

The proliferation of brands and types of processed foods is an ambiguous indicator of technological progress. Many avowedly new products are of doubtful novelty, and some are downright frivolous. The main problem is that some observers equate an increased quantity of goods with an increase in quality. Objective measures of food quality are hard to come by, and mere consumer acceptance (a subjective measure) is not an infallible indicator of superior quality. For example, the arrival of a slew of new products has the effect (sometimes intentional) of bumping some established products

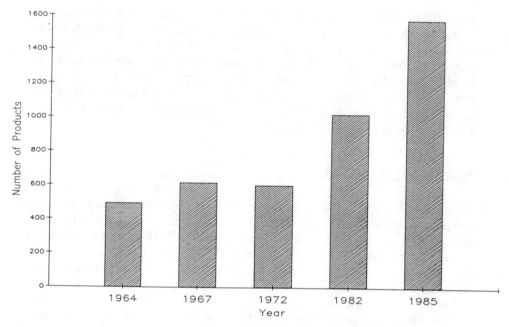

Figure 6–1. New Processed Food Products Introduced Annually, 1964–1985

Source: Data from Appendix Table A11

Note: Includes all new brands and products with new generic descriptions but ignores differences in color, flavor, packaging, size, or formulation.

from the shelves; some customers of the products no longer available may find the new ones less desirable substitutes. Increasingly, newly launched products bite into the sales of brands belonging to the same company. At least one economic analysis (of the breakfast cereal industry) found that new product introductions, because of excessive cannibalization, imposed more costs to society than benefits (Scherer 1979). More than one marketing manager has dreamed of a nonproliferation treaty with rival firms.

Summary

Evidence was assembled on several indicators of technological change in the food processing industries. One set of indicators measures the resources devoted to research and development (R&D) in the industries. For example, R&D expenditures by food processors totaled $834 million in 1984 and had increased at a rate of more than 9 percent per year since 1963. Over 1,000 food processing companies reported having formal R&D programs, and 200 of these had built separate R&D labs for this purpose. Approximately 8,000 scientists and engineers were employed in R&D by food processors in the early 1980s. Well over half of the reported R&D by food processors is concentrated in the twenty largest companies. Government-supported food science research amounted to an additional $170 million in the early 1980s.

Despite total food processing R&D expenditures of more than $1 billion in the mid-1980s, the industry spends less per dollar of sales than any other U.S. manufacturing industry. While the perception is widespread that the need for food scientists and engineers is strong and that the benefits of R&D are obvious, the stark fact is that other industries have bid away many food scientists to work on other matters. The U.S. supply of scientists and engineers has risen about 7 percent per year during the last decade, and although up to 150,000 trained scientists and engineers are employed in food-related jobs, each year sees a smaller proportion devoted to food-related activities. One consequence of this trend is a greater degree of technology transfer from the food machinery, paper, chemicals, plastics, and many other industries, and indeed increasingly from non-U.S. sources.

A minor portion (probably less than 10 percent) of R&D results in innovations that lead to new consumer products. The remainder produces new materials (or new applications of existing materials), machinery, or processes. These industrial process innovations, when adopted, show up as improved productivity. However, labor productivity in food processing has advanced at an annual rate of about 3 percent since 1963, slightly higher than the rest of manufacturing. Labor productivity increases in food processing required substantial increases in capital equipment (about $7 billion per year in the 1980s) and energy; taking these increased input needs into account yields a broader, "multifactor" concept of productivity change that is much lower though still positive.

7
Anticipated Growth of Food Processing

bout 95 percent of the value of foods and beverages purchased by Americans is already processed, so the scope for substitution of processed for unprocessed products is limited. Moreover, homegrown and hunted foods account for at most 3 percent of the value of the U.S. food supply. Neglecting waste and the nonfood uses of processed foods and their by-products, there are basically only four sources of increased demand for the products of the U.S. food processing industries: (1) government, (2) business, (3) domestic households, and (4) exports (table 7–1).

Institutional Demand

Government demand accounts for 3–4 percent of the retail value of food and is expressed by purchases for military, prison, school lunch, food stamp, PL 480 donations, and storage programs (figure 7–1). The first three (military, prison, and school lunch programs) mainly substitute for household purchases; since the early 1970s this institutional channel has been relatively slow growing. The latter three programs, if expanded, would increase the net demand for processed products. At this time significant expansion of the food stamp program is unlikely, and PL 480 donations and storage programs are likely to be reduced.

Businesses purchase food for their employees or as part of a larger package of services (e.g., medical services). Purchases of food by businesses include employee feeding programs in plant or office cafeterias, hospitals, nursing homes, residential care facilities, and in-transit feeding. Business purchases account for 5–6 percent of the retail value of food.

Government and business purchases taken together are termed the *institutional channel* of distribution for food. The institutional channel accounts for about 9 percent of the retail value of U.S. foods and beverages. It is usually considered part of the away-from-home segment of food purchases. The future growth prospects of the institutional channel have not been well studied. Some parts (in-transit and nursing home) will likely grow as fast as restaurant sales, whereas other segments (school lunch) will grow as slowly as grocery store sales unless there are major changes in government policies. Except for exports and institutional sales, all other purchases are made directly by consumers.

Table 7–1
Total U.S. Food and Beverage Demand, 1984

Demand Sector	Place Consumed	Distribution Channel	Places Purchased	Retail Value of Purchases
				$ billion
Households	At-home	Retail	• Retail stores (food, liquor, department)	$274
Households	Away-from-home	Foodservice	• Separate eating & drinking places	146
			• Hotels and motels	13
			• Retail hosts	7
			• Vending machines	5
			• Recreation & entertainment places	4
			• Clubs and associations	2
			• Mobile on street	1
			Total foodservice	176
Business	Away-from-home	Institutional	• Nursing homes & residential care	9
			• Plant & office cafeterias	8
			• Hospitals	7
			• In-transit feeding	3
			• Elderly feeding	1
			Total business	28
Government	Away-from-home	Institutional	• Educational facilities	13
			• Military services	3
			• Correctional facilities	1
			Total government	17
Rest of the World	Outside U.S.	Export	• Free on board ships[a]	11
TOTAL				$505

Sources: Data from USDA, *Food Consumption, Prices, and Expenditures*, Statistical Bulletin 694 (November 1982) and data provided by researchers at the Academy of Food Marketing, St. Joseph's University (September 1986). Excludes alcoholic beverages.

[a]This is the "final" place of purchase as far as U.S. food processors are concerned, but of course the retail value in the importing countries will be much higher.

Consumer Demand and Demographic Factors

Domestic household expenditures account for about 89 percent of total retail value of processed foods. Households are supplied through two marketing channels: retail stores for at-home consumption and foodservice outlets for

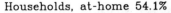

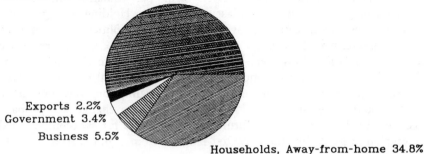

Households, at-home 54.1%

Exports 2.2%
Government 3.4%
Business 5.5%

Households, Away-from-home 34.8%

Figure 7–1. Sources of Demand for Foods and Beverages, Measured at Retail, 1984

away-from-home consumption. Consumers in 1985 spent 60 percent of their food dollars for at-home items and 40 percent for away-from-home meals (figure 7–1). Taking into account household as well as institutional sales of food, some 45 percent of U.S. retail sales now occur in the away-from-home channel. Note, however, because of the much higher wholesale-retail mark-up, away-from-home accounts for only about 20 percent of manufacturer sales.

Given that the total weight of foods and beverages (or perhaps more precisely total caloric intake) will be a constant 1,400 lb. per person in the future, as it has been for decades, then there are four main factors that can influence the value of processed foods demanded: (1) population, (2) trading-up, (3) consumer preferences, and (4) demographic factors (see chapter 2). A fifth factor, changing relative prices among consumer goods and services, also affects the demand for food, but predicting prices far into the future appears to be beyond the abilities of economic science. However, in the post-World War II era at-home food prices and other nondurable goods prices have risen at about the same rate (appendix table A6). At-home food prices increased slightly faster than the prices of furniture and other durable goods, but they increased much more slowly than the prices of private transportation, shelter, and personal services. The prices of foods purchased away from home rose considerably faster (about 5.1 percent per year) than at-home foods and beverages (3.7 percent per year), yet food service prices did not rise as fast as other services. Thus, on the whole, long-term price changes since 1947 have made at-home foods relatively less expensive consumer goods, and away-from-home food became a relatively cheap service for consumers.

Predictions of U.S. population change depend on assumptions about natural birth rates and net immigration. The Census Bureau's assumption about birth rates ("middle series") is 1.9 births per woman of child-bearing age, the average birth rate of the last several years. Holding immigration at historical rates (which can be heavily influenced by political decisions), the U.S. population would reach 297 million by 2020, a 24 percent increase over the 1985 population. However, by varying the birth rate assumption from 1.7 to 2.1 births, population increases from 1985 to 2020 would vary from 11 percent to 45 percent (and under the low assumption, zero population growth would be reached by 2015). Thus, population change will probably affect real food demand in the future by about *+0.6 percent* (compounded) per year on average, but the expected range is from +0.3 percent to +1.1 percent per year.

The second factor influencing food demand is "trading up"; that is, the purchase of more expensive foods per pound (or perhaps per calorie). This is a pervasive trend in a growing economy, and it is driven mainly by rising real incomes (economists call this the "income effect"). During severe recessions, consumers will often try to economize by "trading-down," for example, substituting some dry beans for meat. Blaylock and Smallwood (1986) traced the effects of income changes on food purchases far into the future through an analysis of the food purchasing behavior of thousands of families in the 1980–1981 BLS Continuing Expenditure Survey. They found, in common with many other economic studies, that households spend an additional 2 percent on at-home foods for each additional 10 percent of personal disposable income; for away-from-home foods, there was about a 5.7 percent increase for each increase of 10 percent in income. There are no reliable methods of predicting real income increases decades into the future, but using the post-World War II era as a guide, incomes are likely to increase between 1 percent and 2 percent per year. As can be seen in table 7–2, differences in income growth would have a substantial effect on real food expenditures. With only 1 percent average personal income growth, per capita food and beverage expenditures would grow 16 percent over fifteen years (or 0.4 percent per year), but with an unexpectedly high 3 percent growth rate, food demand would rise 1.2 percent per year.

Perhaps an increase in U.S. income of 1.5 percent per year would represent some sort of consensus forecast. Under this scenario, total food and beverage per capita expenditures would rise about 0.7 percent per year over the next few decades. However, grocery store expenditures would increase only about 0.4 percent per person per year, whereas foodservice and alcoholic beverage expenditures would increase 1.1 percent per year. (These projections assume that no major wars or depressions occur.)

The third major factor affecting per capita demand is changes in tastes and preferences (other than the trading-up phenomenon). These shifts are notoriously difficult to predict. Besides, preference changes would likely

Table 7-2
Predicted Effects on Per Capita Real Food Expenditures of Increases in Personal Income, 1985 to 2020

Category	Increase in Demand Under Alternative Income Growth		
	1% per year	2% per year	3% per year
		Percent	
Food at home	+9	+19	+30
Food away from home	+28	+67	+95
Alcoholic beverages	+29	+74	+98
Total food & beverage	+16	+37	+54

Source: Data from Blaylock and Smallwood (1986).
Note: No changes occur other than income.

affect the *distribution* of food expenditures more than total expenditures on food per person.

The fourth and final major factor influencing food demands are demographic factors. Blaylock and Smallwood (1986) have estimated the impact of three expected demographic shifts on per capita food demand. The impact on demand of the aging of the U.S. population is quite modest. Under the "middle series" assumption of birth rates, the proportion of the population under 30 years will fall from 47.5 percent to 37.6 percent in 2020; the share of the population 45 years or older will rise from 30.7 percent in 1985 to 43.2 percent in 2020. This shifting age profile alone is predicted to increase per capita at-home food expenditures by 5 percent (1985–2020) and decrease away-from-home expenditures by 4 percent. A second demographic change is the regional shift in the U.S. population toward the West and South. Because households in the Northeast buy 6 percent more food per person than other regions, this shift will cause a slight decline in expenditures. Finally, nonblacks spend about 11 percent more per capita on food than blacks (irrespective of region, income, or other factors). The proportion of blacks in the U.S. population is expected to rise from 12 percent in 1985 to 15 percent in 2020, but this change will depress per capita food expenditures by less than 1%.

The combined effects of population increase ("middle series" birth rate assumption), the three demographic changes, and two scenarios of increases in annual household disposable incomes are shown in table 7–3. The table

Table 7–3
Predicted U.S. Real Household Expenditures for Food, 1980 to 2000, 2010, and 2020

	Year					
	2000		2010		2020	
Category	Low growth	High growth	Low growth	High growth	Low growth	High growth
	Percent increase					
Food at-home	26	32	39	48	49	62
Food away-from-home	31	49	46	79	62	112
	Percent per year					
Food at-home	1.2	1.4	1.1	1.3	1.0	1.2
Food away-from-home	1.4	2.0	1.3	2.0	1.2	1.9

Source: Data from Blaylock and Smallwood (1986).

Note: Prediction based on 1.9 births per woman and resulting shifts in regional, racial, and age distributions. High growth scenario assumes 2 percent increase in annual real household disposable incomes; low growth assumes 1 percent growth rate. It assumes no change in preferences, relative prices, or female labor participation rates.

expresses expenditure growth in "real" terms; that is, in the quantity of goods consumed. The predictions assume that no other changes take place, such as major shifts in food preferences or relative prices of food compared to other consumer goods. Food purchased in grocery stores is expected to rise at a rate of between 1.2 to 1.4 percent per year up to the year 2000. Food for away-from-home consumption will increase at 1.4 to 2.0 percent per year. Changes in income account for about one-fourth of at-home demand growth and about one-half of away-from-home growth (see table 7–2). Both types of food demand grow at even slower rates as one looks further into the future, mainly because of a deceleration in population growth.

A BLS study has made predictions of employment growth in the food processing industries from 1992 to 1985 (table 7–4). The method takes into account the number of persons entering the labor force with different education or skill levels and the expected demand for labor by each sector and industry of the U.S. economy. Total employment is expected to remain approximately constant in food processing, but fairly substantial increases are expected for professional and managerial positions. Sales positions are expected to decline.

Foreign Demand

The USDA regularly publishes estimates of foreign demand for U.S. agricultural products. However, these predictions are made only for

Table 7–4
Employment by Occupational Categories in Food and Tobacco Manufacturing, 1982 and 1995

Item	1980	1981	1982	1983	1984	1985
			Million dollars			
Direct foreign investment in United States:						
Food manufacturing	4,869	5,721	6,635	7,447	8,270	11,172
Wholesaling	616	703	705	1,046	1,124	1,151
Food stores and eating & drinking places	1,447	1,966	2,012	2,106	2,174	2,729
Total	6,932	8,390	9,355	10,596	12,168	15,052
Foreign investment by United States:						
Food manufacturing	8,278	9,163	7,630	7,661	8,163	9,297
Wholesaling	601	669	662	801	805	997
Food stores and eating & drinking places	1,259	1,365	1,344	1,483	1,522	1,497
Total	10,138	11,197	9,636	9,945	10,490	11,791

Source: Data from Connor (1986:69) and Appendix Table A13.

unprocessed agricultural commodities and typically extend only a year or so in the future. Other agencies also do not prepare predictions for processed food exports and imports specifically. This type of analysis seems to be particularly complex and subject to many policy decisions. Large portions of U.S. wheat flour, rice, vegetable oils, and dairy products exports were subject to various federal government subsidies. In 1986 the U.S. Export Enhancement, Commodity Credit Corporation export credit and PL 480 food aid programs subsidized over 20 million tons of U.S. farm and food commodities, including over half of the wheat, almost half of the vegetable oil, and one-third of the rice. These sales usually involve government purchasing agencies on the importing end, and at times subsidies are concurrently offered by other exporting countries. When so many political factors influence trade patterns, economic prognostication is dubious.

However, one approach to estimating export demand for processed foods is to examine the growth of the world export market and the U.S. share of that market. Some long-term trends are evident. First, the volume and value of international trade are growing faster than the domestic market. From the early 1960s to 1980, the value of merchandise trade grew at an average annual rate of 16 percent (table 7–5). Excluding seafood, the rate of growth in the value of all food and agricultural exports was about 12 percent per year during the same 1963–1980 period. Adjusting for inflation, the rate of growth of agriculturally related exports was about 6 percent per year—about double the rate of growth of the U.S. market.

Second, after 1980 or 1981 the value of agriculturally related world trade fell sharply until 1984 or 1985. The value of agriculturally related world trade fell by about 25 percent in the early 1980s, and there was overall a

Table 7–5
U.S. and World Exports of Raw Agricultural and Processed Food Products, Selected Years, 1961–1965 to 1985

Export Category	1961-1965	1963-1965	1969-1971	1979-1981	1985
			Billion dollars		
Total merchandise:					
World	157	165	315	1,863	1,587
U.S.	24	25	41	215	214
Total food & agriculture, excluding fish:					
World	39	41	50	239	183E
U.S.	6.0	6.0	7.0	42	30
Total processed food, beverage, tobacco:					
World	--	--	21	95	74
U.S.	--	--	2.1	8.6	8.4
			Percent		
U.S. shares of world trade:					
Total	15	15	13	12	11
Food & agriculture:	16	15	14	18	16
Processed food	--	17	10	9	11
Unprocessed food	--	14E	17	23	20
Ag./total world trade	25	23	19	21	12
Processed food/ agriculture world trade	--	--	42	40	40

Sources: UN trade data; O'Brien et al. (1983); IMF, *Direction of Trade Statistics; Economic Report of the President, 1987;* World Bank, *World Development Report, 1987;* IMF, *Primary Commodities: Market Developments and Outlook.*

Note: "World" excludes USSR and most Eastern European countries.

— = Not available.

E = Estimated.

deflationary tendency as well. However, around 1984 the volume of world trade and U.S. exports of agriculturally related products began to rise again. The major factor influencing the value of world trade is effective demand, that is, the GNPs of importing nations. The severe 1980–1983 worldwide recession crimped exports of all kinds.

Third, processed agricultural products (foods, beverages, feeds, and tobacco products) constitute about 40 percent of world trade of agricultural products. However, only 25–30 percent or less of U.S. agriculturally related exports are processed. The U.S. tends to export more raw agricultural products than other high-income exporting nations.

Fourth, although the U.S. share of world trade in agricultural products has held steady at about 14–18 percent for the last three decades, the U.S. share of world trade in manufactured products has fallen. The U.S. share of world trade in processed foods parallels the U.S. experience in other manufactured goods, whereas the U.S. has a rising share of unprocessed agricultural products trade. The U.S. share of world trade in processed foods is quite a bit below that of the EEC, but it appears to have stabilized at about 10 percent. Should the worldwide recovery continue as it has since 1983, annual increases of 5 percent in the volume of U.S. exports of processed foods would be expected.

8
International Trade and Investment

By nearly all measures, the U.S. economy is developing greater links with the world economy. Imports and exports of goods and services now represent a much higher share of U.S. economic activity than was the case ten or twenty years ago. For example, in 1970 the value of merchandise exports and imports represented only 8 percent of U.S. GNP, but by 1984 trade amounted to 15 percent of GNP, an 80 percent increase in the trade share. The U.S. has borrowed billions of dollars from investors in other countries, so much that around 1985 the United States became a net debtor nation for the first time in over sixty years. Foreign direct investment, both by U.S. investors abroad and by foreign investors into the United States has grown much faster than the general economy. This chapter examines these international linkages with respect to the U.S. food processing industries and processed food products.

Comparisons with Other Countries

The only comprehensive study of the relative economic size of the food processing industries of various countries was published by the United Nations' Centre on Transportational Corporations (1982). This report found that the total 1975 output of the world's processed food and beverage industries was valued at about $700 billion (or $475 billion if one excludes the centrally planned economies). The U.S. food processing industries accounted for 27 percent of world output of the "market-based" (not centrally planned) economies evaluated at official or market rates of currency exchange.[8] In fact, the U.S. food processing industries were only slightly smaller than the combined food industries of the ten countries of the European Economic Community. It is likely that the world share of the U.S. food processing industries has fallen to the 23 to 25 percent range today, but it still ranks number one in output.

Imports and Exports of Processed Food Products

Until the early twentieth century, the exports of agricultural products were crucial to the economic development of the United States. Exports of tobacco, cotton, wheat, and flour contributed mightily to the nation's capital formation. However, from the 1920s to the early 1960s the United States was a net importer of foods and agricultural products except for a brief period during and just after World War II. Since the early 1960s, the United States has been a net exporter of foods and agricultural products, with 1981 a peak year.

Data sources on processed food imports and exports are quite muddled, mainly because of different definitions of what constitutes processed versus unprocessed products. In this report, the SIC definition will be followed as closely as possible, but some products remain difficult to classify. Fish frozen on board boats before being landed is one such ambiguous example. Animal feed, hides, tea, and nuts constitute further examples.

One official series on imports and exports is shown with three-year averages in table 8–1. From the late 1970s to the early 1980s, a period when the U.S. dollar was rising relative to the other currencies, processed food exports rose from $7.5 billion annually to $11.1 billion. Agricultural exports rose (peaking in 1981 or so) as did all other manufacturers in value terms. The three components of export trade rose about 40, 50, and 70 percent, respectively, rates far higher than inflation or general economic growth.

Table 8–1
U.S. Exports and Imports of Processed Foods and Other Manufactures, 1976–1984

	Average 1976-1978		Average 1979-1981		Average 1982-1984	
	Exports	Imports	Exports	Imports	Exports	Imports
			Billion dollars per year			
Agricultural, livestock, and marine products	18.8	8.0	28.8	9.5	26.6	11.0
Processed foods	7.5	7.0	11.9	10.2	11.1	10.6
Other manufactured products	91.9	90.3	154.3	142.3	156.0	207.5
			Percent of total trade			
Agricultural, livestock, and marine products	15.2	5.5	13.8	4.1	13.0	4.0
Processed foods	6.1	4.8	5.7	4.4	5.4	3.9
Other manufactured products	74.1	61.9	74.2	60.6	76.1	75.7

Source: Data from the Bureau of the Census (FT990).
Note: Imports for consumption only. *Marine products* include frozen and packaged fish.

Imports of processed foods increased from $7.0 billion to $10.6 billion over the six year period; agricultural imports increased from $8.0 to $11.0 billion and other manufactures from $90 billion to $208 billion. The increases were 50, 40, and 130, respectively. Thus, imports increased slightly faster than exports for processed foods, but the trade gap was much greater for other manufactures.

Throughout 1977–1983 there was a substantial agricultural trade surplus, a small trade surplus in processed foods, and a widening trade deficit for all other manufactured products. During 1984–1985 a large trade deficit appeared for processed foods, raising some serious concerns (figure 8–1). However, the U.S. dollar exchange rate peaked for most currencies in early 1985 and fell thereafter, and there is some evidence that the huge U.S. trade deficit was beginning to narrow again in 1987.

A fairly clear trend since the late 1970s was the declining relative importance of both agricultural and processed food products in the mix of U.S. trade. Exports of both categories fell from 21 to 18 percent of the value of trade, while imports fell from 10 to 8 percent of total value (table 8–1). It is difficult to say whether this trend is likely to persist.

The data in table 8–2 follows a more careful matching of SIC definitions of food processing. In the early 1970s when the dollar was held to an

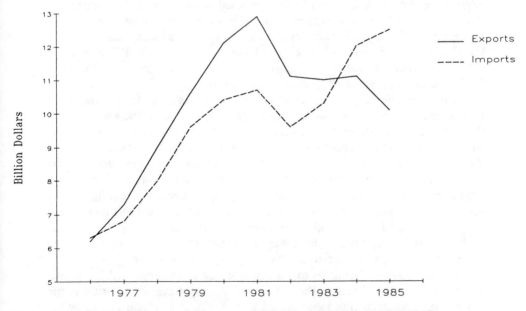

Figure 8–1. U.S. Imports and Exports of Processed Foods, 1976–1985

Source: Data from U.S. Census Bureau, *Statistical Abstract of the United States 1987.*

Table 8-2
U.S. Exports and Imports of Processed Foods, 1970-1972, 1975-1977, and 1980-1982

Trade Item	1970-1972 Average	1975-1977 Average	1980-1982 Average
	Million dollars		
Imports	5,842	7,152	11,419
Exports	2,840	6,270	11,825
Net trade balance	-3,002	-882	+406
	Percent of U.S. shipments		
Imports	5.8	4.3	4.1
Exports	2.8	3.8	4.2
Net trade balance	-3.0	-0.5	+0.1

Source: Data from Appendix Tables A14 and A15.
Note: Follows SIC 20 definition as closely as possible.

artificially low level because it was tied to gold, there was a surprisingly large trade deficit in U.S. trade of processed foods. The deficit narrowed during the mid-1970s and turned to a slight surplus in the early 1980s. As a proportion of total U.S. value of shipments, exports rose substantially over the decade, but imports fell slightly. Thus, from the early 1970s to early 1980s, the trade balance in processed foods was increasingly favorable; after 1983, the trend reversed itself at least up through 1986.

Although the degree of export orientation of the food processing industries is rather modest (about 4 percent of shipments in the early 1980s), the number of jobs dependent upon exports of processed foods is significant. An analysis by the Bureau of the Census using 1981 data traced both the direct and indirect employment created by exports of manufactures, by industry and by state (*Annual Survey of Manufactures*, vol. 5). The direct employment effect came from production workers devoted to making export products. The indirect effects came from activities in other manufacturing industries supplying material inputs for exported product. (The analysis excludes agriculture, wholesale trade, business services, and other sectors supplying materials and services related to export production.)

For the manufacturing sector as a whole one job in eight (12.8 percent) is directly or indirectly related to exports of manufactures. In addition to the 2.6 million manufacturing jobs created by exports, 2.2 million nonmanufacturing jobs were dependent on exports. These 4.8 million jobs represented 5.6 percent of U.S. private-sector employment in 1981. In the case of food processing, 76,000 jobs were created directly or indirectly in manufacturing because of processed food exports, which was 5.1 percent of food industry employment. In just five years, exports of processed foods raised industry employment by 32 percent. In addition, exports of processed foods generated about 60,000 more jobs in agriculture and other input-supply industries in 1981.

In 1981 exports of processed foods reached about $12 billion. However, another $6 billion of indirect materials and services were required from other manufacturing industries to produce those exports. The total exports and indirect requirements of $18 billion placed food processing (SIC 20) *sixth* in size among the twenty major industry groups of the manufacturing industries (figure 8–2). Nonelectrical machinery (SIC 35) is the largest major industry group ($48 billion), followed by transportation equipment (SIC 37) ($38 billion), chemicals (SIC 28) ($36 billion), primary metals (SIC 33) ($28 billion), and electrical equipment (SIC 36) ($23 billion). The direct and indirect value of shipments for processed foods ($18 billion) amounted to 6.4 percent of total food processing shipments in 1981 and also 6.5 percent of total shipments of the manufacturing sector.

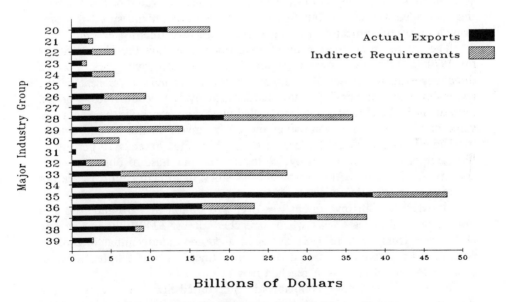

Figure 8–2. Direct Exports and Indirect Requirements to Support Manufactured Exports, 1981

Source: Data from the U.S. Bureau of the Census, *1981 Annual Survey of Manufactures* (M81(AS)-5).

International Direct Investment

International exports are only one way that a food processor can sell in foreign markets. The other two principal methods are licensing and foreign direct investment. In the case of licensing, a U.S. food processor would exchange the right to produce and sell a trademarked product or patented process in a foreign market for a royalty or other form of payment. Very little systematic data are available on foreign licensing arrangements by food processing companies.

Somewhat more is known about foreign direct investment. In this case, a food processor markets a product by establishing or buying a subsidiary manufacturing facility that ships its products to the local foreign market. The parent company may have sole, majority, or minority ownership in the foreign subsidiary and the ownership interest must be large enough that the parent company plays a role in managing the subsidiary. Most countries, in developing data series on foreign direct investment, use an arbitrary 10 percent level of ownership as a dividing line between a mere portfolio investment and direct investment. Therefore, foreign direct investment is measured by the book value of stockholders' equity and long-term debt owned by a parent company in a subsidiary located abroad. Foreign direct investment value usually is much less than the market value of the assets of the controlled subsidiary, but foreign direct investment measured this way provides a useful indicator of changes in foreign investment over time.

The trends in all foreign direct investment affecting the United States for 1970 to 1985 are shown in figure 8–3. There are two types. Foreign direct investment *abroad* (also called *outward* or *outbound investment*) is the ownership value in non-U.S. subsidiaries held by U.S. companies. Foreign investment *in* the United States (also called *inward investment*) is the ownership value of U.S.-registered companies owned by investors that reside outside the United States, where the foreign ownership value exceeds 10 percent of the value of each U.S. company. Note that the purchase of bonds in other countries and the individual ownership of stock in foreign countries are not included in these data on direct investment.

Outward foreign investment was over $70 billion in 1970 and rose at a rapid rate until at least 1981 when it reached almost $240 billion. The rate of increase from 1970 to 1981 averaged a compounded annual rate of 11 percent. The amount of foreign direct investment abroad faltered a bit in 1982–1984, but after 1984 it reached new heights.

Investment by foreign companies in the United States in 1970 was very small by comparison to outward investment—only $15 billion—and it grew to about $35 billion in 1977, a 13 percent annual average rate of increase.

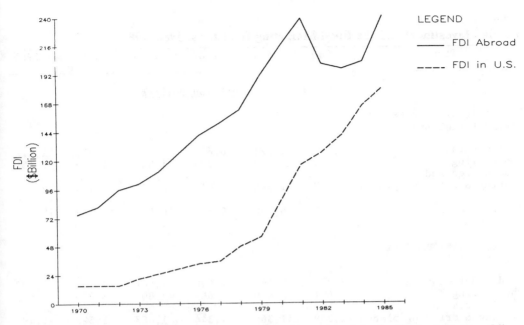

Figure 8–3. Total Foreign Direct Investment Abroad and in the United States, All Industries, 1970–1985

Source: Data from the Bureau of Economic Analysis, Department of Commerce.

After 1977, foreign direct investment in the United States rose even faster, reaching about $110 billion in 1981 (a 33 percent average annual increase from 1977) and about $180 billion in 1985 (a 13 percent rate of increase per year). Therefore, on average, inward foreign direct investment has been growing at a greater rate than outward investment, particularly after 1977 when the inflow grew at 23 percent per year as compared to 6 percent per year of outflow. Also 1981 was a watershed year, the first in which the dollar value of direct investment inflow exceeded the absolute value of the outflow. That is, from 1981 to 1984 the dollar amount of the gap began to narrow, though after 1984 it widened a bit again.

Foreign investment is important to the food processing industries. In 1985, U.S. food processors owned $9.3 billion of equity in and loans to foreign subsidiaries (table 8–3). In 1960 direct investment in food processing abroad totaled $0.9 billion, and by 1977 it was $5.6 billion. Processing formed by far the largest component of foreign direct investment abroad in

Table 8–3
Foreign Investment and the Food Marketing Industries, 1980–1985

Item	1980	1981	1982	1983	1984	1985
			Million dollars			
Direct foreign investment in United States:						
Food manufacturing	4,869	5,721	6,635	7,447	8,270	11,172
Wholesaling	616	703	705	1,046	1,124	1,151
Food stores and eating & drinking places	1,447	1,966	2,012	2,106	2,174	2,729
Total	6,932	8,390	9,355	10,596	12,168	15,052
Foreign investment by United States:						
Food manufacturing	8,278	9,163	7,630	7,661	8,163	9,297
Wholesaling	601	669	662	801	805	997
Food stores and eating & drinking places	1,259	1,365	1,344	1,483	1,522	1,497
Total	10,138	11,197	9,636	9,945	10,490	11,791

Source: Data from the U.S. Department of Commerce, *Survey of Current Business,* various years.

the food marketing industries. However, foreign direct investment into U.S. food processing companies increased much faster than outward investment. In 1984 for the first time, foreign companies owned a greater amount of equity in U.S. food processing subsidiaries than the reverse. Foreign investment in U.S. food wholesaling and retailing companies is also substantial, but food processing still accounts for at least 70 percent of all such investment.

How does direct investment abroad by U.S. food processors compare to their total investment value? Figure 8–4 demonstrates that foreign assets are very important for the average U.S. food processing company. In 1982 about 14 percent of total food processors' assets were located abroad, a ratio considerably higher than that for the food distribution industries. Food processors have committed a smaller proportion of their assets abroad than have other manufactures, and that proportion has declined slightly since

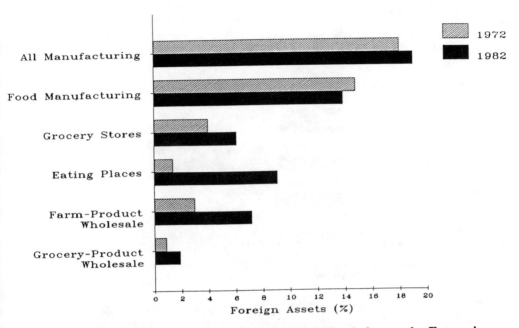

Figure 8–4. Foreign Assets as a Proportion of Total Book Assets, by Enterprise Industry, 1972 and 1982

Source: Data from Connor et al. (1985:Appendix Table C.6) and Table 50.

1972. All the U.S. food distribution industries experienced fairly substantial increases in their foreign assets, particularly the foodservice industry.

Figure 8–5 looks at the proportion of all U.S. assets held by foreign investors. In 1980, foreigners owned about 6 percent of total U.S. food processing assets. However, except for agriculture, foreigners owned higher proportions of the assets of other food marketing industries: about 8 percent of the foodservice, 10 percent of the food wholesaling, and 26 percent of the farm-product wholesaling industries in the United States. The foreign direct investment proportion in U.S. food processing is about the same as the rest of the U.S. economy.

Selling in International Markets: Summary

In the early 1980s foreign firms controlled about 10 percent of the U.S. market for processed foods; four-tenths of that control comes through

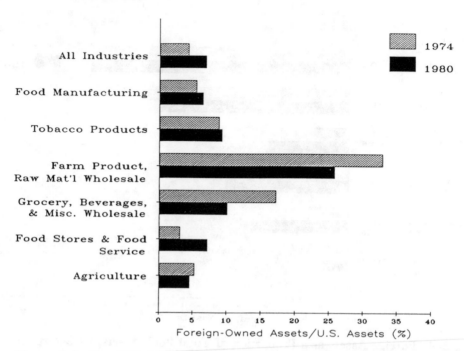

Figure 8–5. Proportion of U.S. Assets Held by Foreign Investors, 1974 and 1980

Source: Data from Connor et al. (1985:Appendix Table C.5).

imports into the United States and six-tenths comes through foreign direct investment in U.S. subsidiaries. In the early 1970s the degree of control was also about 10 percent, but import penetration was greater than sales through investment.

Looking at selling by U.S.-owned food processors in the 1980s, we have seen that about 4 percent of domestic shipments are exported. But considerably more sales abroad are made by U.S. subsidiaries; sales abroad by foreign affiliates of U.S. food processors were over 37 percent of domestic sales or 27 percent of worldwide sales values. Therefore, over 31 percent of the worldwide sales of U.S. food processors occurred in international markets in the early 1980s, up from 29 percent in 1977. Most overseas sales (over 85 percent) are effected through direct investment rather than exports.

The dependence on foreign investment as compared to exports is a matter of some concern, for economic historians have attributed part of the relative decline of England after 1900 to a preference for foreign over domestic industrial investment (Kennedy 1988). Whether such a tendency

Table 8–4
Foreign Versus Domestic New Capital Investment by U.S. Food Processors, 1963–1985

Expenditures for New and Used Capital[a]	1963	1967	1972	1977	1982	1985
	Billion dollars					
U.S. manufacturing companies:						
Foreign[b]	2.3	4.6	7.3	10.5	16.8	15.3
Domestic	11.4	21.5	24.1	47.5	74.6	83.2
U.S. food processors:						
Foreign[b]	--	0.4	0.4	0.8	1.3	1.3
Domestic	1.3	1.7	2.4	4.2	6.7	7.0
	Percent					
Foreign/domestic ratio:						
All manufacturing	20.1	21.4	30.3	22.1	22.5	18.4
Food processing	--	23.5	16.7	19.1	19.4	18.6

Sources: Data from *1985 Annual Survey of Manufactures, 1982 Census of Manufactures, Survey of Current Business,* (October 1986) and previous editions.
[a]Gross capital outlays for adding to or improving property, plant, or equipment.
[b]Majority-owned foreign affiliates of parent firms primarily classified in (food) manufacturing.
— = Not available.

exists can be demonstrated by comparing the annual amounts of foreign versus domestic investment. In 1985 new capital investment abroad by U.S. food processors was $1.3 billion, but domestic capital investment totaled $7.0 billion. Thus, in 1985 the domestic-to-foreign investment ratio for all manufacturers and for food processors was about 5 to 1 (table 8–4). Moreover, this ratio has remained fairly constant since the mid-1960s. So far at least, the opportunities for expansion of capacity in the domestic market are judged to be about four times greater than the opportunities for expansion in foreign markets.

Part II
Size, Growth, and Contribution of Individual Food Processing Industries

Part I examined the national size, growth, and economic contributions made by the food processing industries as a whole. This part repeats the analysis for forty-one individual food processing industries. The industry definitions used correspond to the Standard Industrial Classification (SIC) system, except that six food processing industries were combined with others because of their quite small size or to simplify exposition. For example, plants making raw cane sugar were combined with plants making refined cane sugar. However, it should be noted that SIC definitions change over time. In the food industries three 1963 industries were later split to form six industries: processed poultry products were separated from poultry dressing, pet foods from (commercial) animal feeds, and frozen specialty products (pot pies, pizza, sweet baked goods, etc.) from frozen fruits and vegetables. Therefore, for 1963–1972 changes, we are dealing with thirty-eight observations instead of forty-one.

In the tables that follow, the forty-one food processing industries usually are listed in numerical SIC order. Therefore, the tables list first the four meat-based industries, followed by five dairy industries, six fruit and vegetable industries, seven grain-based industries, and so forth. Occasionally, it is more useful to deal with SIC product classes instead of industries. In 1982 there were about 155 well-defined product classes. Some industries consist of only one product class (e.g., butter), whereas other industries have many (e.g., meatpacking has ten). Thus, product classes are more finely defined in general than industries. Moreover, product class information is available on a "wherever made" basis; for example, dog food made in both pet food plants and meatpacking plants is lumped together. Industry data, on the other hand, treat the plant as the unit of observation.

9
Size and Growth among the Industries

Size Differences

Three measures of industry size are utilized in this report: employment, value added, and shipments value. Each deserves a brief discussion (for a fuller discussion, see appendix C). In the manufacturing sector, the number of production workers are counted four times a year, so employment data are essentially on a full-time-equivalent (FTE) basis. Some unpaid family workers in small companies are excluded. Moreover, in the industry breakdowns that follow, workers outside plants (e.g., those in headquarters establishments) are not distributed by industry. Therefore, employment numbers reported here (FTEs of paid workers in operating establishments) are slightly lower than the actual number of people working in the industry.

Shipments and value added are dollar values. Shipments are measured f.o.b. plant; except for inventory changes, shipments basically correspond to receipts for products as they leave the plant. Generally, taxes and transportation costs are not included in shipments values. Value added is a sort of margin and is sometimes called net product. Value added for an industry is calculated by subtracting the costs of materials, containers, components, supplies, purchased fuel and energy, and certain other purchased production inputs from value of shipments. Therefore, value added includes wages, salaries, fringe benefits, gross operating profits, and many overhead expenses. Value added data are not available for product classes; it is a plant or industry concept. Unless otherwise stated, both shipments and value added are stated in current dollar figures.

Table 9–1 shows the size of the forty-one food processing industries in 1985 ranked by industry value added. Value of shipments and employment totals are also shown. The same data are arranged by SIC in appendix tables A16 and A19.

The top ten food processing industries each had value added of $4 to $9 billion in 1985. These ten industries created 56 percent of the value added of the forty-one food processing industries. A remarkable feature of the high-value-added food industries is that they produce consumer products.[9] Indeed, the highest-ranking food processing industry specializing in producer goods is animal feeds which is ranked eighteenth. The other food processing industries that mainly sell ingredients to industrial customers are wet corn

Table 9–1
The Size of the Food Processing Industries, Ranked by Value Added, 1985

Industry	Measure of Industry Size		
	Value Added	Value of Shipments	Employment
	Million dollars		Thousands
1. Bread, rolls, cakes	8,811	14,389	162.1
2. Soft drinks bottling	7,587	19,358	105.8
3. Miscellaneous prepared foods	7,027	13,708	84.9
4. Meatpacking	5,859	42,554	122.2
5. Confectionery	5,883	11,514	70.7
6. Beer	5,681	12,216	40.3
7. Fluid milk	4,953	19,679	73.2
8. Canned fruits and vegetables	4,448	10,999	67.6
9. Cookies and crackers	4,184	6,446	46.7
10. Breakfast cereals	3,995	5,718	16.3
11. Meat processing	3,705	12,406	64.6
12. Flavorings	3,108	4,840	12.0
13. Pet foods	3,074	5,306	16.7
14. Frozen specialties	2,985	6,508	47.0
15. Poultry dressing	2,859	10,340	104.0
16. Coffee	2,446	6,677	11.4
17. Frozen fruits and vegetables	2,355	5,803	46.1
18. Animal feeds	2,276	10,410	32.0
19. Canned specialties	2,161	4,802	24.2
20. Sauces, pickles	2,116	5,123	22.9
21. Cheese	1,910	11,060	31.5
22. Spirits	1,691	2,763	10.5
23. Prepared milk	1,628	5,288	12.0
24. Wet corn milling	1,363	4,190	8.7
25. Cooking oils and margarine	1,190	5,608	10.7
26. Flour	1,159	5,205	13.3
27. Frozen fish	1,070	3,947	36.0
28. Wine and brandy	1,063	2,763	13.2
29. Ice cream	1,041	3,477	18.9
30. Cane sugar	1,035	3,785	12.6
31. Dried fruits and vegetables	840	1,788	13.2
32. Soybean oil	712	8,629	7.3
33. Flour mixes	700	1,635	7.3
34. Other fats and oils	653	2,386	12.3
35. Pasta	629	1,155	7.7
36. Poultry processing	535	1,839	12.5
37. Beet sugar	524	1,789	7.9
38. Rice	389	1,581	4.9
39. Canned fish	227	697	5.8
40. Cottonseed oil	219	881	3.5
41. Butter	98	1,571	2.0
Total	104,146	301,562	1,422.5

Source: Data from Appendix Tables A16 and A19.

milling (twenty-fourth), flour (twenty-sixth), cane sugar (thirtieth), soybean oil (thirty-second), other fats and oils (thirty-fourth), beet sugar (thirty-seventh), and cottonseed oil (fortieth). In the aggregate, these eight predominantly producer goods industries accounted for 7.6 percent of total value added by the food processing industries.

Industries with high value added generally also have large shipments and employment, but the correspondence is far from perfect. For example, the breakfast foods industry ranks tenth in value added, but it is relatively low in ranking by shipments (seventeenth) and employment (twenty-first). On the other hand, the soybean oil processing industry ranked thirteenth in shipments, but a lowly thirty-second in terms of value added.

Table 9–2 shows the largest processed food products ranked by value of product shipments in 1985. Note that the product definitions used in

Table 9–2
The Twenty Largest Food Product Classes, by 1985 Value of Product Shipments

1985 Rank	Product Class	1963 Rank	Value of Shipments, 1985
			Million dollars
1.	Beef, chilled and frozen	1	20,158
2.	Soft drinks bottling	7	18,100
3.	Canned and cured red meats	2	15,315
4.	Beer	6	12,146
5.	Fluid milk	3	10,046
6.	Confectionery	11	8,982
7.	Poultry, chilled and frozen	9	8,508
8.	Pork, chilled and frozen	5	8,139
9.	Bread and rolls	4	7,809
10.	Cooking oil and margarine	12	6,051
11.	Cookies and crackers	15	6,030
12.	Frozen specialties	25	5,740
13.	Natural cheese	22	5,665
14.	Miscellaneous foods	18	5,339
15.	Pet food	30	4,820
16.	Flour and grain mill products	8	4,585
17.	Chips	29	4,481
18.	Roasted coffee	14	4,386
19.	Breakfast cereals	26	4,379
20.	Refined sugar	10	4,255
	Total	--	164,934

Source: Data from Appendix Table A17.
Note: There are fifty-four product classes grouped altogether.

tables 9–1 and 9–2 differ somewhat (e.g., beef and pork are both parts of the meatpacking industry). There have been several changes in rank of food product classes since 1963. Most less processed, less differentiated products have dropped in rank: fluid milk, pork, bread and rolls, flour, and sugar are examples. The only exceptions to this pattern in table 9–2 are the rise in poultry from nineth to seventh position and natural cheeses from twenty-seventh to thirteenth position. On the other hand, several highly processed foods for which physical and brand differentiation are important have risen in rank: soft drinks, beer, candy, cookies, frozen specialties, pet food, chips, and breakfast cereals are all examples of the latter trend.

Differences in Value Added

Why do industries differ in their rankings by shipments and value added? What is meant by a "high-value added" industry? Some patterns that help answer those questions can be seen in table 9–3. First of all, we again see

Table 9–3
The Food Processing Industries, Ranked by Intensity of Value Added, 1985

Industry	Value Added per Dollar of Shipments	
	1963	1985
	Percent	
1. Breakfast cereals	58.4	69.9
2. Cookies and crackers	54.5	64.9
3. Flavorings	54.8	64.2
4. Bread, rolls, cakes	53.4	61.2
5. Pet foods	NA	57.9
6. Pasta	43.1	54.5
7. Miscellaneous foods	46.8	51.3
8. Confectionery	44.3	50.7
9. Spirits	57.2	48.4
10. Dried fruits and vegetables	36.4	47.0
11. Beer	55.6	46.5
12. Frozen specialties	35.5[a]	45.9
13. Canned specialties	46.3	45.0
14. Flour mixes	44.9	42.8
15. Sauces, pickles	36.8	41.3
16. Frozen fruits and vegetables	35.5[a]	40.6
17. Canned fruits and vegetables	37.6	40.4
18. Soft drinks bottling	35.8	39.2
19. Wine and brandy	37.2	38.5
20. Coffee	33.0	36.6

Table 9–3 continued

Industry	Value Added per Dollar of Shipments	
	1963	1985
	Percent	
21. Canned fish	38.6	32.6
22. Wet corn milling	46.8	32.5
23. Prepared milk	15.4	30.8
24. Ice cream	25.2	29.9
25. Meat processing	26.4	29.9
26. Beet sugar	35.6	29.3
27. Poultry processing	18.3[b]	29.1
28. Poultry dressing	18.3[b]	27.7
29. Other fats and oils	33.3	27.4
30. Cane sugar	23.6	27.3
31. Frozen fish	30.4	27.1
32. Fluid milk	31.4	25.2
33. Cottonseed oil	18.2	24.9
34. Rice	19.2	24.6
35. Flour	17.1	22.3
36. Cooking oils and margarine	25.4	21.9
37. Animal feeds	20.0	21.2
38. Cheese	13.4	17.3
39. Meatpacking	15.3	13.8
40. Soybean oil	10.3	8.3
41. Butter	13.5	6.2
Total	31.9	34.5

Source: Data from Appendix Table A16.

Note: The measure of value added reported here is based on Census of Manufactures data collected at the establishment level. Because it fails to net out certain "overhead" or central office expenses, the value added shown here is slightly overstated. However, it is believed that the degree of overstatement is roughly the same across industries. Thus, the value added intensities displayed here are highly correlated with value added properly calculated.

[a]Frozen fruits and vegetables and frozen specialties were combined in one industry in 1963; the ratio for frozen specialties was probably slightly higher than the ratio reported here.

[b]The two poultry industries were combined in one industry in 1963, but the ratios shown in this table are quite representative of actual values in 1963.

highly processed, highly differentiated, convenient consumer products at the top of the list of value-intensive products. Breakfast cereals have a value added margin of 70 percent; because payroll costs are less than 10 percent of sales for breakfast cereal manufacturers, the remaining 60 percent of sales consists of advertising, promotion, other overhead, and profits. Value added intensity is high for "flavorings" because this is the location of the high-advertising, high-profit soft drink syrup makers; note that the soft drink bottling industry ranks nineteenth on the list. Another aspect of product differentiation that raises value added relative to sales is the practice of direct-store delivery from some food processors' plants. Direct story delivery is a common practice in the cookies and crackers, bread, snacks (in "miscellaneous foods"), confectionery, frozen foods, and many beverage industries. The driver-salesmen employed by processors have two principal functions, transportation and promotion. The delivery function (including store shelf maintenance and returns of stale or damaged merchandise) is a form of forward vertical integration; that is, it is the assumption of a grocery wholesaling-retailing function by a processor. If successful, the promotional activities of driver-salesmen raise and stabilize a firm's market share and customer loyalty. Thus, direct-store delivery raises value added in two ways: through heightened vertical integration (higher labor and transportation-equipment costs) and greater profitability.

A second factor that explains variations in value added is raw material costs. Because the major inputs purchased in the food processing industries are food materials, industries that purchase relatively expensive farm commodities rank quite low in value added intensity. That is, low value added industries add only 10 percent to 30 percent to the price per pound of a processed food compared to the price per pound of the farm commodity. Thus, most of the meat, fish, dairy, sugar, and oilseed industries have very low value added relative to sales. In addition to farm commodities, where semiprocessed ingredients are the principal materials purchased and have relatively high prices per pound, the scope for adding value is more restricted in a percentage sense. Examples of product lines that utilize relatively costly semiprocessed ingredients are processed poultry products, canned milk, catsup, and frozen prepared fish. On the other hand, industries based on fresh fruits and vegetables, water, and grains generally add far more value to their principal inputs.

The inverse relationship between the costliness of product ingredients and value added intensity is not perfect, of course. A third factor that explains differences in the intensity of value added is consumer expectations about how much "value added" must occur in their kitchens. That is, if consumers anticipate combining a nontrivial amount of their own labor with the food being purchased, less value added by the processor is demanded. By and large, convenience foods have more processor value added per dollar than do basic ingredients for labor-intensive household preparations. It is primarily for this reason that refrigerated doughs and pastas have higher value added intensities than family flour; similarly, one can compare yogurt with fluid milk, salad dressings with cooking oils, and ice cream with milk and sugar. In each of these cases, the first item could be (and in some cases is) made by consumers at home, but most prefer to purchase commercially prepared versions. The increasing demand by consumers for inherent "convenience" in foods and the discoveries of food manufacturers of new ways to supply convenience is certainly one force behind the rising intensity of value added in food products.

A fourth factor that appears to raise the intensity of value added is a high level of new product development and introduction. Most of the industries near the top of table 9–4 introduce more varieties annually than the ones near the bottom. A higher margin is needed to cover product development and introductory merchandising costs. One result of the rising number of new product introductions is rising value added ratios in most food industries over time (beverages are exceptions to this rule).

An alternative way of examining value added is relative to the number

Table 9–4
The Food Processing Industries, Ranked by Value Added per Employee, 1963 and 1985

Industry	Value Added per Employee	
	1963	1985
	Dollars	
1. Flavorings	43,978	259,033
2. Breakfast cereals	32,018	245,074
3. Coffee	35,837	214,544
4. Pet foods	23,017[c]	184,054
5. Spirits	34,650	161,038
6. Wet corn milling	22,037	156,713
7. Beer	20,543	140,975
8. Prepared milk	19,203	135,667
9. Soybean oil	23,400	97,493
10. Flour mixes	24,694	95,904
11. Sauces and pickles	13,126	92,384
12. Cookies and crackers	14,514	89,589
13. Canned specialties	21,460	89,306
14. Flour	16,656	87,173
15. Miscellaneous foods	14,684	82,766
16. Confectionery	12,271	82,573
17. Cane sugar	18,845	82,159
18. Pasta	8,351	81,636
19. Wine and brandy	22,508	80,538
20. Rice	18,721	79,347
21. Soft drinks bottling	11,539	71,739
22. Animal feeds	23,017[c]	71,131
23. Fluid milk	11,909	67,657
24. Beet sugar	17,761	66,637
25. Canned fruits and vegetables	10,053	65,803
26. Dried fruits and vegetables	12,586	63,609

Table 9–4 continued

Industry	Value Added per Employee	
	1963	1985
	Dollars	
27. Frozen specialties	11,809[b]	63,513
28. Cottonseed oil	12,000	62,657
29. Cheese	9,983	60,644
30. Meat processing	11,592	57,355
31. Ice cream	14,628	55,069
32. Cooking oils and margarine	19,593	54,919
33. Bread, rolls, cakes	10,143	54,354
34. Frozen fruits and vegetables	11,809[b]	51,087
35. Butter	11,058	48,800
36. Meat packing	10,548	47,949
37. Poultry processing	6,901[a]	42,832
38. Canned fish	10,092	39,207
39. Other fats and oils	14,479	35,917
40. Frozen fish	5,895	29,725
41. Poultry dressing	6,901[a]	27,494
Total	13,188	73,213

Source: Data from Appendix Table A16.

Note: The measure of value added reported here is based on Census of Manufactures data collected at the establishment level. Because it fails to net out certain "overhead" or central office expenses, the value added shown here is slightly overstated. However, it is believed that the degree of overstatement is roughly the same across industries. Thus, the value added intensities displayed here are highly correlated with value added properly calculated.

[a]Frozen fruits and vegetables and frozen specialties were combined in one industry in 1963; the ratio for frozen specialties was probably slightly higher than the ratio reported here.

[b]The two poultry industries were combined in one industry in 1963, but the ratios shown in this table are quite representative of actual values in 1963.

[c]Combined in 1963; pet foods probably had a higher ratio in 1963 than reported here.

of employees in the industry. Recall that value added has two primary components, returns to labor and returns to capital investment (capital depletion and profits). By looking at the ratio of value added to labor, one can observe some of the variation in value added due to plant and equipment investments. This distinction is hardly cut-and-dried, however, because the skills and productivity of workers (their "human capital") can significantly enhance the value added generated by a given stock of capital. Thus, the variations in value added per employee shown in table 9–4 are due not only to the quality and amount of capital employed per worker but also to the synergistic interaction of physical capital with human capital. In short, value added per employee is a special measure of labor productivity.

For most food processing industries, the two value added rankings are quite similar. Most of the meat, poultry, dairy, fish, and oils industries rank quite low by both measures. Most of the beverage industries and others that use flow-type processes (sauces, confectionery) continue to rank high. However, several industries that are heavily capitalized rank much higher based on value added per employee: coffee, corn wet milling, prepared milk, soybean oil, flour, and rice milling. The change in the position of the soybean oil processing industry is particularly striking: its value added intensity ratio was fortieth, but its value added per employee was nineth in 1985. Finally, several labor-intensive food processing industries are much lower in rank using value added per employee: cookies and crackers, bread, dried fruits and vegetables, and frozen foods are the main examples.

Besides value added, the economic impact of an industry on the national economy can be measured with income or employment multipliers (see chapter 1). Recall that the average income multiplier for food processing was 3.81. That is, if demand for processed foods were to increase such that $1 million more wage and salary payments were made in the food processing industries, then an additional $2.81 million in income would be generated in other U.S. industries.

Income multipliers vary considerably within the food processing industries. The multipliers are highest for the meat (7.39), fats and oils (7.02), dairy (5.12), and grain milling (4.43) processing industries. The multipliers are smallest for the bakery (2.02) and beverages (2.28) industries. Therefore, the first group of industries have relatively strong economic linkages with other sectors of the economy, whereas the second group of industries are somewhat self-contained. Employment multipliers tend to follow an analogous ranking. Of course, these multipliers are measured at the national level; the multiplier effects are quite a bit lower within state boundaries. In a study done for Indiana, employment multipliers ranged from 5.2 for fats and oils to 1.7 for canned vegetables (Connor 1987).

High-Growth Industries

Value added is a superior meaure of cross-industry size comparisons, but for comparisons across-time shipments works just as well. Table 9–5 shows the twenty-three (of fifty-four) food product classes that have demonstrated very high rates of growth during at least one of the three time periods selected for study. Specifically, each product class had growth that was at least *double* the average for all food industries during one of the periods 1963–1972,

Table 9–5
Food Processing Product Classes with Historically High Growth,[a] 1963–1985

Product Class	High Rates of Growth[a] During		
	1963-1972	1972-1982	1982-1985
	Percent		
Processed poultry products	1,984	373	50
Processed eggs	--	--	49
Flour mixes and doughs	--	--	41
Ready-to-mix desserts	--	--	41
Cookies and crackers	--	--	40
Fruit juices, refrigerated	--	--	36
Chips and salty snacks	--	--	35
Frozen specialties	177	--	30
Catsup and tomato sauces	--	--	27
Confectionery and chewing gum	--	--	27
Dried soup mixes	182	--	26
Cottage cheese and yogurt	--	--	25
Pickles and relishes	--	--	23
Frozen fruits and juices	--	--	22
Soft drinks	--	--	22
Canned fruits and juices	--	--	21
Sauces and dressings	--	--	19
Natural cheese	--	302	--
Pet food	238	--	--
Process cheese	192	--	--
Fresh and frozen fish	180	--	--
Wine and brandy	141	--	--
Frozen vegetables	130	--	--

Source: Data from Appendix Table A17.
— = Not high growth
[a]"High" growth is a rate that is at least twice the average of all the food processing product classes.

1972–1982, or 1982–1985. For example, the average growth rate in value of product shipments from 1982 to 1985 was 9 percent, so the seventeen classes with a growth rate exceeding 18 percent are listed in table 9–5. This method corrects somewhat for inflation rates, particularly from 1972 to 1982.

The only product class with consistently high growth rates is processed poultry products (chicken hot dogs, smoked turkey breast, and the like). Sales in 1985 were over thirty times the sales in 1963. Two more product classes (frozen specialties and dried soup mixes) had high growth in two periods, but none of the others did. The list is replete with highly processed consumer products that experienced high rates of new product introductions.

Low-Growth Industries

Twenty-three product classes that have experienced extraordinary low growth are shown in table 9–6. What is surprising is that a few of the high-growth classes also appear as low growth classes (for different periods, of course). In some cases, this may be due to price changes rather than quantity changes.

Table 9–6
Food Processing Product Classes with Historically Low Growth,[a] 1963–1985

Product Class	Low Rates of Growth[a] During		
	1963-1972	1972-1982	1982-1985
		Percent	
Canned and cured fish	--	--	-31
Rice	--	--	-16
Butter	-4	--	-7
Baby food, canned	--	--	-5
Fresh and frozen fish	--	--	-3
Beef, fresh and frozen	--	--	-2
Pork, fresh and frozen	--	--	-2
Wine and brandy	--	--	-1
Natural cheese	--	--	1
Sugar, refined	--	56	4
Miscellaneous foods	--	--	4
Veal and lamb	-6	10	--
Cottage cheese and yogurt	--	42	--
Ready-to-mix desserts	--	51	--
Canned and cured meats	30	--	--
Processed eggs	12	--	--
Canned milk	28	--	--
Ice cream	26	--	--
Fluid milk	19	--	--
Jams, jellies, preserves	23	--	--
Flour	9	--	--
Cakes, pies, pastries	28	--	--
Roasted coffee	26	--	--

Source: Data from Appendix Table A17.
— = Not low growth
[a]"Low" growth is a rate that is less than half the average of all the food product classes.

But in many others, changes in consumer preferences appear to be the main source of growth. Diet and health concerns may have slowed growth of foods high in salt, sugar, caffeine, and fats (Kinsey & Heien 1988), but this influence is moderated by desires for variety, simplicity of preparation, conformity with tradition, physical satiation, and several others.

Real Growth Rates

The influence of relative price changes and changes in consumer preference can be seen more clearly in the growth rates assembled in table 9–7. The

Table 9–7
Growth Rates, Sixty-eight Selected Food Processing Product Classes, 1963–1982

Product Class	Growth in Value of Shipments		Growth in Value of Production		Implied Inflation Rate	
	1963-1972	1972-1982	1963-1972	1972-1982	1963-1972	1972-1982
			Percent per year			
Red meats:						
Beef, chilled	8.4	5.8	4.3	-1.2	4.1	7.0
Pork, chilled	6.8	6.6	-6.8	0.2	13.6	6.4
Processed beef and pork	3.0	6.7	4.2	6.0	-1.2	0.7
Poultry and eggs:						
Chickens	5.3	10.0	4.9	3.8	0.4	6.6
Turkeys	5.3	10.0	4.4	1.7	0.9	8.3
Processed poultry products	38.6	16.8	49.5	12.1	-10.9	4.7
Processed eggs	1.3	7.7	2.8	-1.3	-1.5	9.0
Fish:						
Fresh packaged seafood	12.1	13.8	1.1	7.5	11.0	6.3
Frozen packaged seafood	12.1	13.8	9.5	3.3	2.6	10.5
Canned and cured seafood	4.8	8.0	-0.7	-0.4	5.5	8.4
Dairy products:						
Butter	-0.5	9.6	2.2	1.4	2.7	8.2
Natural cheese	8.3	14.9	2.5	7.6	5.8	7.3
Process cheese	12.6	11.7	7.8	1.9	4.8	9.8
Dried milk powder	5.9	11.9	-1.7	2.1	7.6	9.8
Canned milk powder	2.8	10.2	2.0	1.9	0.8	8.3
Ice cream and frozen desserts	2.6	8.0	0.9	1.8	1.7	6.2
Fluid milk	2.0	6.0	0.8	0.4	1.2	5.6
Cottage cheese, buttermilk, and yogurt	6.3	3.6	3.6	2.8	2.7	0.8
Fruits and vegetables:						
Canned fruits	3.7	9.1	-0.9	0.7	4.6	8.2
Canned (dry) beans	8.0	8.0	1.4	0.9	6.6	7.9
Canned vegetables	4.4	6.4	0.1	2.3	4.3	4.1
Dried fruits and vegetables	5.7	11.0	3.9	2.2	5.8	8.8
Pickles	5.3	6.7	1.6	-0.8	3.7	7.5
Grains:						
Flour milling	1.0	7.2	-0.9	1.5	1.9	5.7
Rice milling	5.7	11.0	5.2	3.6	0.5	7.4
Wet corn milling	3.3	14.7	5.4	8.3	-2.1	6.4
Animal feeds	5.8	8.4	4.2	-0.5	1.6	8.9
Pasta	5.1	12.9	3.4	4.8	1.7	8.1
Flour mixes and doughs	5.2	10.0	4.6	2.5	0.6	7.5

Table 9-7 continued

Product Class	Growth in Value of Shipments		Growth in Value of Production		Implied Inflation Rate	
	1963-1972	1972-1982	1963-1972	1972-1982	1963-1972	1972-1982

Percent per year

Product Class	1963-1972	1972-1982	1963-1972	1972-1982	1963-1972	1972-1982
Sugar:						
Cane sugar	3.0	6.8	2.9	-1.9	0.1	4.9
Beet sugar	5.1	5.6	3.7	-2.0	1.4	3.6
Oils:						
Cottonseed	-2.0	7.3	-2.5	2.6	0.5	4.7
Soybean	9.6	9.9	6.6	2.3	3.0	7.6
Animal and marine fats	4.2	8.4	2.7	-0.8	1.5	9.2
Shortening and cooking oils	7.1	8.9	4.2	0.9	2.9	8.0
Margarine	7.1	8.9	3.9	-0.8	3.2	9.7
Bakery products:						
Bread	3.4	7.8	1.1	0.4	2.3	7.4
Rolls	3.4	7.8	1.1	3.6	2.3	4.2
Crackers	4.6	9.8	1.3	3.1	3.3	6.7
Cookies	4.6	9.8	1.9	-0.3	2.7	10.1
Confectionery:						
Chocolate confectionery	2.0	4.8	0.9	2.5	1.1	2.3
Nonchocolate confectionery	5.6	2.5	3.0	3.6	2.6	1.5
Nuts, glace fruits, etc.	--	4.6	9.8	3.1	--	0.6
Chewing gum	7.1	2.3	5.1	-0.3	2.0	2.6
Sweetening syrups	2.2	2.0	3.7	-1.3	-1.5	5.5
Frozen foods:						
Frozen fruits	7.9	9.7	7.9	1.9	0.0	7.8
Frozen vegetables	9.7	13.0	8.3	4.0	1.4	9.0
Frozen specialties	12.0	9.7	13.5	2.5	-1.5	5.2
Beverages:						
Canned fruit juices	7.1	11.3	7.6	5.2	-0.5	6.1
Canned vegetable juices	6.2	0.7	2.9	-1.3	3.3	2.0
Beer	6.5	10.6	5.0	3.8	1.5	6.8
Wine	10.3	12.3	9.0	4.7	1.3	7.6
Spirits	5.5	6.1	4.4	0.1	1.1	6.0
Soft drinks	9.4	12.0	5.9	4.7	3.5	7.3
Roasted coffee	2.6	9.6	-1.8	-0.3	4.4	9.9
Soluble coffee	4.7	11.9	-2.6	1.5	7.3	10.4
Tea	7.9	9.8	7.3	1.2	0.6	11.4
Cocoa	5.6	1.9	4.0	1.6	1.6	0.3
Drink powders	6.5	5.2	4.7	6.9	1.8	-1.7
Highly prepared and convenience:						
Breakfast cereals	5.9	12.8	3.1	4.1	2.8	8.7
Canned baby foods	4.7	5.6	4.6	-0.2	0.1	5.8
Canned soups	8.0	8.0	4.6	1.5	3.4	6.5
Other canned specialties	8.0	8.0	3.9	3.1	4.1	4.9
Catsup and tomato sauces	8.1	13.7	5.2	6.2	2.9	7.5
Dried soup mixes	12.2	10.1	13.7	-1.8	-1.5	11.9
Dog and cat food	14.5	11.8	14.4	3.7	0.1	8.1
Ready-to-mix desserts	3.7	4.2	2.3	-3.5	1.4	7.7
Chips and snacks	9.4	12.3	7.0	4.5	2.4	7.8
Total foods and beverages	5.7	9.3	3.0	2.2	2.7	7.1

Note: Growth in value of shipments from Appendix Table A17 and growth in production (deflated or volume growth) from Appendix Table A18.

first two columns show annual growth rates for two periods in current dollar product shipments (these two columns are consistent with the data presented in tables 9–3 and 9–5). However, the two middle columns apply industry-specific deflation indexes to the product shipments, thus revealing production or quantity growth. The last two columns show changes in prices at the manufacturer's level. Of course, inflation rates were generally higher in the 1972–1982 period than during the earlier period.

Looking first at production changes among the three high-protein food groups—red meats, poultry, and prepared fish—it is clear that a major shift occurred away from fresh red meats (especially pork) and toward poultry and fresh and frozen fish. What is interesting is that *processed* red meat products (hams, bacon, sausage, and cold cuts) experienced above-average real growth, despite their relatively high fat and salt contents. Note that price changes for processed red meats were considerably lower than those of fresh red meats. While the growth of fresh and frozen poultry was high, especially after 1972, the real growth of processed poultry products was extraordinarily high—averaging almost fifty percent per year in the 1960s— as were the very modest price increases for chicken franks, turkey "hams," and other processed poultry products.[10] Within the fish category, there was a notable shift away from smoked and canned seafood toward fresh seafood; even the very rapid growth in frozen fish in the 1960s slowed considerably in the 1970s, again abetted by more rapid price increases for frozen relative to fresh prepared fish.

Except for cheese, the real growth of most dairy products was well below the average growth of processed foods. The slow growth occurred in spite of relatively low price increases; fluid milk grew at annual rates that were 2 percentage points lower than average even though price increases were 1 percentage point lower than average. Demographic and taste changes (such as dietary concerns regarding animal fats) certainly played a role, as did increasing competition from other beverages (see beer and soft drinks growth rates in table 9–7). These observations are reinforced by the fairly rapid growth of such low-fat dairy products as cottage cheese and yogurt, categories that had very low price increases throughout the period. Cheese, however, is a real puzzle. Despite the high fat levels and salt content of most cheeses, process and natural cheeses grew rapidly; real growth of natural cheese was almost 6 percent per year in the 1970s, even though price increases were above average. Although government storage programs explain some of the growth of the natural cheese market, much of the explanation appears to lie with greater variety, improved packaging, an image of convenience, and possibly calcium content.

Most processed foods based on fruits, vegetables, and grains grew quite slowly. Canned and dried fruits and vegetables suffered from intense competition from frozen preparations and to a lesser extent from a shift toward fresh produce. The fairly robust growth of dried fruits and vegetables and rice was driven largely by increased export demand. Two grain products that provide highly convenient product forms and substantial new product development were pasta (including pasta-based entrees) and flour mixes (including refrigerated baking doughs); these product classes experienced relatively rapid real growth in demand, aided by average or below average price increases as well as dietary recommendations in favor of greater grain consumption.

The wet corn milling industry displayed very high production increases, slowing somewhat in the 1970s as the industry raised prices rapidly after 1972. The principal cause of growth was the adoption of high-fructose corn syrup as a replacement for cane- and beet-derived sucrose in industrial uses, especially after 1972. New uses for corn starch, a healthful image for corn oil, and export demand for corn gluten (an animal feed by-product) abetted growth. Note the zero or negative growth of the two sugar industries after 1972, despite relatively slow price increases during 1972–1982. The corn refining and sugar industries have lobbied hard to protect the domestic sugar industry from cheap foreign sugar; high sugar prices keep fructose prices high, too. The imposition of tight sugar import quotas has accelerated the shift from sucrose to fructose, so the sugar program has merely slowed the death of the sugar industries rather than prevented it.[11]

Among the oil processing industries, the cottonseed oil industry has been undergoing a long-term decline, but growth of all the others slowed drastically after 1972. The very high price increases of fats and oils after 1972 (almost 11 percent per year for ten years!) certainly played a major role with perhaps consumer concerns about oil consumption reinforcing the trend. (Note that butter production increased slowly from 1963 to 1982; a major portion of butter output now is sold to the foodservice industry.)

After rather slow growth in the 1960s (about equal to population growth), growth in baked goods except for bread picked up slightly. The increased growth rate for rolls was driven by large demand increases by the foodservice industry. The cracker industry had fairly active new product development as well as slow price increases after 1972.

Except for the increased growth of chocolate-based confectionery in recent years, most candy and confectionery products experienced growth slowdowns after 1972. Price increases for all confectionery products were among the lowest of the food processing industries, so changing consumer tastes and fewer youth must be compelling factors.

With a few exceptions to be noted, the remaining three categories of processed foods (frozen foods, beverages, and highly prepared, convenience-type foods) displayed above average growth in one or both periods. Frozen foods grew at above average paces in all periods, though the novelty of the products and the possibilities of substitution for canned versions (canned fruits, vegetables, stews, ethnic foods, and the like) was clearly becoming exhausted after 1972. The slowdown was more severe for such products as frozen dessert pies (quantity up only 6 percent from 1972 to 1982), frozen beef and pork pies (1972–1982 quantity declined 41 percent), and frozen TV dinners (27 percent decline) than for frozen pizza and other nationality foods (quantity increased 283 percent from 1972 to 1982).

The beverage product classes have in general experienced rapid real growth (fluid milk was discussed earlier), but with the exception of drink powders, all of them slowed down after 1972. The four exceptions to the rule of above-average growth were canned vegetable juices,[12] both kinds of coffee, and spirits after 1972. Health concerns about coffee and drinks high in alcohol were factors in declining consumption, but in the case of coffee, huge price increases (over 16 percent per year for ten years) were probably the major factor. Beer, wine, bottled water, and soft drinks appear to have been substituted by consumers for milk, spirits, and tap water, despite the fact that prices for the former beverages rose faster than prices for the latter; this suggests consumer taste change is responsible. However, except for coffee and tea, beverage prices rose more slowly than most other food categories, thus accounting for some of the rapid growth of the category as a whole.

Highly prepared convenience products generally enjoyed high real production increases from 1963 to 1982. The annual growth rates of breakfast cereals, tomato sauces, mayonnaise and salad dressings, pet foods, and salty snacks were especially buoyant (table 9–7). The moderate growth of canned ethnic foods and other canned specialties was distinctly better than that of most canned foods. Canned baby foods slowed for demographic reasons primarily. Dried soup mixes growth was negative after 1972 mainly because of extraordinarily high price increases. Indeed, what is surprising is how many convenience food product classes grow rapidly in spite of high price increases, especially after 1972 (for example, breakfast cereals, sauces, and pet foods). Probably rapid new product introductions helped counter consumer price resistance.

Summary

This chapter presented data on industry sizes as measured by value of shipments, employment, and value added. The reasons for differences in the intensity of value added (value added relative to shipments) among the forty-one food processing industries were explored in some detail. High-value-added industries had the following characteristics: they are predominantly consumer-goods industries; product differentiation, usually reinforced by advertising, is high; raw materials costs per pound are relatively low;

consumers expect high degrees of convenience in use; new product development is rapid; and the use of capital-intensive, flow-type processes is common.

High rates of output growth have occurred among nearly half of the food product classes since 1963, but it is rare for such extraordinary growth to persist for more than five to ten years. Indeed, it is not unusual for a product class to experience a sudden reversal in its growth pattern. The role of shifting prices and consumer preferences in real growth is studied in some detail for sixty-eight food and beverage classes. Many growth patterns are consistent with consumer desires for less salty, less fatty, fresher, and more convenient foods, but there are major instances that run counter to these preferences.

10
Principal Inputs Utilized

T he focus of this chapter is on differences among several food processing industries with respect to major inputs of production: materials, labor, energy, and capital equipment. Chapter 4 has already introduced these and other inputs in the context of the food processing industries as a whole. In general, the food industries are materials-intensive, capital-intensive, and labor-intensive compared to the rest of the manufacturing sector. That is, materials costs and assets are large relative to industry shipments, whereas labor costs are a relatively small portion of sales. However, these and other inputs vary considerably across the food processing industries.

Materials

The definition of *materials* is broad. It includes raw and semiprocessed agricultural products, containers, packaging, supplies used for repairs or maintenance, and products made under contract or bought and resold. In short, materials are physical goods (other than energy and fuel) "consumed" or used up during production. Land, plant structures, and equipment that depreciate slowly are considered capital.

Figure 10–1 shows how material costs vary widely among four representative food processing industries. Soybean crushing requires expenditures of over 90 percent of sales on materials consumed. Most of the materials are soybeans or semirefined soybean oil for further refining, but there is a considerable amount of contract work and resales (about 10 percent of sales). Soybean crushing is representative of several food processing industries that make industrial products.

The other three industries ship primarily consumer products. Meatpacking is typical of several food industries that make highly standardized products with relatively little value added. Compared to meatpacking, bread baking adds more value to the flour, milk, shortening, salt, and other ingredients it buys from other processors. Meat packing products are generally unbranded, whereas bakery products are a mixture of moderately differentiated branded products and products sold under store labels. The third industry, breakfast foods, is the epitome of the highly differentiated consumer products industry. The value added to the corn, oats, sugar,

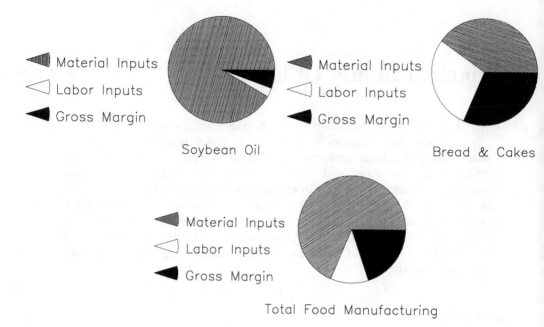

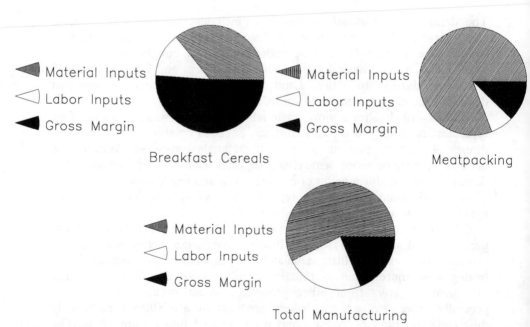

Figure 10–1. Costs and Margins of Selected Food Processing Industries, 1982

Source: Data from Appendix Table A20.

paper, and other ingredients purchased is very large relative to final sales price. As figure 10–1 illustrates, materials costs relative to sales falls as the degree of product differentiation rises. This pattern generally holds across the food processing industries (appendix table A20). If both materials and labor costs are a small portion of sales, as in the case of breakfast cereals, the opportunity for wide margins is great.

A special kind of "material" purchased by food processors is finished goods to be resold as is. That is, some manufacturers essentially carry on wholesaling activities along with their manufacturing activities. In 1982 food processors purchased $15,234 million of goods for resale at $18,993 million (the latter figure is a component of shipments that accounted for 6.6 percent of 1982 shipments value). The gross margin for these wholesaling activities earned by food processors was about 20 percent.

The cost of goods for resale amounted to 5.4 percent of shipments of food processors in 1982, twice as large as the manufacturing sector as a whole. However, this cost ratio varied considerably across various food processing industries (appendix table A20). It rose above 10 percent for meat processing, frozen specialties, miscellaneous vegetable oils, and canned seafood. It was well above average for most of the dairy processing industries, baking, distilling, and soft drinks bottling. In most cases, resold goods are the same type of those manufactured by the industry. The purchase of products for resale appears to allow a manufacturer to make a full line of products available to its customers where self-manufacture is not economical. Note that most of the industries with heavy resales also deliver direct to retail stores. For example, a soft drink bottler may purchase bottled spring water, root beer, or other small-selling lines in order to deliver a full array of flavors to stores it serves. A creamery that makes basic ice cream may purchase frozen novelties from other processors that would be inefficient for the creamery to manufacture itself.

Energy

The prices of petroleum-based fuels reached their post-World War II peak in 1982 at a level 475 percent above 1969 levels. Prices of most other energy sources were also at historical highs. By 1982 the food processing industries were spending over $5 billion per year for energy inputs. Yet, the cost of purchased fuels and electricity used for processing foods amounted to only 1.8 percent of the value of 1982 industry shipments; for all manufacturing energy intensity was 2.9 percent of shipments. Despite energy conservation efforts that intensified after the first "oil shock" of 1973, the intensity of energy costs in 1982 was 50 to 150 percent higher than in 1972 in most food processing industries.

Although energy costs are under 2 percent of shipments in the vast majority of the food processing industries, in a few it is considerably higher (appendix table A20). Drying fruits and vegetables requires significant energy for heating (3.9 percent of 1982 shipments value), as do wet corn milling (9.4 percent), cane sugar (3.8 percent) and beet sugar (12.1 percent) refining, animal fat rendering (8.0 percent), and barley malting (8.0 percent). Fruit and vegetable freezing requires 3.5 percent of shipments value to be used for energy costs. Perhaps one reason for the relative decline of the cottonseed oil industry is the high energy costs (5.6 percent of shipments) of production compared to other oil extraction methods (generally 2.5 to 3.0 percent).

Labor

Labor costs are second only to the costs of materials in the food processing industries, but they are a distant second. In 1982 payroll (wages and salaries) and supplementary wage benefits (social security, workmen's compensation, pensions, profit sharing, and the like) amounted to $32.1 billion or 11.4 percent of the value of food processing industry's shipments (appendix table A20). On average, supplementary wage payments added 22.8 percent to payroll costs. These data apply only to workers in operating food processing establishments. Recall that there are also food processing company employees located outside of plants in separate administrative or auxiliary establishments. These 109,000 employees in 1982 were paid an additional $3.0 billion. So, taking both classes of employees together, food processing companies' labor costs in 1982 were $35.1 billion or 12.5 percent of the value of industry shipments. Food processing is quite labor-extensive (low labor-shipments ratio) compared to the rest of the manufacturing sector. In 1982 the total manufacturing sector paid out 23.5 percent of its receipts in the form of labor costs, double the ratio in the food industries.

Labor cost intensity varies considerably among the food processing industries. Labor costs relative to sales are greatest in the bread baking (30.4 percent), cookies and crackers (21.5 percent), poultry dressing (17.8 percent), poultry processing (17.6 percent), pasta (16.2 percent), frozen specialties (15.6 percent), and soft drink bottling (15.3 percent). Many companies in these industries have direct plant-to-store delivery systems, and the salaries of driver-salesmen are included in payroll costs. Among the least labor-intensive of the food processing industries are butter (3.3 perecent of shipments), soybean oil (2.7 percent), miscellaneous vegetable oils (4.8 percent), coffee (5.6 percent), cheese (5.4 percent), rice (6.0 percent), meatpacking (7.0 percent), and animal feed (6.5 percent). These latter industries tend to be heavily capitalized with large amounts of labor-saving machinery in place to assist worker productivity.

Plant and Equipment

Expenditures for plants, offices, equipment, and other forms of tangible capital are a relatively small proportion of total costs in the food processing industries—about 4 percent in the last decade or more. Capital-related expenditures in 1982 included:

- $1,356 million for new buildings and structures;
- $5,371 million for new machinery and equipment;
- $735 million for used buildings and equipment;
- $306 million for rental of buildings; and
- $543 million for rental of machinery and equipment.

Thus, total expenditures were $8,311 million, of which about 22 percent was used for buildings and 78 percent for equipment. Information is available on two specific types of equipment purchased by the food processing industries: trucks were about 8 percent and data processing equipment about 2 percent of new equipment expenditures. Because of extensive direct-delivery operations, food processors purchased over one-fifth of all trucks bought by manufacturers.

Capital investment rates differ considerably among the food processing industries. Looking only at expenditures on new or used capital (i.e., excluding rentals), the investment rate for 1982 was found to vary from 13.1 percent of sales to 0.6 percent (appendix table A21). High rates of capital expenditure are found in food processing industries with high rates of expected future growth, rapid technological changes that require new equipment, and new product introductions that require changes in production methods or location.

For example, investment expenditures were very high relative to sales in such beverage industries as beer, wine, and soft drinks; rates are low in the fluid milk, spirits, and coffee industries that apparently have low growth prospects. This especially appears in the new plant investment category, where expenditures for the three former beverage industries totaled $297 million compared to $106 million in the three slower growth industries. Similarly, there are high capital investment levels in frozen foods, breakfast cereals, wet corn milling, and pasta industries, each of which had good growth prospects at the time. High investment in equipment is often spurred by new product development, such as sunflower, safflower, and olive oils in the "other vegetable oil" industry, and miscellaneous prepared foods industries. Investment in energy-reduction equipment appears to have been important in the cane sugar, ice, and cottonseed oil industries.

Assets

Annual expenditures in capital accumulate over time on the balance sheets of firms. After subtracting depreciation charges and "retired" capital, one is left with a balance sheet measure of asset values—gross book value of depreciable assets. These are "fixed" assets (plant and equipment), not goodwill assets or inventories. They are evaluated at historical prices rather than more appropriate market prices. Despite these drawbacks, net fixed assets are a conventional and convenient way of comparing asset intensities among industries.

Food processing employed about $58.6 billion in fixed assets at the end of 1982, which was $56,000 of fixed capital per production worker. The degree of capitalization per worker in food processing is about the same as the rest of manufacturing. However, some food industries are very capital intensive: grain products (except flour mixes and animal feeds), sugar, vegetable oils, coffee, and almost all the beverage industries (Connor et al. 1985:67–68). Many of these same industries are the ones with the least use of labor per dollar of shipments. In other words, there appears to be a great deal of substitution of capital for labor in many food industries. Others, such as poultry dressing, remain quite labor intensive.

Summary

In general, relative to comparable manufacturing industries, food processing is capital and materials intensive but labor and energy extensive. However, this section drew out the many variations among the forty-one food processing industries. Energy costs, for example, run as high as 12 percent of sales value in beet processing but are less than 1 percent in several other industries. Labor and salary costs are the second largest component of costs of food processors, amounting to over $35 billion in 1982 or 12.5 percent of industry shipments. Here, too, the range is enormous, from 30 percent for bread to 3 percent for soybean oil crushing.

Capital expenditures totaled $8.3 billion in 1982, but again the range was great. High rates of investment were characteristic of industries with rapid technological change and growth prospects. Indeed, new capital spending by food processing industries is a useful predictive indicator.

11
Organization of the Industries

This chapter parallels chapter 4 in its analysis of several structural features of the food processing industries. In particular, it examines the number of plants, number of companies, and size distribution of companies within each of the forty-one food processing industries. Data are presented on trends of each structural feature, focusing on the period 1963–1982. (More recent information is not obtainable.)

Plants

In 1982 there were 22,130 food and beverage processing plants in the United States (table 11–1). To be counted by the census, the plant must have had one paid employee and a minimal amount of shipments during the calendar year. More than half of the food processing plants had fewer than twenty employees, and many of these operated for only part of the year.[13]

Seven food processing industries had over 1,000 plants each in 1982: meatpacking, meat processing, fluid milk, animal feed, bread, soft drinks, and miscellaneous prepared foods. These seven industries alone accounted for 57 percent of all the food processing plants operating in 1982. Except for the two red meat industries, each serves essentially localized markets. For example there are about 50 to 100 separable fluid milk markets, each with a good sized city within it and each with a few fluid milk bottling plants. The industry with the fewest number of plants is wet corn milling with 42.

Nearly every food processing industry has experienced declining net numbers of food processing plants. The numbers shown in table 11–1 are *net* changes, the difference between gross entry and gross exit of operating plants. For example, a net decline of four plants in an industry during a given period might be the result of four new plants being built while eight were closed. However, a change in ownership of a plant would not affect the numbers shown in table 11–1.

In 1982 there were fifty-six percent fewer plants than in 1947 and 41 percent fewer than in 1963. During the most recent period, 1972–1982, an average of over 600 plants closed each year. The greatest number of plant closings occurred in the local-market industries just noted, probably because the geographic size of these markets has grown. A number of industries

Table 11–1
Numbers of Food Processing Plants, 1947–1982

Industry	Number of Plants				Change in Numbers		
	1947	1963	1972	1982	1947-1963	1963-1972	1972-1982
					- - - - - -Percent- - - - - -		
Meatpacking	2,154	2,992	2,475	1,780	+39	-17	-28
Meat processing	1,088	1,341	1,311	1,311	+23	-2	0
Poultry dressing	553	967	522	375	+75	-33	-28
Processed poultry			130	157			+21
Butter	1,904	766	231	74	-60	-70	-68
Cheese	1,877	1,138	872	704	-39	-23	-19
Prepared milk	451	281	283	204	-38	+1	-28
Ice cream	1,690	1,081	697	552	-36	-36	-21
Fluid milk	9,050	4,619	2,507	1,190	-49	-46	-53
Canned specialties	2,265	173	203	198	-29	+17	-2
Canned fruits and vegetables		1,430	1,038	715		-27	-31
Dry fruits and vegetables	146	176	178	151	+21	+1	-15
Sauces, pickles	742	588	495	376	-21	-16	-24
Frozen fruit and vegetables	291	650	209	264	+23	-1	+26
Frozen specialties			435	389			-11
Flour	1,243	618	457	360	-50	-26	-21
Breakfast cereals	64	48	47	52	-25	-2	+11
Rice	88	74	57	68	-16	-23	+19
Flour mixes	123	165	137	111	+34	-17	-19
Wet corn mills	55	60	41	42	+9	-32	+2
Pet foods			221	285			+29
Animal feeds	2,688	2,590	2,120	1,827	-4	-10	-14
Bread and rolls	6,769	5,010	3,323	2,305	-26	-34	-31
Cookies and crackers	326	356	315	358	+9	-12	+14
Cane sugar	107	99	110	81	-7	+11	-26
Beet sugar	74	65	61	48	-12	-6	-21
Confectionery	1,754	1,263	1,078	904	-28	-15	-16
Cottonseed oil	315	188	115	77	-40	-39	-33
Soybean oil	133	102	94	114	-23	-8	+21
Other fats and oils	728	662	542	415	-9	-18	-23
Cooking oil and margarine	127	115	109	118	-9	-5	+8
Beer	440	222	167	109	-50	-25	-35
Wine and brandy	418	222	210	366	-47	-5	+74
Spirits	226	107	121	104	-53	+13	-14
Soft drinks	5,618	3,905	2,687	1,626	-30	-32	-39
Flavorings	606	520	400	343	-14	-23	-14
Canned fish	254	405	310	204	+59	-23	-34
Frozen fish	--[a]	547	518	783	--	-5	+51
Coffee	--[b]	324	213	152	--	-61	-29
Pasta	226	221	194	230	-2	-12	+19
Miscellaneous prepared foods	5,730	3,431	2,957	2,608	-40	-14	-12
Total food processing[c]	50,350	37,521	28,193	22,130	-25	-25	-22
Rest of manufacturing	190,457	269,096	324,101	335,931	+41	+20	+4

Source: Data from U.S. Bureau of the Census, *1982 Census of Manufactures* (and previous editions).
— = Not available.
[a]Included in frozen fruits, vegetables, and specialties or in wholesale trade.
[b]Included in miscellaneous prepared foods.
[c]Excludes an additional 25 percent of plants for which little data were collected after 1967.

experienced consistently greater *percentage* declines than average; examples are butter, ice cream, fluid milk, canned fruits and vegetables, bread, cottonseed oil, beer, and coffee. Except for brewing, these industries have been growing slowly or not at all. The decline in food plants stands in sharp contrast to the rest of manufacturing where the number of plants increased by 76 percent since 1947.

A few industries have seen net increases in plant numbers during at least one of the three periods shown in table 11–1. For example, all the meat and poultry industries showed growth in plant numbers to 1963, but most declined thereafter. The frozen fruits and vegetables, pet food, wine, and pasta industries—all relatively fast-growing in recent years—have had new plants built in large numbers. Appendix table A24, which contains data on changes on food processing plants with twenty or more employees, shows four other food processing industries increasing in plant numbers: meat processing, cheese, flavorings, and miscellaneous prepared foods. These four industries also have been relatively fast growing. (There is reason to expect that the data presented in appendix table A24 are more accurate representations of the 1963–1972 trends because changes in Census Bureau methods affected only the counts of very small plants.)

Table 11–2 shows the employment size classes of plants by industry.

Table 11–2
Employment Size Distribution of Food Processing Plants, by Industry, 1963 and 1982

	1963			1982		
	Small	Medium	Large	Small	Medium	Large
Industry	(1-19)	(20-99)	(100 +)	(1-19)[a]	(20-99)	(100 +)
			Percent			
Meatpacking	67	23	10	73	17	10
Meat processing	64	26	10	66	24	10
Poultry dressing				29	12	59
	42	31	26			
Poultry processing				47	34	19
Butter	77	22	2	62	34	4
Cheese	82	16	2	64	28	8
Prepared milk	41	48	11	42	47	11
Ice cream	64	30	6	72	23	5
Fluid milk	58	31	11	48	33	19
Canned specialties	55	22	23	69	13	18
Canned fruit and vegetables	42	38	20	50	26	24
Dried fruit and vegetables	55	32	13	57	23	20
Sauces and pickles	69	22	10	71	18	11
Frozen fruits and vegetables				34	25	41
	47	30	23			
Frozen specialties				51	27	22

Table 11–2 continued

Industry	1963			1982		
	Small (1-19)	Medium (20-99)	Large (100 +)	Small (1-19)[a]	Medium (20-99)	Large (100 +)
				Percent		
Flour	65	24	11	63	27	10
Breakfast cereals	38	31	31	41	19	40
Rice	34	51	15	43	35	22
Flour mixes	64	24	13	61	22	17
Wet corn mills	67	10	23	45	18	37
Pet foods	} 73	} 24	} 3	60	27	13
Animal feeds				74	25	1
Bread, rolls	64	23	13	68	17	15
Cookies and crackers	42	35	24	62	21	17
Cane sugar	1	46	53	22	34	44
Beet sugar	5	6	89	8	13	79
Confectionery	64	23	13	70	19	11
Cottonseed oil	19	74	13	33	48	19
Soybean oil	30	57	13	37	44	19
Other fats and oils	65	31	4	59	38	3
Cooking oil and margarine	25	34	41	35	28	37
Beer	19	27	54	47	13	40
Wine	68	27	5	81	14	5
Liquor	17	48	36	35	32	33
Soft drinks	61	34	5	46	38	16
Flavorings	81	15	4	71	23	6
Canned seafood	52	41	7	59	32	9
Frozen seafood	53	39	7	52	38	10
Coffee	59	28	13	50	31	19
Pasta	68	20	12	77	16	7
Miscellaneous prepared foods	79	17	4	76	18	6
Total		.		63	24	13

Source: Data from U.S. Bureau of the Census, *1982 Census of Manufactures* and previous editions.
[a]Includes 7,122 establishments covered by administrative records from other government agencies.

Only one-seventh of all food processing plants are "large"; that is, have at least 100 employees. Only nine of the forty-one industries have at least one-third of their plants in the large category. In general the size of food processing plants, measured by the number of employees per plant, increased from 1963 to 1982. Larger plants are seen in the meat, dairy, frozen foods, sugar, and alcoholic beverages industries, though the shift is not enormous. Moreover, a reverse shift in plant sizes is seen in many industries (sauces, corn wet mills, soft drink bottling, and coffee), and in others the movement has been towards mid-sized plants (canned fruits and vegetables, rice, and vegetable oils).

Companies

The patterns of plant numbers and company numbers[14] are quite similar in most ways. Because of multiple ownership, the number of companies is less than the number of plants in each industry (table 11–3). In 1982 16,800 companies owned at least one operating plant in one food processing industry. The number of food processing companies in each industry varies quite widely—from a high of 2,300 in miscellaneous prepared foods to a low of 14 beet sugar companies. The former industry is quite mixed, of course, including at least 80 firms making potato chips, 36 packaging tea, 23

Table 11–3
Numbers of Food Processing Companies, 1947–1982

Industry	Number of Companies[a]				Change in Numbers		
	1947	1963	1972	1982	1947–1963	1963–1972	1972–1982
					- - - Percent - - -		
Meatpacking	1,999	2,833	2,291	1,658	+42	-19	-28
Meat processing	1,083	1,273	1,207	1,193	+18	-5	-1
Poultry dressing	} 330	} 842	407	231	} +155	} -38	-43
Processed poultry			110	136			+24
Butter	1,583	725	201	61	-54	-72	-70
Cheese	1,313	982	739	575	-25	-25	-22
Prepared milk	182	167	172	132	-8	+3	-23
Ice cream	1,273	901	561	482	-29	-38	-14
Fluid milk	7,875	4,030	2,025	853	-49	-50	-58
Canned specialties	} 1,856	154	178	171	} -31	+16	-4
Canned fruit and vegetables		1,135	765	514		-33	-33
Dried fruit and vegetables	120	126	133	119	+5	+6	-11
Sauces and pickles	637	541	429	325	-15	-21	-24
Frozen fruit and vegetables	254	566	136	195	+123	-7	+43
Frozen specialties			388	318			-18
Flour	1,084	510	340	251	-53	-33	-26
Breakfast cereals	55	35	24	32	-36	-31	+33
Rice	75	62	48	49	-17	-23	+2
Flour mixes	115	140	115	91	+22	-18	-21
Wet corn mills	47	49	26	25	+4	-47	-4
Pet foods	} 2,372	} 2,150	147	222	} -9	} -20	+51
Animal feeds			1,579	1,245			-21
Bread and rolls	5,985	4,339	2,801	1,869	-28	-35	-33
Cookies and crackers	249	286	257	296	+15	-10	+15
Cane sugar	94	66	83	62	-30	+26	-25
Beet sugar	17	11	16	14	-35	+45	-13
Confectionery	1,686	1,186	971	804	-30	-18	-17

Table 11–3 continued

Industry	Number of Companies[a]				Change in Numbers		
	1947	1963	1972	1982	1947–1963	1963–1972	1972–1982
					- - - Percent - - -		
Cottonseed oil	177	115	74	47	-35	-36	-36
Soybean oil	105	68	54	52	-35	-21	-4
Other fats and oils	616	555	430	296	-10	-23	-31
Cooking oil and margarine	68	65	64	79	-4	-2	+23
Beer	404	150	108	67	-63	-28	-38
Wine	379	194	183	324	-49	-6	+77
Spirits	144	70	76	71	-51	+9	-7
Soft drinks	5,169	3,569	2,273	1,236	-31	-36	-46
Flavorings	582	492	350	297	-15	-29	-15
Canned fish	187	345	258	170	+84	-25	-34
Frozen fish[b]	--	528	470	697	--	-11	+48
Coffee[c]	--	261	162	118	--	-38	-27
Pasta	219	207	179	208	-5	-14	+16
Miscellaneous prepared foods	4,286	2,868	2,496	2,300	-33	-13	-8
Total duplicated	42,469	32,342	23,132	17,885	-24	-28	-23
Total unduplicated	--	31,500E	22,349	16,813	--	-29	-25

Sources: Data from Connor (1982b:Appendix Table 11) and *1982 Census of Manufactures*.
E = Estimated.
— = Not available.
[a]Number of companies owning and operating one or more plants in the industry. Companies owning plants in two industries are counted double in "total duplicated" row and in a few combined industries.
[b]In 1963, most companies classified in wholesaling.
[c]In 1963, included in Miscellaneous prepared foods.

fermenting vinegar, 65 assembling refrigerated salads, 111 baking tortillas, 31 blending peanut butter, and so on. Over one-third of all food processing firms serve local markets (ice cream, fluid milk, animal feed, bread, soft drinks, chips, and a few others).

Since 1947 the number of food processing companies has fallen by over 60 percent; since 1963 the drop was about 50 percent. Because of mergers, the decline in company numbers was greater than the decline in plant numbers. The five local-market industries have accounted for a net decline of 17,000 companies since 1947, or about 70 percent of the total loss in company numbers. Moreover, except for animal feed firms, the percentage drop in local-market firms was greater than the drop for all food processing companies. Other industries with especially severe losses in company numbers were butter (96 percent decline from 1947 to 1982), canned fruits and vegetables (about 70 percent), flour (77 percent), cottonseed oil (73 percent), beer (83 percent), and coffee (about 70 percent). In all cases, except for beer, low growth rates contributed to the disappearance of firms in the industry. Another contributing factor in a few food processing industries is the increase in economies of scale of production and distribution: butter, fluid milk, baking, cottonseed oil, and brewing appear to fit this description. As economies of scale and geographic scope increase, there is a need for fewer plants to serve the market (even a growing one), and as most food processing firms operate only a single plant, firm numbers also decline.

Only nine food processing industries had *more* companies in 1982 than in 1947 or 1963: meat processing, poultry processing, frozen foods, breakfast cereals, pet food, cookies and crackers, shortening and cooking oils, and wine. In all cases these industries experienced above-average growth in demand. This allowed some companies to exploit small but stable segments of product demand. In other cases, new companies were founded to serve fast-growing specialty markets. Most of the wineries begun in recent years started by selling only a few thousand cases of high-priced wine made from one or a very few varietal grapes; "granola" cereals encouraged the entry of many small breakfast cereal manufacturers that could sell to health food stores. The start-up of several "microbreweries" that make expensive beers in a European style will probably lead to a slight rise in brewing company numbers after 1982.

Sales Concentration

One effect of lower company numbers, when disappearances occur primarily among lower ranking firms, is a rise in the market shares of the leading firms. That is, industry sales concentration rises. Sales concentration is an important piece of information for business people and public officials alike. High concentration normally is a source of high profit for firms doing business in an industry; on the other hand, high concentration typically signals the presence of problems for firms that are outside the industry but would like to enter it (Connor & Wills 1987). Concentration ratios are used for antitrust enforcement decisions, particularly in the case of mergers. High concentration before or subsequent to a merger is likely to lead the antitrust agencies to mount a legal challenge against the acquiring firm.

Table 11–4 presents levels of concentration for each food processing industry in 1963 and 1982. In 1982 the average national-market four-firm concentration ratio was 49.5 percent; including the five local-market industries would likely raise average four-firm concentration to the 52–56 percent range. The most concentrated industries were soft drinks, breakfast cereals, beer, wet corn milling, canned specialties (soup, baby food, and ethnic foods), and coffee. The least concentrated were fresh and frozen packaged fish, processed red meats, and butter (all below 30 percent). The four-firm concentration ratio is the most conventional measure of concentration, but the Hirshman-Herfindahl index is also given for comparative purposes.[15] This index is currently being used by the Justice Department to decide whether to prosecute or enjoin mergers. If a merger would leave an industry below the 1,000 mark, no action would be taken; if the index would

Table 11–4

Sales Concentration in the Food Processing Industries, 1963 and 1982

Industry	Four-Firm Sales Concentration[a]		Hirschman-Herfindahl Index, 1982[b]
	1963	1982	
	-----Percent-----		
Meatpacking	30.2	42.7	680
Meat processing	25.3	26.8	404
Poultry dressing	17.8	34.5	NA
Poultry processing	33.0	36.3	NA
Butter	37.0*	29.0	377
Cheese	45.6	44.1	844
Prepared milk	34.3	44.3	893
Ice cream (local)	34.0 (62.0)	22.0	214
Fluid milk (local)	24.6 (53.0)	22.7	267
Canned specialties	81.8	71.0	2,594E
Canned fruits and vegetables	36.7	42.7	709
Dried fruits and vegetables	45.1	53.6	1,119
Sauces, pickles	41.8	55.3	1,296
Frozen fruits and vegetables	33.2	37.5	605
Frozen specialties	49.8	46.4	776
Flour	42.2	50.4	872
Breakfast cereals	82.0	81.0	2,058
Rice	46.0	44.0	795
Flour mixes	60.0	59.0	1,141
Wet corn mills	65.0	77.9	1,721
Pet foods	42.0	63.1	1,402
Animal feeds (local)	22.0 (NA)	30.8	412
Bread, rolls (local)	22.0 (43.0)	37.9	581
Cookies and crackers	59.6	62.5	1,599
Cane sugar	58.6	58.6	1,213
Beet sugar	66.0	67.0	1,382
Confectionery	34.0	61.1	1,507

Table 11–4 continued

Industry	Four-Firm Sales Concentration[a]		Hirschman-Herfindahl Index, 1982[b]
	1963	1982	
	- - - - - - -Percent- - - - - - -		
Cottonseed oil	40.0	55.1	981
Soybean oil	48.0	57.0	1,068
Other fats and oils	35.9	37.7	574
Cooking oil and margarine	50.8	48.9	783
Beer	34.0	80.2	2,271
Wine	50.0	52.0	1,008
Spirits	56.8	50.4	822
Soft drinks (local)	89.0 (89.0)	90.0 (90.0)	3,417E
Flavorings	58.6	64.8	1,794
Canned fish	33.0	44.0	582
Frozen fish	34.9*	23.9	266
Coffee	40.5	70.2	1,407
Pasta	28.0	53.9	1,077
Miscellaneous prepared foods	53.6	50.4	1,332
Total, excluding local markets	39.5	49.5	985
Total, including local markets	43.0	--	--

Source: Data from Connor et al. (1985:137–39) and *1982 Census of Manufactures*.

E = Estimated.

*Used earliest year available after 1963 because of definitional changes.

[a]Percent of sales by top four companies in the product classes in the industry, weighted by value of product shipments and excluding "NSK" classes. (Estimates in parentheses are for appropriately defined regional markets.) Estimated a few missing CR4s.

[b]The HHI is the sum of the squared percentage market shares of the fifty leading companies in the product classes. Range is from close to zero up to 10,000 for a monopoly.

be above 1,800, action blocking the merger is virtually certain; index levels between 1,000 and 1,800 is a gray area.

The market definitions used in table 11–4 are the narrowest ones available from public data sources; all food processing output was placed into 170 SIC product classes. However, private market-research companies use even narrower product definitions when they sell market-share information to food processing companies. Companies like A.C. Nielsen and SAMI (Selling-Area Markets, Inc.) divide their data on warehoused foods and beverages into approximately 450 categories. For example, the SIC system recognizes only one class for breakfast cereals, whereas the proprietary companies distinguish ready-to-eat from to-be-cooked breakfast cereals. If the narrower definitions are really the way business people view markets when making competitive decisions, they are superior systems for measuring market shares and concentration levels.

Table 11–5 uses market shares developed from grocery warehouse-withdrawal data compiled by A.C. Nielsen (April–May 1980 *Supermarket Directory*). Although these data have several limitations, the general message is clear. When using narrower and on the whole more appropriate market definitions, concentration is much higher than official data indicate. Two-thirds of the Nielsen edible products categories were dominated (at least 40 percent market share) by a single leading brand (table 11–5). The 204 product categories with dominant brands accounted for 54 percent of retail grocery sales of the sample categories. On the other hand, true monopoly situations are quite rare and involve a negligible share of grocery product sales.

Sales concentration levels for individual Nielsen grocery product categories are shown in appendix table A25. Coverage is incomplete, but it is quite good for many dry groceries and frozen foods. One general observation is that concentration is usually higher for more highly processed products that are newer to the market. For example, in the rice products industry, precooked rice is twice as concentrated as regular packaged rice.

Usually concentration levels are quite stable over the years, but in the food processing industries several changes have recurred (table 11–4). Between 1963 and 1982 overall four-firm concentration rose a hefty 25 percent (that is, 10 percentage points). Three-fourths of the food industries

Table 11–5
Edible Products Categories, by Market Share of the Leading Brand, 1980

Market Share of the Leading Brand	Number of Nielsen Categories	Retail Sales of Categories
	Number	Million dollars
71% to 100%	72	4,194
51% to 70%	66	7,095
40% to 50%	66	11,944
Less than 40%	93	19,904
Total	297	43,137

Source: Adapted from A.C. Nielson Co., *Supermarket Directory*, April–May 1980 (revised 1981 version). See also Appendix Table A25.

Note: Market shares are based on national retail grocery sales (including store brands). In 1980 there were 422 edible product categories. However, 44 categories were severely affected by direct store delivery (a form of delivery omitted by the data source) and in 81 categories private label products were, as a group, market leaders. The latter two types of categories are not included in this table.

rose in concentration. Some of them showed extraordinary increases: beer (+136 percent), coffee (+73 percent), pasta (+93 percent), confectionery (+80 percent), poultry dressing (+94 percent), meatpacking (+41 percent), and pet food (+50 percent) are the outstanding examples. Only frozen fish declined by as much as 30 percent. The major factor affecting concentration change in the food manufacturing industries is advertising intensity. When advertising as a percent of sales is high, concentration rises twice as fast as the average; when it is absent, as in the case of industrial products, concentration is stable (Connor et al. 1985:108–13). High advertising intensity is either a cause or a symptom of factors responsible for discouraging entry into consumer foods processing industries.

Summary

This wide-ranging chapter covered a number of dimensions of the business and competitive organization of the forty-one food processing industries. The greatest net declines in numbers of food plants and companies are found mainly in the slower growing industries serving geographically localized markets. Expanding economies of scale may have contributed to reduced numbers also. Market concentration levels are higher and increasing in industries that produce highly differentiated foods. From 1963 to 1982, the share of the top four firms rose from 39.5 percent on average to 49.5 percent. The greatest increase was in the brewing industry, which saw concentration rise 136 percent. Other commercial market-share sources indicate that half or more of the warehoused product categories are dominated by single brands.

12
Technological Change

Obtaining data on R&D or other evidence of technological progressiveness in individual industries is a daunting task. No government data series exists. R&D is by its very nature a companywide activity, difficult to partition according to company profit centers. The results of R&D activity can be seen in scientific publications, patent awards, and commercialization of product and process innovations. New product introductions, an ambiguous measure of technological progressiveness, can be seen in appendix table A12 for the years 1964–1986.

Table 12–1 assembles four indicators of technological progressiveness among the food processing industries, each keyed to the year 1975 and each divided by company or industry sales to facilitate comparisons. The first two columns refer to R&D expenditures, an input measure of innovative effort. These expenditures are generated by the cash-flow of food processors; unlike most other manufacturing industries, no government funds are received by food processors for research. The last two columns measure two outputs of R&D effort, scientific publications and patents. The latter statistics come from a meticulous study of all publications appearing over eleven years in the *Science Citation Index* that were authored by scientists affiliated with food processing companies and an exhaustive search of U.S. Patent Office records of patents awarded to food processing companies in the United States for a fifteen year period. In each case the company or a subsidiary was assigned to a specific industry. The problem of accurately assigning diversified companies to only one industry affects all the data in table 12–1 except the second column.

There are substantial differences in technological progressiveness among industries, and in general all four indexes tell the same story. The meat and poultry industries display below-average progressiveness in all respects, with the poultry industry particularly retrograde. The dairy industries are also below but closer to the average levels of progressiveness, The canning and freezing industries spend slightly above-average amounts on R&D, but except for canned specialties there is little to show for it by way of output. Perhaps these industries have corporate policies that discourage patenting or publishing. The grain-based industries all spend above-average amounts on R&D; the wet corn milling and breakfast cereals companies had the two highest rates of patenting and publishing of any of the food processing industries. The baking industries showed low to moderate technological

Table 12-1
Technological Progressiveness among the U.S. Food Processing Industries, Selected Periods, 1961–1976

Industry	Company R&D Sales Intensity		Number of Scientific and Technical Publications 1965–1975	Number of Patents Assigned in U.S. 1961–1975
	95 Large Public Companies 1974–75	472 Largest Manufacturers 1974–76		
	Percent of 1975 sales			
Meatpacking	0.1	0.1	1.0	2.6
Meat processing	0.2	0.0	0.2	0.0
Poultry	0.3		0.0	0.0
Butter	NA	0.3	2.6	0.3
Cheese	0.2		1.3	4.4
Prepared milk	NA		0.8	1.5
Fluid milk and ice cream	0.2	0.0	1.0	4.4
Canned specialties	0.7	0.6	6.0	8.7
Canned fruits and vegetables	0.6	0.6	0.0	0.0
Dried fruits and vegetables	0.0		0.0	0.0
Sauces and dressings	0.0		0.0	0.0
Frozen fruits, vegetables, and specialties	0.2	0.5	0.1	1.7
Flour and flour mixes	0.3	0.7	1.9	4.6
Rice	NA		0.1	0.4
Breakfast cereals	1.0	0.8	9.6	56.2
Wet corn milling	0.7	0.7	11.0	32.3
Pet foods and animal feeds	0.4	0.7	1.2	1.3

Bread, rolls, cakes	0.1	0.2	0.4	0.2
Cookies and crackers	0.6	0.3	0.6	3.4
Cane and beet sugar	0.2	0.2	3.4	0.8
Confectionery	0.5	0.4	0.1	0.3
Fats and oils	0.1	0.2	5.0	7.1
Beer and malt	0.4	0.3	1.3	3.3
Wine and spirits	0.3	0.3	1.2	22.8
Soft drinks bottling and flavorings	0.7	0.2	2.0	2.7
Fish products	0.0	NA	0.0	0.0
Coffee	0.7	0.6 ⎱	6.8	24.4
Pasta	0.0	0.6 ⎰	0.0	0.0
Miscellaneous foods	1.3	0.6	1.6	1.1
Total food processing	0.4	0.4	1.5	4.2

Sources: Data from annual reports assembled by the author; Peckham (1980); and FTC (1982).

Note: Data on the ninety-five companies from fiscal 1974 or 1975 annual reports; companies accounted for $84.9 billion in sales, about 52 percent of the total of all food processing companies. Data on the 472 manufacturers is from a special FTC survey that requested R&D and sales data on a line-of-business basis; there were about 360 food business segments reported in 1975. The last two columns are from Peckham; numbers of publications by scientists employed by food processors totalled 2,260 and numbers of patents totalled 6,362; both were divided by 1975 value of shipments in millions of dollars.

NA = Not available

Table 12–2
Multifactor Productivity Change in Food Processing, 1958–1982

Industry Group	1958-1963	1963-1967	1967-1972	1972-1977	1977-1982	1958-1982
			Percent per year			
Meat and poultry	1.7	-0.9	0.7	-0.1	0.6	0.4
Dairy products	-0.6	0.3	0.7	2.1	0.3	0.5
Fruit & vegetable processing	1.8	0.6	-0.2	0.0	0.4	0.5
Grain products	-1.0	-1.4	1.4	-1.1	1.9	0.0
Bakery products	0.4	0.3	1.4	-1.3	0.2	0.2
Sugar and confectionery	0.6	0.5	-0.1	-1.3	1.0	0.1
Fats and oils	1.9	0.2	-1.2	0.1	0.2	0.2
Beverages	0.2	0.4	0.3	0.3	-0.5	0.1
Miscellaneous foods	1.4	-2.8	-0.8	-2.7	2.0	-0.5
Total	0.6	-0.3	0.5	-0.1	0.7	0.3

Source: Data from Lee (1986).

effort, and all the indicators placed cookies and crackers slightly above bread.

The sugar industries have below-average R&D expenditures whereas confectionery is at or above average, yet their positions are reversed when publishing and patenting are taken into account. Perhaps the discrepancy is due to a high level of developmental activity in confectionery (especially chewing gum), whereas the sugar industry performs more basic and applied research. Except for flavorings, the beverage industries all spend below average amounts on R&D, though patent activity is quite high in the wine and spirits industries. All indications are that fish products firms performed no R&D. Of the remaining industries, coffee stands out as relatively progressive, perhaps because of work going on in the crystalization of soluble coffees at that time.

Another indicator of the adoption of process-type innovations in an industry is the rate of productivity change. As was argued in chapter 6, multifactor productivity change is a superior measure. This statistic compares the rate of change in the quantity of output with the rate of change in the use of several inputs (labor, capital, materials, and energy). Lee (1986) calculated multifactor productivity rates for nine food industry groups for the years 1958 to 1982 (table 12–2). For the full period, each of the industry groups except miscellaneous foods had positive, if low, rates of productivity growth. Meats, dairy, and fruits and vegetables had the highest rates of change. However, all the industry groups experienced some periods of negative productivity change.

13
Anticipated Growth

One good source of long-term growth predictions for U.S. food demand is the study by Blaylock and Smallwood (1986), which was explained in chapter 7. This study took into account such expected demographic changes as population growth, age profile, racial composition, and regional distribution. Predictions are made up to the year 2020 for two alternative growth scenarios, 1 percent or 2 percent annual increases per year in real (inflation-adjusted) household disposable income. No account can be taken of changes in relative prices, qualities, or tastes. The results are shown for seventeen food and beverage groups in table 13–1.

Growth in real food demand from the base year 1980 to 2000 is anticipated to be in the range of 27 to 39 percent, or 1.2 to 1.7 percent per year on average. Food eaten away from home is expected to rise faster (1.4 to 2.0 percent per year) than food purchased for at-home use (1.2 to 1.4 percent annually). Among the food groups, 1980–2000 growth in demand is predicted to be highest for fish (32 to 43 percent), alcoholic beverages (29 to 48 percent), and butter and cheese (27 to 37 percent). Growth of demand for milk and cream (19 to 20 percent) is expected to be the lowest category. Most of the others are close to the all-food average. Differences widen (as does the range of prediction) as one moves further out into the future.

The other principal method of making predictions about food demand is through the use of large-scale econometric models. These models are proving fairly accurate for short- to medium-term predictions (two to five years), but often data available on shipments or employment for individual industries are two or three years old, so predictions are actually made only for the current year or a year or two into the future. An example of such a predictive exercise for the food processing industries is given in appendix table A23. Several industry predictions already appear to be inaccurate.

One way of improving upon the predictions of large-scale models is to temper the results with the knowledge of industry experts. This is the approach taken by the U.S. Department of Commerce in its publication *U.S. Industrial Outlook* released in January each year.

Table 13–1
Predicted U.S. Demand for Processed Foods, 2000, 2010, and 2020

Food Product	1980-81 Allocation of of Food Expenditures	Year 2000 Low Growth (1%)	2000 High Growth (2%)	2010 Low Growth (1%)	2010 High Growth (2%)	2020 Low Growth (1%)	2020 High Growth (2%)
	Percent	100 = Expenditures in 1980					
Beef	13.1	126	133	139	150	150	165
Pork	6.9	127	131	140	146	151	157
Other red meats	4.6	123	128	134	141	142	150
Poultry	4.4	126	128	138	141	148	148
Butter	0.6	127	137	140	158	152	176
Cheese	3.6	127	137	139	153	150	168
Milk and cream	7.0	119	120	127	128	133	134
Other dairy products	2.1	126	132	137	147	148	161
Fruit, canned and frozen	3.6	127	133	140	150	151	165
Vegetables, canned & frozen	2.8	127	133	140	149	151	162
Cereal and bakery products	12.7	124	128	134	141	143	151
Sugar and sweeteners	3.6	124	128	134	139	144	149
Fats and oils	2.1	125	129	136	142	146	154
Margarine	0.7	126	127	137	137	146	143
Nonalcoholic beverages	9.0	124	127	134	140	142	150
Alcoholic beverages	10.9	129	148	143	178	158	215
Miscellaneous foods	9.0	125	131	136	147	147	161
Total food at home	67.6	126	132	139	148	149	162
Total food away from home	32.4	131	149	146	179	162	212
Total food	100.0	127	139	142	160	155	182

Source: Data from Blaylock and Smallwood (1986).

Note: The indexes represent levels of real household expenditures relative to 1980; that is, 100 = expenditures in 1980. The "low growth" scenario assumes a 1 percent increase per year in real household disposable incomes, and the "high growth" scenario assumes 2 percent per year. The projections are based on differences in expenditure patterns revealed by the 1980–1981 Continuing Consumer Expenditure Survey. The predictions take into account the demographic changes (population growth, age distribution, regional distribution, and racial distribution) predicted by the U.S. Bureau of the Census ("middle series"). No account is taken of changing tastes, relative prices, quality changes, or female work participation.

14
International Trade and Investment

This section parallels data presented on investment and trade for the food processing industries as a group in Section I.H above. Details are given for imports, exports, and investment flows to the extent possible at the individual industry level.

International Trade

Recent data on U.S. imports and exports of processed foods and beverages is given in table 14–1. In 1986 imports exceeded $16 billion and exports approached $11 billion, leaving a trade deficit of over $5 billion. Except for the early 1980s, it appears that the United States has had a trade deficit in processed foods for the past fifteen years or more (table 8–2). The principal U.S. exports were meatpacking products ($2,340 million in 1986), soybean oil and meal ($1,373), wet corn milling products including corn gluten ($902

Table 14–1
Imports and Exports of Processed Foods and Beverages, 1985 and 1986

Industry	Imports		Exports		Trade Balance	
	1985	1986[a]	1985	1986[a]	1985	1986
	Million dollars					
Meatpacking	1,683	1,729	1,997	2,340	314	611
Processed meats	711	673	40	52	-671	-621
Poultry dressing	19	23	232	274	213	251
Processed poultry	9	11	39	55	30	44
Butter	2	2	71	31	69	29
Cheese	374	387	29	22	-345	-365
Prepared milk	209	212	340	323	131	111
Ice cream	0	0	3	5	3	5
Fluid milk	10	11	25	34	15	23
Canned specialties	28	25	37	33	9	8
Canned fruit and vegetables	1,868	1,556	220	223	-1,648	-1,333
Dry fruit and vegetables	119	84	235	248	116	164
Sauces, pickles	46	51	41	47	-5	-4
Frozen fruit and vegetables	118	128	261	262	143	134
Frozen specialties	0	0	25	27	25	27

Table 14-1 continued

Industry	Imports		Exports		Trade Balance	
	1985	1986[a]	1985	1986[a]	1985	1986
	Million dollars					
Flour	55	51	346	306	291	255
Breakfast cereals	12	11	23	21	11	10
Rice	25	31	659	528	634	497
Flour mixes	7	7	8	7	1	0
Wet corn mills	45	50	693	902	648	852
Pet foods	26	39	89	97	63	58
Animal feeds	60	64	358	349	298	285
Bread, rolls	28	32	15	14	-13	-18
Cookies and crackers	216	259	30	25	-186	-234
Cane sugar	820	670	129	165	-691	-505
Beet sugar	90	79	52	77	-38	-2
Confectionery	975	1,009	210	219	-765	-790
Cottonseed oil	9	8	140	95	131	87
Soybean oil	7	2	1,199	1,373	1,192	1,371
Other fats and oils	706	580	777	654	71	74
Cooking oils and margarine	0	0	203	125	203	125
Beer	654	856	46	38	-608	-818
Wine and brandy	1,185	1,386	28	31	-1,157	-1,355
Spirits	1,021	1,015	89	25	-932	-990
Soft drinks	120	91	22	23	-98	-68
Flavorings	76	89	195	211	119	122
Canned fish	2,422	2,533	106	111	-2,316	-2,422
Frozen fish	1,441	1,675	902	926	-539	-749
Coffee	195	300	91	90	-104	-210
Pasta	63	60	8	7	-55	-53
Miscellaneous foods	522	587	259	299	-281	-288
Total	15,976	16,389	10,254	10,794	-5,722	-5,595

Source: Data from International Trade Administration and Bureau of the Census, in *U.S. Industrial Outlook 1987*, pp. 39-4 to 39-39.
[a]Data for 1986 estimated by the U.S. Department of Commerce.

million), frozen fish ($926 million), other fats and oils ($654 million), and rice ($528 million). These six industries accounted for 62 percent of 1986 U.S. processed food exports. The major processed food and beverage imports are canned and cured fish ($2,533 million), meat ($1,729 million), frozen fish ($1,675 million), canned fruits and vegetables ($1,556 million), distilled spirits ($1,015 million) wine ($1,386 million), and confectionery ($1,009 million). These $7 billion plus industries accounted for 67 percent of 1986 imports. Generally, where imports are absolutely large, there is also a large trade deficit because there are few counterbalancing exports; the prime exception is meatpacking products. The U.S. has a net trade surplus in most of the meat, dairy, grain, and oilseed industries, whereas trade deficits are the rule among the other food industries. Put another way, U.S. exports consist primarily of undifferentiated, low-value-added products, whereas imported processed foods tend to be packaged consumer products with relatively high intensity of value added (to the exporting countries' economies). Import quotas on meat and dairy products and export subsidies for milk powder, flour, and vegetable oils assisted U.S. trade surpluses.

Table 14–2 looks more deeply at product class exports at two time

Table 14–2
Major U.S. Agricultural and Processed Food Exports, 1970–1972 and 1980–1982 Averages

Products	Value Exported 1970-72 Average	Value Exported 1980-82 Average	Proportion of Domestic Production 1970-72	Proportion of Domestic Production 1980-82
	$ Million		Percent	
1. Corn	937	7,387	18	40
2. Wheat	1,127	6,965	52	72
3. Soybeans	1,350	6,107	37	47
4. Cotton	489	2,379	30	59
5. Tobacco	521	1,445	38	45
6. Other farm products	654	4,230	--	--
Total farm products	5,078	28,513	35	53
1. Soybean cake and meal	400	1,607	26	31
2. Rice and rice products	320	1,260	56	63
3. Hides and skins	197	714	56	86
4. Animal fats	198	656	45	61
5. Wet corn mill products	65	613	8	20
6. Beef	85	544	1	3
7. Fresh and frozen fish	38	500	6	31
8. Soybean oil	147	416	18	16
9. Sugar	9	387	0	8
10. Chickens	26	306	1	7
11. Canned seafood	46	296	10	22
12. Dried fruit and vegetables	70	280	16	21
13. Wheat flour	91	279	6	9
14. Flavorings	56	244	11	6
15. Prepared milk	168	236	18	5
16. Pork	49	225	2	3
17. Cooking oils and shortening	73	205	5	5
Total processed foods	2,840	11,825	2.8	4.2

Source: Data from Appendix Table A15.

periods. During 1980–1982 farm-product exports peaked at almost $29 billion with five products (corn, wheat, soybeans, cotton, and tobacco) accounting for most farm exports. In ten years farm product exports had increased in dollar value by 460 percent and accounted for over half of all U.S. farm output. On the processed side, accounting for about 30 percent of U.S. food and agricultural exports, the products shipped abroad are far more diversified. Processed food exports increased by 316 percent over the ten year period. On average only 4.2 percent of domestic output of processed foods were exported, but that ratio was much higher for soybean meal, rice, hides, and animal fats. The list of exported products is dominated by the less processed items.

The detailed picture on imports is quite different. Imports of unprocessed products consists mostly of coffee, bananas, and other so-called noncompetitive products (table 14–3). There was a very favorable trade surplus in farm-

Table 14–3
Major U.S. Agricultural and Processed Foods Imports, 1970–1972 and 1980–1982 Averages

Products	Imports for Consumption		Proportion Domestic Production	
	1970-72	1980-82	1970-72	1980-82
	$ Million		Percent	
1. Tree nuts (incl. coffee)	1,473	3,954	NA	NA
2. Leaf tobacco	135	379	9	12
Total farm products	1,729	4,791	12	9
1. Sugar	824	2,336	23	25
2. Beef	688	1,515	8	7
3. Distilled spirits	524	1,024	26	25
4. Wine and brandy	192	1,022	21	29
5. Canned and frozen fruits and juices	94	635	5	7
6. Other vegetable oils	154	530	4	5
7. Canned meats	308	479	22	23
8. Chocolate and cocoa	51	450	10	17
9. Beer	NA	452	0	5
10. Canned seafood	164	432	25	22
11. Cheese	90	352	3	4
12. Coffee, soluble	59	231	10	14
13. Prepared milk	90	206	NA	5
Total processed foods	5,842	11,419	5.8	4.1

Source: Data from Appendix Table A14.

commodity trade in both periods. Although farm import rose, import value declined as a proportion of domestic farm output.

Most agriculturally related U.S. imports are processed foods and beverages—77 percent in 1970–1972 and 70 percent in 1980–1982. Some imported processed food products are fairly low in value added: beef, sugar, and vegetable oils (palm, coconut, olive, etc.). But for the most part, U.S. imports are at the highly processed end of the spectrum. Without import protection programs, beef, cheese, and dry milk product imports would very likely be much higher. The proportion of the domestic market supplied by imports (called *import penetration*) generally did not change much over the ten year period: beer, soluble coffee, wine, and confectionery penetration increased the most.

The value of products imported and exported is affected by many conditions: exchange rates, excess capacity, tariffs, quotas, and a host of nontarrif barriers to trade (labeling regulations, safety standards, and others). The data presented in table 14–4 examine changes in import penetration (imports relative to domestic supply) and export propensity (exports relative to domestic production). The data are divided into four periods: 1973–1976, 1977–1979, 1981–1984, and 1986. The first period corresponds to a period when the value of the U.S. dollar was virtually constant compared to the value of the currencies of its ten major trading partners. During the second period, the dollar fell (1981 was the trough), and during the third period, the dollar rose rather sharply. The year 1985 was a peak for the dollar, which started falling in mid-1985 until mid-1987. When the dollar falls (as in 1977–1979 and 1986), exports should rise and imports should fall as a proportion of supply, though this often occurs with a lag of six to eighteen months (the so-called J-curve effect). When the dollar rises, the opposite should occur. during these periods, trade barriers did not change appreciably.

Many processed food products follow the expected pattern of import penetration compared to the "normal" 1973–1976 period. In the case of butter, prepared milk products, bread, breakfast cereals, confectionery, spirits and seafood, the classic pattern is observed through 1984. But these seven industries are less than half of those in table 14–4. Moreover, in almost all industries, import penetration increased in 1986 when it should have decreased. Another common pattern is for import penetration to increase throughout the periods, which may be one indicator of loss of competitiveness in international trade; poultry, canned foods, cookies and crackers, beer, wine, and soft drinks fit this pattern.

In the case of export propensity, we should observe a pattern of rising exports in 1977–1979 and falling exports in 1981–1984. Only four industries fit such a temporal pattern: canned foods, prepared milk products, breakfast cereals, and soft drinks. The most common pattern is for export propensity to more or less rise throughout the period; this is the case with red meats,

Table 14-4
Trends in Import Penetration and Export Propensity of Processed Foods, Four Periods, 1973-1986
(percent)

Industry	Import Penetration[a]				Export Propensity[b]			
	1973-1976	1977-1979	1981-1984	1986	1973-1976	1977-1979	1981-1984	1986
				Percent				
Red meats	4.37	4.80	4.17	4.19	2.64	3.68	3.70	4.36
Poultry	0.17	0.17	0.20	0.26	2.07	3.38	3.50	2.55
Canned and dried foods	2.84	4.00	5.27	7.74	3.56	4.00	3.54	2.70
Frozen foods	0.97	1.28	1.46	0.99	1.87	2.34	3.73	2.24
Butter	0.98	0.03	0.10	0.10	0.15	0.10	4.34	1.88
Cheese	3.85	3.57	3.40	3.70	0.20	0.20	0.28	0.22
Prepared milk	3.56	2.62	3.87	4.48	6.20	5.52	5.39	7.13
Ice cream and fluid milk	0.03	0.00	0.00	0.05	0.10	0.10	0.25	0.19
Bread, rolls, cakes	0.12	0.13	0.21	0.25	0.01	0.02	0.04	0.11
Cookies and crackers	2.04	2.26	2.84	3.82	0.51	0.67	0.67	0.44
Breakfast cereals	0.46	0.25	0.29	0.23	4.01	1.32	0.87	0.44
Confectionery	2.52	2.21	2.38	3.44	1.38	2.23	2.29	2.10
Beer	1.93	2.28	4.42	6.49	0.12	0.24	0.32	0.31
Wine and brandy	21.28	24.43	27.01	31.48	0.39	0.81	1.31	1.03
Spirits	25.93	24.68	24.93	26.67	2.30	2.63	2.79	4.48
Soft drinks	0.12	0.31	0.33	0.49	0.05	0.74	0.24	0.13
Processed seafood	45.14	44.44	50.65	59.02	12.06	19.21	19.60	23.15

Source: Data from *U.S. Industrial Outlook, 1987.*

Note: The four periods correspond to the following U.S. dollar exchange rate conditions (from *Economic Report of the President, 1987,* Table B-105): (1) 1973-1976, constant dollar; (2) 1977-1979, falling dollar (real depreciation) with 1980 the trough; (3) 1981-1984, rising dollar (real appreciation) with 1985 the peak; (4) 1986, falling dollar (real depreciation), where the index is the multilateral (ten-country), trade-weighted real value of the U.S. dollar.

[a]The ratio of the value of imports to the "new supply" (value of product shipments plus imports).

[b]The ratio of the value of exports to domestic value of industry shipments.

prepared milk products, bread, beer, spirits, and seafood. In thirteen of seventeen cases, exports dropped in 1986 rather than rise as would be expected. Clearly, changes in exchange rates are poor predictors of changes in both import penetration and export propensity.

Another interesting pattern can be discerned in table 14-4. Import penetration and export propensity tend to go hand in hand. When one is high so is the other in many cases. The main exceptions are poultry and breakfast cereals (positive trade balance) and cheese, cookies and crackers, beer, wine, spirits, and seafood (negative trade balance).

An alternative method of charting the relative importance of U.S. exports is by calculating their share of world trade (tables 14–5 and 14–6). Some writers regard a large or growing share of world trade as a measure of a nation's competitiveness in international trade, but this is probably an over-simplified position. Market shares are affected by government policy interventions of all kinds, historical trading relationships, exchange rates, and other factors that have little to do with the cost-based advantages of exporting countries. Therefore, market shares are at best crude indicators of a country's efficiency, productivity, or comparative cost advantages of internationally traded goods.

One fairly clear pattern is that U.S. shares are highest for what the UN terms *semiprocessed products*. About 45 percent of the value of worldwide trade in processed foods is considered semiprocessed, but the U.S. composition of such trade is about 70–75 percent semiprocessed. The United States has

Table 14–5
The U.S. Share of World Trade, Selected Processed Foods and Tobacco Products, 1985

Product Class[a]	Value of U.S. Exports	U.S. Share of World Trade
	Million dollars	Percent
Semiprocessed foods:		
Beef, fresh and frozen	453.9	7.6
Pork, fresh and frozen	61.7	2.2
Poultry, fresh and frozen	231.7	19.9
Flour and meal	180.0[b]	17.9
Coffee, roasted and extracts	90.8	3.8
Cocoa powder, pastes, and butter	11.9	1.0
Animal feeds	1,800.1	29.0
Animal and marine fats and oils	619.0	46.4
Soybean oil	425.6	26.5
Cottonseed oil	124.8	78.5
Other vegetable oils	169.2	17.0
Subtotal of semiprocessed foods	4,168.7	28.0
Highly processed foods:		
Processed meats	62.1	5.1
Prepared milk	--	--
Fluid milk	6.8	0.8
Butter	71.0	3.4
Cheese	28.5	0.7
Breakfast cereals, including infant	208.8	26.3
Pasta	8.3	2.6
Bakery products	37.0[b]	19.7
Dried fruits and vegetables	231.2	24.1

Table 14–5 continued

Product Class[a]	Value of U.S. Exports	U.S. Share of World Trade
	Million dollars	Percent
Frozen fruits and vegetables	87.0[b]	11.0
Canned fruits and vegetables	20.5	5.5
Chocolate and cocoa	55.8	3.2
Other confectioneory	--	--
Margarine and hydrogenated oils	39.9	4.3
Sauces	41.8	11.5
Soups	15.0	6.1
Soft drinks	22.0[b]	3.3
Beer	45.2	4.2
Wine	24.6	0.6
Spirits	74.8	2.3
Miscellaneous foods	466.5	14.8
Subtotal of highly processed foods	1,546.8	14.1
Tobacco products:		
Tobacco, stemmed and redried	1,520.6	66.6
Cigars	5.1	2.6
Cigarettes	1,180.3	38.1
Other manufactured tobacco	82.5	19.7
Subtotal of tobacco products	2,788.5	53.0
Total food and tobacco	8,504.0	33.7

Source: UN trade data supplied by Lawrence Traub of ERS-USDA.

[a]Definitions follow UN nomenclature.

[b]UN data apparently suppress commodity exports sold on a concessional basis, so for these products FAO data are substituted.

high shares of world trade in animal feed and ingredients (soybean cake, sugar beet by-products, etc.) and in fats and oils (the denominator of the "other vegetable oils" category includes many tropical oils not grown in the United States). The United States also exports a substantial share of the world trade in poultry and beef. However, the United States generally has a much smaller share of world trade in "highly processed" foods. On average, the U.S. shares of world trade in semiprocessed foods are twice as high (28 percent) as is true for highly processed foods (14 percent). Breakfast cereals, dried fruits, sauces, and miscellaneous foods are the main ones with high shares. In most highly processed classes, EEC countries tend to dominate world trade. Except for cigars, U.S. exports of tobacco products are substantial and represent a high share of world trade.

Table 14–6
The U.S. Share of World Trade, Selected Processed Foods, 1985

Standard International Trade Class	Value of U.S. Exports	U.S. Share of World Trade
	Mil. dollars	Percent
Beef, chilled or frozen	454.3	6.7
Lamb, chilled or frozen	2.2	0.2
Pork, chilled or frozen	61.9	1.8
Poultry, chilled or frozen	258.3	15.3
Meat, dried, salted, or smoked	30.5	3.9
Meat, canned	35.3	1.4
Milk, fresh	11.0	1.3
Whey, concentrated	12.2	7.2
Milk, dried	199.3	7.5
Milk canned	11.2	1.4
Butter	71.0	3.3
Cheese	29.4	0.7
Eggs, liquid, dried, or frozen	33.9	15.8
Wheat and wheat flour	378.1	24.8
Wheat flour	179.2	13.4
Rice	664.9	22.4
Malt	13.6	2.1
Bran and milling byproducts	5.3	1.9
Raisins	91.7	23.1
Sugar, refined	6.1	3.0
Honey	4.2	1.8
Cocoa powder, paste, butter	14.2	0.7
Chocolate and chocolate confectionery	57.1	3.1
Soybean cake	87.1	24.7
Cottonseed cake	0.9	1.2
Rendered meat and animal fats	43.6	10.2
Margarine	20.8	4.6
Soybean oil	426.1	19.1
Cottonseed oil	124.8	49.2
Peanut oil	13.9	5.0
Sunflower oil	87.6	6.9
Corn oil	97.1	36.9
Wine	26.7	0.6
Beer	45.8	3.6
Subtotals:		
Agriculture, fisheries, and forestry	370,086	13.6
Food and agricultural products	305,341	14.8
Food products, excluding fish	212,512	15.6

Source: Data from Food and Agriculture Organization of the UN. *FAO Trade Yearbook*, Vol. 39, 1985. Rome: FAO (1986).

International Investment

Foreign direct investment data covering individual industries tend to be available only when infrequent "benchmark surveys" are taken by the Department of Commerce. The results of the two most recent benchmark surveys of inward foreign investment are given in table 14–7. In 1980 117 food processing companies were foreign owned, in part or in whole. Foreign-owned companies constituted less than 0.6 percent of all food processing companies in the United States in that year, but they controlled 6.5 percent of the book assets of all food processors. However, the degree of foreign control was higher in many industries; in the beverage and miscellaneous foods industries, where companies like Unilever (Lipton, Lever Bros.) and Nestlé (Nestlé, Carnation) own affiliates, one-eighth of all assets were foreign owned. Foreign food processors tend to invest in those food industries making the most differentiated products. A careful analysis of 1975 media

Table 14–7
U.S. Assets Held by Foreign Investors, Food Processing Industries, 1974 and 1980

Industry of Foreign-Owned U.S. Affiliates[a]	Number of U.S. Affiliates, 1980	Proportion of Total Industry Assets Owned by Foreign Investors 1974	Proportion of Total Industry Assets Owned by Foreign Investors 1980	Book Assets of Foreign-Owned Affiliates, 1980
		- - - -Percent- - - -		Million dollars
Meat products	11	2.1	4.0	632
Dairy products	8	3.2	1.0	172
Preserved fruits and vegetables	5	4.6	0.5	74
Grain mill products	5	0.4	1.7	296
Bakery products	10	4.5	10.7	577
Beverages	27	9.6	12.0	3,564
Sugar, oils, and miscellaneous	51	7.6	12.0	2,888
Total food processing	117	5.5	6.5	8,203
All manufacturing	1,232	3.0	4.8	81,684

Source: Data from Connor et al. (1985:200–201).
[a]Foreign residents owned 10 percent or more of the voting stock or long-term debt of the U.S. company.

advertising expenditures on food and beverages products found that 11 percent of all such advertising was by foreign companies; the proportion was especially high for coffee, tea, and cocoa (40 percent); alcoholic beverages (36 percent); canned and dry soups (26 percent); wine (17 percent); and cookies and crackers (14 percent) (Connor et al. 1985:209–10). Foreign investment is much less intense in the U.S. industries producing less differentiated products.

Until 1983, U.S. food companies owned more assets abroad than foreign investors own in the United States. In 1982 large U.S.-owned and based parent companies owned at least $21 billion of assets of affiliates located abroad, up from $6 billion in 1972 (table 14–8). These U.S. multinationals owned thousands of subsidiaries abroad in many lines of business. Some, like CPC International, had over half of their business located outside the United States, but the average in 1982 was 14 percent (measured by book assets). Every enterprise industry had some assets located abroad, ranging from only 0.3 percent by butter and cheese processors to 26 percent by grain mill products companies. The amount of foreign investment by U.S. food processors is increasing in most industries. However, the large shifts sometimes seen in table 14–8 often are an artifact of company classification methods; small shifts in sales by a highly diversified company can cause the company to be reclassified from one industry to another. In other cases, the large percentage changes are due to large acquisitions or divestitures of major foreign affiliates. These data are also affected by the exchange value of the dollar.

Summary

In the late 1970s the United States had a small trade surplus in processed foods and beverages. This was reversed in the mid-1980s. U.S. food exports consist primarily of undifferentiated, low-value-added products, whereas imports tend to be packaged consumer products with a relatively high intensity of value added. Many U.S. exports are assisted by export subsidies or other government programs, and several product classes with net imports are protected by U.S. quotas or other barriers to trade.

Import penetration (the value of imports relative to domestic production) has fallen for processed foods from about 6 percent in the early 1970s to 4 percent in the early 1980s. Export propensity rose slightly over the same period, and rose for almost all major exports. These patterns should be affected by the exchange rate of the U.S. dollar, but consistent patterns for processed foods since the early 1970s are difficult to establish.

Not only does the United States export mostly semiprocessed food products, but it also has a higher share of world trade in those products,

Table 14–8
Foreign Assets of Large U.S. Food Processing Companies, 1972–1982

Enterprise Industry	Number of Companies[a]		Percent of Total Worldwide Assets[b]			Value of Net Foreign Assets	
	1972	1982	1972	1977	1982	1972	1982
			- - - Percent - - -			Million dollars	
Meatpacking	47	47	11.8	6.3	10.8	617	3,516
Prepared meats and poultry	41	51	2.9	5.4	3.6	27	205
Fluid milk	34	26	10.2	19.2	18.6	382	2,265
Other dairy products	4	11	19.1	19.4	0.3[d]	277	3[d]
Canned fruits and vegetables	25	22	23.0	27.3	2.6	571	62
Other fruits and vegetables	35	40	13.6	18.8	19.0	422	2,701
Grain mill products	33	22	20.4	17.0	25.7	1,672	5,598
Bakery products[c]	45	43	0.0	14.6	11.1	0	1,004
Cookies and crackers	11	10	0.0	29.0	18.2	0	725
Sugar and confectionery	30	30	6.7	9.0	6.1	222	325
Fats and oils	8	8	21.3	3.3	11.4	255	380
Alcoholic beverages	28	18	11.4	9.2	3.6	620	312
Soft drinks and flavorings	36	44	23.9	22.2	18.0	846	2,342
Miscellaneous foods	24	33	15.0	17.9	15.9	368	1,468
Tobacco manufacturing	14	11	13.3	10.8	7.9	1,090	2,245
Total food processing	401	405	14.8	13.3	13.9	6,280	20,930
Total food and tobacco	415	416	14.5	12.9	13.7	7,370	23,175
All manufacturing	3,406	3,437	18.0	19.8	19.0	104,853	299,105

Sources: Data from Connor et al. (1985:202–203) and U.S. Bureau of the Census *General Report on Industrial Organization, 1982* (Table 7) and previous editions.

[a]Parent companies with 500 or more employees in United States, whether multinational or not.

[b]Includes depreciable net fixed assets, inventories, cash, accounts receivable, depletable assets, and intangible assets.

[c]During 1972–1982 it is evident that ITT Corporation was classified by the Census Bureau as a bread company by virtue of its acquisition of Continental Bakeries. In 1982, ITT's foreign assets were omitted inadvertently. Nearly all of ITT's foreign assets were in industries other than food processing, so in this table the reported foreign assets of ITT Corp. were omitted from this row ($4,379 million in 1972, $6,773 in 1977, and $5,755 in 1982).

[d]Because of the merger between Dart Industries and Kraft in 1980, it is likely that in 1982 the assets of Dart & Kraft, Inc., are classified outside of food processing.

about 28 percent in 1985. In the highly processed category, the U.S. share of world trade is only 14 percent, a situation that is just the reverse of the EEC countries.

Some of the same patterns hold for foreign direct investment. U.S. food processors in the meat, dairy, and grain product industries accounted for most foreign investment. On the other hand, most investment into the United States by foreign food processors occurs in the beverage and miscellaneous foods industries; these companies hold large shares of the U.S. market for coffee, tea, cocoa, alcoholic beverages, soups, and wine.

Part III
Importance of Food Processing to Individual States

This part analyzes patterns of food processing growth among the fifty states plus the District of Columbia. Three tables have been prepared for each state. The first table provides information on employment, shipments, and exports for both food processing and the rest of the manufacturing sector; data were prepared for four years (1963, 1972, 1982, and 1985) where available. Various ratios and growth rates are developed. The second table identifies the ten largest processed food products made in each state in 1982. The proportion of U.S. output represented by state output is calculated for each of the ten product classes. Third, additional details can be found in the fifty-two tables of appendix B. The appendix tables assemble data (some of which had to be estimated) on the number of establishments, employment, value added, and shipments for each of forty-one food processing industries; 1963–1972 and 1972–1982 growth rates were calculated for most of these economic measures. Complete data at this level of detail is unique to this book because of the substantial lack of disclosure in the publications from which the data derive. For an explanation of how the author coped with these disclosure problems, see appendix E.

Part III is arranged into ten chapters. Chapter 15 explores food processing patterns using national maps that convey a great deal of information quite compactly. The following nine chapters discuss the food processing industries of each of the nine census geographic *divisions*, each containing three to nine contiguous states. Moreover, the Census Bureau groups two or three divisions together to form the four *regions* of the United States. For example, the Northeast Region consists of two divisions, the New England and the Middle Atlantic states. New England contains the six states long grouped together under this name, and the Middle Atlantic States are New York, New Jersey, and Pennsylvania. Thus, the Northeast Region includes the nine U.S. states to the north and east of Pennsylvania. Indeed, the Northeast Region is nearly identical with the northern part of the original thirteen colonies of British North America. Most of the divisions define regions that share some similarities in geography, demographics, economic base, or history.

15
United States Patterns

The Top Twenty States

The twenty largest states in terms of employment in food processing in 1982 are listed in table 15–1. These twenty states accounted for 76 percent of U.S. employment in food processing (the ten largest accounted for 51 percent). In 1963 the twenty leading states in food processing employment accounted for a slightly higher share of U.S. employment (78 percent), so U.S. production of processed foods has become more geographically dispersed. State rankings based on 1982 employment and those based on value added correspond quite closely; only one of the top twenty states in value added is missing from the list (Nebraska ranked nineteenth). However, states with a large number of employees working in the low-pay poultry industry (Georgia, North Carolina) will rank higher in employment than in value added; contrariwise, New Jersey, with many high-value-added industries (coffee, canned specialties, bakery products) ranks lower based on employment than value added. Similarly, states like Iowa and Wisconsin heavily dependent on meatpacking or dairy, which have high shipment-employment ratios, typically rank much higher based on shipments than on employment. In short, there is no perfect measure for ranking states.

Several changes in employment rankings took place between 1963 and 1982. California retained its first place, but several states in the Northeast and North Central regions lost ground: Massachusetts, New York, New Jersey, Michigan, Minnesota, Missouri, and Indiana each dropped at least two places in rank. On the other hand, states in the faster-growing South and West moved up in the ranking: Texas, Georgia, Florida, North Carolina, Virginia, Tennessee, and Washington each gained at least two places in state rank between 1963 and 1982. However, a few states in the Northeast and North Central regions managed to remain in about the same rank throughout: Pennsylvania, Illinois, Ohio, Wisconsin, and Iowa are the major examples. These patterns of locational change will be explored more fully in a series of maps that follow.

Manufacturing Intensity

To some extent changes in the location of food processing jobs reflects the changing location of manufacturing generally. One secular trend is the steady

Table 15–1
Twenty Leading U.S. States in Food Processing Activity, 1963 and 1982

State, Ranked by 1982 Employment	1963		1982		
	Employment (rank)	Shipments (rank)	Employment	Value Added (rank)	Shipments (rank)
	'000	$ Mil.	'000	Million dollars	
1. California	155.7 (1)	7,216 (1)	173.5	10,937 (1)	31,263 (1)
2. Texas	75.4 (5)	3,044 (6)	89.9	5,329 (3)	17,303 (3)
3. Illinois	116.1 (3)	5,767 (2)	88.0	6,810 (2)	19,248 (2)
4. Pennsylvania	107.5 (4)	3,785 (4)	85.1	4,950 (4)	13,240 (5)
5. New York	128.2 (2)	4,840 (3)	66.2	4,703 (5)	12,237 (7)
6. Ohio	76.3 (6)	3,014 (7)	62.8	4,260 (6)	11,513 (8)
7. Wisconsin	58.7 (8)	2,716 (9)	56.3	3,324 (7)	13,044 (6)
8. Georgia	41.9 (14)	1,515 (16)	50.6	2,457 (13)	7,386 (15)
9. Florida	39.6 (15)	1,522 (15)	45.3	2,915 (11)	8,717 (11)
10. Iowa	50.4 (10)	3,168 (5)	44.8	3,131 (9)	13,747 (4)
11. North Carolina	32.9 (17)	1,000 (24)	43.9	1,930 (18)	6,319 (18)
12. Michigan	52.5 (9)	2,018 (13)	42.2	2,974 (10)	7,908 (14)
13. Minnesota	48.6 (11)	2,602 (10)	41.0	2,392 (14)	9,307 (10)
14. New Jersey	61.1 (7)	2,864 (8)	39.1	3,266 (8)	8,041 (13)
15. Missouri	48.2 (9)	2,225 (11)	38.8	2,501 (12)	8,549 (12)
16. Virginia	32.0 (19)	1,000 (24)	36.8	2,059 (17)	5,903 (20)
17. Tennessee	31.9 (20)	1,365 (18)	36.3	2,161 (15)	6,557 (17)
18. Indiana	45.4 (13)	2,019 (12)	32.9	2,064 (16)	6,188 (19)
19. Washington	26.7 (22)	1,062 (23)	30.2	1,499 (20)	5,000 (21)
20. Massachusetts	41.0 (16)	1,434 (17)	26.0	1,161 (24)	3,764 (26)
Total U.S.	1,643.0	68,467	1,488.0	88,419	280,529

Source: Data in Appendix B.

dispersal of manufacturing from the Northeast to the West and South. In 1899, 52 percent of all manufacturing employment was in the Northeast; by 1963 the ratio was 32 percent; and by 1982 it was 25 percent. Figures 15–1 and 15–2 show the dependence of each state on manufacturing for its private-sector employment for 1985 and 1963, respectively. In 1985 most of the New England and East North Central states had high (25 percent or more) or very high (30 percent or more) ratios of manufacturing to total employment. Surprisingly, New York, New Jersey, and Illinois were below the U.S. average (25 percent) in 1985. Seven of the seventeen Southern states are heavily industrialized (Delaware, the Carolinas, Tennessee, Alabama, Mississippi, and Arkansas). In the West, *no* states have levels of manufacturing employment above the U.S. average; indeed, except for Utah and the three West Coast states, all the Western States are far below the average.[16]

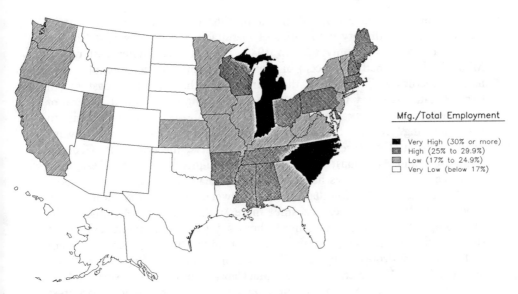

Figure 15–1. Importance of Manufacturing, 1985

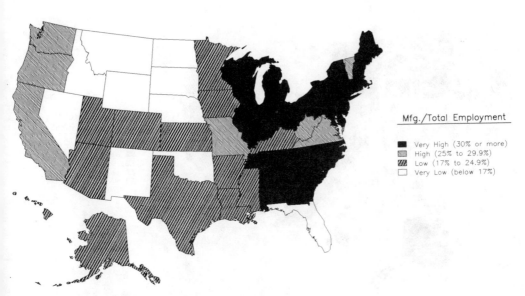

Figure 15–2. Importance of Manufacturing, 1963

The picture looked quite different in 1963 (figure 15–2). There were eighteen states with very high ratios of manufacturing employment (shaded black), as opposed to only four in 1985. All but three states east of the Mississippi River had 25 percent or more of their private-sector employment in manufacturing. Thirteen of the fourteen Northeastern and East North Central states had very high ratios of manufacturing employment, several of them with over forty percent of their private-sector employment in manufacturing. In the South, nine states were heavily oriented toward manufacturing (Delaware, Maryland, the Virginias, the Carolinas, Georgia, Tennessee, and Alabama), five of them very highly so. In the West, only the three West Coast states had above-average manufacturing orientations.

The deindustrialization that occurred between 1963 and 1985 is strikingly general. Only two states became more industrialized: Arkansas and Mississippi. Most states experienced about a 5 percentage point loss in the share of manufacturing jobs; that is, most states that were in the "very high" category dropped to "high," went from "high" to "low," or "low" to "very low." However, one state (Maryland) dropped from very high to very low and several (New York, New Jersey, Illinois, and Georgia) dropped from very high to low. Only four states remained very highly oriented to manufacturing (Michigan, Indiana, and the Carolinas).

The next two figures show the degree of food-industry employment relative to total manufacturing employment (figures 15–3 and 15–4). The

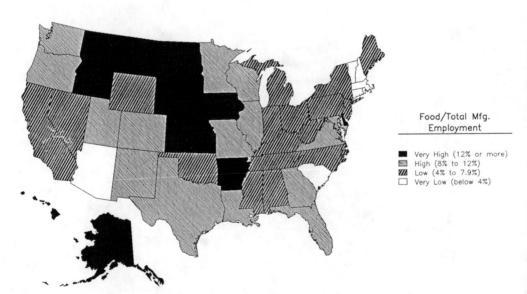

Food/Total Mfg.
Employment

■ Very High (12% or more)
▨ High (8% to 12%)
▨ Low (4% to 7.9%)
☐ Very Low (below 4%)

Figure 15–3. Importance of Food in Manufacturing, 1985

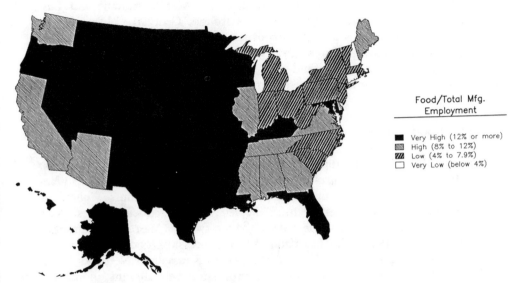

Figure 15–4. Importance of Food in Manufacturing, 1963

pattern of food-processing dependence is quite different from general manufacturing dependence. For example, in 1985 none of the nine Northeastern states had food processing employment above 7.9 percent of manufacturing employment, and in most it was 2 or 3 percent. The most intensive area for food processing employment is a huge swath of the central-west U.S., roughly triangular in shape, with the angles formed by Washington, Wisconsin, and Louisiana. Within this enormous triangle lie twenty-one states, only two of which (Wyoming and Oklahoma) have a below-average food employment-manufacturing employment ratio. In virtually all of the nineteen other states of this triangle, the manufacturing sector is a relatively small source of employment, but food processing is an important segment of that sector. Put another way, without the food processing industries, these states would have a manufacturing sector one-tenth to one-third smaller than it is. Only a few other states fit this pattern: the three poultry states of Maryland, Virginia, and Georgia plus Florida in the South; and Alaska and Hawaii in the West. Hawaii's small manufacturing sector (only 7 percent of state employment) is the most dominated by the food industries (43 percent of manufacturing employment).

The patterns just mentioned for 1985 have persisted for the most part since 1963 (figure 15–4). The degree of food-processing orientation of the manufacturing sector has dropped slightly in most states (only Delaware has bucked this trend). In several other states, the ratio of food processing to total manufacturing was roughly constant: the Middle Atlantic and East North Central States, Virginia, North Carolina, Georgia, California, and Washington. In a few states, the proportion of food jobs in the manufacturing sector dropped a lot: Kentucky (slow growth in distilled whiskeys), Oklahoma (loss of meatpacking and fluid milk jobs), Wyoming (meatpacking), and Arizona (rapid growth in the rest of manufacturing).

The Food Processing Belts

Figure 15–5 shows the top food processing states based on 1982 shipments. Unlike the previous figures based on relative importance, this map gives states' ranks based on an absolute size criterion. Of course, populous industrialized states generally head the list of top-producing states. New England no longer has a single state in the top twenty (Massachusetts ranked seventeenth in 1963). The heartland of food processing production is a wide band stretching from New York in the East to Kansas and Nebraska in the West. The twelve states in this food processing belt all rank in the top twenty; together they shipped $130 billion worth of processed foods—46 percent of the U.S. total in 1982. There is a considerable overlap between this food processing zone and the American Corn Belt.

The second largest concentration in food processing output is the West

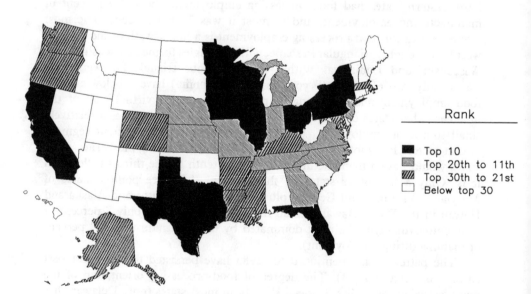

Figure 15–5. Rank of State by Food Processing Shipments, 1982

Coast. California is nearly sui generis, with a dominant national position in several food processing industries because of its ports, unique climate, and agricultural mix—canned and dried fruits, rice, cane sugar, beet sugar, wine, canned tuna, and coffee. Moreover, its large population and remoteness from the Midwest ensure large output of red meat, poultry, dairy, bakery, and beverage products. Washington state has substantial output in the meatpacking, dairy, frozen vegetable, and fish industries. Oregon is a leader in frozen vegetables. These three Pacific states accounted for 14 percent of U.S. food processing production in 1985.

The third most important zone for food processing are the five most populous states of the South: Virginia, North Carolina, Georgia, Florida, and Texas. Except for the gap in South Carolina, one might speak of a South Atlantic belt as well. These six states made 12 percent of the nation's processed foods in 1985. It is noteworthy that all these top-ranking states border the ocean—the source of fish, raw sugar, green coffee, and other water-borne material inputs for food and beverage processing.

Change in Food Processing Employment

The next three maps focus on employment growth rates by state for the years 1963–1972, 1972–1982, and 1982–1985 (figures 15–6, 15–7, and 15–

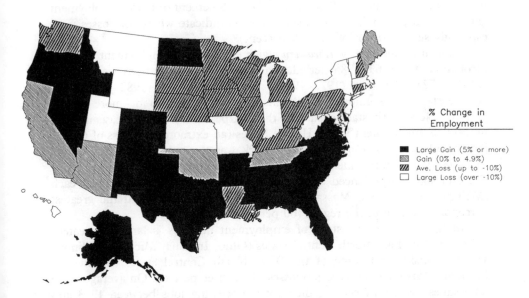

Figure 15–6. Change in Food Processing Employment, 1963–1972

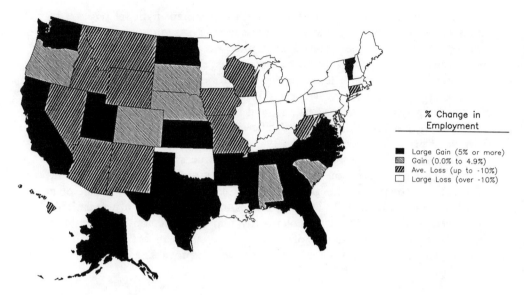

% Change in
Employment

■ Large Gain (5% or more)
▨ Gain (0.0% to 4.9%)
▨ Ave. Loss (up to -10%)
☐ Large Loss (over -10%)

Figure 15-7. Change in Food Processing Employment, 1972-1982

8). In each of those three periods, U.S. employment in food processing fell by about 5 percent. Therefore, the heavily shaded portions of the map indicate moderate (up to 4.9 percent) or large (5 percent or more) employment gains in food processing; the unshaded areas indicate where job losses were especially severe (drops of over 10 percent).

As a rule, the nine *Northeastern* states experienced employment declines throughout the 1963-1985 period. The only (brief) exceptions were Maine (1963-1972), Vermont (1972-1982), and New Jersey (1982-1985). No Northeastern state enjoyed employment growth for two or more of the periods. New York state sustained the sharpest absolute decrease in food processing employment in the United States (an extraordinary loss of 65,000 jobs or 50 percent). Moreover, New York was the only Northeastern state to suffer large employment losses in all three time periods. Three New England states experienced employment losses of about forty percent each (Maine, Vermont, and Massachusetts), and Rhode Island had the greatest percentage decline in the region (60 percent).

In the *Midwest*, the story of employment declines is largely repeated. All of the five East North Central states (Ohio, Indiana, Michigan, Illinois, and Wisconsin) and three of the West North Central states (Minnesota, Iowa, and Missouri) suffered job losses in all three periods. On average these nine states lost 23 percent of their food processing jobs between 1963 and 1985, though the loss rate was larger for Ohio, Indiana, Michigan, and

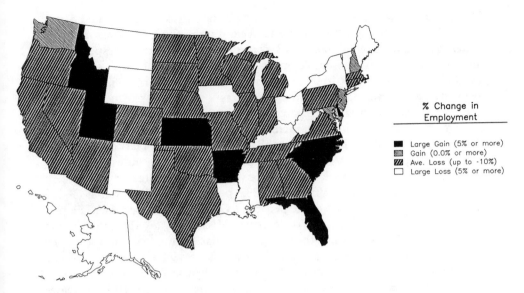

Figure 15–8. Change in Food Processing Employment, 1982–1985

Illinois (−27 percent average) and smallest for Wisconsin (−13 percent). The four remaining North Central states did much better. South Dakota and Nebraska had nearly constant levels of employment. North Dakota and Kansas generated 23 percent and 17 percent *increases* in 1963–1985 employment in food processing—the only states in the North Central region to do so. Population increases played no role in the two states' success; employment increases were found in processed red meats, frozen foods, animal feeds, beet sugar, and miscellaneous foods.

The *South* was the major area of expansion for the food processing industries. The states recording 1963–1985 employment increases were Delaware (+54 percent), Virginia (+8 percent), North Carolina (+42 percent), South Carolina (+20 percent), Georgia (+20 percent), Florida (+13 percent), Tennessee (+9 percent), Alabama (+9 percent), Mississippi (+11 percent), Arkansas (+79 percent), and Texas (+13 percent). Thus, eleven of the seventeen Southern states had increased employment, and only five states in the South had large (over 30 percent) decreases (Maryland, D.C., West Virginia, Kentucky, and Louisiana).

Most of the states in the South with increases in food processing employment were helped by large population increases that led to increased demand for local-market consumer foods (milk, bread, soft drinks, and the like). For ten of the eleven fast-growing Southern states (Delaware is the exception), personal incomes grew an average of 817 percent from 1963 to

1985, and this was a 49 percent *faster* growth rate than for the United States generally. For example, Florida and Texas were the two fastest-growing states (personal incomes rose 1,213 percent and 933 percent, respectively). In those two states the employment in the bread, beer, and soft drink bottling industries grew from 30,500 in 1963 to 37,500 in 1982, or by 23 percent; by contrast, for the United States as a whole, employment in these three industries *declined* by 17 percent in the same period.

In addition to population increases, the eleven fast-growing Southern states were assisted by the rapid growth of certain national-market industries. For example, the poultry dressing and poultry processing industries greatly assisted employment growth in Delaware (employment increased 172 percent between 1963 and 1982), Virginia (+232 percent), North Carolina (+113 percent), South Carolina (+100 percent), Georgia (+88 percent), Florida (+100 percent), Alabama (+70 percent), Mississippi (+81 percent), and Arkansas (+175 percent). Other industries that have expanded within the South include frozen foods, rice, cookies and crackers, confectionery, soybean oil crushing, beer, wine, frozen fish, coffee, and miscellaneous foods.

The *Western* region also contains some states with very large increases in population and, hence, effective demand for food products. The fastest-growing states have been Alaska (personal income growth was 1,257 percent between 1963 and 1985), Nevada (+1,033 percent), Arizona (+1,136 percent), and Colorado (+898 percent); these four Western states grew on average at almost twice the U.S. rate. Five other Western states grew at moderately high rates (personal income grew about 30 percent faster than the U.S. average): Hawaii, California, Washington, Utah, and Wyoming. Population increases accounted for most of the growth in food processing employment in Arizona, Nevada, Colorado, and Hawaii.

Besides the four states just mentioned, growth in food processing employment occurred in California (+2 percent from 1963 to 1985), Oregon (+7 percent), Alaska (+31 percent), Washington (+15 percent), and Idaho (+48 percent). In each of these five Western states, except California, employment growth in only one or a few industries was responsible for overall food processing growth. In California the major growth industries were poultry, cheese, canned specialties, frozen foods, confectionary, wine, fish, and miscellaneous prepared foods. In Oregon the principal source of growth was frozen foods; in Alaska, it was frozen fish; in Washington, frozen foods and miscellaneous prepared foods; and in Idaho, dried vegetables and beet sugar.

Changes in Food Processing Output

Focusing on changes in employment would leave the incorrect impression that the food processing industries are in decline in most states. Just the opposite is true. Because of substantial increases in labor productivity, real output levels increased from 1963 to 1985 in all but one of the 50 states. Real production (value of shipments corrected for inflation) increased by an average of 111 percent in the United States during the period, and in eight states the output of the food processing industries more than tripled. This story is told in four maps (figures 15–9 through 15–12).

Figure 15–2 illustrates relative state rates of production change from 1963 to 1972, when the U.S. average increase was 36 percent; figure 15–10 shows the same information for the ten years 1972–1982, a period that also had a 36 percent national increase in food processing output; and figure 15–11 covers the three year period 1982–1985, when wholesale food prices declined slightly and unit production rose 14 percent. Finally, figure 15–12 summarizes growth during the entire twenty-two-year period.

From 1963 to 1972 positive growth was observed in all but three states with small populations (West Virginia, Wyoming, and Hawaii) and the District of Columbia (figure 15–12). For other subperiods, too, production declines were quite unusual and confined to states with very small or quite specialized food processing industries, such as Rhode Island, Montana, and Alaska. The only exception to this rule is the 1982–1985 drop in Iowa's production. No jurisdiction sustained production declines in all three subperiods.

In *New England* real growth averaged only a little over 1 percent per

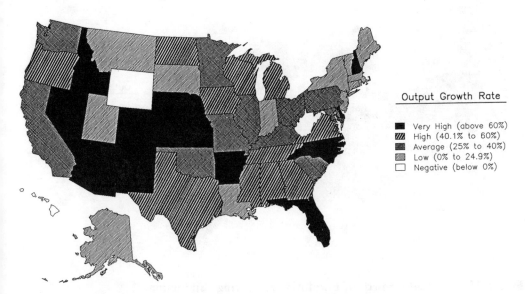

Output Growth Rate

■ Very High (above 60%)
▨ High (40.1% to 60%)
▨ Average (25% to 40%)
▨ Low (0% to 24.9%)
☐ Negative (below 0%)

Figure 15–9. Real Growth of Food Manufacturing Production, 1963–1972

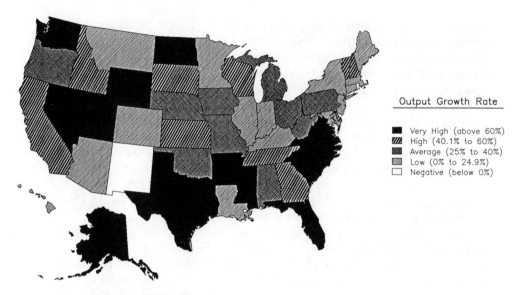

**Figure 15–10. Real Growth of Food Manufacturing Production,
1972–1982**

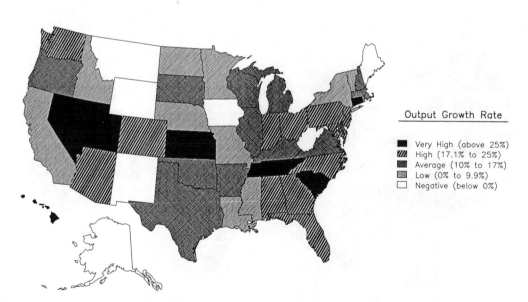

**Figure 15–11. Real Growth of Food Manufacturing Production,
1982–1985**

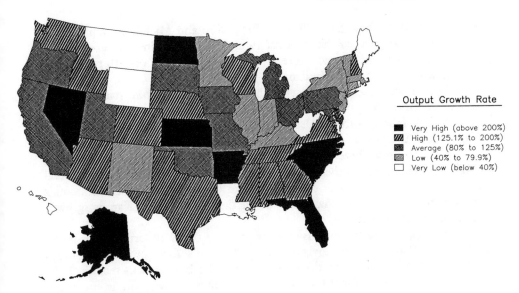

Output Growth Rate

■ Very High (above 200%)
▨ High (125.1% to 200%)
▦ Average (80% to 125%)
▨ Low (40% to 79.9%)
□ Very Low (below 40%)

**Figure 15–12. Real Growth of Food Manufacturing Production,
1963–1985**

year from 1963 to 1982, less than half the U.S. average. However, a reversal of this pattern is seen after 1982 when the division's growth was actually a bit above the national rate; Connecticut in particular enjoyed a robust growth rate in its food processing industries of nearly 40 percent or over 11 percent per year. However, for the entire 1963–1985 period, New Hampshire was the shining exception to the lackluster growth of the New England division, led mainly by its brewing industry. Rhode Island's food processing output was nearly flat from 1963 to 1985.

In the *Middle Atlantic* states, overall growth patterns were very similar to that of the New England states. Food processing output grew at less than half the U.S. rate from 1963 to 1982 but then turned about after 1982, rising slightly faster than the United States as a whole. From 1963 to 1985 Pennsylvania's food processing production almost doubled, while New Jersey's grew at half that rate. New York's processed food output expanded very slowly, by 24 percent over the twenty-two year period, the sixth slowest rate of the fifty states. Unlike Pennsylvania and New Jersey, New York's food processing industries did not accelerate after 1982.

The *East North Central* division experienced below-average growth in its food processing production throughout 1963–1982. However, from 1982 to 1985 unit output increased by 20 percent, well above the U.S. average. Growth rates varied greatly among the five East North Central states. The Wisconsin food processing industries expanded about 30 percent faster than the country as a whole from 1963 to 1985; Ohio and Michigan both grew at about the same pace as the national rate; Illinois and Indiana grew about two-thirds as fast. In the most recent (1982–1985) period, growth rebounded to high levels in Ohio and Indiana.

Food processing production in the *West North Central* states grew at about the same pace as the United States as a whole; however, the rate of growth has fallen with each successive subperiod. Within the division, Kansas had the best overall growth record, followed by North Dakota and Nebraska. In these three states, the quantity of food processed tripled from 1963 to 1985. In three other states (Iowa, Missouri, and South Dakota), real growth was about one-fifth slower than the U.S. average, and Minnesota's growth was a bit slower than that. In all the states except Kansas, growth rates decelerated after 1982.

The first of the three divisions constituting the Southern Region is the eight-state *South Atlantic* division. This division's food processing output rose 50 percent faster than the U.S. average, the best growth record of the nine U.S. divisions. North Carolina had the fastest growth rate in the South and second highest in the nation; production increased 250 percent from 1963 to 1985. Output tripled in South Carolina, Florida, and Virginia. Real production also rose well above average in Delaware and Georgia. However, in Maryland food processing output increased only 85 percent, while West Virginia experienced practically no growth in output. In the most recent period (1982–1985), food processing production showed no signs of slackening; indeed, it rose almost 20 percent, the highest increase of the nine divisions. All the states except West Virginia enjoyed average or above average growth after 1982.

The four *East South Central* states also enjoyed growth in their food processing industries that was well above the 1963–1985 U.S. average, and except for Kentucky each state was also well above the U.S. rate. Tennessee had the best growth record in the division, over 50 percent higher than the U.S. average; Alabama and Mississippi were about 25 percent higher. Kentucky grew about three-fifths as fast as the country as a whole.

The four *West South Central* states had, as a group, the second highest rate of increase in food processing output from 1963 to 1985, but the variation in growth among the states was the greatest observed. Arkansas, propelled by its poultry industry, grew by over 230 percent, the third-best record among the fifty states. Production tripled in Texas, was a bit below average in Oklahoma, and only achieved one-third the U.S. rate in Louisiana. Over time, food processing growth has slowed in most of the states; after 1982 output increased at a rate slightly slower than the nation as a whole.

The *Mountain* states were the third-fastest growing division in the United States from 1963 to 1985. However, the pattern of growth has been quite uneven and sporadic. From 1963 to 1972, the eight Mountain states had by far the highest rate of real growth (68 percent of food processing industries in the United States; the rate dropped to one of the lowest (twenty-two percent during 1972–1982 but then bounced back after 1982 to achieve the highest growth outside the South. The individual states also displayed the greatest range in 1963–1985 growth—from a 360 percent increase in Nevada to a 13 percent drop in Wyoming. Production in Idaho tripled over the period, increased 150 percent in Colorado and Arizona, and increased 125 percent in Utah. New Mexico had negative growth after 1972, and Montana's food industries were stagnant. Thus, except for New Mexico, the southern Mountain states displayed robust growth during 1963–1985, while the northernmost had relatively weak growth records.

Except for Hawaii, the five *Pacific* division states each experienced above-average rates of real growth in food processing from 1963 to 1985. Alaska's growth was the greatest, but virtually all its growth occurred during 1972–1982 oil boom when the food industries grew at eleven percent per year in real terms. Washington state had a 160 percent increase in output during 1963–1982, but Oregon and California's growth were only slightly above average. Hawaii's food processing output grew on average less than 1 percent per year from 1963 to 1985, however, nearly all the growth took place since 1982, when the state had an impressive 26 percent real growth in output in three years. Otherwise, the division's growth has faltered a bit since 1982.

Exports of Processed Foods

A careful study of the geographical origins of the U.S. exports of manufactures was published by the Census Bureau in 1984 (*1981 Annual Survey of Manufactures*). This study traced processed food exports to each state for the year 1981 and estimated the employment generated directly in food processing plants as well as indirectly in the industries that supply inputs to food processing plants.

Figure 15–13 shows the proportion of exports to total value of state shipments of processed foods (export propensity). States that produce highly exported products and are near ports or major waterways generally have high export propensities. Recall that the United States exported substantial shares of domestic output of pork, hides, broilers, canned and dried fruits and vegetables, frozen fruits, wet corn milling products, rice, fats and oils, and processed seafood products (appendix table A15). The Mississippi River and its tributaries provide relative inexpensive transportation to foreign ports for these products.

It is clear that mere proximity to ocean ports does not guarantee high export propensities (figure 15–13). Except for the borderline case of

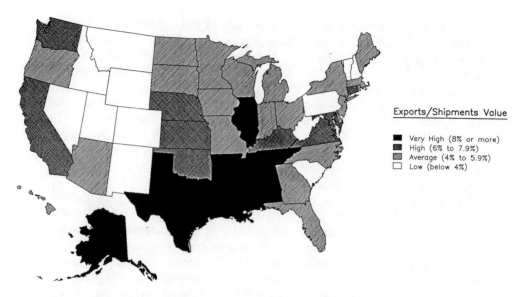

Exports/Shipments Value

■ Very High (8% or more)
▨ High (6% to 7.9%)
▧ Average (4% to 5.9%)
□ Low (below 4%)

Figure 15–13. Export Propensity of the Food Processing Industries, 1981

Connecticut, export propensities are low to average for all the Northeastern states. In the North Central region, Illinois, Nebraska, and Kansas stand out. The poultry, rice, and vegetable oil industries appear to account for the high degree of exports from Delaware, Virginia, and the Southern states on the Gulf of Mexico. California, of course, produces many exported processed foods (rice, dried fruit, canned fruit, canned tuna, and others). Alaska and Washington export seafood and frozen fruit.

The picture is slightly different when the dollar value of exports is displayed (figure 15–14). Seven states each had food processing exports of $400 million or more. California is far and away the largest state in this respect, with over $1,800 million of processed food exports in 1981. Texas was second with $1,243 million and Illinois third with $1,170 million. The top seven states shipped a total of $6,200 million of processed foods, about half the U.S. total. Most exports come from states bordering on the oceans, but several major exporters are in "landlocked" areas (Iowa and the Great Lakes states form a principal group).

The pattern of employment created by processed food exports is similar to the pattern for total export values (figure 15–15). Two states (California and Texas) have over 5,000 jobs dependent on these exports. The other states with large numbers of jobs created by exports are in the Mid-Atlantic (New York and Pennsylvania), East North Central (Indiana, Illinois, and

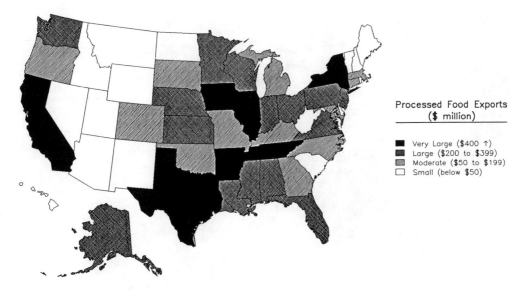

Figure 15–14. Value of Exports of Processed Foods, 1981

Wisconsin) and Southern (North Carolina, Florida, Alabama, and Arkansas). A breakdown in international trading arrangements would have strong negative impacts on employment in these states.

Future Expected Growth

One way of determining future growth of the food processing industries in each state is simply to project forward from past trends. Projection is analogous to predicting tomorrow's weather from today's conditions. This method is quite naive, in the sense that one must assume the comparative economic advantages of each state will remain about the same in the future as it was in the past. While naive, simple projection from past growth trends usually proves more often right than wrong. However, projection requires that the forecaster choose the correct past period. Thus, a choice must be made between a fairly short time period such as 1982–1985, a much longer period such as 1963–1985, or some intermediate period. Based on 1982–1985 real output growth, there would be three areas where high future growth of food processing is concentrated: (1) the four Northeastern states between Indiana on the west and New Jersey on the east, (2) the six Southern states to the south of Virginia, and (3) most of the states in the southern part of the Mountain division.

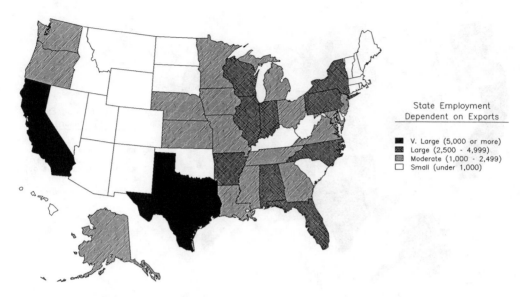

Figure 15–15. Employment Generated by Processed Foods Exports, 1981

A superior indicator of expected future growth is the capital investment plans of the business firms operating in an industry. Investment plans are not compiled for individual industries by state, but the next-best alternative (actual recent capital investment expenditures) is available. New capital expenditures for food processing in each state are published by the Census Bureau with a lag of two or three years. Because most capital investment in food processing is for equipment rather than structures, the expected life of capital installed in 1985 probably averages about ten years (1995). New capital expenditures represent the informed estimates of thousands of food processing managers about likely trends in regional demand and relative regional cost levels through at least 1995, and in the case of structures farther into the future. One possible disadvantage to capital expenditures as a predictive device is that in states with recent slow growth some of the expenditures will be devoted to modernization too long delayed.

Figure 15–16 shows the expected future growth of the food processing industries in each state projected from new capital investment expenditures in 1984–1985. The expenditures were converted to a common yardstick by dividing by value of processed food shipments from each state; the 1984–1985 U.S. average was 2.2 percent of shipments (see appendix table A26). Future growth is expected to be high if capital expenditures exceeded 2.5 percent and low if below 1.5 percent of shipments. The capital expenditures

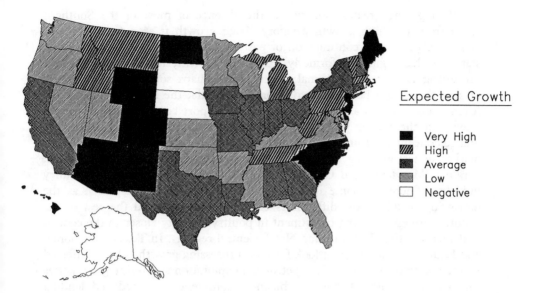

Figure 15–16. Future Growth of Food Processing

approach leads to projections that are not correlated with mere growth projection.

Using this standard future output growth is expected to be above average, say above 3 percent per year, in three goegraphic areas. First, perhaps as a result of renewed optimism engendered by its recent industrial renaissance, New England (except for Rhode Island) is expected to see a turnabout in its fortunes. This recovery of New England's food processing industries is consistent with 1982–1985 output growth of its four most populous states. A second area of average to very high expected expansion is the major part of the historical U.S. "food processing belt" identified earlier, running from Illinois in the west to New Jersey in the east. Except for Wisconsin, all eight of the East North Central and Middle Atlantic states have average to very high expected growth. Like New England, this represents a reversal of long-term growth trends, but it is consistent with the high output growth during 1982–1985 in Indiana, Ohio, Pennsylvania, and New Jersey.

The third large zone of expected high growth is virtually the whole Mountain division. Only in Nevada and Utah is growth indicated to be less than high. This future trend is of course simply a continuation of the very rapid growth of food processing in the Mountain states that occurred since the mid-1960s. It does however, signal a turning point for Montana and Wyoming.

Perhaps the greatest surprise is the absence of most of the Southern states from the high growth category. High growth *is* seen for Tennessee and the Carolinas, a continuation of past trends. But for all the rest of the states in this region of formerly exuberant growth, the outlook for food processing is average to dismal. There are perhaps some industry-specific reasons that might be speculated upon. In Florida, the fruit juice industries (canned and frozen) are under considerable import competition at present; freezes in the recent past have encouraged large increases in imports of orange concentrate from Brazil, much of it now being packaged for the U.S. market in fast-growing Delaware. The low growth prospects in Arkansas, Virginia, Maryland, and Georgia probably can be attributed to the poultry industry. There are some indications that economic changes, such as the narrowing of labor cost differences between the South and the rest of the country, are encouraging investment in poultry capacity closer to the centers of demand in the Northeast and North Central regions. In Texas, Oklahoma, and Louisiana, the bleak outlook for food processing growth is likely affected by the severe contraction of the petroleum exploration and refining industries that has apparently shaken the business confidence and reduced lending capacity in these and other oil producing states. Similarly, the poor expected growth in the formerly expansive High Plains states, especially Kansas and Nebraska, may be traced to overcapacity in the beef packing industry.

The following chapters trace the historic food processing growth of the nine U.S. geographical divisions. The order followed is from the Northeastern to the North Central, Southern, and Western Regions.

16
New England States

The New England division is the smallest in area of the nine geographic divisions demarcated by the Census Bureau. The New England states as a group contained about 6 percent of the U.S. population. The largest of the six states is Massachusetts, with a population of 6 million. The three southernmost states of the division (Massachusetts, Connecticut, and Rhode Island) are densely populated, highly urbanized, and highly industrialized, whereas the three northern states of the division (Maine, New Hampshire, and Vermont) retain a more rural character. The agriculture of the region is dominated by dairy operations, and its long coastline and many ports support a large fisheries industry. Maine has significant poultry, egg, and potato production.

During the immediate post-World War II region the New England states experienced substantial loss of manufacturing jobs, relatively high unemployment, and emigration. However, in the 1980s the region enjoyed a robust resurgence in industrial growth spearheaded by several high-technology and defense industries. In 1963 the New England states had 1.425 million manufacturing jobs (8.4 percent of the U.S. jobs), dropped to 1.363 million in 1972 (7.2 percent of the U.S. jobs), and rebounded by 1985 to 1.430 million jobs (7.6 percent of the U.S. jobs). In 1985, New England shipped $126 billion of manufactures, 5.5 percent of the U.S. total (see table 16–1).

Despite the loss of manufacturing capacity to other parts of the country, manufacturing remains a relatively important source of employment in the division. In every state but Vermont, the proportion of private-sector employment in manufacturing was well above the U.S. average. In 1963 the six New England states had an average of 41.4 percent of its private-sector employment in manufacturing (compared to 38.4 percent for the United States); by 1985 this ratio had fallen to 28.0 percent in New England (compared to 23.9 percent for the United States). During 1963–1985 total private-sector employment rose 50 percent in New England, compared to a 45 percent rise in the United States.

In 1985 food manufacturing provided 47,000 jobs, 3.3 percent of the U.S. total. Value of processed food shipments in 1985 was $7,975 million, 2.6 percent of the U.S. total. Between 1963 and 1985, food manufacturing employment fell by 32 percent, more than twice as fast as the United States as a whole. Although employment fell drastically, production levels grew by 46 percent over the same period. This growth rate was less than half the

Table 16–1
United States: Importance and Growth of the Food Manufacturing Industries, 1963, 1972, 1982, and 1985

Measures (units)	Year			
	1963	1972	1982[b]	1985
Value of Shipments ($ billions):				
Food manufacturing	68.47	115.06	280.53	301.56
All manufacturing	420.53	756.53	1,960.21	2,279.13
U.S. Personal Income ($ billion)	461.6	932.4	2,571.6	3,310.5
Employment (thousands):				
Food manufacturing	1,643	1,569	1,488	1,423
All manufacturing	16,961	19,029	19,094	18,791
Total, private sector[a]	53,946	64,714	77,843	84,020
Export Dependence:				
Value of processed foods ($ million)	--	--	12,100	12,500
Employment created (thousands)	--	--	77.0	--
Growth Rates and Ratios:				
Food manufacturing shipments growth (%)	--	68.1	143.8	7.5
Total manufacturing shipments growth (%)	--	79.9	159.1	16.3
Food manufacturing output growth (%)	--	36.0	36.0	14.1
Food mfg. shipments/mfg. shipments (%)	16.3	15.2	14.3	13.2
Food mfg. VA/mfg. VA (%)	11.4	10.1	10.7	10.4
Food manufacturing employment growth (%)	--	-4.5	-5.2	-4.4
Total manufacturing employment growth (%)	--	12.2	0.3	-1.6
Food mfg. employment/mfg. employment (%)	9.7	8.2	7.8	7.6
Mfg. employment/total employment (%)	31.4	29.4	24.5	22.4
Exports/total processed foods shipped (%)	--	--	6.4	4.2

Sources: Data from *Statistical Abstract of the United States* (various years); State Appendix Tables, *Employment and Earnings*, States and Areas, 1978, 1983; *1981 Annual Survey of Manufactures: Origin of Exports of Manufactured Products; Agricultural Statistics*, USDA, 1964, 1973, 1983; Appendix Table A1 for production index.
— = Not applicable
[a]From Bureau of Labor Statistics data on all nonagricultural employees minus government employment (all levels).
[b]Used 1981 data for export values and employment dependence.

U.S. average of 111 percent, but there was a noticeable surge in output after 1982, especially in Connecticut.

By 1985 the six New England states had only 3.6 percent of their manufacturing employment in food processing, which is about half the U.S. ratio. Such a low food processing dependence has been true for some time. In 1963 food processing provided 4.8 percent of all manufacturing jobs, slightly less than half the U.S. proportion. All six New England states had below-average ratios in 1985, and only Maine was above the U.S. average in 1963.

The food industries found in New England are generally of the highly processed, consumer products types: milk, baking, confectionery, and beverages. The states are leading U.S. processors for only a few commodities. Fish processing is a prominent industry in Maine, Massachusetts, and Rhode Island. Maine processes significant quantities of frozen potatoes and broilers. Massachusetts is a leading state in production of chocolate confectionery and cane sugar. Vermont is a leader in cheese. Only Massachusetts ranks in the top thirty states in value of food shipments.

Maine

Maine had 167 food processing plants in 1982 employing 9,200 persons (appendix table B–2). From 1963 to 1982 the number of plants in operation dropped 51 percent and employment 21 percent (table 16–2). Another 2,000 food processing jobs were lost between 1982 and 1985. The 1963–1985 fall in Maine's food processing employment of 38 percent was almost *three times* the U.S. decline. Real output of processed foods rose by 32 percent from 1963 to 1982, but then fell by 7 percent in the next three years. The net increase in production of 25 percent was less than one-fourth of the U.S. average.

In 1982 Maine's food processing plants shipped $948 million of products. This was only 0.3 percent of the U.S. output of processed foods, placing Maine fortieth among the states. Although very small by U.S. standards, Maine's food processing industry is an important segment of the state's manufacturing sector, accounting for eleven percent of shipments in 1982 (slightly below the U.S. average). However, it used to be far more important; in 1963 food constituted 20 percent of Maine's manufacturing output, a ratio considerably above the U.S. average.

Ten processed foods accounted for over half of the state's 1982 value of product shipments (table 16–3). Maine has only 0.4 percent of U.S. personal income, but in at least eight products Maine accounts for over 1 percent of U.S. production. These food products draw on agricultural supplies of broilers, potatoes, blueberries, and seafood. Moreover, Maine ranks among the top ten states in at least five processed food products: frozen vegetables ($105 million and seventh in the United States in 1982), canned seafood ($69 million and fifth), frozen fish ($32 million and ninth), canned soup ($25 million and ninth), and frozen fruit ($21 million and eighth). The three largest employers in food processing in 1982 were frozen fruit and vegetables (2,100), bread (1,700), and canned fish (1,000) (appendix table B–2).

Table 16–2
Maine: Importance and Growth of the Food Manufacturing Industries, 1963, 1972, 1982, and 1985

Measures (units)	Year			
	1963	1972	1982	1985
Value of Shipments ($ millions):				
Food manufacturing	325	493	948	835
All manufacturing	--	2,879	8,649	9,778
State Personal Income ($ billion)	2.0	3.7	10.2	13.8
Employment (thousands):				
Food manufacturing	11.7	11.8	9.2	7.2
All manufacturing	100	100	110	105.9
State total, private sector	260.1	291.9	352.2	387.9
Export Dependence:				
Value of processed foods ($ million)	--	--	21.4	--
Employment created (thousands)	--	--	0.3	--
Growth Rates and Ratios:				
Food manufacturing shipments growth (%)	--	51.7	92.3	-11.9
Total manufacturing shipments growth (%)	--	--	200.4	13.1
Food manufacturing output growth (%)	--	22.8	7.3	-6.6
Food manufacturing shipments/manufacturing shipments (%)	20.1	17.1	11.0	8.5
Food manufacturing VA/manufacturing VA (%)	13.9	11.9	8.2	6.3
Food manufacturing employment growth (%)	--	0.9	-22.0	-21.7
Total manufacturing employment growth (%)	--	0.0	10.0	-3.7
Food manufacturing employment/manufacturing employment (%)	11.7	11.8	8.4	6.8
Manufacturing employment/state employment (%)	38.4	34.3	31.2	27.3
Exports/total processed foods shipped (%)	--	--	4.3	--

Note: See Table 16–1 for sources and notes applicable to this table.

Table 16–3
Maine: The Top Ten Manufactured Food Products by 1982 Value of Product Shipments

Product Class	Value of Shipments	Proportion of State Food Manufacturing	Proportion of Total U.S. Production	Rank in U.S.
	$ Million	- - - - - - - - Percent - - - - - - - -		Rank
1. Frozen vegetables	105	11.1	3.4	7
2. Young chickens	98E	10.3	1.6	16
3. Canned seafoods	69E	7.3	3.7	5
4. Bread	50E	5.3	1.1	33
5. Packaged fluid milk	44	4.6	0.5	40
6. Bottled soft drinks	35	3.7	0.3	42
7. Frozen fish	32	3.4	3.1	9
8. Rolls	26E	2.7	1.1	27
9. Canned soup and specialties	25E	2.6	1.2	9
10. Frozen fruits	21	2.2	1.1	8
Top 10 products	505	53.2	--	--
Total food manufacturing	948	100.0	0.34	40

Sources: *Statistical Abstract of the United States* (various years) and Appendix Table B–2.

E = Estimated from four-digit SIC shipments.

— = Not applicable.

New Hampshire

New Hampshire had sixty-seven food processing plants in 1982 employing 2,500 employees. From 1963 to 1982 the number of food processing plants in operation dropped fifty-five percent and employment fourteen percent (appendix table B–3). Between 1982 and 1985 food processing employment held steady (table 16–4). The 1963–1985 drop in New Hampshire's food processing employment was just equal to the U.S. decline and was the best record of any of the New England states. Moreover, value of shipments adjusted for inflation increased by 185 percent from 1963 to 1985, with most of this increase occurring in the 1960s. This growth was much higher than the U.S. average and was three times the rate of growth of the division. Growth appeared to be slowing in the 1980s.

In 1982, New Hampshire received 0.4 percent of U.S. personal income, but the state's food processing plants accounted for only 0.2 percent of U.S. output of processed foods. Food processing is also a very small proportion of the state's manufacturing sector, accounting for only 7.7 percent of total manufacturing shipments in 1982, a ratio that was about the same in 1963. These ratios were about half the U.S. proportions in both years.

New Hampshire's food processing output is notably concentrated in just a few lines. Eight processed food products accounted for 70 percent of the state's 1982 value of product shipments (table 16–5). New Hampshire accounts for over 1 percent of U.S. processed food output in only two products: beer and frozen fish. However, New Hampshire is not among the top ten producing states in any product. The two largest employers in New Hampshire's food processing industries in 1982 were brewing (600 employees) and meatpacking (400).

Vermont

Vermont's food processing industries are similar to New Hampshire's in several respects. Vermont had seventy-seven food processing plants in 1982 employing 2,300 persons (appendix table B–4). From 1963 to 1982 the number of food processing plants in operation has dropped by 42 percent and employment by 15 percent (table 16–6). Another 400 food processing jobs were lost between 1982 and 1985. The 1963–1985 drop in Vermont's food processing employment of 41 percent was over *three times* the U.S. decline. Despite such large employment losses, real output in food processing rose 60 percent from 1963 to 1985, with practically all the increase accruing in the 1970s.

In 1982 Vermont's food processing plants shipped $502 million of

Table 16-4
New Hampshire: Importance and Growth of the Food Manufacturing Industries, 1963, 1972, 1982, and 1985

Measures (units)	Year			
	1963	1972	1982	1985
Value of Shipments ($ millions):				
Food manufacturing	105	232	587	625
All manufacturing	1,269	2,289	7,636	9,050
State Personal Income ($ billion)	1.5	3.2	10.2	14.9
Employment (thousands):				
Food manufacturing	2.9	2.8	2.5	2.5
All manufacturing	84	90	107	108.7
State total, private sector	190.8	243.5	343.9	411.3
Export Dependence:				
Value of processed foods ($ million)	--	--	1.9	--
Employment created (thousands)	--	--	0.0	--
Growth Rates and Ratios:				
Food manufacturing shipments growth (%)	--	121.0	153.0	6.5
Total manufacturing shipments growth (%)	--	80.4	233.6	18.5
Food manufacturing output growth (%)	--	78.8	41.2	13.0
Food manufacturing shipments/manufacturing shipments (%)	8.3	10.1	7.7	6.9
Food manufacturing VA/manufacturing VA (%)	5.0	6.7	4.7	4.8
Food manufacturing employment growth (%)	--	-3.4	-10.7	0.0
Total manufacturing employment growth (%)	--	7.1	18.9	1.6
Food manufacturing employment/manufacturing employment (%)	3.5	3.1	2.3	2.3
Manufacturing employment/state employment (%)	44.0	37.0	31.1	26.4
Exports/total processed foods shipped (%)	--	--	2.4	--

Note: See Table 16-1 for sources and notes applicable to this table.

Table 16–5
New Hampshire: The Top Eight Manufactured Food Products by 1982 Value of Product Shipments

Product Class	Value of Shipments	Proportion of State Food Manufacturing	Proportion of Total U.S. Production	Rank in U.S.
	$ Million	- - - - - Percent - - - - -		Rank
1. Beer	190E	32.4	1.7	15
2. Bottled soft drinks	88E	15.0	0.8	33
3. Beef	45E	7.7	0.2	34
4. Packaged fluid milk	33E	5.6	0.4	45
5. Sausages	22E	3.8	0.6	33
6. Processed pork	14E	2.4	0.6	22
7. Frozen fish	11E	1.9	1.1	13
8. Bread	5E	0.9	0.1	49
Top 8 products	408	69.5	--	--
Total food manufacturing	587	100.0	0.21	43

Sources: Data from *Statistical Abstract of the United States* (various years) and Appendix Table B–3.

E = Estimated from four-digit SIC shipments.

— = Not applicable.

Table 16-6
Vermont: Importance and Growth of the Food Manufacturing Industries, 1963, 1972, 1982, and 1985

Measures (units)	Year			
	1963	1972	1982	1985
Value of Shipments ($ millions):				
Food manufacturing	148	191	502	493
All manufacturing	667	1,229	3,730	3,574
State Personal Income ($ billion)	0.8	1.8	4.9	6.5
Employment (thousands):				
Food manufacturing	2.7	2.0	2.3	1.6
All manufacturing	34	37	47	43.7
State total, private sector	116.6	138.5	180.9	198.1
Export Dependence:				
Value of processed foods ($ million)	--	--	2.2	--
Employment created (thousands)	--	--	0.1	--
Growth Rates and Ratios:				
Food manufacturing shipments growth (%)	--	29.1	162.8	-1.8
Total manufacturing shipments growth (%)	--	84.3	203.5	-4.2
Food manufacturing output growth (%)	--	4.5	46.6	4.2
Food manufacturing shipments/manufacturing shipments (%)	22.2	15.5	13.5	13.8
Food manufacturing VA/manufacturing VA (%)	11.3	6.9	4.6	7.5
Food manufacturing employment growth (%)	--	-25.9	15.0	-30.4
Total manufacturing employment growth (%)	--	8.8	27.0	-7.0
Food manufacturing employment/manufacturing employment (%)	7.9	5.4	4.9	3.7
Manufacturing employment/state employment (%)	29.2	26.7	26.0	22.1
Exports/total processed foods shipped (%)	--	--	2.5	--

Note: See Table 16-1 for sources and notes applicable to this table.

products, less than 0.2 percent of total U.S. output of processed foods but about equal to the state's share of U.S. personal income. Although small by U.S. standards (forty-fifth in rank), Vermont's food processing industries are a large segment of the state's small manufacturing sector. In 1982, food accounted for 13 percent of all manufacturing shipments, about the same as the U.S. ratio. However, food processing used to be much more important to Vermont. In 1963 food was almost one-fourth of Vermont's manufacturing output, a proportion well above the U.S. average.

Ten processed foods accounted for over 80 percent of the state's 1982 value of product shipments (table 16–7), of which four represented over 1 percent of U.S. output. Processing is strongly linked to Vermont's dairy industry: milk, cheese, and dairy feed alone had $330 million in shipments value. In two processed food products, natural cheese and dairy cattle feed, Vermont ranked seventh among the U.S. states. The two largest employers in food processing in 1982 were fluid milk (600 employees) and cheese (400).

Massachusetts

Massachusetts is by far the largest state in New England in economic terms. Households in the state received 47 percent of the division's personal income in 1985 (and 2.9 percent of the U.S. total). Massachusetts also accounts for half of New England's food processing and total manufacturing output.

Massachusetts had 570 food processing plants in 1982 employing 26,000 persons. From 1963 to 1982 the number of plants in operation has dropped by 48 percent and employment by 37 percent. Another 1,700 food processing jobs were lost between 1982 and 1985 (table 16–8). The 1963–1985 fall in Massachusetts' food processing employment of 41 percent was over *three times* the U.S. decline. During the same period, production increased by 36 percent, about one-third the U.S. average increase for food processing.

In 1982, Massachusetts' food processing plants shipped $3,764 million of products, which was 1.3 percent of total U.S. production of processed foods. Massachusetts ranked twenty-sixth in value of food product shipments in 1982. The food industries are a relatively small segment of the state's manufacturing sector, constituting about 8 percent of output in 1982, down from about 12 percent in 1963. In both years, this share was far below the U.S. averages.

Massachusetts has a fairly diversified mix of food processing industries. The top ten processed foods accounted for about half of Massachusetts' output in 1982. In eight cases the state's value of shipments represented 3 percent or more of national output (table 16–9). In two cases (frozen fish and fresh packaged fish), Massachusetts' output was one-fourth of U.S.

Table 16–7
Vermont: The Top Ten Manufactured Food Products by 1982 Value of Product Shipments

Product Class	Value of Shipments $ Million	Proportion of State Food Manufacturing Percent	Proportion of Total U.S. Production Percent	Rank in U.S. Rank
1. Natural cheese	168	33.5	3.0	7
2. Dairy cattle feed	64	12.7	4.4	7
3. Packaged fluid milk	54	10.8	0.6	38
4. Bulk fluid milk	44	8.8	1.4	14
5. Bottled soft drinks	24E	4.8	0.2	45
6. Ice cream	19E	3.8	0.6	32
7. Beef	14E	2.8	0.1	38
8. Bread	10E	2.0	0.2	45
9. Butter	9E	1.8	0.5	14
10. Other vegetable oils	6E	1.2	1.6	—
Top 10 products	412	82.1	—	—
Total food manufacturing	502	100.0	0.18	45

Sources: Data from *Statistical Abstract of the United States* (various years) and Appendix Table B3.

E = Estimated from four-digit SIC shipments.

— = Not applicable.

Table 16–8
Massachusetts: Importance and Growth of the Food Manufacturing Industries, 1963, 1972, 1982, and 1985

Measures (units)	Year			
	1963	1972	1982	1985
Value of Shipments ($ millions):				
Food manufacturing	1,434	1,901	3,764	4,056
All manufacturing	12,081	19,134	48,204	60,610
State Personal Income ($ billion)	14.9	28.2	69.9	95.4
Employment (thousands):				
Food manufacturing	41.0	32.7	26.0	24.3
All manufacturing	674	619	643	649.6
State total, private sector	1,709.4	1,934.4	2,284.9	2,560.9
Export Dependence:				
Value of processed foods ($ million)	--	--	65.3	--
Employment created (thousands)	--	--	0.8	--
Growth Rates and Ratios:				
Food manufacturing shipments growth (%)	--	32.6	98.0	7.8
Total manufacturing shipments growth (%)	--	58.4	151.9	25.7
Food manufacturing output growth (%)	--	7.3	10.5	14.3
Food manufacturing shipments/manufacturing shipments (%)	11.9	9.9	7.8	6.7
Food manufacturing VA/manufacturing VA (%)	7.9	6.0	4.5	4.3
Food manufacturing employment growth (%)	--	-20.2	-20.5	-6.5
Total manufacturing employment growth (%)	--	-8.2	3.9	1.0
Food manufacturing employment/manufacturing employment (%)	6.1	5.3	4.0	3.7
Manufacturing employment/state employment (%)	39.4	32.0	28.1	25.4
Exports/total processed foods shipped (%)	--	--	3.8	--

Note: See Table 16–1 for sources and notes applicable to this table.

Table 16–9
Massachusetts: The Top Ten Manufactured Food Products by 1982 Value of Product Shipments

Product Class	Value of Shipments $ Million	Proportion of State Food Manufacturing Percent	Proportion of Total U.S. Production Percent	Rank in U.S. Rank
1. Packaged fluid milk	409	10.9	4.5	6
2. Frozen fish	286	7.6	27.6	1
3. Ice cream	244E	6.5	8.5	3
4. Cane sugar	197E	5.2	4.7	8
5. Bottled soft drinks	151	4.0	1.4	26
6. Fresh packaged fish	142	3.8	24.5	1
7. Bread	122	3.3	2.6	14
8. Chocolate confectionery	114	3.0	3.0	4
9. Sausages	110	2.9	1.7	17
10. Frozen shellfish	77	2.1	5.5	7
Top 10 products	1,852	49.2	--	--
Total food manufacturing	3,764	100.0	1.34	26

Sources: Data from *Statistical Abstract of the United States* (various years) and Appendix Table B–5.
E = Estimated from four-digit SIC shipments.
— = Not applicable.

output and ranked first in the nation. The dairy, fish, and sugar-based industries dominate Massachusetts' food processing industries. In five other product classes Massachusetts ranked high nationally: fluid milk (sixth), ice cream (third), cane sugar (eighth), chocolate (fourth), and frozen shellfish (seventh). In terms of employment, the principal food processing industries were bread (5,100), frozen fish (4,200), fluid milk (2,800), confectionery (2,700), and soft drinks (2,000).

Rhode Island

By far the smallest of the New England states in geographic size, Rhode Island also has one of the smallest of the division's food processing industries. In 1982, Rhode Island had 110 operating food processing plants employing 2,600 persons (appendix table B–6). From 1963 to 1982 the number of food processing plants has dropped by 49 percent and employment by 57 percent. Another 200 food processing jobs were lost between 1982 and 1985 (table 16–10). The 60 percent drop in Rhode Island's food processing employment between 1963 and 1985 was over *four times* the U.S. rate. Moreover, real production remained virtually constant during the period, the lowest growth rate in New England and the second-lowest in the nation. However, after 1982 growth picked up to an average of 4 percent per year, which was close to the national average.

In 1982 Rhode Island's food processing plants shipped $374 million of products, which is only 0.1 percent of total U.S. output of processed foods. Rhode Island's food processing shipments were more than $100 million below those of any of the other New England states. Rhode Island also has the smallest plants on average in the division, with only about $3 million of annual output per plant in 1982. Food processing is a very small segment of the state's manufacturing sector, making up only 4.6 percent of manufacturing output in 1982, which was less than one-third the ratio of the typical state. Measured by value added, the drop in food in the manufacturing mix was even steeper.

Most of Rhode Island's major food industries serve local markets. Milk, ice cream, bread, rolls, soft drinks, and sausage accounted for 29 percent of the state's 1982 food processing output (table 16–11). The principal nationally oriented industries were shortening ($60 million in 1982 shipments), frozen fish ($15 million), and margarine ($15 million), and these three industries are the only ones that had over 1 percent of national production located in the state. In terms of employment, the major Rhode Island food industries in 1982 were baking (500 employees), frozen fish (400), confectionery (300), and miscellaneous prepared foods (300).

Table 16–10
Rhode Island: Importance and Growth of the Food Manufacturing Industries, 1963, 1972, 1982, and 1985

Measures (units)	Year			
	1963	1972	1982	1985
Value of Shipments ($ millions):				
Food manufacturing	174	219	352	374
All manufacturing	1,880	3,219	7,652	8,238
State Personal Income ($ billion)	2.2	4.3	10.3	13.5
Employment (thousands):				
Food manufacturing	6.0	5.0	2.6	2.4
All manufacturing	114	118	114	110.5
State total, private sector	258.7	302.9	334.5	369.4
Export Dependence:				
Value of processed foods ($ million)	--	--	10.0	--
Employment created (thousands)	--	--	0.2	--
Growth Rates and Ratios:				
Food manufacturing shipments growth (%)	--	25.9	60.7	6.3
Total manufacturing shipments growth (%)	--	71.2	137.7	7.7
Food manufacturing output growth (%)	--	1.9	-10.3	12.7
Food manufacturing shipments/manufacturing shipments (%)	9.3	6.8	4.6	4.5
Food manufacturing VA/manufacturing VA (%)	6.4	6.0	3.1	1.8
Food manufacturing employment growth (%)	--	-16.7	-48.0	-7.7
Total manufacturing employment growth (%)	--	3.5	-3.4	-3.1
Food manufacturing employment/manufacturing employment (%)	5.3	4.2	2.3	2.2
Manufacturing employment/state employment (%)	44.1	39.0	34.1	29.9
Exports/total processed foods shipped (%)	--	--	4.9	--

Note: See Table 16–1 for sources and notes applicable to this table.

Table 16-11
Rhode Island: The Top Ten Manufactured Food Products by 1982 Value of Product Shipments

Product Class	Value of Shipments $ Million	Proportion of State Food Manufacturing - - - - - Percent - - - - -	Proportion of Total U.S. Production	Rank in U.S. Rank
1. Shortening & Cooking Oils	59E	16.8	1.5	10
2. Packaged fluid milk	33	9.3	0.4	46
3. Bottled soft drinks	27E	7.7	0.2	42
4. Frozen fish	15E	4.3	1.5	11
5. Bread	15E	4.3	0.3	44
6. Margarine	15E	4.3	1.2	4
7. Beer	13E	3.7	0.1	26
8. Ice cream	10E	2.8	0.3	36
9. Rolls	8E	2.3	0.3	40
10. Sausage	8E	2.3	0.2	37
Top 10 products	203	57.7	--	--
Total food manufacturing	352	100.0	0.13	48

Sources: Data from *Statistical Abstract of the United States* (various years) and Appendix Table B–6.

E = Estimated from four-digit SIC shipments.

— = Not applicable.

Table 16-12
Connecticut: Importance and Growth of the Food Manufacturing Industries, 1963, 1972, 1982, and 1985

Measures (units)	Year			
	1963	1972	1982	1985
Value of Shipments ($ millions):				
Food manufacturing	429	556	1,218	1,592
All manufacturing	7,999	12,121	30,067	34,980
State Personal Income ($ billion)	8.5	16.5	43.4	57.4
Employment (thousands):				
Food manufacturing	11.4	10.5	9.5	9.2
All manufacturing	419	399	424	410.6
State total, private sector	904.3	1,058.7	1,264.8	1,391.5
Export Dependence:				
Value of processed foods ($ million)	--	--	64.0	--
Employment created (thousands)	--	--	0.4	--
Growth Rates and Ratios:				
Food manufacturing shipments growth (%)	--	29.6	119.1	30.7
Total manufacturing shipments growth (%)	--	51.5	148.1	16.3
Food manufacturing output growth (%)	--	4.9	22.2	38.7
Food manufacturing shipments/manufacturing shipments (%)	5.4	4.6	4.1	4.6
Food manufacturing VA/manufacturing VA (%)	3.8	3.6	3.3	3.5
Food manufacturing employment growth (%)	--	-7.9	-9.5	-3.2
Total manufacturing employment growth (%)	--	-4.8	6.3	-3.2
Food manufacturing employment/manufacturing employment (%)	2.7	2.6	2.2	2.2
Manufacturing employment/state employment (%)	46.3	37.7	33.5	29.5
Exports/total processed foods shipped (%)	--	--	7.5	--

Note: See Table 16-1 for sources and notes applicable to this table.

Table 16–13

Connecticut: The Top Ten Manufactured Food Products by 1982 Value of Product Shipments

Product Class	Value of Shipments $ Million	Proportion of State Food Manufacturing Percent	Proportion of Total U.S. Production Percent	Rank in U.S. Rank
1. Bread	146	12.0	3.1	9
2. Rolls	85	7.0	3.5	9
3. Packaged fluid milk	79	6.5	0.9	34
4. Ice cream	78E	6.4	2.7	15
5. Bottled soft drinks	69	5.6	0.6	36
6. Bottled liquors	62E	5.1	2.6	7
7. Frozen dinners	60E	5.0	2.6	11
8. Sausage	25	2.1	0.4	32
9. Dried vegetables	17E	1.4	1.3	4
10. Soft cakes	12	1.0	1.0	16
Top 10 products	633	52.0	--	--
Total food manufacturing	1,218	100.0	0.43	37

Sources: Data from *Statistical Abstract of the United States* (various years) and Appendix Table B6.

E = Estimated from four-digit SIC shipments.

— = Not applicable.

Connecticut

The last of the New England states, Connecticut is the second largest in terms of population and the size of its manufacturing and food manufacturing industries. Almost 30 percent of the personal income of New England residents is received by Connecticut residents.

In 1982, Connecticut had 199 operating food processing plants employing 9,500 persons (appendix table B–7). From 1963 to 1982 the number of plants has dropped by 52 percent and employment by 17 percent (table 16–2). Between 1982 and 1985 Connecticut lost a further 300 jobs in food processing. The 19 percent decline in Connecticut's food processing employment was only slightly steeper than the U.S. average. Real output rose 78 percent during the period, the second best rate in New England. Output appears to be accelerating; the 1982–1985 increase was the second largest in the United States.

Connecticut's food processing plants shipped products worth $1,281 billion in 1982, about 0.4 percent of the U.S. total. Despite this large value of food product shipments, the state's industrial base was so diversified that food represented only 4 percent of manufacturing output in 1982, though it rose closer to 5 percent in 1985, about the same ratio as in 1963. Food processing is less than one-third as important a segment of the manufacturing sector here than in the typical U.S. state.

The top ten processed food products accounted for over half of Connecticut's food manufacturing shipments in 1982 (table 16–13). Most of these leading products served fairly localized markets: baked goods, milk, ice cream, sausage, and soft drinks accounted for about 40 percent of state food processing production. Indeed, Connecticut ranks among the top ten states in shipments of baked goods, bottled liquors, and dried vegetables. Connecticut also ranks in the top twenty in output of ice cream and frozen entrees. The principal employers in food processing were baking (4,000 employees), fluid milk (1,000), frozen specialties (900), soft drinks bottling (600), confectionery (600), and ice cream (500).

17
Mid-Atlantic States

The three Mid-Atlantic states (New York, Pennsylvania, and New Jersey) constitute the eastern core of the U.S. industrial belt that stretches from Boston to Milwaukee. Each of the three states ranks high on the list of states in terms of population, per capita income, and manufacturing output. Until a decade or two ago, when surpassed by California, for over a century New York had reigned first among the states in industrial might and population. New York City, still the largest American city, lies at the center of a multi-state urban conurbation of 20 to 25 million people. The city is home to more leading U.S. corporations than any other and contains most of the country's major financial institutions.

The three Mid-Atlantic states contain about 16 percent of the U.S. population and work force—over double the size of the six New England states—but down from about 20 percent in 1963. In 1985, residents of the three Mid-Atlantic states earned over 17 percent of U.S. personal income. Industrial and population growth has been relatively slow in the post-World War II era. Like New England, the Mid-Atlantic division has an agriculture dominated by dairy enterprises, though fruits and vegetables are important products in upstate New York and parts of Pennsylvania and New Jersey. The proximity of ocean ports has encouraged the growth of certain food processing industries that require imported ingredients such as cane sugar refining, coffee roasting, and chocolate confectionery. Many other highly processed consumer foods and beverages are produced in the region for historical reasons. Dairy cows and modest hog production support moderate sized meatpacking and meat processing industries.

Manufacturing is the largest sector of the economies of the Mid-Atlantic states. Manufacturing provided 3.353 million jobs in 1982, which was 27 percent of total private-sector employment in the region and over 2 percentage points higher than the U.S. average. However, the number of manufacturing jobs has declined in all three states. In 1963 there were 4.075 million manufacturing jobs that provided 38 percent of the region's private-sector employment. Thus, between 1963 and 1982 the number of manufacturing jobs dropped by 18 percent while overall private-sector employment rose by 17 percent. Furthermore, the Mid-Atlantic region's manufacturing employment did not recover in the 1980s; from 1982 to 1985, there was a further loss of 250,000 jobs.

As a result, the region's share of national manufacturing employment fell from 24 percent in 1963 to 14 percent in 1985; its shipments share also fell from 21 to 14 percent, respectively. The Mid-Atlantic states are outstanding examples of the relative deindustrialization and geographic shifts in industrial capacity that have characterized the U.S. since the mid-1960s. However, deindustrialization in an absolute sense did not occur. Production levels in 1985 were more than 50 percent above 1963 levels, with most of the increase accruing to Pennsylvania. Since 1982, production increases were well above the U.S. average in New Jersey and Pennsylvania.

In 1985 food manufacturing in the Mid-Atlantic division provided 186,400 jobs, 13 percent of the U.S. total. The value of processed food shipments in 1985 was $36.4 billion, or 12 percent of the U.S. total. Pennsylvania is the leading state in the division, with 40 percent of production of processed foods; New York has about one-third and New Jersey one-fourth. Between 1963 and 1985, employment in food processing fell by 37 percent in the region, about three times as fast as that in the United States as a whole. By 1985 the three Mid-Atlantic states had only 6 percent of their manufacturing employment in food processing, which was 1.6 percentage points lower than the U.S. average. In 1963 this ratio was 7.3 percent or about 2 percentage points below the U.S. average. Pennsylvania comes close to the U.S. average and New York is the farthest below it.

The Mid-Atlantic states' food industries are highly diversified. They are prominent manufacturers of processed meats, dairy products, canned vegetables, frozen foods, confectionery, snacks, and all types of beverages. New York is a leading processor of over a dozen food products and Pennsylvania and New Jersey of ten or more. In value of food product shipments, New York, New Jersey, and Pennsylvania rank seventh, thirteenth, and fifth, respectively.

New York

Before World War II, New York was the leading state in the production of processed foods; by 1960 it had slipped behind California to second place; and by 1982 it ranked seventh. New York has almost half of the region's personal income and 40 percent of its manufacturing shipments.

New York had 1,434 food processing plants operating in 1982 employing 66,200 persons. From 1963 to 1982 the number of food processing plants dropped by 52 percent and employment by 49 percent (table 17–1). Another 2,300 food processing jobs were lost between 1963 and 1985. The 1963–1985 drop in food processing employment of 50 percent was almost *four times* the U.S. rate. Production increased by a weak 24 percent during the period, less than a fourth the U.S. rate.

In 1982, New York's food processing plants shipped $12,237 million of

Table 17-1
New York: Importance and Growth of the Food Manufacturing Industries, 1963, 1972, 1982, and 1985

Measures (units)	Year			
	1963	1972	1982	1985
Value of Shipments ($ millions):				
Food manufacturing	4,840	6,092	12,237	12,531
All manufacturing	39,247	58,559	121,469	138,217
State Personal Income ($ billion)	53.4	97.7	217.5	285.4
Employment (thousands):				
Food manufacturing	128.8	92.3	66.2	63.9
All manufacturing	1,853	1,679	1,419	1,304.6
State total, private sector	5,519.5	5,882.6	6,051.9	6,476.9
Export Dependence:				
Value of processed foods ($ million)	--	--	419.6	--
Employment created (thousands)	--	--	2.9	--
Growth Rates and Ratios:				
Food manufacturing shipments growth (%)	--	25.9	100.9	2.4
Total manufacturing shipments growth (%)	--	49.2	107.4	13.8
Food manufacturing output growth (%)	--	1.9	12.1	8.7
Food manufacturing shipments/manufacturing shipments (%)	12.3	10.4	10.1	9.1
Food manufacturing VA/manufacturing VA (%)	9.4	7.7	7.5	6.8
Food manufacturing employment growth (%)	--	-28.3	-28.3	-3.5
Total manufacturing employment growth (%)	--	-9.4	-15.5	-8.1
Food manufacturing employment/manufacturing employment (%)	7.0	5.5	4.7	4.9
Manufacturing employment/state employment (%)	33.6	28.5	23.4	20.1
Exports/total processed foods shipped (%)	--	--	5.6	--

Note: See Table 16-1 for sources and notes applicable to this table.

products, which was 4.4 percent of total U.S. production of processed foods. The food industries are a modest segment of the state's manufacturing sector, accounting for 9 percent of 1985 and 12 percent of 1963 manufacturing output, ratios 4 percentage points lower than the U.S. average.

New York has a very diversified set of food processing industries. The ten leading products of the state accounted for less than 40 percent of the state's food processing output in 1982. In many cases New York also has a leading position nationally (table 17–2). New York supplies over 10 percent of the nation's refined cane sugar (third largest state), wheat flour (first), and processed tomato products (second); it produces over 5 percent of bottled soft drinks (third), beer (eighth), fluid milk (third), natural cheese (second), bread (third), roasted coffee (seventh), and wine (second). The principal food processing industries in New York were baking (13,000 employees), soft drinks (5,100), processed meats (4,600), fluid milk (4,400), canned fruits and vegetables (4,400), miscellaneous prepared foods (4,100), confectionery (3,500), beer (2,800), frozen specialties (2,300), and cheese (2,100).

New Jersey

New Jersey is the smallest of the three Mid-Atlantic states. The state has about 22 percent of the region's personal income and 24 percent of its manufacturing output; nationally the respective shares are about 3.2 and 3.1 percent. Like the Northeast generally, New Jersey's manufacturing growth has lagged behind national growth rates, and this is reflected in its food processing activity.

In 1982 New Jersey had 621 food processing plants employing 39,100 persons. From 1963 to 1982, the number of food processing plants dropped by 45 percent and employment by 36 percent (table 17–3). There was a slight rise in employment between 1982 and 1985, but the 34 percent decline in 1963–1985 food processing employment was more than double the U.S. average. Production rose a modest 52 percent from 1963 to 1985, somewhat less than half the U.S. growth rate. However, the 20 percent surge in output after 1982 was well above national levels.

New Jersey's food processing plants shipped $8,041 million in products in 1982, placing the state thirteenth in the United States. Because of the state's relatively rich mix of high-value-added products, its 1982 value-added rank was eighth. Food is an important segment of the state's manufacturing sector, accounting for 12 percent of shipments in 1985, down from 14 percent in 1963. This ratio was slightly below the typical U.S. state in both years. Measured by value added, food processing has become more important to New Jersey's manufacturing mix over time, contrary to the U.S. trend.

Table 17–2
New York: The Top Ten Manufactured Food Products by 1982 Value of Product Shipments

Product Class	Value of Shipments	Proportion of State Food Manufacturing	Proportion of Total U.S. Production	Rank in U.S.
	$ Million	- - - - - - Percent - - - - - -		Rank
1. Bottled soft drinks	821	6.7	7.4	3
2. Cane sugar	611	5.0	14.7	2
3. Beer	600E	4.9	5.4	8
4. Packaged fluid milk	547	4.5	6.0	3
5. Natural cheese	497	4.1	8.8	2
6. Wheat flour	327	2.7	10.5	1
7. Bread	287	2.3	6.1	3
8. Sausage	282	2.3	4.3	8
9. Catsup and tomato sauce	225	1.8	10.4	2
10. Roasted coffee	210	1.7	5.6	7
Top 10 products	4,407	36.0	--	--
Total food manufacturing	12,237	100.0	4.36	7

Sources: Data from *Statistical Abstract of the United States* (various years) and Appendix Table B–8.

E = Estimated from four-digit SIC shipments.

— = Not applicable.

Table 17–3
New Jersey: Importance and Growth of the Food Manufacturing Industries, 1963, 1972, 1982, and 1985

Measures (units)	Year			
	1963	1972	1982	1985
Value of Shipments ($ millions):				
Food manufacturing	2,864	3,849	8,041	9,063
All manufacturing	19,925	32,410	70,420	75,554
State Personal Income ($ billion)	18.9	37.8	97.4	130.2
Employment (thousands):				
Food manufacturing	61.1	53.7	39.1	40.5
All manufacturing	829	836	754	710.8
State total, private sector	1,896.2	2,284.4	2,586.5	2901.1
Export Dependence:				
Value of processed foods ($ million)	--	--	298.5	--
Employment created (thousands)	--	--	2.0	--
Growth Rates and Ratios:				
Food manufacturing shipments growth (%)	--	34.4	108.9	12.7
Total manufacturing shipments growth (%)	--	62.7	117.3	7.3
Food manufacturing output growth (%)	--	8.8	16.6	19.6
Food manufacturing shipments/manufacturing shipments (%)	14.4	11.9	11.4	12.0
Food manufacturing VA/manufacturing VA (%)	10.4	9.2	10.3	10.8
Food manufacturing employment growth (%)	--	-12.1	-27.2	3.6
Total manufacturing employment growth (%)	--	0.8	-9.8	-5.7
Food manufacturing employment/manufacturing employment (%)	7.4	6.4	5.2	5.7
Manufacturing employment/state employment (%)	43.7	36.6	29.2	24.5
Exports/total processed foods shipped (%)	--	--	5.8	--

Note: See Table 16–1 for sources and notes applicable to this table.

Table 17–4
New Jersey: The Top Ten Manufactured Food Products by 1982 Value of Product Shipments

Product Class	Value of Shipments	Proportion of State Food Manufacturing	Proportion of Total U.S. Production	Rank in U.S.
	$ Million	– – – – – Percent – – – – –		Rank
1. Roasted coffee	699.1	8.7	18.5	2
2. Beer	523.0E	6.5	4.7	10
3. Packaged fluid milk	257.1	3.2	2.8	10
4. Cookies	243.1	3.0	9.8	2
5. Canned soups	210.2	2.6	10.3	3
6. Bottled & canned soft drinks	199.9	2.5	1.8	19
7. Processed pork	196.8	2.4	3.7	8
8. Bottled liquors	192.2	2.4	8.0	3
9. Crackers	161.2	2.0	8.8	3
10. Shortening and cooking oils	149.3	1.9	3.7	6
Top 10 products	2,832	35.2	– –	– –
Total food manufacturing	8,041	100.0	2.87	13

Sources: Data from *Statistical Abstract of the United States* (various years) and Appendix Table B–9.

E = Estimated from four-digit SIC shipments.

— = Not applicable.

Table 17–5
Pennsylvania: Importance and Growth of the Food Manufacturing Industries, 1963, 1972, 1982, and 1985

Measures (units)	Year			
	1963	1972	1982	1985
Value of Shipments ($ millions):				
Food manufacturing	3,587	5,785	13,240	14,776
All manufacturing	30,034	48,345	102,940	110,319
State Personal Income ($ billion)	28.0	53.0	130.0	159.3
Employment (thousands):				
Food manufacturing	107.5	99.1	85.1	82.0
All manufacturing	1,393	1,418	1,180	1,086.3
State total, private sector	3,379.2	3,834.0	4,009.6	4,139.2
Export Dependence:				
Value of processed foods ($ million)	--	--	335.1	--
Employment created (thousands)	--	--	3.7	--
Growth Rates and Ratios:				
Food manufacturing shipments growth (%)	--	61.3	128.9	11.6
Total manufacturing shipments growth (%)	--	61.0	112.9	7.2
Food manufacturing output growth (%)	--	30.5	27.7	18.4
Food manufacturing shipments/manufacturing shipments (%)	11.9	12.0	12.9	13.4
Food manufacturing VA/manufacturing VA (%)	9.7	8.8	11.0	11.9
Food manufacturing employment growth (%)	--	-7.8	-14.1	-3.6
Total manufacturing employment growth (%)	--	1.8	-16.8	-7.9
Food manufacturing employment/manufacturing employment (%)	7.7	7.0	7.2	7.5
Manufacturing employment/state employment (%)	41.2	37.0	29.4	26.2
Exports/total processed foods shipped (%)	--	--	3.6	--

Note: See Table 16–1 for sources and notes applicable to this table.

Table 17-6
Pennsylvania: The Top Ten Manufactured Food Products by 1982 Value of Product Shipments

Product Class	Value of Shipments	Proportion of State Food Manufacturing	Proportion of Total U.S. Production	Rank in U.S.
	$ Million	- - - - - - - Percent - - - - - - -		Rank
1. Chocolate confectionery	1,126	8.5	29.9	1
2. Bottled soft drinks	436	3.3	3.9	6
3. Packaged fluid milk	432	3.3	4.7	5
4. Beer	415	3.1	3.7	13
5. Chips	397	3.0	11.9	2
6. Beef	388	2.9	1.9	12
7. Canned specialties	325E	2.5	16.0	2
8. Sausage	304	2.3	4.7	7
9. Dog food	288	2.2	10.8	2
10. Bread	283	2.1	6.0	4
Top 10 products	4,394	33.2	--	--
Total food manufacturing	13,240	100.0	4.72	5

Sources: Data from *Statistical Abstract of the United States* (various years) and Appendix Table B–10.

E = Estimated from four-digit SIC shipments.

— = Not applicable.

Within food processing, New Jersey has one of the most diversified set of industries in the U.S., with the top ten processed foods accounting for only 35 percent of 1982 state output (table 17–4). Also, the state is a leading producer of several processed foods, notably roasted coffee (second in the United States), cookies (second), canned soups (third), spirits (third), and crackers (third). These are all high-value-added products. The leading employers in New Jersey in 1982 were bread (4,200 employees), cookies and crackers (3,700), meat processing (2,900), coffee (2,700), candy (2,700), and brewing (2,200).

Pennsylvania

Pennsylvania surpassed New York as the leading Northeastern state in food processing around 1980. Pennsylvania is now fourth in the nation in terms of employment and value added in the food processing industries, a rank that it has held most years since 1963 (table 13–1). Moreover, unlike any other Northeastern state, Pennsylvania's food industries now account for a markedly higher share of both shipments and value added in manufacturing than at any time since 1963. Pennsylvania's success in food processing is unique among the nine Northeastern states.

In 1982, the state's 1,225 food processing plants shipped $13,240 million of products, which was 4.7 percent of U.S. production (table 17–5). Despite a substantial 97 percent growth in output, food processing employment slipped from 107,500 in 1963 to 82,000 persons in 1985, a drop of 24 percent (almost twice the U.S. rate of decline). Nevertheless, this was among the slowest employment declines in the Northeast. Food is an important component (13.4 percent of shipments) of the manufacturing sector—the only Northeastern state above the U.S. average. Moreover, food is increasing in importance; in 1963 food accounted for only 12 percent of manufacturing output, over 4 percentage points below the U.S. average.

Pennsylvania's extraordinary record of growth was helped by its diverse mix of fast growing industries (table 17–6). The ten leading food products amounted to only one-third of 1982 food processing production. Pennsylvania was the leading state by far in chocolate confectionery (centered in Hershey), and ranked second in canned specialties, salty snacks, and dog food. Soft drinks, beer, and sausage processing also aided growth. In 1982, the major food processing industries in Pennsylvania were confectionery (13,300), bread (11,100), miscellaneous foods (5,900), soft drinks bottling (5,400), cookies and crackers (5,000), and fluid milk bottling (4,500).

18
East North Central States

The East North Central division is the largest of the nine divisions in terms of manufacturing output and population. The five East North Central states (Ohio, Indiana, Illinois, Michigan, and Wisconsin) constitute the western half of the historical U.S. industrial belt. Each of the states ranks high on the list of the states in terms of population, per capita income, and manufacturing output. Manufacturing is dominated by such heavy industries as steel, automobiles, machinery, and chemicals. The East North Central states are located in the Eastern Corn Belt, an agricultural region specialized in corn, soybeans, and hogs; in addition, Michigan and Wisconsin have important dairy, fruit, and vegetables output.

The East North Central states had 42 million residents in 1985, which was 17.6 percent of the U.S. total population. Since 1963 the division's population grew by 13.5 percent, about a half of the U.S. rate. The division's residents received 17 percent of 1985 U.S. total income, placing it second, just below the Mid-Atlantic division.

Manufacturing is the largest economic sector in the division. In 1963 the East North Central states had 4.483 million manufacturing jobs, but by 1985 the number had dropped to 4.161 million jobs, 26.4 and 22.1 percent of the U.S. total, respectively. In 1985, the division shipped $450 billion of manufactures, which was 22 percent of the U.S. manufacturing shipments. However, the division's manufacturing used to be relatively more important; in 1963 the division's five states accounted for 29 percent of total U.S. manufacturing shipments. So, like the Northeast, these North Central states deindustrialized but at a much slower rate.

In 1985 food manufacturing provided 261,600 jobs for the East North Central five states, 18.4 percent of the U.S. total (decreased from 21.2 percent in 1963). The value of processed food shipments in 1985 was $64,131 million, 21.3 percent of that in the United States. Between 1963 and 1985, food manufacturing employment fell by 25 percent, almost twice as fast as the United States as a whole. Despite substantial employment losses, the East North Central states' food processing industries grew by over 100 percent from 1963 to 1985. Generally, output growth was a little slower than the U.S. average up to 1982, but after 1982 real growth averaged over 6 percent per year. Output growth in Wisconsin was well above U.S. levels, whereas Illinois and Indiana were the slowest in the division.

By 1985 the five East North Central states had only 6.3 percent of their manufacturing employment in food processing, which was slightly below the U.S. ratio. In 1963 food processing provided 7.8 percent of all manufacturing jobs, almost 2 percentage points below the U.S. average. So, in general, food jobs have held up somewhat better than other manufacturing jobs. And, unlike most areas, food has retained its share of value added in the manufacturing sector.

In terms of value of food product shipments, all five of the East North Central states ranked in the top twenty in 1982. Illinois had by far the greatest production—over $20 billion in 1985. Ohio and Wisconsin were in the $13–14 billion range, while Michigan ($9 billion) and Indiana ($7 billion) ranked lower. Collectively, these five states produce substantial national shares of such food products as pork, sausage, cheese, canned vegetables, frozen specialties, wet corn mill products, soybean oil products, candy, and beer.

Ohio

Ohio is the second largest state in the division and sixth largest in the United States in terms of food processing employment. By 1983 Ohio had surpassed Illinois to become the largest manufacturing state in the division. Ohio had 860 food processing plants with 62,800 employees in 1982 (table 18–1). From 1963 to 1982 the number of food processing plants in operation dropped 50 percent and employment 18 percent. Another 7,300 food processing jobs were lost between 1982 and 1985. The 1963–1985 drop in food processing employment of 27 percent was about twice the U.S. decline. Real output grew 107 percent, which about equals the U.S. rate.

In 1982 Ohio's food processing plants shipped $11,513 million of products, which was 4.1 percent of total U.S. production of processed foods (eighth largest in the United States). The food processing industries accounted for 10.3 percent of the state's total manufacturing shipments in 1982. This ratio was 4 percentage points lower than the U.S. average. In 1982 Ohio's food processing employment was about 6 percent of total manufacturing employment, about 2 percentage points lower than the U.S. average. The proportion of value added originating from food processing is low but rising over time.

Ohio had a very diversified mix of food industries in 1982 (table 18–2). In eight cases the state's value of processed food shipments represent 4 percent or more of the nation's output. Ohio supplies over 10 percent of the nation's breakfast food (third largest state) and frozen dinners (first) and over 5 percent of U.S. packaged fluid milk (fourth), sausages (fourth), processed pork (second), soybean cake and meal (fourth).

In terms of employment, Ohio's principal food processing industries

Table 18-1
Ohio: Importance and Growth of the Food Manufacturing Industries, 1963, 1972, 1982, and 1985

Measures (units)	Year			
	1963	1972	1982	1985
Value of Shipments ($ millions):				
Food manufacturing	3,014	4,868	11,513	13,191
All manufacturing	32,475	55,025	112,278	145,482
State Personal Income ($ billion)	25.2	48.7	115.2	142.1
Employment (thousands):				
Food manufacturing	76.3	73.5	62.8	55.5
All manufacturing	1,240	1,346	1,102	1,114.8
State total, private sector	2,930.4	3,497.2	3,593.6	3,804.0
Export Dependence:				
Value of processed foods ($ million)	--	--	220.4	--
Employment created (thousands)	--	--	2.2	--
Growth Rates and Ratios:				
Food manufacturing shipments growth (%)	--	61.5	136.5	14.6
Total manufacturing shipments growth (%)	--	69.4	104.0	29.6
Food manufacturing output growth (%)	--	30.7	30.2	21.6
Food manufacturing shipments/manufacturing shipments (%)	9.3	8.8	10.3	9.1
Food manufacturing VA/manufacturing VA (%)	6.8	6.4	8.6	8.5
Food manufacturing employment growth (%)	--	-3.7	-14.6	-11.6
Total manufacturing employment growth (%)	--	8.5	-18.1	1.2
Food manufacturing employment/manufacturing employment (%)	6.2	5.5	5.7	5.0
Manufacturing employment/state employment (%)	42.3	38.5	30.7	29.3
Exports/total processed foods shipped (%)	--	--	4.0	--

Note: See Table 16–1 for sources and notes applicable to this table.

Table 18–2
Ohio: The Top Ten Manufactured Food Products by 1982 Value of Product Shipments

Product Class	Value of Shipments	Proportion of State Food Manufacturing	Proportion of Total U.S. Production	Rank in U.S.
	$ Million	- - - - Percent - - - -		Rank
1. Bottled soft drinks	525	4.6	4.7	4
2. Breakfast foods	508E	4.4	12.3	3
3. Beer	476E	4.1	4.3	11
4. Packaged fluid milk	461	4.0	5.1	4
5. Sausages	365	3.2	5.6	4
6. Frozen dinners	343	3.0	14.5	1
7. Processed pork	326	2.8	6.1	2
8. Pork	278	2.4	3.4	10
9. Soybean cake and meal	276	2.4	5.7	4
10. Beef	270	2.3	1.3	16
Top 10 products	3,828	33.2	--	--
Total food manufacturing	11,513	100.0	4.10	8

Sources: Data from *Statistical Abstract of the United States* (various years) and Appendix Table B–11.
E = Estimated from four-digit SIC shipments.
— = Not applicable.

were baking (9,800 employees), fluid milk (9,500), soft drinks (6,400), meat packing (6,000), meat processing (3,200), miscellaneous foods (3,200), frozen specialties (3,100), canned fruits and vegetables (2,800), and canned specialties (2,500). These ten leading industries account for 72 percent of the state's food processing employment.

Indiana

Indiana is the smallest of the five East North Central states. The state has 3.4 percent of the nation's manufacturing output. Indiana had 446 food processing plants in 1982 employing 32,900 persons. From 1963 to 1982 the number of plants in operation dropped 50 percent and employment 28 percent. Between 1982 and 1985 food processing employment held steady. The 1963–1985 drop in Indiana's food processing employment of 29 percent was about double the U.S. decline (table 18–3). However, production levels in 1985 were 71 percent above 1963 levels. The rates of increase in Indiana were far lower than U.S. rates up to 1982, but after 1982 growth was almost double the national rate.

In 1982, Indiana's food processing plants shipped $6,188 million of products, which was 2.2 percent of total U.S. production of processed foods. Indiana's food processing value of shipments ranked nineteenth in the United States. The food processing industries shipped 10 percent of the state's total manufactures in 1982. This rate is 4 percentage points lower than the U.S. average and decreased from 12 percent in 1963. Indiana's food processing employment formed 7.4 percent of the total manufacturing employment in 1963 and declined to 5.6 percent in 1982.

Indiana has the most diversified set of food processing industries in the United States. The ten leading food products of the state accounted for less than a third of the state's food processing products in 1982. Indiana has at least four industries that represent 4 percent or more of national output (table 18–4). Indiana supplies over 10 percent of the nation's flour mixes (second largest state) and over 5 percent of the U.S. soybean cake and meal (sixth), dry milk products (sixth), and bottled liquors (fifth). In terms of employment, the principal food processing industries in the state were bread and rolls (4,600 employees), soft drinks (3,400), meatpacking (2,800), and miscellaneous foods (2,200).

Illinois

Illinois is the second leading state in the production of processed foods, a position it has held since 1963. Illinois ranked sixth in total manufacturing

Table 18–3
Indiana: Importance and Growth of the Food Manufacturing Industries, 1963, 1972, 1982, and 1985

Measures (units)	Year			
	1963	1972	1982	1985
Value of Shipments ($ millions):				
Food manufacturing	2,019	2,765	6,188	7,192
All manufacturing	16,527	29,168	63,332	76,654
State Personal Income ($ billion)	11.6	23.2	54.8	68.4
Employment (thousands):				
Food manufacturing	45.4	37.0	32.9	32.4
All manufacturing	610	704	585	587.4
State total, private sector	1,488.0	1,762.6	1,790.3	1,906.5
Export Dependence:				
Value of processed foods ($ million)	--	--	210.3	--
Employment created (thousands)	--	--	3.7	--
Growth Rates and Ratios:				
Food manufacturing shipments growth (%)	--	36.9	123.8	15.9
Total manufacturing shipments growth (%)	--	76.5	117.1	21.0
Food manufacturing output growth (%)	--	10.8	24.9	23.3
Food manufacturing shipments/manufacturing shipments (%)	12.2	9.5	9.8	9.4
Food manufacturing VA/manufacturing VA (%)	8.3	6.9	8.0	8.4
Food manufacturing employment growth (%)	--	-18.5	-11.1	-1.5
Total manufacturing employment growth (%)	--	15.4	-16.9	0.4
Food manufacturing employment/manufacturing employment (%)	7.4	5.3	5.6	5.5
Manufacturing employment/state employment (%)	41.0	39.9	32.7	30.8
Exports/total processed foods shipped (%)	--	--	5.1	--

Note: See Table 16–1 for sources and notes applicable to this table.

Table 18–4
Indiana: The Top Ten Manufactured Food Products by 1982 Value of Product Shipments

	Product Class	Value of Shipments	Proportion of State Food Manufacturing	Proportion of Total U.S. Production	Rank in U.S.
		$ Million	Percent		Rank
1.	Bottled soft drinks	335	5.4	3.0	11
2.	Pork	259	4.2	3.2	6
3.	Soybean cake and meal	240	3.9	5.0	6
4.	Packaged fluid milk	215	3.5	2.4	13
5.	Dry milk products	180E	2.9	7.4	6
6.	Bottled liquors	178E	2.9	7.4	5
7.	Flour mixes	157	2.5	11.1	2
8.	Beer	145	2.3	1.3	18
9.	Beef	127	2.0	0.6	23
10.	Poultry feed	102	1.6	2.8	13
	Top 10 products	1,938	31.3	--	--
	Total food manufacturing	6,188	100.0	2.21	19

Sources: Data from *Statistical Abstract of the United States* (various years) and Appendix Table B–12.

E = Estimated from four-digit SIC shipments.

— = Not applicable.

in the U.S. in 1985. Within the East North Central region, Illinois is the largest state in food processing manufactures and third in total manufactures after Ohio and Michigan.

Illinois had 1,055 food processing plants operating in 1982 employing 88,000 persons. From 1963 to 1982 the number of food processing plants has dropped by 44 percent and employment by 24 percent (table 18–5). Another 4,700 food processing jobs were lost between 1982 and 1985. The 1963–1985 drop in food processing employment of 28 percent was twice the U.S. decline; unit output, however, increased 76 percent.

In 1982 Illinois' food processing plants shipped $19,248 million of products, which was 6.9 percent of total U.S. production of processed foods. Food processing is very important to Illinois. The food processing industries composed 17 percent of the state's total manufacturing output in 1982. This is about 3 percentage points higher than the U.S. average. In 1963 the ratio was 2 points above the U.S. average.

Illinois has a very diversified mix of food processing industries. The top ten processed foods account for only a third of the state's output in 1982 (table 18–6). In many products, Illinois has a leading position nationally. The state supplies over 30 percent of the nation's packaged candy (top state); over 20 percent of the soybean cake and meal (first), shortening and cooking oils (first), soybean oil (first); and over 10 percent of the chocolate confectionery (second). In terms of employment, the principal food processing industries in Illinois were confectionery (14,100 employees), bread (9,500), meat processing (6,800), miscellaneous foods (6,500), cookies and crackers (5,300), meat packing (4,900), soft drinks (4,500), sauces and pickles (3,100), wet corn mills (3,000), and frozen specialties (2,900). These ten industries generated 69 percent of Illinois' food processing employment.

Michigan

Michigan ranked fourth and fourteenth in food processing value of shipments in the East North Central region and in the United States, respectively. The state had 626 food processing plants in operation in 1982 employing 42,200 persons. From 1963 to 1982 the number of food processing plants dropped 53 percent and employment 20 percent. Another 2,700 food processing jobs were lost between 1982 and 1985 (table 18–7). The 1963–1985 fall in food processing employment of 25 percent was twice the U.S. decline, but output increased 104 percent, which was about the same as the U.S. average.

In 1982 Michigan's food processing plants shipped $7,908 million of products, which was 2.8 percent of total U.S. food processing products. Food processing is a very small proportion of the state's manufacturing sector, accounting for 6.4 percent of total manufacturing shipments in 1985.

Table 18–5
Illinois: Importance and Growth of the Food Manufacturing Industries, 1963, 1972, 1982, and 1985

Measures (units)	Year			
	1963	1972	1982	1985
Value of Shipments ($ millions):				
Food manufacturing	5,767	9,110	19,248	21,161
All manufacturing	31,354	53,553	112,929	124,402
State Personal Income ($ billion)	30.0	57.7	138.5	170.0
Employment (thousands):				
Food manufacturing	116.1	112.3	88.0	83.3
All manufacturing	1,211	1,306	1,069	1,016.9
State total, private sector	3,374.7	3,816.2	4,006.4	4,165.4
Export Dependence:				
Value of processed foods ($ million)	--	--	1,169.8	--
Employment created (thousands)	--	--	4.6	--
Growth Rates and Ratios:				
Food manufacturing shipments growth (%)	--	58.0	111.3	9.9
Total manufacturing shipments growth (%)	--	70.8	77.7	10.2
Food manufacturing output growth (%)	--	27.9	17.9	16.7
Food manufacturing shipments/manufacturing shipments (%)	18.4	17.0	17.0	17.0
Food manufacturing VA/manufacturing VA (%)	14.1	12.1	14.3	14.2
Food manufacturing employment growth (%)	--	-3.3	-21.6	-5.3
Total manufacturing employment growth (%)	--	7.8	-18.1	-4.9
Food manufacturing employment/manufacturing employment (%)	9.6	8.6	8.2	8.2
Manufacturing employment/state employment (%)	35.9	34.2	26.7	24.4
Exports/total processed foods shipped (%)	--	--	8.3	--

Note: See Table 16–1 for sources and notes applicable to this table.

Table 18–6
Illinois: The Top Ten Manufactured Food Products by 1982 Value of Product Shipments

Product Class	Value of Shipments	Proportion of State Food Manufacturing	Proportion of Total U.S. Shipments	Rank in U.S.
	$ Million	Percent		Rank
1. Soybean cake and meal	1,114	5.8	23.0	1
2. Shortening and cooking oil	931	4.8	23.1	1
3. Beef	703	3.7	3.4	7
4. Chocolate confectionery	656	3.4	17.5	2
5. Soybean oil	647	3.4	27.2	1
6. Pork	586	3.0	7.3	2
7. Breakfast foods	522	2.7	12.6	2
8. Sausage	507	2.6	7.8	2
9. Packaged candy	486	2.5	30.5	1
10. Bottled soft drinks	438	2.3	3.9	5
Top 10 products	6,590	34.2	–	––
Total food manufacturing	19,248	100.0	6.86	2

Sources: Data from *Statistical Abstract of the United States* (various years) and Appendix Table B–13.

E = Estimated from four-digit SIC shipments.

— = Not applicable.

Table 18-7
Michigan: Importance and Growth of the Food Manufacturing Industries, 1963, 1972, 1982, and 1985

Measures (units)	Year			
	1963	1972	1982	1985
Value of Shipments ($ millions):				
Food manufacturing	2,018	3,586	7,908	8,631
All manufacturing	31,165	54,039	99,715	134,043
State Personal Income ($ billion)	20.6	43.7	99.8	123.7
Employment (thousands):				
Food manufacturing	52.5	48.1	42.2	39.5
All manufacturing	961	1,076	884	952.1
State total, private sector	2,259.1	2,715.7	2,733.5	3,003.7
Export Dependence:				
Value of processed foods ($ million)	--	--	174.0	--
Employment created (thousands)	--	--	1.6	--
Growth Rates and Ratios:				
Food manufacturing shipments growth (%)	--	77.7	120.6	9.1
Total manufacturing shipments growth (%)	--	73.4	84.5	34.4
Food manufacturing output growth (%)	--	43.1	23.1	15.8
Food manufacturing shipments/manufacturing shipments (%)	6.5	6.6	7.9	6.4
Food manufacturing VA/manufacturing VA (%)	5.6	5.6	7.6	6.7
Food manufacturing employment growth (%)	--	-7.8	-12.3	-6.4
Total manufacturing employment growth (%)	--	12.0	-17.8	7.7
Food manufacturing employment/manufacturing employment (%)	5.5	4.5	4.8	4.1
Manufacturing employment/state employment (%)	42.5	39.6	32.3	31.7
Exports/total processed foods shipped (%)	--	--	4.3	--

Note: See Table 16-1 for sources and notes applicable to this table.

This ratio was the lowest in the East North Central region and is virtually unchanged since 1963. These ratios were less than half of the U.S. proportions in both years. The employment of food processing industries constituted 4.8 percent of the state's total manufacturing employment in 1982. This ratio is 3 percentage points lower than the U.S. average.

Michigan has a diversified set of food processing industries. The top ten processed food products accounted for 48 percent of the state's food processing shipments in 1982 (table 18–8). The state supplies over 20 percent of the nation's breakfast foods (state ranks first) and pickles (first) and over 5 percent of the nation's pork (fourth), sausages (fifth), processed pork (fourth), and dry milk products (fifth). In terms of employment, Michigan's principal food processing industries were breakfast foods (4,500 employees), bread and rolls (4,500), meat processing (3,700), meatpacking (3,000), soft drinks (2,800), fluid milk (2,600), canned fruits and vegetables (2,100), cookies and crackers (2,000), and sauces and pickles (1,900). These ten leading industries accounted for 69 percent of the state's food processing employment (appendix table B–14).

Wisconsin

The food processing industry is an important segment of the state's manufacturing sector. The state ranked second and sixth in food processing value of shipments in the East North Central and the United States, respectively. Wisconsin had 998 food processing plants with 56,300 employees in 1982 (table 18–9). Since 1963, the number of food processing plants has dropped 45 percent but employment only 4 percent. However, 5,400 food processing jobs were lost between 1982 and 1985. The 1963–1985 drop in food processing employment of 13 percent was equal to the U.S. average, but the 146 percent increase in real production was 30 percent higher than the average.

In 1982 Wisconsin's food processing plants shipped $13,044 million of products, which was 4.7 percent of the total U.S. food processing products and sixth largest in the United States. Food processing is a very large proportion of the state's manufacturing sector, accounting for 25 percent of total manufacturing shipments in 1982. This ratio increased from 23 percent in 1963. The 1982 ratio was 10 percentage points higher than the U.S. average. Employment in the food processing industries composed 8.1 percent of the state's total manufacturing employment in 1982.

Food processing in Wisconsin is concentrated in relatively few products. Ten processed foods accounted for over 60 percent of the state's 1982 value of product shipments. The state is a leading producer of many foods, especially dairy products (table 18–10). Wisconsin supplies over 30 percent

Table 18–8
Michigan: The Top Ten Manufactured Food Products by 1982 Value of Product Shipments

	Product Class	Value of Shipments	Proportion of State Food Manufacturing	Proportion of Total U.S. Shipments	Rank in U.S.
		$ Million	– – – – – Percent – – – – –		Rank
1.	Breakfast foods	1,001E	12.7	24.2	1
2.	Pork	565E	7.1	7.0	4
3.	Beer	429E	5.4	3.8	12
4.	Sausages	347	4.4	5.3	5
5.	Packaged fluid milk	322	4.1	3.5	9
6.	Processed pork	289	3.7	5.4	4
7.	Bottled soft drinks	252	3.2	2.3	17
8.	Beef	216	2.7	1.0	19
9.	Dry milk products	200	2.5	8.3	5
10.	Pickles	189	2.4	26.9	1
	Top 10 products	3,810	48.2	–	–
	Total food manufacturing	7,908	100.0	2.82	14

Sources: Data from *Statistical Abstract of the United States* (various years) and Appendix Table B–14.

E = Estimated from four-digit SIC shipments.

— = Not applicable.

Table 18–9
Wisconsin: Importance and Growth of the Food Manufacturing Industries, 1963, 1972, 1982, and 1985

Measures (units)	Year			
	1963	1972	1982	1985
Value of Shipments ($ millions):				
Food manufacturing	2,716	4,844	13,044	13,956
All manufacturing	11,952	21,246	52,448	62,837
State Personal Income ($ billion)	9.6	19.0	51.3	62.8
Employment (thousands):				
Food manufacturing	58.7	56.5	56.3	50.9
All manufacturing	462	501	697	489.5
State total, private sector	1,309.8	1,484.0	1,742.6	1,781.7
Export Dependence:				
Value of processed foods ($ million)	--	--	312.6	--
Employment created (thousands)	--	--	2.6	--
Growth Rates and Ratios:				
Food manufacturing shipments growth (%)	--	78.4	169.3	7.0
Total manufacturing shipments growth (%)	--	77.8	146.8	19.8
Food manufacturing output growth (%)	--	44.3	50.2	13.5
Food manufacturing shipments/manufacturing shipments (%)	22.7	22.8	24.9	22.2
Food manufacturing VA/manufacturing VA (%)	14.1	14.0	14.7	14.6
Food manufacturing employment growth (%)	--	-3.6	-0.4	-9.6
Total manufacturing employment growth (%)	--	8.4	39.1	-29.8
Food manufacturing employment/manufacturing employment (%)	12.7	11.3	8.1	10.4
Manufacturing employment/state employment (%)	35.3	33.8	40.0	27.5
Exports/total processed foods shipped (%)	--	--	4.4	--

Note: See Table 16–1 for sources and notes applicable to this table.

Table 18–10
Wisconsin: The Top Ten Manufactured Food Products by 1982 Value of Product Shipments

Product Class	Value of Shipments	Proportion of State Food Manufacturing	Proportion of Total U.S. Shipments	Rank in U.S.
	$ Million	Percent		Rank
1. Natural cheese	2,097	16.1	37.3	1
2. Processed cheese	996	7.6	31.2	1
3. Beer	987	7.6	8.8	3
4. Beef	655	5.0	3.2	8
5. Pork	600E	4.6	7.4	2
6. Butter	553	4.2	32.8	1
7. Bulk fluid milk	526	4.0	8.8	2
8. Dry milk products	525	4.0	21.6	1
9. Sausages	522	4.0	8.0	1
10. Canned vegetables	511	3.9	24.9	1
Top 10 products	7,972	61.1	--	--
Total food manufacturing	13,044	100.0	4.65	6

Sources: Data from *Statistical Abstract of the United States* (various years) and Appendix Table B–15.

E = Estimated from four-digit SIC shipments.

— = Not applicable.

of the nation's natural cheese (state ranked first), processed cheese (first), and butter (first); over 20 percent of the nation's dry milk products (first) and canned vegetables (first); over 7 percent of the beer (third), pork (second), bulk fluid milk (second), and sausages (first). In terms of employment, Wisconsin's principal food processing industries were cheese (10,400 employees), meatpacking (6,700), canned fruits and vegetables (6,000), beer (5,200), bread and rolls (4,100), soft drinks (2,700), meat processing (2,600), miscellaneous foods (2,500), processed milk (2,100), and fluid milk (1,900). These ten leading industries constitute about 80 percent of the state's food processing employment.

19
West North Central

The seven West North Central states had 18 million residents in 1985, which was 7.5 percent of the U.S. total population. Since 1963 the division's population had grown 12.5 percent, the second lowest growth rate among the nine divisions and less than a half of the U.S. rate. The division's residents received $233 billions of income in 1985, which was 7 percent of the U.S. total income (third smallest of the nine divisions).

Nevertheless, the division contains four fairly populous, moderately industrialized states. Missouri, Minnesota, Iowa, and Kansas each have over $30 billion in shipments of manufactures. Each of these four states contains portions of the Western Corn Belt (especially Iowa), dominated by corn, soybeans, hogs, and feed cattle. Minnesota has an agricultural sector very much like that of Wisconsin. The three remaining states (Nebraska and the Dakotas) are much more sparsely populated and less industrialized; their agriculture verges into that of the High Plains, concentrating more on wheat and range cattle. The Red River Valley is an important area for sugar beet production.

In 1963 the West North Central states had 1.014 million manufacturing jobs but by 1985 the number had risen to 1.293 million jobs, 6.0 and 6.9 percent of the U.S. total in their respective years. The number of manufacturing jobs grew in every state. In 1985 the division shipped $182.4 billions of manufactures, which was 8.0 percent of the U.S. manufacturing shipments (increased from 7.4 percent in 1963). The 1963–1985 increase in the division's manufacturing shipments of 487 percent was 45 percentage points above the U.S. average.

In 1985 food manufacturing provided 176,000 jobs to the seven West North Central states, 12.4 percent of the U.S. total (about the same percentage as in 1963). The value of processed food shipments in 1985 was $50,362 million, 16.7 percent of the U.S. value. Between 1963 and 1985 food manufacturing employment fell by 15 percent, about the same as the U.S. decline. However, during the same period real output grew 113 percent, which was slightly higher than the national average. Divisional growth was well above average in the 1960s but slipped below the average in the 1980s. In this division, 1985 output in Kansas, North Dakota, and Nebraska was triple the 1963 levels.

By 1985 the seven West North Central states had 13.6 percent of their manufacturing employment in food processing, which was slightly higher than the U.S. average. In 1963 food processing provided 20.3 percent of all manufacturing jobs, 4 percentage points above the U.S. proportion.

The food processing industries of the West North Central division are strongly tied to the kind of agriculture practiced in the region. Beef, pork, and processed meats are leading industries in several of these states; turkey and dairy products processing is important in Minnesota. Soybean crushing, breakfast foods, and wet corn milling are major industries in Iowa but not in other states. Sugar beet processing is prominent in South Dakota. Minnesota, headquarters for Pillsbury and General Mills, is a leading state in flour milling, though most of the supply comes from states to the west. Missouri is prominent as a major producer of beer, mainly because the headquarters and major plant of Anheuser-Busch is located in St. Louis.

Minnesota

Food processing is an important segment of Minnesota's manufacturing sector. In 1982 Minnesota ranked second in food processing employment and third in value of shipments in the West North Central region. Nationally it ranked tenth in processed food shipments (3.3 percent of the U.S. total). Minnesota had 559 food processing plants operating in 1982 employing 41,000 persons (table 19–1). From 1963 to 1982 the number of food processing plants dropped by 49 percent and employment by 16 percent. Between 1982 and 1985, food processing jobs decreased by 2,200. The 1963–1985 decrease in food processing employment of 20 percent was almost twice the U.S. decline; real output rose 76 percent, but this was well below the U.S. average increase and was the smallest increase in the division.

In 1982 Minnesota's food processing plants shipped $9,307 million of products. Food processing is a very large proportion of the state's manufacturing sector, accounting for 23 percent of total manufacturing shipments in 1985. However, it used to be far more important; in 1963 Minnesota's food processing output was 38 percent of total manufacturing output, over twice the national percentage. The proportion of the food processing employment is also high.

Minnesota has a fairly diversified mix of food processing industries. The top ten processed foods accounted for 44 percent of the state's output in 1982, and in eight cases, Minnesota ranked among the top three states in the United States (table 19–2). Minnesota supplies over 20 percent of the nation's processed cheese (second largest state) and butter (second); over 10 percent of the turkeys (first), bulk fluid milk (second), wheat flour (second), dry milk products (second); and over 6 percent of pork (fifth), natural cheese (third), and soybean cake and meal (third). Minnesota's major food processing industries were meatpacking (4,400 employees in 1982), poultry dressing

Table 19–1
Minnesota: Importance and Growth of the Food Manufacturing Industries, 1963, 1972, 1982, and 1985

Measures (units)	Year			
	1963	1972	1982	1985
Value of Shipments ($ millions):				
Food manufacturing	2,602	4,295	9,307	9,549
All manufacturing	6,804	12,901	35,321	42,532
State Personal Income ($ billion)	8.2	16.9	46.2	59.1
Employment (thousands):				
Food manufacturing	48.6	45.6	41.0	38.8
All manufacturing	246	302	350	366.8
State total, private sector	1,087.0	1,283.5	1,631.4	1,706.7
Export Dependence:				
Value of processed foods ($ million)	--	--	285.7	--
Employment created (thousands)	--	--	1.7	--
Growth Rates and Ratios:				
Food manufacturing shipments growth (%)	--	65.1	116.7	2.6
Total manufacturing shipments growth (%)	--	89.6	173.8	20.4
Food manufacturing output growth (%)	--	33.6	20.9	8.9
Food manufacturing shipments/manufacturing shipments (%)	38.2	33.3	26.3	22.5
Food manufacturing VA/manufacturing VA (%)	21.0	16.7	15.6	13.3
Food manufacturing employment growth (%)	--	-6.2	-10.1	-5.4
Total manufacturing employment growth (%)	--	22.8	15.9	4.8
Food manufacturing employment/manufacturing employment (%)	19.8	15.1	11.7	10.6
Manufacturing employment/state employment (%)	22.6	23.5	21.5	21.5
Exports/total processed foods shipped (%)	--	--	5.1	--

Note: See Table 16–1 for sources and notes applicable to this table.

Table 19–2
Minnesota: The Top Ten Manufactured Food Products by 1982 Value of Product Shipments

Product Class	Value of Shipments	Proportion of State Food Manufacturing	Proportion of Total U.S. Production	Rank in U.S.
	$ Million	- - - - - - - Percent - - - - - - -		Rank
1. Processed cheese	657	7.1	20.6	2
2. Pork	531	5.7	6.6	5
3. Beef	497	5.3	2.4	9
4. Natural cheese	441	4.7	7.8	3
5. Bulk fluid milk	406	4.4	13.4	2
6. Butter	375	4.0	22.2	2
7. Wheat flour	324	3.5	10.5	2
8. Soybean cake and meal	307	3.3	6.3	3
9. Dry milk products	304	3.3	12.5	2
10. Turkeys	292	3.1	18.5	1
Top 10 products	4,134	44.4	--	--
Total food manufacturing	9,307	100.0	3.32	10

Sources: Data from *Statistical Abstract of the United States* (various years) and Appendix Table B–16.
E = Estimated from four-digit SIC shipments.
— = Not applicable.

(3,600), soft drinks (3,400), bread (2,800), cheese (2,600), canned vegetables (2,300), frozen specialties (2,100), beet sugar (1,900), fluid milk (1,900), and poultry processing (1,900).

Iowa

Iowa is a leading state in the production of processed foods. Iowa ranked tenth in 1982 food processing employment and fourth in value of shipments in the United States. With barely 1 percent of the U.S. population, Iowa processes almost 5 percent of the country's food. Within the West North Central region, Iowa ranked first both in food processing employment and production.

Iowa had 484 food processing plants operating with 44,800 employees in 1982. From 1963 to 1982 the number of food processing plants declined by 47 percent and employment by 11 percent, about the same as the U.S. averages. Another 500 food processing jobs were lost between 1982 and 1985. The 1963–1985 drop in food processing employment of 21 percent was considerably more than the U.S. decline. Although production increased by 90 percent from 1963 levels, this was 20 percent lower than the national average and shows signs of deceleration in recent periods (table 19–3).

In 1982 Iowa's food processing plants shipped $13,747 million of products. The food processing industries are an important segment of the state's manufacturing sector, accounting for 39 percent of 1985 manufacturing output. This ratio was one of the highest in the U.S. However, the food processing industries used to be even more important; in 1963 food processing output constituted 50 percent of the manufacturing sector.

Ten processed foods accounted for 60 percent of the state's 1982 value of shipments. In many products Iowa has a leading position nationally (table 19–4). The state supplies over 30 percent of the nation's corn sweeteners (the leading state) and canned meats (first); over 20 percent of the pork (first) and cat food (first); and over 10 percent of the beef (fourth), soybean cake and meal (second), processed pork (first), breakfast foods (fourth), and soybean oil (second). In terms of employment, Iowa's principal food processing industries were meatpacking (17,900 employees), animal feed (3,900), wet corn mills (3,200), meat processing (2,300), and bread and rolls (2,100). These five leading industries accounted for 66 percent of the state's total food processing employees in 1982.

Missouri

In 1982 Missouri ranked twelfth in food processing production in the U.S. and fourth in the West North Central region (after Iowa, Minnesota, and

Table 19-3
Iowa: Importance and Growth of the Food Manufacturing Industries, 1963, 1972, 1982, and 1985

Measures (units)	1963	1972	1982	1985
Value of Shipments ($ millions):				
Food manufacturing	3,168	5,829	13,747	12,562
All manufacturing	6,294	12,600	31,397	32,237
State Personal Income ($ billion)	6.4	12.4	31.3	36.3
Employment (thousands):				
Food manufacturing	50.4	49.6	44.8	39.7
All manufacturing	178	216	213	198.2
State total, private sector	854.9	960.1	1,024.9	1,012.8
Export Dependence:				
Value of processed foods ($ million)	--	--	450.4	--
Employment created (thousands)	--	--	2.0	--
Growth Rates and Ratios:				
Food manufacturing shipments growth (%)	--	84.0	135.8	-8.6
Total manufacturing shipments growth (%)	--	100.2	149.2	2.6
Food manufacturing output growth (%)	--	48.9	31.6	-3.1
Food manufacturing shipments/manufacturing shipments (%)	50.3	46.3	43.8	39.0
Food manufacturing VA/manufacturing VA (%)	28.6	23.4	25.9	25.0
Food manufacturing employment growth (%)	--	-1.6	-9.7	-11.4
Total manufacturing employment growth (%)	--	21.3	-1.4	-6.9
Food manufacturing employment/manufacturing employment (%)	28.3	23.0	21.0	20.0
Manufacturing employment/state employment (%)	20.8	22.5	20.8	19.6
Exports/total processed foods shipped (%)	--	--	5.3	--

Note: See Table 16-1 for sources and notes applicable to this table.

Table 19–4
Iowa: The Top Ten Manufactured Food Products by 1982 Value of Product Shipments

Product Class	Value of Shipments	Proportion of State Food Manufacturing	Proportion of Total U.S. Production	Rank in U.S.
	$ Million	– – – – Percent – – – –	– – – – – –	Rank
1. Pork	2,188	15.9	27.1	1
2. Beef	2,121	15.4	10.3	4
3. Soybean cake and meal	757	5.5	15.6	2
4. Processed pork	623	4.5	11.7	1
5. Corn sweeteners	604	4.4	37.5	1
6. Canned meats	495	3.6	31.9	1
7. Breakfast foods	490E	3.6	11.9	4
8. Sausages	348	2.5	5.3	5
9. Soybean oil	347	2.5	14.6	2
10. Cat food	327	2.4	29.2	1
Top 10 products	8,300	60.4	– –	– –
Total food manufacturing	13,747	100.0	4.90	4

Sources: Data from *Statistical Abstract of the United States* (various years) and Appendix Table B–17.

E = Estimated from four-digit SIC shipments.

— = Not applicable.

Nebraska). It had 537 food processing plants in operation in 1982 employing 38,800 persons (table 19–5). From 1963 to 1982 the number of food processing plants dropped by 36 percent and employment by 20 percent. Another 1,800 food processing jobs were lost between 1982 and 1985. The 1963–1985 drop in food processing employment of 23 percent was more than twice the U.S. decline. Food processing production increased by a relatively slow 89 percent from 1963 to 1985; growth was slightly below average in all subperiods.

Missouri's food processing plants shipped $8,549 million of products in 1982, which was 3.1 percent of total U.S. food processing products. The food processing industries are an important segment of the state's manufacturing sector. From 1963 to 1982 Missouri's food processing output composed about 20 percent of the state's total manufacturing output. This ratio was about 5 percentage points higher than the U.S. average. The proportion of the food processing employment was 12 percent in 1963 and 10 percent in 1982.

Missouri has a very diversified mix of food processing industries. The ten leading products of the state accounted for 39 percent of the state's 1982 food processing output (table 19–6). In six product areas, Missouri ranks among the top ten states. Missouri supplies about 35 percent of the nation's frozen specialties (leading state); 19 percent of processed cheese (third); and over 4 percent of the beer (fourth), soybean cake and meal (eighth), and wheat flour (fifth). In terms of employment, Missouri's principal food processing industries were bread and rolls (4,700 employees), beer (3,400), meatpacking (3,200), soft drinks (3,100), poultry dressing (2,800), cheese (2,700), frozen specialties (2,400), miscellaneous foods (2,300), fluid milk (2,100), and animal feeds (1,500). These ten industries accounted for over 70 percent of the state's food processing employment.

North Dakota

North Dakota is the smallest state in the West North Central region in terms of food processing and manufacturing generally. Households in the state received only 3.6 percent of the division's personal income in 1985, the second lowest in the region. In 1982 North Dakota ranked forty-first in value of food processing production in the United States.

North Dakota had ninety-three food processing plants in operation with 4,100 employees in 1982 (table 19–7). From 1963 to 1982 the number of food processing plants dropped by 48 percent; but the number of employees in food processing increased by 23 percent from 1963 to 1985 at a time when national employment fell by 13 percent. Manufacturing employment doubled in the state during the same period. Real output of processed foods grew an

Table 19–5
Missouri: Importance and Growth of the Food Manufacturing Industries, 1963, 1972, 1982, and 1985

Measures (units)	Year			
	1963	1972	1982	1985
Value of Shipments ($ millions):				
Food manufacturing	2,225	3,567	8,549	8,779
All manufacturing	10,773	18,774	44,459	54,872
State Personal Income ($ billion)	10.9	20.0	50.3	66.6
Employment (thousands):				
Food manufacturing	48.2	41.6	38.8	37.0
All manufacturing	391	434	406	413.6
State total, private sector	1,431.3	1,585.1	1,753.2	1,892.2
Export Dependence:				
Value of processed foods ($ million)	--	--	196.5	--
Employment created (thousands)	--	--	1.3	--
Growth Rates and Ratios:				
Food manufacturing shipments growth (%)	--	60.3	139.7	2.7
Total manufacturing shipments growth (%)	--	74.3	120.8	32.4
Food manufacturing output growth (%)	--	29.8	33.7	9.0
Food manufacturing shipments/manufacturing shipments (%)	20.7	19.0	20.6	16.0
Food manufacturing VA/manufacturing VA (%)	14.7	12.4	13.6	13.5
Food manufacturing employment growth (%)	--	-13.7	-6.7	-4.6
Total manufacturing employment growth (%)	--	11.0	-6.5	1.9
Food manufacturing employment/manufacturing employment (%)	12.3	9.6	9.6	8.9
Manufacturing employment/state employment (%)	27.3	27.4	23.2	21.9
Exports/total processed foods shipped (%)	--	--	4.5	--

Note: See Table 16–1 for sources and notes applicable to this table.

Table 19–6
Missouri: The Top Ten Manufactured Food Products by 1982 Value of Product Shipments

Product Class	Value of Shipments	Proportion of State Food Manufacturing	Proportion of Total U.S. Production	Rank in U.S.
	$ Million	- - - - - - - - Percent - - - - - - - -		Rank
1. Beer	786	9.2	7.0	4
2. Processed cheese	598	7.0	18.7	3
3. Beef	430	5.0	2.1	12
4. Bottled soft drinks	336	3.9	3.0	10
5. Soybean cake and meal	230	2.7	4.8	8
6. Frozen specialties	215	2.5	34.5	1
7. Packaged fluid milk	214	2.5	2.3	14
8. Wheat flour	211	2.5	6.8	5
9. Natural cheese	140	1.6	2.5	9
10. Bread	135	1.6	2.9	12
Top 10 products	3,295	38.5	--	--
Total food manufacturing	8,549	100.0	3.05	12

Sources: Data from *Statistical Abstract of the United States* (various years) and Appendix Table B–18.

E = Estimated from four-digit SIC shipments.

— = Not applicable.

Table 19-7
North Dakota: Importance and Growth of the Food Manufacturing Industries, 1963, 1972, 1982, and 1985

Measures (units)	Year			
	1963	1972	1982	1985
Value of Shipments ($ millions):				
Food manufacturing	135	261	870	878
All manufacturing	251	594	2,465	2,493
State Personal Income ($ billion)	1.3	2.4	7.3	8.3
Employment (thousands):				
Food manufacturing	3.1	3.6	4.1	3.8
All manufacturing	7	10	15	14.1
State total, private sector	182.7	184.1	235.2	223.0
Export Dependence:				
Value of processed foods ($ million)	--	--	14.7	--
Employment created (thousands)	--	--	0.1	--
Growth Rates and Ratios:				
Food manufacturing shipments growth (%)	--	93.3	233.3	0.9
Total manufacturing shipments growth (%)	--	136.7	315.0	0.1
Food manufacturing output growth (%)	--	56.5	86.0	7.1
Food manufacturing shipments/manufacturing shipments (%)	54.8	43.9	35.3	35.2
Food manufacturing VA/manufacturing VA (%)	51.4	33.3	35.0	28.2
Food manufacturing employment growth (%)	--	16.1	13.9	-7.3
Total manufacturing employment growth (%)	--	42.9	50.0	-6.0
Food manufacturing employment/manufacturing employment (%)	44.3	36.0	27.3	27.0
Manufacturing employment/state employment (%)	3.8	5.4	6.4	6.3
Exports/total processed foods shipped (%)	--	--	4.2	--

Note: See Table 16-1 for sources and notes applicable to this table.

impressive 212 percent from 1963 to 1982, making the state the sixth-fastest growing in food processing in the United States.

North Dakota's food processing plants shipped $870 million of products in 1982, which was only 0.3 percent of total U.S. output of processed foods. However, food processing industry is an important segment of total manufacturing in the state, accounting for 35 percent of manufacturing output in 1982, almost triple the U.S. ratio. Food processing used to be more important; in 1963 food processing output was 55 percent of North Dakota's manufacturing output, well over three times the U.S. average. Food processing employment constituted 27 percent of the state's total manufacturing employment, a proportion more than three times the U.S. share.

North Dakota's process is highly concentrated in meat and sugar products. The top ten processed foods accounted for nearly 70 percent of the state's 1982 value of shipments (table 19–8). In three of the ten products, North Dakota accounted for over 1 percent of U.S. production. The state ranked among the top ten states in only two processed food products: beet sugar (fourth largest state, 11 percent of the nation's supply), and nuts and seeds (ninth). The two largest employers in food processing in 1982 were beet sugar (1,100) and fluid milk (500).

South Dakota

In economic terms South Dakota is the smallest state in the West North Central region, though it is very close in size to North Dakota. Households in the state received 3.4 percent of the region's personal income in 1985. Like North Dakota, the state's manufacturing sector is growing rapidly.

South Dakota had 100 food processing plants operating with 7,500 employees in 1982 (table 19–9). From 1963 to 1982 the number of food processing plants dropped by 40 percent, the same as the U.S. average. Food processing employment has ranged from 7,200 to 7,900 throughout the period. The 1963–1985 drop in food processing employment of 500 (9 percent) was less than the U.S. decline, but output grew a relatively slow 90 percent.

South Dakota's food processing plants shipped $1,702 million of products in 1982, which was 0.6 percent of the total U.S. output of processed foods, placing the state thirty-third in the United States. However, the food processing industry is an extremely important segment of the state's manufacturing sector, accounting for 51 percent of shipments in 1982 (almost *four times* the U.S. average). Food processing employment constituted 30 percent of the state's total manufacturing employment, also about four times the U.S. average. The food processing industries used to be even more

Table 19–8
North Dakota: The Top Ten Manufactured Food Products by 1982 Value of Product Shipments

Product Class	Value of Shipments	Proportion of State Food Manufacturing	Proportion of Total U.S. Production	Rank in U.S.
	$ Million	– – – – Percent – – – –		Rank
1. Beet sugar	162E	18.6	10.7	4
2. Sausages	132E	15.2	2.0	14
3. Processed pork	83E	9.5	1.6	17
4. Packaged fluid milk	71E	8.2	0.8	35
5. Beef	51E	5.9	0.2	33
6. Natural cheese	45	5.2	0.8	18
7. Bottled soft drinks	18	2.1	0.2	48
8. Shortening and cooking oil	15E	1.7	0.4	13
9. Chips	14E	1.6	0.4	20
10. Nuts and seeds	12	1.4	0.8	9
Top 10 products	603	69.3	--	--
Total food manufacturing	870	100.0	0.31	41

Sources: Data from *Statistical Abstract of the United States* (various years) and Appendix Table B–19.

E = Estimated from four-digit SIC shipments.

— = Not applicable.

Table 19–9
South Dakota: Importance and Growth of the Food Manufacturing Industries, 1963, 1972, 1982, and 1985

Measures (units)	Year			
	1963	1972	1982	1985
Value of Shipments ($ millions):				
Food manufacturing	460	640	1,702	1,822
All manufacturing	536	937	3,005	3,585
State Personal Income ($ billion)	1.4	2.5	6.7	7.9
Employment (thousands):				
Food manufacturing	7.9	7.3	7.5	7.2
All manufacturing	13	17	25	26.1
State total, private sector	195.6	197.2	220.9	226.2
Export Dependence:				
Value of processed foods ($ million)	--	--	54.1	--
Employment created (thousands)	--	--	0.4	--
Growth Rates and Ratios:				
Food manufacturing shipments growth (%)	--	39.1	165.9	7.1
Total manufacturing shipments growth (%)	--	74.8	220.7	19.3
Food manufacturing output growth (%)	--	12.6	48.4	13.6
Food manufacturing shipments/manufacturing shipments (%)	85.8	68.3	56.6	50.8
Food manufacturing VA/manufacturing VA (%)	67.9	44.6	38.5	34.9
Food manufacturing employment growth (%)	--	-7.6	2.7	-4.0
Total manufacturing employment growth (%)	--	30.8	47.1	4.4
Food manufacturing employment/manufacturing employment (%)	60.8	42.9	30.0	27.6
Manufacturing employment/state employment (%)	6.6	8.6	11.3	11.5
Exports/total processed foods shipped (%)	--	--	5.5	--

Note: See Table 16–1 for sources and notes applicable to this table.

important; in 1963 food processing production provided 86 percent of South Dakota's manufacturing output, the highest in the United States at the time.

Despite the dependence on beef and dairy products, South Dakota has very diversified food processing industries. The top ten processed foods accounted for only 36 percent of the state's output in 1982 (table 19–10). In five of the ten products, South Dakota accounted for over 1 percent of the U.S. production. The state ranked among the top ten states in four processed food products: dry milk product (ninth largest state), swine feed supplements (ninth), processed cheese (seventh), and beef cattle feed supplements (tenth). The two largest employers in food processing in 1982 were meatpacking (4,100) and fluid milk (500).

Nebraska

Nebraska in 1982 ranked ninth in the value of food processing production in the United States and second in the West North Central division. It had 342 food processing plants operating with 25,900 employees in 1982 (table 19–11). From 1963 to 1982, the number of food processing plants dropped by 29 percent; employment fell by 3 percent, a third the U.S. rate of decline. Between 1982 and 1985, food processing employment decreased another 5 percent as 1,300 jobs were lost. Even so, the 1963–1985 drop of 8 percent in food processing employment was lower than the U.S. decline.

Although employment fell slightly, shipments growth was impressive, especially in the late 1960s as IBP expanded. Real output increased 97 percent from 1963 to 1972, but decelerated after 1972; for 1963–1985, real output grew 190 percent, well above the U.S. average.

Nebraska's food processing plants shipped $9,432 million of products in 1982, which was 3.4 percent of total U.S. food processing production. The food processing industry is an extremely important segment of the state's manufacturing sector, accounting for 55 percent of shipments in 1985, over *four times* the U.S. average. Nebraska's food processing employment comprised 27 percent of 1985 manufacturing employment, down from 41 percent in 1963.

The state's food industries are highly concentrated in beef and pork products. Ten processed foods accounted for 60 percent of the state's 1982 value of shipments (table 19–12). In seven of the top ten product classes, the state's value of shipments represent 4 percent or more of the nation's output. Nebraska supplies 21 percent of the nation's beef (the leading state); over 10 percent of the hides and skins (first), swine feed supplements (third), and probably other vegetable oils (third); and over 4 percent of the pork (fifth), breakfast foods (eighth), dog food (seventh), and beet sugar (fifth). In terms of employment, Nebraska's principal food processing industries in

Table 19–10
South Dakota: The Top Ten Manufactured Food Products by 1982 Value of Product Shipments

Product Class	Value of Shipments	Proportion of State Food Manufacturing	Proportion of Total U.S. Production	Rank in U.S.
	$ Million	Percent	Percent	Rank
1. Beef	328	19.3	1.6	13
2. Natural cheese	94	5.5	1.7	12
3. Dry milk products	37	2.2	1.5	9
4. Packaged fluid milk	37	2.1	0.4	42
5. Swine feed supplements	23	1.3	2.0	9
6. Bottled and canned soft drinks	22	1.3	0.2	40
7. Processed cheese	19	1.1	0.6	7
8. Crackers	17E	1.0	0.9	11
9. Beef cattle feed supplements	15	0.9	2.5	10
10. Wheat flour	14E	0.8	0.5	24
Top 10 products	606	35.6	--	--
Total food manufacturing	1,702	100.0	0.61	33

Sources: Data from *Statistical Abstract of the United States* (various years) and Appendix Table B–20.

E = Estimated from four-digit SIC shipments.

— = Not applicable.

Table 19-11
Nebraska: Importance and Growth of the Food Manufacturing Industries, 1963, 1972, 1982, and 1985

Measures (units)	Year			
	1963	1972	1982	1985
Value of Shipments ($ millions):				
Food manufacturing	1,549	3,774	9,432	8,422
All manufacturing	2,448	5,898	15,143	15,215
State Personal Income ($ billion)	3.4	6.6	16.9	21.3
Employment (thousands):				
Food manufacturing	26.7	25.4	25.9	24.6
All manufacturing	65	85	92	89.8
State total, private sector	458.0	518.0	583.5	593.7
Export Dependence:				
Value of processed foods ($ million)	--	--	382.8	--
Employment created (thousands)	--	--	1.3	--
Growth Rates and Ratios:				
Food manufacturing shipments growth (%)	--	148.5	150.0	-10.7
Total manufacturing shipments growth (%)	--	140.9	156.5	0.5
Food manufacturing output growth (%)	--	97.2	39.4	5.3
Food manufacturing shipments/manufacturing shipments (%)	62.1	63.9	62.3	55.4
Food manufacturing VA/manufacturing VA (%)	42.4	33.5	35.0	35.4
Food manufacturing employment growth (%)	--	-4.9	2.0	-5.0
Total manufacturing employment growth (%)	--	25.0	8.2	-2.4
Food manufacturing employment/manufacturing employment (%)	41.1	29.9	28.2	27.4
Manufacturing employment/state employment (%)	14.2	16.4	15.8	15.1
Exports/total processed foods shipped (%)	--	--	6.1	--

Note: See Table 16-1 for sources and notes applicable to this table.

Table 19–12
Nebraska: The Top Ten Manufactured Food Products by 1982 Value of Product Shipments

Product Class	Value of Shipments	Proportion of State Food Manufacturing	Proportion of Total U.S. Production	Rank in U.S.
	$ Million	- - - - - - Percent - - - - - -		Rank
1. Beef	4,225	44.8	20.5	1
2. Pork	344	3.6	4.3	5
3. Breakfast foods	198E	2.1	4.8	8
4. Hides and skins	149	1.6	17.2	1
5. Swine feed supplements	148	1.6	13.2	3
6. Processed pork	144	1.5	2.7	13
7. Other vegetable oils	140E	1.5	--	--
8. Dog food	119E	1.3	4.5	7
9. Beet sugar	103E	1.1	6.8	5
10. Wheat flour	100	1.1	3.2	11
Top 10 products	5,670	60.1	--	--
Total food manufacturing	9,432	100.0	3.36	9

Sources: Data from *Statistical Abstract of the United States* (various years) and Appendix Table B–21.

E = Estimated from four-digit SIC shipments.

— = Not applicable.

Table 19–13
Kansas: Importance and Growth of the Food Manufacturing Industries, 1963, 1972, 1982, and 1985

Measures (units)	Year			
	1963	1972	1982	1985
Value of Shipments ($ millions):				
Food manufacturing	1,245	2,571	6,891	8,350
All manufacturing	3,945	8,063	26,753	31,630
State Personal Income ($ billion)	5.0	10.4	28.3	33.8
Employment (thousands):				
Food manufacturing	21.2	18.9	21.5	24.9
All manufacturing	114	137	171	184.4
State total, private sector	600.3	658.8	847.6	868.1
Export Dependence:				
Value of processed foods ($ million)	--	--	293.3	--
Employment created (thousands)	--	--	1.2	--
Growth Rates and Ratios:				
Food manufacturing shipments growth (%)	--	101.7	174.4	21.2
Total manufacturing shipments growth (%)	--	104.4	231.8	18.2
Food manufacturing output growth (%)	--	67.1	49.5	28.6
Food manufacturing shipments/manufacturing shipments (%)	31.6	31.1	25.8	26.4
Food manufacturing VA/manufacturing VA (%)	16.4	15.0	14.2	13.6
Food manufacturing employment growth (%)	--	-10.8	13.8	15.8
Total manufacturing employment growth (%)	--	20.2	24.8	7.8
Food manufacturing employment/manufacturing employment (%)	18.6	13.8	12.6	13.5
Manufacturing employment/state employment (%)	19.0	20.8	20.2	21.2
Exports/total processed foods shipped (%)	--	--	7.1	--

Note: See Table 16–1 for sources and notes applicable to this table.

Table 19–14
Kansas: The Top Ten Manufactured Food Products by 1982 Value of Product Shipments

Product Class	Value of Shipments	Proportion of State Food Manufacturing	Proportion of Total U.S. Production	Rank in U.S.
	$ Million	Percent		Rank
1. Beef	2,912	42.3	14.1	3
2. Wheat flour	320	4.6	10.3	3
3. Sausages	272	3.9	4.2	10
4. Dog food	265	3.8	10.0	3
5. Soybean cake and meal	182	2.6	3.8	10
6. Processed pork	168	2.4	3.2	11
7. Bottled and canned soft drinks	137	2.0	1.2	29
8. Packaged fluid milk	108	1.6	1.2	30
9. Hides and skins	106	1.5	12.3	3
10. Soybean oil	86	1.2	3.6	8
Top 10 products	4,556	66.1	––	––
Total food manufacturing	6,891	100.0	2.46	16

Sources: Data from *Statistical Abstract of the United States* (various years) and Appendix Table B–22.
E = Estimated from four-digit SIC shipments.
— = Not applicable.

1982 were meatpacking (12,100 employees), bread and rolls (1,800), meat processing (1,600), animal feed (1,600), and poultry processing (1,100). These top five industries provided 70 percent of the state's food processing employment in 1982.

Kansas

Kansas is a demographically small state, with only about 1 percent of the U.S. population, yet it had 303 food processing plants in operation employing 21,500 persons in 1982 (table 19–13). From 1963 to 1982 the number of food processing plants declined by 44 percent, slightly faster than the U.S. average, but employment increased 1.4 percent. Between 1982 and 1985, food processing employment increased by 16 percent and more than 3,000 jobs were created. The 1963–1985 increase of 17 percent is very impressive, as U.S. employment fell by 13 percent in that period. Moreover, real output expanded by 221 percent from 1963 to 1985, a rate that was double the U.S. average, the highest in the Midwest region, and fifth-highest in the United States. Kansas ranked sixteenth in 1982 food processing production in the United States (table 19–14).

In 1982 Kansas' food processing plants shipped $6,891 million of products, which was 2.5 percent of total U.S. food processing. The food processing industry is a very important segment of the state's manufacturing sector, producing 26 percent of manufacturing output in 1985, double the U.S. average. Kansas's food processing employment was 14 percent of manufacturing employment, almost double the U.S. average. In 1963 food employment was 19 percent of that of total manufacturing.

Production is highly concentrated in beefpacking. The top ten processed foods accounted for 66 percent of the state's 1982 value of shipments. In eight cases, the state's value of shipments represented 3 percent or more of the nation's output. Seven Kansas products ranked top ten of the U.S. food processing industries. Kansas supplies over 10 percent of the nation's beef (third largest state), wheat flour (third), dog food (third), and hides and skins (third); it makes over 3 percent of the sausages (tenth), soybean cake and meal (tenth), processed pork (eleventh), and soybean oil (eighth). In terms of employment, Kansas' principal food processing industries were meatpacking (6,700 employees), bread and rolls (2,200), soft drinks (1,700), flour (1,200), fluid milk (1,000), frozen specialties (1,000), and animal feed (1,000).

20
South Atlantic States

The eight states of the South Atlantic division—from Delaware in the north to Florida in the south—had 38 million people in 1985, which was 16.7 percent of the U.S. population. Since 1963 the division's population had grown by 43 percent (fourth highest growth among the nine divisions and 16 percentage points higher than the U.S. average). This division is now the second largest division in the United States, rising from third place in 1963. The division's residents received $532 billion in income in 1985, which was 16 percent of U.S. income; in both 1963 and 1985, the division was in fourth place among the nine divisions. Average personal incomes are now only about 4 percent below the U.S. average. Florida is by far the largest state in the division, with almost 30 percent of the division's income; Virginia, Georgia, and North Carolina are each about half the size of Florida.

Manufacturing was relatively unimportant to most of the states of the South Atlantic division just after World War II. Even by 1963 the 2.125 million manufacturing jobs in the division represented only 13 percent of the U.S. total. However, the division experienced considerable growth in its manufacturing sector throughout the post-World War II era. By 1985 manufacturing was generating 2.984 million jobs in the division; this was 16 percent of the U.S. total, almost the same proportion as population. The 40 percent increase in manufacturing employment in the South Atlantic division was almost *four times* the U.S. growth rate. In terms of unit production, the South Atlantic division's growth was the highest in the United States: 171 percent from 1963 to 1985. Production tripled in four states: the Carolinas, Virginia, and Florida. Growth decelerated in the 1980s but was still at or above the national level in nearly all the states.

While the dependence on manufacturing employment has fallen in the division, as has happened in the United States generally, the decline has been a bit slower than nationally. In 1963 some 29 percent of all private sector jobs in the South Atlantic division were in manufacturing (3 percentage points below the U.S. average), but by 1985 only 21 percent were (almost the same as the U.S. average). Like many other parts of the South, this division has attracted a broad array of industries: textiles, chemicals, paper, furniture, and some heavy industries as well.

The South Atlantic division has diversified agriculture and marine sectors. All the states have ocean coastlines or access (except West Virginia), with especially rich fishing grounds around the Chesapeake Bay and the Gulf of Mexico. Corn is the principal grain grown in the division, and soybean production has been moving southward from the Eastern Corn Belt for several decades. The division produces large shares of the nation's hogs and broiler chickens, but in most states dairy and cattle raising are relatively small. Florida is one of the few subtropical states in the United States, with cane sugar and citrus fruits providing a base for some nearly unique food processing industries.

From 211,000 employees in 1963, the South Atlantic division in 1985 had 225,000 food processing employees, a 7 percent growth rate (compared to a 13 percent U.S. decline). This division now employs about 16 percent of all U.S. food processing employees, up from 13 percent in 1963. However, because general manufacturing growth has been so rapid, food has only an average share of all manufacturing jobs. That is, food provided 10 percent of all manufacturing jobs in 1963 and only 7.5 percent in 1985—just about the U.S. average.

The division is a leading producer of only a few processed foods. A very large share of U.S. broilers are processed in the Delmarva peninsula, Georgia, and North Carolina. Canned and frozen fish processing is important in Delaware, Maryland, and Florida. Cane sugar refining is significant in Delaware (imported) and Florida (mostly local supply). Florida processes a great deal of fruit into juices. And of course, the large population of the region supports such regionalized food processing industries as bread, milk, sausage, and beer.

Delaware

From a very small base, Delaware has had one of the fastest growing food processing industries in the United States. Moreover, unlike most states, Delaware's food processing industry has become a more important part of the state's manufacturing sector.

The state had sixty-three food processing plants in 1982 employing 8,400 person (table 20–1). From 1963 to 1982 the number of food processing plants dropped by 34 percent, but food processing employment increased by 38 percent. Between 1982 and 1985, another 1,000 food processing jobs were created. Thus, 1963–1985 job growth was an impressive 54 percent. The proportion of food processing employment to total manufacturing increased from 11 to 14 percent from 1963 to 1982, bucking the downward U.S. trend—that 14 percent is nearly double the U.S. average for 1985.

In 1982 Delaware's food processing plants shipped $1,298 million of products, which was 0.5 percent of the U.S. output of processed foods. Output grew 169 percent in real terms from 1963 to 1982, well above the U.S. average, but apparently slowing down over time. Although very small

Table 20-1
Delaware: Importance and Growth of the Food Manufacturing Industries, 1963, 1972, 1982, and 1985

Measures (units)	Year			
	1963	1972	1982	1985
Value of Shipments ($ millions):				
Food manufacturing	253	507	1,298	1,423
All manufacturing	1,815	3,388	8,383	10,789
State Personal Income ($ billion)	1.6	2.8	7.1	8.9
Employment (thousands):				
Food manufacturing	6.1	8.2	8.4	9.4
All manufacturing	58	69	68	69.5
State total, private sector	152.8	202.6	222.8	253.4
Export Dependence:				
Value of processed foods ($ million)	--	--	31.4	--
Employment created (thousands)	--	--	0.4	--
Growth Rates and Ratios:				
Food manufacturing shipments growth (%)	--	100.4	156.0	9.6
Total manufacturing shipments growth (%)	--	86.7	147.4	28.7
Food manufacturing output growth (%)	--	62.2	42.8	16.3
Food manufacturing shipments/manufacturing shipments (%)	13.9	15.0	15.5	13.2
Food manufacturing VA/manufacturing VA (%)	8.4	16.3	19.3	14.0
Food manufacturing employment growth (%)	--	34.4	2.4	11.9
Total manufacturing employment growth (%)	--	19.0	-1.4	2.2
Food manufacturing employment/manufacturing employment (%)	10.5	11.9	12.4	13.5
Manufacturing employment/state employment (%)	38.0	34.1	30.5	27.4
Exports/total processed foods shipped (%)	--	--	4.1	--

Note: See Table 16-1 for sources and notes applicable to this table.

by U.S. standards (it ranked thirty-sixth in the United States), the state's food processing industry is an important segment of the state's manufacturing sector, accounting for 16 percent of shipments in 1982 (slightly above the U.S. average). Moreover, manufacturing is a relatively large source of employment in the state, providing 27 percent of all private-sector jobs in 1985.

Ten processed foods accounted for 58 percent of the state's 1982 value of product shipments (table 20–2). Delaware supplies 5 percent of the nation's young chickens (ninth largest state) and over 3 percent of the poultry feed (tenth) and canned fish (sixth). The state's other major processed food products were other vegetable oils (2.6 percent and seventh), frozen fish (1.7 percent and tenth), and frozen vegetables (0.5 percent and tenth). The three largest employers in food processing in 1982 were poultry dressing (3,800 employees), miscellaneous foods (1,400), and canned fruits and vegetables (1,000).

Maryland

Maryland is an average size U.S. state, with about 2 percent of the U.S. population in 1985. Maryland's food processing production ranked twenty-fourth in the United States and fifth in the South Atlantic division in 1982. The state had 365 food processing plants in operation with 23,300 employees (table 20–3). From 1963 to 1982 the number of plants in operation dropped by 15 percent, less than half the U.S. rate. However, the 1963–1985 fall in Maryland's fall in food processing employment of 35 percent was almost three times the U.S. average. Although 1963–1982 growth in production was a relatively low 55 percent, growth since 1982 has been quite rapid.

In 1982 Maryland's food processing plants shipped $3,935 million of products, which was 1.4 percent of total U.S. production of processed foods. Food processing is an important segment of the state's manufacturing sector, accounting for 18 percent of output in 1963 and 1982. In 1982 this share was 4 percentage points above the U.S. average. Food processing employment provided 10 percent of the total manufacturing employment in 1982, down from about 14 percent in 1963. Maryland has deindustrialized at a rapid rate since 1963, when manufacturing accounted for 30 percent of private sector employment; now it is 15 percent.

Maryland has a fairly diversified mix of food processing industries. The top ten processed foods accounted for a half of Maryland's output in 1982 (table 20–4). In eight cases, the state's value of shipments represented 3 to 9 percent of national output. These product classes were bottled soft drinks (seventh in the nation), cane sugar (seventh), young chickens (tenth), bottled liquor (third), poultry feed (seventh), ice cream (sixth), and frozen fish

Table 20–2
Delaware: The Top Ten Manufactured Food Products by 1982 Value of Product Shipments

Product Class	Value of Shipments	Proportion of State Food Manufacturing	Proportion of Total U.S. Production	Rank in U.S.
	$ Million	- - - - - - - Percent - - - - - - -		Rank
1. Young chickens	310	23.9	5.2	9
2. Poultry feed	129	10.0	3.6	10
3. Other vegetable oils	60E	4.6	2.6	7
4. Chips	60E	4.6	1.8	13
5. Canned fish	56	4.3	3.0	6
6. Miscellaneous prepared foods	43E	3.3	1.7	17
7. Canned vegetables	30E	2.3	1.5	13
8. Bottled soft drinks	27E	2.1	0.2	42
9. Frozen fish	18E	1.4	1.7	10
10. Frozen vegetables	17	1.3	0.5	10
Top 10 products	750	57.8	--	--
Total food manufacturing	1,298	100.0	0.46	36

Sources: Data from *Statistical Abstract of the United States* (various years) and Appendix Table B–23.

E = Estimated from four-digit SIC shipments.

— = Not applicable.

Table 20-3
Maryland: Importance and Growth of the Food Manufacturing Industries, 1963, 1972, 1982, and 1985

Measures (units)	Year			
	1963	1972	1982	1985
Value of Shipments ($ millions):				
Food manufacturing	1,148	1,834	3,935	4,434
All manufacturing	6,401	9,963	21,282	25,328
State Personal Income ($ billion)	9.2	19.9	52.2	69.7
Employment (thousands):				
Food manufacturing	35.9	30.4	23.3	23.3
All manufacturing	264	256	234	225.4
State total, private sector	867.3	1,122.8	1,315.6	1,516.2
Export Dependence:				
Value of processed foods ($ million)	--	--	191.3	--
Employment created (thousands)	--	--	1.3	--
Growth Rates and Ratios:				
Food manufacturing shipments growth (%)	--	59.8	114.6	12.7
Total manufacturing shipments growth (%)	--	55.6	113.6	19.0
Food manufacturing output growth (%)	--	29.3	19.7	19.6
Food manufacturing shipments/manufacturing shipments (%)	17.9	18.4	18.5	17.5
Food manufacturing VA/manufacturing VA (%)	14.0	14.4	13.2	14.3
Food manufacturing employment growth (%)	--	-15.3	-23.4	0.0
Total manufacturing employment growth (%)	--	-3.0	-8.6	-3.7
Food manufacturing employment/manufacturing employment (%)	13.6	11.9	10.0	10.3
Manufacturing employment/state employment (%)	30.4	22.8	17.9	14.9
Exports/total processed foods shipped (%)	--	--	6.7	--

Note: See Table 16-1 for sources and notes applicable to this table.

Table 20–4
Maryland: The Top Ten Manufactured Food Products by 1982 Value of Product Shipments

Product Class	Value of Shipments	Proportion of State Food Manufacturing	Proportion of Total U.S. Production	Rank in U.S.
	$ Million	- - - - - Percent - - - - -		Rank
1. Bottled soft drinks	399	10.1	3.6	7
2. Cane sugar	256	6.5	6.2	7
3. Young chickens	223	5.7	3.7	10
4. Bottled liquor	207E	5.3	8.6	3
5. Poultry feed	202	5.1	5.5	7
6. Packaged fluid milk	201	5.1	2.2	17
7. Ice cream	199E	5.1	7.0	6
8. Chips	95E	2.4	2.9	10
9. Frozen fish	90E	2.3	8.7	5
10. Shortening and cooking oils	90E	2.3	2.2	8
Top 10 products	1,962	49.9	--	--
Total food manufacturing	3,935	100.0	1.40	24

Sources: Data from *Statistical Abstract of the United States* (various years) and Appendix Table B–24.
E = Estimated from four-digit SIC shipments.
— = Not applicable.

(fifth). In terms of 1982 employment, Maryland's principal food processing industries were poultry dressing (3,100 employees), bread and rolls (2,800), soft drinks (2,200), fluid milk (1,700), and frozen fish (1,500). Together, these five industries accounted for 49 percent of state food processing employment.

District of Columbia

The District of Columbia has the smallest group of food processing industries in the nation. In 1982 District of Columbia had only sixteen food processing plants employing 1,200 persons (table 20–5). From 1963 to 1982 the number of food processing plants dropped by 67 percent and employment by 73 percent. From 1963 to 1985, D.C. lost 3,400 of its 4,500 jobs, or 76 percent. This drop was the highest in the nation (about six times the U.S. decline). The District also has a very small manufacturing sector (mostly printing) that supplies only 4 percent of all private sector employment.

From 1963 to 1982 real output in food processing fell by an extraordinary 70 percent. However, the industries experienced a modest recovery after 1982.

In 1982, District of Columbia's food processing plants shipped $94 million of products, which was only 0.03 percent of total U.S. products of processed foods. District of Columbia's principal food processing industries were bread and rolls, which accounted for about 64 percent of output and 90 percent of employment in the District's food processing industries (table 20–6).

Virginia

Virginia ranked twentieth in food processing production in the United States and fourth in the South Atlantic region in 1982. The state had 445 food processing plants operating with 36,800 employees in 1982 (table 20–7). From 1963 to 1982 the number of plants dropped by 33 percent, less than the U.S. average. Food processing employment increased 15 percent up to 1982, but between 1982 and 1985 more than 2,000 food processing jobs were lost. From 1963 to 1985 employment increased 8 percent, and output tripled in real terms, making it the ninth-fastest growing state in processed foods.

In 1982 Virginia's food processing plants shipped $5,903 million of products, which was 2.1 percent of the nation's production of processed foods. Food processing is an important segment of the state's manufacturing sector, accounting for 16 percent of total Virginia's manufacturing products

Table 20–5
District of Columbia: Importance and Growth of the Food Manufacturing Industries, 1963, 1972, 1982, and 1985

Measures (units)	Year			
	1963	1972	1982	1985
Value of Shipments ($ millions):				
Food manufacturing	153	106	94	101
All manufacturing	467	617	1,537	1,787
State Personal Income ($ billion)	2.6	4.8	9.2	11.4
Employment (thousands):				
Food manufacturing	4.5	1.5	1.2	1.1
All manufacturing	22	19	17	16.5
State total, private sector	293.8	313.4	337.1	366.0
Export Dependence:				
Value of processed foods ($ million)	--	--	0.5	--
Employment created (thousands)	--	--	0.0	--
Growth Rates and Ratios:				
Food manufacturing shipments growth (%)	--	-31.4	-11.4	8.6
Total manufacturing shipments growth (%)	--	32.1	149.1	16.3
Food manufacturing output growth (%)	--	-43.9	-50.5	14.0
Food manufacturing shipments/manufacturing shipments (%)	32.8	17.0	6.1	5.7
Food manufacturing VA/manufacturing VA (%)	21.8	12.8	6.2	4.7
Food manufacturing employment growth (%)	--	-66.7	-20.0	-8.3
Total manufacturing employment growth (%)	--	-13.6	-10.5	-2.9
Food manufacturing employment/manufacturing employment (%)	20.5	7.9	7.1	6.7
Manufacturing employment/state employment (%)	7.5	6.1	5.0	4.5
Exports/total processed foods shipped (%)	--	--	2.5	--

Note: See Table 16–1 for sources and notes applicable to this table.

Table 20-6
District of Columbia: The Top Ten Manufactured Food Products by 1982 Value of Product Shipments

Product Class	Value of Shipments	Proportion of State Food Manufacturing	Proportion of Total U.S. Production	Rank in U.S.
	$ Million	---- Percent ----		Rank
1. Bread	37E	39.8	0.8	36
2. Rolls	22E	23.7	0.9	32
3. Packaged fluid milk	10E	10.8	0.1	48
4. Soft cakes	9E	9.7	0.7	17
5. Roasted coffee	4E	4.3	0.1	12
6. Miscellaneous prepared foods	4E	4.3	0.2	27
7. Chips	2E	2.2	0.1	25
8. Bottled soft drinks	1E	1.1	0.0	50
9. Other vegetable oils	1E	1.1	--	--
10. Crackers	1E	1.1	0.1	12
Top 10 products	91	97.8	--	--
Total food manufacturing	93	100.0	0.03	51

Sources: Data from *Statistical Abstract of the United States* (various years) and Appendix Table B–25.

E = Estimated from four-digit SIC shipments.

— = Not applicable.

Table 20-7
Virginia: Importance and Growth of the Food Manufacturing Industries, 1963, 1972, 1982, and 1985

Measures (units)	Year			
	1963	1972	1982	1985
Value of Shipments ($ millions):				
Food manufacturing	1,000	1,964	5,903	6,195
All manufacturing	6,611	12,824	36,803	45,554
State Personal Income ($ billion)	8.9	20.3	60.1	83.0
Employment (thousands):				
Food manufacturing	32.0	33.6	36.8	34.5
All manufacturing	302	375	391	408.7
State total, private sector	1,078.1	1,370.5	1,747.3	1,968.8
Export Dependence:				
Value of processed foods ($ million)	--	--	246.6	--
Employment created (thousands)	--	--	1.8	--
Growth Rates and Ratios:				
Food manufacturing shipments growth (%)	--	96.4	200.6	4.9
Total manufacturing shipments growth (%)	--	94.0	187.0	23.8
Food manufacturing output growth (%)	--	59.0	67.7	11.3
Food manufacturing shipments/manufacturing shipments (%)	15.1	15.3	16.0	13.6
Food manufacturing VA/manufacturing VA (%)	10.7	9.9	11.9	9.6
Food manufacturing employment growth (%)	--	5.0	9.5	-6.3
Total manufacturing employment growth (%)	--	24.2	4.3	4.5
Food manufacturing employment/manufacturing employment (%)	10.6	9.0	9.4	8.4
Manufacturing employment/state employment (%)	28.0	27.4	22.4	20.8
Exports/total processed foods shipped (%)	--	--	6.8	--

Note: See Table 16-1 for sources and notes applicable to this table.

in 1982, 2 percentage points higher than the U.S. average. Virginia's food processing employment accounted for 9 percent of the total manufacturing employment in 1982, equal to the U.S. average. However, since 1982 Virginia has experienced very rapid industrial growth (24 percent increase in shipments up to 1985), and food processing has not kept pace. By 1985 the value of food shipments had fallen to 13.6 percent of total manufactures, which is about the U.S. average.

Virginia has a diversified set of food processing industries. The top ten products of the state accounted for 44 percent of the state's value of food processing output in 1982 (table 20–8). Virginia made six food products that represent 4 percent or more of national output; shipments of these products placed Virginia in top ten states in the United States. Virginia supplies 20 percent of the nation's roasted nuts and seeds (second largest state) and over 4 percent of the young chickens (fifth), pork (seventh), processed pork (fifth), chips (fifth), poultry feed (ninth). In terms of employment, Virginia's principal food processing industries are poultry dressing (7,100 employees), meatpacking (4,600), frozen fish (3,700), bread and rolls (3,000), and soft drinks (2,900).

West Virginia

West Virginia had 100 food processing plants in 1982 employing 5,700 persons (table 20–9). From 1963 to 1982 the number of plants in operation has dropped about 60 percent and employment 22 percent. Another 600 food processing jobs were lost between 1982 and 1985. The 1963–1985 drop in West Virginia's food processing employment of 30 percent was over twice the U.S. rate of decline. Output grew by an anemic 18 percent from 1963 to 1985, the third-slowest rate in the nation. The state ranked forty-fourth in 1982 food processing production.

In 1982 West Virginia's food processing plants shipped $559 million of products, which accounted for only 0.2 percent of the U.S. output of processed foods. Processed foods accounted only for 5 percent of the state's total manufacturing output in 1985, far below the U.S. average. In 1963 the ratio was 6 percent. These ratios are less than half the U.S. average in both years.

Ten processed foods accounted for about a half of the state's 1982 value of product shipments (table 20–10). In three of the ten products, West Virginia accounted for over 1 percent of the U.S. production. One product ranked top ten in the nation: processed poultry (2.1 percent of the U.S. product, tenth largest state). The three largest employers in food processing industry in 1982 served local consumers: bread and rolls (1,900 employees), soft drinks (1,300), and fluid milk (800). These three leading industries represented 70 percent of the state's food processing employment.

Table 20–8
Virginia: The Top Ten Manufactured Food Products by 1982 Value of Product Shipments

Product Class	Value of Shipments	Proportion of State Food Manufacturing	Proportion of Total U.S. Production	Rank in U.S.
	$ Million	- - - - - Percent - - - - -		Rank
1. Young chickens	460	7.8	7.6	5
2. Pork	350E	5.9	4.3	7
3. Nuts and seeds	296	5.0	19.8	2
4. Bottled soft drinks	276	4.7	2.5	15
5. Processed pork	261	4.4	4.9	5
6. Beef	250E	4.2	1.2	18
7. Packaged fluid milk	188	3.2	2.1	18
8. Chips	188E	3.2	5.7	5
9. Beer	179	3.0	1.6	17
10. Poultry feed	164	2.8	4.5	9
Top 10 products	2,612	44.2	--	--
Total food manufacturing	5,903	100.0	2.10	20

Sources: Data from *Statistical Abstract of the United States* (various years) and Appendix Table B–26.
E = Estimated from four-digit SIC shipments.
— = Not applicable.

Table 20-9
West Virginia: Importance and Growth of the Food Manufacturing Industries, 1963, 1972, 1982, and 1985

Measures (units)	Year			
	1963	1972	1982	1985
Value of Shipments ($ millions):				
Food manufacturing	200	245	559	494
All manufacturing	3,270	5,022	9,869	10,603
State Personal Income ($ billion)	3.3	6.4	17.1	19.7
Employment (thousands):				
Food manufacturing	7.3	5.8	5.7	5.1
All manufacturing	117	121	96	84.9
State total, private sector	434.8	475.1	517.2	491.3
Export Dependence:				
Value of processed foods ($ million)	--	--	5.7	--
Employment created (thousands)	--	--	0.1	--
Growth Rates and Ratios:				
Food manufacturing shipments growth (%)	--	22.5	128.2	-11.6
Total manufacturing shipments growth (%)	--	53.6	96.5	7.4
Food manufacturing output growth (%)	--	-0.9	27.3	-6.2
Food manufacturing shipments/manufacturing shipments (%)	6.1	4.9	5.7	4.7
Food manufacturing VA/manufacturing VA (%)	3.8	3.8	5.6	4.1
Food manufacturing employment growth (%)	--	-20.5	-1.7	-10.5
Total manufacturing employment growth (%)	--	3.4	-20.7	-11.6
Food manufacturing employment/manufacturing employment (%)	6.2	4.8	5.9	6.0
Manufacturing employment/state employment (%)	26.9	25.5	18.6	17.3
Exports/total processed foods shipped (%)	--	--	3.1	--

Note: See Table 16–1 for sources and notes applicable to this table.

Table 20–10
West Virginia: The Top Ten Manufactured Food Products by 1982 Value of Product Shipments

Product Class	Value of Shipments	Proportion of State Food Manufacturing	Proportion of Total U.S. Production	Rank in U.S.
	$ Million	‑ ‑ ‑ ‑ Percent ‑ ‑ ‑ ‑		Rank
1. Bottled soft drinks	59	10.6	0.5	37
2. Bread	52	9.3	1.1	32
3. Packaged fluid milk	44	7.8	0.5	41
4. Processed poultry	25E	4.5	2.1	10
5. Young chickens	24E	4.3	0.4	23
6. Beef	22E	3.9	0.1	36
7. Canned fruit juices	20E	3.6	1.4	12
8. Rolls	17	3.0	0.7	34
9. Pork	8E	1.4	0.1	19
10. Sausages	7E	1.3	0.1	38
Top 10 products	278	49.7	‑‑	‑‑
Total food manufacturing	559	100.0	0.20	44

Sources: Data from *Statistical Abstract of the United States* (various years) and Appendix Table B–27.

E = Estimated from four-digit SIC shipments.

— = Not applicable.

North Carolina

North Carolina is a highly industrialized state. From 1963 to 1985 at least 35 percent of its private sector employment was in manufacturing occupations, a ratio 12 percentage points higher than the 1985 average. Food processing has followed this general trend.

North Carolina ranked eighteenth in food processing value of shipments in the United States and third in the South Atlantic division in 1982. In that year the state had 544 food processing plants employing 43,900 persons (table 20–11). From 1963 to 1982 the number of food processing plants dropped by 37 percent, but food processing employment increased by 33 percent. Another 3,000 food processing jobs were created between 1982 and 1985. The 42 percent increase in 1963–1985 food processing employment was one of the largest in the United States; output increased by 250 percent in the same period, second fastest in the country.

In 1982 North Carolina's food processing plants shipped $6,319 million of products, which was 2.3 percent of the nation's production and up from 1.5 percent in 1963. Food processing produced about 9 percent of the state's total manufacturing output in 1985, about 4 percentage points below the U.S. average. North Carolina has experienced rapid manufacturing growth since 1963, but since 1972 food processing created jobs much faster than the rest of manufacturing, which is a very unusual pattern.

Ten processed foods accounted for over a half of the state's 1982 value of shipments (table 20–12). In 1982 the state supplied over 10 percent of the nation's young chickens (third largest state), poultry feed (second), and other vegetable oils (second); 7 percent or more of the beer (fifth) and crackers (third); over 3 percent of bottled soft drinks (twelfth), processed pork (sixth), soybean cake and meal (eleventh). In terms of employment, North Carolina's principal food processing industries are poultry dressing (9,900 employees), cookies and crackers (5,300), bread and rolls (4,900), soft drinks (3,800), meatpacking (3,200), fluid milk (2,700).

South Carolina

South Carolina had 195 food processing plants in operation with 12,200 employees in 1982 (table 20–13). From 1963 to 1982, the number of plants in operation dropped by 46 percent, but food processing employment has increased 11 percent. Between 1982 and 1985, another 1,000 food processing jobs were created; the 1963–1985 increase in South Carolina's food processing employment was 20 percent. South Carolina ranked thirty-fourth in 1982 U.S. food processing production.

In 1982 South Carolina's food processing plants shipped $1,666 million

Table 20–11
North Carolina: Importance and Growth of the Food Manufacturing Industries, 1963, 1972, 1982, and 1985

Measures (units)	Year			
	1963	1972	1982	1985
Value of Shipments ($ millions):				
Food manufacturing	1,000	2,025	6,319	7,285
All manufacturing	10,989	24,124	64,176	81,985
State Personal Income ($ billion)	8.6	19.4	54.4	72.7
Employment (thousands):				
Food manufacturing	32.9	37.4	43.9	46.8
All manufacturing	531	744	799	812.1
State total, private sector	1,520.0	1,858.8	2,190.7	2,319.2
Export Dependence:				
Value of processed foods ($ million)	--	--	141.6	--
Employment created (thousands)	--	--	4.4	--
Growth Rates and Ratios:				
Food manufacturing shipments growth (%)	--	102.5	212.0	15.3
Total manufacturing shipments growth (%)	--	119.5	166.1	27.8
Food manufacturing output growth (%)	--	63.9	74.1	22.3
Food manufacturing shipments/manufacturing shipments (%)	9.1	8.4	9.8	8.9
Food manufacturing VA/manufacturing VA (%)	7.1	5.8	6.8	7.0
Food manufacturing employment growth (%)	--	13.7	17.4	6.6
Total manufacturing employment growth (%)	--	40.1	7.4	1.6
Food manufacturing employment/manufacturing employment (%)	6.2	5.0	5.5	5.8
Manufacturing employment/state employment (%)	34.9	40.0	36.5	35.0
Exports/total processed foods shipped (%)	--	--	4.5	--

Note: See Table 16–1 for sources and notes applicable to this table.

Table 20–12
North Carolina: The Top Ten Manufactured Food Products by 1982 Value of Product Shipments

Product Class	Value of Shipments	Proportion of State Food Manufacturing	Proportion of Total U.S. Production	Rank in U.S.
	$ Million	- - - - - Percent - - - - -		Rank
1. Beer	782E	12.4	7.0	5
2. Young chickens	644	10.2	10.7	3
3. Poultry feed	371	5.9	10.2	2
4. Bottled soft drinks	328	5.2	3.0	12
5. Processed pork	247	3.9	4.6	6
6. Pork	225E	3.6	2.8	12
7. Other vegetable oils	208E	3.3	38.5	2
8. Packaged fluid milk	204	3.2	2.2	16
9. Crackers	165E	2.6	9.0	3
10. Soybean cake and meal	165	2.6	3.4	11
Top 10 products	3,339	52.8	--	--
Total food manufacturing	6,319	100.0	2.25	18

Sources: Data from *Statistical Abstract of the United States* (various years) and Appendix Table B–28.
E = Estimated from four-digit SIC shipments.
— = Not applicable.

Table 20–13
South Carolina: Importance and Growth of the Food Manufacturing Industries, 1963, 1972, 1982, and 1985

Measures (units)	Year			
	1963	1972	1982	1985
Value of Shipments ($ millions):				
Food manufacturing	361	574	1,666	2,345
All manufacturing	4,912	10,721	27,836	33,869
State Personal Income ($ billion)	3.9	9.2	27.2	35.4
Employment (thousands):				
Food manufacturing	11.0	12.1	12.2	13.2
All manufacturing	262	345	368	350.7
State total, private sector	689.5	826.7	988.3	1,081.3
Export Dependence:				
Value of processed foods ($ million)	--	--	22.8	--
Employment created (thousands)	--	--	0.2	--
Growth Rates and Ratios:				
Food manufacturing shipments growth (%)	--	59.0	190.2	40.8
Total manufacturing shipments growth (%)	--	118.3	159.6	21.7
Food manufacturing output growth (%)	--	28.7	61.9	49.3
Food manufacturing shipments/manufacturing shipments (%)	7.3	5.4	6.0	6.9
Food manufacturing VA/manufacturing VA (%)	4.6	3.5	4.4	4.9
Food manufacturing employment growth (%)	--	10.0	0.8	8.2
Total manufacturing employment growth (%)	--	31.7	6.7	-4.7
Food manufacturing employment/manufacturing employment (%)	4.2	3.5	3.3	3.8
Manufacturing employment/state employment (%)	38.0	41.7	37.2	32.4
Exports/total processed foods shipped (%)	--	--	3.6	--

Note: See Table 16–1 for sources and notes applicable to this table.

of products, but this was only 0.7 percent of U.S. output of processed foods. Food processing is also a very small proportion of the state's manufacturing sector, accounting for only 6 percent of total manufacturing shipments in 1985, about half the U.S. average. In 1963 this ratio was about the same. Since 1972 growth in food processing shipments and employment has been more rapid than in the rest of South Carolina's manufacturing sector. In real terms, food processing output rose 211 percent from 1963 to 1985, almost twice as fast as the country generally and the seventh-fastest in the nation. Indeed, from 1982 to 1985 production increased by an astounding 49 percent, the fastest rate in the United States.

Ten processed foods accounted for over a half of the state's 1982 value of product shipments (table 20–14). South Carolina accounts for over 1 percent of U.S. processed food output in eight products: frozen dinners (4.5 percent of the nation's output, sixth largest state), bottled soft drinks (1.5 percent, twenty-fourth), packaged fluid milk (1.3 percent, twenty-ninth), soybean cake and meal (2.2 percent, thirteenth), young chickens (1.5 percent, eighteenth), bread (1.3 percent, twenty-ninth), soybean oil (2.1 percent, twelfth), and ice cream (1.5 percent, twenty-fourth). The four largest food processing employers in 1982 were soft drinks (2,100 employees), bread and rolls (2,000), meatpacking (1,200), and poultry dressing (1,200). These four industries accounted for 53 percent of state food processing employment.

Georgia

Georgia is the second largest state in the South Atlantic division in food processing production and third in terms of personal income (after Florida and Virginia). The state had 501 food processing plants in 1982 employing 50,600 persons (table 20–15). From 1963 to 1982 the number of plants in operation dropped by 39 percent, but the food processing employment has increased 21 percent. Between 1982 and 1985, food processing employment held steady. General manufacturing employment has also increased rapidly, by 52 percent from 1963 to 1985, which was five times the U.S. average. Production of processed foods increased 165 percent from 1963 to 1985, rather slow for a Southern state but above the U.S. average.

In 1982 Georgia's food processing plants shipped $7,386 million of products, which was 2.6 percent of total U.S. production of processed foods and up from 2.2 percent in 1963. Georgia ranked fifteenth in value of food product shipments in the United States in 1982. The food industries are an important segment of the state's manufacturing sector, producing 15 percent of output, down from 18 percent in 1963. These ratios are slightly above the U.S. averages. Food processing employment accounted for 10 percent of

Table 20–14
South Carolina: The Top Ten Manufactured Food Products by 1982 Value of Product Shipments

Product Class	Value of Shipments	Proportion of State Food Manufacturing	Proportion of Total U.S. Production	Rank in U.S.
	$ Million	– – – – – – Percent – – – – – –		Rank
1. Bottled soft drinks	171	10.3	1.5	24
2. Packaged fluid milk	116	7.0	1.3	29
3. Soybean cake and meal	107	6.4	2.2	13
4. Frozen dinners	105E	6.3	4.5	6
5. Young chickens	91E	5.5	1.5	18
6. Pork	75E	4.5	0.9	18
7. Bread	62	3.7	1.3	29
8. Soybean oil	50	3.0	2.1	12
9. Ice cream	44E	2.6	1.5	24
10. Sausages	35	2.1	0.5	29
Top 10 products	856	51.4	– –	– –
Total food manufacturing	1,666	100.0	0.59	34

Sources: Data from *Statistical Abstract of the United States* (various years) and Appendix Table B–29.

E = Estimated from four-digit SIC shipments.

— = Not applicable.

Table 20–15
Georgia: Importance and Growth of the Food Manufacturing Industries, 1963, 1972, 1982, and 1985

Measures (units)	Year			
	1963	1972	1982	1985
Value of Shipments ($ millions):				
Food manufacturing	1,515	2,640	7,386	8,368
All manufacturing	8,508	18,374	48,056	63,057
State Personal Income ($ billion)	7.7	18.2	54.0	75.0
Employment (thousands):				
Food manufacturing	41.9	46.2	50.6	50.3
All manufacturing	354	468	503	539.2
State total, private sector	1,105.7	1,480.2	1,881.5	2,178.5
Export Dependence:				
Value of processed foods ($ million)	--	--	188.0	--
Employment created (thousands)	--	--	2.3	--
Growth Rates and Ratios:				
Food manufacturing shipments growth (%)	--	74.3	179.8	13.3
Total manufacturing shipments growth (%)	--	116.0	161.6	31.2
Food manufacturing output growth (%)	--	41.0	56.1	20.2
Food manufacturing shipments/manufacturing shipments (%)	17.8	14.4	15.4	13.3
Food manufacturing VA/manufacturing VA (%)	13.6	11.3	12.8	11.3
Food manufacturing employment growth (%)	--	10.3	9.1	-0.6
Total manufacturing employment growth (%)	--	32.2	7.5	7.2
Food manufacturing employment/manufacturing employment (%)	11.8	9.9	10.1	9.3
Manufacturing employment/state employment (%)	32.0	31.6	26.7	24.8
Exports/total processed foods shipped (%)	--	--	4.8	--

Note: See Table 16–1 for sources and notes applicable to this table.

Georgia's total manufacturing employment in 1982, down from 12 percent in 1963. In both years, these shares were slightly above the U.S. averages.

The top ten processed foods accounted for over a half of the state's 1982 value of product shipments (table 20–16). In many cases, Georgia has a leading position nationally. Georgia supplies over 50 percent of the nation's processed poultry (largest of all states); over 10 percent of U.S. young chickens (first), crackers (second); and over 5 percent of the beer (ninth), poultry feed (third), shortening and cooking oils (sixth), other vegetable oils (first), and cookies (fourth). In terms of 1982 employment, the state's principal food processing industries were poultry dressing (12,900 employees), bread and rolls (5,200), soft drinks (2,800), meatpacking (2,700), miscellaneous food (2,300), fluid milk (2,200), and meat processing (2,100). These nine leading food processing industries represent over 70 percent of the state's food processing employment.

Florida

Florida is the largest state in the South Atlantic Division in food processing production and in general economic terms. The state ranks fifth in U.S. population and ranked eleventh in the processed food value of shipments in the nation in 1982. Florida accounts for one-quarter of South Atlantic food processing output, much of which serves the local population.

Florida had 716 food processing plants in 1982 employing 45,300 persons (table 20–17). From 1963 to 1982 food processing plants in operation declined by 20 percent, half the U.S. average. Food processing employment increased 12 percent from 1963 to 1972. Since then, food processing employment has been virtually constant. However, output of processed foods more than tripled from 1963 to 1985, the eighth-fastest growth record in the nation.

In 1982 Florida's food processing plants shipped $8,717 million of products, which was 3.1 percent of the nation's production of processed foods. The food industries are an important segment of the state's manufacturing sector, accounting for 20 percent of the state's total manufacturing output in 1985, down from 31 percent in 1963. In both years, these shares were much higher than the U.S. average. Food processing provided 10 percent of the state's total manufacturing employment in 1982, down from 18 percent in 1963. These ratios are also far above the U.S. average shares.

The top ten processed foods accounted for 58 percent of Florida's 1982 value of product shipments (table 20–18). Florida has many leading processed food industries nationally. The state supplies 70 percent of the nation's frozen fruit and juices; 36 percent of the U.S. canned fruit juices and nectars

Table 20–16
Georgia: The Top Ten Manufactured Food Products by 1982 Value of Product Shipments

Product Class	Value of Shipments $ Million	Proportion of State Food Manufacturing Percent	Proportion of Total U.S. Production Percent	Rank in U.S. Rank
1. Young chickens	866	11.7	14.4	1
2. Processed poultry	660E	8.9	55.0	1
3. Beer	565E	7.6	5.1	9
4. Poultry feed	319	4.3	8.8	3
5. Bottled soft drinks	306	4.1	2.8	13
6. Crackers	267	3.6	14.6	2
7. Shortening and cooking oils	257	3.5	6.4	6
8. Other vegetable oils	210E	2.8	9.1	1
9. Soybean cake and meal	200	2.7	4.1	9
10. Cookies	182	2.5	7.3	4
Top 10 products	3,832	51.9	--	--
Total food manufacturing	7,386	100.0	2.63	15

Sources: Data from *Statistical Abstract of the United States* (various years) and Appendix Table B–30.

E = Estimated from four-digit SIC shipments.

— = Not applicable.

Table 20–17

Florida: Importance and Growth of the Food Manufacturing Industries, 1963, 1972, 1982, and 1985

Measures (units)	Year			
	1963	1972	1982	1985
Value of Shipments ($ millions):				
Food manufacturing	1,522	3,020	8,717	9,767
All manufacturing	4,976	11,958	38,683	49,691
State Personal Income ($ billion)	11.9	30.4	114.3	156.2
Employment (thousands):				
Food manufacturing	39.6	44.3	45.3	44.7
All manufacturing	215	343	454	475.7
State total, private sector	1,305.9	2,150.7	3,201.4	3,853.0
Export Dependence:				
Value of processed foods ($ million)	--	--	248.3	--
Employment created (thousands)	--	--	2.5	--
Growth Rates and Ratios:				
Food manufacturing shipments growth (%)	--	98.4	188.6	12.6
Total manufacturing shipments growth (%)	--	140.3	223.5	28.5
Food manufacturing output growth	--	60.6	61.1	19.1
Food manufacturing shipments/manufacturing shipments (%)	30.6	25.3	22.5	19.7
Food manufacturing VA/manufacturing VA (%)	21.3	16.7	16.1	15.1
Food manufacturing employment growth (%)	--	11.9	2.3	-7.9
Total manufacturing employment growth (%)	--	59.5	32.4	4.8
Food manufacturing employment/manufacturing employment (%)	18.4	12.9	10.0	8.8
Manufacturing employment/state employment (%)	16.5	15.9	14.2	12.3
Exports/total processed foods shipped (%)	--	--	4.8	--

Note: See Table 16–1 for sources and notes applicable to this table.

Table 20-18
Florida: The Top Ten Manufactured Food Products by 1982 Value of Product Shipments

Product Class	Value of Shipments	Proportion of State Food Manufacturing	Proportion of Total U.S. Production	Rank in U.S.
	$ Million	- - - - Percent - - - -		Rank
1. Frozen fruits and juices	1,303	14.9	70.0	1
2. Beer	637E	7.3	5.7	7
3. Roasted coffee	520	6.0	13.8	3
4. Canned fruit juices and nectars	505	5.7	35.8	1
5. Cane sugar	501E	5.7	12.1	3
6. Packaged fluid milk	398	4.6	4.4	7
7. Bottled soft drinks	376	4.3	3.4	8
8. Frozen shellfish	375	4.3	21.8	1
9. Fresh fruit juices and nectars	218	2.5	33.4	1
10. Bread	188	2.2	4.0	7
Top 10 products	5,021	57.6	--	--
Total food manufacturing	8,717	100.0	3.11	11

Sources: Data from *Statistical Abstract of the United States* (various years) and Appendix Table B–31.

E = Estimated from four-digit SIC shipments.

— = Not applicable.

(first); 33 percent of fresh fruit juices and nectars (first); 22 percent of frozen shellfish (first); over 10 percent of roasted coffee (third), cane sugar (third); over 4 percent of beer (seventh), packaged fluid milk (seventh), bread (seventh). The major food processing employers in the state in 1982 were frozen fruits (6,400), bread (5,900), frozen fish (5,200), soft drinks (5,100), and canned fruits and juices (4,500).

21
East South Central

The East South Central Division consists of four Southern states: Kentucky, Tennessee, Alabama, and Mississippi. The division had 15 million people in 1985, which was only 6 percent of the U.S. population. From 1963 to 1982 the division's population grew 15 percent, about 12 percentage points below U.S. population growth. Throughout the 1963–1985 period, the division remained the third smallest in population. The division's residents received $161 billion of 1985 personal income, which was only 5 percent of the U.S. income and the smallest of the nine divisions of the United States. Alabama and Mississippi are among the poorest U.S. states.

In 1963 the four East South Central states had 892,000 manufacturing jobs, but by 1985 the number had risen to 1.250 million jobs, 5.3 and 6.7 percent of the U.S. total in their respective years. The increase in manufacturing employment was almost four times the U.S. average. In 1985 the division shipped $148 billion of manufactures, which was 6.5 percent of the U.S. manufacturing shipments (increased from 5.0 percent in 1963). The 1963–1985 increase in the division's manufacturing shipments of 600 percent compared to the U.S. average increase of 440 percent.

The states of the East South Central division have a diversified agricultural and fisheries sector. Beef and dairy enterprises are relatively small, but the area produces a significant portion of the nation's hogs and chickens. Corn is a principal food crop, but soybean production has been moving south from the eastern Corn Belt for several decades. Mississippi is a leading producer of rice. For historical reasons and because of ample local supplies of corn and oak, Kentucky is the leading state for whisky distillation. The two Gulf shore states land a large share of the U.S. shrimp catch.

In 1985 food manufacturing provided 91,000 jobs for the four East South Central states, which was 6.4 percent of the U.S. total (increased from 5.3 percent in 1963). The value of processed food shipments in the division in 1985 was $18,306 million, 6.1 percent of the U.S. total food manufacturing shipments. Between 1963 and 1985 food manufacturing employment was virtually constant, compared to the 13 percent U.S. decline. Growth in real output levels was generally well above the national average. From 1963 to 1985, output increased 131 percent on average, ranging from 173 percent in Tennessee to 68 percent in Kentucky.

By 1985 the four East South Central states had 7.3 percent of their manufacturing employment in food processing, which was about the same as the U.S. average. In 1963 food processing provided 10.4 percent of the division's manufacturing jobs, which was only slightly above the U.S. proportion.

The mix of food processing industries reflects in part the agricultural base of the division. The four states of the division are leaders in the processing of poultry, pork, soybean, and shellfish products. There is also a surprisingly large share of U.S. production of soft drinks in the division, 8.3 percent in 1982. Tennessee is twice the size of the other three states in terms of food processing shipments value.

Kentucky

Kentucky had 272 food processing plants in 1982 employing 19,100 persons (table 21–1). The state ranked twenty-seventh in food processing products in the United States and the second in the East South Central division. From 1963 to 1982 food processing plants in operation dropped by 45 percent and employment by 20 percent. Another 3,200 food processing jobs were lost between 1982 and 1985. The 1963–1985 drop in Kentucky's food processing employment of 33 percent was two and one-half times the U.S. decline. Despite the steep drop in employment, Kentucky's food processing output increased by 68 percent from 1963 to 1985, a rate that was about three-fifths of the national average and by far the slowest in the division.

In 1982 Kentucky's food processing plants shipped $3,676 million of products, which was 1.3 percent of total U.S. production of processed foods. The food industries are an important but declining segment of the state's manufacturing sector, constituting 10 percent of output in 1985, down from 19 percent in 1963. These shares were 3 points below and 3 points above the respective U.S. averages. Food processing employment accounted for 7.7 percent of Kentucky's manufacturing employment, down from 13 percent in 1963. General manufacturing supplied 22 percent of the state's private sector jobs in both 1963 and 1985.

The top ten processed foods accounted for 57 percent of Kentucky's output in 1982 (table 21–2). Among these ten, Kentucky had two leading processed foods in the nation: bottled liquors (27 percent of U.S. production) and distilled liquors (35 percent). Kentucky also supplies 7.2 percent of the nation's miscellaneous food preparations (third) and 4.7 percent of the pork (sixth). The three largest food processing employers are: spirits (3,800 employees), soft drinks (2,900), and meatpacking (2,800). These three industries represented 50 percent of the state's food processing employment.

Table 21-1
Kentucky: Importance and Growth of the Food Manufacturing Industries, 1963, 1972, 1982, and 1985

Measures (units)	Year			
	1963	1972	1982	1985
Value of Shipments ($ millions):				
Food manufacturing	1,109	1,772	3,676	3,884
All manufacturing	5,797	12,360	26,929	38,404
State Personal Income ($ billion)	5.5	11.9	32.8	40.3
Employment (thousands):				
Food manufacturing	23.8	21.8	19.1	15.9
All manufacturing	180	259	247	246.7
State total, private sector	815.7	951.2	1,068.8	1,101.8
Export Dependence:				
Value of processed foods ($ million)	--	--	183.5	--
Employment created (thousands)	--	--	0.7	--
Growth Rates and Ratios:				
Food manufacturing shipments growth (%)	--	59.8	107.4	5.7
Total manufacturing shipments growth (%)	--	113.2	118.0	42.6
Food manufacturing output growth (%)	--	29.3	15.7	12.1
Food manufacturing shipments/manufacturing shipments (%)	19.1	14.3	13.6	10.1
Food manufacturing VA/manufacturing VA (%)	17.4	12.4	11.4	8.4
Food manufacturing employment growth (%)	--	-8.4	-12.4	-16.8
Total manufacturing employment growth (%)	--	43.9	-4.6	-0.1
Food manufacturing employment/manufacturing employment (%)	13.2	8.4	7.7	6.4
Manufacturing employment/state employment (%)	22.1	27.2	23.1	22.4
Exports/total processed foods shipped (%)	--	--	7.3	--

Note: See Table 16-1 for sources and notes applicable to this table.

Table 21-2
Kentucky: The Top Ten Manufactured Food Products by 1982 Value of Product Shipments

Product Class	Value of Shipments	Proportion of State Food Manufacturing	Proportion of Total U.S. Production	Rank in U.S.
	$ Million	- - - - - Percent - - - - -		Rank
1. Bottled liquors	638	17.4	26.5	1
2. Pork	380E	10.3	4.7	6
3. Miscellaneous food preparations	186	5.0	7.2	3
4. Bottled soft drinks	174	4.7	1.6	23
5. Sausages	145	3.9	2.2	13
6. Packaged fluid milk	139	3.8	1.5	23
7. Soybean cake and meal	129E	3.5	2.7	12
8. Distilled liquors	122	3.3	35.2	1
9. Processed pork	95	2.6	1.8	16
10. Natural cheese	80	2.2	1.4	14
Top 10 products	2,088	56.8	--	--
Total food manufacturing	3,676	100.0	1.31	27

Sources: Data from *Statistical Abstract of the United States* (various years) and Appendix Table B–32.

E = Estimated from four-digit SIC shipments.

— = Not applicable.

Tennessee

Tennessee is the largest state in the East South Central in general economic terms and in food processing production. A third of the personal income of the East South Central residents was received by Tennessee residents in 1985. In 1982 the state had 431 food processing plants employing 36,300 persons (table 21–3). From 1963 to 1982 the number of food processing plants dropped by 38 percent, about the same as the U.S. decline. Food processing employment increased by 14 percent from 1963 to 1982, but 1,500 food processing jobs were lost in the period of 1982–1985. Overall, from 1963 to 1985, the state gained 9 percent in food processing jobs, while output rose a healthy 173 percent.

In 1982 Tennessee's food processing plants shipped $6,557 million of products, which was 2.3 percent of the total U.S. production of processed foods. The value of processed foods accounted for 15 percent of the state's total manufacturing products in 1985, down from 19 percent in 1963. These shares were slightly higher than the U.S. averages. Food processing employment accounted for 7 percent of the state's 1985 manufacturing employment, down from 9 percent in 1963; these ratios were almost the same as the U.S. averages.

Tennessee has a fairly diversified mix of food processing industries. The top ten processed foods accounted for only 38 percent of the state's output in 1982 (table 21–4). Six of Tennessee's top ten processed food products also ranked among the top ten in the United States. The state supplies 10 percent of the nation's shortening and cooking oils (fourth largest state); over 5 percent of the breakfast foods (sixth), chips (fourth), wheat flour (sixth), soybean cake and meal (seventh); and 3 percent of bottled soft drinks (ninth). In terms of employment, Tennessee's principal food processing industries were bread and rolls (5,800 employees), soft drinks (4,100), meatpacking (3,500), miscellaneous foods (2,200), and fluid milk (2,000). These five leading industries accounted for about 50 percent of the state's total food processing employment in 1982.

Alabama

Alabama had 286 food processing plants in operation employing 24,900 persons in 1982 (table 21–5). From 1963 to 1982 the number of food processing plants decreased by 46 percent, slightly faster than the U.S. decline. However, the food processing employment increased 9 percent, including the 500 food processing jobs lost between 1982 and 1985. In the same period output grew an above-average 137 percent. Alabama ranked

Table 21–3
Tennessee: Importance and Growth of the Food Manufacturing Industries, 1963, 1972, 1982, and 1985

Measures (units)	Year			
	1963	1972	1982	1985
Value of Shipments ($ millions):				
Food manufacturing	1,365	2,595	6,557	7,778
All manufacturing	7,390	16,129	40,777	50,611
State Personal Income ($ billion)	6.6	14.7	41.4	53.5
Employment (thousands):				
Food manufacturing	31.9	32.8	36.3	34.8
All manufacturing	339	467	462	468.2
State total, private sector	1,074.0	1,363.7	1,523.4	1,631.2
Export Dependence:				
Value of processed foods ($ million)	--	--	497.8	--
Employment created (thousands)	--	--	1.5	--
Growth Rates and Ratios:				
Food manufacturing shipments growth (%)	--	90.1	152.7	18.6
Total manufacturing shipments growth (%)	--	118.3	152.8	24.1
Food manufacturing output growth (%)	--	53.9	41.0	25.9
Food manufacturing shipments/manufacturing shipments (%)	18.5	16.1	16.1	15.4
Food manufacturing VA/manufacturing VA (%)	10.6	9.0	12.1	11.9
Food manufacturing employment growth (%)	--	2.8	10.7	-4.1
Total manufacturing employment growth (%)	--	37.8	-1.1	1.3
Food manufacturing employment/manufacturing employment (%)	9.4	7.0	7.9	7.4
Manufacturing employment/state employment (%)	31.6	34.2	30.3	28.7
Exports/total processed foods shipped (%)	--	--	9.6	--

Note: See Table 16–1 for sources and notes applicable to this table.

Table 21–4
Tennessee: The Top Ten Manufactured Food Products by 1982 Value of Product Shipments

Product Class	Value of Shipments	Proportion of State Food Manufacturing	Proportion of Total U.S. Production	Rank in U.S.
	$ Million	- - - - - - Percent - - - - - -		Rank
1. Shortening and cooking oils	406	6.2	10.1	4
2. Bottled soft drinks	353	5.4	3.2	9
3. Beef	325E	5.0	1.6	15
4. Breakfast foods	264E	4.0	6.4	6
5. Soybean cake and meal	239	3.6	4.9	7
6. Chips	230	3.5	6.9	4
7. Packaged fluid milk	221	3.4	2.4	12
8. Sausages	165	2.5	2.5	11
9. Wheat flour	163	2.5	5.2	6
10. Pork	149	2.3	1.9	16
Top 10 products	2,515	38.4	--	--
Total food manufacturing	6,557	100.0	2.34	17

Sources: Data from *Statistical Abstract of the United States* (various years) and Appendix Table B–33.

E = Estimated from four-digit SIC shipments.

— = Not applicable.

Table 21-5
Alabama: Importance and Growth of the Food Manufacturing Industries, 1963, 1972, 1982, and 1985

Measures (units)	Year			
	1963	1972	1982	1985
Value of Shipments ($ millions):				
Food manufacturing	778	1,356	3,270	3,840
All manufacturing	5,451	11,240	29,794	36,635
State Personal Income ($ billion)	5.5	11.7	34.1	42.9
Employment (thousands):				
Food manufacturing	22.4	24.7	24.9	24.4
All manufacturing	244	323	330	330.6
State total, private sector	778.5	933.4	1,084.1	1,157.2
Export Dependence:				
Value of processed foods ($ million)	--	--	247.7	--
Employment created (thousands)	--	--	2.5	--
Growth Rates and Ratios:				
Food manufacturing shipments growth (%)	--	74.3	141.2	17.4
Total manufacturing shipments growth (%)	--	106.2	165.1	23.0
Food manufacturing output growth (%)	--	41.1	34.6	24.6
Food manufacturing shipments/manufacturing shipments (%)	14.3	12.1	11.0	10.5
Food manufacturing VA/manufacturing VA (%)	8.1	7.3	7.0	6.5
Food manufacturing employment growth (%)	--	10.3	0.8	-2.0
Total manufacturing employment growth (%)	--	32.4	2.2	0.2
Food manufacturing employment/manufacturing employment (%)	9.2	7.6	7.5	7.4
Manufacturing employment/state employment (%)	31.3	34.6	30.4	28.6
Exports/total processed foods shipped (%)	--	--	9.7	--

Note: See Table 16-1 for sources and notes applicable to this table.

twenty-eighth in food processing value of product shipments in 1982 in the United States.

In 1982 Alabama's food processing plants shipped products worth $3,270 million, which was 1.2 percent of the U.S. total. Alabama's food processing industry accounted for 11 percent of the state's manufacturing output in 1982, down from 14 percent in 1963. These ratios were 3 percentage below the U.S. averages in both years. Food processing provided about 8 percent of the state's total manufacturing employment, down from 9 percent in 1963. These shares were almost the same as the U.S. shares.

Ten processed foods accounted for over a half of the state's 1982 value of product shipments (table 21–6). Alabama supplies 10 percent of the nation's young chickens (fourth largest state) and over 5 percent of poultry feed (fifth) and frozen shellfish (eighth). Alabama's mayonnaise output ranked seventh in the U.S. The three largest food processing employers were poultry dressing (7,600 employees), bread and rolls (3,100), and soft drinks (2,300). These three industries accounted for 52 percent of the state's employment in food processing.

Mississippi

Mississippi is the smallest state in East South Central in economic terms. The state also has the smallest of the division's food processing industries (table 21–7). In 1982 Mississippi had 266 food processing plants employing 19,400 persons. From 1963 to 1982 the number of plants dropped by 37 percent. However, during that period food processing employment increased 33 percent. The upward trend was suddenly reversed when 3,200 food processing jobs were lost between 1982 and 1985, a loss of 17 percent. From 1963 to 1985 output of food processing plants increased by 145 percent, about 30 percent faster than the national rate. Until 1982 the state's food processing industries grew well above average, but after 1982 growth was virtually negligible.

In 1982 Mississippi's food processing plants shipped $2,848 million of products, which was 1 percent of total U.S. output of processed foods. Mississippi's food processing industry is an important segment of the state's manufacturing sector, accounting for 15 percent of shipments in 1982 (slightly above the U.S. average) and 12 percent in 1985 (below the U.S. average). However, it used to be more important; in 1963 food represented 22 percent of the state's manufacturing output, a ratio 4 percentage points above the U.S. average. Food processing employment accounted for 10 percent of the state's total manufacturing employment in 1982, 2 percentage points above the U.S. share.

Table 21–6
Alabama: The Top Ten Manufactured Food Products by 1982 Value of Product Shipments

Product Class	Value of Shipments $ Million	Proportion of State Food Manufacturing Percent	Proportion of Total U.S. Production Percent	Rank in U.S. Rank
1. Young chickens	612.0	18.7	10.2	4
2. Bottled soft drinks	256.3	7.8	2.3	16
3. Poultry feed	210.7	6.4	5.8	5
4. Packaged fluid milk	138.3	4.2	1.5	24
5. Sausages	114.0	3.5	1.8	15
6. Breads	101.7	3.1	2.2	17
7. Frozen shellfish	72.8	2.2	5.2	8
8. Rolls	68.6	2.1	2.8	12
9. Mayonnaise	52.8	1.6	2.9	7
10. Dog food	49.3	1.5	1.9	12
Top 10 products	1,676.5	51.3	--	--
Total food manufacturing	3,270	100.0	1.17	28

Sources: Data from *Statistical Abstract of the United States* (various years) and Appendix Table B–34.

E = Estimated from four-digit SIC shipments.

— = Not applicable.

Table 21-7
Mississippi: Importance and Growth of the Food Manufacturing Industries, 1963, 1972, 1982, and 1985

Measures (units)	Year			
	1963	1972	1982	1985
Value of Shipments ($ millions):				
Food manufacturing	552	956	2,848	2,804
All manufacturing	2,552	6,541	19,488	22,723
State Personal Income ($ billion)	3.2	6.9	19.8	24.0
Employment (thousands):				
Food manufacturing	14.6	17.0	19.4	16.2
All manufacturing	129	200	202	204.0
State total, private sector	557.5	614.5	674.4	694.1
Export Dependence:				
Value of processed foods ($ million)	--	--	206.0	--
Employment created (thousands)	--	--	1.3	--
Growth Rates and Ratios:				
Food manufacturing shipments growth (%)	--	73.2	197.9	-1.5
Total manufacturing shipments growth (%)	--	156.3	197.9	16.6
Food manufacturing output growth (%)	--	40.2	66.2	4.5
Food manufacturing shipments/manufacturing shipments (%)	21.6	14.6	14.6	12.3
Food manufacturing VA/manufacturing VA (%)	12.9	7.9	9.8	7.6
Food manufacturing employment growth (%)	--	16.4	14.1	-16.5
Total manufacturing employment growth (%)	--	55.0	1.0	1.0
Food manufacturing employment/manufacturing employment (%)	11.3	8.5	9.6	7.9
Manufacturing employment/state employment (%)	23.1	32.5	30.0	29.4
Exports/total processed foods shipped (%)	--	--	10.5	--

Note: See Table 16-1 for sources and notes applicable to this table.

Table 21-8
Mississippi: The Top Ten Manufactured Food Products by 1982 Value of Product Shipments

Product Class	Value of Shipments	Proportion of State Food Manufacturing	Proportion of Total U.S. Production	Rank in U.S.
	$ Million	- - - - - - - - Percent - - - - - - - -		Rank
1. Pork	340E	11.9	4.2	9
2. Young chickens	326	11.4	5.4	8
3. Bottled soft drinks	130	4.6	1.2	30
4. Poultry feed	125	4.4	3.4	11
5. Beef	98	3.5	0.5	26
6. Packaged fluid milk	89	3.1	1.0	31
7. Rice milling	87	3.1	4.5	5
8. Frozen shellfish	83	2.9	5.9	6
9. Soybean cake and meal	60E	2.1	1.2	15
10. Other vegetable oils	59E	2.1	2.6	7
Top 10 products	1,397	49.1	--	--
Total food manufacturing	2,848	100.0	1.02	29

Sources: Data from *Statistical Abstract of the United States* (various years) and Appendix Table B–35.

E = Estimated from four-digit SIC shipments.

— = Not applicable.

The ten leading processed foods represented 49 percent of the state's 1982 value of product shipments (table 21–8). Five of Mississippi's top ten products ranked among the top ten nationally. The state in 1982 supplied over 5 percent of the nation's young chickens (eighth largest state) and frozen shellfish (sixth); and over 3 percent of pork (ninth), poultry feed (eleventh), and rice (fifth). Mississippi's two leading food processing employers are poultry dressing (5,700 employees) and meatpacking (3,200), and these accounted for 46 percent of the total.

22
West South Central

The West South Central division includes four states (Arkansas, Louisiana, Oklahoma, and Texas) with 27 million people in 1985, which was about 11 percent of the U.S. population. From 1963 to 1982 the division's population grew 50 percent (the third highest growth among the nine divisions and about two times the U.S. average). The division's residents received $336 billions of income in 1985, which was more than 10 percent of the U.S. total income, ranking fifth place among the nine divisions. Texas dominates the division with 66 percent of its personal income.

In 1963 the four West South Central states had 865,000 manufacturing jobs, but by 1985 the number had risen to 1.486 million jobs, 5.1 and 7.9 percent of the U.S. total manufacturing employment in their respective years. The 1963–1985 increase in the division's manufacturing employment of 72 percent was the highest among the nine divisions. In 1985 the West South Central division shipped $271 billions of manufactures, which was 11.9 percent of U.S. manufacturing shipments (increased from 6.8 percent in 1963). The 1963–1985 increase in the division's manufacturing shipments of 852 percent was the highest growth among the nine divisions.

The principal animal enterprises are beef in the two westernmost states of the division and poultry in Arkansas. There is also a modest dairy industry in each state. The major food crops are winter wheat, rice, cane sugar, and some soybeans in Arkansas. Louisiana and Texas have substantial fishing activity. Oil is extracted from cottonseeds from the cotton industry centered in the Mississippi delta region.

In 1985 food manufacturing provided 149,000 jobs for the four West South Central states, which was 10.5 percent of the U.S. total. The value of processed food shipments in 1985 was $30,114 million, 10 percent of the U.S. food processing shipments. Between 1963 and 1985, food processing employment rose by 9 percent, with all the increase in Arkansas and Texas. Real output rose by 157 percent over the same period, the second highest divisional increase. Output tripled in Arkansas and Texas, but grew a paltry 39 percent in Louisiana. Growth rates have decelerated in the division over time.

By 1985 the four West South Central states had 10 percent of their manufacturing employment in food processing, which was quite a bit higher than the U.S. average. In 1963 food processing provided 16 percent of the division's all manufacturing jobs, 6 percentage points above the U.S. share.

The division leads in production of several food processing industries: chickens, turkeys, rice, cane sugar, soft drinks, chips, and rendering.

Arkansas

Arkansas is the smallest state in the West South Central division in economic terms, with only 7 percent of the region's personal income in 1985. Arkansas had 288 food processing plants in 1982 employing 30,400 persons (table 22–1). From 1963 to 1982, the number of plants dropped by 37 percent (5 percentage points less than the U.S. decline). Food processing employment increased by 70 percent, which was the highest increase in food processing employment in the nation. The state got another 1,600 food processing jobs between 1982 and 1985. From 1963 to 1985 food processing employment rose by 79 percent, while production increased 234 percent.

In 1982 Arkansas' food processing plants shipped $4,766 million of products, which was 1.8 percent of the nation's food processing value of shipments. The food industries are an important segment of the state's manufacturing sector, accounting for 24 percent of 1982 manufacturing output, a ratio 10 percentage points above the U.S. average. It used to be even more important; in 1963 the share was 29 percent. Food processing employment accounted for 17 percent of the state's 1985 manufacturing employment, over twice the U.S. average.

Ten processed foods represented a very high 63 percent of the state's 1982 value of product shipments (table 22–2). Arkansas supplies 31 percent of the nation's milled rice (largest state); over 10 percent of the young chickens (second), poultry feed (first), and processed poultry (second); over 5 percent of soybean cake and meal (fifth), frozen dinners (third), and turkeys (4th); and over 3 percent of the canned specialties (sixth), and soybean oil (eleventh). In terms of employment, Arkansas' principal food processing industries were poultry dressing (13,000 employees), frozen specialties (2,100), rice (1,900), bread and rolls (1,800), and soft drinks (1,600). These five leading industries represented 67 percent of the state's food processing employment in 1982. Arkansas exports a very high proportion of its processed foods, 17 percent in 1981.

Louisiana

Louisiana is the second smallest state in the West South Central division in terms of food processing. Louisiana had 423 food processing plants in 1982 employing 23,000 persons (table 22–3). From 1963 to 1982 the number of food processing plants dropped by 39 percent (slightly below the U.S.

Table 22–1
Arkansas: Importance and Growth of the Food Manufacturing Industries, 1963, 1972, 1982, and 1985

Measures (units)	Year			
	1963	1972	1982	1985
Value of Shipments ($ millions):				
Food manufacturing	744	1,608	4,766	5,193
All manufacturing	2,607	6,504	19,747	21,840
State Personal Income ($ billion)	3.0	6.6	19.4	24.7
Employment (thousands):				
Food manufacturing	17.9	25.3	30.4	32.0
All manufacturing	114	181	190	190.2
State total, private sector	530.2	607.9	650.1	703.9
Export Dependence:				
Value of processed foods ($ million)	--	--	619.4	--
Employment created (thousands)	--	--	2.5	--
Growth Rates and Ratios:				
Food manufacturing shipments growth (%)	--	116.1	196.4	9.0
Total manufacturing shipments growth (%)	--	149.5	203.6	10.6
Food manufacturing output growth (%)	--	74.9	65.4	15.6
Food manufacturing shipments/manufacturing shipments (%)	28.5	24.7	24.1	23.8
Food manufacturing VA/manufacturing VA (%)	16.2	13.0	14.1	14.6
Food manufacturing employment growth (%)	--	41.3	20.2	5.3
Total manufacturing employment growth (%)	--	58.8	5.0	0.1
Food manufacturing employment/manufacturing employment (%)	15.7	14.0	16.0	16.8
Manufacturing employment/state employment (%)	21.5	30.0	29.2	27.0
Exports/total processed foods shipped (%)	--	--	16.6	--

Note: See Table 16–1 for sources and notes applicable to this table.

Table 22–2
Arkansas: The Top Ten Manufactured Food Products by 1982 Value of Product Shipments

Product Class	Value of Shipments	Proportion of State Food Manufacturing	Proportion of Total U.S. Production	Rank in U.S.
	$ Million	– – – – – – Percent – – – – – –		Rank
1. Young chickens	810	17.0	13.5	2
2. Rice milling	608	12.8	31.4	1
3. Poultry feed	539	11.3	14.8	1
4. Soybean cake and meal	251	5.3	5.2	5
5. Frozen dinners	177	3.7	7.5	3
6. Processed poultry	152	3.2	12.7	2
7. Bottled soft drinks	148	3.1	1.3	28
8. Turkeys	115	2.4	7.3	4
9. Canned specialties	100E	2.1	4.9	6
10. Soybean oil	78	1.6	3.3	11
Top 10 products	2,978	62.5	– –	– –
Total food manufacturing	4,766	100.0	1.70	22

Sources: Data from *Statistical Abstract of the United States* (various years) and Appendix Table B–36.
E = Estimated from four-digit SIC shipments.
— = Not applicable.

Table 22–3
Louisiana: Importance and Growth of the Food Manufacturing Industries, 1963, 1972, 1982, and 1985

Measures (units)	Year			
	1963	1972	1982	1985
Value of Shipments ($ millions):				
Food manufacturing	1,277	1,936	3,913	3,694
All manufacturing	5,299	11,265	57,058	52,828
State Personal Income ($ billion)	6.1	13.1	44.6	50.5
Employment (thousands):				
Food manufacturing	29.6	28.1	23.0	20.3
All manufacturing	140	179	202	170.9
State total, private sector	799.6	982.0	1,347.7	1,307.1
Export Dependence:				
Value of processed foods ($ million)	--	--	391.6	--
Employment created (thousands)	--	--	1.7	--
Growth Rates and Ratios:				
Food manufacturing shipments growth (%)	--	51.6	102.1	-5.6
Total manufacturing shipments growth (%)	--	112.6	406.5	-7.4
Food manufacturing output growth (%)	--	22.7	12.8	0.2
Food manufacturing shipments/manufacturing shipments (%)	24.1	17.2	6.9	7.0
Food manufacturing VA/manufacturing VA (%)	19.2	13.6	9.4	9.7
Food manufacturing employment growth (%)	--	-5.1	-18.1	-11.7
Total manufacturing employment growth (%)	--	27.9	12.8	-15.4
Food manufacturing employment/manufacturing employment (%)	21.1	15.7	11.4	11.9
Manufacturing employment/state employment (%)	17.5	18.2	15.0	13.1
Exports/total processed foods shipped (%)	--	--	10.9	--

Note: See Table 16–1 for sources and notes applicable to this table.

decline) and employment fell 22 percent. Another 2,700 food processing jobs were lost between 1982 and 1985. The 1982–1985 drop in food processing employment of 31 percent was over twice the U.S. average rate. Despite the large employment loss in food processing, the industries maintained a relatively low 39 percent real growth from 1963 to 1985.

In 1982 Louisiana's food processing plants shipped $3,913 million products, which was 1.4 percent of the nation's food processing value of shipments. Despite this large value of food product shipments, the state's industrial base was so diversified that food represented only 7 percent of manufacturing output in 1982, half of the U.S. average. The food processing industry used to be far more important; in 1963 the share was 24 percent. This drop from 24 to 7 percent is one of the largest of any state, but it is due as much to the rapid growth of the chemical and petroleum industries as it is to the very slow growth of food manufacturing. For example, from 1972 to 1982 the rest of manufacturing grew four times faster than food processing. Food processing employment represented 11 percent of the state's manufacturing employment in 1982, 3 percentage points above the U.S. average.

The top ten processed food products accounted for a high 58 percent of Louisiana's processed foods in 1982 (table 22–4). Louisiana supplies 35 percent of the nation's animal and marine oils (largest state); 22 percent of the cane sugar (first); and over 9 percent of the roasted coffee (sixth), and milled rice (fourth). The state also ranked among the top ten states in shortening and cooking oils (ninth) and canned vegetables (tenth). Louisiana's three leading employers are cane sugar (3,800 employees), soft drinks (3,800), and bread and rolls (2,800).

Oklahoma

Oklahoma had 231 food processing plants in 1982 employing 12,500 persons (table 22–5). From 1963 to 1982 the number of plants dropped by 50 percent and employment by 12 percent, about the same rate as the United States as a whole. Another 800 food processing jobs were lost between 1982 and 1985. The 1963–1985 drop in Oklahoma's food processing employment of 18 percent was more rapid than the U.S. decline. Although employment decreased, output of processed foods managed to increase 102 percent in real terms, a rate that was a bit less than the U.S. average.

In 1982 Oklahoma's food processing plants shipped $2,164 million of products, but this was only 0.8 percent of the U.S. output of processed foods. Although very small by U.S. standards, Oklahoma's food processing industries are an important segment of the state's manufacturing sector, producing 9 percent of output in 1982 (5 percentage points below the U.S.

Table 22–4
Louisiana: The Top Ten Manufactured Food Products by 1982 Value of Product Shipments

Product Class	Value of Shipments	Proportion of State Food Manufacturing	Proportion of Total U.S. Production	Rank in U.S.
	$ Million	- - - - Percent - - - -		Rank
1. Cane sugar	923	23.6	22.2	1
2. Roasted coffee	373	9.5	9.9	6
3. Bottled soft drinks	202	5.2	1.8	18
4. Rice milling	175	4.5	9.0	4
5. Packaged fluid milk	155	3.9	1.7	21
6. Young chickens	121	3.1	2.0	12
7. Bread	100	2.6	2.1	18
8. Shortening and cooking oils	85E	2.2	2.1	9
9. Animal and marine oils	72	1.8	35.1	1
10. Canned vegetables	44	1.1	2.2	10
Top 10 products	2,250	57.5	--	--
Total food manufacturing	3,913	100.0	1.39	25

Sources: Data from *Statistical Abstract of the United States* (various years) and Appendix Table B–37.

E = Estimated from four-digit SIC shipments.

— = Not applicable.

Table 22-5
Oklahoma: Importance and Growth of the Food Manufacturing Industries, 1963, 1972, 1982, and 1985

Measures (units)	Year			
	1963	1972	1982	1985
Value of Shipments ($ millions):				
Food manufacturing	546	926	2,164	2,307
All manufacturing	2,439	5,348	23,116	25,025
State Personal Income ($ billion)	4.9	10.0	36.1	40.4
Employment (thousands):				
Food manufacturing	14.2	14.4	12.5	11.7
All manufacturing	98	143	197	170.3
State total, private sector	614.1	746.6	1,076.3	1,011.4
Export Dependence:				
Value of processed foods ($ million)	--	--	131.4	--
Employment created (thousands)	--	--	0.8	--
Growth Rates and Ratios:				
Food manufacturing shipments growth (%)	--	69.6	133.7	6.6
Total manufacturing shipments growth (%)	--	119.3	332.2	8.3
Food manufacturing output growth (%)	--	37.3	30.4	13.1
Food manufacturing shipments/manufacturing shipments (%)	22.4	17.3	9.4	9.2
Food manufacturing VA/manufacturing VA (%)	15.1	10.6	7.2	8.0
Food manufacturing employment growth (%)	--	1.4	-13.2	-6.4
Total manufacturing employment growth (%)	--	45.9	37.8	-13.6
Food manufacturing employment/manufacturing employment (%)	14.5	10.1	6.3	6.9
Manufacturing employment/state employment (%)	16.0	19.2	18.3	16.8
Exports/total processed foods shipped (%)	--	--	7.8	--

Note: See Table 16-1 for sources and notes applicable to this table.

share). However, it used to be far more important; in 1963, this share was 22 percent, about 6 percentage points above the U.S. average. Until 1982 Oklahoma had enjoyed very rapid growth in its manufacturing industries.

The top ten processed foods accounted for half of Oklahoma's output in 1982 (table 22–6). In the case of four of the ten products, Oklahoma accounts for over 2 percent of the U.S. production. Oklahoma supplies 11 percent of the nation's beef cattle feed (second largest state) and over 2 percent of young chickens (eleventh), wheat flour (fourteenth), and dog food (tenth). Oklahoma's four leading employers were the soft drinks (2,100 employees), bread and rolls (1,600), meatpacking (1,300), and fluid milk (1,200) industries.

Texas

Texas is the third largest state in the United States in population and in food processing production. The state dominates the West South Central division, with about 66 percent of the region's personal income and 63 percent of its processed food production. In 1963 the state was the seventh largest in economic terms.

In 1982 Texas had 1,224 food processing plants in operation employing 89,900 persons (table 22–7). From 1963 to 1982 the number of plants dropped by 35 percent. In contrast, food processing employment grew 19 percent between 1963 and 1982. But between 1982 and 1985, food processing jobs decreased by 5 percent (4,700 jobs were lost), for a net increase of 13 percent. In the 1963–1985 period real output of food processing increased by 198 percent, the ninth-fastest rate in the nation.

Texas' food processing plants shipped $17,303 million of products in 1982, which was 6.2 percent of the nation's total output of processed foods. The state exported over $1 billion of processed foods in 1981. Although very large by U.S. standards, the state's industrial base was so diversified that food represented only 11 percent of manufacturing output in 1985, 2 percentage points below the U.S. share. In 1963 this share was 17 percent, slightly above the U.S. average. Food processing employment represented 8.5 percent of the state's manufacturing employment in 1982, slightly above the U.S. average.

The ten leading products of the state accounted for half of the state's food processing output in 1982 (table 22–8). In many cases, Texas has a leading position nationally. Texas supplied over 20 percent of the nation's milled rice (second largest state) and flavoring for bottlers (first); over 10 percent of U.S. beef (second), roasted coffee (fifth), chips (first), and canned

Table 22–6
Oklahoma: The Top Ten Manufactured Food Products by 1982 Value of Product Shipments

Product Class	Value of Shipments	Proportion of State Food Manufacturing	Proportion of Total U.S. Production	Rank in U.S.
	$ Million	- - - - - Percent - - - - -		Rank
1. Beef	260	12.0	1.3	17
2. Bottled soft drinks	188	8.7	1.7	20
3. Packaged fluid milk	135	6.3	1.5	25
4. Young chickens	125E	5.8	2.1	11
5. Wheat flour	82	3.8	2.6	14
6. Dog food	70E	3.2	2.6	10
7. Poultry feed	59	2.7	1.6	17
8. Processed pork	55E	2.5	1.0	21
9. Beef cattle feed	55	2.5	10.7	2
10. Bread	55	2.5	1.2	30
Top 10 products	1,084	50.1	--	--
Total food manufacturing	2,164	100.0	0.77	32

Sources: Data from *Statistical Abstract of the United States* (various years) and Appendix Table B–38.

E = Estimated from four-digit SIC shipments.

— = Not applicable.

Table 22-7
Texas: Importance and Growth of the Food Manufacturing Industries, 1963, 1972, 1982, and 1985

Measures (units)	Year			
	1963	1972	1982	1985
Value of Shipments ($ millions):				
Food manufacturing	3,044	5,573	17,303	18,920
All manufacturing	18,165	36,148	171,674	171,543
State Personal Income ($ billion)	21.4	47.1	174.5	220.7
Employment (thousands):				
Food manufacturing	75.4	77.5	89.9	85.2
All manufacturing	514	736	1,059	955.4
State total, private sector	2,608.4	3,451.0	5,458.5	5,774.6
Export Dependence:				
Value of processed foods ($ million)	--	--	1,243.4	--
Employment created (thousands)	--	--	5.4	--
Growth Rates and Ratios:				
Food manufacturing shipments growth (%)	--	83.1	210.5	9.3
Total manufacturing shipments growth (%)	--	101.8	368.4	-0.1
Food manufacturing output growth (%)	--	48.2	73.2	16.0
Food manufacturing shipments/manufacturing shipments (%)	16.8	15.2	10.1	11.0
Food manufacturing VA/manufacturing VA (%)	13.1	11.3	10.0	11.5
Food manufacturing employment growth (%)	--	27.9	16.0	-5.2
Total manufacturing employment growth (%)	--	43.2	43.9	-9.8
Food manufacturing employment/manufacturing employment (%)	14.7	10.5	8.5	8.9
Manufacturing employment/state employment (%)	19.7	21.3	19.4	16.5
Exports/total processed foods shipped (%)	--	--	9.3	--

Note: See Table 16-1 for sources and notes applicable to this table.

Table 22-8
Texas: The Top Ten Manufactured Food Products by 1982 Value of Product Shipments

Product Class	Value of Shipments	Proportion of State Food Manufacturing	Proportion of Total U.S. Production	Rank in U.S.
	$ Million	- - - - - - - Percent - - - - - - -		Rank
1. Beef	3,210	18.6	15.6	2
2. Bottled soft drinks	1,087	6.3	9.8	2
3. Beer	1,048	6.1	9.4	2
4. Packaged fluid milk	650	3.8	7.1	2
5. Rice milling	534	3.1	27.6	2
6. Young chickens	435	2.5	7.2	6
7. Roasted coffee	427	2.5	11.3	5
8. Chips	413	2.4	12.4	1
9. Flavoring for bottlers	405	2.3	21.9	1
10. Canned specialties	377	2.2	18.5	1
Top 10 products	8,586	49.6	--	--
Total food manufacturing	17,303	100.0	6.17	3

Sources: Data from *Statistical Abstract of the United States* (various years) and Appendix Table B-39.

E = Estimated from four-digit SIC shipments.

— = Not applicable.

specialties (first); and over 7 percent of bottled soft drinks (second), beer (second), packaged fluid milk (second), and young chickens (sixth). In terms of employment, Texas' principal food processing industries were meatpacking (12,300 employees), bread and rolls (11,100), soft drinks (10,900), miscellaneous food (9,500), and fluid milk (5,400).

23
Mountain States

The Mountain and Pacific divisions encompass the twelve states that make up the Western region of the United States. The Mountain division consists of eight states, ranging from Montana in the north to Arizona and New Mexico in the south. It is by far the largest division in terms of land area, but it is also the most rural and sparsely populated of the nine U.S. divisions. The only cities of large size in the division are Denver, Salt Lake City, and Tucson. Colorado and Arizona are the largest states in the division in terms of population and eocnomic activity, each of them with 25 percent or more of 1985 personal incomes. Wyoming is demographically the smallest state in the division, indeed it is the smallest in the United States, with only 0.2 percent of U.S. personal income and population.

The Mountain division had 13 million people in 1985, which was only 5.4 percent of the U.S. population. It is the second smallest of the nine U.S. divisions. Though small by the U.S. standards, Mountain's population has grown fast. Since 1963 the division's population had grown by 63 percent (the highest growth of all the divisions and more than twice the rate of U.S. population growth). Mountain's residents received $162 billions of income in 1985, which was 4.9 percent of U.S. total income. Average incomes are quite low by U.S. standards.

The division has rapidly industrialized from a very small base. In 1963 the nine Mountain states had 284,000 manufacturing jobs, but by 1985 the number had risen to 575,000 jobs, 1.7 and 3.1 percent of the U.S. manufacturing employment in their respective years. Thus, even today the degree of industrialization is quite low by U.S. standards. In 1985 the Mountain division shipped $66 billion of manufactures, which was 2.9 percent of U.S. manufacturing shipments (increased from 1.9 percent in 1963). The 1963–1985 increase in the division's manufacturing shipments of 733 percent was 66 percent above the U.S. average.

In 1985 food manufacturing provided 58,000 jobs to the nine Mountain states, which was 4.1 percent of U.S. food processing jobs. The value of processed food shipments in 1985 was $11,216 million, 3.7 percent of the U.S. processed foods production. Between 1963 and 1985 food processing employment rose by 9 percent, which was considerably better than the 13 percent U.S. decline. Output rose by 137 percent, the third-fastest U.S. division. The division has both the fastest growing state in food processing (Nevada, 360 percent) and the only state that declined (Wyoming). Growth is also subject to very wide swings over time.

Food processing is a relatively large source of manufacturing employment in this division. By 1985 the nine Mountain states had 10 percent of their manufacturing employment in food processing, which was almost 3 percentage points above the U.S. average. In 1963 food processing provided 19 percent of the division's manufacturing jobs, almost double the U.S. average.

The Mountain division is a difficult area for agricultural and ranching enterprises, mainly because of the low rainfall in most parts. There are some fruits and vegetables grown in restricted areas of Idaho and Utah. Sugar beets are grown in river valleys in several of the Mountain states. The winter wheat and irrigated corn grown in flatter areas of the north, mostly east of the Rocky Mountains, does not provide a large enough base for much grain milling. By far the largest animal enterprise is raising beef cattle, most of which is range-fed. The center of the small U.S. lamb industry is in Idaho. Dairy, pork, and poultry enterprises are small or nonexistent in this division. Fishing resources are nil. Thus, except for bread or other local-market industries, the range of food processing industries in the Mountain states is quite narrow, and the leading ones revolve around cattle and sugar beets. The main exceptions are canned, frozen, and dried fruit in Idaho and Utah; beer in Colorado; and cottonseed oil processing in Arizona.

Montana

Montana had 116 food processing plants in 1982 employing 3,200 persons (table 23–1). From 1963 to 1982 the number of plants in operation dropped by 41 percent (the same as the U.S. rate of decline) and employment fell 20 percent. Another 400 food processing jobs were lost between 1982 and 1985. The 1963–1985 drop in Montana's food processing employment of 30 percent was more than twice the U.S. decline. The 1963–1982 growth of food processing output was a meagre 7 percent, third weakest in the United States.

In 1982 Montana's food processing plants shipped $494 million of products, but this was only 0.2 percent of U.S. output of processed foods. Montana ranked forty-fifth in 1982 food processing output in the United States. Although very small by U.S. standards, Montana's food processing industry is an important segment of the state's manufacturing sector, accounting for 12 percent of shipments (the same as the U.S. average) in 1985. However, it used to be more important; in 1963 foods produced 21 percent of Montana's manufacturing output, about 5 percentage points above the U.S. average.

Ten processed foods accounted for 54 percent of the state's 1982 value of product shipments (table 23–2). In only two cases did Montana account for over 1 percent of U.S. production. The state supplies 4 percent of the

Table 23-1
Montana: Importance and Growth of the Food Manufacturing Industries, 1963, 1972, 1982, and 1985

Measures (units)	Year			
	1963	1972	1982	1985
Value of Shipments ($ millions):				
Food manufacturing	181	258	494	404
All manufacturing	878	1,597	3,668	3,510
State Personal Income ($ billion)	1.6	2.8	7.7	9.1
Employment (thousands):				
Food manufacturing	4.0	3.4	3.2	2.8
All manufacturing	20	21	20	21.0
State total, private sector	179.6	203.7	237.6	234.9
Export Dependence:				
Value of processed foods ($ million)	--	--	7.1	--
Employment created (thousands)	--	--	0.1	--
Growth Rates and Ratios:				
Food manufacturing shipments growth (%)	--	42.5	91.5	-18.2
Total manufacturing shipments growth (%)	--	81.9	129.4	-4.3
Food manufacturing output growth (%)	--	15.4	6.8	-13.2
Food manufacturing shipments/manufacturing shipments (%)	20.6	16.2	13.5	11.5
Food manufacturing VA/manufacturing VA (%)	20.3	14.3	19.9	14.6
Food manufacturing employment growth (%)	--	-15.0	-5.9	-12.5
Total manufacturing employment growth (%)	--	5.0	-4.8	5.0
Food manufacturing employment/manufacturing employment (%)	20.0	16.2	16.0	13.3
Manufacturing employment/state employment (%)	11.1	10.3	8.4	8.9
Exports/total processed foods shipped (%)	--	--	3.2	--

Note: See Table 16-1 for sources and notes applicable to this table.

Table 23–2
Montana: The Top Ten Manufactured Food Products by 1982 Value of Product Shipments

Product Class	Value of Shipments	Proportion of State Food Manufacturing	Proportion of Total U.S. Production	Rank in U.S.
	$ Million	--- Percent ---		Rank
1. Beef	70E	14.2	0.3	29
2. Beet sugar	60E	12.1	4.0	9
3. Packaged fluid milk	39	7.9	0.4	42
4. Wheat flour	30E	6.1	0.1	23
5. Bread	23E	4.7	0.5	42
6. Bottled soft drinks	13	2.6	0.1	49
7. Rolls	11E	2.2	0.5	36
8. Beef cattle feed supplements	10	2.0	1.6	11
9. Bulk fluid milk	6	1.2	0.2	29
10. Beef cattle feed	4	0.8	0.6	27
Top 10 products	266	53.8	--	--
Total food manufacturing	494	100.0	0.18	46

Sources: Data from *Statistical Abstract of the United States* (various years) and Appendix Table B–40.

E = Estimated from four-digit SIC shipments.

— = Not applicable.

nation's refined beet sugar (ninth largest state) and 1.6 percent of beef cattle feed supplements (eleventh). The four largest employers in food processing in 1982 were meatpacking (700 employees), bread and rolls (700), fluid milk (500), and soft drinks (500). These four industries represented 75 percent of the state's food processing employment.

Idaho

Idaho is the second largest state in the Mountain division in food processing production. Idaho had 138 food processing plants in 1982 with 13,500 employees (table 23–3). From 1963 to 1982 the number of plants in operation has dropped by 38 percent. However, food processing employment increased by an impressive 36 percent. Another 1,200 food processing jobs were created between 1982 and 1985. Thus, from 1963 to 1985, food processing employment escalated by 48 percent, one of the greatest increases in the United States. Moreover, food processing production climbed 195 percent from 1963 to 1985, second only to Nevada in the Mountain division. Growth slowed markedly after 1982.

In 1982 Idaho's food processing plants shipped $2,300 million of products, which was 0.8 percent of the U.S. output of processed foods. Although small by U.S. standards, Idaho's food processing industries are an extremely large segment of the state's small manufacturing sector. In 1985 processed foods accounted for 38 percent of all manufacturing shipments, down slightly from 40 percent in 1963. The 1985 ratio was *three times* the U.S. share. Food processing shipments made up 29 percent of the state's total manufacturing employment in 1985, almost four times the U.S. average share.

Processing is highly concentrated in four or five industries. Ten processed foods accounted for 82 percent of the state's 1982 value of product shipments (table 23–4). Idaho supplied 18 percent of the nation's dried fruits and vegetables in 1982 (second largest state); 15 percent of the frozen vegetables (fourth), and refined beet sugar (second); and over 2 percent of the beef (eleventh), natural cheese (sixth), canned vegetables (ninth), and hides and skins (twelfth). Idaho's three largest employers were frozen fruit and vegetables (5,700 employees), dry fruit and vegetables (2,600), and beet sugar (1,500). These three industries represented 67 percent of the state's food processing employment in 1982.

Wyoming

Wyoming had forty-four food processing plants in 1982 employing 1,000 employees (table 23–5). From 1963 to 1982 the number of plants in operation

Table 23-3
Idaho: Importance and Growth of the Food Manufacturing Industries, 1963, 1972, 1982, and 1985

Measures (units)	Year			
	1963	1972	1982	1985
Value of Shipments ($ millions):				
Food manufacturing	363	805	2,300	2,237
All manufacturing	913	2,069	5,370	5,821
State Personal Income ($ billion)	1.4	2.7	8.7	11.2
Employment (thousands):				
Food manufacturing	9.9	13.9	13.5	14.7
All manufacturing	30	43	48	50.5
State total, private sector	193.9	223.5	299.4	313.6
Export Dependence:				
Value of processed foods ($ million)	--	--	20.5	--
Employment created (thousands)	--	--	0.4	--
Growth Rates and Ratios:				
Food manufacturing shipments growth (%)	--	121.8	185.7	-2.7
Total manufacturing shipments growth (%)	--	126.6	159.5	8.4
Food manufacturing output growth (%)	--	79.5	59.4	3.2
Food manufacturing shipments/manufacturing shipments (%)	39.8	38.9	42.8	38.4
Food manufacturing VA/manufacturing VA (%)	30.3	31.3	31.6	29.8
Food manufacturing employment growth (%)	--	40.4	-2.9	8.9
Total manufacturing employment growth (%)	--	43.3	11.6	5.2
Food manufacturing employment/manufacturing employment (%)	33.0	32.3	28.1	29.1
Manufacturing employment/state employment (%)	15.5	19.2	16.0	16.1
Exports/total processed foods shipped (%)	--	--	3.2	--

Note: See Table 16-1 for sources and notes applicable to this table.

Table 23-4
Idaho: The Top Ten Manufactured Food Products by 1982 Value of Product Shipments

Product Class	Value of Shipments	Proportion of State Food Manufacturing	Proportion of Total U.S. Production	Rank in U.S.
	$ Million	– – – – – – Percent – – – – – –		Rank
1. Frozen vegetables	474	20.6	15.4	4
2. Beef	456	19.6	2.2	11
3. Natural cheese	249	10.8	4.4	6
4. Dried fruits and vegetables	233	10.1	17.6	2
5. Beet sugar	221E	9.6	14.6	2
6. Packaged fluid milk	146	6.4	1.6	22
7. Canned vegetables	55	2.4	2.7	9
8. Canned specialties	20E	0.9	0.2	47
9. Bottled soft drinks	20	0.9	0.2	47
10. Hides and skins	18	0.8	2.1	12
Top 10 products	1,886	82.0	– –	– –
Total food manufacturing	2,300	100.0	0.82	31

Sources: Data from *Statistical Abstract of the United States* (various years) and Appendix Table B–41.

E = Estimated from four-digit SIC shipments.

— = Not applicable.

Table 23–5
Wyoming: Importance and Growth of the Food Manufacturing Industries, 1963, 1972, 1982, and 1985

Measures (units)	Year			
	1963	1972	1982	1985
Value of Shipments ($ millions):				
Food manufacturing	58	64	184	105
All manufacturing	241	451	2,558	2,311
State Personal Income ($ billion)	0.8	1.5	6.2	6.7
Employment (thousands):				
Food manufacturing	1.5	1.1	1.0	0.4
All manufacturing	7	7	10	7.6
State total, private sector	91.8	102.2	183.2	161.5
Export Dependence:				
Value of processed foods ($ million)	--	--	2.7	--
Employment created (thousands)	--	--	0.0	--
Growth Rates and Ratios:				
Food manufacturing shipments growth (%)	--	10.3	187.5	-42.9
Total manufacturing shipments growth (%)	--	87.1	467.2	-9.7
Food manufacturing output growth (%)	--	-10.7	60.4	-39.5
Food manufacturing shipments/manufacturing shipments (%)	24.1	14.2	7.2	4.5
Food manufacturing VA/manufacturing VA (%)	20.7	13.2	15.9	10.6
Food manufacturing employment growth (%)	--	-26.7	-9.1	-60.0
Total manufacturing employment growth (%)	--	0.0	42.9	-24.0
Food manufacturing employment/manufacturing employment (%)	21.4	15.7	10.0	5.3
Manufacturing employment/state employment (%)	7.6	6.8	5.5	4.7
Exports/total processed foods shipped (%)	--	--	3.0	--

Note: See Table 16–1 for sources and notes applicable to this table.

dropped by 27 percent (14 percentage points less than the U.S. decline) and employment by 33 percent. Another 600 food processing jobs were lost between 1982 and 1985. Employment loss was disastrous. The 1963–1985 drop in Wyoming's food processing employment of 73 percent was more than *six times* the U.S. decline and was the worst record of any of the state in the United States. On top of that, the state suffered a 13 percent loss of food processing output from 1963 to 1985, the worst growth record in the United States except for the District of Columbia.

In 1982 Wyoming's food processing plants shipped $184 million of products, which was only 0.07 percent of the U.S. output of processed foods. This was the smallest share of any of the fifty states. Food processing is also a very small proportion of the state's manufacturing sector, accounting for a mere 4.5 percent of the state's total manufacturing shipments in 1985, *half* the U.S. average. But it used to be far more important; in 1963 this share was 24 percent, 8 percentage points *above* the U.S. average. Food processing employment made up 5.3 percent of the state's manufacturing employment in 1985, down from 21 percent in 1963. Wyoming's food processing industries have declined rapidly.

The ten leading processed foods represented 98 percent of the state's 1982 value of products (table 23–6). Wyoming accounts for over 1 percent of U.S. processed food output in only two products: refined beet sugar and beef cattle feed. Beet sugar ranked eighth in the United States in 1982 and is the principal food processing industry in Wyoming, employing 700 persons in 1982.

Colorado

Colorado is the largest state in the Mountain division in economic terms. Households in the state received almost 30 percent of the division's personal income in 1985. Colorado also accounts for 43 percent of the food processing and 31 percent of manufacturing output of the division.

Colorado had 337 food processing plants in 1982 employing 22,200 persons (table 23–7). From 1963 to 1982 the number of food processing plants dropped by 27 percent, 14 percentage points below the U.S. decline. On the other hand, food processing employment bucked national trends by increasing 19 percent in that period. But between 1982 and 1985 food processing employment dropped by 5 percent. The net 1963–1985 increase in employment was a healthy 13 percent, and output rose 151 percent. Most growth occurred in the 1960s and 1980s.

In 1982 Colorado's food processing plants shipped $4,123 million of products, which was 1.5 percent of total U.S. production of processed foods. The food industries are a very important part of the state's manufacturing

Table 23–6
Wyoming: The Top Ten Manufactured Food Products by 1982 Value of Product Shipments

Product Class	Value of Shipments $ Million	Proportion of State Food Manufacturing Percent	Proportion of Total U.S. Production Percent	Rank in U.S. Rank
1. Beet sugar	63E	34.2	4.2	8
2. Bottled soft drinks	38E	20.7	0.3	39
3. Beef	25E	13.6	0.1	35
4. Other vegetable oils	20E	10.9	0.9	10
5. Ice cream	11E	6.0	0.4	35
6. Beef cattle feed	9E	4.9	1.8	21
7. Bread	7E	3.8	0.1	47
8. Canned vegetables	3E	1.6	0.1	19
9. Sausages	2E	1.1	0.0	39
10. Natural cheese	2E	1.1	0.0	20
Top 10 products	180	97.8	--	--
Total food manufacturing	184	100.0	0.07	50

Sources: Data from *Statistical Abstract of the United States* (various years) and Appendix Table B–42.

E = Estimated from four-digit SIC shipments.

— = Not applicable.

Table 23-7
Colorado: Importance and Growth of the Food Manufacturing Industries, 1963, 1972, 1982, and 1985

Measures (units)	Year			
	1963	1972	1982	1985
Value of Shipments ($ millions):				
Food manufacturing	912	2,191	4,123	4,782
All manufacturing	2,350	5,793	17,963	20,619
State Personal Income ($ billion)	4.8	10.5	37.5	47.9
Employment (thousands):				
Food manufacturing	18.6	21.6	22.2	21.1
All manufacturing	94	133	192	188.6
State total, private sector	500.6	723.6	1,123.0	1,219.4
Export Dependence:				
Value of processed foods ($ million)	--	--	73.7	--
Employment created (thousands)	--	--	0.7	--
Growth Rates and Ratios:				
Food manufacturing shipments growth (%)	--	140.2	88.2	16.0
Total manufacturing shipments growth (%)	--	146.5	210.1	14.8
Food manufacturing output growth (%)	--	94.4	5.0	23.1
Food manufacturing shipments/manufacturing shipments (%)	38.8	37.8	23.0	23.2
Food manufacturing VA/manufacturing VA (%)	21.1	20.4	13.2	16.3
Food manufacturing employment growth (%)	--	16.1	2.8	-5.0
Total manufacturing employment growth (%)	--	41.5	44.4	-1.8
Food manufacturing employment/manufacturing employment (%)	19.8	16.2	11.6	11.2
Manufacturing employment/state employment (%)	18.8	18.4	17.1	15.5
Exports/total processed foods shipped (%)	--	--	3.7	--

Note: See Table 16-1 for sources and notes applicable to this table.

sector, accounting for 23 percent of 1985 manufacturing output, 10 percentage points above the U.S. average. However, in 1963 Colorado's food processing industries produced 39 percent of manufacturing output, more than two times the U.S. share. Food processing employment accounted for 12 percent of the state's manufacturing employment in 1982, down from 20 percent in 1963. These ratios are also well above the U.S. averages.

Beer and beef account for nearly half the state's food processing output (table 23–8). The ten leading processed foods of the state accounted for 64 percent of the state's food processing output in 1982. Colorado supplied 7 percent of the nation's beer (sixth largest state) and over 3 percent of the beef (fifth), dog food (ninth), and beet sugar (seventh). In terms of employment, Colorado's principal food processing industries were beer (5,200 employees), meatpacking (3,000), bread and rolls (2,300), miscellaneous food (1,600), fluid milk (1,500), and soft drinks (1,500).

New Mexico

New Mexico had 104 food processing plants in 1982 employing 3,600 persons (table 23–9). From 1963 to 1982 the number of plants in operation dropped by 33 percent, 8 percentage points less than the U.S. decline. Between 1963 and 1982, food processing employment held steady. But New Mexico lost 900 jobs in food processing between 1982 and 1985. The net 1963–1985 drop was 25 percent, double the U.S. average loss.

Despite the large employment losses, New Mexico's food processing industries grew by 90 percent in real terms from 1963 to 1972; however, output declines after 1972 brought the net growth rate for 1963–1985 to only 65 percent, very low by Western region standards.

In 1982 New Mexico's food processing plants shipped $458 million products, which was only 0.2 percent of the U.S. total output of processed foods. New Mexico's processed foods shipments ranked forty-seventh in the U.S. in 1982. Although small by U.S. standards, New Mexico's food processing industries are a large segment of the state's manufacturing sector. In 1985 processed foods still accounted for 10 percent of manufacturing shipments, 3 percentage points below the U.S. ratio. However, in 1963 processed foods were 30 percent of the state's processed food output, double the U.S. average. Food processing employment accounted for 9 percent of the state's manufacturing employment in 1985, down from 24 percent in 1963.

Ten processed foods accounted for 65 percent of the state's processed foods in 1982 (table 23–10). Two out of the state's top ten products represented over 1 percent of U.S. output: beef cattle feed (2.9 percent of the U.S. supply and ranked eleventh), and cottage cheese (1 percent, twenty-

Table 23–8
Colorado: The Top Ten Manufactured Food Products by 1982 Value of Product Shipments

Product Class	Value of Shipments	Proportion of State Food Manufacturing	Proportion of Total U.S. Production	Rank in U.S.
	$ Million	– – – – – – Percent – – – – – –		Rank
1. Beef	1,161	28.2	5.6	5
2. Beer	757	18.4	6.8	6
3. Bottled soft drinks	149	3.6	1.3	27
4. Packaged fluid milk	129	3.1	1.4	22
5. Dog food	101E	2.4	3.8	9
6. Bread	95E	2.3	2.0	21
7. Young chickens	75E	1.8	1.2	20
8. Beet sugar	73E	1.8	4.8	7
9. Wheat flour	44E	1.1	1.4	20
10. Sausages	40E	1.0	0.6	24
Top 10 products	2,624	63.6	– –	– –
Total food manufacturing	4,123	100.0	1.47	23

Sources: Data from *Statistical Abstract of the United States* (various years) and Appendix Table B–43.

E = Estimated from four-digit SIC shipments.

— = Not applicable.

Table 23–9
New Mexico: Importance and Growth of the Food Manufacturing Industries, 1963, 1972, 1982, and 1985

Measures (units)	Year			
	1963	1972	1982	1985
Value of Shipments ($ millions):				
Food manufacturing	115	270	458	397
All manufacturing	382	910	3,815	4,074
State Personal Income ($ billion)	2.0	3.9	12.5	15.8
Employment (thousands):				
Food manufacturing	3.6	3.8	3.6	2.7
All manufacturing	15	24	33	31.7
State total, private sector	212.3	251.6	363.3	402.6
Export Dependence:				
Value of processed foods ($ million)	--	--	7.8	--
Employment created (thousands)	--	--	0.1	--
Growth Rates and Ratios:				
Food manufacturing shipments growth (%)	--	134.8	69.6	-13.3
Total manufacturing shipments growth (%)	--	138.2	319.8	6.8
Food manufacturing output growth (%)	--	90.0	-5.4	-8.0
Food manufacturing shipments/manufacturing shipments (%)	30.1	29.7	12.0	9.7
Food manufacturing VA/manufacturing VA (%)	23.3	19.0	9.5	9.9
Food manufacturing employment growth (%)	--	5.6	-5.3	-25.0
Total manufacturing employment growth (%)	--	60.0	37.5	-3.9
Food manufacturing employment/manufacturing employment (%)	24.0	15.8	10.9	8.5
Manufacturing employment/state employment (%)	7.1	9.5	9.1	7.9
Exports/total processed foods shipped (%)	--	--	3.5	--

Note: See Table 16–1 for sources and notes applicable to this table.

Table 23–10
New Mexico: The Top Ten Manufactured Food Products by 1982 Value of Product Shipments

Product Class	Value of Shipments	Proportion of State Food Manufacturing	Proportion of Total U.S. Production	Rank in U.S.
	$ Million	- - - - - Percent - - - - -		Rank
1. Beef	84	18.3	0.4	28
2. Bottled soft drinks	75	16.4	0.7	35
3. Packaged fluid milk	49	10.7	0.5	39
4. Bread	20E	4.4	0.4	43
5. Sausages	16E	3.5	0.2	35
6. Beef cattle feed	15E	3.3	2.9	11
7. Frozen dinners	13E	2.8	0.6	13
8. Rolls	10E	2.2	0.4	39
9. Dog food	10E	2.2	0.4	21
10. Cottage cheese	7	1.5	1.0	21
Top 10 products	299	65.3	--	--
Total food manufacturing	458	100.0	0.16	47

Sources: Data from *Statistical Abstract of the United States* (various years) and Appendix Table B–44.

E = Estimated from four-digit SIC shipments.

— = Not applicable.

first). New Mexico's three leading employers in the food processing industry were soft drinks (600 employees), meatpacking (500 employees), and baking (500).

Arizona

Arizona had 188 food processing plants in 1982 employing 6,600 persons (table 23–11). From 1963 to 1982, the number of plants in operation has dropped by 18 percent, less than a half of the U.S. decline. Food processing employment held steady between 1963 and 1982, and fell only slightly after 1982. The 1963–1985 drop in Arizona's food processing employment was just 3 percent, a third of the U.S. average. Real output of processed foods grew 151 percent from 1963 to 1985, more than one-third faster than the nation as a whole. Like New Mexico, growth was very rapid before 1972 but very slow during the next decade; rapid growth resumed after 1982.

In 1982 Arizona's food processing plants shipped $1,087 million of products, which was only 0.4 percent of the U.S. output of processed foods. Food processing is a small proportion of the state's manufacturing sector, accounting for 8 percent of total manufacturing shipments, down from 17 percent in 1963. The 1982 ratio was 6 percentage points below the U.S. average. Food processing employment made up 4 percent of the state's manufacturing employment in 1985, a half of the U.S. share. The state's food processing industries have grown fast by U.S. standards, but their growth has been greatly overshadowed by a boom in the rest of manufacturing. General manufacturing employment grew 186 percent from a small base in 1963 to 1985, a rate that was *seventeen times* the U.S. average.

The top ten processed foods accounted for 56 percent of the state's 1982 value of product shipments, of which eight accounted for over 1 percent of U.S. output (table 23–12). Arizona supplies 7 percent of the nation's cottonseed cake and meal (fourth largest state) and 6 percent of the beef cattle feed (fifth). Arizona also ranked among top ten states in canned fruit juices. Arizona's two leading food processing employers were baking (1,500 employees) and soft drinks (1,400).

Utah

Utah had 158 food processing plants with 7,600 employees in 1982 (table 23–13). From 1963 to 1982, the number of plants in operation dropped by 18 percent (less than a half of the U.S. decline) and employment by 11 percent (about the U.S. average). However, food processing employment increased 13 percent between 1982 and 1985, with 1,000 new jobs created

Table 23–11
Arizona: Importance and Growth of the Food Manufacturing Industries, 1963, 1972, 1982, and 1985

Measures (units)	Year			
	1963	1972	1982	1985
Value of Shipments ($ millions):				
Food manufacturing	244	573	1,087	1,279
All manufacturing	1,426	4,041	12,907	16,721
State Personal Income ($ billion)	3.3	8.4	29.1	40.8
Employment (thousands):				
Food manufacturing	6.6	6.7	6.6	6.4
All manufacturing	57	94	150	163.0
State total, private sector	334.6	544.1	857.9	1,090.4
Export Dependence:				
Value of processed foods ($ million)	--	--	33.4	--
Employment created (thousands)	--	--	0.2	--
Growth Rates and Ratios:				
Food manufacturing shipments growth (%)	--	134.8	89.7	17.7
Total manufacturing shipments growth (%)	--	183.3	219.5	29.5
Food manufacturing output growth (%)	--	90.0	5.8	24.8
Food manufacturing shipments/manufacturing shipments (%)	17.1	14.2	8.4	7.6
Food manufacturing VA/manufacturing VA (%)	12.4	7.2	5.7	6.3
Food manufacturing employment growth (%)	--	1.5	-1.5	-3.0
Total manufacturing employment growth (%)	--	64.9	59.6	8.7
Food manufacturing employment/manufacturing employment (%)	11.6	7.1	4.4	3.9
Manufacturing employment/state employment (%)	17.0	17.3	17.5	14.9
Exports/total processed foods shipped (%)	--	--	5.1	--

Note: See Table 16–1 for sources and notes applicable to this table.

Table 23–12
Arizona: The Top Ten Manufactured Food Products by 1982 Value of Product Shipments

Product Class	Value of Shipments $ Million	Proportion of State Food Manufacturing Percent	Proportion of Total U.S. Production Percent	Rank in U.S. Rank
1. Bottled soft drinks	166	15.3	1.5	25
2. Packaged fluid milk	127	11.7	1.4	28
3. Beef	100E	9.2	0.5	25
4. Bread	44	4.0	0.9	34
5. Dog food	35E	3.2	1.3	16
6. Beef cattle feed	30E	2.8	5.9	5
7. Beet sugar	28	2.6	1.8	12
8. Cottonseed cake and meal	25E	2.3	6.9	4
9. Canned fruit juices	25E	2.3	1.8	10
10. Rolls	24	2.2	1.0	29
Top 10 products	604	55.6	--	--
Total food manufacturing	1,087	100.0	0.39	38

Sources: Data from *Statistical Abstract of the United States* (various years) and Appendix Table B–45.

E = Estimated from four-digit SIC shipments.

— = Not applicable.

Table 23-13
Utah: Importance and Growth of the Food Manufacturing Industries, 1963, 1972, 1982, and 1985

Measures (units)	Year			
	1963	1972	1982	1985
Value of Shipments ($ millions):				
Food manufacturing	364	464	1,389	1,694
All manufacturing	1,512	2,632	8,960	10,941
State Personal Income ($ billion)	2.1	4.2	13.8	17.3
Employment (thousands):				
Food manufacturing	8.5	7.0	7.6	8.6
All manufacturing	54	57	83	93.1
State total, private sector	254.1	309.9	449.8	502.8
Export Dependence:				
Value of processed foods ($ million)	--	--	0.0	--
Employment created (thousands)	--	--	0.0	--
Growth Rates and Ratios:				
Food manufacturing shipments growth (%)	--	27.5	199.4	22.0
Total manufacturing shipments growth (%)	--	74.1	240.4	22.1
Food manufacturing output growth (%)	--	3.2	67.0	29.4
Food manufacturing shipments/manufacturing shipments (%)	24.1	17.6	15.5	15.5
Food manufacturing VA/manufacturing VA (%)	13.9	13.4	9.8	8.9
Food manufacturing employment growth (%)	--	-17.6	8.6	13.2
Total manufacturing employment growth (%)	--	5.6	45.6	12.2
Food manufacturing employment/manufacturing employment (%)	15.7	12.3	9.2	9.2
Manufacturing employment/state employment (%)	21.3	18.4	18.5	18.5
Exports/total processed foods shipped (%)	--	--	0.0	--

Note: See Table 16-1 for sources and notes applicable to this table.

in the food processing industries. Thus, employment just about held steady from 1963 to 1985. Production in the industries grew 124 percent from 1963 to 1985; since 1972 Utah has been among the fastest growing states in processed food products.

In 1982 Utah's food processing plants shipped $1,389 million of products, which was only 0.5 percent of total U.S. output of processed foods. However, the food processing industries are an important segment of the state's manufacturing sector, making up 16 percent of manufacturing output in 1985, 3 percentage points above the U.S. share. Food processing provided 9 percent of the state's manufacturing employment in 1982. However, it used to be far more important; in 1963, the value of food products accounted for 24 percent of the state's total manufacturing output and 16 percent of manufacturing employment, both of these ratios well above the U.S. average.

The top ten food products accounted for 53 percent of the state's processed food products in 1982 (table 23–14). Six products of Utah's top ten represented over 1 percent of U.S. production: natural cheese (2.7 percent of the U.S. products and eighth rank), packaged fluid milk (1 percent, thirty-second), wheat flour (2.4 percent, sixteenth), frozen fruit (3 percent, fifth), ice cream (1.8 percent, twentieth), and dog food (1.1 percent, seventeenth). Utah's five leading employers in food processing were baking (1,300 employees), cheese (1,100), fluid milk (800), meatpacking (700), and frozen specialties (700).

Nevada

Nevada is the second smallest state in food processing products in the United States and in the Mountain division. Nevada had forty-five food processing plants in 1982 employing 1,300 persons (table 23–15). From 1963 to 1982, the number of plants has dropped by 40 percent (almost the same as the U.S. average). However, food processing employment increased by a remarkable 20 percent between 1963 and 1985. Even more impressive was the 362 percent rise in food processing output from 1963 to 1985, by far the most rapid rate of growth in the nation. Moreover, Nevada's food processing growth has been very high in all three subperiods. Output has raced along at an average compounded rate of 7.2 percent per year.

In 1982 Nevada's food processing plants shipped $259 million of products, which was only 0.09 percent of the U.S. total output of processed foods. Although very small by U.S. standards, Nevada's food processing industries are an important segment of the state's manufacturing sector. Processed foods were 16 percent of the state's total manufacturing output in 1985, more than double the U.S. average. Moreover, unlike almost all other U.S. states, that ratio has risen since 1963.

Table 23–14
Utah: The Top Ten Manufactured Food Products by 1982 Value of Product Shipments

Product Class	Value of Shipments	Proportion of State Food Manufacturing	Proportion of Total U.S. Production	Rank in U.S.
	$ Million	- - - - - - - Percent - - - - - - -		Rank
1. NAtural cheese	152	11.0	2.7	8
2. Beef	141E	10.2	0.7	20
3. Packaged fluid milk	88	6.3	1.0	32
4. Bottled soft drinks	81	5.8	0.7	34
5. Wheat flour	75	5.4	2.4	16
6. Frozen fruits	55E	4.0	3.0	5
7. Ice cream	51E	3.7	1.8	20
8. Bread	36	2.6	0.8	39
9. Dog food	30E	2.2	1.1	17
10. Sausages	20E	1.4	0.3	33
Top 10 products	729	52.5	--	--
Total food manufacturing	1,389	100.0	0.50	35

Sources: Data from *Statistical Abstract of the United States* (various years) and Appendix Table B–46.

E = Estimated from four-digit SIC shipments.

— = Not applicable.

Table 23–15
Nevada: Importance and Growth of the Food Manufacturing Industries, 1963, 1972, 1982, and 1985

Measures (units)	Year			
	1963	1972	1982	1985
Value of Shipments ($ millions):				
Food manufacturing	33	78	259	318
All manufacturing	221	423	1,756	1,946
State Personal Income ($ billion)	1.2	2.7	10.6	13.6
Employment (thousands):				
Food manufacturing	1.0	1.4	1.3	1.2
All manufacturing	7	10	20	20.0
State total, private sector	123.8	188.6	346.6	389.8
Export Dependence:				
Value of processed foods ($ million)	--	--	2.1	--
Employment created (thousands)	--	--	0.0	--
Growth Rates and Ratios:				
Food manufacturing shipments growth (%)	--	136.4	221.1	22.8
Total manufacturing shipments growth (%)	--	91.4	315.1	10.8
Food manufacturing output growth (%)	--	91.3	85.3	30.3
Food manufacturing shipments/manufacturing shipments (%)	14.9	18.4	14.7	16.3
Food manufacturing VA/manufacturing VA (%)	11.3	14.4	14.7	15.0
Food manufacturing employment growth (%)	--	40.0	-7.1	-7.7
Total manufacturing employment growth (%)	--	42.9	100.0	0.0
Food manufacturing employment/manufacturing employment (%)	14.3	14.0	6.5	6.0
Manufacturing employment/state employment (%)	5.7	5.3	5.8	5.1
Exports/total processed foods shipped (%)	--	--	3.0	--

Note: See Table 16–1 for sources and notes applicable to this table.

Table 23-16
Nevada: The Top Ten Manufactured Food Products by 1982 Value of Product Shipments

Product Class	Value of Shipments	Proportion of State Food Manufacturing	Proportion of Total U.S. Production	Rank in U.S.
	$ Million	--- Percent ---		Rank
1. Dog food	40E	15.4	1.5	13
2. Packaged fluid milk	37	14.3	0.4	43
3. Bottled soft drinks	26	10.0	0.2	44
4. Cat food	15E	5.8	1.2	4
5. Dried fruits and vegetables	13E	5.0	1.0	5
6. Beef	12E	4.6	0.1	39
7. Beef cattle feed	11E	4.2	2.2	15
8. Sausages	10E	3.9	0.2	36
9. Chips	10E	3.9	0.3	21
10. Bread	4E	1.5	0.1	50
Top 10 products	178	68.7	--	--
Total food manufacturing	259	100.0	0.09	49

Sources: Data from *Statistical Abstract of the United States* (various years) and Appendix Table B-47.

E = Estimated from four-digit SIC shipments.

— = Not applicable.

Nevada's top ten processed foods represented 69 percent of the state's value of product shipments in 1982 (table 23–16). Nevada has only two of its top ten products in leading positions in the U.S.: cat food (1.2 percent, fourth largest state) and dried fruit and vegetables (1 percent, fifth). The state's three principal employers in food processing are fluid milk (300 employees), soft drinks (300), and pet food (200).

24
Pacific States

The Pacific and Mountain divisions together form the Western Region of the United States. The five Pacific states (California, Oregon, Washington, Alaska, and Hawaii) are considerably larger in population and economic activity than the eight Mountain states. Indeed, the Pacific area is the third largest U.S. division in terms of 1985 personal income—just a few percentage points smaller than the Middle Atlantic and East North Central divisions. Because of the faster population and income growth (50 percent faster from 1963 to 1985), it is likely that the Pacific division will overtake the other two leading divisions between 1990 and the year 2000. While the overall growth has been fastest in the two demographically smallest states of the Pacific division (Alaska and Hawaii), California dominates the statistics for the region. California residents earned about 80 percent of the personal income of the division, and the state's manufacturing sector had almost as large a share.

The Pacific division had 35 million people in 1985, which was 14.6 percent of the U.S. population. From 1963 to 1982 the division's population grew 52 percent (the second highest growth among the nine divisions and about twice the U.S. population growth). Pacific residents received $543 billions of personal income in 1985, which was more than 16 percent of U.S. income.

In 1963 the five Pacific states had 1.799 million manufacturing jobs, but by 1985 the number had risen to 2.510 million jobs, 10.6 and 13.4 percent of the U.S. total, respectively. The 1963–1985 increase in Pacific's manufacturing employment of 40 percent was the second highest growth among the nine U.S. divisions, and was almost four times the U.S. rate. In 1985 the division shipped $295 billions of manufactures, which has 12.9 percent of U.S. manufacturing shipments (increased from 10.9 percent in 1963). The 1963–1985 increase in the division's manufacturing shipments of 540 percent was 22 percent faster than the U.S. average.

Food processing is an important industry in the division. In 1985 food manufacturing provided 222,000 jobs to the five Pacific states, which was 15.6 percent of the U.S. total (increased from 10.6 percent in 1963). The value of processed food shipments in 1985 was $42,698 million, 14.3 percent of the U.S. total. Between 1963 and 1985 food manufacturing employment was virtually constant in the Pacific division. However, real production increased by 115 percent over the same period, ranging from 227 percent in

Alaska to only 22 percent in Hawaii. Oregon and California grew at rates slightly above the U.S. average. By 1985 the five Pacific states had 9 percent of their manufacturing employment in food processing, slightly above the U.S. average. In 1963 food processing provided 12 percent of the division's manufacturing jobs, which was over 2 percentage points above the U.S. average.

The Pacific division has the most diversified agricultural and marine sector in the nation. Alaska has the coldest U.S. climate, and Hawaii is the only tropical state, uniquely growing coffee and other tropical fruit and nuts. Southern and central California is the country's largest subtropical zone and produces large shares of the U.S. supply of fruit, nuts, vegetables, rice, and cotton, much of it under irrigation. In addition, because the West Coast is so remote from other food processing centers, the Pacific states are nearly self-sufficient in meat, dairy products, bakery products, sugar, and beverages. The region does obtain a good deal of its food grain, feed, and oil, as well as some specialty items, from other U.S. regions. The marine and fisheries industries export a high proportion of its production to foreign nations as well as other U.S. regions.

As a result of its great population and agricultural diversity, the Pacific division is a leading processor of scores of foods: canned fruit and vegetables, frozen foods of all kinds, canned and frozen fish, beer, wine, coffee, sugar, rice, and dairy products, to name but a few.

Washington

Washington is the second largest state within the Pacific division in economic terms. The state ranked twenty-first in food processing production in the nation. In 1982 Washington had 532 operating food processing plants employing 30,200 persons (table 24–1). From 1963 to 1982 the number of food processing plants dropped 22 percent, about a half of the U.S. decline. However, food processing employment grew an impressive 15 percent between 1963 and 1985. In the same period, food processing output grew by 159 percent, the second-fastest rate in the Pacific division and almost 50 percent faster than the national rate.

In 1985 Washington's food processing plants shipped $5,736 million of products, which was 1.9 percent of U.S. output of processed foods, up from 1.6 percent in 1963. Food processing is an important segment of Washington's manufacturing sector, accounting for 14 percent of the state's 1985 manufacturing output, 1 percentage point above the U.S. average. Food processing employment was 11 percent of the state's manufacturing employment in 1985, 3.5 percentage points above the U.S. average. In 1963

Table 24-1
Washington: Importance and Growth of the Food Manufacturing Industries, 1963, 1972, 1982, and 1985

Measures (units)	Year			
	1963	1972	1982	1985
Value of Shipments ($ millions):				
Food manufacturing	1,062	1,682	5,000	5,736
All manufacturing	6,359	10,016	34,665	40,458
State Personal Income ($ billion)	7.6	15.4	49.1	61.2
Employment (thousands):				
Food manufacturing	26.7	25.6	30.2	30.7
All manufacturing	224	226	291	275.9
State total, private sector	781.7	918.3	1,324.3	1,410.4
Export Dependence:				
Value of processed foods ($ million)	--	--	240.2	--
Employment created (thousands)	--	--	2.1	--
Growth Rates and Ratios:				
Food manufacturing shipments growth (%)	--	58.4	197.3	14.7
Total manufacturing shipments growth (%)	--	70.1	220.5	16.7
Food manufacturing output growth (%)	--	28.2	65.9	21.7
Food manufacturing shipments/manufacturing shipments (%)	16.7	15.6	14.4	14.2
Food manufacturing VA/manufacturing VA (%)	11.9	11.8	11.9	13.1
Food manufacturing employment growth (%)	--	-4.1	18.0	1.7
Total manufacturing employment growth (%)	--	0.8	28.8	-5.2
Food manufacturing employment/manufacturing employment (%)	11.9	11.3	10.4	11.1
Manufacturing employment/state employment (%)	28.7	24.6	22.0	19.6
Exports/total processed foods shipped (%)	--	--	6.4	--

Note: See Table 16-1 for sources and notes applicable to this table.

these shares were slightly higher than in 1982 but closer to the national average.

Washington has a diversified mix of food processing industries. The ten leading processed foods accounted for 46 percent of the state's 1982 value of product shipments (table 24–2). Washington supplies 18 percent of the nation's frozen vegetables (second largest state); 11 percent of U.S. frozen shellfish (third); and over 4 percent of the butter (third), ice cream (ninth), and canned fruits (fourth). The five leading employers in the state were frozen fruit and vegetables (6,200 employees), baking (3,200), canned fruit and vegetables (2,800), meatpacking (2,700), and frozen fish (2,700). These five industries accounted for 58 percent of the state's 1982 food processing employment.

Oregon

Oregon had 352 food processing plants in operation with 22,600 employees in 1982 (table 24–3). From 1963 to 1982 the number of food processing plants dropped by 31 percent, 10 percentage points below the U.S. decline. Food processing employment grew 14 percent between 1963 and 1982, but 1,300 food processing jobs were lost between 1982 and 1985 in Oregon. The 1963–1985 drop in Oregon's food processing employment of 7 percent was about half of the U.S. decline. In the same years, output rose 120 percent, which was somewhat above the U.S. average. However, since 1972, Oregon's production growth has slipped below the U.S. average.

In 1982 Oregon's food processing plants shipped $2,830 million of products, which was 1 percent of the value of U.S. processed foods. The state ranked thirtieth in the U.S. in 1982. The food processing industries are an important segment of the state's manufacturing sector, producing 14 percent of the state's 1985 manufacturing output, 1 percentage point above the U.S. average. Food processing employment accounted for 12 percent of the state's 1985 manufacturing jobs, which was 4 percentage points above the U.S. average. The food processing industries used to be more important, for in 1963 food processing represented 18 percent of the state's manufacturing shipments and 14 percent of employment, both ratios well above the U.S. average.

Oregon has fairly diversified set of food processing industries. The top ten processed foods accounted for only 45 percent of the state's 1982 value of processed foods (table 24–4). Oregon supplies 18 percent of the nation's frozen vegetables (the largest state) and over 3 percent of the cookies (ninth), canned vegetables (seventh), and crackers (eighth). Oregon's two leading employers in the food processing industries are frozen fruit and vegetables

Table 24–2
Washington: The Top Ten Manufactured Food Products by 1982 Value of Product Shipments

Product Class	Value of Shipments	Proportion of State Food Manufacturing	Proportion of Total U.S. Production	Rank in U.S.
	$ Million	Percent	Percent	Rank
1. Frozen vegetables	562	11.2	18.2	2
2. Beef	465E	9.3	2.3	10
3. Beer	289	5.8	2.6	14
4. Packaged fluid milk	187	3.7	2.0	19
5. Bottled soft drinks	182	3.6	1.6	21
6. Frozen shellfish	146	2.9	10.5	3
7. Butter	131	2.6	7.8	3
8. Ice cream	131	2.6	4.6	9
9. Canned fruit juices and nectars	125	2.5	2.9	3
10. Canned fruits	102	2.0	6.4	4
Top 10 products	2,320	46.4	—	—
Total food manufacturing	5,000	100.0	1.78	21

Sources: Data from *Statistical Abstract of the United States* (various years) and Appendix Table B–48.

E = Estimated from four-digit SIC shipments.

— = Not applicable.

Table 24–3
Oregon: Importance and Growth of the Food Manufacturing Industries, 1963, 1972, 1982, and 1985

Measures (units)	Year			
	1963	1972	1982	1985
Value of Shipments ($ millions):				
Food manufacturing	657	1,174	2,830	3,014
All manufacturing	3,654	7,571	17,897	21,004
State Personal Income ($ billion)	4.6	9.4	27.4	33.9
Employment (thousands):				
Food manufacturing	19.9	21.9	22.6	21.3
All manufacturing	145	179	185	183.6
State total, private sector	557.1	698.6	862.6	891.6
Export Dependence:				
Value of processed foods ($ million)	--	--	95.2	--
Employment created (thousands)	--	--	1.0	--
Growth Rates and Ratios:				
Food manufacturing shipments growth (%)	--	78.2	141.1	6.5
Total manufacturing shipments growth (%)	--	107.2	136.4	17.4
Food manufacturing output growth (%)	--	44.6	34.5	13.0
Food manufacturing shipments/manufacturing shipments (%)	18.0	15.5	15.8	14.3
Food manufacturing VA/manufacturing VA (%)	14.9	12.0	14.1	12.1
Food manufacturing employment growth (%)	--	10.1	3.2	-5.8
Total manufacturing employment growth (%)	--	23.4	3.4	-0.8
Food manufacturing employment/manufacturing employment (%)	13.7	12.2	12.2	11.6
Manufacturing employment/state employment (%)	26.0	25.6	21.4	20.6
Exports/total processed foods shipped (%)	--	--	5.8	--

Note: See Table 16–1 for sources and notes applicable to this table.

Table 24–4
Oregon: The Top Ten Manufactured Food Products by 1982 Value of Product Shipments

Product Class	Value of Shipments	Proportion of State Food Manufacturing	Proportion of Total U.S. Production	Rank in U.S.
	$ Million	Percent		Rank
1. Frozen vegetables	567	20.0	18.3	1
2. Packaged fluid milk	132	4.7	1.4	26
3. Cookies	82E	2.9	3.3	9
4. Canned vegetables	80	2.8	3.9	7
5. Young chickens	80E	2.8	1.3	19
6. Beer	77E	2.7	0.7	21
7. Bread	64	2.3	1.4	28
8. Crackers	62E	2.2	3.4	8
9. Sausages	60E	2.1	0.9	23
10. Shortening and cooking oils	59E	2.1	1.5	10
Top 10 products	1,263	44.6	--	--
Total food manufacturing	2,830	100.0	1.01	30

Sources: Data from *Statistical Abstract of the United States* (various years) and Appendix Table B–49.

E = Estimated from four-digit SIC shipments.

— = Not applicable.

(7,700 employees) and baking (3,000), and they account for 47 percent of total food processing employment.

California

California is the leading state in food processing and general manufacturing production. In 1963 the state ranked second place (behind New York) in manufacturing shipments and employment but was already in first place in food processing. Personal income of Californians in 1985 was about 13 percent of the nation's income. Within the Pacific division, California has 78 percent of the region's personal income and manufacturing shipments.

In 1982 California had 2,536 food processing plants employing 173,500 persons (table 24–5). From 1963 to 1982 the number of food processing plants dropped by 17 percent, one-third the U.S. rate of decline. Food processing employment grew by 11 percent. However, between 1982 and 1985, California lost 14,000 food processing jobs. The net 1963–1985 rise in California's food processing employment was 2 percent. In terms of food processing output, California's growth was 113 percent, just about the same as the country as a whole. However, growth before and after the 1972–1982 decade was significantly below average.

California's food processing plants shipped $32,057 million of products in 1985, which was 11 percent of the U.S. total. In 1981 almost $2 billion of processed foods were exported from California. The food processing industries are an important segment of the state's manufacturing sector, accounting for 14 percent of 1985 manufacturing output, a ratio 1 percentage point above the U.S. average. However, in 1963 California's food processing output was 20.5 percent of manufacturing output, 4 points above the national average. Food processing employment represented 9 percent of the total manufacturing employment in 1982 and 11 percent in 1963.

California has an extremely diversified set of food processing industries. The ten leading products of the state accounted for only 37 percent of the state's food processing output in 1982 (table 24–6). In about twenty food product classes, California is the leading state nationally. California supplies 86 percent of the nation's wine and brandy (the largest state); 67 percent of the U.S. dried fruit and vegetables; 62 percent of the canned seafood; and over 50 percent of the tomato sauces and canned fruit. California also is the number-one producer of beer, soft drinks, fluid milk, coffee, and many other consumer food products.

In terms of employment, California's principal food processing industries were canned fruit and vegetables (21,000 employees), baking (21,300), miscellaneous foods (14,000), wine and brandy (9,300), confectionery (9,000), soft drinks (8,900), frozen fruit and vegetables (8,600), poultry dressing

Table 24–5
California: Importance and Growth of the Food Manufacturing Industries, 1963, 1972, 1982, and 1985

Measures (units)	Year			
	1963	1972	1982	1985
Value of Shipments ($ millions):				
Food manufacturing	7,216	11,795	31,263	32,057
All manufacturing	35,215	62,903	199,695	227,086
State Personal Income ($ billion)	52.3	102.4	310.7	423.6
Employment (thousands):				
Food manufacturing	155.7	156.1	173.5	159.5
All manufacturing	1,399	1,546	2,005	2,016.6
State total, private sector	4,744.7	6,002.1	8,405.6	9,387.0
Export Dependence:				
Value of processed foods ($ million)	--	--	1,814.2	--
Employment created (thousands)	--	--	9.9	--
Growth Rates and Ratios:				
Food manufacturing shipments growth (%)	--	63.5	165.1	2.5
Total manufacturing shipments growth (%)	--	78.6	217.5	13.7
Food manufacturing output growth (%)	--	32.3	47.9	8.8
Food manufacturing shipments/manufacturing shipments (%)	20.5	18.8	15.7	14.1
Food manufacturing VA/manufacturing VA (%)	14.1	13.0	11.6	10.9
Food manufacturing employment growth (%)	--	0.3	11.1	-8.1
Total manufacturing employment growth (%)	--	10.5	29.7	0.6
Food manufacturing employment/manufacturing employment (%)	11.1	10.1	8.7	7.9
Manufacturing employment/state employment (%)	29.5	25.8	23.9	21.5
Exports/total processed foods shipped (%)	--	--	7.9	--

Note: See Table 16–1 for sources and notes applicable to this table.

Table 24–6
California: The Top Ten Manufactured Food Products by 1982 Value of Product Shipments

Product Class	Value of Shipments	Proportion of State Food Manufacturing	Proportion of Total U.S. Shipments	Rank in U.S.
	$ Million	Percent		Rank
1. Wine and brandy	2,407	7.7	86.4	1
2. Beer	1,263E	4.0	11.3	1
3. Catsup and other tomato sauces	1,197	3.8	55.0	1
4. Bottled soft drinks	1,190	3.8	10.7	1
5. Canned seafood	1,147	3.7	62.0	1
6. Packaged fluid milk	1,011	3.2	11.1	1
7. Beef	887	2.8	4.3	6
8. Dried fruits and vegetables	886	2.8	66.9	1
9. Canned fruits	793	2.5	49.9	1
10. Roasted coffee	743	2.4	19.7	1
Top 10 products	11,524	36.9	--	--
Total food manufacturing	31,263	100.0	11.14	1

Sources: Data from *Statistical Abstract of the United States* (various years) and Appendix Table B–50.

E = Estimated from four-digit SIC shipments.

— = Not applicable.

(8,200), dry fruit and vegetables (7,900), and fluid milk (6,800). These ten leading industries represented 65 percent of the state's food processing employment in 1982.

Alaska

Alaska had 121 food processing plants in 1982 employing 5,400 persons (table 24–7). From 1963 to 1982 the number of food processing plants grew by 14 percent (the only state that had an increase) and employment grew 86 percent (the highest increase in the United States). However, food processing employment dropped by 30 percent between 1982 and 1985, the largest drop in the country.

The output growth of Alaska's food processing industries has been quite variable. From 1963 to 1972, output rose a slow 2 percent annually; from 1972 to 1982 growth spurted to an amazing 11 percent per year; and after 1982 real output fell. For the whole period 1963–1985, production increased by 227 percent, which was the fourth-fastest rate in the nation.

In 1982 Alaska's food processing plants shipped $662 million of products, which was 0.24 percent of the nation's processed foods. Although small by U.S. standards (forty-second in rank), Alaska's food processing industries are a very important segment of the state's small manufacturing sector. In 1982 processed foods accounted for 26 percent of the state's manufacturing shipments and 42 percent of the employment. These shares were *two times* and *five times* the U.S. averages, respectively. And the food processing industries used to be even more important. In 1963 processed foods represented 47 percent of the state's manufacturing output and 48 percent of the employment.

The state's food industries are highly concentrated in seafood (table 24–8). Alaska's top ten processed foods accounted for about 80 percent of the state's processed foods. The state supplies 13 percent of the nation's frozen shellfish (second largest state); 16 percent of the frozen fish (second), and 8 percent of the canned seafoods (second). The processed fish industry employed over 90 percent of the state's food processing employment in 1982.

Hawaii

Hawaii had 221 food processing plants in 1982 employing 11,100 persons (table 24–9). The number of food processing plants dropped by 22 percent (half the U.S. rate) and employment by 27 percent from 1963 to 1982 (three times the U.S. rate). Another 1,300 food processing jobs were lost between 1982 and 1985. The 1963–1985 drop in Hawaii's food processing employment

Table 24-7
Alaska: Importance and Growth of the Food Manufacturing Industries, 1963, 1972, 1982, and 1985

Measures (units)	Year			
	1963	1972	1982	1985
Value of Shipments ($ millions):				
Food manufacturing	90	133	662	614
All manufacturing	191	366	2,580	2,512
State Personal Income ($ billion)	0.7	1.7	7.1	9.5
Employment (thousands):				
Food manufacturing	2.9	3.3	5.4	3.8
All manufacturing	6	8	13	9.7
State total, private sector	35.0	63.8	140.8	163.0
Export Dependence:				
Value of processed foods ($ million)	--	--	210.5	--
Employment created (thousands)	--	--	1.6	--
Growth Rates and Ratios:				
Food manufacturing shipments growth (%)	--	47.8	397.7	-7.3
Total manufacturing shipments growth (%)	--	91.6	604.9	-2.6
Food manufacturing output growth (%)	--	19.6	177.7	-1.6
Food manufacturing shipments/manufacturing shipments (%)	47.1	36.3	25.7	24.4
Food manufacturing VA/manufacturing VA (%)	47.1	34.1	24.1	23.5
Food manufacturing employment growth (%)	--	13.8	63.6	-29.6
Total manufacturing employment growth (%)	--	33.3	62.5	-25.4
Food manufacturing employment/manufacturing employment (%)	48.3	41.3	41.5	39.2
Manufacturing employment/state employment (%)	17.1	12.5	9.2	6.0
Exports/total processed foods shipped (%)	--	--	30.2	--

Note: See Table 16–1 for sources and notes applicable to this table.

Table 24–8
Alaska: The Top Ten Manufactured Food Products by 1982 Value of Product Shipments

Product Class	Value of Shipments	Proportion of State Food Manufacturing	Proportion of Total U.S. Production	Rank in U.S.
	$ Million	- - - - - - - Percent - - - - - - -		Rank
1. Frozen shellfish	180	27.2	12.9	2
2. Frozen fish	167	25.2	16.2	2
3. Canned seafood	139	21.0	7.5	2
4. Packaged fluid milk	10E	1.5	0.1	48
5. Chips	6E	1.0	0.2	23
6. Bread	6E	1.0	0.1	48
7. Natural cheese	4E	0.6	0.1	19
8. Miscellaneous prepared food	4E	0.6	0.2	27
9. Fresh packaged fish	4	0.6	0.7	17
10. Dairy cattle feed	3E	0.5	0.2	31
Top 10 products	523	79.0	--	--
Total food manufacturing	662	100.0	0.24	42

Sources: Data from *Statistical Abstract of the United States* (various years) and Appendix Table B–51.

E = Estimated from four-digit SIC shipments.

— = Not applicable.

Table 24–9
Hawaii: Importance and Growth of the Food Manufacturing Industries, 1963, 1972, 1982, and 1985

Measures (units)	Year			
	1963	1972	1982	1985
Value of Shipments ($ millions):				
Food manufacturing	501	513	1,080	1,277
All manufacturing	599	956	3,443	3,477
State Personal Income ($ billion)	1.7	4.0	11.6	14.6
Employment (thousands):				
Food manufacturing	15.2	11.9	11.1	9.8
All manufacturing	25	25	24	23.0
State total, private sector	146.7	233.2	326.0	343.0
Export Dependence:				
Value of processed foods ($ million)	--	--	38.1	--
Employment created (thousands)	--	--	0.6	--
Growth Rates and Ratios:				
Food manufacturing shipments growth (%)	--	2.4	110.5	18.2
Total manufacturing shipments growth (%)	--	59.6	260.1	1.0
Food manufacturing output growth (%)	--	-17.1	17.5	25.5
Food manufacturing shipments/manufacturing shipments (%)	83.6	53.7	31.4	36.7
Food manufacturing VA/manufacturing VA (%)	64.0	52.4	35.6	46.1
Food manufacturing employment growth (%)	--	-21.7	-6.7	-11.7
Total manufacturing employment growth (%)	--	0.0	-4.0	-4.2
Food manufacturing employment/manufacturing employment (%)	60.8	47.6	46.3	42.6
Manufacturing employment/state employment (%)	17.0	10.7	7.3	6.7
Exports/total processed foods shipped (%)	--	--	5.3	--

Note: See Table 16–1 for sources and notes applicable to this table.

Table 24-10
Hawaii: The Top Ten Manufactured Food Products by 1982 Value of Product Shipments

Product Class	Value of Shipments	Proportion of State Food Manufacturing	Proportion of Total U.S. Production	Rank in U.S.
	$ Million	- - - - - - - Percent - - - - - - -		Rank
1. Cane sugar	356	33.0	8.6	5
2. Canned fruits	126	11.7	7.9	2
3. Canned fruit juices and nectars	76	7.0	5.4	6
4. Bottled soft drinks	38E	3.5	0.3	39
5. Bread	37	3.4	0.8	38
6. Ice cream	28E	2.6	1.0	27
7. Packaged fluid milk	25E	2.3	0.3	47
8. Beef	22E	2.0	0.1	36
9. Canned seafood	20	1.9	1.1	10
10. Chocolate confectionery	19	1.8	--	--
Top 10 products	747	69.2	--	--
Total food manufacturing	1,080	100.0	0.38	39

Sources: Data from *Statistical Abstract of the United States* (various years) and Appendix Table B–52.

E = Estimated from four-digit SIC shipments.

— = Not applicable.

of 36 percent was *three times* the U.S. decline. Output increased only by 22 percent from 1963 to 1985, but the pattern of growth is a strong acceleration in the rate. Prior to 1972 output fell 1.6 percent per year, whereas after 1972 annual growth averaged 8 percent.

In 1982 Hawaii's food processing plants shipped $1,080 million of products, which was 0.4 percent of the nation's total processed foods. Hawaii ranked thirty-ninth in the value of 1982 processed food shipments in the United States. Although small by U.S. standards, Hawaii's food processing industries are an important segment of the state's small manufacturing sector. Processed foods provided 31 percent of the state's manufacturing shipments and 46 percent of employment in 1982; however, it used to be far more important. In 1963 processed food industries accounted for 84 percent of the state's manufacturing output and 61 percent of employment. These ratios are more than five times the U.S. average.

Hawaii's two leading food processing employers in 1982 were canned fruit and vegetables (3,100 employees) and cane sugar (3,000). In four product classes, Hawaii's output put it among the top ten states in 1982 (table 24–10). Hawaii made more than 5 percent of the canned fruit (second state), cane sugar (fifth), and canned fruit juices (sixth); and it supplied about 1 percent of U.S. canned fish (tenth).

25
Summary

It is hopeless to attempt to summarize the discussions of food processing growth trends in individual states, but an attempt will be made to relate the major patterns for the four geographical regions of the United States and their constituent divisions. Growth is measured using changes in employment and production of food processing plants.

Like the U.S. population, food processing activity has become more geographically dispersed since the early 1960s. In general, both have moved toward the West and the South. However, even in 1985, half of the employment and value of shipments remained concentrated in just ten states. The major zone for food and beverage processing is a narrow belt running from Kansas and Nebraska in the west to the New York metropolitan area in the east. The twelve states in this, the U.S. industrial heartland, accounted for 46 percent of the 1985 value of food products shipped. All twelve states ranked in the top twenty food processing states. The second largest area of food processing activity is the West Coast. The three continental states bordering the Pacific produced 14 percent of the country's processed foods. The third most important area for food processing is the six southern Atlantic states from Virginia to Florida; these states accounted for 12 percent of the value of processed foods shipped in the United States in 1985. Except for Texas, the three groups of states contain all of the nation's top producing states.

Just as the national share of total employment in manufacturing has diminished, so has the share of food processing in manufacturing. Nevertheless, as recently as 1985, most states west of the Mississippi River had a fairly high (10 percent or more) share of their manufacturing sector in food processing occupations. In the East only states with large poultry processing industries were highly dependent on food processing jobs.

Food processing employment fell about 10 percent from 1963 to 1982 nationally. However, all but two of the states in the South had increases in food processing jobs (the two exceptions were Oklahoma and Louisiana). A few Western states also had employment gains. However, after 1982 this pattern was not repeated; more Southern states lost food processing jobs than gained them.

Although job losses were widespread, substantial gains in labor productivity permitted output growth in all but one of the states. Thus, deindustrialization in this sense was quite rare, with output rising 111 percent from 1963 to 1985. The Northeast grew at less than half the national rate from 1963 to 1982, but after 1982 a growth spurt well above national levels is evident in many states. The East North Central states generally had growth below the U.S. average, but after 1982 output jumped to a 6 percent annual rate. Production in the West North Central states grew at about the national average but was highest in the 1960s and lowest in the early 1980s.

The fastest growth in food processing production occurred in the Southern region. Within the region, output rose fastest in the South Atlantic Division (the states from the Virginias south), which grew more than 50 percent faster than the U.S. average. North Carolina was the star performer, with a 250 percent increase in real production from 1963 to 1985. Other Southern states outside the South Atlantic division whose production of food processing tripled include Tennessee, Arkansas, and Texas. Growth in the South since 1982 was quite rapid, except in the West South Central states.

The West was the second fastest growing region for food processing, with the southern Mountain states growing as a group significantly faster than the five Pacific states. Indeed, growth in the Pacific division has decelerated since 1982.

The discussion of the patterns of growth among states concluded with an analysis of expected future growth of food processing output, roughly for the period 1985–1995. This analysis leads to patterns of growth that represent a departure from past growth rates for several regions. In particular, states in the traditional U.S. manufacturing heartland (pejoratively known as the Rust Belt) appear to be poised for a comeback. Most states from Illinois in the west to New England in the east are expected to display above-average growth of their food processing plants. The Mountain states, including those in the northern part of the Mountain division, are predicted to continue their rapid growth. Somewhat contrary to expectations is the average to below-average future growth of all the Southern states except Tennessee and the Carolinas. Also slated for reversals in formerly rapid growth are some of the states of the High Plains.

Notes

1. Simply stated, value of shipments is the net amount received (or receivable) for products sold as they leave the plant. Except in a few industries (e.g., canning), no adjustment is made for inventories. *Industry* shipments include finished foods, semiprocessed food ingredients, nonfood byproducts, resales, contract work, and miscellaneous receipts. Value of shipments is roughly the same as company sales plus the value of interplant transfers within the company. See appendix C.

2. The costs subtracted include the cost of all purchased materials, components, supplies, containers, fuel, purchased electricity, and contract work attributed to the activities of operating establishments. This approach of the Census Bureau yields a measure of *gross* value added that includes certain business services purchased by firms (e.g., legal and accounting services). Subtracting these latter services would yield *net* value added, the appropriate measure of the contribution of an industry to Gross Domestic Product. In the food processing industries gross value added is about 25–30 percent higher than net value added. However, the two value added measures are highly correlated across industries.

3. One disadvantage of value added is that it is sensitive to the degree of vertical integration within manufacturing plants. For example, a bread bakery that also mills its own wheat within the plant will have a larger value added (relative to shipments) than a bakery that buys flour (even if that flour comes from a plant owned by the bakery).

4. Unless otherwise stated this report uses Census Bureau counts of employment—a full-time-equivalent concept averaged across four times of the year. The other main source of employment data, the Bureau of Labor Statistics (BLS), essentially counts *jobs*, whether full- or part-time. Thus, BLS data show higher totals for food-processing employment: 1.8 million in 1963 and 1.7 million in 1982.

5. The GNP can also be calculated by adding personal consumption expenditures, gross private domestic investment, government purchases, and net exports. In practice, the two approaches usually yield totals that are quite close.

6. Data supplied to the author by the Quarterly Financial Reports Program of the U.S. Bureau of the Census.

7. Patent practices vary by industry; patent counts make no adjustment for quality; many patents are never commercialized; many others have multiindustry applications or when commercialized involve multiindustry transfers.

8. The U.S. industries were slightly smaller in output compared to the USSR industries, but many economists believe that the ruble is overvalued relative to the U.S. dollar.

9. Another feature of several top-ranked food industries is the use of plant employees for transporting products directly to grocery stores. The bread, soft drinks, fluid milk, and cookies and crackers industries all use this system of direct delivery. This demonstrates that value added is influenced by the degree of vertical integration in an industry. That is, the more functions performed by an industry, the greater its value added.

10. The large price decreases for processed poultry during 1963–1972 can be attributed in part to a reduction in canned poultry compared to rapid growth in cured poultry products.

11. Of course, some small niches may remain for crystalized sucrose (in baking, for example, or candy), but technological developments in the wet corn milling industry make even this prospect uncertain.

12. The decline in canned vegetable juices after 1972 is puzzling. Low price increases and health image should have been positive factors. Perhaps being canned was alone to cause the demand slowdown.

13. In addition, 7,122 food processing plants were too small to have complete census data collected for them.

14. Companies may be organized as corporations, cooperatives, partnerships, proprietorships, trusts, or other legal forms. For data on multiplant ownership, see appendix table A22.

15. This HHI index is the sum of the squared percentage market shares of the top 50 firms in the product class. A monopoly (100 percent market share) has HHI = $100 \times 100 = 10,000$. If 100 firms share the market equally, the HHI = $50 \times 1 \times 1 = 50$.

16. Shipments, employment, and growth data are all taken from the state tables in each chapter and appendix B.

Appendix A: Detailed Industry Tables

Appendix Table A–1
Measures of Size, U.S. Food Manufacturing Industries, 1947–1985

Measure (units)[a]	1947[b]	1954	1963	1972	1977	1982	1985
Net value added ($ bil.)	6.2	7.9	13.4	20.3	33.5	46	53
Proportion of all manufacturing (%)	10.2	8.8	9.3	8.1	8.1	8.4	7.6
Proportion of U.S. GNP (%)	2.64	2.12	2.21	1.67	1.68	1.45	1.33
Value of industry shipments ($ bil.)	--	47.7	68	115	193	281	302
Proportion of all manufacturing (%)	--	--	16.3	15.2	14.2	14.3	13.2
Value of food product shipments							
($ bil.)	41	48	65	107	177	259	282
Proportion of all manufacturing (%)	21.7	16.8	15.5	14.4	13.8	13.2	12.3
Index of production							
1977 = 100	40	45	62	84	100	115	130
1963 = 100	65	73	100	136	162	185	211
1947 = 100	100	113	154	209	248	285	323
Total employment ('000)	1,421	1,738	1,725	1,663	1,622	1,597	1,545
Production workers ('000)	1,021	1,169	1,098	1,085	1,072	1,048	994
Nonproduction workers ('000)	386	518	555	484	448	440	429
Offices and auxiliaries ('000)	32E	51E	72	94	102	109	122
Gross value added ($ bil.)	11.6	13.8	21.8	35.6	56.0	88.4	104.1
Proportion of all manufacturing (%)	15.7	11.8	11.4	10.1	9.6	10.7	10.4
New capital investment ($ bil.)	0.7	0.8	1.3	2.4	4.2	6.7	7.0
Proportion of all manufacturing (%)	11.3	10.6	11.0	9.8	8.9	9.0	8.5

Sources: Data from *Statistical Abstract of the United States 1986, 1982 Census of Manufactures, 1985 Annual Survey of Manufactures,* and previous editions.

[a] For definitions of terms see Appendix C.

[b] Definition not comparable to later years, except value of product shipments.

Appendix Table A–2
Industrial Production Indexes, Selected Manufactures, 1947–1985
(1977 = 100)

Year	Foods	Apparel products	Printing & publishing	Chemicals & products	Automotive products	Home goods	Primary metals	Fabricated metal products	Nonelectrical machinery	Electrical machinery	Total manufacturing	Total industrial production
								1977 = 100				
1947	41.9	47.0	34.3	10.4	25.8	26.1	57.8	40.4	26.7	14.5	28.9	29.0
1948	41.5	49.1	36.0	11.3	27.0	27.2	60.1	41.2	26.8	15.1	30.0	30.2
1949	41.9	48.6	37.0	11.1	26.7	25.2	50.5	37.2	22.9	14.1	28.3	28.6
1950	43.4	52.3	38.8	13.9	33.6	34.7	63.6	45.5	25.7	19.4	33.0	33.1
1951	44.3	51.3	39.5	15.7	29.8	29.9	69.2	48.6	32.6	19.5	35.6	35.9
1952	45.2	54.0	39.4	16.5	26.8	29.9	63.2	47.4	35.5	22.3	37.1	37.2
1953	46.1	54.7	41.2	17.8	33.9	33.9	71.6	53.5	36.9	25.6	40.4	40.4
1954	47.0	54.1	42.9	18.1	31.5	31.3	57.9	48.2	31.6	22.8	37.8	38.2
1955	49.8	59.7	47.2	21.1	41.9	36.9	75.3	55.0	34.6	26.1	42.6	43.0
1956	52.6	61.1	50.2	22.6	34.5	38.8	74.8	55.8	39.7	28.3	44.4	44.9
1957	53.4	60.9	51.9	23.9	36.1	38.0	71.6	57.1	39.6	28.1	44.9	45.5
1958	54.7	59.2	50.7	24.7	28.7	35.8	56.8	51.3	33.2	25.7	41.7	42.6
1959	57.4	65.2	54.1	28.8	36.0	41.1	66.4	57.6	38.8	31.2	47.0	47.7
1960	59.0	66.5	56.3	29.9	41.2	41.4	66.1	57.6	39.0	33.8	48.0	48.8
1961	60.7	66.9	56.5	31.4	37.6	42.7	64.9	56.2	37.9	35.9	48.1	49.1
1962	62.6	69.6	58.6	34.8	45.6	46.4	69.6	61.1	42.5	41.3	52.4	53.2
1963	64.9	72.5	61.7	38.1	49.9	50.0	75.1	63.1	45.4	42.4	55.5	56.3
1964	67.8	75.0	65.5	41.7	52.3	54.6	84.7	67.0	51.7	44.9	59.3	60.1
1965	69.4	79.3	69.7	46.5	64.4	61.9	93.2	73.6	58.2	53.5	65.7	66.1
1966	72.0	81.3	75.0	50.7	64.2	68.2	98.9	78.8	67.6	64.2	71.7	72.0
1967	75.2	80.9	79.1	53.0	56.4	69.1	91.4	82.5	68.9	64.5	73.1	73.5
1968	77.2	82.9	80.4	59.6	67.2	74.0	94.7	86.9	69.5	68.1	77.2	77.6
1969	79.8	85.6	84.3	64.5	67.5	78.9	101.9	88.4	75.2	72.5	80.6	81.2

Year												
1970	81.0	82.2	82.0	67.1	56.8	76.5	94.8	81.9	72.8	69.3	77.0	78.5
1971	83.6	83.2	82.7	71.4	72.4	81.0	89.9	81.5	67.6	69.6	78.2	79.6
1972	88.0	88.3	88.2	80.3	78.1	92.7	100.7	89.4	78.5	79.7	86.4	87.3
1973	89.8	89.0	90.6	87.8	86.2	98.1	114.3	99.4	91.7	90.7	94.0	94.4
1974	91.0	85.0	89.2	91.0	74.5	90.7	110.7	95.4	97.7	89.8	92.6	93.0
1975	90.4	77.6	83.5	82.9	70.2	79.9	88.2	82.7	84.5	77.2	83.4	84.8
1976	95.6	91.5	91.2	92.8	87.1	89.5	98.7	91.6	88.8	86.8	91.9	92.6
1977	100.0	100.0	100.0	100.0	100.0	100.0	100.0	100.0	100.0	100.0	100.0	100.0
1978	104.3	103.1	107.8	106.8	102.4	104.7	107.0	105.7	111.7	112.9	107.1	106.5
1979	106.7	98.3	112.7	111.4	94.9	103.7	108.5	109.4	122.6	125.7	111.5	110.7
1980	111.4	97.3	115.1	106.4	76.1	97.7	90.4	101.8	123.3	130.3	108.2	108.6
1981	113.7	96.1	118.6	112.6	78.8	98.1	95.0	101.6	129.8	134.1	110.5	111.0
1982	114.9	87.3	120.2	103.8	78.1	86.5	65.8	86.6	115.6	128.4	102.2	103.1
1983	120.4	95.3	129.8	114.0	95.1	101.1	73.0	89.1	118.3	143.8	110.2	109.2
1984	126.9	102.7	146.5	121.6	109.4	114.3	82.3	102.6	141.8	170.5	123.4	121.4
1985	130.2	100.9	153.9	127.1	114.0	112.2	80.5	107.3	145.3	168.4	126.3	123.8

Source: Data from *Economic Report of the President, 1987* (Table B–47).

Appendix Table A–3
Number of Employees in U.S. Food Marketing, 1963–1985

Year	Food processing	Food wholesaling	Eating & drinking places[a]	Retailing Food stores	Grocery stores	Total
			Thousands			
1963	1,752.0	472.9	1,747.9	1,383.8	--	5,356.6
1967	1,786.3	513.0	2,191.4	1,571.6	--	6,062.3
1972	1,745.2	536.3	2,860.2	1,805.1	1,577.8	6,946.8
1977	1,711.0	611.7	3,948.6	2,106.3	1,837.2	8,377.3
1982	1,635.9	666.9	4,831.2	2,477.6	2,152.8	9,611.6
1983	1,614.8	682.4	5,041.8	2,556.2	2,234.6	9,895.2
1984	1,612.2	707.3	5,388.0	2,637.1	2,298.1	10,344.6
1985	1,607.9	734.3	5,715.1	2,778.6	2,427.0	10,835.9

Source: Data from National Economics Division (1987:72).

— = Not available.

[a]Excludes all noncommercial eating facilities and such commercial outlets as hotel restaurants, department store coffee shops, and ballpark food concessions. These eating facilities numbered over 397,000 in 1982 and over 343,000 in 1977.

Appendix Table A–4
Number of Production Workers in U.S. Food Marketing, 1963–1985

Year	Food processing	Food wholesaling	Eating & drinking places[a]	Retailing Food stores	Grocery stores	Total
			Thousands			
1963	1,157.3	411.3	--	1,289.9	--	2,858.5
1967	1,187.3	442.3	2,047.8	1,456.6	--	5,134.0
1972	1,191.8	462.3	2,673.7	1,676.1	1,467.3	6,003.8
1977	1,161.0	526.3	3,665.4	1,942.1	1,697.4	7,294.8
1982	1,125.6	575.3	4,444.1	2,294.0	2,016.5	8,439.0
1983	1,113.7	588.4	4,632.9	2,374.0	2,085.0	8,709.0
1984	1,119.5	598.3	4,925.9	2,441.7	2,139.7	9,085.4
1985	1,121.9	621.9	5,199.2	2,569.6	2,258.0	9,512.6

Source: Same as Appendix Table A–5.

— = Not available.

[a]Excludes all noncommercial eating facilities and such commercial outlets as hotel restaurants, department store coffee shops, and ballpark food concessions. These eating facilities numbered over 397,000 in 1982 and over 343,000 in 1977.

Appendix Table A–5
Producer Price Indexes by Stage of Processing, 1947–1986

Year	Prices received by farmers: All farm products	Crops	Livestock & products	Crude foodstuffs and feedstuffs	Intermediate materials, supplies, and components: Total	Foods and feeds	Materials & components for manufacturing	Processed fuels & lubricants	Containers	Supplies	Finished goods: Consumer foods Total	Crude	Processed	Total	Consumer goods Durable	Non-durable
1947	60	61	60	111.7	72.4	--	72.1	85.5	66.8	77.5	82.8	99.4	80.2	79.0	74.6	80.7
1948	63	59	65	120.8	78.3	--	77.8	96.9	69.8	81.0	90.4	107.1	87.6	84.0	79.7	85.8
1949	55	52	56	100.3	75.2	--	74.5	88.2	70.1	76.3	83.1	101.3	80.1	82.2	81.8	82.3
1950	56	54	58	107.6	78.6	--	78.1	89.9	72.0	78.9	84.7	92.2	83.4	83.5	82.7	83.6
1951	66	61	70	124.5	88.1	--	88.5	93.9	84.5	88.8	95.2	105.9	93.2	89.5	88.9	90.0
1952	63	62	64	117.2	85.5	--	84.8	92.8	79.9	88.8	94.3	112.8	91.3	88.3	88.9	87.8
1953	56	55	56	104.9	86.0	--	86.2	93.4	80.0	84.3	89.4	105.2	86.7	89.1	89.6	88.6
1954	54	56	52	104.9	86.5	--	86.3	93.3	81.5	86.3	88.7	94.7	87.6	89.4	90.3	88.9
1955	51	53	49	95.1	88.1	--	88.4	93.3	82.6	84.8	86.5	98.8	84.4	90.1	91.2	89.4
1956	50	54	47	93.1	92.0	--	92.6	96.2	88.6	87.1	86.3	98.7	84.3	92.3	94.3	91.1
1957	51	52	51	97.2	94.1	--	94.8	101.9	92.5	88.0	89.3	97.4	87.9	94.6	97.1	93.2
1958	55	52	57	103.0	94.3	--	95.2	96.0	94.7	90.0	94.5	103.5	93.1	94.7	98.4	92.6
1959	53	51	53	96.2	95.6	--	96.5	95.6	94.2	91.2	90.1	94.3	89.5	95.9	99.6	94.0
1960	52	51	53	95.1	95.6	--	96.5	98.2	95.5	90.7	92.1	100.6	90.7	96.3	99.2	94.7
1961	53	52	52	93.8	95.0	--	95.3	99.4	94.7	91.8	91.7	96.1	90.9	96.2	98.8	94.7
1962	53	54	53	95.7	94.9	--	94.7	99.0	95.9	93.8	92.5	97.0	91.7	96.0	98.3	94.8
1963	53	55	51	92.9	95.2	--	94.9	98.1	94.7	95.2	91.4	95.5	90.7	96.0	97.8	95.1
1964	52	55	49	90.8	95.5	--	95.9	96.0	94.0	94.3	91.9	98.2	90.8	95.9	98.2	94.8
1965	54	53	54	97.1	96.8	--	97.4	97.4	95.8	95.2	95.4	98.6	94.9	96.6	97.9	95.9
1966	58	55	60	105.9	99.2	--	99.3	99.2	98.4	99.4	101.6	104.8	101.0	98.1	98.5	97.8
1967	55	52	57	100.0	100.0	100.0	100.0	100.0	100.0	100.0	100.0	100.0	100.0	100.0	100.0	100.0
1968	56	52	60	101.3	102.3	99.4	102.2	97.6	102.4	101.0	103.6	107.5	103.0	102.1	102.2	102.2
1969	59	50	67	109.3	105.8	102.7	105.8	98.5	106.3	102.8	110.0	116.0	108.9	104.6	104.0	105.0

Appendix Table A–5 continued

Year	Prices received by farmers			Crude foodstuffs and feedstuffs	Intermediate materials, supplies, and components						Finished goods: Consumer foods			Finished goods: Consumer goods		
	All farm products	Crops	Livestock & products		Total	Foods and feeds	Materials & components for manufacturing	Processed fuels & lubricants	Containers	Supplies	Total	Crude	Processed	Total	Durable	Non-durable
1970	60	52	67	112.0	109.9	109.1	110.0	105.0	111.4	108.0	113.5	116.3	113.1	107.7	106.9	108.3
1971	62	56	67	114.2	114.1	111.7	112.8	115.2	116.6	111.0	115.3	115.8	115.1	111.4	110.8	111.7
1972	69	60	77	127.5	118.7	118.5	117.0	118.9	121.9	115.6	121.7	121.2	121.7	113.5	113.3	113.6
1973	98	91	104	180.0	131.6	168.4	127.7	131.5	129.2	140.6	146.4	160.7	143.9	118.6	115.4	120.5
1974	105	117	94	189.4	162.9	200.2	162.2	199.1	152.2	154.5	166.9	180.8	164.6	138.6	125.9	146.8
1975	101	105	98	191.8	180.0	195.3	178.7	233.0	171.4	168.1	181.0	181.2	181.3	153.1	138.2	163.0
1976	102	102	101	190.2	189.1	185.3	185.4	250.1	180.2	179.0	180.4	193.9	177.8	162.6	144.5	174.8
1977	100	100	100	192.1	201.5	190.5	195.4	282.5	188.3	188.7	189.9	201.0	187.3	174.3	152.8	189.3
1978	115	105	124	216.2	215.6	203.1	208.7	295.3	202.8	198.5	207.2	216.8	204.6	186.7	166.9	200.0
1979	132	116	147	247.9	243.2	226.1	234.4	364.8	226.8	218.2	226.2	233.1	223.8	211.5	183.2	231.3
1980	134	125	144	259.2	280.3	252.6	265.7	503.0	254.5	244.5	239.5	237.2	237.8	250.8	206.2	283.9
1981	139	134	143	257.4	306.0	250.3	286.1	595.4	276.1	263.8	253.6	263.8	250.6	276.5	218.6	319.6
1982	133	121	145	247.8	310.4	239.4	289.8	591.7	285.6	272.1	259.3	252.7	257.7	287.8	226.7	333.6
1983	135	128	141	252.2	312.3	247.9	293.4	564.8	286.6	277.1	261.8	258.7	260.0	291.4	233.1	335.3
1984	142	139	146	259.5	318.7	253.1	301.8	566.2	302.3	283.4	273.3	281.6	270.0	294.1	236.8	337.3
1985	128	120	136	235.0	307.6	232.8	299.5	548.9	311.2	284.2	271.2	260.0	270.0	297.3	241.5	339.3
1986	123	106	138	230.6	304.3	230.2	296.1	430.3	315.1	287.3	278.0	265.6	276.7	283.4	246.9	311.1

Source: Data from *Economic Report of the President, 1987* (Table B–60).

Appendix Table A-6
Consumer Price Indexes, Selected Expenditure Classes, 1947–1986

Year	Food			Shelter			Private transportation				Medical care			Services less medical care	Commodities less food		
	Total	At-home	Away from home	Total	Rent, residential	Maintenance and repairs	Total	New cars	Used cars	Motor fuel	Total	Medical care commodities	Medical care services		All	Durable	Non-durable
1947	70.6	73.5	--	--	61.1	--	61.5	69.2	--	62.2	48.1	81.8	43.5	--	76.8	80.3	72.2
1948	76.6	79.8	--	--	65.1	--	68.2	75.6	--	70.4	51.1	86.1	46.4	--	82.7	86.2	77.8
1949	73.5	76.7	--	--	68.0	--	72.3	82.8	--	72.3	52.7	87.4	48.1	--	81.5	87.4	76.3
1950	74.5	77.6	--	--	70.4	--	72.5	83.4	--	71.8	53.7	88.5	49.2	--	81.4	88.4	76.2
1951	82.8	86.3	--	--	73.2	--	75.8	87.4	--	73.9	56.3	91.0	51.7	--	87.5	95.1	82.0
1952	84.3	87.8	--	--	76.2	--	80.8	94.9	--	75.8	59.3	91.8	55.0	--	88.3	96.4	82.4
1953	83.0	86.2	68.9	76.5	80.3	71.2	82.4	95.8	89.2	80.3	61.4	92.6	57.0	--	88.5	95.7	83.5
1954	82.8	85.8	70.1	78.2	83.2	72.4	80.3	94.3	75.9	82.5	63.4	93.7	58.7	--	87.5	93.3	83.1
1955	81.6	84.1	70.8	79.1	84.3	74.1	78.9	90.9	71.8	83.6	64.8	94.7	60.4	--	86.9	91.5	83.5
1956	82.2	84.4	72.2	80.4	85.9	77.2	80.1	93.5	69.1	86.5	67.2	96.7	62.8	--	87.8	91.5	85.3
1957	84.9	87.2	74.9	83.4	87.5	80.5	84.7	98.4	77.4	90.0	69.9	99.3	65.5	77.6	90.5	94.4	87.6
1958	88.5	91.0	77.2	85.1	89.1	81.8	87.4	101.5	80.2	88.8	73.2	102.8	68.7	80.4	91.5	95.9	88.2
1959	87.1	88.8	79.3	86.0	90.4	83.2	91.1	105.9	89.5	89.9	76.4	104.4	72.0	82.5	92.7	97.3	89.3
1960	88.0	89.6	81.4	87.8	91.7	84.6	90.6	104.5	83.6	92.5	79.1	104.5	74.9	85.2	93.1	96.7	90.7
1961	89.1	90.4	83.2	88.5	92.9	85.9	91.3	104.5	86.9	91.4	81.4	103.3	77.7	86.7	93.4	96.6	91.2
1962	89.9	91.0	85.4	89.6	94.0	86.5	93.0	104.1	94.8	91.9	83.5	101.7	80.2	88.1	94.1	97.6	91.8
1963	91.2	92.2	87.3	90.7	95.0	87.7	93.4	103.5	96.0	91.8	85.6	100.8	82.6	89.6	94.8	97.9	92.7
1964	92.4	93.2	88.9	92.2	95.9	89.5	94.7	103.2	100.1	91.4	87.3	100.5	84.6	91.2	95.6	98.8	93.5
1965	94.4	95.5	90.9	93.8	96.9	91.3	96.3	100.9	99.4	94.9	89.5	100.2	87.3	93.2	96.2	98.4	94.8
1966	99.1	100.0	95.1	96.8	98.2	95.2	97.5	99.1	97.0	97.0	93.4	100.0	92.0	96.4	97.5	98.5	97.0
1967	100.0	100.0	100.0	100.0	100.0	100.0	100.0	100.0	100.0	100.0	100.0	100.0	100.0	100.0	100.0	100.0	100.0
1968	103.6	103.2	105.2	104.8	102.4	106.1	103.0	102.8	(4)	101.4	106.1	100.2	107.3	104.9	103.7	103.1	104.1
1969	108.9	108.2	111.6	113.3	105.7	115.0	106.5	104.4	103.1	104.7	113.4	101.3	116.0	112.0	108.1	107.0	108.8

Appendix Table A-6 continued

Year	Food Total	Food At-home	Food Away from home	Shelter Total	Shelter Rent, residential	Shelter Maintenance and repairs	Private transportation Total	New cars	Used cars	Motor fuel	Total	Medical care commodities	Medical care services	Services less medical care	All	Durable	Non-durable
1970	114.9	113.7	119.9	123.6	110.1	124.0	111.1	107.6	104.3	105.6	120.6	103.6	124.2	121.3	112.5	111.8	113.1
1971	118.4	116.4	126.1	128.8	115.2	133.7	116.6	112.0	110.2	106.3	128.4	105.4	133.3	127.7	116.8	116.5	117.0
1972	123.5	121.6	131.1	134.5	119.2	140.7	117.5	111.0	110.5	107.6	132.5	105.6	138.2	132.6	119.4	118.9	119.8
1973	141.4	141.4	141.4	140.7	124.3	151.0	121.5	111.1	117.6	118.1	137.7	105.9	144.3	138.3	123.5	121.9	124.8
1974	161.7	162.4	159.4	154.4	130.6	171.6	136.6	117.5	122.6	159.9	150.5	109.6	159.1	151.0	136.6	130.6	140.9
1975	175.4	175.8	174.3	169.7	137.3	187.6	149.8	127.6	146.4	170.8	168.6	118.8	179.1	164.7	149.1	145.5	151.7
1976	180.8	179.5	186.1	179.0	144.7	199.6	164.6	135.7	167.9	177.9	184.7	126.0	197.1	177.7	156.6	154.3	158.3
1977	190.2	190.2	200.3	191.1	153.5	214.7	176.6	142.9	182.8	188.2	202.4	134.1	216.7	190.6	165.1	163.2	166.5
1978	211.4	210.2	218.4	210.4	164.0	233.0	185.0	153.8	186.5	196.3	219.4	143.5	235.4	206.9	174.7	173.9	174.3
1979	234.5	232.9	242.9	239.7	176.0	256.4	212.3	166.0	201.0	265.6	239.7	153.8	258.3	230.1	195.1	191.1	198.7
1980	254.6	251.5	267.0	281.7	191.6	285.7	249.2	179.3	208.1	369.1	265.9	168.1	287.4	266.6	222.0	210.4	235.2
1981	274.6	269.9	291.0	314.7	208.2	314.4	277.5	190.2	256.9	410.9	294.5	186.5	318.2	302.2	241.2	227.1	257.5
1982	285.7	279.2	306.5	337.0	224.0	334.1	287.5	197.6	296.4	389.4	328.1	205.7	356.0	328.6	250.9	241.1	261.6
1983	291.7	282.2	319.9	344.8	236.9	346.3	293.9	202.6	329.7	376.4	357.3	223.3	387.0	338.1	259.0	253.0	266.3
1984	302.9	292.6	333.4	361.7	249.3	359.2	306.6	208.5	375.7	370.7	379.5	239.7	410.3	355.6	267.0	266.5	270.8
1985	309.8	296.8	346.6	382.0	264.6	368.9	314.2	215.2	379.7	373.8	403.1	256.7	435.1	373.3	272.5	270.7	277.2
1986	319.7	305.3	360.1	402.9	280.0	373.8	299.5	224.4	363.2	292.1	433.5	273.6	468.6	390.6	263.4	270.2	262.2

Source: Data from *Economic Report of the President, 1987* (Table B-56).

— = Not available

Appendix Table A-7
Prices, Wages, and Salaries, U.S. Food Manufacturing, 1947-1985

	Producer price index		Wages and salaries,[a] annual average			Wages in food as a proportion of all manufacturing		
Year	Farm goods[b]	Processed foods[c]	Production workers	Nonproduction workers in plants	Workers in headquarters & auxiliaries	Production workers	Nonproduction workers in plants	Workers in headquarters & auxiliaries
	1967 = 100		- - - - - Dollars - - - - - -			Mfg. = 100		
1947	109	83	2,340	3,548	--	92	89	--
1954	98	89	3,303	4,798	--	92	86	--
1958	100	95	3,957	5,439	6,984	93	84	94
1963	96	91	4,498	6,382	8,347	93	82	92
1967	100	100	5,405	7,604	10,022	93	82	95
1972	125	122	7,378	10,153	12,570	95	83	91
1973	178	146	--	--	--	--	--	--
1974	190	167	--	--	--	--	--	--
1975	184	181	--	--	--	--	--	--
1976	185	180	--	--	--	--	--	--
1977	182	190	10,943	15,201	18,912	95	86	92
1978	209	207	11,727	16,542	19,865	95	85	91
1979	240	226	12,569	17,391	20,535	97	83	87
1980	244	240	13,576	18,845	22,545	95	84	89
1981	253	254	14,697	20,314	24,986	94	82	89
1982	242	259	15,705	21,883	27,834	95	87	93
1983	245	262	16,428	23,076	30,039	94	82	93
1984	258	273	16,900	24,045	31,960	92	80	93
1985	233	271	17,540	24,825	33,670	91	79	89
1986	224	278	--	--	--	--	--	--

Sources: Same as Appendix Table A-3 and data from *Economic Report of the President*, January 1987 and previous editions.

— = Not available

[a]Payroll only; in 1984 industry workers got 24 percent in fringe benefits.

[b]Index of prices received by farmers (Table B-96 in 1987 *Economic Report*).

[c]Producer price index for finished goods, consumer foods, total crude and processed (Table B-60 in 1987 *Economic Report*).

Appendix Table A–8
Number of U.S. Food Marketing Companies, 1963–1982

Year	Food processing	Food wholesaling	Foodservice	Food retailing	Total
			Number		
1963	32,617	35,666	--	--	--
1967	26,549	33,848	--	--	--
1972	21,171	32,053	221,883	218,320	494,427
1977	20,616	31,670	226,421	200,486	478,590
1982	16,800	31,290	198,088	198,815	444,993
1987[a]	12,100	29,600	191,700	188,200	421,600

Source: Data from National Economics Division (1987:67).

— = Not available.

[a]Estimates made by projecting forward from data in this table using ordinary least-squares linear regression.

Appendix Table A–9
Profits and Stockholders' Equity, U.S. Food Processing, Tobacco Manufacturing, and All Other Manufacturing, 1950–1985

Year[a]	Net income after tax			Stockholders' equity, at end of second quarter			Profits over equity	
	Food	Tobacco	Other mfg.	Food	Tobacco	Other mfg.	Food & tobacco	Other mfg.
	- - - - - - - -Billion dollars- - - - - - - - -						- - -Percent- - -	
1950-54	4.49	0.70	52.8	51.2	7.1	445.8	8.90	11.84
1955-59	5.79	1.11	68.8	60.6	8.8	623.0	9.94	11.04
1960	1.22	0.28	13.7	13.9	2.1	148.5	9.42	9.22
1961	1.33	0.30	13.7	14.8	2.2	154.5	9.56	8.86
1962	1.37	0.31	16.1	15.4	2.3	162.8	9.46	9.86
1963	1.45	0.33	17.7	16.0	2.4	170.6	9.64	10.38
1964	1.69	0.35	21.2	16.7	2.6	179.3	10.58	11.81
1965	1.90	0.35	25.3	17.5	2.6	189.5	11.19	13.33
1966	2.10	0.39	28.4	18.7	2.8	207.1	11.61	13.74
1967	2.13	0.42	26.5	19.6	2.9	223.1	11.22	11.86
1968	2.21	0.44	29.4	20.3	2.9	240.1	11.36	12.25
1969	2.38	0.48	30.4	21.8	3.2	263.0	11.43	11.56
1970	2.46	0.57	25.5	23.5	3.5	279.0	11.55	9.12
1971	2.75	0.64	27.6	24.4	4.1	290.5	11.92	9.51
1972	3.02	0.68	32.8	26.9	4.3	309.2	11.83	10.60
1973	3.72	0.73	43.8	29.3	4.7	336.8	13.14	13.00
1974	4.60	0.80	53.3	32.5	5.1	352.4	14.39	15.14
1975	4.15	0.92	44.1	35.2	5.7	379.4	14.87	11.35
1976	5.81	1.01	57.6	38.6	6.3	415.2	15.18	13.88
1977	5.55	1.24	63.7	41.9	7.0	444.6	13.87	14.32
1978	6.21	1.41	73.7	44.1	7.6	481.6	14.75	15.29
1979	7.36	1.75	89.2	49.1	8.9	534.3	15.67	16.69
1980	8.22	2.06	82.2	54.7	10.3	593.1	15.81	13.85
1981	9.11	2.20	90.0	64.1	11.0	664.3	15.06	13.55
1982	8.38	2.46	60.2	63.8	12.7	688.5	16.66	8.74
1983	9.44	2.60	73.8	76.0	13.9	714.3	13.39	10.33
1984	9.76	3.07	94.8	73.5	14.8	768.7	14.53	12.34
1985[b]	12.80	--	74.9	81.8	--	782.2	15.64	9.57
1986	13.29	--	69.8	82.5	--	794.5	16.12	8.79

Source: Data from U.S. Bureau of the Census, *Quarterly Financial Report for Manufacturing, Mining, and Trade Corporations.*
— = Not available.
[a]For dollars annual totals.
[b]Tobacco included in food after 1984.

Appendix Table A–10
Administrative and Auxiliary Establishments,[a] U.S. Food Manufacturing, 1963–1982

Type of establishment	1963	1967	1972	1977	1982
	- - - -number, employment (thousands)- - - -				
Administrative	} 625	} 585	} 872	} 1,061	989
	60.4	68.0	80.6	76.8	49.2
Office and clerical					744
					30.4
Research, development, and testing	40	52	57	215	208
	4.4	4.0	4.9	8.0	7.1
Warehousing	113	117	191	270	284
	2.1	1.9	4.7	3.9	4.0
Electronic data processing	--	--	6	261	288
			0.2	5.7	5.7
Other activities	288	206	144	422	530
	4.6	2.3	3.2	7.7	12.4
TOTAL[b]	1,066	960	1,270	1,341	1,219
	71.5	76.3	93.7	102.1	108.9

Source: Data from U.S. Bureau of the Census, *1982 Census of Manufactures* and previous editions.

— = Not available.

[a]Separate establishments (not an integral part of an operating plant) primarily for administrative or centralized activities of a food manufacturing company.

[b]Establishments above may be classified into more than one type of activity.

Appendix Table A-11
Interindustry Technology Flows Involving the U.S. Food System, Company-Financed R&D Expenditures, 1974

Industries of Origin	Industries of Use								
	Agricultural & Forestry	Food Manufacturing	Tobacco Manufacturing	Agricultural Chemicals	Leather Products	Farm Machinery	Wholesale and Retail	Food-service & Final Demand	Total Origin R & D
Agriculture and forestry	32E	0	0	0	0	0	0	96E	128
Food & tobacco manufacturing	8	258	20	0	0	0	16	143	445
Paper products	6	26	0	0	0	0	15	73	202
Agricultural chemicals	143	0	(D)	34	0	0	0	80	187
Pharmaceuticals	32	0	0	0	0	0	22	462	557
Rubber and plastic	14	18	1	0	0	0	12	112	420
Fabricated metals	5	28	0	1	0	0	12	107	553
Engines	10	2	0	0	0	0	(D)	60	282
Farm machinery	165	0	0	0	0	3	77	33	199
Other machinery	25	62	2	2	2	4	98	128	1,164
Computers, office equipment	3	16	1	1	2	2	289	45	1,153
Motor vehicles	78	25	1	1	1	1	33	1,346	1,518
Instruments	6	8	1	1	0	9	150	343	1,036
Other manufacturing	67	49	4	6	12	0	0	1,050E	6,462
Trade, finance, real estate	0	0	0	0	0	0	4	0	40
Other sectors	1	1	0	0	0	0		(D)	374
Total R & D Used	562	493	30	46	16	19	728	4,111	14,700

Source: Data from Scherer (1984).

(D) = Data suppressed because fewer than four firms in cell.

Note: These data exclude $8 billion in publicly financed R&D. Inventions with consumer goods applications were treated as public goods (the *total* R&D cost of the relevant patent was assigned to final demand, with part of the cost counted as industrial use). However, in this table all patents with only industrial uses are treated as only private goods (associated R&D costs are fully allocated among the using industries). Diagonal elements of the matrix represent approximate process inventions utilized within the same industry.

Appendix Table A–12
Number of New Grocery Products Introduced in Twenty-two Selected Categories, 1964–1986

Category	1964	1967	1972	1982	1983	1984	1985	1986P
				Number				
Baby food	6	10	2	5	5	8	4	
Baking ingredients	44	35	25	40	30	36	28	
Beverages	62	75	39	61	81	137	147	
Breads, cakes, cookies	20	30	38	81	106	103	103	
Breakfast cereals	10	11	19	11	19	21	23	
Candy and gum	37	25	36	90	122	123	136	
Canned fruit, vegetable juices	14	22	21	52	84	69	74	
Canned meat and fish	17	17	14	15	23	23	13	
Dairy foods	28	38	40	91	115	158	167	
Desserts, sugar, syrup	19	22	13	10	16	11	12	
Fresh meats and fish	15	11	6	48	87	78	96	
Frozen foods	72	145	165	207	251	286	322	
Household & beauty aids*	121	125	86	369	362	411	474	
Household supplies*	65	65	49	85	89	91	105	
Low-calorie foods	28	39	17	60	91	93	71	
Macaroni, potatoes, rice	27	20	27	30	35	23	42	
Paper products*	16	21	21	19	16	20	26	
Pet products	17	7	46	33	28	40	51	
Sauces, spices, condiments	48	55	50	71	94	109	127	
Snacks, crackers, nuts	16	41	33	102	102	123	130	
Soups	13	12	10	13	25	15	29	
Tobacco products*	20	35	17	17	19	14	26	
Total food products	493	615	601	1,020	1,305	1,452	1,575	1,810
Total grocery products	715	861	774	1,510	1,791	1,988	2,206	2,500

Source: Data from National Economics Division (1987:77).
* = Nonfood grocery product.
P = Preliminary.

Appendix Table A–13
Employment by Occupational Categories in the Food and Tobacco Manufacturing Industries,[b] Numbers in 1982 and BLS Projections for 1995

Occupational Category[a]	Meat		Dairy		Fruit and Vegetable		Grains		Bakery		Sugar and Candy		Beverages		Oils and Misc.		Tobacco		Food and Tobacco	
	1982	% Change	1982	% Change	1982	% Change	1982	% Change	1982	% Change	1982	% Change	1982	% Change	1982	% Change	1982	% Change	1982	% Change
Scientists & engineers	2	+50	2	0	2	0	2	0	2	-50	2	0	2	0	2	0	0	0	17	0
Other professional & technical	6	0	5	-40	6	+17	5	0	4	-50	4	-33	6	+17	6	0	4	-25	39	+8
Managers	15	+13	12	-33	13	+31	12	+8	13	-23	6	0	19	+11	15	+20	4	-25	109	+5
Sales workers	9	0	8	-25	2	+50	5	-25	20	+25	3	-50	13	-8	5	0	1	-99	64	-8
Clerical workers	27	+7	22	+38	20	+25	17	+6	21	-19	12	0	26	+15	22	+5	7	-14	172	+2
Craft & related workers	26	+8	18	+29	36	+25	22	+5	27	-22	18	-6	34	+6	24	0	14	-21	219	-1
Meat cutters & butchers	45	+9	0	0	3	0	0	0	--	0	--	0	0	0	7	+14	--	0	55	+9
Packers, graders, inspectors	23	+4	14	-36	22	+23	12	0	24	-25	18	-6	27	+7	29	+17	8	-25	176	+1

Manufacturing Industry Group[b]

Appendix Table A–13 continued

	Manufacturing Industry Group[b]																			
	Meat		Dairy		Fruit and Vegetable		Grains		Bakery		Sugar and Candy		Beverages		Oils and Misc.		Tobacco		Food and Tobacco	
Occupational Category[a]	1982	% Change	1982	% Change	1982	% Change	1982	% Change	1982	% Change	1982	% Change	1982	% Change	1982	% Change	1982	% Change	1982	% Change
Drivers	15	+13	32	-28	12	+33	14	+7	38	-24	3	0	49	+6	18	+6	2	-50	183	-5
All other operatives	109	+6	21	+5	28	+29	24	+4	42	-21	19	-11	19	+5	37	+3	12	-17	321	-1
Service workers	11	0	4	-25	6	+33	4	0	10	-20	4	0	5	+20	6	0	2	0	53	-4
Laborers, except farm	55	+7	21	-24	83	+23	21	0	18	-28	18	-17	33	-3	37	+8	12	-25	299	+3
Total	342	+8	168	-26	232	+20	137	+4	217	-23	107	-7	233	+6	208	+7	66	-21	1710	+0.

Source: Data from Bureau of Labor Statistics, *Monthly Labor Review* (November 1983).

[a]Categories listed according to BLS occupational codes.

[b]Industries follow SIC system. Workers in thousands, therefore where numbers small, change is exaggerated.

— = Less than 1,000 workers.

Appendix Table A-14
U.S. Food Imports, 1970-1972, 1975-1977, and 1980-1982 Average

SIC	Products	Annual Value 1970-1972	1975-1977	1980-1982	Proportion of Domestic Value 1970-1972	1975-1977	1980-1982
		$ million			Percent		
0111	Wheat	1	4	3	0	0	0
0115	Corn	7	14	13	0	0	0
0116	Soybeans	0	0	2	0	0	0
0119	Other cash grains	22	64	75	0	NA	NA
0131	Cotton and cottonseed	16	17	NA	1	1	NA
0132 } 2141	Leaf tobacco	135	290	379	9	11	12
0139	Other field crops	62	114	281	NA	NA	NA
0172	Grapes	4	19	71	1	3	9
0173	Tree nuts	1,473	3,365	3,954	NA	29	27
0174	Citrus fruit	9	14	13	1	1	1
20111	Beef	688	838	1,515	8	5	7
20112	Veal	18	17	25	8	6	7
20113	Lamb and mutton	29	21	37	8	5	11
20114	Pork	26	20	179	1	0	3
20115	Lard	0	0	0	0	0	0
20116-36	Processed pork	3	2	5	0	0	0
20117-37	Sausage	5	10	13	0	0	0
20118-38	Canned meat	308	504	479	22	28	23
20119	Hides, skins	55	92	91	14	13	10
20110	Miscellaneous meat products	24	38	24	NA	NA	NA
20139	Natural sausage casings	27	39	55	16	36	59
20162-62	Chickens	4	9	14	0	0	0
20163	Turkeys	4	NA	NA	0	NA	NA
20164	Other poultry	4	7	13	0	0	0
20171	Processed poultry	1	2	2	0	0	0
20172	Processed eggs	0	0	0	0	0	0
20210	Butter	1	1	3	0	0	0
20220	Cheese	90	215	352	3	4	4
20221	Natural cheese	NA	NA	NA	NA	NA	NA
20222	Processed cheese	NA	NA	NA	NA	NA	NA
20231	Dry milk	38	60 }		NA	NA }	
20232	Canned milk	1	1	206			5
20233	Concentrated milk	NA	NA		NA	NA	
20261-2	Fluid milk	3	5	7	0	0	0
20264	Buttermilk, yogurt	0	0	0	0	0	0
20263	Cottage cheese	0	NA	NA	0	NA	NA
20320	Canned specialties	220	NA	NA	(X)	NA	NA
20321	Canned baby food	NA	NA	NA	NA	NA	NA
20323	Canned dry beans	NA	NA	1	NA	NA	0
20322	Canned soups	3	10	22	NA	NA	NA
20324	Canned specialties	NA	NA	NA	NA	NA	NA

Appendix Table A–14 continued

SIC	Products	Annual Value			Proportion of Domestic Value		
		1970–1972	1975–1977	1980–1982	1970–1972	1975–1977	1980–1982
		$ million			Percent		
20331+71	Frozen & canned fruits	94	208	635	5	6	7
20334	Frozen & canned juices						
20332	Canned vegetables	104	229	117	3	5	6
20336	Catsup, tomato sauces	15	14	39	3	1	3
20338	Jams, jellies	3	5	6	1	1	1
20335	Canned vegetable juices	1	1	1	0	0	0
20341	Dried fruits & vegetables	14	46	48	4	6	4
20342	Soup mixes, dried						
20353	Meat sauces	5	14	34	1	1	1
20354	Mayonnaise						
20372	Frozen vegetables	NA	NA	38	NA	NA	1
20381	Frozen pies	NA	NA	NA	NA	NA	NA
20382	Frozen dinners	NA	NA	NA	NA	NA	NA
20411	Wheat flour	18	40	56	1	1	1
20412	Wheat mill products						
20415,45	Flour mixes, doughs						
20416	Other grain mill products						
20413	Corn mill products						
20460	Wet corn millings	11	23	22	1	1	1
20430	Breakfast cereals	2	5	9	0	0	0
20440	Milled rice products	4	1	6	1	0	0
20471	Dog and cat foods	23	12	13	1	0	0
20480	Prepared feeds	7	18	44	NA	0	0
2051–52	Bread, cake, and cookies	36	66	127	1	1	1
2061,2,3	Sugar	824	1,574	2,336	23	24	25
2065–662	Candy	54	107	153	2	3	2
20661	Chocolate	51	268	450	10	20	17
20668	Cocoa						
20670	Chewing gum	3	9	11	1	2	1
20741	Crude cottonseed oil	0	0	0	0	0	0
20742	Refined cottonseed oil						
20743	Cotton linters	3	3	6	9	8	6
20744	Cottonseed oil mill by-products	0	1	1	0	0	0

Appendix Table A–14 continued

SIC	Products	Annual Value ($ million)			Proportion of Domestic Value (Percent)		
		1970-1972	1975-1977	1980-1982	1970-1972	1975-1977	1980-1982
20751	Soybean oil	0	0	0	0	0	0
20752	Soybean cake meal	NA	NA	NA	NA	NA	NA
20762	Vegetable oil	154	513	530	4	5	5
20770	Animal fats	53	41	35	6	3	1
20791	Shortening	NA	NA	NA	NA	NA	NA
20792	Margarine	0	0	0	0	0	0
20820	Malt beverage	--	--	452	--	--	5
20830	Malt	42	174	20	1	3	3
20840	Wine, brandy	192	407	1,022	21	25	29
20850	Distilled liquor	524	665	1,024	26	27	25
20860	Canned soft drinks	1	6	43	0	0	0
20871	Flavorings						
20872	Liquid base, not soft drink	10	31	52	1	1	1
20873-4	Others						
20910	Canned and cured seafood	164	256	432	25	23	22
20922-3	Fresh and frozen fish	NA	NA	NA	NA	NA	NA
20924	Frozen shellfish	NA	NA	NA	NA	NA	NA
20950	Coffee	70	247	266	3	6	4
20951	Coffee, roasted	11	58	61	1	2	2
20952	Coffee, concentrated	59	190	231	10	13	14
20980	Pasta products	6	22	45	2	3	4
20990	Food prep.	NA	NA	NA	NA	NA	NA
20992	Chips	NA	NA	NA	NA	NA	NA
20994	Baking powder	1	3	8	1	3	3
20996	Vinegar	1	2	3	1	2	2
20993	Syrups	1	2	NA	0	0	NA
20	Total	5,842	7,152	11,419	5.8	4.3	4.1

Sources: Data from U.S. Bureau of the Census, *U.S. Imports* (FT 210) for years 1980–1982 and U.S. Bureau of the Census, *U.S. Commodity Exports and Imports as Related to Output, 1976 and 1977* (and earlier years).

Appendix Table A–15
U.S. Food Exports, 1970–1972, 1975–1977, and 1980–1982 Average

SIC	Products	Annual Value			Proportion of Domestic Value		
		1970–1972	1975–1977	1980–1982	1970–1972	1975–1977	1980–1982
		$ million			Percent		
0111	Wheat	1,127	3,910	6,965	52	64	72
0115	Corn	937	4,604	7,387	18	34	40
0116	Soybeans	1,350	3,525	6,107	37	40	47
0119	Other cash grains	336	939	2,558	NA	NA	NA
0131 0132	Cotton and cottonseed	489	1,197	2,379	30	38	59
2141	Leaf tobacco	521	931	1,445	38	39	45
0139	Other field crops	105	318	757	NA	NA	NA
0172	Grapes	35	55	91	10	8	7
0173	Tree nuts	65	168	371	31	41	64
0174	Citrus fruit	113	259	453	16	25	22
20111	Beef	85	194	544	1	2	3
20112	Veal	2	5	7	1	2	2
20113	Lamb and mutton	4	8	20	1	3	6
20114	Pork	49	243	225	2	4	3
20115	Lard	33	33	31	17	14	14
20116-36	Processed pork	6	13	24	0	0	1
20117-37	Sausage	2	4	8	0	0	1
20118-38	Canned meat	8	16	17	1	2	1
20119	Hides, skins	197	462	714	56	70	86
20110	Miscellaneous meat products	14	9	55	NA	NA	NA
20139	Natural sausage casings	12	24	20	8	40	54
20162-62	Chickens	26	110	306	1	3	7
20163	Turkeys	13	32	42	2	4	3
20164	Other poultry	2	7	16	9	10	27
20171	Processed poultry	2	3	NA	1	1	NA
20172	Processed eggs	2	14	NA	1	4	NA
20210	Butter	24	1	69	4	0	5
20220	Cheese	5	12	--	0	0	--
20221	Natural cheese	2	5	24	0	0	0
20222	Processed cheese	3	6	--	0	0	--
20231	Dry milk	153	173	--	19	11	--
20232	Canned milk	12	13	236	3	2	5
20233	Concentrated milk	0	0	--	0	0	--
20261-2	Fluid milk	3	5	9	0	0	0
20264	Buttermilk, yogurt	2	2	11	0	1	0
20263	Cottage cheese	0	0	NA	0	0	NA
20320	Canned specialties	13	35	45	1	2	2
20321	Canned baby food	4	10	9	1	3	2
20323	Canned dry beans	1	2	3	0	0	0
20322	Canned soups	4	8	13	1	0	1
20324	Canned specialties	4	15	20	1	1	1

Appendix Table A–15 continued

SIC	Products	Annual Value			Proportion of Domestic Value		
		1970-1972	1975-1977	1980-1982	1970-1972	1975-1977	1980-1982
		$ million			Percent		
20331	Canned fruits	54	79	115	6	7	7
20332	Canned vegetables	11	38	90	1	2	5
20334	Canned fruit juices	23	48	85	5	4	4
20335	Canned vegetable juices	3	9	8	3	3	3
20336	Catsup, tomato sauces	4	18	24	1	1	1
20338	Jams, jellies	2	4	9	1	1	2
20341	Dried fruits and vegs.	70	182	280	16	21	21
20342	Soup mixes, dried	1	2	3	1	1	1
20352	Pickles	5	12	9	1	3	1
20353	Meat sauces	2	6	16	1	3	4
20354	Mayonnaise	4	9	16	1	1	1
20371	Frozen fruit & juice	29	81	168	5	8	10
20372	Frozen vegetables	4	27	88	1	2	4
20381	Frozen pies	2	6	9	NA	1	1
20382	Frozen dinners	3	3	9	NA	0	0
20411	Wheat flour	91	159	279	6	7	9
20412	Wheat mill products	2	17	15	1	3	3
20415+45	Flour mixes, doughs	2	5	10	0	0	1
20416	Other grain mill products	2	15	23	2	11	11
20413	Corn mill products	11	19	44	6	4	8
20460	Wet corn milling	65	217	613	8	11	20
20430	Breakfast cereals	30	64	26	4	4	2
20440	Milled rice products	320	733	1,260	56	59	63
20471	Dog and cat foods	10	21	154	--	NA	4
2048-472	Prepared feeds	60	121	NA	1	2	NA
20481-83	Poultry feed	19	47	58	NA	2	2
20484	Dairy feed	5	6	7	NA	0	0
20485-88	Livestock feed	8	26	47	NA	1	1
20489-472	Other feeds	27	51	217	NA	NA	58
2051-52	Bread, cake, and cookies	5	17	33	0	0	0
2061,2,3	Sugar	9	65	387	0	2	8
2065-662	Candy	24	61	188	1	2	3
20661	Chocolate	1	9	38	0	1	1
20668	Cocoa	3	9	16	1	1	1
20670	Chewing gum	5	13	16	NA	3	3
20741	Crude cottonseed oil	8	6	16	7	3	10
20742	Refined cottonseed oil	47	162	178	69	82	73
20743	Cotton linters	5	9	19	6	21	26
20744	Cottonseed oil mill by-products	1	5	14	1	3	4
20751	Soybean oil	147	266	416	18	13	16
20752	Soybean cake meal	400	831	1,607	26	24	31
20761	Linseed oil	8	14	14	20	15	19
20762	Vegetable oil	27	82	139	16	28	33

Appendix Table A–15 continued

SIC	Products	Annual Value			Proportion of Domestic Value		
		1970-1972	1975-1977	1980-1982	1970-1972	1975-1977	1980-1982
		$ million			Percent		
20763	Other oils	31	32	46	56	37	49
20770	Animal fats	198	413	656	45	45	61
20791	Cooking oils and shortening	73	90	205	5	3	5
20792	Margarine	1	2	6	0	0	1
20820	Malt beverage	2	12	45	0	0	0
20830	Malt	5	7	12	3	1	2
20840	Wine, brandy	1	7	38	0	1	2
20851	Distilled liquor, bulk	12	24	85	NA	12	3
20852	Bottled liquor	28	23	--	NA	1	--
20860	Canned soft drinks	3	22	55	0	1	1
20871	Flavorings	10	19	--	7	9	--
20872	Liquid base, not soft drink	26	40	244	20	18	6
20873-4	Other flavorings	20	39	--	2	2	--
20910	Canned and cured seafood	46	12	296	10	13	22
20922-3	Fresh and frozen fish	38	141	500	6	11	31
20924	Frozen shellfish	32	85	178	7	13	15
20951	Coffee, roasted	13	48	63	1	2	2
20952	Coffee, concentrated	12	22	62	2	2	4
20980	Pasta products	1	1	5	0	0	0
20992	Chips	1	10	25	0	1	1
20994	Baking powder	3	5	6	4	4	3
20996	Vinegar	1	1	4	1	1	2
20993	Syrups	5	15	NA	3	5	NA
20999	Miscellaneous food preparations	NA	NA	NA	NA	NA	NA
20	Total	2,840	6,270	11,825	2.8	3.8	4.2

Sources: Data from U.S. Bureau of the Census, *U.S. Exports* (FT 610) for years 1980–1982 and U.S. Bureau of the Census, *U.S. Commodity Exports and Imports as Related to Output, 1976 and 1977* (and earlier years).

Appendix Table A–16
Value Added by the U.S. Food Processing Industries, 1963–1985

Industry	Value Added				Ratio of Value Added to Shipments	
	1963	1972	1982	1985	1963	1985
	Million dollars				Percent	
Meat packing	1,908	2,968	5,825	5,859	15.3	13.8
Meat processing	563	1,100	2,901	3,705	26.4	29.9
Poultry dressing		724	1,888	2,859		27.7
	411				18.3	
Poultry processing		169	389	535		29.1
Butter	133	82	136	98	13.5	6.2
Cheese	180	492	1,777	1,910	13.4	17.3
Prepared milk	236	467	1,448	1,628	15.4	30.8
Ice cream	433	460	910	1,041	25.2	29.9
Fluid milk	2,203	2,552	4,171	4,953	31.4	25.2
Canned specialties	541	815	1,769	2,161	46.3	45.0
Canned fruits and vegetables	1,030	1,625	3,553	4,448	37.6	40.4
Dried fruits and vegetables	116	236	790	840	36.4	47.0
Sauces, pickles	249	428	1,737	2,116	36.8	41.3
Frozen fruits and vegetables		695	2,409	2,355		40.6
	550				35.5	
Frozen specialties		716	2,066	2,985		45.9
Flour	373	510	1,094	1,159	17.1	22.3
Breakfast cereals	365	688	2,623	3,995	58.4	69.9
Rice	81	148	380	389	19.2	24.6
Flour mixes	123	307	609	700	44.9	42.8
Wet corn milling	291	331	1,157	1,363	46.8	32.5
Pet food		614	2,281	3,074		57.9
	984				25.4	
Animal feeds		1,101	2,188	2,276		21.9
Bread, rolls, cakes	2,404	3,518	7,861	8,811	53.4	61.2
Cookies and crackers	627	1,019	2,789	4,184	54.5	64.9
Cane sugar	390	536	920	1,035	23.6	27.3
Beet sugar	201	311	432	524	35.6	29.3
Confectionery	956	1,627	4,882	5,838	44.3	50.7
Cottonseed oil	101	88	203	219	18.2	24.9
Soybean oil	152	350	678	712	10.3	8.3
Other fats and oils	236	342	643	653	33.3	27.4
Cooking oils and margarine	265	513	1,262	1,190	20.0	21.2
Beer	1,286	1,994	4,535	5,681	55.6	46.5
Wine and brandy	137	408	997	1,063	37.2	38.5
Spirits	624	1,024	1,460	1,691	57.2	48.4
Soft drinks bottling	1,234	2,337	6,856	7,587	55.8	39.2
Flavorings	400	872	2,670	3,108	54.8	64.2
Canned fish	175	231	613	227	38.6	32.6
Frozen fish	119	288	967	1,070	30.4	27.1
Coffee	616	826	2,070	2,446	33.0	36.6
Pasta	96	156	551	629	43.1	54.5
Miscellaneous foods	984	1,952	5,982	7,027	46.8	51.3
Total	21,825	35,617	88,419	104,146	31.9	34.5

Sources: Data from Bureau of the Census, *1985 Annual Survey of Manufactures* and *1982 Census of Manufactures* (and previous editions).

Appendix Table A–17
Changes in Values of Manufacturers' Shipments of Foods, Fifty-four Product Classes, 1963, 1972, 1982, and 1985

Consumer Product Class (Number of 1985 classes)	Value of Shipments[a]				Growth Rates		
	1963	1972	1982	1985	1963–1972	1972–1982	1982–1985
	Million dollars				Percent		
Beef (1)	5,708	11,790	20,607	20,158	107	75	-2
Veal and lamb (2)	611	572	632	678	-6	10	7
Pork and lard (2)	2,427	4,392	8,311	8,139	81	89	-2
Canned and cured meats (7)	5,213	6,785	12,967	15,315	30	91	18
Poultry, chilled and frozen (8)	1,886E	2,909	7,524	8,508	54E	159	13
Poultry, processed (2)	19E	358	1,692	2,546	1,984E	373	50
Eggs, processed (1)	140	157	330	491	12	110	49
Butter (1)[b]	820	791	1,976	1,839	-4	150	-7
Natural cheese (1)[b]	682	1,400	5,626	5,665	105	302	1
Process cheese (2)	389	1,134	3,434	3,763	192	203	10
Dried milk (3)[b]	662	1,108	3,400	3,492	67	207	3
Canned milk (2)	438	560	1,486	1,771	28	165	19
Ice cream and frozen desserts (1)	1,210	1,519	3,281	3,882	26	116	18
Fluid milk, packaged (1)	4,285	5,079	9,115	10,046	19	79	10
Cottage cheese and yogurt (2)	442	764	1,087	1,359	73	42	25
Baby food, canned (1)	230	347	596	567	51	72	-5
Canned soup and specialties (2)	643	1,283	2,771	3,022	100	116	9
Fruit juices, refrigerated (1)	--	--	652	889	--	--	36
Canned fruits and juices (2)	1,103	1,538	3,001	3,620	39	138	21
Canned vegetables and juices (3)	898	1,321	2,456	2,603	47	86	6
Catsup and tomato sauces (1)	298	603	2,174	2,825	102	261	30
Jams, jellies, preserves (1)	227	280	603	637	23	115	6
Dried fruits and vegetables (1)	285	466	1,325	1,530	64	184	15
Dried soup mixes (1)	45	127	333	422	182	162	26
Pickles (1)	228	363	695	854	59	91	23
Sauces and dressings (2)	373	727	2,355	2,802	95	224	19
Frozen fruits and juices (1)	436	734	1,860	2,270	68	153	22
Frozen vegetables (1)	396	915	3,090	3,297	130	238	7
Frozen specialties (3)	629	1,743	4,417	5,740	177	153	30
Flour and grain mill products (4)	1,951	2,136	4,301	4,585	9	101	7
Flour mixes (2)	505	797	2,073	2,345	58	160	13
Breakfast cereals (1)	561	935	3,112	4,379	67	233	41
Rice (1)	407	671	1,897	1,588	65	183	-16
Pet food (4)	442	1,451	4,287	4,820	238	206	12
Bread and rolls (2)	2,497	3,373	7,136	7,809	35	112	9
Cakes, pies, pastries (5)	1,119	1,435	2,890	3,171	28	101	10
Cookies and crackers (2)	1,130	1,691	4,309	6,030	50	155	40
Sugar, refined (2)	1,809	2,613	4,083	4,255	44	156	4
Candy, chocolate, chewing gum (6)	1,601	2,720	7,071	8,982	70	160	27
Cooking oil and margarine (2)	1,231	2,275	5,341	6,051	85	135	13

Appendix Table A–17 continued

Consumer Product Class (Number of 1985 classes)	Value of Shipments[a]				Growth Rates		
	1963	1972	1982	1985	1963-1972	1972-1982	1982-1985
	Million dollars				Percent		
Beer (5)	2,282	4,039	11,106	12,146	77	175	9
Wine and brandy (3)	353	851	2,720	2,696	141	220	-1
Distilled liquor (x)	960	1,557	2,809	3,126	62	80	11
Soft drinks (3)	2,136	4,807	14,892	18,100	125	210	22
Flavorings (3)	474	744	2,282	2,631	57	207	15
Canned fish (1)	384	588	1,267	869	53	115	-31
Fresh and frozen fish (4)	363	1,017	3,714	3,615	180	265	-3
Roasted coffee (1)	1,206	1,518	3,773	4,386	26	149	16
Concentrated coffee (1)	396	599	1,250	1,308	51	209	5
Pasta (3)	216	355	1,193	1,367	64	236	15
Ready-to-mix desserts (1)	192	267	402	568	39	51	41
Chips (1)	466	1,042	3,322	4,481	124	219	35
Tea (1)	181	360	913	1,162	99	154	27
Miscellaneous foods (7)[c]	1,025	1,746	5,147	5,339	70	195	4
Total food[d]	65,134	106,780	259,473	281,595	64	143	9

Sources: Data from Bureau of the Census, *1982 Census of Manufactures* and previous years and *1985 Annual Survey of Manufactures.*

[a]Value of product shipments, excluding NSK classes unless whole SIC included in class, for comparably defined SIC consumer product classes. Some values estimated.

[b]Affected upward by increases in government-held inventories.

[c]Includes sweetening syrups, molasses, baking powder, yeast, vinegar, cider, cocoa, canned chocolate syrups, dry prepared foods (salad mixes, sauce mixes, seasoning mixes, boullion, frosting mixes, etc.), refrigerated perishable foods (dairy substitutes, salads, sandwiches, pies, dips, etc.), coconut, spices, peanut butter, honey, pectin, popping corn, and other prepared foods.

[d]Includes industrial, by-product, and NSK product classes.

Appendix Table A–18
Average Annual Change in Production Level, Selected Food Processing Industries and Product Classes, 1963–1987

Industry or Product Class	Change in Production Level				
	1963-1967[a]	1967-1972[a]	1972-1977[a]	1977-1982[b]	1982-1987[b]
	Percent per year				
Meatpacking:	2.5	2.7	0.3	-2.0	0.8
Beef	4.6	4.0	-0.1	-2.2	0.9
Veal	-3.9	-9.2	4.7	-2.2	0.9
Lamb	-3.2	1.5	-9.4	-9.3	--
Pork	1.9	4.5	-1.2	1.6	0.2
Meat processing:	4.4	4.1	5.2	6.8	2.0
Processed pork (hams, etc.)	0.6	-0.8	-2.7	3.8	--
Sausage	2.1	1.7	3.9	3.0	--
Canned meats	-0.4	0.8	-2.5	-1.6	--
Poultry products:	8.7	1.5	3.9	5.0	5.4
Dressed chickens	6.2	3.7	4.6	3.0	--
Dressed turkeys	11.2	-1.0	2.7	0.6	--
Other poultry	3.4	-1.3	12.2	-5.3	--
Processed poultry products	79.2	25.8	7.9	16.3	--
Processed egg products	5.7	0.4	2.2	-4.7	--
Butter	-2.8	-1.7	-0.3	3.0	-2.5
Cheese:	4.8	7.7	1.6	6.2	3.2
Natural cheese	-0.3	4.7	4.1	11.1	--
Processed cheese	5.0	10.0	4.8	-1.1	--
Preserved milk:	2.7	-1.9	-0.1	4.1	0.7
Dried milk powder	-1.5	-4.7	0.0	4.1	--
Canned milk, consumer	2.7	-5.2	-2.1	5.9	--
Canned milk, bulk	-3.2	6.1	2.8	1.0	--
Ice cream and frozen desserts	-0.6	2.1	0.3	3.3	4.8
Fluid milk products	0.6	1.7	0.3	2.1	1.2
Packaged fluid milk	-0.6	1.9	0.2	0.6	--
Cottage cheese	0.1	8.5	-3.9	0.8	--
Buttermilk	0.4	5.7	8.0	-1.7	--
Yogurt				9.0	--
Canned specialties:	1.3	3.0	1.5	0.9	--
Canned baby foods	-1.0	9.0	-2.5	2.1	--
Canned soups	5.5	3.9	1.4	1.5	--
Canned beans	2.5	0.6	2.1	-0.3	--
Other canned specialties	--	3.9	4.4	1.8	--
Canned fruits and vegetables:	4.0	-0.4	1.7	3.0	--
Canned fruits	1.0	-2.4	0.0	1.4	--
Canned vegetables	1.5	-1.1	1.0	3.6	--
Canned mushrooms	8.0	32.9	-0.5	-4.5	--
Canned fruit juices	8.9	6.5	3.6	6.8	--
Canned vegetable juices	-2.5	7.3	-0.3	-2.3	--
Tomato catsup and sauces	9.1	2.1	6.4	5.9	--
jams, jellies, preserves	-1.8	0.1	-3.1	4.7	--
Dried fruits and vegetables:	7.3	3.5	2.7	1.7	--
Dried fruits and vegetables	4.5	3.5	4.4	2.0	--
Dried soup mixes	17.6	10.5	-4.6	1.0	--

Appendix Table A–18 continued

Industry or Product Class	Change in Production Level				
	1963-1967[a]	1967-1972[a]	1972-1977[a]	1977-1982[b]	1982-1987[b]
	Percent per year				
Pickles, sauces, and dressings:	4.7	4.1	6.8	1.6	--
Pickles	1.3	1.8	-0.4	-1.2	--
Meat sauces	5.4	12.7	-0.1	9.0	--
Mayonnaise and dressings	8.8	6.7	7.2	1.0	--
Frozen fruits and vegetables:	10.8	6.6	3.3	3.0	6.9
Frozen fruits and juices	9.1	6.9	1.4	2.4	--
Frozen vegetables	9.9	7.0	4.2	3.7	--
Frozen specialties:	10.8	15.6	2.6	2.5	--
Frozen baked goods		12.2	3.1	4.7	--
Frozen entrees and dinners	10.2	10.3	5.4	6.3	--
Other frozen specialties		--	0.0	-8.3	--
Flour milling:	1.5	-2.0	2.8	0.1	4.8
Wheat flour	-1.4	-0.5	2.1	1.0	5.8
Flour mixes	7.0	1.6	4.2	0.8	2.3
Breakfast cereals	3.9	2.1	3.4	4.9	2.3
Rice milling	9.1	2.1	4.6	2.7	2.3
Wet corn milling	4.6	6.0	8.4	8.1	9.5
Pet foods:	?	10.5	6.5	0.8	3.2
Dog and cat food	12.7	15.7	5.4	--	--
Other pet food	--	5.1	3.7	--	--
Animal feeds	5.6	3.1	0.3	-1.3	--
Bakery products:	1.4	0.5	-0.2	2.4	3.4
Bread			-1.1	1.8	--
	1.5	0.7			
Rolls			3.9	3.3	--
Sweet yeast goods	3.0	-1.2	-0.4	1.0	--
Cakes	-0.2	-0.2	0.5	1.1	--
Pies	-1.4	-3.0	-2.8	1.6	--
Crackers and cookies:	2.3	1.3	0.8	2.4	3.4
Crackers	-1.0	3.2	3.9	2.2	--
Cookies	4.4	-0.1	-2.8	2.3	--
Refined cane sugar	4.6	1.6	-0.4	-3.3	-2.5
Refined beet sugar	-0.8	7.3	-0.7		
Confectionery:					
Chocolate	2.3	-0.2	1.8	3.2	5.3
Nonchocolate confectionery	4.3	1.9	2.7	-0.8	--
Nuts, glace fruits, etc.	10.1	9.6	3.7	4.3	--
Cocoa and other chocolate products	5.4	2.8	7.1	-3.8	--
Chewing gum	8.9	2.1	0.5	-1.2	--
Cottonseed oil	-9.1	2.7	1.0	4.1	2.6
Soybean oil	8.8	4.9	0.5		
Other vegetable oils	-1.3	2.1	-9.4		
Animal and marine fats and oils	4.0	1.7	-1.3	-0.3	-1.6

Appendix Table A–18 continued

Industry or Product Class	Change in Production Level				
	1963-1967[a]	1967-1972[a]	1972-1977[a]	1977-1982[b]	1982-1987[b]
	Percent per year				
Cooking oils and margarine:	4.4	0.4	1.6	3.4	3.7
Shortening and cooking oils	4.9	3.6	0.8	1.0	--
Margarine	7.5	1.0	2.6	-1.1	--
Beer	4.7	5.3	4.9	2.6	0.1
Malt	2.0	2.6	0.6	0.0	--
Wine and brandy	4.3	12.7	5.2	4.2	9.8
Distilled spirits	5.7	3.4	0.0	0.1	-2.1
Soft drinks bottling	6.6	5.4	4.7	4.6	3.5
Flavorings:	8.4	6.4	5.9	4.6	3.5
Liquid flavorings	--	1.7	8.3	2.5	--
Liquid beverage bases	27.9	-5.1	11.8	8.7	--
Flavorings for bottlers	2.8	9.9	3.0	8.2	--
Other flavoring agents	7.8	2.3	9.7	4.0	--
Canned and cured seafood	-1.5	-0.1	0.8	-1.6	--
Fresh and frozen seafood	7.7	4.4	6.9	2.5	--
Fresh packaged seafood	-4.8	5.8	16.2	-1.3	--
Frozen packaged fish	11.8	7.6	5.8	0.8	--
Frozen packaged shellfish	11.8	0.0	2.8	3.3	--
Coffee:	-0.4	-2.6	-5.3	6.6	1.7
Roasted coffee	-0.5	-2.9	-8.0	7.6	--
Soluble coffee	-0.2	4.6	-2.6	5.6	--
Manufactured ice	-2.3	-2.4	-6.2	3.8	--
Pasta	0.6	6.8	6.1	3.5	--
Miscellaneous prepared foods:	7.6	5.2	2.8	4.0	5.9
Ready-to-mix desserts	1.7	2.7	-0.2	-6.8	--
Chips	10.0	4.6	2.9	6.1	--
Sweetening syrups	-1.7	8.0	-0.1	-2.5	--
Baking powder and yeast	0.6	0.8	5.0	3.1	--
Tea	--	7.3	0.9	1.4	--
Vinegar and cider	1.8	2.3	-2.7	2.1	--
Other prepared foods, NEC	2.3	7.3	1.0	1.0	--
Total food processing	3.3	2.8	1.6	2.8	4.0

Sources: Data from Bureau of the Census, *1977 Census of Manufactures*, Volume IV, *Indexes of Production*, Table 1c (and previous years) and *1982 Census of Manufactures*, Industry Reports, Table 6a.

[a]Production indexes are developed from individual product (7-digit SIC) dollar shipments deflated by Census Bureau unit value relatives or by Bureau of Labor Statistics wholesale (produce) price indexes. Product class (5-digit SIC) production indexes are weighted averages of the product indexes, with dollar shipments used as weights. Industry production indexes are weighted averages of product class indexes, resales, and receipts, all weighted by gross value added; each type of receipt is separately deflated. There are no adjustments for quality change or product-mix change at the 7-digit level.

[b]Production indexes supplied by Mr. Kenneth Armitage of the Federal Reserve Board for the years 1977-1987, for a mixture of four- and five-digit SIC categories. Where such indexes were unavailable, product-class-shipments growth was deflated for 1977-1982 with the PPI for finished processed foods (38.8%). If only four-digit indexes were given, the five digit product classes were adjusted proportionately.

Appendix Table A-19
Changes in Values of Manufacturers' Shipments, Food Manufacturing
Industries, 1963, 1972, 1982, and 1985

Industry[a]	Value of Shipments				Growth Rates		
					1963– 1972	1972– 1982	1982– 1985
	1963	1972	1982	1985	1972	1982	1985
	Million dollars				Percent		
Meatpacking	12,436	23,003	44,854	42,554	85	95	-5
Meat processing	2,130	4,632	12,278	12,406	117	165	1
Poultry dressing	2,066E	3,254	9,045	10,340	58	178	14
Poultry processing	175E	588	1,427	1,839	236	143	29
Butter	989	808	1,687	1,571	-18	109	-7
Cheese	1,171	3,195	10,763	11,060	173	237	3
Processed milk	938	1,668	4,731	5,288	78	184	12
Ice cream	1,077	1,245	2,855	3,477	16	129	22
Fluid milk	7,026	9,396	18,736	19,679	34	99	5
Canned specialties	1,169	1,877	4,141	4,802	61	121	16
Canned fruit and vegetables	2,743	4,044	9,283	10,999	47	130	18
Dry fruit and vegetables	319	607	1,745	1,788	90	187	2
Sauces, pickles	677	1,167	4,269	5,123	72	266	20
Frozen fruit and vegetables	} 1,549	1,849	5,375	5,803	} 144	191	8
Frozen specialties		1,936	5,061	6,508		161	29
Flour	2,177	2,380	4,933	5,205	9	107	6
Breakfast foods	625	1,126	4,132	5,718	80	267	38
Rice	423	681	1,934	1,581	61	184	-18
Flour mixes	434	705	1,419	1,635	62	101	15
Wet corn mills	622	832	3,268	4,190	34	293	28
Pet foods	} 3,880	1,402	4,402	5,306	} 66	214	21
Animal feeds		5,037	11,298	10,410		124	-8
Bread, rolls	4,506	6,132	13,143	14,389	36	111	9
Cookies and crackers	1,150	1,764	4,665	6,446	53	164	38
Cane sugar	1,650	2,150	4,154	3,785	30	93	-9
Beet sugar	564	880	1,516	1,789	56	72	18
Confectionery	2,159	3,592	9,906	11,514	66	176	16
Cottonseed oil	555	459	933	881	-17	103	-6
Soybean oil	1,473	3,357	8,604	8,629	128	156	0
Other fats and oils	708	1,026	2,309	2,386	45	125	3
Cooking oils and margarine	1,324	2,068	4,906	5,608	56	137	14
Beer	2,315	4,054	11,183	12,216	75	176	9
Wine and brandy	368	865	2,786	2,763	135	222	-1
Spirits	1,091	1,798	3,126	3,495	65	74	12
Soft drinks	2,211	5,454	16,808	19,358	147	208	15
Flavorings	730	1,472	4,237	4,840	102	188	14
Canned fish	453	810	1,849	697	79	128	-62
Frozen fish	391	1,084	4,010	3,947	177	270	-2
Coffee	1,868	2,329	5,827	6,677	25	150	15
Pasta	223	348	1,065	1,155	56	206	8
Miscellaneous foods[b]	2,104	3,990	11,870	13,708	90	197	15
Total	68,467	115,060	280,529	301,562	68	144	8

Sources: Same as Table A-1.

[a]Listed by four-digit SIC code. See Appendix D for definitions of industries.

[b]Includes SICs 2083 (Malt), 2097 (Ice), and 2099 (Miscellaneous).

Appendix Table A–20
Materials, Resales, Energy, Contract Work, and Labor Costs of the Food Processing Industries, 1982

Industry	Materials	Resales	Energy Fuels	Energy Electricity	Contract Work	Labor Costs Payroll	Labor Costs Supplementals
				Percent of shipments			
Meatpacking	79.5	0.4	0.4	0.4	0.1	5.7	1.3
Meat processing	64.4	10.6	0.5	0.7	0.1	9.8	2.2
Poultry dressing	74.4	2.1	1.0	1.4	0.4	15.2	2.6
Poultry processing	90.3	7.2	1.1	1.3	0.2	14.9	2.7
Butter	95.8	3.0	0.8	0.3	0.1	2.6	0.7
Cheese	76.9	5.5	0.9	0.4	0.9	4.4	1.0
Prepared milk	63.1	4.0	1.6	0.6	0.4	5.5	1.3
Ice cream	56.9	9.0	0.5	1.7	0.1	11.0	2.3
Fluid milk	68.1	8.6	0.6	0.8	0.1	8.0	1.8
Canned specialties	53.0	2.3	1.4	0.6	0.0	9.5	2.3
Canned fruits and vegetables	58.0	1.5	1.7	0.8	0.1	11.2	2.7
Dried fruits and vegetables	51.6	0.9	2.8	1.1	0.0	12.4	3.5
Sauces and pickles	53.1	5.3	0.5	0.5	0.0	8.7	2.0
Frozen fruits and vegetables	48.8	2.8	1.8	1.7	0.1	12.0	3.2
Frozen specialties	46.9	10.1	0.6	1.3	0.1	12.9	2.7
Flour	72.7	3.0	0.4	1.4	0.1	6.5	1.5
Breakfast cereals	30.3	4.0	0.8	0.7	0.0	10.3	2.8
Rice	70.0	5.4	0.8	1.0	0.2	4.9	1.1
Flour mixes	51.9	5.4	0.3	0.5	0.4	9.2	2.0
Wet corn milling	53.0	1.6	6.4	3.0	0.3	7.8	2.1
Pet foods	44.6	2.2	0.8	0.8	0.1	7.7	1.7
Animal feeds	74.5	4.8	0.5	0.7	0.1	5.5	1.0
Bread, rolls, cake	28.4	9.8	1.0	0.8	0.2	24.7	5.7
Cookies and crackers	33.9	4.3	0.9	0.7	0.5	17.1	4.4
Raw cane sugar	63.7	0.8	2.5	0.7	0.1	12.0	2.6
Refined cane sugar	74.8	0.6	3.6	0.2	0.5	6.5	1.7
Beet sugar	60.0	0.4	11.3	0.8	0.3	11.1	2.3
Confectionery	47.1	4.1	0.6	0.8	0.2	12.7	3.1
Chocolate	52.3	0.5	0.6	0.8	0.6	9.3	2.1
Chewing gum	31.4	1.4	0.3	0.7	0.1	10.6	2.8
Cottonseed oil	62.5	8.5	2.1	3.5	0.1	8.1	1.9
Soybean oil	81.0	8.3	1.7	0.8	0.0	2.2	0.5
Other vegetable oil	64.3	16.7	1.8	1.1	0.1	4.0	0.8
Animal and marine fats	54.7	4.8	5.9	2.1	0.4	12.3	2.6
Shortening and cooking oils	69.9	1.9	1.6	1.1	0.2	5.5	1.3
Beer	56.8	0.4	1.4	1.0	0.1	11.7	2.8
Wine and brandy	60.7	1.3	0.5	0.7	0.1	8.8	2.2
Malt	64.2	0.3	4.4	3.6	0.0	6.5	1.9
Distilled spirits	44.9	7.4	1.2	0.5	0.4	8.4	2.2
Soft drink bottling	50.0	8.1	0.4	0.6	0.2	12.8	2.5
Flavorings	35.2	1.0	0.5	0.3	0.1	5.6	1.2
Canned seafood	46.0	19.3	0.8	0.6	0.1	10.5	1.9
Fresh and frozen fish	67.5	6.2	0.6	1.0	0.4	10.2	1.7
Coffee	57.6	5.4	0.7	0.5	0.2	4.6	1.0
Ice	19.3	1.3	0.5	13.0	0.1	28.3	3.8
Pasta	43.1	3.4	0.8	1.0	0.0	13.6	2.6
Miscellaneous prepared foods	44.7	2.1	1.0	0.7	0.2	11.1	2.6
Processed foods	61.1	5.4	1.0	0.8	0.2	9.3	2.1
Total manufacturing	50.5	2.7	1.5	1.4	1.6	19.4	4.1

Source: Data from Bureau of the Census, *1982 Census of Manufactures.*

Appendix Table A-21
Capital Expenditures by the Food Processing Industries, 1982

Industry	Capital Expenditures			Capital Expend. ÷ Shipments	Plant ÷ Equipment Expenditures
	New or Expanded Plants	New Machinery or Equipment	Used Capital		
	- - - Million dollars - - -			- - - Percent - - -	
Meatpacking	84	206	13	0.7	41
Meat processing	42	133	15	1.6	32
Poultry dressing	41	157	12	2.3	26
Poultry processing	5	28	3	2.5	16
Butter	2	7	2	0.6	29
Cheese	37	124	9	1.6	30
Prepared milk	27	72	4	2.2	38
Ice cream	80	16	64	3.1	500
Fluid milk	56	311	28	2.1	18
Canned specialties	48	107	6	3.9	45
Canned fruits and vegetables	55	209	37	3.2	26
Dried fruits and vegetables	8	44	5	3.2	18
Sauces, pickles	11	57	9	1.8	19
Frozen fruits and vegetables	42	194	10	4.6	22
Frozen specialties	30	131	10	3.4	23
Flour	21	70	32	2.5	30
Breakfast cereals	13	153	0	4.0	9
Rice	21	20	11	2.7	105
Flour mixes	6	23	4	2.3	26
Wet corn milling	35	292	0	10.0	12
Pet foods	20	82	8	2.5	24
Animal feeds	30	101	17	1.3	30
Bread, rolls, cakes	92	290	38	3.2	32
Cookies and crackers	27	81	4	2.5	33
Raw cane sugar	16	74	2	8.3	22
Refined cane sugar	18	52	7	2.5	35
Beet sugar	6	27	3	2.4	22
Confectionery	36	172	12	3.3	21
Chocolate	10	44	1	2.5	23
Chewing gum	4	13	1	1.9	31
Cottonseed oil	8	52	2	6.5	15
Soybean oil	32	81	58	2.0	40
Other vegetable oil	8	59	6	13.1	14
Animal and marine fats	8	49	9	3.7	16
Shortening and cooking oils	12	85	1	2.0	14
Beer	154	511	237	8.1	30
Malt	5	25	0	4.5	20
Wine	30	107	8	5.2	28
Spirits	21	69	2	2.9	30
Soft drinks bottling	113	537	45	4.1	21
Flavorings	11	47	14	1.7	23
Canned seafood	4	17	4	1.4	24
Frozen fish	20	42	7	1.8	48
Coffee	5	75	2	1.4	7
Ice	2	11	4	7.5	18
Pasta	11	38	2	4.8	29
Miscellaneous prepared foods	60	236	23	2.9	25
Total food processing	1,356	5,371	735	2.7	25

Source: Data from U.S. Census Bureau, *1982 Census of Manufactures*, Table 3a.

Appendix Table A–22
Number of Establishments Owned by Food and Tobacco Manufacturing Companies,
by Sales Size of Company within Category, 1977

Enterprise Industry Category	Sales Size of Company Within Category				
	1st to 4th	5th to 8th	9th to 20th	21st to 50th	Below 50th
	Establishments per firm[1]				
Meatpacking	942	111	20	5	1.1
Prepared meats and poultry	45	42	10	7	1.2
Fluid milk	445	40	13	15	1.4
Other dairy products	140	34	7	6	1.1
Canned fruits and vegetables	276	13	8	3	1.1
Preserved fruits and vegetables	301	57	15	3	1.2
Grain mill products	621	117	64	8	1.3
Bread and cake	649	230	18	17	1.2
Cookies and crackers	86	9	2	2	1.0
Sugar and confectionery	67	86[3]	9	7	1.2
Fats and oils	155	29	6	4	1.1
Alcoholic beverages	61	22	17	3	1.1
Soft drinks and flavorings	692	58	21	7	1.3
Miscellaneous foods	104	27	15	9	1.1
Tobacco	161	41	13	2	1.0
Food and tobacco[2]	316	61	16	7	1.2

Source: Data from Connor (1982b:Table 18).
[1]Average number of establishments per company in size class, including separate central administrative offices and auxiliary establishments.
[2]Average of the 60 largest, 61–120 largest, 121–300 largest, 301–750 largest, and all others.
[3]SIC 2065.

Appendix Table A-23
Annual Real Growth Rates of the U.S. Food Manufacturing Industries, Historical and Projected[a]

Industry	Data Resources, Inc. National Econometric Forecasting Model, 1983-1989	
	Output	Employment
	Percent per year	
Meatpacking	2.6	0.8
Meat processing	2.7	1.1
Poultry	3.6	2.5
Poultry and egg processing	3.5	1.2
Butter	1.2	-0.7
Cheese	4.1	2.5
Prepared milk	2.4	2.3
Ice cream	3.9	1.1
Fluid milk	2.4	1.4
Canned specialties	2.9	1.3
Canned fruit and vegetables	2.6	-0.2
Dried fruit and vegetables	3.8	4.2
Pickles, sauces	3.9	1.9
Frozen fruits and vegetables	3.7	1.7
Frozen specialties	---	---
Flour milling	3.2	1.2
Breakfast cereal	2.7	0.7
Rice milling	7.6	5.9
Flour mixes	3.2	2.2
Wet corn milling	5.1	1.9
Pet foods	2.8	0.9
Animal feeds, prepared	3.7	2.1
Bread, cake	2.7	0.6
Cookies and crackers	2.9	2.4
Sugar refining	2.1	0.9
Candy	3.1	1.1
Chocolate	3.3	1.5
Chewing gum	2.3	1.5
Cottonseed oil refining	4.7	3.5
Soybean oil refining	2.8	1.1
Other vegetable oil refining	3.5	3.0
Animal fats	5.2	3.3
Shortening and cooking oils	3.3	1.9
Beer	3.0	0.0
Malt	3.5	1.2
Wine and brandy	5.1	3.0
Distilled liquor	3.6	2.2
Soft drinks bottling	4.2	1.7
Flavorings	4.5	2.5
Manufactured ice	2.4	1.0
Pasta	3.8	1.2
Miscellaneous prepared foods	3.3	1.2
Frozen fish and seafood	3.5	1.8
Coffee	2.7	2.7
Canned seafood	4.0	2.8

Source: Data Resources, Inc., forecasts of June 1984 and DOC estimates.

[a]According to Data Resources, Inc., National Econometric Forecasting Model, 1983–1989.

Appendix Table A-24
Number of Food Processing Plants with Twenty or More Employees, 1947-1982

Industry	Number of Plants				Change		
	1947	1963	1972	1982	1947- 1963	1963- 1972	1972- 1982
					- - - Percent - - -		
Meatpacking	832	976	863	668	+17	-12	-23
Meat processing	511	483	557	613	-5	+15	+10
Poultry dressing	} 428	} 559	369	302	} +30	} -17	-18
Poultry processing			93	99			+6
Butter	261	178	63	35	-32	-65	-44
Cheese	161	206	281	319	+28	+36	+14
Prepared milk	250	166	163	125	-34	-2	-23
Ice cream	443	387	273	219	-13	-29	-20
Fluid milk	2,329	1,948	1,287	751	-16	-34	-42
Canned specialties	} 1,238	77	88	88	} -26	14	0
Canned fruit & vegetables		836	621	451		-26	-27
Dried fruit & vegetables	50	80	88	85	+60	+10	-3
Sauces, pickles	249	184	191	155	-26	+4	-19
Frozen fruits & vegetables	} 179	} 346	190	199	} +93	} +16	+5
Frozen specialties			211	251			+19
Flour	383	218	181	174	-43	-17	-4
Breakfast foods	30	30	26	37	0	-13	+42
Rice	59	49	35	44	-17	-29	+26
Flour mixes	31	60	57	55	+94	-5	-4
Wet corn mills	21	20	37	27	-5	+85	-27
Pet foods	} 670	} 711	113	142	} +6	} +8	+26
Animal feeds			654	584			-11
Bread and rolls	2,319	1,904	1,374	1,074	-18	-28	-28
Cookies and crackers	187	208	177	187	+11	-15	+6
Cane sugar	87	98	90	69	+13	-8	-23
Beet sugar	74	62	54	44	-16	-13	-19
Confectionery	603	451	440	393	-25	-2	-11
Cottonseed oil	262	153	84	59	-42	-45	-30
Soybean oil	78	71	74	84	-9	+4	+14
Other fats and oils	265	233	213	204	-12	-9	-4
Cooking oil and margarine	72	86	86	85	+19	0	-1
Beer	393	180	130	73	-54	-28	-44
Wine and brandy	104	70	74	103	-33	+6	+39
Spirits	164	89	96	75	-46	+8	-22
Soft drinks	1,002	1,530	1,552	1,094	+53	+1	-30
Flavorings	122	97	115	131	-20	+19	+14
Canned fish	206	196	139	107	-5	-29	-23
Frozen fish	--[a]	255	257	433	--	+1	+68
Coffee	--[b]	133	104	85	--	-22	-18
Pasta	91	70	64	79	-23	-9	+23
Miscellaneous foods	1,204	713	771	879	-41	+8	+14
Total food processing	15,358	14,113	12,235	10,681	-8	-13	-13
Rest of manufacturing	69,675	85,008	97,471	112,482	+22	+15	+15

Source: Data from Connor (1982b:137-38) and *1982 Census of Manufactures*.
[a]Included in other frozen foods industries or in wholesale trade.
[b]Included in miscellaneous prepared foods.

Appendix Table A–25
Sales Concentration in Nielsen Grocery Product Categories, 1980

Industry	Nielsen Product Category	Sales Concentration		Industry Four-Firm Concentration
		Four-Firm Concentration Ratio	Hirschman-Herfindahl Index	
		Percent	Index	Percent
Meatpacking:	Frozen pet food	100.0	10,000	--
Meat processing:	Refrigerated pork tidbits feet	87.6	2,283	88
	Canned corn beef	63.8	1,764	
	Canned beef hash	78.3	1,705	
	Canned roast beef	73.8	1,399	
	Canned roast beef hash	98.9	4,535	
	Canned dried sliced beef	91.5	6,394	
	Canned barbecued beef & pork	77.8	1,772	
	Canned beef stew	78.2	3,936	
	Canned ham loaf	100.0	6,953	
	Canned deviled ham	100.0	9,129	
	Canned potted meat	83.8	3,041	
	Canned meat & fish spread	98.6	3,685	
	Canned Vienna sausage	82.2	2,321	
	Canned spiced lunch meat	90.3	5,598	
	Canned sausage	98.8	6,207	
	Canned scrapple	100.0	5,078	
	Canned pigs feet	89.6	2,659	
Poultry dressing:	None	--	--	--
Poultry processing:	Canned chicken	90.7	3,763	96
	Canned chicken stew	95.0	2,346	
	Canned turkey	100.0	6,226	
	Dry egg mixes	96.6	8,086	
Butter:	Refrigerated butter	38.9	899	39
Cheese:	Refrigerated cheese spreads	82.8	4,239	79
	Refrigerated packaged cheese, American type	62.0	2,906	
	Refrigerated packaged cheese, Swiss type	69.6	3,844	
	Refrigerated packaged cheese, other types	43.7	870	
	Refrigerated grated & shredded cheese	57.7	1,979	
Prepared milk:	Canned milk	60.1	1,177	78
	Canned egg nog	100.0	10,000	
	Powdered milk	45.6	1,209	
	Modified milk products, including infant formulas	99.4	4,716	
	Cream substitutes, including nondairy	63.5	2,550	
	Instant breakfast powders	83.1	5,118	
	Ice cream mixes	100.0	10,000	
	Frozen cream substitute	68.1	2,597	
Ice cream:	None	--	--	--
Fluid milk:	Cream cheese	69.1	3,982	69
Canned specialties:	Canned baby food, strained	99.4	5,405	90
	Canned baby food, strained meat	100.0	7,051	
	Canned baby food, strained hi-protein	99.1	6,569	
	Canned baby food, junior	99.0	6,081	
	Canned baby food, junior meat	99.9	7,161	
	Canned baby food, junior hi-protein	98.8	7,881	
	Canned jelled aspic salad	100.0	7,551	
	Canned baked beans with meat	64.2	1,764	
	Canned soup	84.5	6,397	
	Canned tamales	62.0	1,187	
	Canned chili	60.1	1,143	
	Canned ravioli	94.5	5,601	
	Canned macaroni products	97.9	5,864	
	Canned spaghetti	94.0	5,196	
	Canned pizza pie mixes	94.3	5,203	
	Canned lasagna	99.9	8,097	

Appendix Table A–25 continued

Industry	Nielsen Product Category	Sales Concentration		Industry Four-Firm Concentration
		Four-Firm Concentration Ratio	Hirschman-Herfindahl Index	
		Percent	Index	Percent
	Canned rice	92.1	5,257	
	Canned pudding and sauce	79.2	2,348	
	Canned chop suey & chow mein	100.0	5,181	
	Canned Oriental noodles	67.6	1,302	
	Canned bean sprouts	96.0	5,606	
	Canned Oriental sauces	89.8	2,893	
	Canned mincemeat	100.0	10,000	
Canned fruits & vegetables:	Pie and pastry fillings	78.8	1,577	55
	Apple sauce	44.2	753	
	Canned applies	79.7	2,070	
	Canned apricots	28.0	409	
	Canned berries	74.6	2,377	
	Canned cranberries	68.5	5,660	
	Canned figs	49.7	1,903	
	Canned fruit cocktail	49.2	903	
	Canned salad fruits	80.9	3,205	
	Canned grapefruit	16.0	79	
	Canned oranges	31.9	289	
	Canned freestone peaches	36.0	537	
	Canned cling peaches	43.4	979	
	Canned spiced peaches	67.3	3,122	
	Canned pears	38.8	830	
	Canned pineapple	68.6	2,264	
	Canned grapes	64.7	2,381	
	Canned cherries	55.5	814	
	Canned plums	28.4	928	
	Canned prunes	99.8	9,747	
	Canned artichokes	67.0	1,539	
	Canned asparagus	58.3	1,210	
	Canned green beans	46.6	800	
	Canned wax beans	33.9	397	
	Canned lima beans	39.1	585	
	Canned beets	34.6	378	
	Canned cabbage	79.2	2,095	
	Canned carrots	41.8	486	
	Canned creamed corn	50.7	852	
	Canned whole corn	51.1	929	
	Canned okra	72.2	2,500	
	Canned onions	81.6	2,177	
	Canned peas	46.1	852	
	Canned peas and carrots	55.5	1,209	
	Canned mixed vegetables	61.0	1,724	
	Canned potatoes	16.6	83	
	Canned sweet potatoes	53.0	834	
	Canned pumpkin	91.8	5,435	
	Canned sauerkraut	47.1	611	
	Canned spinach	54.8	2,306	
	Canned squash	91.1	5,662	
	Canned succotash	85.5	2,879	
	Canned greens	52.9	1,118	
	Canned Italian tomatoes	76.2	1,736	
	Canned tomatoes	28.0	239	
	Canned chilies	93.0	4,492	
	Canned pimentoes	87.6	2,886	
	Canned olives, green	31.5	389	
	Canned olives, stuffed	24.1	201	
	Canned olives, ripe	57.0	1,384	
	Canned olives, miscellaneous	34.3	380	
	Canned capers	91.3	3,148	
	Canned cocktail onions	66.7	1,449	
	Canned peppers	48.4	904	
	Canned mushrooms	38.2	457	
	Canned hominy	62.0	2,264	
	Canned apple juice	38.9	442	
	Canned grape juice	80.7	5,504	

Appendix Table A-25 continued

Industry	Nielsen Product Category	Sales Concentration		Industry Four-Firm Concentration
		Four-Firm Concentration Ratio	Hirschman-Herfindahl Index	
		Percent	Index	Percent
	Canned grapefruit juice	42.7	542	
	Canned lemon and lime juice	75.2	4,726	
	Canned orange juice	36.9	366	
	Canned pineapple juice	69.9	2,775	
	Canned prune juice	78.6	3,562	
	Canned other fruit juices	78.5	5,373	
	Canned nectars	85.6	2,320	
	Canned tomato juice	53.5	864	
	Canned vegetable juice	95.0	7,335	
	Canned tomato puree	63.8	1,203	
	Canned tomato paste	71.7	3,505	
	Canned tomato sauce	53.2	1,875	
	Canned barbecue sauce	80.1	2,662	
	Canned fish and cocktail sauce	67.1	1,442	
	Canned pizza sauce	75.3	1,649	
	Canned spaghetti sauce	75.5	3,838	
	Canned marinara sauce	87.1	2,568	
	Jams	65.3	1,352	
	Jelly	59.0	1,281	
	Marmalade	53.1	1,028	
	Preserves	35.0	631	
	Fruit butter	50.3	956	
	Maraschino cherries, canned	21.3	126	
	Diet fruit spreads	82.5	2,886	
Dried fruits & vegetables:	Dried prunes	65.7	1,861	65
	Dried raisins	67.3	3,197	
	Dried fruit, other	54.4	963	
	Dried dates	56.4	1,682	
	Dried potatoes	75.6	2,225	
	Dried onions	47.4	667	
	Dried seasonings	56.7	966	
	Dried soup mixes	95.6	5,285	
Pickles, sauces, and dressings:	Pickled salad vegetables	35.2	311	78
	Hot dog sauce	70.9	1,135	
	Relish	48.8	706	
	Sweet pickles	49.7	986	
	Dill pickles	44.4	981	
	Spoonable salad dressing	84.5	6,778	
	Mayonnaise	76.6	2,849	
	Liquid salad dressings	78.1	2,098	
	Sandwich spreads	76.6	2,629	
	Garlic spreads	100.0	8,694	
	Mustard	72.2	2,119	
	Hot sauces	59.7	1,017	
	Meat sauces and ham glaze	90.1	3,903	
	Mushroom sauce	100.0	8,221	
	Worchestershire sauce	94.5	3,431	
	Meat cooking sauce	94.3	6,221	
	Gravy aids and beef extract	99.0	5,729	
	Canned gravy	99.3	4,721	
	Fondue and fondue sauce	100.0	4,912	
	Canned Oriental sauces	89.8	2,893	
	Diet liquid salad dressing	90.4	3,885	
	Diet spoonable salad dressing	63.2	2,105	
Frozen fruits & vegetables:	Frozen potatoes	56.4	2,331	52
	Frozen vegetables	20.7	159	
	Frozen formulated vegetables	76.5	2,271	
	Frozen fruits	20.0	110	
	Frozen coconut	100.0	4,364	
	Frozen orange juice	34.7	530	
	Frozen juices, other	66.3	1,200	
	Frozen drinks	40.2	570	

Appendix Table A–25 continued

Industry	Nielsen Product Category	Sales Concentration		Industry Four-Firm Concentration
		Four-Firm Concentration Ratio	Hirschman-Herfindahl Index	
		Percent	Index	Percent
Frozen specialties:	Frozen dinners	83.6	2,503	77
	Frozen pot pies	81.9	2,179	
	Frozen meat entrees	74.5	1,571	
	Frozen poultry entrees	74.8	1,889	
	Frozen Oriental entrees	83.4	2,623	
	Frozen Italian entrees	53.8	884	
	Frozen Mexican entrees	43.9	498	
	Frozen hors d'oeurve & snacks	84.2	2,799	
	Frozen breakfasts	97.9	3,104	
	Frozen pizza	67.7	1,307	
	Frozen biscuits, rolls, muffins	65.4	2,510	
	Frozen breakfast cakes	87.3	3,506	
	Frozen cobbler, dumpling, strudel	89.0	3,494	
	Frozen dessert cakes	88.1	3,336	
	Frozen cream pies	73.8	1,516	
	Frozen fruit pies	65.3	2,016	
	Frozen desserts	94.1	8,863	
Flour mill products:	Wheat germ	98.7	8,812	82
	Hominy grits	86.4	3,639	
	Corn meal	61.8	1,015	
	Cake flour	98.9	4,513	
	All purpose flour	64.6	1,681	
Breakfast cereals:	Ready-to-eat cereals	83.7	2,396	84
	Natural granola cereals	81.9	2,564	
	To-be-cooked cereals	85.2	4,006	
Rice:	Packaged rice	43.9	632	74
	Precooked rice	91.2	5,706	
	Rice-based dry dinners	88.1	3,294	
Flour mixes and doughs:	Cake mix	89.4	2,592	87
	Brownie mix	89.1	2,643	
	Bread and muffin mixes	72.0	1,932	
	Coffee cake mixes	99.8	5,046	
	Gingerbread mix	95.8	3,718	
	Roll and biscuit mix	93.2	5,920	
	Cookie mix	98.2	3,364	
	Pie crust mix	72.1	2,075	
	Pancake flour and mixes	77.8	2,407	
	Pizza pie mixes	94.3	5,203	
	Cake and pastry shells	100.0	9,985	
	Refrigerated cookies and brownies	93.6	8,411	
	Refrigerated doughnuts and sweet rolls	83.8	6,244	
	Refrigerated biscuits, breads, rolls	65.0	3,177	
	Frozen pancake batter	83.1	2,255	
Wet corn milling products:	Corn starch	95.3	4,338	81
	Salad and cooking oils (part)	65.7	1,197	
Pet foods:	Bird food	27.9	222	72
	Wet cat food	72.6	1,566	
	Moist cat food	98.0	5,435	
	Dry cat food	80.0	1,996	
	Wet dog food	60.4	945	
	Moist dog food	94.5	4,477	
	Dry dog food	61.9	2,000	
	Pet treats, snacks, candy	82.5	2,520	
Bread, rolls, and cakes:	Frozen bread and bread dough	53.4	814	--
	Frozen buiscuits, rolls, muffins	65.4	2,510	
	Brown bread and nut rolls	96.6	6,291	
	Breading products	83.0	3,266	
	Croutons and stuffing	81.8	4,163	

Appendix Table A–25 continued

Industry	Nielsen Product Category	Sales Concentration		Industry Four-Firm Concentration
		Four-Firm Concentration Ratio	Hirschman-Herfindahl Index	
		Percent	Index	Percent
Cookies and crackers:	Toaster pastries	74.0	4,629	--
Sugar:	Brown sugar	57.6	1,312	57
	Powdered sugar	49.0	953	
	Cube sugar	87.1	3,270	
	Granulated sugar	33.5	323	
Confectionery:	Chewing gum	72.0	2,430	88
	Breath sweeteners	99.6	4,532	
	Cough drops	97.5	4,367	
	Marshmallows	70.1	2,814	
	Baking chocolate	99.6	3,934	
	Chocolate chips	81.4	3,721	
	Nonchocolate baking chips	96.0	4,380	
	Cocoa	99.4	9,884	
	Sweetened milk additives	76.3	2,057	
	Glazed fruit	70.0	1,491	
	Breakfast bars	95.9	3,253	
	Chocolate syrup	95.3	5,315	
Shortening & cooking oils:	Olive oil	76.1	1,502	73
	Salad and cooking oils	65.7	1,197	
	Peanut oil	98.3	5,625	
	Safflower oil	94.7	5,639	
	Soybean oil	56.8	3,226	
	Shortening	67.5	3,667	
	Margarine	52.3	736	
Beer:	None	--	--	--
Malt:	None	--	--	--
Wine:	None	--	--	--
Spirits:	None	--	--	--
Soft drinks:	Bottled water	29.9	268	--
	Canned tea	100.0	3,823	
	Isotonic drinks	99.9	9,282	
	Fruit flavored beverages	66.2	1,625	
Flavorings:	Fruit punch syrups	63.1	2,483	72
	Powdered breakfast drinks	81.9	5,832	
	Chocolate drinks	94.5	4,732	
	Soft drink powders	70.4	2,238	
	Cocktail mix	59.1	1,081	
	Food colorings	61.8	1,058	
Canned seafood:	Anchovies	42.1	647	53
	Clams and clam juice	71.0	1,424	
	Canned oysters	50.6	667	
	Canned salmon	38.9	442	
	Canned sardines	42.7	492	
	Canned shrimp	53.4	1,091	
	Canned tuna	73.4	1,892	
Frozen and fresh packaged fish:	Frozen shrimp	31.3	261	48
	Frozen seafood	63.4	1,221	
Coffee:	Ground coffee	55.6	1,097	59
	Instant coffee	62.3	1,017	

Appendix Table A–25 continued

Industry	Nielsen Product Category	Sales Concentration		Industry Four-Firm Concentration
		Four-Firm Concentration Ratio	Hirschman-Herfindahl Index	
		Percent	Index	Percent
Pasta products:	Macaroni	43.9	519	62
	Spaghetti	36.5	373	
	Noodles and dumplings	41.0	557	
	Pastina	88.4	4,318	
	Instant lunch	85.5	2,670	
	Pasta-based dry dinners	76.9	2,215	
Ready-to-mix desserts:	Flavored gelatin	88.5	5,439	93
	Pudding mix	91.9	5,532	
	Custard, rennet, tapioca	96.6	4,949	
Chips and salty snacks:	Potato sticks	76.5	2,027	--
Sweetening syrups:	Table syrup, plain	54.9	850	70
	Table syrup, berry flavored	83.8	5,857	
Baking powder and yeast:	Baking powder	97.8	3,246	98
	Baking soda	93.3	8,699	
	Dry yeast	100.0	7,078	
	Refrigerated yeast	100.0	5,365	
Tea, packaged:	Packaged tea	85.6	5,953	79
	Tea bags	72.0	2,696	
	Instant tea	69.8	3,684	
	Iced tea mixes	88.0	1,893	
Vinegar and cider:	Cider	46.4	710	48
	Vinegar	48.7	1,230	
Miscellaneous prepared foods:	Coconut, dry	74.5	3,947	71
	Honey	41.9	611	
	Pepper	40.6	537	
	Other spices, bottled	69.2	1,199	
	Liquid seasonings	94.4	2,894	
	Dry seasonings	56.7	966	
	Meat flavor and tenderizers	77.9	2,806	
	Monosodium glutamate	92.5	7,776	
	Refrigerated fruit and fruit drinks	64.1	1,266	
	Refrigerated vegetable salad	32.2	348	
	Refrigerated sauerkraut	40.2	517	
	Refrigerated pudding	96.2	7,989	
	Refrigerated horseradish and mustard	56.2	1,077	
	Refrigerated pickles and relish	88.1	5,005	
	Refrigerated herring and seafood snacks	80.2	2,144	
	Refrigerated pressure topping	55.7	1,958	
	Frosting and fudge mix	88.2	4,153	
	Gravy mixes, dry packaged	71.6	1,415	
	Sauce mix, spaghetti	75.7	1,539	
	Sauce mix, cheese	95.2	2,334	
	Chili mix, packaged	63.8	1,386	
	Sauce mix, sour cream	78.9	2,175	
	Sauce mix, meat loaf	65.7	1,199	
	Sloppy Joe seasoning	76.4	1,865	
	Fondue sauces and mixes	100.0	4,912	
	Unfrozen popsicles	75.9	2,467	

Source: Adapted from A.C. Nielsen, *Supermarket Directory* (April–May 1980) by Robert L. Wills.

— = Not applicable.

Note: Includes food and beverages primarily distributed through grocery warehouses. The two sales concentration ratios are based on the market shares of manufacturers' brands only; in cases where private-label products would rank among the leading brands, the ratios are understated (unless the branded and private-label segments fall into separate markets). Definitions of the two concentration ratios are given in the text. Nielsen product categories are classified according to census SIC principles.

Appendix Table A–26
New Capital Expenditures in Food Manufacturing as Indicators of Future Growth, by State, 1984 and 1985

| State | New Capital Expenditures in Food Manufacturing | | | |
| | Total | | Per Dollar of State Shipments | |
	1984	1985	1984	1985
	Million dollars		- - - Percent - - -	
AL	63.1	97.9	1.62	2.55
AK	10.6	8.2	1.74	1.34
AZ	41.0	76.6	3.43	5.99
AR	81.4	124.2	1.53	2.39
CA	708.7	664.1	2.21	2.07
CO	200.8	119.1	3.56	2.49
CN	33.8	31.9	2.50	2.00
DE	44.5	62.2	2.93	4.37
FL	165.8	214.6	1.78	2.20
GA	135.1	204.6	1.62	2.45
HI	40.6	38.5	3.02	3.02
ID	51.2	82.9	1.99	3.71
IL	430.5	583.5	2.00	2.76
IN	138.2	178.9	2.23	2.49
IA	122.4	334.9	1.79	2.67
KS	153.8	64.3	1.77	0.77
KY	63.8	92.1	1.61	2.37
LA	103.6	71.1	2.68	1.92
ME	54.4	32.3	7.92	3.87
MD	67.7	74.2	1.58	1.67
MA	119.3	111.4	2.85	2.75
MI	232.6	269.6	2.80	3.12
MN	170.4	185.0	1.78	1.94
MS	45.2	61.8	1.55	2.20
MO	193.7	163.7	2.25	1.86
MT	10.9	12.4	2.32	3.07
NE	66.1	81.7	0.79	0.97
NV	4.6	5.7	1.61	1.79
NH	14.5	15.4	2.29	2.46
NJ	309.4	367.0	3.50	4.05
NM	17.4	14.0	4.13	3.53
NY	268.3	274.2	2.16	2.19
NC	215.9	246.1	3.03	3.38
ND	27.8	37.3	3.13	4.25
OH	262.1	286.5	2.11	2.17
OK	38.9	42.8	1.70	1.86
OR	54.9	58.3	1.87	1.93
PA	318.5	451.1	2.21	3.05
RI	3.3	5.7	0.82	1.52
SC	89.9	59.5	4.12	2.54

Appendix Table A–26 continued

State	New Capital Expenditures in Food Manufacturing			
	Total		Per Dollar of State Shipments	
	1984	1985	1984	1985
	Million dollars		- - - Percent - - -	
SD	26.3	30.1	1.42	1.65
TN	211.0	214.2	2.83	2.75
TX	527.7	408.8	2.80	2.16
UT	35.2	22.1	2.23	1.30
VT	16.2	12.0	3.28	2.43
VA	121.4	126.1	1.92	2.04
WA	105.2	91.9	1.95	1.60
WV	13.1	12.9	2.48	2.61
WI	235.9	220.8	1.72	1.58
WY	5.9	3.8	3.49	3.62
U.S.	6,433.2	7,048.7	2.14	2.34

Source: Data from Bureau of the Census, *1985 Annual Survey of Manufactures* (M85(AS)-5).

Appendix B: Detailed State Tables

Note: The states are arranged by census regions and divisions:

Region	Division	Table
United States, total		B–1
Northeast	New England	B–2 to B–7
Northeast	Middle Atlantic	B–8 to B–10
North Central	East North Central	B–11 to B–15
North Central	West North Central	B–16 to B–22
South	South Atlantic	B–23 to B–31
South	East South Central	B–32 to B–35
South	West South Central	B–36 to B–39
West	Mountain	B–40 to B–47
West	Pacific	B–48 to B–52

Appendix Table B–1
United States: Basic Economic Data on Food Manufacturing Industries, 1963, 1972, 1982, and 1985

INDUSTRY 1/	1982 Totals				Growth Rates					
	EST	EMP	VA	VS	EST	EMP		VS		
					1963-1982	1963-1972	1972-1982	1963-1972	1972-1982	1982-1985
	No.	'00	$ million		- - - - - - - - - - Percent - - - - - - - - - -					
Meatpacking	1780	1344	5825	44854	-40.5	-12.9	-14.7	85.0	95.0	-5.1
Meat processing	1311	655	2901	12278	-2.2	19.5	-88.8	117.5	165.0	1.0
Poultry dressing	375	1044	1880	9045	-45.0	31.5	34.8	71.5	178.0	14.3
Poultry processing	157	133	397	1427			-9.6		142.7	28.9
Butter	74	22	136	1687	-90.3	-66.7	-45.0	-18.3	108.7	-6.8
Cheese	704	296	1777	10763	-38.1	40.0	17.5	172.9	236.9	2.8
Processed milk	204	122	1448	4731	-27.4	0.0	-0.8	77.8	183.6	11.8
Ice cream	552	178	910	2855	-48.9	-28.7	-15.6	15.6	129.4	21.8
Fluid milk	1190	782	4089	18736	-74.2	-31.9	-40.0	33.7	99.4	5.0
Canned specialties	198	234	1769	4141	14.5	-15.5	-19.6	60.5	120.7	16.0
Canned fruit & veg.	715	705	3553	9283	-50.0	-12.3	-21.5	47.4	129.6	18.5
Dry fruit & veg.	151	136	792	1745	-14.2	34.8	9.7	90.6	187.4	2.5
Sauces, pickles	376	220	1737	4269	-36.1	9.5	5.8	72.3	265.9	20.0
Frozen fruit & veg.	264	477	2409	5375	0.5	56.6	11.5	144.4	190.7	8.0
Frozen specialties	389	424	2094	5061			10.7		161.4	28.6
Flour	360	151	1094	4933	-41.7	-27.7	-6.2	9.3	107.3	5.5
Breakfast foods	52	156	3623	4132	8.3	13.2	20.9	80.1	267.1	38.4
Rice	68	56	380	1934	-8.1	-7.0	40.0	60.9	184.1	-18.3
Flour mixes	111	68	609	1419	-32.7	9.7	-13.9	62.4	101.4	15.2
Wet corn mills	42	95	1157	3268	-30.0	-8.3	-21.5	33.7	292.7	28.2
Pet foods	285	174	2281	4402	-18.5	6.8	21.7	65.9	214.0	20.5
Animal feeds	1827	375	2188	11298			-14.8		124.3	-7.9
Bread, rolls	2305	1709	7861	13143	-54.0	-18.0	-11.7	36.1	114.3	9.6
Cookies & crackers	358	456	2789	4665	0.6	-4.6	10.9	53.4	164.5	38.2
Cane sugar	81	158	920	4154	-18.2	-13.0	-12.2	30.3	93.3	-8.9
Beet sugar	48	103	432	1516	-26.2	17.7	-10.4	56.0	72.2	18.0
Confectionary	904	697	4882	9906	-28.4	-0.4	-10.2	100.3	129.1	16.2
Cottonseed oil	77	52	203	933	-59.0	-34.5	-5.5	-17.4	103.5	-5.6
Soybean oil	114	89	678	8604	11.8	40.0	-2.2	127.9	156.3	0.3
Other fats & oils	415	121	643	2309	-37.3	-21.5	-5.5	44.8	125.2	3.3
Cooking oil & marg.	118	125	1262	4906	2.6	-4.4	-3.1	56.2	137.2	14.3
Beer	109	430	4535	11183	-50.9	-16.1	-16.5	75.1	175.8	9.2
Wine & brandy	366	118	997	2786	64.9	54.1	25.5	222.4	222.0	-0.8
Spirits	104	122	1460	3126	-2.8	2.2	-33.7	64.9	73.9	11.8
Soft drinks	1626	1138	6856	16808	-58.4	13.3	2.2	146.7	208.2	15.2
Flavorings	343	116	2670	4237	-34.0	11.0	14.9	101.7	187.8	14.2
Canned fish	204	139	613	1849	-49.6	-7.5	-13.1	79.0	128.3	-62.3
Frozen fish	783	375	967	4010	43.1	24:4	50.0	177.2	269.7	-1.6
Coffee	152	118	2070	5827	-53.1	-25.0	-8.5	24.7	150.2	14.6
Pasta	230	84	551	1065	4.1	0.0	15.1	56.3	205.8	8.5
Miscellaneous foods	2608	881	5982	11870	-24.0	11.5	19.7	89.7	197.5	15.5
Total	22130	14877	88419	280529	-41.0	-4.5	-5.2	68.1	143.8	7.5

Source: Data from Bureau of the Census reports.

Note: Industries are listed by four-digit SIC code, see Appendix C for definitions of terms.

E = Estimated. EST = Establishments. EMP = Employment. VA = Value added. VS = Value of shipments.

Appendix Table B–2
Maine: Basic Economic Data on Food Manufacturing Industries, 1963, 1972, 1982, and 1985

INDUSTRY 1/	1982 Totals EST	EMP	VA	VS	Growth Rates EST 1963-1982	EMP 1963-1972	EMP 1972-1982	VS 1963-1972	VS 1972-1982	VS 1982-1985
	No.	'00	$ million		– – – – – – – – – Percent – – – – – – – – –					
Meatpacking	6E	P	0.4	2	-66.7	0.0	-90.0	-36.2	-59.1	
Meat processing	4	3	12E	55E	-33.3	200.0	0.0	198.2	237.8	
Poultry dressing	4	7	28E	129E	} -55.6	} 40.0	} -66.7	} 61.1	} 40.4	
Poultry processing	0E	0	0	0						
Butter	0E	0	0	0	-100.0	-100.0	0.0	-100.0	0.0	
Cheese	4E	Z	1	4	300.0	100.0	-75.0	-25.0	500.0	
Processed milk	1E	P	0.2	1	inf.	0.0	inf.	0.0	inf.	
Ice cream	4E	Z	1	4	-50.0	-95.0	400.0	-91.8	500.0	
Fluid milk	18	6	26	115	-71.9	0.0	-50.0	57.1	60.8	
Canned specialties	2	3	20E	42E	0.0	-25.0	0.0	-28.0	216.4	
Canned fruit & veg.	6	2	13E	28E	-73.9	-57.1	-33.3	52.3	111.2	
Dry fruit & veg.	0E	0	0	0	0.0	0.0	0.0	0.0	0.0	
Sauces, pickles	2E	Z	3	7	0.0	0.0	-50.0	1025.0	57.8	
Frozen fruit & veg.	12	21	55	127	} 27.3	} 9.5	} -8.7	} 115.0	} 73.3	
Frozen specialties	2E	Z	3	7						
Flour	4E	Z	3	14	inf.	0.0	inf.	0.0	inf.	
Breakfast foods	0E	0	0	0	0.0	0.0	0.0	0.0	0.0	
Rice	0E	0	0	0	0.0	0.0	0.0	0.0	0.0	
Flour mixes	1E	P	1	3	inf.	0.0	0.0	0.0	inf.	
Wet corn mills	0E	0	0	0	-100.0	0.0	-100.0	19.0	-100.0	
Pet foods	1E	Z	3	14	} -11.1	} 100.0	} -25.0	} -16.1	} 81.7	
Animal feeds	7E	1	6	28						
Bread, rolls	18	17	64	117	-60.0	-25.0	13.3	29.0	115.7	
Cookies & crackers	0	0	0	0	0.0	0.0	0.0	0.0	0.0	
Cane sugar	0E	0	0	0	0.0	0.0	0.0	0.0	0.0	
Beet sugar	0E	0	0	0	0.0	0.0	0.0	0.0	0.0	
Confectionary	3E	Z	3	6	-25.0	0.0	0.0	81.8	210.0	
Cottonseed oil	0E	0	0	0	0.0	0.0	0.0	0.0	0.0	
Soybean oil	0E	0	0	0	0.0	0.0	0.0	0.0	0.0	
Other fats & oils	3E	Z	3	8	-66.7	0.0	-75.0	266.7	-38.6	
Cooking oil & marg.	0E	0	0	0	0.0	inf.	-100.0	inf.	-100.0	
Beer	0E	0	0	0	0.0	0.0	0.0	0.0	0.0	
Wine & brandy	1E	Z	3	6	inf.	0.0	inf.	0.0	inf.	
Spirits	0E	0	0	0	-100.0	-100.0	0.0	-100.0	0.0	
Soft drinks	12	7	35E	89E	-70.7	-40.0	133.3	53.2	360.6	
Flavorings	1E	Z	3	6	-66.7	0.0	0.0	-20.0	100.0	
Canned fish	18	10	32	69	-55.0	0.0	-28.6	63.3	93.3	
Frozen fish	20	7	7	55	66.7	33.3	-12.5	57.3	200.0	
Coffee	0E	0	0	0	0.0	-80.0	0.0	-50.0	100.0	
Pasta	1	P	0.3	1	inf.	0.0	inf.	0.0	inf.	
Miscellaneous foods	14	3	9	19	-6.7	0.0	0.0	48.3	112.8	
Total	167	92	331	948	-51.0	0.9	-22.0	51.5	92.4	-11.9

Source: Data from Bureau of the Census reports.

Note: Industries are listed by four-digit SIC code, see Appendix C for definitions of terms.

EST = Establishments. EMP = Employment. VA = Value added. VS = Value of shipments. inf. = Infinity. P = Less than 20. Z = 20 to 99.

Appendix Table B–3
New Hampshire: Basic Economic Data on Food Manufacturing Industries, 1963, 1972, 1982, and 1985

INDUSTRY 1/	1982 Totals				Growth Rates					
	EST	EMP	VA	VS	EST	EMP		VS		
					1963–1982	1963–1972	1972–1982	1963–1972	1972–1982	1982–1985
	No.	'00	$ million		- - - - - - - - - - - Percent - - - - - - - - - - -					
Meatpacking	6	4	12E	85E	50.0	50.0	33.3	2400.0	126.7	
Meat processing	4	3	9E	64E	-60.0	-33.3	50.0	52.4	154.8	
Poultry dressing	0	0	0	0	-100.0	-100.0	0.0	-100.0	0.0	
Poultry processing	0	0	0	0						
Butter	0E	0	0	0	0.0	0.0	0.0	0.0	0.0	
Cheese	1E	P	0.3	2	0.0	400.0	-80.0	100.0	28.6	
Processed milk	0E	0	0	0	0.0	0.0	0.0	0.0	0.0	
Ice cream	1E	P	0.3	2	-83.3	0.0	-80.0	-22.2	28.6	
Fluid milk	9	3	10E	55	-83.6	-50.0	-40.0	-23.2	86.6	
Canned specialties	0E	0	0	0	-100.0	0.0	-100.0	39.1	-100.0	
Canned fruit & veg.	2E	Z	3	7	-33.3	0.0	0.0	76.9	187.0	
Dry fruit & veg.	0	0	0	0	0.0	0.0	0.0	0.0	0.0	
Sauces, pickles	1E	P	1	2	inf.	0.0	inf.	0.0	inf.	
Frozen fruit & veg.	0E	0	0	0	-100.0	0.0	-100.0	33.3	-100.0	
Frozen specialties	0E	0	0	0						
Flour	1E	D	1	3	inf.	0.0	inf.	0.0	inf.	
Breakfast foods	0E	0	0	0	0.0	0.0	0.0	0.0	0.0	
Rice	0E	0	0	0	0.0	0.0	0.0	0.0	0.0	
Flour mixes	0E	0	0	0	0.0	0.0	0.0	0.0	0.0	
Wet corn mills	0E	0	0	0	0.0	0.0	0.0	0.0	0.0	
Pet foods	0E	0	0	0	-60.0	0.0	100.0	-5.0	429.8	
Animal feeds	2E	2	12	60						
Bread, rolls	16	2	6E	11E	-36.0	-20.0	-50.0	15.5	-13.4	
Cookies & crackers	1	P	0.3E	1E	inf.	0.0	inf.	0.0	inf.	
Cane sugar	0E	0	0	0	0.0	0.0	0.0	0.0	0.0	
Beet sugar	0E	0	0	0	0.0	0.0	0.0	0.0	0.0	
Confectionary	2E	P	1	1	100.0	0.0	0.0	250.0	71.4	
Cottonseed oil	0E	0	0	0	0.0	0.0	0.0	0.0	0.0	
Soybean oil	0E	0	0	0	0.0	0.0	0.0	0.0	0.0	
Other fats & oils	0E	0	0	0	-100.0	-100.0	0.0	-100.0	0.0	
Cooking oil & marg.	0E	0	0	0	0.0	0.0	0.0	0.0	0.0	
Beer	1	6	88E	197E	inf.	inf.	100.0	inf.	404.1	
Wine & brandy	2E	P	2	3	inf.	0.0	inf.	0.0	inf.	
Spirits	1E	P	2	3	0.0	0.0	0.0	116.7	153.8	
Soft drinks	5	3	44E	98E	-75.0	-20.0	-25.0	273.3	89.4	
Flavorings	1E	P	2	3	-50.0	0.0	0.0	62.5	153.8	
Canned fish	0E	0	0	0	0.0	0.0	0.0	0.0	0.0	
Frozen fish	5	2	5E	21E	25.0	500.0	-33.3	1200.0	64.6	
Coffee	0E	0	0	0	-100.0	0.0	-100.0	63.6	-100.0	
Pasta	1E	P	1	1	inf.	inf.	0.0	inf.	160.0	
Miscellaneous foods	5E	1	7	14	-37.5	20.0	83.3	-52.9	1650.0	
Total	67	25	188	587	-55.3	-3.4	-10.7	120.3	153.1	6.5

Source: Data from Bureau of the Census reports.

Note: Industries are listed by four-digit SIC code, see Appendix C for definitions of terms.

EST = Establishments. EMP = Employment. VA = Value added. VS = Value of shipments. inf. = Infinity. P = Less than 20. Z = 20 to 99.

Appendix Table B–4
Vermont: Basic Economic Data on Food Manufacturing Industries, 1963, 1972, 1982, and 1985

INDUSTRY 1/	1982 Totals				Growth Rates					
	EST	EMP	VA	VS	EST	EMP		VS		
					1963-1982	1963-1972	1972-1982	1963-1972	1972-1982	1982-1985
	No.	'00	$ million		- - - - - - - - - - Percent - - - - - - - - - -					
Meatpacking	7	1	4E	27E	0.0	100.0	0.0	329.4	87.0	
Meat processing	0	0	0	0	0.0	0.0	0.0	0.0	0.0	
Poultry dressing	0	0	0	0	-100.0	100.0	-100.0	162.5	-100.0	
Poultry processing	0	0	0	0						
Butter	2E	Z	1	9	inf.	inf.	400.0	inf.	683.3	
Cheese	9	4	34	172	-10.0	0.0	100.0	54.2	626.7	
Processed milk	1	Z	1	9	0.0	0.0	400.0	500.0	683.3	
Ice cream	2E	1	3	19	100.0	0.0	900.0	500.0	1466.7	
Fluid milk	15	6	16E	113E	-73.7	-30.0	-14.3	-5.3	87.4	
Canned specialties	0	0	0	0	0.0	0.0	0.0	0.0	0.0	
Canned fruit & veg.	2E	Z	3	7	100.0	0.0	400.0	66.7	1220.0	
Dry fruit & veg.	0	0	0	0	0.0	0.0	0.0	0.0	0.0	
Sauces, pickles	0	0	0	0	0.0	0.0	0.0	0.0	0.0	
Frozen fruit & veg.	0	0	0	0	0.0	0.0	0.0	0.0	0.0	
Frozen specialties	0	0	0	0						
Flour	0	0	0	0	0.0	0.0	0.0	0.0	0.0	
Breakfast foods	0	0	0	0	-100.0	-100.0	0.0	-100.0	0.0	
Rice	0	0	0	0	0.0	0.0	0.0	0.0	0.0	
Flour mixes	0	0	0	0	0.0	0.0	0.0	0.0	0.0	
Wet corn mills	0	0	0	0	0.0	0.0	0.0	0.0	0.0	
Pet foods	0	0	0	0	-10.0	-33.3	-25.0	44.8	69.2	
Animal feeds	9	3	12	104						
Bread, rolls	9	3	14E	23E	-35.7	-25.0	0.0	20.3	143.2	
Cookies & crackers	1	P	1E	1E	inf.	0.0	inf.	0.0	inf.	
Cane sugar	0E	0	0	0	0.0	0.0	0.0	0.0	0.0	
Beet sugar	0E	0	0	0	0.0	0.0	0.0	0.0	0.0	
Confectionary	5E	P	1	1	150.0	0.0	-80.0	81.8	-40.0	
Cottonseed oil	0E	0	0	0	0.0	0.0	0.0	0.0	0.0	
Soybean oil	0E	0	0	0	0.0	0.0	0.0	0.0	0.0	
Other fats & oils	2E	Z	3	8	100.0	0.0	0.0	94.1	145.5	
Cooking oil & marg.	0E	0	0	0	0.0	0.0	0.0	0.0	0.0	
Beer	0	0	0	0	0.0	0.0	0.0	0.0	0.0	
Wine & brandy	0	0	0	0	0.0	0.0	0.0	0.0	0.0	
Spirits	0	0	0	0	0.0	0.0	0.0	0.0	0.0	
Soft drinks	6	3	12	27	-57.1	-50.0	200.0	9.8	502.2	
Flavorings	0	0	0	0	0.0	0.0	0.0	0.0	0.0	
Canned fish	0E	0	0	0	0.0	0.0	0.0	0.0	0.0	
Frozen fish	0E	0	0	0	0.0	0.0	0.0	0.0	0.0	
Coffee	0E	0	0	0	0.0	0.0	0.0	0.0	0.0	
Pasta	0E	0	0	0	0.0	0.0	0.0	0.0	0.0	
Miscellaneous foods	7E	1	4	7	-41.7	-45.5	0.0	-11.8	140.0	
Total	77	23	93	502	-41.7	-25.9	15.0	28.8	163.5	-1.8

Source: Data from Bureau of the Census reports.

Note: Industries are listed by four-digit SIC code, see Appendix C for definitions of terms.

EST = Establishments. EMP = Employment. VA = Value added. VS = Value of shipments. inf. = Infinity. P = Less than 20. Z = 20 to 99.

Appendix Table B–5
Massachusetts: Basic Economic Data on Food Manufacturing Industries, 1963, 1972, 1982, and 1985

INDUSTRY 1/	1982 Totals				Growth Rates					
	EST	EMP	VA	VS	EST	EMP		VS		
					1963–1982	1963–1972	1972–1982	1963–1972	1972–1982	1982–1985
	No.	'00	$ million		– – – – – – – – – – Percent – – – – – – – – – –					
Meatpacking	12	7	26E	112E	-52.0	-33.3	250.0	-58.8	690.8	
Meat processing	47	17	66	247	-26.6	-5.6	-50.0	67.3	-18.6	
Poultry dressing	3E	P	0.4	2	-70.0	-33.3	-95.0	5.2	-88.7	
Poultry processing	0E	0	0	0						
Butter	1E	P	0.4	2	0.0	400.0	-80.0	275.0	-26.7	
Cheese	3	Z	2	11E	-50.0	0.0	-50.0	-7.6	70.8	
Processed milk	1E	P	0.4	2	0.0	400.0	-80.0	275.0	-26.7	
Ice cream	35	11	46	244E	-34.0	35.7	-42.1	70.9	93.3	
Fluid milk	45	28	137	610	-80.0	-38.6	-20.0	8.4	131.5	
Canned specialties	1E	Z	2	5	-66.7	0.0	-75.0	1.1	-50.5	
Canned fruit & veg.	9	3	12	42	-60.9	-33.3	-50.0	17.4	13.2	
Dry fruit & veg.	1E	Z	2	5	0.0	0.0	400.0	66.7	820.0	
Sauces, pickles	10	3	27	61	0.0	0.0	0.0	30.8	335.7	
Frozen fruit & veg.	2E	1	3	9	0.0	50.0	0.0	81.7	156.0	
Frozen specialties	12	2	6E	19E						
Flour	4E	Z	3	8	300.0	0.0	400.0	-30.0	1014.3	
Breakfast foods	3	2	10E	31E	200.0	0.0	0.0	2.7	131.1	
Rice	0E	0	0	0	0.0	0.0	0.0	0.0	0.0	
Flour mixes	2	Z	3	8E	-50.0	-95.0	400.0	-94.2	1014.3	
Wet corn mills	0	0	0	0	-100.0	-100.0	0.0	-100.0	0.0	
Pet foods	3E	Z	3	8	-52.2	-20.0	-62.5	3.8	-22.0	
Animal feeds	8	1	5	16						
Bread, rolls	94	51	230	373	-57.3	-29.9	-16.4	24.8	80.4	
Cookies & crackers	15	2	7	13	66.7	-36.4	-71.4	-15.7	-47.3	
Cane sugar	3	7	39E	197E	50.0	0.0	0.0	10.3	148.1	
Beet sugar	0	0	0	0	0.0	0.0	0.0	0.0	0.0	
Confectionary	46	27	111	274	-16.4	-31.7	-34.1	1.3	68.7	
Cottonseed oil	0	0	0	0	0.0	0.0	0.0	0.0	0.0	
Soybean oil	1	P	1E	1E	inf.	inf.	-80.0	inf.	-36.4	
Other fats & oils	5	2	11E	28E	-66.7	-33.3	-50.0	6.1	62.6	
Cooking oil & marg.	0	0	0	0	-100.0	400.0	-100.0	120.0	-100.0	
Beer	1	Z	3	9	-83.3	-14.3	-91.7	50.2	-77.6	
Wine & brandy	2	Z	3	9	inf.	0.0	inf.	0.0	inf.	
Spirits	5	3	19E	52E	66.7	-14.3	-50.0	-8.3	34.7	
Soft drinks	41	20	113	366	-65.3	4.2	-20.0	190.1	144.3	
Flavorings	8	7	44E	122E	-61.9	50.0	133.3	118.0	529.9	
Canned fish	6	Z	3E	7E	-45.5	-33.3	-75.0	80.3	-35.5	
Frozen fish	74	42	137	642	32.1	11.5	44.8	118.0	253.2	
Coffee	4	2	11E	28E	-69.2	-100.0	-33.3	-32.9	38.2	
Pasta	13	7	37E	99E	-23.5	0.0	133.3	79.3	498.8	
Miscellaneous foods	50	12	44	105	-47.4	-30.0	-24.8	31.0	29.3	
Total	570	260	1161	3764	-48.6	-20.2	-20.5	32.6	98.0	7.8

Source: Data from Bureau of the Census reports.

Note: Industries are listed by four-digit SIC code, see Appendix C for definitions of terms.

EST = Establishments. EMP = Employment. VA = Value added. VS = Value of shipments. inf. = Infinity. P = Less than 20. Z = 20 to 99.

Appendix Table B-6
Rhode Island: Basic Economic Data on Food Manufacturing Industries, 1963, 1972, 1982, and 1985

INDUSTRY 1/	EST No.	EMP '00	VA $ million	VS	EST 1963-1982	EMP 1963-1972	EMP 1972-1982	VS 1963-1972	VS 1972-1982	VS 1982-1985
Meatpacking	2E	P	0.2	1	-33.3	300.0	-95.0	758.8	-95.9	
Meat processing	10	2	5E	24E	-9.1	100.0	100.0	263.6	203.8	
Poultry dressing	0E	0	0	0	-100.0	-100.0	0.0	-100.0	0.0	
Poultry processing	0E	0	0	0						
Butter	0E	0	0	0	0.0	0.0	0.0	0.0	0.0	
Cheese	1E	Z	3	10	inf.	inf.	0.0	inf.	209.4	
Processed milk	0E	0	0	0	0.0	0.0	0.0	0.0	0.0	
Ice cream	5	Z	3E	10	-64.3	-75.0	0.0	-47.5	209.4	
Fluid milk	9	2	11E	40E	-79.1	-25.0	-77.8	16.0	-12.2	
Canned specialties	0E	0	0	0	-100.0	-100.0	0.0	-100.0	0.0	
Canned fruit & veg.	2	Z	3E	13E	-60.0	400.0	0.0	666.7	473.9	
Dry fruit & veg.	0E	0	0	0	0.0	0.0	0.0	0.0	0.0	
Sauces, pickles	0E	0	0	0	-100.0	-100.0	0.0	-100.0	0.0	
Frozen fruit & veg.	2E	Z	3	6	inf.	inf.	0.0	inf.	146.8	
Frozen specialties	2E	Z	3	6						
Flour	0E	0	0	0	-100.0	-100.0	0.0	-100.0	0.0	
Breakfast foods	0E	0	0	0	0.0	0.0	0.0	0.0	0.0	
Rice	0E	0	0	0	0.0	0.0	0.0	0.0	0.0	
Flour mixes	0E	0	0	0	-100.0	-100.0	0.0	-100.0	0.0	
Wet corn mills	0E	0	0	0	0.0	0.0	0.0	0.0	0.0	
Pet foods	0E	0	0	0	-50.0	-80.0	0.0	-69.4	172.7	
Animal feeds	2E	P	1	3						
Bread, rolls	20	5	19	36	-64.3	-33.3	-64.3	54.4	-42.2	
Cookies & crackers	0	0	0	0	-100.0	-80.0	-100.0	-69.2	-100.0	
Cane sugar	0	0	0	0	0.0	0.0	0.0	0.0	0.0	
Beet sugar	0	0	0	0	0.0	0.0	0.0	0.0	0.0	
Confectionary	5	3	18E	38E	0.0	75.0	-57.1	213.2	31.6	
Cottonseed oil	0	0	0	0	0.0	0.0	0.0	0.0	0.0	
Soybean oil	0	0	0	0	0.0	0.0	0.0	0.0	0.0	
Other fats & oils	0	0	0	0	-100.0	-80.0	-100.0	-76.5	-100.0	
Cooking oil & marg.	1	2	20E	79	0.0	300.0	0.0	83.7	772.2	
Beer	2	Z	5E	13E	100.0	-25.0	-91.7	11.8	-60.7	
Wine & brandy	3E	P	1	2	inf.	inf.	0.0	inf.	300.0	
Spirits	0E	0	0	0	0.0	0.0	0.0	0.0	0.0	
Soft drinks	8	2	12E	30E	-70.4	-25.0	-33.3	98.8	78.8	
Flavorings	0E	0	0	0	-100.0	-80.0	-100.0	-85.0	-100.0	
Canned fish	2E	Z	1	4	inf.	inf.	400.0	inf.	760.0	
Frozen fish	13	4	9	31	160.0	0.0	300.0	126.3	623.3	
Coffee	1E	P	0.2	1	inf.	0.0	inf.	0.0	inf.	
Pasta	2E	P	0.2	1	100.0	0.0	0.0	66.7	80.0	
Miscellaneous foods	14	3	10	19	-12.5	-16.0	19.0	55.6	72.3	
Total	110	26	118	352	-48.8	-16.7	-48.0	26.4	60.4	6.2

Source: Data from Bureau of the Census reports.

Note: Industries are listed by four-digit SIC codes, see Appendix C for definitions of terms.

EST = Establishments. EMP = Employment. VA = Value added. VS = Value of shipments. inf. = Infinity. P = Less than 20. Z = 20 to 99.

Appendix Table B-7
Connecticut: Basic Economic Data on Food Manufacturing Industries, 1963, 1972, 1982, and 1985

INDUSTRY 1/	1982 Totals				Growth Rates					
	EST	EMP	VA	VS	EST	EMP		VS		
					1963-1982	1963-1972	1972-1982	1963-1972	1972-1982	1982-1985
	No.	'00	$ million		- - - - - - - - - - Percent - - - - - - - - - -					
Meatpacking	8	1	2E	11E	-11.1	-66.7	-50.0	-62.4	-15.9	
Meat processing	20	4	10	44	-25.0	0.0	0.0	-14.9	89.3	
Poultry dressing	0	0	0	0	} -80.0	} -96.7	} 900.0	} -94.7	} 1485.7	
Poultry processing	1	1	2E	11E						
Butter	0	0	0	0	0.0	0.0	0.0	0.0	0.0	
Cheese	4	1	2E	6E	-42.9	100.0	0.0	78.8	1.7	
Processed milk	0	0	0	0	-100.0	-100.0	0.0	-100.0	0.0	
Ice cream	10	5	23	78	-41.2	150.0	0.0	181.4	107.4	
Fluid milk	17	10	38	170	-84.4	-31.3	-68.8	-15.1	30.0	
Canned specialties	1E	P	1	1	-50.0	0.0	0.0	100.0	10.0	
Canned fruit & veg.	5	1	6E	12E	-44.4	0.0	0.0	31.2	13.9	
Dry fruit & veg.	1	2	12E	23E	inf.	inf.	1900.0	inf.	2190.0	
Sauces, pickles	2E	P	1	1	-66.7	-80.0	0.0	-44.4	10.0	
Frozen fruit & veg.	1E	P	1	1	} 125.0	} 320.0	} 333.3	} 266.7	} 2000.0	
Frozen specialties	8	9	57	114						
Flour	2E	P	1	3	inf.	inf.	0.0	inf.	120.0	
Breakfast foods	0E	0	0	0	0.0	0.0	0.0	0.0	0.0	
Rice	0E	0	0	0	0.0	0.0	0.0	0.0	0.0	
Flour mixes	0E	0	0	0	0.0	0.0	0.0	0.0	0.0	
Wet corn mills	0E	0	0	0	0.0	0.0	0.0	0.0	0.0	
Pet foods	1E	P	1	3	} 0.0	} -40.0	} 0.0	} -5.6	} 162.7	
Animal feeds	4	Z	3E	15E						
Bread, rolls	44	40	157	303	-56.0	25.8	2.6	109.8	145.5	
Cookies & crackers	0	0	0	0	-100.0	0.0	-100.0	33.3	-100.0	
Cane sugar	0	0	0	0	0.0	0.0	0.0	0.0	0.0	
Beet sugar	0	0	0	0	0.0	0.0	0.0	0.0	0.0	
Confectionary	11	6	59E	91E	37.5	131.4	-24.7	250.5	173.9	
Cottonseed oil	0	0	0	0	0.0	0.0	0.0	0.0	0.0	
Soybean oil	0	0	0	0	0.0	0.0	0.0	0.0	0.0	
Other fats & oils	1	Z	3E	8E	-66.7	-50.0	0.0	0.0	145.5	
Cooking oil & marg.	0	0	0	0	0.0	0.0	0.0	0.0	0.0	
Beer	0	0	0	0	-100.0	-100.0	0.0	-100.0	0.0	
Wine & brandy	0	0	0	0	0.0	0.0	0.0	0.0	0.0	
Spirits	1	3	38E	72E	-66.7	0.0	0.0	47.3	167.2	
Soft drinks	28	6	77E	143E	-55.6	-30.8	-33.3	170.7	78.1	
Flavorings	5	2	26E	48E	-16.7	300.0	0.0	347.5	166.5	
Canned fish	3E	P	0.4	1	200.0	400.0	-80.0	110.0	-38.1	
Frozen fish	1	2	5E	21E	inf.	inf.	100.0	inf.	422.0	
Coffee	2E	P	2	5	-50.0	0.0	-80.0	50.0	133.3	
Pasta	4	P	1	1	0.0	-75.0	-80.0	-65.6	-38.1	
Miscellaneous foods	14	3	15E	30E	-17.6	28.6	-44.4	91.8	58.6	
Total	199	95	546	1218	-51.5	-7.9	-9.5	29.6	119.3	30.6

Source: Data from Bureau of the Census reports.

Note: Industries are listed by four-digit SIC code, see Appendix C for definitions of terms.

EST = Establishments. EMP = Employment. VA = Value added. VS = Value of shipments. inf. = Infinity. P = Less than 20. Z = 20 to 99.

Appendix Table B-8
New York: Basic Economic Data on Food Manufacturing Industries, 1963, 1972, 1982, and 1985

INDUSTRY 1/	EST	EMP	VA	VS	EST 1963-1982	EMP 1963-1972	EMP 1972-1982	VS 1963-1972	VS 1972-1982	VS 1982-1985
	No.	'00	$ million		---	---	Percent	---	---	---
Meatpacking	44	9	47	292	-55.6	-29.3	-69.0	13.2	3.1	
Meat processing	111	46	205	873	-42.2	-18.6	-19.3	37.6	101.8	
Poultry dressing	9	6	14	42						
					-55.6	16.7	-35.7	58.4	21.3	
Poultry processing	7	3	10	31						
Butter	3	2	9E	60	-62.5	-80.0	1900.0	-73.2	5309.1	
Cheese	35	21	101	590	-32.7	0.0	75.0	121.7	363.1	
Processed milk	20	5	41	304	0.0	16.7	-28.6	114.4	209.9	
Ice cream	48	17	75E	208E	-42.9	-29.4	-29.2	-1.9	53.3	
Fluid milk	105	44	232	1046	-79.3	-42.8	-47.0	7.9	45.6	
Canned specialties	11	11	84	156	-38.9	-44.4	-21.4	22.3	1.4	
Canned fruit & veg.	49	44	311	764	-62.9	-32.9	-6.4	28.5	196.0	
Dry fruit & veg.	4	2	9E	21E	-69.2	120.0	-81.8	235.3	-63.3	
Sauces, pickles	41	7	30	75E	-32.8	30.8	-58.8	118.3	-34.7	
Frozen fruit & veg.	10	11	54	137						
					-13.8	33.3	36.0	148.8	166.8	
Frozen specialties	40	23	216	426						
Flour	17	9	63	389	-26.1	-52.6	0.0	-16.9	111.2	
Breakfast foods	4	7	113E	170E	0.0	25.0	-53.3	53.2	69.0	
Rice	0	0	0	0	0.0	0.0	0.0	0.0	0.0	
Flour mixes	6	3	48E	73E	-60.0	-28.6	-40.0	64.3	72.2	
Wet corn mills	3	7	113E	170E	300.0	-100.0	inf.	-100.0	inf.	
Pet foods	14	10	201	300						
					-26.7	-35.5	-10.0	1.3	162.1	
Animal feeds	52	8	37	273						
Bread, rolls	288	130	617	1034	-54.1	-41.2	-54.2	-10.1	102.3	
Cookies & crackers	41	16	71	120	-6.8	-48.0	23.1	-19.4	187.7	
Cane sugar	6	16	160	611	150.0	-43.2	-5.9	-26.0	273.6	
Beet sugar	0	0	0	0	0.0	inf.	-100.0	inf.	-100.0	
Confectionary	71	35	307	572	-43.2	-45.7	-49.3	77.9	36.6	
Cottonseed oil	0	0	0	0	-100.0	-100.0	0.0	-100.0	0.0	
Soybean oil	1E	P	1	2	-66.7	0.0	0.0	228.6	-4.3	
Other fats & oils	7	3	22E	65E	-75.0	-50.5	-40.0	-3.5	137.6	
Cooking oil & marg.	6	3	22E	65E	20.0	0.0	0.0	129.9	-3.7	
Beer	10	28	246E	600E	-37.5	-22.2	-55.6	38.7	53.3	
Wine & brandy	32	15	132E	321E	18.5	60.0	-6.3	150.2	155.7	
Spirits	0	0	0	0	-100.0	-33.3	-100.0	8.2	-100.0	
Soft drinks	89	51	416	1071	-64.7	-6.5	-28.2	179.7	140.4	
Flavorings	38	6	317	395	-51.9	-29.4	-50.0	33.5	134.8	
Canned fish	10	3	11	51	-63.0	-14.3	-50.0	11.1	36.9	
Frozen fish	16	3	13	41	-36.0	66.7	-40.0	117.6	51.5	
Coffee	17	6	54	236	-55.3	-50.0	-14.3	-38.0	150.2	
Pasta	38	12	66	133	2.7	-12.5	-14.3	42.4	114.3	
Miscellaneous foods	131	41	243	521	-45.0	2.0	-18.0	30.7	99.3	
Total	1434	662	4703	12237	-52.1	-28.3	-28.3	25.9	100.9	2.4

Source: Data from Bureau of the Census reports.

Note: Industries are listed by four-digit SIC code, see Appendix C for definitions of terms.

EST = Establishments. EMP = Employment. VA = Value added. VS = Value of shipments. inf. = Infinity. P = Less than 20. Z = 20 to 99.

Appendix Table B–9
New Jersey: Basic Economic Data on Food Manufacturing Industries, 1963, 1972, 1982, and 1985

INDUSTRY 1/	1982 Totals				Growth Rates						
	EST	EMP	VA	VS	EST	EMP			VS		
					1963–1982	1963–1972	1972–1982	1963–1972	1972–1982	1982–1985
	No.	'00	$ million		- - - - - - - - - - Percent - - - - - - - - - -						
Meatpacking	9	3	13	136	-79.5	-53.6	-76.9	-6.2	-50.4	
Meat processing	54	29	128	566	-14.3	50.0	-3.3	145.5	183.8	
Poultry dressing	6	9	12	48	-33.3	50.0	77.8	122.0	334.5	
Poultry processing	6	7	26	114						
Butter	1E	P	1	2	-50.0	400.0	-80.0	412.5	-43.9	
Cheese	14	4	19	140	75.0	200.0	33.3	172.5	464.1	
Processed milk	1E	P	1	2	-50.0	400.0	-80.0	412.5	-43.9	
Ice cream	26	5	33E	117E	-18.8	-45.5	-16.7	-13.2	250.0	
Fluid milk	24	17	133	516	-83.7	-61.5	-15.0	-3.2	152.1	
Canned specialties	7	18	184E	364	-12.5	-17.9	-43.8	7.1	87.9	
Canned fruit & veg.	19	13	126	311	-55.8	8.0	-51.9	75.4	108.0	
Dry fruit & veg.	5	7	72	142E	400.0	2900.0	133.3	5966.7	678.6	
Sauces, pickles	11	7	68	171	-54.2	50.0	-53.3	26.3	88.3	
Frozen fruit & veg.	4	3	12	32	50.0	91.7	-4.3	138.4	141.5	
Frozen specialties	23	19	74	174						
Flour	2E	1	5	15	-50.0	-80.0	900.0	-77.6	1245.4	
Breakfast foods	0	0	0	0	-100.0	-100.0	0.0	-100.0	0.0	
Rice	0E	0	0	0	-100.0	-100.0	0.0	-100.0	0.0	
Flour mixes	3	2	11E	30E	-62.5	-80.0	100.0	-62.5	161.9	
Wet corn mills	0E	0	0	0	-100.0	-100.0	0.0	-100.0	0.0	
Pet foods	6	3	16E	45E	-36.7	50.0	-44.4	49.9	49.3	
Animal feeds	13	2	3	54						
Bread, rolls	102	42	345	507	-57.3	-20.7	-39.1	35.7	106.0	
Cookies & crackers	23	37	261	413	4.5	2.1	-24.5	78.9	76.2	
Cane sugar	0	0	0	0	0.0	0.0	0.0	0.0	0.0	
Beet sugar	0	0	0	0	0.0	0.0	0.0	0.0	0.0	
Confectionary	41	27	281	657	-40.6	-7.5	-27.0	64.3	248.1	
Cottonseed oil	0	0	0	0	-100.0	-100.0	0.0	-100.0	0.0	
Soybean oil	0	0	0	0	0.0	0.0	0.0	0.0	0.0	
Other fats & oils	11	5	30E	127E	-57.7	-44.4	0.0	-64.2	138.0	
Cooking oil & marg.	6	5	17	171	-45.5	-32.0	-70.6	2.6	-5.6	
Beer	7	22	222	523	-22.2	-34.9	-46.3	37.7	91.2	
Wine & brandy	4	Z	11E	18E	-66.7	0.0	-83.3	68.2	-20.3	
Spirits	7	6	131E	212E	16.7	0.0	-14.3	-10.8	461.4	
Soft drinks	37	19	189	460	-63.7	21.7	-32.1	266.2	109.6	
Flavorings	33	15	140	283	22.2	100.0	25.0	113.4	137.6	
Canned fish	9	4	11	30	-35.7	-22.2	-42.9	74.1	18.5	
Frozen fish	11	2	16E	27E	-8.3	0.0	-33.3	174.4	156.1	
Coffee	12	27	475	1191	-40.0	2.9	-25.0	39.5	87.1	
Pasta	8	7	54E	96E	0.0	-16.7	0.0	-56.5	796.3	
Miscellaneous foods	74	24	150	346	-16.9	-4.4	-2.1	40.9	111.9	
Total	621	391	3266	8041	-44.7	-12.1	-27.2	34.4	108.9	12.7

Source: Data from Bureau of the Census reports.

Note: Industries are listed by four-digit SIC code, see Appendix C for definitions of terms.

EST = Establishments. EMP = Employment. VA = Value added. VS = Value of shipments. P = Less than 20. Z = 20 to 99.

Appendix Table B-10
Pennsylvania: Basic Economic Data on Food Manufacturing Industries, 1963, 1972, 1982, and 1985

INDUSTRY 1/	1982 Totals				Growth Rates					
	EST	EMP	VA	VS	EST	EMP		VS		
					1963-1982	1963-1972	1972-1982	1963-1972	1972-1982	1982-1985
	No.	'00	$ million		- - - - - - - - - - - Percent - - - - - - - - - - -					
Meatpacking	97	38	149	1022	-54.0	-32.0	-25.5	36.5	58.6	
Meat processing	80	47	221	907	-9.1	40.0	-4.1	182.8	109.0	
Poultry dressing	16	39	84	316	-37.5	47.8	50.0	110.3	200.8	
Poultry processing	14	12	40	174						
Butter	4	1	2	90	-66.7	-95.0	900.0	-92.7	7366.7	
Cheese	25	14	56	367	13.6	62.8	7.7	181.5	130.0	
Processed milk	8	3	38	198	-33.3	66.7	-40.0	173.8	215.2	
Ice cream	33	17	76	244	-63.7	-33.3	-15.0	21.0	94.3	
Fluid milk	108	45	214	833	-77.2	-37.4	-57.9	18.8	35.9	
Canned specialties	6	35	289	541	-40.0	53.3	-23.9	88.8	105.8	
Canned fruit & veg.	26	32	156	466	-59.4	4.8	-27.3	84.7	103.9	
Dry fruit & veg.	2	Z	4E	11E	100.0	300.0	-75.0	570.6	-0.9	
Sauces, pickles	14	15	119E	340E	-41.7	16.7	114.3	73.9	749.3	
Frozen fruit & veg.	8	7	56E	159E	5.3	137.5	-5.3	258.2	189.5	
Frozen specialties	32	29	160	337						
Flour	30	3	22	109	-31.8	-25.0	0.0	37.2	243.8	
Breakfast foods	2	7	101E	214E	-33.3	0.0	133.3	92.1	575.4	
Rice	0	0	0	0	0.0	0.0	0.0	0.0	0.0	
Flour mixes	7	3	43E	92E	0.0	-25.0	0.0	31.5	189.6	
Wet corn mills	1	3	43E	92E	-50.0	300.0	50.0	783.3	333.0	
Pet foods	20	16	174	373	-19.7	42.9	3.3	150.8	157.7	
Animal feeds	90	15	82	460						
Bread, rolls	160	111	497	803	-68.0	-34.1	-22.4	4.6	90.8	
Cookies & crackers	45	50	316	532	-26.2	2.0	-2.0	68.3	136.6	
Cane sugar	1	3	18E	38E	-50.0	0.0	-80.0	-1.9	-66.8	
Beet sugar	0	0	0	0	0.0	0.0	0.0	0.0	0.0	
Confectionary	110	133	910	1919	-35.7	107.1	-2.2	-43.5	170.4	
Cottonseed oil	0	0	0	0	-100.0	-100.0	0.0	-100.0	0.0	
Soybean oil	0	0	0	0	0.0	0.0	0.0	0.0	0.0	
Other fats & oils	19	6	33E	117E	-62.7	-36.4	-14.3	53.4	148.8	
Cooking oil & marg.	3	2	11E	39E	0.0	-50.0	100.0	-65.8	483.6	
Beer	10	23	189	415	-65.5	-20.8	-39.5	30.5	153.2	
Wine & brandy	8E	1	2	5	166.7	0.0	900.0	100.0	562.5	
Spirits	4	6	44	126	-42.9	-31.3	-45.5	-12.2	48.5	
Soft drinks	95	54	292	796	-63.2	1.8	-5.3	137.3	189.7	
Flavorings	15	4	26	49	-50.0	0.0	33.3	80.6	149.2	
Canned fish	1	Z	2E	7E	0.0	-80.0	400.0	-81.8	1016.6	
Frozen fish	12	12	65	238	50.0	250.0	-14.3	396.7	161.7	
Coffee	9	Z	2E	7E	350.0	-96.7	400.0	-98.2	1016.6	
Pasta	11	6	56	107	-26.7	0.0	-14.3	100.4	134.9	
Miscellaneous foods	99	59	359	698	-44.4	26.7	12.3	101.6	228.6	
Total	1225	851	4950	13240	-53.4	-7.8	-14.1	61.3	128.9	11.6

Source: Data from Bureau of the Census reports.

Note: Industries are listed by four-digit SIC code, see Appendix C for definitions of terms.

EST = Establishments. EMP = Employment. VA = Value added. VS = Value of shipments. P = Less than 20. Z = 20 to 99.

Appendix Table B-11
Ohio: Basic Economic Data on Food Manufacturing Industries, 1963, 1972, 1982, and 1985

INDUSTRY 1/	1982 Totals				Growth Rates					
	EST	EMP	VA	VS	EST	EMP		VS		
					1963-1982	1963-1972	1972-1982	1963-1972	1972-1982	1982-1985
	No.	'00	$ million					Percent		
Meatpacking	101	60	257	1401	-46.0	-15.2	-23.1	41.8	75.8	
Meat processing	50	32	124	433	-10.7	55.6	14.3	162.3	122.5	
Poultry dressing	15	7	9E	69E	-66.7	-8.3	-18.2	71.6	20.7	
Poultry processing	5	2	3E	20E						
Butter	2	Z	2E	9E	-80.0	-50.0	-75.0	-33.0	-55.6	
Cheese	23	9	39	207	-32.4	12.5	0.0	129.4	167.3	
Processed milk	10	11	120	387	-16.7	0.0	22.2	59.8	281.6	
Ice cream	28	8	38E	145E	-60.0	-46.2	14.3	-2.8	242.5	
Fluid milk	50	95	352	1321	-80.1	-21.1	-20.8	27.9	108.9	
Canned specialties	9	15	113E	264E	28.6	10.5	-28.6	92.6	55.5	
Canned fruit & veg.	33	28	170	472	-53.5	26.1	-3.4	125.4	145.8	
Dry fruit & veg.	3	2	15E	35	inf.	inf.	1900.0	inf.	4300.0	
Sauces, pickles	18	4	29	62	-41.9	-12.5	-42.9	205.9	9.5	
Frozen fruit & veg.	3	12	90	211	-9.5	55.5	151.5	168.5	599.8	
Frozen specialties	16	31	233E	546E						
Flour	10	4	24	171	-54.5	-20.0	0.0	14.5	112.1	
Breakfast foods	3	12	272E	508E	0.0	0.0	2300.0	114.8	8658.6	
Rice	0	0	0	0	0.0	0.0	0.0	0.0	0.0	
Flour mixes	6	4	59	121	-25.0	27.3	-71.4	146.9	-26.1	
Wet corn mills	3	3	68E	127E	-40.0	-75.0	500.0	-38.3	2089.7	
Pet foods	14	10	148	280	-28.9	4.5	-21.7	36.1	103.7	
Animal feeds	50	8	51	233						
Bread, rolls	82	71	371	592	-68.5	-14.0	-42.3	46.6	49.3	
Cookies & crackers	20	27	191	335	-33.3	-11.1	12.5	37.4	179.9	
Cane sugar	1	2	12E	22E	inf.	inf.	300.0	inf.	484.2	
Beet sugar	0	0	0	0	-100.0	66.7	-100.0	153.3	-100.0	
Confectionary	53	14	83E	156E	-34.6	19.4	-34.9	33.1	130.0	
Cottonseed oil	0	0	0	0	0.0	0.0	0.0	0.0	0.0	
Soybean oil	8	4	39	463	14.3	50.0	-33.3	-6.3	444.8	
Other fats & oils	14	3	34E	96E	-36.4	0.0	-57.1	282.9	-3.1	
Cooking oil & marg.	4	12	134E	383E	-33.3	20.0	0.0	84.4	111.5	
Beer	5	17	227E	476	-50.0	-34.8	13.3	85.1	286.8	
Wine & brandy	2E	P	1	3	-77.8	-75.0	-80.0	-78.8	-31.7	
Spirits	4	7	93E	196E	0.0	100.0	-50.0	84.8	56.9	
Soft drinks	56	64	373	816	-63.2	30.9	-11.1	143.1	188.1	
Flavorings	19	5	171	256	-40.6	33.3	25.0	149.7	253.9	
Canned fish	0	0	0	0	-100.0	0.0	-100.0	100.0	-100.0	
Frozen fish	7	2	24E	57E	40.0	50.0	-33.3	232.7	230.6	
Coffee	7	7	84E	200E	53.3	0.0	0.0	88.7	76.3	
Pasta	8	1	12E	29E	0.0	100.0	0.0	286.7	393.1	
Miscellaneous foods	108	32	197	413	-32.1	3.0	-6.2	-43.5	148.5	
Total	860	628	4260	11513	-50.2	-3.7	-14.6	61.5	136.5	14.6

Source: Data from Bureau of the Census reports.

Note: Industries are listed by four-digit SIC code, see Appendix C for definitions of terms.

EST = Establishments. EMP = Employment. VA = Value added. VS = Value of shipments. inf. = Infinity. P = Less than 20. Z = 20 to 99.

Appendix Table B–12
Indiana: Basic Economic Data on Food Manufacturing Industries, 1963, 1972, 1982, and 1985

INDUSTRY 1/	EST	EMP	VA	VS	EST 1963-1982	EMP 1963-1972	EMP 1972-1982	VS 1963-1972	VS 1972-1982	VS 1982-1985
	No.	'00	$ million		\- \- \- \- \- \- \- \- \- Percent \- \- \- \- \- \- \- \- \-					
Meatpacking	51	28	88	606	-54.5	-51.3	-24.3	-11.7	47.0	
Meat processing	21	11	40	189	-19.2	-10.0	22.2	114.0	146.1	
Poultry dressing	10	14	33	125	} -60.5	} -20.0	} 16.7	} 48.1	} 153.9	
Poultry processing	5	1	4	17						
Butter	2	1	10E	24E	-81.8	-33.3	-50.0	34.3	-30.0	
Cheese	7	4	39E	94E	-36.4	-25.0	33.3	100.6	164.4	
Processed milk	4	16	157E	378E	-50.0	50.0	433.3	277.6	646.4	
Ice cream	13	3	29E	71E	-63.9	12.5	-66.7	29.2	72.3	
Fluid milk	22	16	71	349	-77.8	-39.2	-48.4	31.6	56.5	
Canned specialties	7	17	102	252	40.0	33.3	-29.2	54.6	84.5	
Canned fruit & veg.	19	6	21	75	-70.3	-52.9	-62.5	-17.2	19.8	
Dry fruit & veg.	3	P	1E	1E	200.0	0.0	0.0	100.0	83.3	
Sauces, pickles	6	5	23E	57E	-45.5	-22.2	-28.6	13.8	36.8	
Frozen fruit & veg.	2	2	9E	23E	} 42.9	} 400.0	} 100.0	} 930.0	} 238.8	
Frozen specialties	8	8	43	82						
Flour	11	5	27	143	-38.9	-22.2	-28.6	-20.2	113.4	
Breakfast foods	1E	P	1	2	-50.0	-100.0	inf.	-100.0	inf.	
Rice	0E	0	0	0	0.0	0.0	0.0	0.0	0.0	
Flour mixes	2	7	75E	157E	0.0	0.0	0.0	59.0	134.3	
Wet corn mills	4	17	174	499	100.0	30.8	0.0	165.9	205.9	
Pet foods	4	2	21E	45E	} -19.2	} -5.3	} -38.9	} 38.2	} 98.3	
Animal feeds	55	9	74	296						
Bread, rolls	30	46	251	438	-74.8	-22.8	4.5	31.3	207.4	
Cookies & crackers	8	3	19	32	14.3	-60.0	50.0	-49.2	393.8	
Cane sugar	0	0	0	0	0.0	0.0	0.0	0.0	0.0	
Beet sugar	0	0	0	0	0.0	0.0	0.0	0.0	0.0	
Confectionary	18	14	75E	151E	38.5	45.5	-15.6	59.1	144.6	
Cottonseed oil	1E	1	1	51	inf.	0.0	inf.	0.0	inf.	
Soybean oil	6	7	4E	357E	100.0	14.3	-12.5	23.9	81.4	
Other fats & oils	9	3	2E	153E	-59.1	33.3	-25.0	127.3	579.1	
Cooking oil & marg.	4	3	2E	153E	33.3	0.0	-57.1	150.5	-11.2	
Beer	3	7	81E	145E	40.0	-46.2	0.0	7.3	183.0	
Wine & brandy	3E	P	1	2	inf.	inf.	0.0	inf.	200.0	
Spirits	2	10	115E	207E	0.0	41.2	-58.3	70.6	17.8	
Soft drinks	41	34	215	525	-57.7	3.2	6.3	154.3	222.2	
Flavorings	8	7	81E	145E	-11.1	-66.7	800.0	-69.7	1884.9	
Canned fish	0E	0	0	0	0.0	0.0	0.0	0.0	0.0	
Frozen fish	0E	0	0	0	0.0	0.0	0.0	0.0	0.0	
Coffee	1E	P	0.2	0.3	0.0	0.0	0.0	81.8	50.0	
Pasta	0E	0	0	0	-100.0	0.0	-100.0	-42.6	-100.0	
Miscellaneous foods	55	22	177	345	-24.7	12.5	22.2	82.0	280.0	
Total	446	329	2064	6188	-49.5	-18.5	-11.1	36.9	123.8	15.9

Source: Data from Bureau of the Census reports.

Note: Industries are listed by four-digit SIC code, see Appendix C for definitions of terms.

EST = Establishments. EMP = Employment. VA = Value added. VS = Value of shipments. inf. = Infinity. P = Less than 20. Z = 20 to 99.

Appendix Table B–13
Illinois: Basic Economic Data on Food Manufacturing Industries, 1963, 1972, 1982, and 1985

INDUSTRY 1/	1982 Totals				Growth Rates					
	EST	EMP	VA	VS	EST	EMP		VS		
					1963–1982	1963–1972	1972–1982	1963–1972	1972–1982	1982–1985
	No.	'00	\$ million		— — — — — — — — — Percent — — — — — — — — —					
Meatpacking	86	49	221	1866	-35.8	-27.3	-31.9	57.9	67.4	
Meat processing	90	68	298	1286	-28.0	5.3	-13.9	88.9	97.3	
Poultry dressing	6	3	5	20	-68.8	55.6	-42.9	38.0	91.6	
Poultry processing	4	5	14	59						
Butter	2	P	0.4E	1E	-84.6	-33.3	-95.0	22.1	-94.5	
Cheese	30	8	40	256	-47.4	133.3	-61.9	327.6	1.2	
Processed milk	13	7	103	243	-45.8	0.0	-22.2	74.8	112.7	
Ice cream	25	12	43E	162E	-56.1	-38.1	-7.7	2.9	105.3	
Fluid milk	32	21	144	564	-80.0	-28.8	-59.6	35.6	24.0	
Canned specialties	13	11	62	149	-31.6	-39.4	-45.0	-26.0	31.2	
Canned fruit & veg.	23	15	67	201	-54.0	-20.0	-37.5	3.4	90.1	
Dry fruit & veg.	6	6	36	68	50.0	-33.3	200.0	-33.7	887.0	
Sauces, pickles	20	31	382	1032	-50.0	0.0	210.0	78.5	1235.2	
Frozen fruit & veg.	6	6	36	72	2.4	100.0	-27.1	238.0	53.1	
Frozen specialties	37	29	148	306						
Flour	16	15	149	501	-30.4	-26.1	-11.8	402.2	145.7	
Breakfast foods	5	21	323	522	66.7	114.3	66.7	161.2	420.1	
Rice	0	0	0	0	0.0	0.0	0.0	0.0	0.0	
Flour mixes	15	12	125E	319E	15.4	128.6	-25.0	198.2	219.8	
Wet corn mills	4	30	312E	796E	-20.0	-27.9	-38.8	2.2	143.1	
Pet foods	15	15	186	376	-4.9	31.7	-33.3	83.1	68.0	
Animal feeds	83	21	213	693						
Bread, rolls	103	95	448	766	-64.0	-12.7	-18.8	50.5	95.9	
Cookies & crackers	23	53	380	635	9.5	4.8	-18.5	54.9	100.0	
Cane sugar	2	2	26E	46E	0.0	5.0	-4.8	8.3	105.9	
Beet sugar	0	0	0	0	0.0	0.0	0.0	0.0	0.0	
Confectionary	75	141	1136	2036	-33.6	7.7	-15.6	101.8	152.4	
Cottonseed oil	0	0	0	0	0.0	inf.	-100.0	inf.	-100.0	
Soybean oil	16	26	235	2289	-23.8	13.6	4.0	57.6	190.5	
Other fats & oils	16	5	32	113	-44.8	-49.5	-2.0	8.1	129.8	
Cooking oil & marg.	15	23	284	1040	-6.3	-9.5	21.1	53.9	164.2	
Beer	3	3	16E	49E	-80.0	-53.3	-78.6	-2.2	-56.4	
Wine & brandy	1	1	5E	16E	-80.0	50.0	175.0	-32.2	
Spirits	7	4	56	114	16.7	15.0	-82.6	93.2	-51.1	
Soft drinks	68	45	274	758	-60.9	7.7	-19.6	96.6	178.9	
Flavorings	32	18	400	650	-45.8	33.3	-25.0	102.7	98.5	
Canned fish	3	2	5	17	-72.7	-33.3	0.0	69.7	34.1	
Frozen fish	4	P	1E	1E	0.0	-80.0	0.0	-88.9	125.0	
Coffee	7	5	15	90	-61.1	-68.4	-16.7	-59.6	18.7	
Pasta	13	6	58	105	-40.9	28.6	-33.3	103.9	186.4	
Miscellaneous foods	136	65	531	1030	-19.5	11.5	-4.4	72.3	99.0	
Total	1055	880	6810	19248	-44.2	-3.3	-21.6	58.0	111.3	9.9

Source: Data from Bureau of the Census reports.

Note: Industries are listed by four-digit SIC code, see Appendix C for definitions of terms.

EST = Establishments. EMP = Employment. VA = Value added. VS = Value of shipments. inf. = Infinity. P = Less than 20. Z = 20 to 99.

Appendix Table B–14
Michigan: Basic Economic Data on Food Manufacturing Industries, 1963, 1972, 1982, and 1985

INDUSTRY 1/	1982 Totals EST	EMP	VA	VS	Growth Rates EST 1963-1982	EMP 1963-1972	EMP 1972-1982	VS 1963-1972	VS 1972-1982	VS 1982-1985
	No.	'00	\$ million		— — — — — — — Percent — — — — — — —					
Meatpacking	61	30	119	1163	-57.6	25.9	-11.8	144.9	77.1	
Meat processing	54	37	191E	693E	-33.3	0.0	19.4	130.1	146.6	
Poultry dressing	0	0	0	0	-90.5	0.0	100.0	124.2	779.8	
Poultry processing	2	7	36E	131E						
Butter	2	Z	2E	10E	-92.0	-33.3	-75.0	68.7	-77.4	
Cheese	8	3	14E	60E	-63.6	50.0	0.0	56.9	166.8	
Processed milk	9	12	227	526	-52.6	-9.1	20.0	29.6	437.1	
Ice cream	21	6	32	88	-64.4	-41.7	-14.3	-14.0	101.4	
Fluid milk	39	56	135	697	-82.4	-38.8	-36.6	36.3	86.8	
Canned specialties	5	7	48E	113E	-16.7	-22.2	0.0	3.3	161.3	
Canned fruit & veg.	36	21	115	325	-45.5	-3.1	-32.3	64.4	119.5	
Dry fruit & veg.	1	P	1E	2E	-50.0	0.0	0.0	100.0	166.7	
Sauces, pickles	32	19	121	228	-36.0	4.8	-13.6	84.5	137.4	
Frozen fruit & veg.	17	13	75	158	3.3	109.1	13.0	304.6	174.5	
Frozen specialties	14	13	90E	210E						
Flour	11	6	51	156	-42.1	-12.5	-14.3	-25.2	168.3	
Breakfast foods	5	45	672E	1001E	0.0	-5.2	-18.2	43.5	119.4	
Rice	0	0	0	0	0.0	0.0	0.0	0.0	0.0	
Flour mixes	6	2	12	36	-33.3	0.0	100.0	167.7	328.9	
Wet corn mills	0	0	0	0	0.0	0.0	0.0	0.0	0.0	
Pet foods	8	2	30E	45E	37.8	66.7	-20.0	342.1	82.4	
Animal feeds	20	2	7	53						
Bread, rolls	74	45	206	312	-64.4	-23.2	-38.4	52.2	32.2	
Cookies & crackers	11	20	91	174	-31.3	-12.5	42.9	44.4	282.2	
Cane sugar	0E	0	0	0	0.0	0.0	0.0	0.0	0.0	
Beet sugar	5	7	47E	96E	0.0	0.0	0.0	-16.6	235.1	
Confectionary	24E	13	85	176	-11.1	14.3	57.5	108.1	-74.8	
Cottonseed oil	0	0	0	0	0.0	0.0	0.0	0.0	0.0	
Soybean oil	0	0	0	0	0.0	0.0	0.0	0.0	0.0	
Other fats & oils	8	3	15E	65E	-27.3	-40.0	0.0	62.3	164.3	
Cooking oil & marg.	4	3	15E	65E	33.3	0.0	0.0	-17.0	164.3	
Beer	4	18	185E	429E	-50.0	-23.1	-10.0	158.5	128.4	
Wine & brandy	8	1	10E	24E	33.3	0.0	0.0	74.0	153.2	
Spirits	2	3	31E	72E	0.0	50.0	0.0	133.1	153.5	
Soft drinks	41	28	132	362	-55.4	23.5	-33.3	239.8	44.0	
Flavorings	7	2	21E	48E	-72.0	300.0	0.0	370.0	153.7	
Canned fish	3E	P	1	2	-57.1	-80.0	0.0	-46.2	128.6	
Frozen fish	9E	2	12	31	800.0	0.0	1900.0	250.0	4357.1	
Coffee	4	1	6E	16E	-60.0	50.0	-66.7	-9.2	-20.8	
Pasta	5	2	12E	31E	-37.5	-50.0	100.0	127.6	372.7	
Miscellaneous foods	64	20	113E	228E	-29.7	-18.3	5.2	63.4	141.8	
Total	626	422	2974	7908	-53.4	-8.4	-12.3	77.8	120.6	9.1

Source: Data from Bureau of the Census reports.

Note: Industries are listed by four-digit SIC code, see Appendix C for definitions of terms.

EST = Establishments. EMP = Employment. VA = Value added. VS = Value of shipments. P = Less than 20. Z = 20 to 99.

Appendix Table B–15
Wisconsin: Basic Economic Data on Food Manufacturing Industries, 1963, 1972, 1982, and 1985

INDUSTRY 1/	1982 Totals EST	EMP	VA	VS	Growth Rates EST 1963-1982	EMP 1963-1972	EMP 1972-1982	VS 1963-1972	VS 1972-1982	VS 1982-1985
	No.	'00	$ million		- - - - - - - - - Percent - - - - - - - - - -					
Meatpacking	48	67	289	1774	-36.0	5.9	-6.9	100.6	100.3	
Meat processing	48	26	166	637	-21.3	-13.3	100.0	45.8	804.3	
Poultry dressing	4	7	7E	57E	-70.8	-15.4	27.3	35.9	69.3	
Poultry processing	3	7	7E	57E						
Butter	14	6	38	553	-84.3	-82.6	50.0	-50.1	337.3	
Cheese	324	104	645	4116	-50.2	25.7	18.2	156.5	242.5	
Processed milk	33	21	211	716	-26.7	-8.7	0.0	108.0	100.1	
Ice cream	17	5	25	79	-45.2	0.0	0.0	25.0	235.7	
Fluid milk	47	19	109	619	-77.8	-38.2	-44.1	67.1	58.2	
Canned specialties	4	2	9E	42E	inf.	inf.	0.0	inf.	462.3	
Canned fruit & veg.	65	60	239	586	-36.3	9.9	-23.0	110.6	85.7	
Dry fruit & veg.	1	3	14E	63E	inf.	inf.	0.0	inf.	468.2	
Sauces, pickles	12	10	52	125	-50.0	-36.4	42.9	35.8	382.9	
Frozen fruit & veg.	7	12	80	135	109.1	650.0	86.7	2607.1	269.3	
Frozen specialties	16	16	72	145						
Flour	6	3	14E	51E	-25.0	-25.0	0.0	6.9	21.9	
Breakfast foods	1E	2	9	34	inf.	inf.	1900.0	inf.	2314.3	
Rice	1E	P	1	2	inf.	inf.	0.0	inf.	21.4	
Flour mixes	1E	P	1	2	-75.0	-80.0	0.0	-53.3	21.4	
Wet corn mills	0E	0	0	0	0.0	0.0	0.0	0.0	0.0	
Pet foods	26	7	83	158	31.0	30.8	0.0	175.8	107.0	
Animal feeds	67	10	64	306						
Bread, rolls	42	41	128	235	-60.7	-25.9	-4.7	8.3	97.0	
Cookies & crackers	10	6	20	44	100.0	-70.0	100.0	-67.6	431.3	
Cane sugar	1E	2	23	50	0.0	0.0	300.0	21.6	704.8	
Beet sugar	0E	0	0	0	0.0	0.0	0.0	0.0	0.0	
Confectionary	20	14	163E	349E	-9.1	40.0	0.0	334.4	214.0	
Cottonseed oil	1E	P	1	3	inf.	inf.	0.0	inf.	383.3	
Soybean oil	1E	P	1	3	inf.	0.0	inf.	0.0	inf.	
Other fats & oils	13	3	26E	86E	-35.0	-33.3	50.0	-3.1	580.2	
Cooking oil & marg.	1E	P	1	3	inf.	0.0	inf.	0.0	inf.	
Beer	7	52	410	987	-75.0	-5.9	-35.0	73.3	86.6	
Wine & brandy	8	Z	2E	4E	166.7	0.0	400.0	50.0	583.3	
Spirits	2	P	0.3E	1E	100.0	0.0	0.0	0.0	33.3	
Soft drinks	59	27	149	421	-54.3	20.0	12.5	137.2	328.6	
Flavorings	10	2	18	28	150.0	0.0	100.0	-17.5	319.7	
Canned fish	1E	P	1	2	-83.3	-80.0	0.0	-76.9	433.3	
Frozen fish	10	3	6	21	233.3	100.0	200.0	220.0	550.0	
Coffee	1E	P	1	2	-50.0	0.0	0.0	-92.9	433.3	
Pasta	2	Z	3E	8E	100.0	-50.0	-50.0	-95.2	146.8	
Miscellaneous foods	64	25	240	547	-14.7	-1.9	19.0	-9.4	379.8	
Total	998	563	3324	13044	-45.0	-3.7	-0.4	78.3	169.3	7.0

Source: Data from Bureau of the Census reports.

Note: Industries are listed by four-digit SIC code, see Appendix C for definitions of terms.

EST = Establishments. EMP = Employment. VA = Value added. VS = Value of shipments. inf. = Infinity. P = Less than 20. Z = 20 to 99.

Appendix Table B–16
Minnesota: Basic Economic Data on Food Manufacturing Industries, 1963, 1972, 1982, and 1985

INDUSTRY 1/	1982 Totals				Growth Rates					
	EST	EMP	VA	VS	EST	EMP		VS		
					1963-1982	1963-1972	1972-1982	1963-1972	1972-1982	1982-1985
	No.	'00	$ million				Percent			
Meatpacking	29	44	385	1699	-39.6	-34.1	-55.1	63.3	21.9	
Meat processing	17	9	35	132	-10.5	-30.0	28.6	52.4	146.1	
Poultry dressing	14	36	98	394	8.3	28.2	6.0	71.9	159.1	
Poultry processing	12	17	42	152						
Butter	12	4	37	375	-95.0	-57.7	-63.6	17.0	37.7	
Cheese	28	26	273	1385	47.4	100.0	52.5	225.0	340.3	
Processed milk	21	11	70E	290E	-38.2	-53.3	57.1	-10.0	169.1	
Ice cream	5	3	19E	79E	-80.0	-16.7	-40.0	84.4	109.3	
Fluid milk	64	19	98	653	-68.0	0.0	-47.2	98.9	94.9	
Canned specialties	2E	P	1	1	100.0	-57.1	-96.7	-47.7	-91.8	
Canned fruit & veg.	19	23	95	239	-29.6	42.3	-37.8	103.8	76.0	
Dry fruit & veg.	2	P	1	1	0.0	300.0	-95.0	3666.7	-87.6	
Sauces, pickles	5	2	6	23	-61.5	50.0	-33.3	139.4	34.1	
Frozen fruit & veg.	5	15	67	132	69.2	72.2	16.1	225.7	228.8	
Frozen specialties	17	21	107	244						
Flour	23	10	79	418	4.5	-23.1	0.0	28.9	87.1	
Breakfast foods	6	5	54E	89E	100.0	50.0	66.7	85.5	335.9	
Rice	9	Z	5E	9E	200.0	0.0	400.0	-30.0	1171.4	
Flour mixes	6	1	11E	18E	50.0	300.0	-50.0	353.3	30.9	
Wet corn mills	1	P	1E	2E	inf.	inf.	0.0	inf.	157.1	
Pet foods	10	5	48	101	-28.9	-3.1	16.1	37.0	188.1	
Animal feeds	54	13	73	346						
Bread, rolls	34	28	109E	187E	-66.3	-24.3	0.0	33.2	134.0	
Cookies & crackers	3	2	8E	13E	-50.0	-50.0	0.0	-44.1	135.1	
Cane sugar	0	0	0	0	0.0	0.0	0.0	0.0	0.0	
Beet sugar	4	19	77E	201E	0.0	-57.1	533.3	-45.6	958.9	
Confectionary	13	16	65E	170E	-45.8	16.7	105.9	170.4	91.1	
Cottonseed oil	0	0	0	0	0.0	0.0	0.0	0.0	0.0	
Soybean oil	4	3	10	348	-20.0	33.3	-25.0	105.8	104.0	
Other fats & oils	20	6	45E	315E	-25.9	-12.5	-14.3	74.0	118.0	
Cooking oil & marg.	2	4	27E	147E	inf.	0.0	inf.	0.0	inf.	
Beer	5	9	76E	184E	-58.3	-25.0	-50.0	40.8	46.8	
Wine & brandy	3E	P	1	2	inf.	inf.	0.0	inf.	300.0	
Spirits	1E	P	1	2	inf.	inf.	0.0	inf.	inf.	
Soft drinks	39	34	202	477	-46.6	46.7	54.5	298.0	279.9	
Flavorings	3	2	17E	41E	0.0	900.0	100.0	575.0	655.6	
Canned fish	2	Z	4E	9E	-50.0	0.0	0.0	123.1	203.4	
Frozen fish	6	2	16E	35E	200.0	0.0	300.0	50.0	11666.7	
Coffee	5	2	16E	35E	-44.4	0.0	0.0	-46.1	201.7	
Pasta	3	3	24E	53E	-50.0	0.0	50.0	91.8	352.1	
Miscellaneous foods	49	15	95	306	40.0	26.1	4.1	-24.3	313.1	
Total	559	410	2392	9307	-49.1	-6.2	-1.0	65.1	116.7	2.6

Source: Data from Bureau of the Census reports.

Note: Industries are listed by four-digit SIC code, see Appendix C for definitions of terms.

EST = Establishments. EMP = Employment. VA = Value added. VS = Value of shipments. inf. = Infinity. P = Less than 20. Z = 20 to 99.

Appendix Table B–17
Iowa: Basic Economic Data on Food Manufacturing Industries, 1963, 1972, 1982, and 1985

INDUSTRY 1/	1982 Totals				Growth Rates						
	EST	EMP	VA	VS	EST	EMP		VS			
					1963-1982	1963-1972	1972-1982	1963-1972	1972-1982	1982-1985	
	No.	'00	$ million		- - - - - - - - - - Percent - - - - - - - - - -						
Meatpacking	65	179	847	6462	-9.7	1.7	-25.4	94.3	82.0		
Meat processing	37	23	104	473	131.3	300.0	91.7	878.3	482.9		
Poultry dressing	8	15	40	179	-53.3	27.8	-8.7	79.5	118.0		
Poultry processing	6	6	22	66							
Butter	2	P	1E	3E	-98.4	-81.3	-96.7	-58.7	-94.2		
Cheese	16	8	50	421	-65.2	50.0	33.3	205.8	370.2		
Processed milk	13	7	85	320	8.3	125.0	-22.2	873.7	83.7		
Ice cream	8	2	12E	55E	-65.2	-60.0	0.0	-32.1	378.9		
Fluid milk	17	12	86	404	-87.3	-24.1	-45.5	57.7	124.6		
Canned specialties	4	3	17E	37E	100.0	40.0	-25.0	94.4	-17.1		
Canned fruit & veg.	2	10	57E	125E	-77.8	-50.0	233.3	78.0	295.6		
Dry fruit & veg.	1	P	1E	1E	inf.	inf.	0.0	inf.	140.0		
Sauces, pickles	3	Z	3E	6E	-70.0	0.0	0.0	55.6	121.4		
Frozen fruit & veg.	2	2	12E	25E	-16.7	-57.1	200.0	-27.3	474.3		
Frozen specialties	3	7	40E	87E							
Flour	7	4	54E	103E	-22.2	-50.0	100.0	-56.8	442.6		
Breakfast foods	2	19	259E	490E	0.0	25.0	26.7	116.9	243.2		
Rice	0E	0	0	0	0.0	0.0	0.0	0.0	0.0		
Flour mixes	1E	P	1	3	-66.7	0.0	0.0	66.7	160.0		
Wet corn mills	6	32	416	1182	100.0	25.0	-8.6	152.3	254.8		
Pet foods	14	15	390	626	-4.5	10.0	22.7	63.8	270.3		
Animal feeds	135	39	217	817							
Bread, rolls	22	21	80E	153E	-72.8	-22.6	-12.5	33.3	113.0		
Cookies & crackers	3	3	11E	22E	-25.0	-12.5	-57.1	25.4	33.7		
Cane sugar	0E	0	0	0	0.0	0.0	0.0	0.0	0.0		
Beet sugar	0E	0	0	0	-100.0	-50.0	-100.0	-23.0	-100.0		
Confectionary	6	2	13E	27E	-50.0	-33.3	5.0	17.4	235.8		
Cottonseed oil	0E	0	0	0	0.0	0.0	0.0	0.0	0.0		
Soybean oil	17	11	110	1219	-5.6	-11.1	37.5	57.5	211.0		
Other fats & oils	16	4	16E	77E	-46.7	-25.0	33.3	91.8	230.3		
Cooking oil & marg.	1E	1	4	19	inf.	0.0	inf.	0.0	inf.		
Beer	1E	P	0.1	0.4	-50.0	-80.0	0.0	-50.0	-55.6		
Wine & brandy	2E	Z	1	2	100.0	0.0	400.0	125.0	77.8		
Spirits	0E	0	0	0	-100.0	-98.3	-100.0	-97.5	-100.0		
Soft drinks	27	14	75	174	-55.0	30.8	-17.6	150.2	158.5		
Flavorings	2E	Z	1	2	-60.0	0.0	0.0	10.0	-63.6		
Canned fish	1E	P	0.4	0.5	0.0	0.0	0.0	0.0	66.7		
Frozen fish	3E	P	0.3	1	inf.	inf.	0.0	inf.	266.7		
Coffee	0E	0	0	0	0.0	0.0	0.0	0.0	0.0		
Pasta	4	2	13E	25E	100.0	0.0	300.0	0.0	8366.7		
Miscellaneous foods	27	8	109	172	-35.7	-27.8	24.6	112.2	295.6		
Total	484	448	3131	13747	-47.4	-1.6	-9.7	84.0	135.8	-8.6	

Source: Data from Bureau of the Census reports.

Note: Industries are listed by four-digit SIC code, see Appendix C for definitions of terms.

EST = Establishments. EMP = Employment. VA = Value added. VS = Value of shipments. inf. = Infinity. P = Less than 20. Z = 20 to 99.

Appendix Table B–18
Missouri: Basic Economic Data on Food Manufacturing Industries, 1963, 1972, 1982, and 1985

INDUSTRY 1/	1982 Totals EST	EMP	VA	VS	Growth Rates EST 1963-1982	EMP 1963-1972	1972-1982	VS 1963-1972	1972-1982	1982-1985
	No.	'00	$ million		- - - - - - - - - - Percent - - - - - - - - - -					
Meatpacking	78	32	134	1219	-12.4	-50.6	-15.8	13.6	100.5	
Meat processing	29	14	103	350	20.8	9.1	16.7	114.4	200.8	
Poultry dressing	15	28	37	231						
Poultry processing	7	11	41	105	-43.6	13.0	50.0	39.7	229.0	
Butter	0	0	0	0	-100.0	-66.7	-100.0	-40.7	-100.0	
Cheese	16	27	229	1057	-51.5	42.9	35.0	159.0	212.6	
Processed milk	7	5	19	162	-12.5	12.5	-44.4	81.2	73.2	
Ice cream	9	5	24	55	-67.9	-33.3	25.0	53.1	60.6	
Fluid milk	21	21	114	612	-63.8	-30.8	-22.2	61.9	179.3	
Canned specialties	2E	P	1	2	100.0	0.0	0.0	20.0	183.3	
Canned fruit & veg.	5	Z	3	9	-54.5	0.0	0.0	76.9	269.6	
Dry fruit & veg.	1E	P	1	2	inf.	inf.	0.0	inf.	240.0	
Sauces, pickles	9	7	43E	118E	-40.0	-25.0	133.3	-27.9	604.8	
Frozen fruit & veg.	3E	P	1	2						
Frozen specialties	16	24	147E	406E	35.7	61.7	-17.2	173.0	177.6	
Flour	9	8	67	270	-25.0	-26.7	-27.3	11.6	30.0	
Breakfast foods	1	7	75E	170E	0.0	6900.0	0.0	10560.0	219.3	
Rice	1E	P	1	2	inf.	inf.	0.0	inf.	200.0	
Flour mixes	4	3	32E	73E	-42.9	-50.0	500.0	-36.7	1818.4	
Wet corn mills	1	3	32E	73E	-50.0	-22.2	-57.1	25.7	36.8	
Pet foods	7	6	86	170						
Animal feeds	64	15	102	472	-19.3	4.3	-12.5	66.2	193.3	
Bread, rolls	47	47	177	306	-53.0	-23.6	-14.5	28.4	-18.8	
Cookies & crackers	11	7	41	74	-21.4	-11.1	-12.5	31.9	97.6	
Cane sugar	1	Z	3E	7E	0.0	0.0	0.0	56.9	78.1	
Beet sugar	0	0	0	0	0.0	0.0	0.0	0.0	0.0	
Confectionary	20	10	58E	130E	-23.1	0.0	-33.3	175.2	113.1	
Cottonseed oil	2E	1	4	18	-50.0	-95.0	900.0	-82.6	665.2	
Soybean oil	6	3	13	353	50.0	-25.0	0.0	11.6	401.7	
Other fats & oils	9	2	8E	35E	-43.8	-4.8	0.0	551.4	-24.9	
Cooking oil & marg.	2	2	8E	35E	-33.3	0.0	-33.3	139.1	-49.9	
Beer	1	34	352E	786E	-83.3	-24.1	-17.1	52.2	116.9	
Wine & brandy	5	1	10E	23E	inf.	inf.	100.0	inf.	425.0	
Spirits	3	2	21E	46E	50.0	300.0	0.0	490.0	161.0	
Soft drinks	45	31	203	440	-51.1	0.0	-6.1	109.7	233.4	
Flavorings	11	7	73E	162E	-59.3	0.0	40.0	87.6	136.9	
Canned fish	0	0	0	0	0.0	0.0	0.0	0.0	0.0	
Frozen fish	0	0	0	0	-100.0	200.0	-100.0	478.9	-100.0	
Coffee	9	3	51E	139E	-18.2	-55.6	-25.0	20.6	82.0	
Pasta	4	2	34E	93E	-20.0	50.0	-33.3	80.3	744.5	
Miscellaneous foods	56	23	154	344	-37.8	11.1	15.0	117.3	260.3	
Total	537	388	2501	8549	-36.4	-13.7	-6.7	60.3	139.7	2.7

Source: Data from Bureau of the Census reports.

Note: Industries are listed by four-digit SIC code, see Appendix C for definitions of terms.

EST = Establishments. EMP = Employment. VA = Value added. VS = Value of shipments. inf. = Infinity. P = Less than 20. Z = 20 to 99.

Appendix Table B–19
North Dakota: Basic Economic Data on Food Manufacturing Industries, 1963, 1972, 1982, and 1985

INDUSTRY 1/	1982 Totals EST	EMP	VA	VS	Growth Rates EST 1963-1982	EMP 1963-1972	EMP 1972-1982	VS 1963-1972	VS 1972-1982	VS 1982-1985
	No.	'00	$ million		- - - - - - - - - - - Percent - - - - - - - - - - -					
Meatpacking	11	3	13E	100E	-8.3	0.0	50.0	232.1	120.0	
Meat processing	4	2	89E	378E	100.0	100.0	100.0	931.8	1564.3	
Poultry dressing	0	0	0	0	-100.0	-100.0	0.0	-100.0	0.0	
Poultry processing	0	0	0	0						
Butter	1E	P	1	8E	-98.4	-85.7	-90.0	-88.8	75.0	
Cheese	8	1	6E	36E	-20.0	500.0	-66.7	772.7	26.4	
Processed milk	4E	P	1	4	300.0	-100.0	inf.	-100.0	inf.	
Ice cream	1	Z	3E	8E	-50.0	-100.0	inf.	-100.0	inf.	
Fluid milk	8	5	26	120E	-55.6	200.0	-16.7	472.5	161.6	
Canned specialties	0	0	0	0	0.0	0.0	0.0	0.0	0.0	
Canned fruit & veg.	0	0	0	0	-100.0	-100.0	0.0	-100.0	0.0	
Dry fruit & veg.	2	1	6E	14E	-33.3	0.0	-50.0	42.0	45.9	
Sauces, pickles	0	0	0	0	0.0	0.0	0.0	0.0	0.0	
Frozen fruit & veg.	2	2	12E	29E	300.0	2900.0	0.0	4233.3	230.0	
Frozen specialties	2	1	6E	14E						
Flour	3	Z	3	14	-25.0	-66.7	-50.0	-63.9	36.2	
Breakfast foods	0	0	0	0	0.0	0.0	0.0	0.0	0.0	
Rice	0	0	0	0	0.0	0.0	0.0	0.0	0.0	
Flour mixes	0	0	0	0	0.0	0.0	0.0	0.0	0.0	
Wet corn mills	0	0	0	0	-100.0	-100.0	0.0	-100.0	0.0	
Pet foods	1	Z	3E	14E	22.2	300.0	25.0	480.6	242.6	
Animal feeds	10	2	12E	57E						
Bread, rolls	11	3	14E	23E	-57.7	16.7	-57.1	115.5	4.1	
Cookies & crackers	0	0	0	0	0.0	0.0	0.0	0.0	0.0	
Cane sugar	0E	0	0	0	-100.0	0.0	0.0	0.0	0.0	
Beet sugar	3	11	46E	162E	200.0	300.0	450.0	2960.0	958.2	
Confectionary	1E	P	1	1	0.0	0.0	0.0	100.0	200.0	
Cottonseed oil	0E	0	0	0	0.0	0.0	0.0	0.0	0.0	
Soybean oil	1E	P	1	10	inf.	0.0	inf.	0.0	inf.	
Other fats & oils	3E	Z	3	8	0.0	0.0	0.0	94.1	145.5	
Cooking oil & marg.	1	Z	5E	20E	inf.	inf.	0.0	inf.	145.0	
Beer	0	0	0	0	-100.0	-100.0	0.0	-100.0	0.0	
Wine & brandy	0	0	0	0	0.0	0.0	0.0	0.0	0.0	
Spirits	0	0	0	0	0.0	0.0	0.0	0.0	0.0	
Soft drinks	6	3	16E	74E	-60.0	0.0	0.0	100.0	757.0	
Flavorings	0	0	0	0	0.0	0.0	0.0	0.0	0.0	
Canned fish	0E	0	0	0	0.0	0.0	0.0	0.0	0.0	
Frozen fish	2E	Z	3	9	inf.	0.0	inf.	0.0	inf.	
Coffee	0E	0	0	0	0.0	0.0	0.0	0.0	0.0	
Pasta	1	Z	3E	9E	inf.	inf.	0.0	inf.	254.2	
Miscellaneous foods	6	3	13E	48E	50.0	83.3	90.9	216.7	526.3	
Total	93	41	228	870	-48.3	16.1	13.9	92.8	233.2	0.9

Source: Data from Bureau of the Census reports.

Note: Industries are listed by four-digit SIC code, see Appendix C for definitions of terms.

EST = Establishments. EMP = Employment. VA = Value added. VS = Value of shipments. inf. = Infinity. P = Less than 20. Z = 20 to 99.

Appendix Table B–20
South Dakota: Basic Economic Data on Food Manufacturing Industries, 1963, 1972, 1982, and 1985

INDUSTRY 1/	EST	EMP	VA	VS	EST 1963- 1982	EMP 1963- 1972	EMP 1972- 1982	VS 1963- 1972	VS 1972- 1982	VS 1982- 1985
	No.	'00	$ million							
Meatpacking	12	41	276	1139	-40.0	-8.7	-2.4	35.4	168.9	
Meat processing	3	P	0.2E	1E	200.0	0.0	0.0	150.0	-10.0	
Poultry dressing	1	2	5E	18E	} -20.0	} 0.0	} 33.3	} 252.3	} 16.8	
Poultry processing	3	2	5E	18E						
Butter	0	0	0	0	-100.0	-97.5	-100.0	-97.6	-100.0	
Cheese	17	4	17	141	112.5	200.0	33.3	160.0	734.9	
Processed milk	3	1	6E	25E	200.0	300.0	-50.0	197.4	123.0	
Ice cream	0	0	0	0	-100.0	-80.0	-100.0	-66.7	-100.0	
Fluid milk	10	5	28E	126E	-70.6	-12.5	-28.6	5.3	219.0	
Canned specialties	0	0	0	0	0.0	0.0	0.0	0.0	0.0	
Canned fruit & veg.	0	0	0	0	0.0	0.0	0.0	0.0	0.0	
Dry fruit & veg.	0	0	0	0	0.0	0.0	0.0	0.0	0.0	
Sauces, pickles	0	0	0	0	0.0	0.0	0.0	0.0	0.0	
Frozen fruit & veg.	1	2	10E	23E	} -50.0	} 0.0	} 300.0	} 33.3	} 5525.0	
Frozen specialties	0	0	0	0						
Flour	1E	1	6	23	0.0	100.0	0.0	61.2	191.1	
Breakfast foods	0	0	0	0	0.0	0.0	0.0	0.0	0.0	
Rice	0	0	0	0	0.0	0.0	0.0	0.0	0.0	
Flour mixes	0	0	0	0	0.0	0.0	0.0	0.0	0.0	
Wet corn mills	0	0	0	0	0.0	0.0	0.0	0.0	0.0	
Pet foods	1E	1	6	23	} 20.0	} 36.7	} -2.4	} 53.5	} 182.0	
Animal feeds	23	3	16E	69E						
Bread, rolls	6	3	14E	23E	-71.4	-40.0	0.0	0.0	143.2	
Cookies & crackers	1	3	18E	31E	inf.	0.0	inf.	0.0	inf.	
Cane sugar	0	0	0	0	0.0	0.0	0.0	0.0	0.0	
Beet sugar	0	0	0	0	0.0	0.0	-100.0	53.0	-100.0	
Confectionary	0	0	0	0	-100.0	0.0	-100.0	76.1	-100.0	
Cottonseed oil	0	0	0	0	0.0	0.0	0.0	0.0	0.0	
Soybean oil	0	0	0	0	0.0	0.0	0.0	0.0	0.0	
Other fats & oils	5	1	5E	16E	66.7	0.0	100.0	94.1	390.9	
Cooking oil & marg.	0	0	0	0	0.0	0.0	0.0	0.0	0.0	
Beer	0	0	0	0	0.0	0.0	0.0	0.0	0.0	
Wine & brandy	0	0	0	0	0.0	0.0	0.0	0.0	0.0	
Spirits	0	0	0	0	0.0	0.0	0.0	0.0	0.0	
Soft drinks	9	3	12E	28E	-30.8	50.0	0.0	81.0	265.8	
Flavorings	1	Z	2E	5E	0.0	0.0	400.0	-62.5	1433.3	
Canned fish	0	0	0	0	-100.0	0.0	-100.0	0.0	-100.0	
Frozen fish	0	0	0	0	0.0	0.0	0.0	0.0	0.0	
Coffee	0	0	0	0	0.0	0.0	0.0	0.0	0.0	
Pasta	0	0	0	0	0.0	0.0	0.0	0.0	0.0	
Miscellaneous foods	3	Z	4E	7E	-40.0	0.0	-16.7	66.7	123.3	
Total	100	75	423	1702	-39.8	-7.6	2.7	39.3	165.8	7.0

Source: Data from Bureau of the Census reports.

Note: Industries are listed by four-digit SIC code, see Appendix C for definitions of terms.

EST = Establishments. EMP = Employment. VA = Value added. VS = Value of shipments. inf. = Infinity. P = Less than 20. Z = 20 to 99.

Appendix Table B–21
Nebraska: Basic Economic Data on Food Manufacturing Industries, 1963, 1972, 1982, and 1985

INDUSTRY 1/	1982 Totals EST	EMP	VA	VS	Growth Rates EST 1963-1982	EMP 1963-1972	EMP 1972-1982	VS 1963-1972	VS 1972-1982	VS 1982-1985
	No.	'00	$ million		— — — — — — — — — Percent — — — — — — — — —					
Meatpacking	64	121	642	6514	-19.0	-8.7	28.7	200.0	152.6	
Meat processing	23	16	54	259	109.1	175.0	45.5	232.0	247.0	
Poultry dressing	4	2	6E	18E	-52.6 }	-4.5 }	-31.9 }	54.5 }	80.0	
Poultry processing	5	11	32E	96E						
Butter	1	Z	3E	15E	-96.7	-57.1	-83.3	-55.7	-28.2	
Cheese	12	5	14	149	200.0	500.0	66.7	545.5	597.2	
Processed milk	2	1	5E	31E	inf.	inf.	900.0	inf.	4257.1	
Ice cream	4	Z	3E	15E	-55.6	-75.0	0.0	-69.6	337.1	
Fluid milk	12	7	18	117	-64.7	-16.7	-53.3	102.5	9.4	
Canned specialties	0	0	0	0	-100.0	-100.0	0.0	-100.0	0.0	
Canned fruit & veg.	2	P	1	1	100.0	0.0	0.0	66.7	160.0	
Dry fruit & veg.	0	0	0	0	0.0	0.0	0.0	0.0	0.0	
Sauces, pickles	0	0	0	0	-100.0	-80.0	-100.0	-66.7	-100.0	
Frozen fruit & veg.	2	3	15E	34E	-14.3 }	50.0 }	-33.3 }	148.5 }	58.0	
Frozen specialties	4	7	35E	84E						
Flour	6	4	30	182	-45.5	-37.5	-20.0	27.7	83.0	
Breakfast foods	2	7	115E	198E	0.0	133.3	0.0	367.3	156.8	
Rice	1E	1	17	28	inf.	inf.	900.0	inf.	2472.7	
Flour mixes	1	2	33E	57E	-66.7	0.0	0.0	81.8	157.3	
Wet corn mills	0E	0	0	0	0.0	0.0	0.0	0.0	0.0	
Pet foods	5	7	115E	198E	-13.3 }	13.0 }	-11.5 }	96.8 }	181.5	
Animal feeds	106	16	156	456						
Bread, rolls	16	18	61E	101	-44.8	-25.0	20.0	18.7	124.2	
Cookies & crackers	2	p	0.3E	1E	100.0	-80.0	0.0	-76.9	100.0	
Cane sugar	0	0	0	0	0.0	0.0	0.0	0.0	0.0	
Beet sugar	4	7	29E	103E	-20.0	0.0	0.0	53.6	92.2	
Confectionary	2	2	12E	25E	-60.0	-46.7	-75.0	-5.0	-23.3	
Cottonseed oil	1E	Z	3	34	inf.	0.0	inf.	0.0	inf.	
Soybean oil	3	2	11E	137E	50.0	300.0	0.0	356.6	165.9	
Other fats & oils	13	3	17E	206E	-40.9	0.0	-3.2	654.7	157.3	
Cooking oil & marg.	2	Z	3E	34E	100.0	-80.0	400.0	-46.9	1219.2	
Beer	1	2	12E	29E	-50.0	-57.1	-33.3	-35.5	70.7	
Wine & brandy	1E	Z	3	7	inf.	0.0	inf.	0.0	inf.	
Spirits	1E	Z	3	7	inf.	0.0	inf.	0.0	inf.	
Soft drinks	20	7	42E	100E	-58.3	0.0	0.0	187.5	155.2	
Flavorings	1E	Z	3	7	-66.7	-100.0	inf.	-100.0	inf.	
Canned fish	0E	0	0	0	0.0	0.0	0.0	0.0	0.0	
Frozen fish	2E	P	1	3	inf.	0.0	inf.	0.0	inf.	
Coffee	1	Z	7E	16E	0.0	0.0	0.0	9.3	222.4	
Pasta	2	3	42E	95E	-33.3	0.0	0.0	217.4	225.0	
Miscellaneous foods	14	4	19	36	0.0	28.6	-8.9	305.6	-17.8	
Total	342	259	1557	9432	-28.6	-4.9	2.0	148.4	150.0	-10.7

Source: Data from Bureau of the Census reports.

Note: Industries are listed by four-digit SIC code, see Appendix C for definitions of terms.

EST = Establishments. EMP = Employment. VA = Value added. VS = Value of shipments. inf. = Infinity. P = Less than 20. Z = 20 to 99.

Appendix Table B–22
Kansas: Basic Economic Data on Food Manufacturing Industries, 1963, 1972, 1982, and 1985

INDUSTRY 1/	1982 Totals EST	EMP	VA	VS	Growth Rates EST 1963-1982	EMP 1963-1972	EMP 1972-1982	VS 1963-1972	VS 1972-1982	VS 1982-1985
	No.	'00	\$ million		- - - - - - - - - Percent - - - - - - - - -					
Meatpacking	44	67	233	3686	-47.0	-33.3	24.1	175.4	159.4	
Meat processing	21	19	107E	471E	425.0	150.0	90.0	286.9	595.4	
Poultry dressing	2	2	11E	50E	} -86.7	} -20.0	} -37.5	} -23.1	} 404.1	
Poultry processing	2	Z	3E	12E						
Butter	1	P	1E	5E	-90.9	-33.3	-95.0	4.7	-69.7	
Cheese	8	3	8	91	-11.1	300.0	50.0	697.0	246.8	
Processed milk	0	0	0	0	-100.0	-100.0	0.0	154.1	501.9	
Ice cream	6	2	13E	93E	-66.7	0.0	0.0	-100.0	0.0	
Fluid milk	13	10	23	169	-82.9	-26.9	-47.4	0.0	75.4	
Canned specialties	1	2	9E	25E	-66.7	0.0	0.0	38.7	91.5	
Canned fruit & veg.	2E	P	0.4	1	0.0	0.0	-80.0	115.4	-57.1	
Dry fruit & veg.	0E	0	0	0	0.0	0.0	0.0	0.0	0.0	
Sauces, pickles	4	2	9E	25E	-20.0	900.0	100.0	1300.0	341.1	
Frozen fruit & veg.	1E	P	0.4	1	} inf.	} inf.	} 153.7	} inf.	} 506.3	
Frozen specialties	1	10	43E	124E						
Flour	24	12	91	459	-29.4	-39.1	-14.3	-9.6	69.0	
Breakfast foods	2	2	34E	53E	0.0	0.0	300.0	100.0	5200.0	
Rice	0	0	0	0	0.0	0.0	0.0	0.0	0.0	
Flour mixes	0	0	0	0	-100.0	-80.0	-100.0	-66.7	-100.0	
Wet corn mills	0	0	0	0	0.0	0.0	0.0	0.0	0.0	
Pet foods	8	9	169	279	} -17.2	} 28.6	} 5.6	} 74.9	} 211.5	
Animal feeds	64	10	59	263						
Bread, rolls	16	22	125E	196E	-71.9	26.7	15.8	122.1	210.0	
Cookies & crackers	2	7	40E	62E	-33.3	0.0	0.0	30.2	167.8	
Cane sugar	0	0	0	0	0.0	0.0	0.0	0.0	0.0	
Beet sugar	1	Z	2E	7E	inf.	inf.	400.0	inf.	825.0	
Confectionary	1	Z	3E	6E	-75.0	-80.0	400.0	-63.6	1450.0	
Cottonseed oil	0	0	0	0	0.0	0.0	0.0	0.0	0.0	
Soybean oil	4	3	24	349	0.0	0.0	50.0	207.9	149.8	
Other fats & oils	9	2	12E	46E	0.0	100.0	0.0	109.3	304.4	
Cooking oil & marg.	1	Z	3E	11E	inf.	0.0	inf.	0.0	inf.	
Beer	1E	P	1	1	inf.	0.0	inf.	0.0	inf.	
Wine & brandy	1E	P	1	1	inf.	inf.	0.0	inf.	250.0	
Spirits	1	3	20E	42E	0.0	50.0	0.0	5.0	203.7	
Soft drinks	25	17	108E	238E	-49.0	9.1	41.7	121.9	370.9	
Flavorings	1E	P	1	1	-66.7	0.0	-80.0	-47.5	-33.3	
Canned fish	2E	P	0.4	1	100.0	0.0	0.0	0.0	333.3	
Frozen fish	6E	P	0.3	1	inf.	inf.	0.0	inf.	266.7	
Coffee	1E	P	2	5	0.0	0.0	0.0	-72.7	1533.3	
Pasta	1	Z	3E	6E	0.0	-75.0	0.0	-72.1	270.6	
Miscellaneous foods	26	8	56E	108E	-44.7	83.3	-26.4	298.2	145.2	
Total	303	215	1202	6891	-43.7	-10.8	13.8	101.7	174.4	21.2

Source: Data from Bureau of the Census reports.

Note: Industries are listed by four-digit SIC code, see Appendix C for definitions of terms.

EST = Establishments. EMP = Employment. VA = Value added. VS = Value of shipments. inf. = Infinity. P = Less than 20. Z = 20 to 99.

Appendix Table B–23
Delaware: Basic Economic Data on Food Manufacturing Industries, 1963, 1972, 1982, and 1985

INDUSTRY 1/	EST	EMP	VA	VS	EST 1963-1982	EMP 1963-1972	EMP 1972-1982	VS 1963-1972	VS 1972-1982	VS 1982-1985
	No.	'00	\$ million				Percent			
Meatpacking	1E	P	0.1	1	-80.0	0.0	-80.0	0.0	-76.5	
Meat processing	3	Z	1	4	-50.0	0.0	-75.0	242.5	-69.3	
Poultry dressing	7	38	45	321	} 0.0	} 21.4	} 123.5	} 26.3	} 370.7	
Poultry processing	0E	0	0	0						
Butter	0	0	0	0	0.0	0.0	0.0	0.0	0.0	
Cheese	1E	P	1	4	0.0	0.0	0.0	-93.8	800.0	
Processed milk	0	0	0	0	0.0	0.0	0.0	0.0	0.0	
Ice cream	1E	P	1	2	-50.0	-50.0	-90.0	-47.9	-57.9	
Fluid milk	3	Z	3E	12E	-83.3	-75.0	-50.0	-75.0	215.8	
Canned specialties	1	Z	2E	4E	0.0	0.0	0.0	-56.5	270.0	
Canned fruit & veg.	8	10	33E	75E	-52.9	14.3	-37.5	20.0	65.6	
Dry fruit & veg.	0	0	0	0	0.0	0.0	0.0	0.0	0.0	
Sauces, pickles	3	3	10E	22E	0.0	200.0	0.0	350.0	255.6	
Frozen fruit & veg.	2	2	7E	15E	} -33.3	} -66.7	} 100.0	} -54.3	} 254.8	
Frozen specialties	2	2	7E	15E						
Flour	2	P	1	2	-50.0	-80.0	0.0	-57.1	4.8	
Breakfast foods	0	0	0	0	0.0	0.0	0.0	0.0	0.0	
Rice	0	0	0	0	0.0	0.0	0.0	0.0	0.0	
Flour mixes	0	0	0	0	0.0	0.0	0.0	0.0	0.0	
Wet corn mills	0	0	0	0	0.0	0.0	0.0	0.0	0.0	
Pet foods	1E	P	1	2	} -46.2	} -60.0	} 5.0	} -22.7	} 226.4	
Animal feeds	6	2	17	138						
Bread, rolls	4	3	14E	23E	-66.7	-40.0	0.0	-28.6	143.2	
Cookies & crackers	0	0	0	0	-100.0	-100.0	0.0	-100.0	0.0	
Cane sugar	0	0	0	0	0.0	0.0	0.0	0.0	0.0	
Beet sugar	0	0	0	0	0.0	0.0	0.0	0.0	0.0	
Confectionary	2E	P	1	1	100.0	0.0	0.0	100.0	200.0	
Cottonseed oil	0	0	0	0	0.0	0.0	0.0	0.0	0.0	
Soybean oil	0	0	0	0	-100.0	6900.0	-100.0	11126.1	-100.0	
Other fats & oils	3E	2	13	88	-25.0	-100.0	inf.			
Cooking oil & marg.	0	0	0	0	0.0	0.0	0.0	0.0	0.0	
Beer	0	0	0	0	0.0	0.0	0.0	0.0	0.0	
Wine & brandy	0	0	0	0	0.0	0.0	0.0	0.0	0.0	
Spirits	0	0	0	0	0.0	0.0	0.0	0.0	0.0	
Soft drinks	2	2	12E	30E	-80.0	50.0	-33.3	229.3	118.5	
Flavorings	0	0	0	0	0.0	0.0	0.0	0.0	0.0	
Canned fish	3	4	19	56	200.0	50.0	33.3	192.3	267.8	
Frozen fish	2	2	5E	21E	-33.3	0.0	300.0	120.0	872.7	
Coffee	0E	0	0	0	0.0	0.0	0.0	0.0	0.0	
Pasta	1E	P	1	1	inf.	inf.	0.0	inf.	160.0	
Miscellaneous foods	5	14	98E	189E	-28.6	1950.0	-31.2	4344.0	70.4	
Total	63	84	477	1298	-48.8	34.4	2.4	100.2	155.9	9.7

Source: Data from Bureau of the Census reports.

Note: Industries are listed by four-digit SIC code, see Appendix C for definitions of terms.

EST = Establishments. EMP = Employment. VA = Value added. VS = Value of shipments. inf. = Infinity. P = Less than 20. Z = 20 to 99.

Appendix Table B-24
Maryland: Basic Economic Data on Food Manufacturing Industries, 1963, 1972, 1982, and 1985

INDUSTRY 1/	1982 Totals EST	EMP	VA	VS	Growth Rates EST 1963-1982	EMP 1963-1972	EMP 1972-1982	VS 1963-1972	VS 1972-1982	VS 1982-1985
	No.	'00	$ million		— — — — — — — — — Percent — — — — — — — — —					
Meatpacking	15	12	37	177	-51.7	-16.7	-40.0	40.4	35.6	
Meat processing	22	9	39E	120E	15.8	5.6	-52.6	60.6	7.5	
Poultry dressing	9	31	33	244	-50.0	-38.2	61.9	-20.5	239.7	
Poultry processing	2	3	13E	40E						
Butter	1E	P	1	4	0.0	100.0	-90.0	148.8	-60.8	
Cheese	1E	P	1	4	inf.	0.0	inf.	0.0	inf.	
Processed milk	2	Z	5E	20	-33.3	50.0	-83.3	99.3	-34.8	
Ice cream	12	5	48E	199	-25.0	-37.5	0.0	23.7	479.1	
Fluid milk	18	17	66	367	-57.1	-33.3	-22.7	55.1	105.0	
Canned specialties	2	2	10E	30	-33.3	200.0	-33.3	226.1	102.0	
Canned fruit & veg.	30	7	35E	106	-62.0	-65.0	-50.0	-24.7	170.0	
Dry fruit & veg.	1	P	1E	2E	inf.	0.0	inf.	0.0	inf.	
Sauces, pickles	8	7	35E	106	-46.7	-14.3	16.7	64.8	305.0	
Frozen fruit & veg.	3	3	15E	46E	0.0	0.0	-15.4	72.5	192.1	
Frozen specialties	4	8	40E	121E						
Flour	4E	Z	2	7	-42.9	0.0	0.0	51.0	-4.1	
Breakfast foods	0E	0	0	0	0.0	0.0	0.0	0.0	0.0	
Rice	0E	0	0	0	0.0	0.0	0.0	0.0	0.0	
Flour mixes	2	2	8E	28E	-33.3	0.0	0.0	147.1	59.0	
Wet corn mills	1E	P	0.4	1	0.0	-80.0	0.0	-70.8	100.0	
Pet foods	3	Z	2E	7E	-22.7	-66.7	175.0	-54.4	1273.4	
Animal feeds	14	5	64	307						
Bread, rolls	51	28	128E	238E	-27.1	-2.2	-37.8	60.8	70.7	
Cookies & crackers	2	2	9E	17E	-77.8	-60.0	0.0	-43.1	174.2	
Cane sugar	1	7	53E	256E	0.0	0.0	0.0	55.8	129.1	
Beet sugar	0E	0	0	0	0.0	0.0	0.0	0.0	0.0	
Confectionary	16E	3	9	18	-38.5	0.0	-40.0	32.1	65.8	
Cottonseed oil	0	0	0	0	0.0	0.0	0.0	0.0	0.0	
Soybean oil	0	0	0	0	0.0	inf.	-100.0	inf.	-100.0	
Other fats & oils	8	3	14E	54E	-11.1	50.0	-16.7	291.8	41.8	
Cooking oil & marg.	1	2	30E	118E	0.0	0.0	0.0	29.3	209.7	
Beer	3	3	46E	80E	-62.5	-15.8	-81.3	50.1	-17.2	
Wine & brandy	2E	Z	8	13	100.0	300.0	-75.0	904.5	-39.4	
Spirits	6	9	139E	241E	0.0	8.3	-30.8	97.9	67.7	
Soft drinks	25	22	209	449	-45.7	20.0	-26.7	201.3	167.6	
Flavorings	7	2	31E	54E	-36.4	0.0	-33.3	37.8	61.4	
Canned fish	6E	Z	4	12	-50.0	-30.0	-92.9	71.0	-73.0	
Frozen fish	41	15	26	200	-40.6	-42.1	36.4	117.7	353.4	
Coffee	4	1	7E	24E	-33.3	300.0	-50.0	137.0	88.3	
Pasta	2E	P	1	2	0.0	0.0	-80.0	113.3	-25.0	
Miscellaneous foods	36	21	163	318	-12.2	57.7	2.4	92.5	164.6	
Total	365	233	1337	3935	-38.4	-15.3	-23.4	59.9	114.5	12.7

Source: Data from Bureau of the Census reports.

Note: Industries are listed by four-digit SIC code, see Appendix C for definitions of terms.

EST = Establishments. EMP = Employment. VA = Value added. VS = Value of shipments. inf. = Infinity. P = Less than 20. Z = 20 to 99.

Appendix Table B–25
District of Columbia: Basic Economic Data on Food Manufacturing Industries, 1963, 1972, 1982, and 1985

INDUSTRY 1/	1982 Totals EST	EMP	VA	VS	Growth Rates EST 1963–1982	EMP 1963–1972	1972–1982	VS 1963–1972	1972–1982	1982–1985
	No.	'00	\$ million		- - - - - - - - - - Percent - - - - - - - - - -					
Meatpacking	0E	0	0	0	0.0	0.0	0.0	0.0	0.0	
Meat processing	0E	0	0	0	-100.0	-100.0	0.0	-100.0	0.0	
Poultry dressing	0E	0	0	0	-100.0	-100.0	0.0	-100.0	0.0	
Poultry processing	0E	0	0	0						
Butter	0E	0	0	0	0.0	0.0	0.0	0.0	0.0	
Cheese	0E	0	0	0	0.0	0.0	0.0	0.0	0.0	
Processed milk	0E	0	0	0	0.0	0.0	0.0	0.0	0.0	
Ice cream	0E	0	0	0	-100.0	-66.7	-100.0	35.5	-100.0	
Fluid milk	1E	Z	3	12	-66.7	-86.7	-75.0	-38.8	-58.5	
Canned specialties	0E	0	0	0	0.0	0.0	0.0	0.0	0.0	
Canned fruit & veg.	0E	0	0	0	0.0	0.0	0.0	0.0	0.0	
Dry fruit & veg.	0E	0	0	0	0.0	0.0	0.0	0.0	0.0	
Sauces, pickles	0E	0	0	0	-100.0	-80.0	-100.0	-66.7	-100.0	
Frozen fruit & veg.	0E	0	0	0	0.0	0.0	0.0	0.0	0.0	
Frozen specialties	0E	0	0	0						
Flour	0E	0	0	0	-100.0	0.0	-100.0	52.6	-100.0	
Breakfast foods	0E	0	0	0	0.0	0.0	0.0	0.0	0.0	
Rice	0E	0	0	0	0.0	0.0	0.0	0.0	0.0	
Flour mixes	0E	0	0	0	0.0	0.0	0.0	0.0	0.0	
Wet corn mills	0E	0	0	0	0.0	0.0	0.0	0.0	0.0	
Pet foods	0E	0	0	0	0.0	0.0	0.0	0.0	0.0	
Animal feeds	0E	0	0	0						
Bread, rolls	6	11	51E	85E	-68.4	-61.1	57.1	-46.6	281.1	
Cookies & crackers	1	P	1E	1E	inf.	0.0	inf.	0.0	inf.	
Cane sugar	0E	0	0	0	0.0	0.0	0.0	0.0	0.0	
Beet sugar	0E	0	0	0	0.0	0.0	0.0	0.0	0.0	
Confectionary	0E	0	0	0	-100.0	0.0	-100.0	100.0	inf.	
Cottonseed oil	0E	0	0	0	0.0	0.0	0.0	0.0	0.0	
Soybean oil	0E	0	0	0	0.0	0.0	0.0	0.0	0.0	
Other fats & oils	1E	P	1	2	0.0	-80.0	0.0	-58.8	128.6	
Cooking oil & marg.	0E	0	0	0	0.0	0.0	0.0	0.0	0.0	
Beer	0E	0	0	0	0.0	0.0	0.0	0.0	0.0	
Wine & brandy	0E	0	0	0	0.0	0.0	0.0	0.0	0.0	
Spirits	0E	0	0	0	0.0	0.0	0.0	0.0	0.0	
Soft drinks	1E	P	1	2	-75.0	0.0	-95.0	119.5	-83.3	
Flavorings	0E	0	0	0	-100.0	-100.0	0.0	-100.0	0.0	
Canned fish	0E	0	0	0	0.0	0.0	0.0	0.0	0.0	
Frozen fish	0E	0	0	0	0.0	0.0	0.0	0.0	0.0	
Coffee	1E	P	2	5	-85.7	-95.0	0.0	-96.5	880.0	
Pasta	1E	P	1	1	-50.0	0.0	0.0	0.0	0.0	
Miscellaneous foods	4	Z	4E	7E	-42.9	-6.3	-60.0	35.2	-1.4	
Total	16	12	58	93	-71.4	-66.7	-20.0	-31.6	-10.8	9.0

Source: Data from Bureau of the Census reports.

Note: Industries are listed by four-digit SIC code, see Appendix C for definitions of terms.

EST = Establishments. EMP = Employment. VA = Value added. VS = Value of shipments. inf. = Infinity. P = Less than 20. Z = 20 to 99.

Appendix Table B–26
Virginia: Basic Economic Data on Food Manufacturing Industries, 1963, 1972, 1982, and 1985

INDUSTRY 1/	1982 Totals				Growth Rates					
	EST	EMP	VA	VS	EST	EMP		VS		
					1963–1982	1963–1972	1972–1982	1963–1972	1972–1982	1982–1985
	No.	'00	$ million		- - - - - - - - - Percent - - - - - - - - - -					
Meatpacking	39	46	187	896	-18.8	7.7	9.5	83.6	13.5	
Meat processing	16	8	26E	112E	-15.8	50.0	166.7	89.5	586.5	
Poultry dressing	14	71	142	697	-27.3	117.4	48.0	280.7	188.9	
Poultry processing	2	3	10E	42E						
Butter	0E	0	0	0	-100.0	-80.0	-100.0	-78.0	-100.0	
Cheese	2	P	2	4	0.0	-80.0	0.0	-72.7	311.1	
Processed milk	1	5	102E	187E	-75.0	0.0	150.0	11.8	995.3	
Ice cream	8	3	61E	112E	-38.5	-62.5	0.0	-21.3	507.6	
Fluid milk	19	15	86E	340	-64.2	-24.2	-40.0	58.6	103.4	
Canned specialties	0E	0	0	0	0.0	inf.	-100.0	inf.	-100.0	
Canned fruit & veg.	19	17	49	135	-58.7	-14.3	-5.6	91.8	104.6	
Dry fruit & veg.	0E	0	0	0	0.0	0.0	0.0	0.0	0.0	
Sauces, pickles	6	Z	2E	4E	-14.3	0.0	-50.0	12.1	0.0	
Frozen fruit & veg.	3E	1	3	7	0.0	-4.8	-10.0	16.4	106.0	
Frozen specialties	5	17	57	143						
Flour	14	2	7	64	-51.7	-25.0	-33.3	99.3	124.0	
Breakfast foods	1E	Z	2	6	inf.	0.0	inf.	0.0	inf.	
Rice	1E	P	1	1	inf.	0.0	inf.	0.0	inf.	
Flour mixes	1	Z	2E	6E	-50.0	0.0	0.0	60.0	27.1	
Wet corn mills	0E	0	0	0	0.0	0.0	0.0	0.0	0.0	
Pet foods	3	Z	2E	6E	-17.0	-12.5	-21.4	40.8	179.0	
Animal feeds	36	5	25	236						
Bread, rolls	35	30	203E	318E	-43.5	-2.5	-23.1	67.3	149.7	
Cookies & crackers	3	15	102E	159E	0.0	0.0	114.3	27.9	593.9	
Cane sugar	0	0	0	0	0.0	0.0	0.0	0.0	0.0	
Beet sugar	0	0	0	0	0.0	0.0	0.0	0.0	0.0	
Confectionary	21	21	132E	428E	0.0	12.2	-25.5	232.2	88.2	
Cottonseed oil	0E	0	0	0	0.0	0.0	0.0	0.0	0.0	
Soybean oil	2E	Z	3	17	100.0	0.0	0.0	-9.7	63.7	
Other fats & oils	8	6	33E	200E	-42.9	-19.6	46.3	471.2	140.3	
Cooking oil & marg.	2E	Z	3	17	100.0	0.0	0.0	108.2	63.7	
Beer	2	7	80E	179E	0.0	50.0	75.0	575.7	258.4	
Wine & brandy	6	Z	6E	13E	inf.	inf.	0.0	inf.	103.2	
Spirits	1	Z	6E	13E	0.0	50.0	-50.0	316.7	2.4	
Soft drinks	31	29	330E	743E	-67.0	-8.6	-9.4	73.6	500.7	
Flavorings	4	Z	6E	13E	-33.3	0.0	0.0	57.5	103.2	
Canned fish	5	2	3	7	-68.8	-16.7	-60.0	-29.9	-38.2	
Frozen fish	86	37	42	158	-3.4	4.5	60.9	85.7	279.1	
Coffee	3	1	3E	14E	0.0	0.0	0.0	-79.8	527.3	
Pasta	3	P	0.3E	1E	200.0	0.0	0.0	-50.0	600.0	
Miscellaneous foods	44	24	344	627	-13.7	18.5	46.9	86.9	345.1	
Total	445	368	2059	5903	-33.3	5.0	9.5	96.4	200.6	5.0

Source: Data from Bureau of the Census reports.

Note: Industries are listed by four-digit SIC code, see Appendix C for definitions of terms.

EST = Establishments. EMP = Employment. VA = Value added. VS = Value of shipments. inf. = Infinity. P = Less than 20. Z = 20 to 99.

Appendix Table B–27
West Virginia: Basic Economic Data on Food Manufacturing Industries, 1963, 1972, 1982, and 1985

INDUSTRY 1/	EST	EMP	VA	VS	EST 1963-1982	EMP 1963-1972	EMP 1972-1982	VS 1963-1972	VS 1972-1982	VS 1982-1985
	No.	'00	\$ million							
Meatpacking	14	3	7	44	-57.6	-14.3	-50.0	259.0	-49.4	
Meat processing	4	2	7E	21E	100.0	-80.0	300.0	-63.6	2550.0	
Poultry dressing	2	3	11E	32E	-50.0	100.0	200.0	162.5	657.1	
Poultry processing	1	3	11E	32E						
Butter	0E	0	0	0	0.0	0.0	0.0	0.0	0.0	
Cheese	0E	0	0	0	0.0	0.0	0.0	0.0	0.0	
Processed milk	0E	0	0	0	-100.0	100.0	-100.0	28.9	-100.0	
Ice cream	1E	P	0.3	1	-80.0	-100.0	inf.	-100.0	inf.	
Fluid milk	11	8	21E	93E	-71.1	-47.1	-11.1	-6.9	110.4	
Canned specialties	0E	0	0	0	0.0	0.0	0.0	0.0	0.0	
Canned fruit & veg.	3	2	10E	26E	-62.5	-50.0	-33.3	-16.1	94.8	
Dry fruit & veg.	0E	0	0	0	0.0	0.0	0.0	0.0	0.0	
Sauces, pickles	0E	0	0	0	-100.0	0.0	-100.0	50.0	-100.0	
Frozen fruit & veg.	1E	P	1	1	-50.0	400.0	-96.0	720.0	-91.1	
Frozen specialties	0E	0	0	0						
Flour	1E	P	1	3	-75.0	0.0	0.0	50.0	120.0	
Breakfast foods	0E	0	0	0	0.0	0.0	0.0	0.0	0.0	
Rice	0E	0	0	0	0.0	0.0	0.0	0.0	0.0	
Flour mixes	1	Z	5	10	-50.0	-100.0	inf.	-100.0	inf.	
Wet corn mills	0E	0	0	0	0.0	0.0	0.0	0.0	0.0	
Pet foods	0E	0	0	0	-75.0	-90.0	0.0	-83.8	172.7	
Animal feeds	2E	P	1	3						
Bread, rolls	16	19	74	115	-65.2	-21.7	5.5	46.2	70.2	
Cookies & crackers	0	0	0	0	0.0	0.0	0.0	0.0	0.0	
Cane sugar	0	0	0	0	0.0	0.0	0.0	0.0	0.0	
Beet sugar	0	0	0	0	0.0	0.0	0.0	0.0	0.0	
Confectionary	1	P	1E	1E	-75.0	0.0	0.0	100.0	200.0	
Cottonseed oil	0E	0	0	0	0.0	0.0	0.0	0.0	0.0	
Soybean oil	0E	0	0	0	0.0	0.0	0.0	0.0	0.0	
Other fats & oils	2	Z	3E	8E	0.0	0.0	400.0	133.3	1057.1	
Cooking oil & marg.	0E	0	0	0	0.0	0.0	0.0	0.0	0.0	
Beer	0E	0	0	0	-100.0	-100.0	0.0	-100.0	0.0	
Wine & brandy	0E	0	0	0	0.0	0.0	0.0	0.0	0.0	
Spirits	0E	0	0	0	0.0	0.0	0.0	0.0	0.0	
Soft drinks	28	13	66E	145E	-54.1	-17.6	-7.1	35.5	204.0	
Flavorings	1E	P	1	1	0.0	-100.0	inf.	-100.0	inf.	
Canned fish	0E	0	0	0	0.0	0.0	0.0	0.0	0.0	
Frozen fish	0E	0	0	0	0.0	0.0	0.0	0.0	0.0	
Coffee	0E	0	0	0	0.0	0.0	0.0	0.0	0.0	
Pasta	0E	0	0	0	0.0	0.0	0.0	0.0	0.0	
Miscellaneous foods	11	3	6E	12E	-26.7	50.0	66.7	178.3	82.8	
Total	100	57	225	559	-58.7	-20.5	-1.7	22.3	128.1	-11.7

Source: Data from Bureau of the Census reports.

Note: Industries are listed by four-digit SIC code, see Appendix C for definitions of terms.

EST = Establishments. EMP = Employment. VA = Value added. VS = Value of shipments. inf. = Infinity. P = Less than 20. Z = 20 to 99.

Appendix Table B–28

North Carolina: Basic Economic Data on Food Manufacturing Industries, 1963, 1972, 1982, and 1985

INDUSTRY 1/	1982 Totals				Growth Rates					
	EST	EMP	VA	VS	EST	EMP		VS		
					1963-1982	1963-1972	1972-1982	1963-1972	1972-1982	1982-1985
	No.	'00	$ million		- - - - - - - - - Percent - - - - - - - - -					
Meatpacking	48	32	100	569	-43.5	20.0	33.3	146.8	175.4	
Meat processing	45	19	75E	362	32.4	225.0	46.2	651.4	349.6	
Poultry dressing	23	99	140	81	-52.9	62.5	30.8	96.0	177.4	
Poultry processing	1	3	12E	57E						
Butter	0	0	0	0	-100.0	-100.0	0.0	-100.0	0.0	
Cheese	2E	Z	5E	23E	100.0	0.0	0.0	6.1	542.9	
Processed milk	1E	Z	5E	23E	0.0	-100.0	inf.	-100.0	inf.	
Ice cream	8	3	14	39	-46.7	0.0	0.0	91.7	84.7	
Fluid milk	20	27	107	441	-57.4	-35.6	-6.9	37.7	116.0	
Canned specialties	4	8	84	164	100.0	75.0	14.3	135.5	274.9	
Canned fruit & veg.	6	3	16E	50E	-60.0	-50.0	50.0	135.8	298.4	
Dry fruit & veg.	1E	P	1	2	-50.0	-80.0	0.0	-64.7	183.3	
Sauces, pickles	5	6	26	51	-44.4	16.7	-14.3	117.1	89.5	
Frozen fruit & veg.	1E	1	5	17	-80.0	-83.3	100.0	-65.6	435.5	
Frozen specialties	0E	0	0	0						
Flour	21	6	23	134	-61.1	-40.0	100.0	60.2	307.0	
Breakfast foods	1E	P	1	2	0.0	-100.0	inf.	-100.0	inf.	
Rice	0E	0	0	0	0.0	0.0	0.0	0.0	0.0	
Flour mixes	3	2	11E	46E	-25.0	0.0	0.0	-9.3	155.6	
Wet corn mills	0E	0	0	0	0.0	0.0	0.0	0.0	0.0	
Pet foods	3	2	11E	46E	-30.4	-22.7	11.8	49.1	179.4	
Animal feeds	91	17	110	661						
Bread, rolls	46	49	186	325	-44.6	13.8	-25.8	88.0	71.7	
Cookies & crackers	8	53	187	291	33.3	33.3	65.6	77.3	276.3	
Cane sugar	0E	0	0	0	0.0	0.0	0.0	0.0	0.0	
Beet sugar	0E	0	0	0	0.0	0.0	0.0	0.0	0.0	
Confectionary	13	4	19	39	-18.8	-20.0	0.0	132.8	189.6	
Cottonseed oil	1	Z	4E	42E	-90.0	-75.0	-50.0	76.7	48.0	
Soybean oil	4	2	14E	166E	100.0	300.0	0.0	398.2	195.0	
Other fats & oils	15	9	41E	277E	-28.6	1.7	47.5	154.7	635.8	
Cooking oil & marg.	1	Z	4E	42E	-50.0	0.0	-50.0	186.7	48.0	
Beer	3	19	327E	782E	inf.	inf.	171.4	inf.	2019.2	
Wine & brandy	2E	P	2	4	inf.	inf.	0.0	inf.	720.0	
Spirits	0E	0	0	0	0.0	0.0	0.0	0.0	0.0	
Soft drinks	66	38	208	484	-48.4	8.5	-25.5	188.3	80.1	
Flavorings	5	Z	9E	21E	0.0	0.0	0.0	-35.0	692.3	
Canned fish	6	2	7E	16E	0.0	200.0	-33.3	1420.0	6.6	
Frozen fish	28	9	15	55	47.4	-25.0	200.0	333.3	322.3	
Coffee	2	3	11E	24E	0.0	0.0	500.0	66.7	170.0	
Pasta	0	0	0	0	0.0	0.0	0.0	0.0	0.0	
Miscellaneous foods	61	20	154	269	-39.0	61.5	-4.8	429.9	148.5	
Total	544	439	1930	6319	-36.9	13.7	17.4	102.5	212.0	15.3

Source: Data from Bureau of the Census reports.

Note: Industries are listed by four-digit SIC code, see Appendix C for definitions of terms.

EST = Establishments. EMP = Employment. VA = Value added. VS = Value of shipments. inf. = Infinity. P = Less than 20. Z = 20 to 99.

Appendix Table B-29
South Carolina: Basic Economic Data on Food Manufacturing Industries, 1963, 1972, 1982, and 1985

INDUSTRY 1/	1982 Totals EST	1982 Totals EMP	1982 Totals VA	1982 Totals VS	Growth Rates EST 1963-1982	Growth Rates EMP 1963-1972	Growth Rates EMP 1972-1982	Growth Rates VS 1963-1972	Growth Rates VS 1972-1982	Growth Rates VS 1982-1985
	No.	'00	$ million		- - - - - - - - - - Percent - - - - - - - - - -					
Meatpacking	32	12	32	183	-20.0	-14.3	0.0	63.0	94.9	
Meat processing	8	1	5	16	-11.1	-75.0	100.0	-80.7	817.6	
Poultry dressing	7	12	28	120	-46.2	50.0	33.3	118.7	229.8	
Poultry processing	0	0	0	0						
Butter	0	0	0	0	-100.0	-100.0	0.0	-100.0	0.0	
Cheese	0	0	0	0	0.0	0.0	0.0	0.0	0.0	
Processed milk	1	Z	4E	11E	-50.0	0.0	0.0	-2.6	197.3	
Ice cream	4	2	15E	44E	-42.9	-33.3	0.0	88.6	195.3	
Fluid milk	12	8	59E	176E	-61.3	-12.5	-42.9	72.0	68.7	
Canned specialties	2	3	12E	36E	inf.	inf.	50.0	inf.	414.3	
Canned fruit & veg.	4	2	8	24E	-66.7	-50.0	0.0	-36.2	700.0	
Dry fruit & veg.	1E	P	0.4	1	inf.	0.0	inf.	0.0	inf.	
Sauces, pickles	3	Z	2E	6E	-62.5	0.0	-75.0	-1.4	-14.3	
Frozen fruit & veg.	2E	P	0.4	1	100.0	4900.0	6.7	17466.6	266.8	
Frozen specialties	2	2	66E	192E						
Flour	5	1	5E	12E	-68.8	-50.0	0.0	0.0	124.5	
Breakfast foods	0E	0	0	0	0.0	0.0	0.0	0.0	0.0	
Rice	0E	0	0	0	0.0	0.0	0.0	0.0	0.0	
Flour mixes	1	1	5E	12E	inf.	0.0	inf.	0.0	inf.	
Wet corn mills	0E	0	0	0	0.0	0.0	0.0	0.0	0.0	
Pet foods	2E	P	1	1	-39.4	-42.9	-22.5	23.8	84.5	
Animal feeds	18	3	10	60						
Bread, rolls	12	20	101	183	-47.8	-5.6	17.6	43.8	298.5	
Cookies & crackers	0	0	0	0	0.0	0.0	0.0	0.0	0.0	
Cane sugar	0	0	0	0	0.0	0.0	0.0	0.0	0.0	
Beet sugar	0	0	0	0	0.0	0.0	0.0	0.0	0.0	
Confectionary	2	3	18E	38E	-60.0	600.0	-57.1	1139.1	31.6	
Cottonseed oil	5	2	6E	26E	-54.5	-33.3	0.0	4.4	58.1	
Soybean oil	4	2	17	180	33.3	-50.0	100.0	-18.5	388.6	
Other fats & oils	0	0	0	0	-100.0	0.0	-100.0	94.1	-100.0	
Cooking oil & marg.	3	2	6E	26E	200.0	0.0	300.0	63.3	230.0	
Beer	0E	0	0	0	0.0	0.0	0.0	0.0	0.0	
Wine & brandy	3	Z	1E	4E	inf.	0.0	inf.	0.0	inf.	
Spirits	0E	0	0	0	0.0	0.0	0.0	0.0	0.0	
Soft drinks	28	21	121	280	-63.6	4.3	-12.5	96.2	199.3	
Flavorings	1E	Z	1	4	0.0	0.0	400.0	-50.0	1000.0	
Canned fish	2E	P	0.4	1	-60.0	0.0	-95.0	531.3	-87.1	
Frozen fish	10	5	9	26	42.9	0.0	150.0	123.1	202.3	
Coffee	1E	P	2	5	-50.0	0.0	0.0	63.6	172.2	
Pasta	0E	0	0	0	0.0	0.0	0.0	0.0	0.0	
Miscellaneous foods	20	3	10	20	-60.8	20.0	-16.7	117.1	125.8	
Total	195	122	535	1666	-46.4	10.0	-0.8	58.8	190.5	40.8

Source: Data from Bureau of the Census reports.

Note: Industries are listed by four-digit SIC code, see Appendix C for definitions of terms.

EST = Establishments. EMP = Employment. VA = Value added. VS = Value of shipments. inf. = Infinity. P = Less than 20. Z = 20 to 99.

Appendix Table B–30

Georgia: Basic Economic Data on Food Manufacturing Industries, 1963, 1972, 1982, and 1985

INDUSTRY 1/	EST	EMP	VA	VS	EST 1963-1982	EMP 1963-1972	EMP 1972-1982	VS 1963-1972	VS 1972-1982	VS 1982-1985
	No.	'00	\$ million		- - - - - - - - Percent - - - - - - - -					
Meatpacking	47	27	60	474	-46.6	9.4	-22.9	73.7	78.8	
Meat processing	39	21	60	235	50.0	100.0	110.0	253.9	244.1	
Poultry dressing	33	129	209	1013	9.8	32.9	41.2	50.4	208.0	
Poultry processing	12	8	21	848						
Butter	0E	0	0	0	-100.0	-100.0	0.0	-100.0	0.0	
Cheese	2E	P	1	1	-33.3	75.0	-98.6	212.3	-98.5	
Processed milk	0E	0	0	0	-100.0	0.0	-100.0	-50.0	-100.0	
Ice cream	7	5	27E	62E	-50.0	0.0	66.7	532.7	77.6	
Fluid milk	17	22	65	271	-72.6	-40.0	4.8	-12.1	132.3	
Canned specialties	1	P	0.2E	1E	inf.	inf.	0.0	inf.	100.0	
Canned fruit & veg.	12	7	15E	43E	-42.9	-10.0	-22.2	-6.4	148.0	
Dry fruit & veg.	1	Z	1E	3E	0.0	50.0	-83.3	21.7	-63.1	
Sauces, pickles	9	15	117	311	-30.8	-30.8	66.7	-34.1	1129.2	
Frozen fruit & veg.	4	11	24	68	-18.2	128.6	18.8	178.5	164.4	
Frozen specialties	5	8	50	86						
Flour	11	2	15	55	-71.8	-33.3	0.0	-69.4	516.9	
Breakfast foods	0	0	0	0	-100.0	-100.0	0.0	-100.0	0.0	
Rice	0	0	0	0	0.0	0.0	0.0	0.0	0.0	
Flour mixes	2	3	37E	65E	-33.3	100.0	50.0	45.9	628.1	
Wet corn mills	0	0	0	0	-100.0	-100.0	0.0	-100.0	0.0	
Pet foods	7	6	74E	130E	-37.0	27.8	-8.7	74.8	123.1	
Animal feeds	61	15	64	533						
Bread, rolls	32	52	255	392	-43.9	-2.2	15.6	49.4	185.7	
Cookies & crackers	16	39	269	442	100.0	36.0	14.7	93.8	172.6	
Cane sugar	1	7	42E	136E	0.0	0.0	0.0	-28.8	-99.8	
Beet sugar	0E	0	0	0	0.0	0.0	0.0	0.0	0.0	
Confectionary	24	28	169	537	0.0	20.3	-0.3	317.6	158.5	
Cottonseed oil	2	Z	7E	34E	-80.0	-50.0	-75.0	-39.4	188.9	
Soybean oil	3	3	43E	203E	200.0	500.0	0.0	611.5	152.1	
Other fats & oils	9	5	64E	307E	-30.8	-42.9	150.0	264.6	473.1	
Cooking oil & marg.	4	3	43E	203E	-42.9	-28.6	-40.0	21.5	139.3	
Beer	2	15	239E	565E	100.0	50.0	400.0	598.6	991.9	
Wine & brandy	2E	Z	8E	19E	100.0	0.0	0.0	83.0	118.6	
Spirits	2	Z	8E	19E	100.0	0.0	0.0	186.7	118.6	
Soft drinks	50	28	145	390	-60.0	10.0	-36.4	100.0	184.3	
Flavorings	10	7	111E	263E	-9.1	0.0	0.0	114.8	118.6	
Canned fish	1E	P	0.3	1	0.0	3100.0	-99.4	3469.2	-98.9	
Frozen fish	13	15	20	72	-7.1	-95.5	1400.0	-91.0	2235.5	
Coffee	2E	P	0.3	1	-50.0	-100.0	inf.	-100.0	inf.	
Pasta	0E	0	0	0	0.0	0.0	0.0	0.0	0.0	
Miscellaneous foods	58	23	197	357	-45.3	28.2	-14.8	123.0	191.8	
Total	501	506	2457	7386	-38.8	10.3	9.5	74.3	179.7	13.3

Source: Data from Bureau of the Census reports.

Note: Industries are listed by four-digit SIC code, see Appendix C for definitions of terms.

EST = Establishments. EMP = Employment. VA = Value added. VS = Value of shipments. inf. = Infinity. P = Less than 20. Z = 20 to 99.

Appendix Table B–31
Florida: Basic Economic Data on Food Manufacturing Industries, 1963, 1972, 1982, and 1985

INDUSTRY 1/	1982 Totals				Growth Rates					
	EST	EMP	VA	VS	EST	EMP		VS		
					1963-1982	1963-1972	1972-1982	1963-1972	1972-1982	1982-1985
	No.	'00	$ million		- - - - - - - - - - Percent - - - - - - - - - -					
Meatpacking	37	18	37	350	5.7	-10.5	5.9	70.4	86.1	
Meat processing	46	14	53	341	84.0	111.1	-26.3	205.1	118.0	
Poultry dressing	3	14	16	106	-50.0	76.3	13.5	99.2	157.3	
Poultry processing	6	2	4	18						
Butter	0E	0	0	0	0.0	0.0	0.0	0.0	0.0	
Cheese	5E	P	1	2	66.7	0.0	0.0	-50.0	666.7	
Processed milk	2	1	6E	23E	-33.3	100.0	0.0	-34.2	800.0	
Ice cream	15	4	22	67	-28.6	-40.0	-33.3	-22.8	89.2	
Fluid milk	32	28	210	717	-47.5	-8.9	-31.7	94.3	126.6	
Canned specialties	8E	1	4	10	33.3	0.0	0.0	441.2	4.3	
Canned fruit & veg.	40	45	264	838	-50.0	-17.7	-11.8	50.7	193.9	
Dry fruit & veg.	1E	P	0.4	1	0.0	0.0	-80.0	170.6	-78.3	
Sauces, pickles	8	1	4E	10E	60.0	100.0	0.0	411.1	4.3	
Frozen fruit & veg.	34	64	576	1661	22.5	30.2	-2.9	86.9	167.8	
Frozen specialties	15	3	9	19						
Flour	4	Z	3E	15E	-50.0	0.0	-50.0	52.9	198.1	
Breakfast foods	0E	0	0	0	0.0	0.0	0.0	0.0	0.0	
Rice	0E	0	0	0	0.0	0.0	0.0	0.0	0.0	
Flour mixes	3	Z	3E	16E	50.0	300.0	-75.0	1633.3	49.0	
Wet corn mills	1E	Z	3	16	0.0	-100.0	inf.	-100.0	inf.	
Pet foods	2E	Z	3	16	-14.3	12.5	-22.2	59.7	179.5	
Animal feeds	34	7	37	221						
Bread, rolls	101	59	248	420	-9.0	7.3	0.0	67.3	140.2	
Cookies & crackers	16	3	8	16	300.0	50.0	0.0	74.5	77.5	
Cane sugar	13	21	107E	501E	44.4	0.0	23.5	87.1	201.3	
Beet sugar	0E	0	0	0	0.0	0.0	0.0	0.0	0.0	
Confectionary	18	5	21E	100E	-18.2	66.7	2.0	82.9	677.3	
Cottonseed oil	0E	0	0	0	0.0	0.0	0.0	0.0	0.0	
Soybean oil	0E	0	0	0	0.0	0.0	0.0	0.0	0.0	
Other fats & oils	14	4	23E	70E	-33.3	-30.0	14.3	-20.1	161.3	
Cooking oil & marg.	0E	0	0	0	-100.0	0.0	-100.0	80.0	-100.0	
Beer	4	15	288E	637E	-20.0	50.0	25.0	163.4	337.8	
Wine & brandy	3	Z	10E	21E	-40.0	0.0	0.0	177.3	247.5	
Spirits	3E	Z	10	21	200.0	0.0	0.0	103.3	247.5	
Soft drinks	47	51	302	809	-65.2	-2.4	24.4	171.2	304.5	
Flavorings	9	3	58E	127E	-40.0	500.0	0.0	780.0	261.6	
Canned fish	3	2	6E	11E	-72.7	-50.0	100.0	7.1	260.0	
Frozen fish	75	52	144	529	56.3	65.2	36.8	343.8	272.3	
Coffee	20	13	347	839	-4.8	66.7	30.0	137.6	251.6	
Pasta	3	1	3E	5E	50.0	0.0	100.0	0.0	260.0	
Miscellaneous foods	91	18	86	169	-33.1	13.3	5.9	223.3	148.6	
Total	716	453	2915	8717	-20.3	11.9	2.3	98.4	188.6	12.1

Source: Data from Bureau of the Census reports.

Note: Industries are listed by four-digit SIC code, see Appendix C for definitions of terms.

EST = Establishments. EMP = Employment. VA = Value added. VS = Value of shipments. P = Less than 20. Z = 20 to 99.

Appendix Table B–32
Kentucky: Basic Economic Data on Food Manufacturing Industries, 1963, 1972, 1982, and 1985

INDUSTRY 1/	1982 Totals				Growth Rates					
	EST	EMP	VA	VS	EST	EMP		VS		
					1963-1982	1963-1972	1972-1982	1963-1972	1972-1982	1982-1985
	No.	'00	$ million		- - - - - - - - - - Percent - - - - - - - -					
Meatpacking	41	28	143	634	-43.8	0.0	3.7	93.7	133.7	
Meat processing	13	3	8E	27E	18.2	100.0	50.0	200.0	276.4	
Poultry dressing	2	2	5E	18E	} -77.8	} -60.0	} 0.0	} -56.9	} 150.0	
Poultry processing	0	0	0	0						
Butter	2	1	7E	40E	-50.0	200.0	-66.7	411.0	-5.0	
Cheese	8	5	16	102	-50.0	-20.0	25.0	1.6	222.2	
Processed milk	6	2	14E	80E	20.0	-50.0	0.0	-8.2	184.3	
Ice cream	6	1	7E	40E	-50.0	-33.3	-50.0	31.0	328.0	
Fluid milk	18	13	51	240	-70.5	-20.0	-35.0	61.1	90.2	
Canned specialties	1	Z	7E	12E	0.0	0.0	0.0	4.3	395.8	
Canned fruit & veg.	4	3	40E	72E	100.0	0.0	50.0	74.1	661.7	
Dry fruit & veg.	0	0	0	0	0.0	0.0	0.0	0.0	0.0	
Sauces, pickles	2	3	40E	72E	-50.0	0.0	0.0	0.0	0.0	
Frozen fruit & veg.	0	0	0	0	} -80.0	} -75.0	} 0.0	} -41.5	} 395.8	
Frozen specialties	1	Z	7E	12E						
Flour	11	2	15E	65E	-59.3	-60.0	0.0	-51.8	493.6	
Breakfast foods	0	0	0	0	0.0	0.0	0.0	0.0	0.0	
Rice	0	0	0	0	0.0	0.0	0.0	0.0	0.0	
Flour mixes	1	P	1E	2E	-50.0	-66.7	-900.0	-69.6	-61.8	
Wet corn mills	0	0	0	0	0.0	0.0	0.0	0.0	0.0	
Pet foods	2	P	1E	3E	} 6.1	} 2.0	} 0.0	} 61.4	} 205.0	
Animal feeds	33	5	29E	151E						
Bread, rolls	15	18	84E	160E	-60.5	-21.7	0.0	44.9	152.9	
Cookies & crackers	3	11	51E	98E	0.0	75.0	57.1	141.1	297.6	
Cane sugar	0E	0	0	0	0.0	0.0	0.0	0.0	0.0	
Beet sugar	0E	0	0	0	0.0	0.0	0.0	0.0	0.0	
Confectionary	4E	1	6E	13E	-69.2	0.0	0.0	192.9	204.9	
Cottonseed oil	0	0	0	0	0.0	0.0	0.0	0.0	0.0	
Soybean oil	2	2	15E	193E	-33.3	0.0	0.0	44.2	196.0	
Other fats & oils	4	Z	3E	8E	-20.0	0.0	0.0	858.8	-50.3	
Cooking oil & marg.	3	3	30E	118E	200.0	0.0	0.0	233.0	20.2	
Beer	2	3	28E	49E	-60.0	-50.0	-57.1	134.7	-36.8	
Wine & brandy	2E	Z	5	8	100.0	400.0	0.0	1200.0	55.8	
Spirits	19	38	362	811	-47.2	-7.9	-34.5	62.1	35.5	
Soft drinks	36	29	268E	471E	-53.2	34.8	-6.5	12.2	253.1	
Flavorings	4	Z	5E	8E	33.3	0.0	0.0	30.0	55.8	
Canned fish	0E	0	0	0	0.0	0.0	0.0	0.0	0.0	
Frozen fish	2E	3	29	59	0.0	0.0	2900.0	0.0	29400.0	
Coffee	0E	0	0	0	-100.0	-100.0	0.0	-100.0	0.0	
Pasta	1	2	19	39E	0.0	0.0	0.0	-21.3	718.8	
Miscellaneous foods	25	12	110E	226E	-41.9	0.0	22.2	83.3	234.8	
Total	272	191	1347	3676	-45.4	-8.4	-12.4	59.7	107.5	5.7

Source: Data from Bureau of the Census reports.

Note: Industries are listed by four-digit SIC code, see Appendix C for definitions of terms.

EST = Establishments. EMP = Employment. VA = Value added. VS = Value of shipments. P = Less than 20. Z = 20 to 99.

Appendix Table B-33
Tennessee: Basic Economic Data on Food Manufacturing Industries, 1963, 1972, 1982, and 1985

INDUSTRY 1/	1982 Totals				Growth Rates					
	EST	EMP	VA	VS	EST	EMP		VS		
					1963-1982	1963-1972	1972-1982	1963-1972	1972-1982	1982-1985
	No.	'00	\$ million		- - - - - - - - - - Percent - - - - - - - - - -					
Meatpacking	46	35	133	703	-37.0	13.0	-32.7	114.8	27.2	
Meat processing	29	14	41	284	45.0	125.0	55.6	450.6	221.9	
Poultry dressing	6	17	22	130	-25.0	-45.4	153.5	-22.5	307.6	
Poultry processing	3	1	3	9						
Butter	2	1	9E	64E	-33.3	100.0	0.0	180.5	458.3	
Cheese	10	3	24	145	-37.5	-40.0	0.0	36.5	320.9	
Processed milk	5	1	9E	64E	-28.6	-40.0	-66.7	11.3	72.1	
Ice cream	8	4	16	51	-75.8	-45.5	-33.3	9.6	54.2	
Fluid milk	13	20	120	361	-78.0	-24.1	-9.1	40.2	154.6	
Canned specialties	8	8	28E	76E	166.7	333.3	-38.5	329.5	26.8	
Canned fruit & veg.	9	5	22	50	-30.8	-55.6	25.0	-31.6	283.1	
Dry fruit & veg.	0	0	0	0	0.0	0.0	0.0	0.0	0.0	
Sauces, pickles	6	2	10	29	20.0	0.0	300.0	27.8	1143.5	
Frozen fruit & veg.	2	7	25E	66E	11.1	-65.0	300.0	-46.2	1470.2	
Frozen specialties	8	14	82	187						
Flour	18	9	116	350	-53.8	33.3	-25.0	56.3	156.0	
Breakfast foods	2	8	124E	264E	100.0	40.0	14.3	167.2	260.8	
Rice	1	2	31E	66E	0.0	300.0	0.0	326.5	215.8	
Flour mixes	4	3	47E	99E	33.3	0.0	500.0	73.3	1803.8	
Wet corn mills	3	3	47E	99E	inf.	0.0	inf.	0.0	inf.	
Pet foods	0	0	0	0	-89.5	-28.9	-11.1	2.2	89.5	
Animal feeds	6	3	17	53						
Bread, rolls	43	58	228E	410E	-43.4	0.0	16.0	66.8	174.7	
Cookies & crackers	3	15	59E	106E	-72.7	87.5	0.0	282.9	136.8	
Cane sugar	0	0	0	0	0.0	0.0	0.0	0.0	0.0	
Beet sugar	0	0	0	0	0.0	0.0	0.0	0.0	0.0	
Confectionary	12	12	61E	111E	-36.8	33.3	58.3	64.6	346.1	
Cottonseed oil	3	2	4	42E	-75.0	-50.0	-33.3	121.3	-58.8	
Soybean oil	6	6	90	508	20.0	50.0	0.0	70.6	151.7	
Other fats & oils	11	2	4E	42E	10.0	0.0	0.0	191.5	141.9	
Cooking oil & marg.	4	10	67	433	0.0	0.0	42.9	242.6	84.0	
Beer	1	6	48E	112E	inf.	inf.	100.0	inf.	551.2	
Wine & brandy	1E	P	1	2E	inf.	0.0	inf.	0.0	inf.	
Spirits	2	7	56E	131E	0.0	50.0	133.2	42.1	659.3	
Soft drinks	51	41	327E	765E	-48.0	31.3	-2.4	263.1	218.3	
Flavorings	5	2	19	34	-16.7	-33.3	0.0	-52.7	198.2	
Canned fish	0	0	0	0	0.0	0.0	0.0	0.0	0.0	
Frozen fish	0	0	0	0	0.0	0.0	0.0	0.0	0.0	
Coffee	2	1	7E	18E	-66.7	-50.0	-50.0	-9.4	-14.7	
Pasta	3	3	21E	54E	200.0	-50.0	200.0	73.8	409.4	
Miscellaneous foods	43	22	152	309	-50.0	29.4	0.0	189.9	225.1	
Total	431	363	2161	6557	-37.5	2.8	10.7	90.1	152.7	18.6

Source: Data from Bureau of the Census reports.

Note: Industries are listed by four-digit SIC code, see Appendix C for definitions of terms.

EST = Establishments. EMP = Employment. VA = Value added. VS = Value of shipments. inf. = Infinity. P = Less than 20. Z = 20 to 99.

Appendix Table B-34
Alabama: Basic Economic Data on Food Manufacturing Industries, 1963, 1972, 1982, and 1985

INDUSTRY 1/	1982 Totals				Growth Rates					
	EST	EMP	VA	VS	EST	EMP		VS		
					1963-1982	1963-1972	1972-1982	1963-1972	1972-1982	1982-1985
	No.	'00	$ million		- - - - - - - - - Percent - - - - - - - - -					
Meatpacking	33	18	88	284	-40.0	0.0	-14.3	42.5	104.5	
Meat processing	13	3	4	22	30.0	0.0	0.0	15.9	-28.6	
Poultry dressing	20	76	84	653	-18.2	48.9	13.4	150.1	123.7	
Poultry processing	7	7	6	54						
Butter	0E	0	0	0	-100.0	-80.0	-100.0	-70.7	-100.0	
Cheese	2E	P	0.4	1	-33.3	-80.0	0.0	-63.6	8.3	
Processed milk	0E	0	0	0	-100.0	-80.0	-100.0	-68.4	-100.0	
Ice cream	4	5	19E	65E	-75.0	0.0	0.0	30.8	174.4	
Fluid milk	14	16	55	223	-67.4	-11.8	-46.7	60.7	54.8	
Canned specialties	0	0	0	0	0.0	0.0	0.0	0.0	0.0	
Canned fruit & veg.	1	2	17E	44E	-75.0	133.3	-71.4	220.0	70.3	
Dry fruit & veg.	0	0	0	0	0.0	inf.	-100.0	inf.	-100.0	
Sauces, pickles	4	3	25E	66E	-33.3	33.3	-25.0	225.7	171.8	
Frozen fruit & veg.	0	0	0	0	-33.3	50.0	-66.7	83.3	98.2	
Frozen specialties	2	1	8E	22E						
Flour	6	1	5E	19E	-53.8	0.0	100.0	44.9	169.0	
Breakfast foods	0	0	0	0	-100.0	-100.0	0.0	-100.0	0.0	
Rice	0	0	0	0	0.0	0.0	0.0	0.0	0.0	
Flour mixes	0	0	0	0	0.0	0.0	0.0	0.0	0.0	
Wet corn mills	0	0	0	0	0.0	0.0	0.0	0.0	0.0	
Pet foods	6	7	35E	134E	-30.0	0.0	-5.6	52.2	91.9	
Animal feeds	43	10	44	357						
Bread, rolls	19	31	163E	271E	-63.5	-18.8	19.2	56.3	203.8	
Cookies & crackers	1	2	11E	18E	-80.0	-33.3	0.0	25.5	153.6	
Cane sugar	0	0	0	0	0.0	0.0	0.0	0.0	0.0	
Beet sugar	0	0	0	0	0.0	0.0	0.0	0.0	0.0	
Confectionary	5	6	34	75	-54.5	0.0	20.0	194.4	134.6	
Cottonseed oil	6	1	4E	44E	-50.0	-25.0	-66.7	137.6	-6.0	
Soybean oil	2	2	9E	88E	100.0	0.0	300.0	-30.4	5400.0	
Other fats & oils	11	4	16	116	0.0	-22.5	29.0	-53.0	97.9	
Cooking oil & marg.	1	3	13E	132E	0.0	0.0	50.0	59.2	323.1	
Beer	0E	0	0	0	0.0	0.0	0.0	0.0	0.0	
Wine & brandy	1E	P	1	1	inf.	0.0	inf.	0.0	inf.	
Spirits	0E	0	0	0	0.0	0.0	0.0	0.0	0.0	
Soft drinks	26	23	134E	313E	-73.5	11.5	-20.7	158.7	183.7	
Flavorings	2E	P	1	1	0.0	0.0	-80.0	-52.5	-26.3	
Canned fish	1E	Z	2	5	0.0	0.0	0.0	15.4	226.7	
Frozen fish	22	11	15	114	340.0	0.0	450.0	166.7	919.6	
Coffee	2	2	8E	19E	-66.7	300.0	0.0	11.1	223.2	
Pasta	1E	Z	2	5	inf.	inf.	0.0	inf.	226.7	
Miscellaneous foods	31	13	53E	126E	-55.1	22.2	18.2	85.7	246.7	
Total	286	249	845	3270	-46.3	10.3	0.8	74.2	141.3	17.4

Source: Data from Bureau of the Census reports.

Note: Industries are listed by four-digit SIC code, see Appendix C for definitions of terms.

EST = Establishments. EMP = Employment. VA = Value added. VS = Value of shipments. inf. = Infinity. P = Less than 20. Z = 20 to 99.

Appendix Table B–35
Mississippi: Basic Economic Data on Food Manufacturing Industries, 1963, 1972, 1982, and 1985

INDUSTRY 1/	1982 Totals				Growth Rates					
	EST	EMP	VA	VS	EST	EMP		VS		
					1963-1982	1963-1972	1972-1982	1963-1972	1972-1982	1982-1985
	No.	'00	$ million		- - - - - - - - - - Percent - - - - - - - - - -					
Meatpacking	31	32	88	633	-35.4	38.1	10.3	85.9	216.0	
Meat processing	16	2	8E	30E	128.6	900.0	100.0	1600.0	333.8	
Poultry dressing	19	57	155	446	0.0	71.9	5.5	128.8	114.8	
Poultry processing	4	1	4E	15E						
Butter	0	0	0	0	-100.0	0.0	-100.0	-2.4	-100.0	
Cheese	3	Z	5E	12E	-57.1	-66.7	-50.0	129.0	55.0	
Processed milk	1	Z	5E	12E	-66.7	-75.0	0.0	-73.7	210.0	
Ice cream	4	2	19E	50E	-63.6	0.0	0.0	130.0	664.6	
Fluid milk	13	10	45	140	-68.3	-13.3	-23.1	129.0	121.2	
Canned specialties	0	0	0	0	0.0	0.0	0.0	0.0	0.0	
Canned fruit & veg.	4	2	10E	26E	300.0	900.0	100.0	-33.3	1095.5	
Dry fruit & veg.	0	0	0	0	-100.0	0.0	-100.0	-33.3	-100.0	
Sauces, pickles	2	3	24E	58E	0.0	0.0	50.0	-38.0	1222.7	
Frozen fruit & veg.	0	0	0	0	0.0	-80.0	2900.0	-86.7	17800.0	
Frozen specialties	2	3	15E	36E						
Flour	2E	1	5	29	-33.3	0.0	900.0	0.0	2800.0	
Breakfast foods	0E	0	0	0	0.0	0.0	0.0	0.0	0.0	
Rice	3	3	16E	87E	inf.	0.0	inf.	0.0	inf.	
Flour mixes	0E	0	0	0	0.0	0.0	0.0	0.0	0.0	
Wet corn mills	0E	0	0	0	0.0	0.0	0.0	0.0	0.0	
Pet foods	7	5	26E	145	-6.3	0.0	20.0	47.6	253.7	
Animal feeds	38	7	31	238						
Bread, rolls	13	11	47	82	-51.9	-6.7	-21.4	74.4	65.2	
Cookies & crackers	0	0	0	0	-100.0	-100.0	0.0	-100.0	0.0	
Cane sugar	0	0	0	0	0.0	0.0	0.0	0.0	0.0	
Beet sugar	0	0	0	0	0.0	0.0	0.0	0.0	0.0	
Confectionary	1	P	1	1	-80.0	-95.0	0.0	-91.3	200.0	
Cottonseed oil	10	6	15	77	-52.4	-20.0	-25.0	1.0	20.7	
Soybean oil	4	2	16E	88E	100.0	200.0	-66.7	360.2	-15.9	
Other fats & oils	6	2	16E	88E	-40.0	-42.9	0.0	141.0	152.2	
Cooking oil & marg.	1	Z	4E	22E	inf.	0.0	inf.	0.0	inf.	
Beer	0	0	0	0	0.0	0.0	0.0	0.0	0.0	
Wine & brandy	2	P	1	1	inf.	inf.	0.0	inf.	200.0	
Spirits	0	0	0	0	0.0	0.0	0.0	0.0	0.0	
Soft drinks	32	18	89E	221E	-63.6	5.0	-14.3	109.0	239.5	
Flavorings	2	1	5E	12E	-60.0	-80.0	900.0	-90.0	2975.0	
Canned fish	5	Z	5E	8E	-54.5	-75.0	-50.0	-61.4	196.3	
Frozen fish	20	15	40	170	566.7	300.0	650.0	440.0	3051.9	
Coffee	1E	P	1	2	-75.0	-80.0	0.0	-94.4	433.3	
Pasta	2E	P	1	2	inf.	inf.	0.0	inf.	433.3	
Miscellaneous foods	18	10	91E	160E	-62.5	-16.0	-79.0	58.3	2705.3	
Total	266	194	766	2848	-37.3	16.4	14.1	73.4	197.8	-1.5

Source: Data from Bureau of the Census reports.

Note: Industries are listed by four-digit SIC code, see Appendix C for definitions of terms.

EST = Establishments. EMP = Employment. VA = Value added. VS = Value of shipments. inf. = Infinity. P = Less than 20. Z = 20 to 99.

Appendix Table B–36
Arkansas: Basic Economic Data on Food Manufacturing Industries, 1963, 1972, 1982, and 1985

	1982 Totals				Growth Rates					
	EST	EMP	VA	VS	EST	EMP		VS		
INDUSTRY 1/					1963-1982	1963-1972	1972-1982	1963-1972	1972-1982	1982-1985
	No.	'00	$ million		- - - - - - - - - - Percent - - - - - - - - - -					
Meatpacking	31	7	20	105	-43.6	-9.1	-30.0	24.6	78.0	
Meat processing	6	11	56	184	200.0	0.0	inf.	50.0	inf.	
Poultry dressing	32	130	266	1133	} -13.5	} 76.9	} 55.4	} 149.5	} 239.6	
Poultry processing	9	13	33	146						
Butter	1	Z	4E	21E	0.0	-100.0	inf.	-100.0	inf.	
Cheese	3	1	7E	41E	-62.5	0.0	-50.0	30.0	143.8	
Processed milk	0	0	0	0	-100.0	-80.0	-100.0	-78.9	-100.0	
Ice cream	6	2	4	14	-40.0	0.0	0.0	131.5	-20.1	
Fluid milk	11	7	17	96	-60.7	-22.2	0.0	53.2	88.6	
Canned specialties	3	8	55E	132E	200.0	200.0	33.3	322.6	236.4	
Canned fruit & veg.	11	6	10	48	-26.7	54.5	-64.7	139.6	-18.7	
Dry fruit & veg.	0	0	0	0	0.0	0.0	0.0	0.0	0.0	
Sauces, pickles	3	2	14E	33E	-40.0	0.0	-33.3	84.1	68.0	
Frozen fruit & veg.	3	2	5	12	} -45.5	} 150.0	} -23.3	} 297.5	} 65.5	
Frozen specialties	3	21	69	225						
Flour	4E	1	4	10	100.0	400.0	100.0	590.0	49.3	
Breakfast foods	0E	0	0	0	0.0	0.0	0.0	0.0	0.0	
Rice	10	19	129	608	-23.1	10.0	72.7	53.5	302.9	
Flour mixes	2	Z	2E	5E	-84.6	0.0	400.0	133.3	271.4	
Wet corn mills	0	0	0	0	0.0	0.0	0.0	0.0	0.0	
Pet foods	6	Z	2E	5E	} -1.9	} 22.7	} -29.6	} 136.5	} 144.0	
Animal feeds	45	9	48	605						
Bread, rolls	15	18	69E	132E	-58.3	14.3	12.5	106.0	141.4	
Cookies & crackers	2	3	11E	21E	0.0	0.0	50.0	33.3	225.0	
Cane sugar	0E	0	0	0	0.0	0.0	0.0	0.0	0.0	
Beet sugar	0E	0	0	0	0.0	0.0	0.0	0.0	0.0	
Confectionary	6	3	19E	40E	50.0	0.0	3000.0	100.0	450.0	
Cottonseed oil	6	3	7E	52E	-53.8	0.0	-57.1	33.3	-12.2	
Soybean oil	5	6	47	436	25.0	133.3	-14.3	141.9	164.8	
Other fats & oils	5	2	5E	43E	-16.7	0.0	0.0	623.1	-7.7	
Cooking oil & marg.	1	2	5E	43E	0.0	0.0	300.0	140.8	267.8	
Beer	0E	0	0	0	0.0	0.0	0.0	0.0	0.0	
Wine & brandy	2E	P	1	2	-50.0	-80.0	0.0	-86.4	533.3	
Spirits	1	2	11E	37E	inf.	inf.	-71.4	inf.	2380.0	
Soft drinks	27	16	84E	298E	-63.0	17.6	-20.0	127.6	-52.0	
Flavorings	2	2	11E	37E	100.0	0.0	300.0	-62.5	2380.0	
Canned fish	0	0	0	0	0.0	0.0	0.0	0.0	0.0	
Frozen fish	5E	P	0.3	1	inf.	0.0	inf.	0.0	inf.	
Coffee	0E	0	0	0	-100.0	-100.0	0.0	-100.0	0.0	
Pasta	0E	0	0	0	0.0	0.0	0.0	0.0	0.0	
Miscellaneous foods	22	7	43E	83E	-66.2	-50.0	85.7	107.1	377.6	
Total	288	304	1096	4766	-36.6	41.3	20.2	116.1	196.4	9.0

Source: Data from Bureau of the Census reports.

Note: Industries are listed by four-digit SIC code, see Appendix C for definitions of terms.

EST = Establishments. EMP = Employment. VA = Value added. VS = Value of shipments. inf. = Infinity. P = Less than 20. Z = 20 to 99.

Appendix Table B-37
Louisiana: Basic Economic Data on Food Manufacturing Industries, 1963, 1972, 1982, and 1985

INDUSTRY 1/	1982 Totals EST	EMP	VA	VS	Growth Rates EST 1963-1982	EMP 1963-1972	EMP 1972-1982	VS 1963-1972	VS 1972-1982	VS 1982-1985
	No.	'00	\$ million		- - - - - - - - - Percent - - - - - - - - - -					
Meatpacking	31	6	11E	58E	-56.3	0.0	-40.0	39.1	-11.9	
Meat processing	23	7	25	78	35.3	-14.3	16.7	14.0	121.7	
Poultry dressing	3	10	19E	97E	-37.5 }	80.0 }	-33.3 }	191.8 }	9.0	
Poultry processing	2	2	4E	19E						
Butter	0	0	0	0	-100.0	100.0	-100.0	80.5	-100.0	
Cheese	0	0	0	0	0.0	0.0	0.0	0.0	0.0	
Processed milk	1	Z	1	4E	inf.	0.0	inf.	0.0	inf.	
Ice cream	8	1	2E	8E	-52.9	-40.0	-66.7	1.0	-16.3	
Fluid milk	22	18	73	338	-62.7	4.2	-28.0	112.4	170.0	
Canned specialties	0	0	0	0	-100.0	0.0	-100.0	-30.4	-100.0	
Canned fruit & veg.	8	8	27	63	-55.6	-6.3	-46.7	17.4	68.3	
Dry fruit & veg.	2	1	2E	4E	100.0	0.0	100.0	-5.9	162.5	
Sauces, pickles	8	5	32	62	-27.3	20.0	-16.7	5.1	229.4	
Frozen fruit & veg.	3E	P	0.2	0.4	25.0 }	3.3 }	0.0 }	76.4 }	35.1	
Frozen specialties	2	3	7E	13E						
Flour	3	2	10E	58E	0.0	0.0	300.0	30.0	4384.6	
Breakfast foods	0	0	0	0	0.0	0.0	0.0	0.0	0.0	
Rice	16	7	39	175	-44.8	-25.0	-22.2	29.5	46.9	
Flour mixes	0	0	0	0	-100.0	-100.0	0.0	-100.0	0.0	
Wet corn mills	0	0	0	0	0.0	0.0	0.0	0.0	0.0	
Pet foods	0	0	0	0	-26.7 }	0.0 }	-33.3 }	72.0 }	117.9	
Animal feeds	22	4	21E	117E						
Bread, rolls	27	28	168	923	-58.5	-11.1	-12.5	21.9	105.5	
Cookies & crackers	1	2	7E	12E	-66.7	-75.0	100.0	-74.5	369.2	
Cane sugar	34	38	168	923	-30.6	-18.3	-22.4	17.1	77.2	
Beet sugar	0E	0	0	0	0.0	0.0	0.0	0.0	0.0	
Confectionary	7	2	9E	16E	-36.4	-50.0	5.0	-4.0	245.8	
Cottonseed oil	5	3	24E	169E	-44.4	-33.3	50.0	104.5	318.3	
Soybean oil	1E	P	1	6E	inf.	0.0	inf.	0.0	inf.	
Other fats & oils	12	5	19	75	-20.0	0.0	-9.1	51.9	135.8	
Cooking oil & marg.	1	2	16E	113E	-66.7	0.0	-33.3	106.1	86.3	
Beer	2	2	11E	24E	-33.3	-33.3	-80.0	64.3	-73.7	
Wine & brandy	0	0	0	0	-100.0	-100.0	0.0	-100.0	0.0	
Spirits	0	0	0	0	-100.0	0.0	-100.0	53.3	-100.0	
Soft drinks	32	38	213E	456E	-55.6	29.6	22.6	197.1	274.4	
Flavorings	6	Z	3E	6E	-45.5	500.0	-83.3	585.0	-78.1	
Canned fish	15	5	10	72	-50.0	-30.8	-44.4	345.1	-12.1	
Frozen fish	48	12	19	102	84.6	-11.1	50.0	746.5	40.5	
Coffee	10	7	182	584	-41.2	-11.1	-12.5	-36.4	702.7	
Pasta	5	3	9E	16E	0.0	0.0	50.0	506.7	-14.3	
Miscellaneous foods	63	9	40	75	-34.4	-28.6	-10.0	109.2	31.0	
Total	423	230	1105	3913	-38.9	-5.1	-18.1	51.6	102.1	-5.6

Source: Data from Bureau of the Census reports.

Note: Industries are listed by four-digit SIC code, see Appendix C for definitions of terms.

EST = Establishments. EMP = Employment. VA = Value added. VS = Value of shipments. inf. = Infinity. P = Less than 20. Z = 20 to 99.

Appendix Table B–38
Oklahoma: Basic Economic Data on Food Manufacturing Industries, 1963, 1972, 1982, and 1985

INDUSTRY 1/	1982 Totals				Growth Rates					
	EST	EMP	VA	VS	EST	EMP		VS		
					1963-1982	1963-1972	1972-1982	1963-1972	1972-1982	1982-1985
	No.	'00	$ million		- - - - - - - - - Percent - - - - - - - - - - -					
Meatpacking	52	13	30E	308E	-23.5	-4.3	-40.9	141.4	8.4	
Meat processing	11	7	16E	166E	0.0	0.0	250.0	190.9	548.4	
Poultry dressing	2	7	16E	166E	-77.8	68.3	-30.7	112.9	338.0	
Poultry processing	0	0	0	0						
Butter	0E	0	0	0	-100.0	0.0	-100.0	41.5	-100.0	
Cheese	3E	Z	3	21	50.0	100.0	-50.0	251.5	78.4	
Processed milk	1E	P	1	4	-75.0	0.0	-80.0	52.6	-29.3	
Ice cream	5	Z	3E	21E	-44.4	0.0	-50.0	157.8	78.4	
Fluid milk	10	12	54	216	-66.7	-46.2	-7.7	11.9	124.8	
Canned specialties	0	0	0	0	-100.0	-95.0	-100.0	-93.5	-100.0	
Canned fruit & veg.	4	2	10E	21E	-66.7	83.3	-81.8	53.6	24.3	
Dry fruit & veg.	0	0	0	0	0.0	inf.	-100.0	inf.	-100.0	
Sauces, pickles	3	2	10E	21E	-25.0	0.0	300.0	50.0	3400.0	
Frozen fruit & veg.	2	3	15E	32E	-25.0	103.3	63.9	297.8	194.1	
Frozen specialties	4	7	35	74						
Flour	4	3	48E	118E	-60.0	-50.0	0.0	-31.0	194.0	
Breakfast foods	0	0	0	0	-100.0	-100.0	0.0	-100.0	0.0	
Rice	0	0	0	0	0.0	0.0	0.0	0.0	0.0	
Flour mixes	0	0	0	0	-100.0	-100.0	0.0	-100.0	0.0	
Wet corn mills	0	0	0	0	0.0	0.0	0.0	0.0	0.0	
Pet foods	4	3	48E	118E	0.0	37.5	9.1	131.5	207.9	
Animal feeds	35	9	40	237						
Bread, rolls	15	16	75E	130E	-80.3	-27.3	0.0	34.7	130.7	
Cookies & crackers	2	3	14E	24E	-50.0	50.0	0.0	105.9	131.4	
Cane sugar	0	0	0	0	0.0	inf.	-100.0	inf.	-100.0	
Beet sugar	0	0	0	0	0.0	0.0	0.0	0.0	0.0	
Confectionary	9	5	9	28	-35.7	0.0	0.0	137.2	35.8	
Cottonseed oil	3	2	10E	34E	-40.0	0.0	0.0	18.2	117.9	
Soybean oil	2	2	10E	34E	100.0	0.0	300.0	-65.2	4150.0	
Other fats & oils	5	Z	3E	9E	-37.5	-50.0	0.0	62.5	117.9	
Cooking oil & marg.	2	2	10E	34E	100.0	0.0	0.0	-20.4	117.9	
Beer	0	0	0	0	-100.0	-100.0	0.0	-100.0	0.0	
Wine & brandy	1E	P	0.4	1	inf.	0.0	inf.	0.0	inf.	
Spirits	0	0	0	0	0.0	0.0	0.0	0.0	0.0	
Soft drinks	25	21	91E	246E	-65.8	40.0	0.0	106.3	313.8	
Flavorings	0E	0	0	0	-100.0	0.0	-100.0	-65.0	-100.0	
Canned fish	0	0	0	0	0.0	0.0	0.0	0.0	0.0	
Frozen fish	1E	P	1	2	inf.	0.0	inf.	0.0	inf.	
Coffee	1	2	16E	47E	-66.7	50.0	-33.3	149.8	-13.3	
Pasta	0	0	0	0	0.0	0.0	0.0	0.0	0.0	
Miscellaneous foods	24	4	20E	52E	-53.8	14.3	-33.3	284.2	43.6	
Total	231	125	588	2164	-49.5	1.4	-13.2	69.6	133.8	6.6

Source: Data from Bureau of the Census reports.

Note: Industries are listed by four-digit SIC code, see Appendix C for definitions of terms.

EST = Establishments. EMP = Employment. VA = Value added. VS = Value of shipments. inf. = Infinity. P = Less than 20. Z = 20 to 99.

Appendix Table B–39
Texas: Basic Economic Data on Food Manufacturing Industries, 1963, 1972, 1982, and 1985

INDUSTRY 1/	1982 Totals				Growth Rates					
	EST	EMP	VA	VS	EST	EMP		VS		
					1963–1982	1963–1972	1972–1982	1963–1972	1972–1982	1982–1985
	No.	'00	$ million		- - - - - - - - - - Percent - - - - - - - - - -					
Meatpacking	139	123	576	4446	-37.7	4.2	23.0	134.8	240.7	
Meat processing	80	39	125	665	40.4	5.9	116.7	198.1	432.9	
Poultry dressing	19	48	82	463	-59.7	26.4	-7.7	45.7	252.3	
Poultry processing	6	1	0.1	12E						
Butter	2E	P	1	3	-50.0	-80.0	0.0	-85.7	300.0	
Cheese	4	2	15E	57E	100.0	900.0	100.0	842.9	762.1	
Processed milk	4	2	15E	57E	-20.0	0.0	0.0	61.0	331.1	
Ice cream	20	9	67E	256E	-60.8	-25.0	0.0	81.9	331.9	
Fluid milk	55	54	282	1102	-45.0	-27.9	-12.9	23.4	212.6	
Canned specialties	12	21	191	486	-36.8	460.0	-25.0	1052.9	201.4	
Canned fruit & veg.	22	21	105	280	-48.8	-28.6	40.0	22.9	387.7	
Dry fruit & veg.	1	1	8E	18E	0.0	900.0	0.0	1833.3	203.4	
Sauces, pickles	15	10	76E	176E	-54.5	10.0	-9.1	98.1	135.6	
Frozen fruit & veg.	6	5	38E	88E	35.3	-6.7	28.6	100.9	332.4	
Frozen specialties	17	13	48	118						
Flour	15	10	49	219	-40.0	-47.1	11.1	-26.6	121.1	
Breakfast foods	0	0	0	0	-100.0	0.0	-100.0	20.0	-100.0	
Rice	12	15	124	534	-25.0	8.3	15.4	124.8	110.8	
Flour mixes	7	6	72	134	-41.7	80.0	-33.3	187.5	142.2	
Wet corn mills	1	2	13E	27E	-66.7	0.0	-33.3	30.5	45.1	
Pet foods	10	6	40E	80E	-22.9	16.7	2.4	87.8	120.5	
Animal feeds	121	37	138	719						
Bread, rolls	118	111	532E	894E	-38.9	-8.5	14.4	56.2	200.1	
Cookies & crackers	7	15	72E	121E	-30.0	-46.2	114.3	-47.7	462.3	
Cane sugar	2	14	76E	293E	100.0	7.1	86.7	-28.6	470.8	
Beet sugar	1	2	11E	42E	0.0	1900.0	0.0	2640.0	205.1	
Confectionary	30	17	164	355	-50.8	12.5	-5.6	285.0	188.2	
Cottonseed oil	21	20	71	331	-62.5	-37.5	33.3	-22.8	127.9	
Soybean oil	3E	1	4	12	50.0	0.0	100.0	-79.6	342.9	
Other fats & oils	28	7	28E	87E	-30.0	-20.0	16.7	38.0	156.2	
Cooking oil & marg.	8	13	122	442	-33.3	-18.8	0.0	33.0	129.1	
Beer	7	30	428	1048	-12.5	22.2	36.4	345.9	252.9	
Wine & brandy	3E	Z	0.3	1	inf.	inf.	400.0	inf.	-46.2	
Spirits	1E	Z	0.3	1	inf.	0.0	inf.	0.0	inf.	
Soft drinks	100	109	601	1388	152.0	25.0	14.7	153.1	327.3	
Flavorings	20	11	376	534	-9.1	75.0	57.1	194.4	464.9	
Canned fish	2	1	2E	5E	-50.0	0.0	100.0	7.7	278.6	
Frozen fish	24	12	28	159	-7.7	21.1	-47.8	263.4	5.7	
Coffee	7	15	233	744	-53.3	0.0	15.4	33.0	138.6	
Pasta	6	Z	1E	3E	20.0	-50.0	0.0	-54.8	92.9	
Miscellaneous foods	268	95	516	906	-20.0	15.7	61.0	126.3	211.6	
Total	1224	899	5329	17303	-35.1	2.8	16.0	83.1	210.5	9.3

Source: Data from Bureau of the Census reports.

Note: Industries are listed by four-digit SIC code, see Appendix C for definitions of terms.

EST = Establishments. EMP = Employment. VA = Value added. VS = Value of shipments. inf. = Infinity. P = Less than 20. Z = 20 to 99.

Appendix Table B–40
Montana: Basic Economic Data on Food Manufacturing Industries, 1963, 1972, 1982, and 1985

INDUSTRY 1/	1982 Totals				Growth Rates					
	EST	EMP	VA	VS	EST	EMP		VS		
					1963–1982	1963–1972	1972–1982	1963–1972	1972–1982	1982–1985
	No.	'00	$ million		– – – – – – – – – Percent – – – – – – – – –					
Meatpacking	21	7	22E	110E	-32.3	14.3	-12.5	146.2	6.1	
Meat processing	4	1	3E	16E	300.0	0.0	900.0	225.0	1107.7	
Poultry dressing	0	0	0	0	-100.0	0.0	-100.0	333.3	inf.	
Poultry processing	0	0	0	0						
Butter	0E	0	0	0	-100.0	-80.0	-100.0	-87.8	inf.	
Cheese	4E	1	1	6	33.3	0.0	100.0	-24.2	120.0	
Processed milk	1E	Z	1	3	inf.	inf.	0.0	inf.	8.0	
Ice cream	3E	Z	1	3	-62.5	0.0	0.0	38.9	8.0	
Fluid milk	11	5	22	80	-71.1	-12.5	-28.6	-64.7	121.9	
Canned specialties	0E	0	0	0	0.0	0.0	0.0	0.0	0.0	
Canned fruit & veg.	2E	Z	3	7	-60.0	-80.0	400.0	-61.5	1200.0	
Dry fruit & veg.	0E	0	0	0	0.0	0.0	0.0	0.0	0.0	
Sauces, pickles	0E	0	0	0	0.0	0.0	0.0	0.0	0.0	
Frozen fruit & veg.	0E	0	0	0	0.0	0.0	0.0	0.0	0.0	
Frozen specialties	0E	0	0	0						
Flour	3	2	13E	46E	-40.0	0.0	0.0	24.7	108.1	
Breakfast foods	0	0	0	0	-100.0	-100.0	0.0	inf.	0.0	
Rice	0	0	0	0	0.0	0.0	0.0	0.0	0.0	
Flour mixes	0	0	0	0	0.0	0.0	0.0	0.0	0.0	
Wet corn mills	0	0	0	0	0.0	0.0	0.0	0.0	0.0	
Pet foods	0	0	0	0	-91.7	5.0	-4.8	22.5	165.5	
Animal feeds	23	2	13E	46E						
Bread, rolls	14	7	32E	54E	-50.0	-28.6	40.0	36.2	240.5	
Cookies & crackers	0	0	0	0	0.0	0.0	0.0	0.0	0.0	
Cane sugar	0E	0	0	0	0.0	0.0	0.0	0.0	0.0	
Beet sugar	2	4	17E	60E	-50.0	-28.6	-20.0	23.2	53.8	
Confectionary	1E	P	1	1	inf.	0.0	inf.	0.0	inf.	
Cottonseed oil	1E	P	0.4	2	inf.	0.0	inf.	0.0	inf.	
Soybean oil	1E	P	0.2	2	inf.	0.0	inf.	0.0	inf.	
Other fats & oils	3E	Z	1	2	-57.1	-90.0	400.0	-90.8	142.9	
Cooking oil & marg.	1E	Z	1	5	inf.	0.0	inf.	0.0	inf.	
Beer	0E	0	0	0	-100.0	-95.0	-100.0	-93.2	inf.	
Wine & brandy	1E	P	1	1	inf.	0.0	inf.	0.0	inf.	
Spirits	0E	0	0	0	-100.0	-100.0	0.0	-100.0	0.0	
Soft drinks	12	5	24E	57E	-45.5	0.0	66.7	126.7	321.3	
Flavorings	1E	P	1	1	inf.	0.0	inf.	0.0	inf.	
Canned fish	0E	0	0	0	0.0	inf.	-100.0	inf.	-100.0	
Frozen fish	0E	0	0	0	0.0	inf.	-100.0	inf.	-100.0	
Coffee	0E	0	0	0	0.0	inf.	-100.0	inf.	-100.0	
Pasta	0E	0	0	0	0.0	inf.	-100.0	inf.	-100.0	
Miscellaneous foods	5E	P	1	1	-50.0	0.0	-83.3	66.7	-56.7	
Total	116	32	142	494	-41.4	-15.0	-5.9	42.5	88.5	-18.2

Source: Data from Bureau of the Census reports.

Note: Industries are listed by four-digit SIC code, see Appendix C for definitions of terms.

EST = Establishments. EMP = Employment. VA = Value added. VS = Value of shipments. inf. = Infinity. P = Less than 20. Z = 20 to 99.

Appendix Table B–41
Idaho: Basic Economic Data on Food Manufacturing Industries, 1963, 1972, 1982, and 1985

INDUSTRY 1/	1982 Totals				Growth Rates					
	EST	EMP	VA	VS	EST	EMP		VS		
					1963-1982	1963-1972	1972-1982	1963-1972	1972-1982	1982-1985
	No.	'00	$ million		- - - - - - - - - - Percent - - - - - - - - - -					
Meatpacking	25	11	46	537	-34.2	12.5	22.2	151.4	230.5	
Meat processing	3E	P	0.2	1	inf.	inf.	0.0	inf.	-61.1	
Poultry dressing	1E	P	0.2	1	-20.0	-95.0	0.0	-71.0	-61.1	
Poultry processing	0E	0	0	0						
Butter	2	P	1E	2	-77.8	-60.0	-95.0	-16.2	-93.5	
Cheese	14	6	34	193	-26.3	75.0	-14.3	145.5	171.6	
Processed milk	0E	0	0	0	-100.0	-80.0	-100.0	-60.5	inf.	
Ice cream	2E	1	5	19	-75.0	-50.0	0.0	104.2	29.9	
Fluid milk	11	4	51	373	-81.8	-16.7	-20.0	50.5	1026.9	
Canned specialties	1	3	10E	26E	0.0	0.0	2900.0	20.0	4300.0	
Canned fruit & veg.	4	7	24E	61E	-42.9	40.0	-14.3	148.0	94.3	
Dry fruit & veg.	10	26	109	227	42.9	210.0	-16.1	338.7	49.4	
Sauces, pickles	1E	P	0.3E	1E	0.0	0.0	0.0	50.0	50.0	
Frozen fruit & veg.	9	50	248	492	-37.5	93.9	-95.9	354.1	77.4	
Frozen specialties	1E	P	0.3E	1E						
Flour	4E	P	0.4	2	-20.0	-90.0	0.0	-96.3	500.0	
Breakfast foods	0E	0	0	0	0.0	0.0	0.0	0.0	0.0	
Rice	0E	0	0	0	0.0	0.0	0.0	0.0	0.0	
Flour mixes	0E	0	0	0	0.0	0.0	0.0	0.0	0.0	
Wet corn mills	0E	0	0	0	-100.0	0.0	-100.0	-42.3	-100.0	
Pet foods	3	1	4E	18E	-31.6	50.0	-33.3	79.7	85.1	
Animal feeds	10	2	6	28						
Bread, rolls	7	3	13E	23E	-66.7	-20.0	-25.0	1054.5	81.9	
Cookies & crackers	0	0	0	0	0.0	0.0	0.0	0.0	0.0	
Cane sugar	0E	0	0	0	0.0	0.0	0.0	0.0	0.0	
Beet sugar	3	15	63E	221E	-40.0	57.1	36.4	141.3	162.1	
Confectionary	3E	2	12E	25E	inf.	0.0	inf.	0.0	inf.	
Cottonseed oil	0	0	0	0	0.0	0.0	0.0	0.0	0.0	
Soybean oil	0	0	0	0	0.0	0.0	0.0	0.0	0.0	
Other fats & oils	2	Z	3E	8E	-60.0	0.0	0.0	94.1	145.5	
Cooking oil & marg.	0	0	0	0	0.0	0.0	0.0	0.0	0.0	
Beer	0E	0	0	0	0.0	0.0	0.0	0.0	0.0	
Wine & brandy	1E	1	6	19	inf.	0.0	inf.	0.0	inf.	
Spirits	0E	0	0	0	0.0	0.0	0.0	0.0	0.0	
Soft drinks	7	2	13E	37E	-61.1	33.3	-50.0	117.5	200.8	
Flavorings	1E	P	1	2	inf.	0.0	inf.	0.0	inf.	
Canned fish	0E	0	0	0	0.0	0.0	0.0	0.0	0.0	
Frozen fish	2E	P	0.3	1	100.0	-100.0	inf.	-100.0	inf.	
Coffee	0E	0	0	0	0.0	0.0	0.0	0.0	0.0	
Pasta	0E	0	0	0	0.0	0.0	0.0	0.0	0.0	
Miscellaneous foods	11	3	21E	41E	0.0	363.6	-39.2	694.3	47.5	
Total	138	135.	657	2300	-38.4	40.4	-2.9	121.9	185.9	-2.7

Source: Data from Bureau of the Census reports.

Note: Industries are listed by four-digit SIC code, see Appendix C for definitions of terms.

EST = Establishments. EMP = Employment. VA = Value added. VS = Value of shipments. inf. = Infinity. P = Less than 20. Z = 20 to 99.

Appendix Table B–42
Wyoming: Basic Economic Data on Food Manufacturing Industries, 1963, 1972, 1982, and 1985

INDUSTRY 1/	1982 Totals				Growth Rates					
	EST	EMP	VA	VS	EST	EMP		VS		
					1963-1982	1963-1972	1972-1982	1963-1972	1972-1982	1982-1985
	No.	'00	$ million		- - - - - - - - - Percent - - - - - - - - - -					
Meatpacking	13	1	4E	34E	-7.1	0.0	-50.0	113.1	15.8	
Meat processing	6E	P	5E	19E	inf.	inf.	0.0	inf.	2262.5	
Poultry dressing	0E	0	0	0	0.0	0.0	0.0	0.0	0.0	
Poultry processing	0E	0	0	0						
Butter	0E	0	0	0	-100.0	-100.0	0.0	-100.0	0.0	
Cheese	1	Z	1E	5E	0.0	0.0	0.0	-21.2	107.7	
Processed milk	0E	0	0	0	0.0	0.0	0.0	0.0	0.0	
Ice cream	1E	1	2	11	-50.0	400.0	100.0	550.0	315.4	
Fluid milk	4	Z	1E	5E	-71.4	-33.3	-75.0	-8.0	-48.1	
Canned specialties	0E	0	0	0	0.0	0.0	0.0	0.0	0.0	
Canned fruit & veg.	1	Z	3E	7E	0.0	-80.0	400.0	-64.3	1220.0	
Dry fruit & veg.	0E	0	0	0	0.0	0.0	0.0	0.0	0.0	
Sauces, pickles	0E	0	0	0	0.0	0.0	0.0	0.0	0.0	
Frozen fruit & veg.	0E	0	0	0	0.0	0.0	0.0	0.0	0.0	
Frozen specialties	0E	0	0	0						
Flour	0E	0	0	0	-100.0	-80.0	-100.0	-69.4	-100.0	
Breakfast foods	0E	0	0	0	0.0	0.0	0.0	0.0	0.0	
Rice	0E	0	0	0	0.0	0.0	0.0	0.0	0.0	
Flour mixes	0E	0	0	0	0.0	0.0	0.0	0.0	0.0	
Wet corn mills	0E	0	0	0	0.0	0.0	0.0	0.0	0.0	
Pet foods	0E	0	0	0	0.0	0.0	400.0	57.1	1272.7	
Animal feeds	2E	Z	3	15						
Bread, rolls	2E	2	10	15	-84.6	-50.0	100.0	39.1	381.3	
Cookies & crackers	0E	0	0	0	0.0	0.0	0.0	0.0	0.0	
Cane sugar	0	0	0	0	0.0	0.0	0.0	0.0	0.0	
Beet sugar	4	7	29E	103E	-33.3	66.7	40.0	155.3	168.9	
Confectionary	0	0	0	0	-100.0	-100.0	0.0	-100.0	0.0	
Cottonseed oil	0E	0	0	0	0.0	0.0	0.0	0.0	0.0	
Soybean oil	0E	0	0	0	0.0	0.0	0.0	0.0	0.0	
Other fats & oils	1E	2	10	33	0.0	0.0	300.0	133.3	4542.9	
Cooking oil & marg.	0E	0	0	0	0.0	0.0	0.0	0.0	0.0	
Beer	0E	0	0	0	0.0	0.0	0.0	0.0	0.0	
Wine & brandy	0E	0	0	0	0.0	0.0	0.0	0.0	0.0	
Spirits	0E	0	0	0	0.0	0.0	0.0	0.0	0.0	
Soft drinks	4	3	18E	44E	-66.7	-50.0	200.0	87.5	884.4	
Flavorings	0	0	0	0	0.0	0.0	0.0	0.0	0.0	
Canned fish	0E	0	0	0	0.0	0.0	0.0	0.0	0.0	
Frozen fish	0E	0	0	0	0.0	0.0	0.0	0.0	0.0	
Coffee	0E	0	0	0	0.0	0.0	0.0	0.0	0.0	
Pasta	0E	0	0	0	0.0	0.0	0.0	0.0	0.0	
Miscellaneous foods	5E	P	1	1	-16.7	-66.7	-50.0	-11.1	62.5	
Total	44	10	65	184	-38.9	-26.7	-9.0	11.3	187.4	-43.0

Source: Data from Bureau of the Census reports.

Note: Industries are listed by four-digit SIC code, see Appendix C for definitions of terms.

EST = Establishments. EMP = Employment. VA = Value added. VS = Value of shipments. inf. = Infinity. P = Less than 20. Z = 20 to 99.

Appendix Table B–43
Colorado: Basic Economic Data on Food Manufacturing Industries, 1963, 1972, 1982, and 1985

INDUSTRY 1/	1982 Totals				Growth Rates					
	EST	EMP	VA	VS	EST	EMP			VS		
					1963–1982	1963–1972	1972–1982	1963–1972	1972–1982	1982–1985
	No.	'00	$ million		- - - - - - - - - - Percent - - - - - - - - - -					
Meatpacking	43	30	59	1536	-23.2	30.2	-42.3	190.8	24.9	
Meat processing	17	8	21E	94E	142.9	66.7	60.0	61.9	316.9	
Poultry dressing	3	8	21E	94E	-72.7	33.3	100.0	136.8	421.1	
Poultry processing	0	0	0	0						
Butter	2	Z	4E	12E	-77.8	-80.0	400.0	-82.9	1542.9	
Cheese	4E	P	1	2	300.0	900.0	-90.0	871.4	-66.2	
Processed milk	1E	P	1	2	-50.0	-80.0	0.0	-81.6	228.6	
Ice cream	8	2	15E	46E	-20.0	0.0	100.0	41.7	577.9	
Fluid milk	18	15	59	259	-72.7	-36.4	7.1	23.3	156.6	
Canned specialties	8	2	4E	13E	300.0	400.0	300.0	160.0	876.9	
Canned fruit & veg.	7	3	7E	19E	-50.0	-55.6	-25.0	-23.8	74.3	
Dry fruit & veg.	3	1	2E	6E	200.0	0.0	900.0	0.0	2000.0	
Sauces, pickles	5	5	11E	32E	-50.0	50.0	66.7	9.9	305.1	
Frozen fruit & veg.	1	Z	1E	3E	-33.3	400.0	-40.0	333.3	46.2	
Frozen specialties	3	1	2E	6E						
Flour	3	2	32E	67E	-57.1	-100.0	100.0	-62.9	833.3	
Breakfast foods	0	0	0	0	0.0	inf.	-100.0	inf.	-100.0	
Rice	0	0	0	0	0.0	inf.	-100.0	inf.	-100.0	
Flour mixes	2	P	2	3	-60.0	0.0	-80.0	20.0	-5.6	
Wet corn mills	0	0	0	0	-100.0	300.0	-100.0	500.0	-100.0	
Pet foods	9	5	80E	168E	-7.8	14.3	25.0	42.0	353.6	
Animal feeds	38	5	21	110						
Bread, rolls	44	23	137E	214E	-31.3	0.0	-8.0	90.1	136.7	
Cookies & crackers	3	7	42E	65E	-40.0	0.0	0.0	41.3	157.3	
Cane sugar	1E	P	0.4	1	inf.	0.0	inf.	0.0	inf.	
Beet sugar	6	7	27E	73E	-53.8	-14.3	-61.1	-8.4	-23.9	
Confectionary	15	7	27E	74E	25.0	40.0	1.4	418.1	98.7	
Cottonseed oil	0	0	0	0	0.0	0.0	0.0	0.0	0.0	
Soybean oil	0	0	0	0	0.0	0.0	0.0	0.0	0.0	
Other fats & oils	6	2	11E	35E	-25.0	100.0	0.0	287.2	90.7	
Cooking oil & marg.	3	3	17E	52E	inf.	0.0	inf.	0.0	inf.	
Beer	3	52	294E	757E	0.0	100.0	73.3	325.0	225.3	
Wine & brandy	1E	Z	28E	73E	inf.	inf.	400.0	inf.	9000.0	
Spirits	0E	0	0	0	0.0	0.0	0.0	0.0	0.0	
Soft drinks	22	15	85E	219E	-50.0	66.7	0.0	533.9	85.3	
Flavorings	1E	Z	28	73E	-66.7	0.0	400.0	0.0	9000.0	
Canned fish	0	0	0	0	0.0	inf.	-100.0	inf.	-100.0	
Frozen fish	0	0	0	0	0.0	inf.	-100.0	inf.	-100.0	
Coffee	0	0	0	0	-100.0	0.0	-100.0	-37.0	-100.0	
Pasta	3	Z	2E	5E	-33.3	100.0	-50.0	353.3	-23.5	
Miscellaneous foods	54	16	76	142	14.9	-5.6	82.4	81.4	367.7	
Total	337	222	1065	4123	-27.4	16.1	2.8	140.2	88.2	16.0

Source: Data from Bureau of the Census reports.

Note: Industries are listed by four-digit SIC code, see Appendix C for definitions of terms.

EST = Establishments. EMP = Employment. VA = Value added. VS = Value of shipments. inf. = Infinity. P = Less than 20. Z = 20 to 99.

Appendix Table B–44
New Mexico: Basic Economic Data on Food Manufacturing Industries, 1963, 1972, 1982, and 1985

INDUSTRY 1/	1982 Totals				Growth Rates					
	EST	EMP	VA	VS	EST	EMP		VS		
					1963–1982	1963–1972	1972–1982	1963–1972	1972–1982	1982–1985
	No.	'00	$ million		– – – – – – – – – Percent – – – – – – – – –					
Meatpacking	15	5	11E	77E	-25.0	66.7	-50.0	252.0	-44.6	
Meat processing	2	3	7E	46E	-33.3	100.0	200.0	531.8	231.7	
Poultry dressing	0	0	0	0	-100.0	-100.0	0.0	-100.0	0.0	
Poultry processing	0	0	0	0						
Butter	0E	0	0	0	0.0	0.0	0.0	0.0	0.0	
Cheese	1E	Z	3	12	inf.	inf.	0.0	inf.	190.0	
Processed milk	0E	0	0	0	0.0	0.0	0.0	0.0	0.0	
Ice cream	1	Z	3E	12E	-50.0	0.0	0.0	122.2	190.0	
Fluid milk	6	3	15E	69E	-66.7	-42.9	-25.0	33.2	116.2	
Canned specialties	0E	0	0	0	0.0	0.0	0.0	0.0	0.0	
Canned fruit & veg.	2E	P	1	1	inf.	inf.	0.0	inf.	160.0	
Dry fruit & veg.	0E	0	0	0	0.0	0.0	0.0	0.0	0.0	
Sauces, pickles	0E	0	0	0	0.0	0.0	0.0	0.0	0.0	
Frozen fruit & veg.	0E	0	0	0	inf.	inf.	300.0	inf.	856.0	
Frozen specialties	2	2	10E	24E						
Flour	1E	P	0.2	1	-50.0	0.0	-80.0	-46.9	-73.1	
Breakfast foods	0E	0	0	0	0.0	0.0	0.0	0.0	0.0	
Rice	0E	0	0	0	0.0	0.0	0.0	0.0	0.0	
Flour mixes	0E	0	0	0	0.0	0.0	0.0	0.0	0.0	
Wet corn mills	0E	0	0	0	0.0	0.0	0.0	0.0	0.0	
Pet foods	3	2	5E	15E	-35.7	25.0	100.0	81.7	190.7	
Animal feeds	6	3	7E	23E						
Bread, rolls	14	5	27	44	-50.0	-22.2	-28.6	37.2	123.1	
Cookies & crackers	0	0	0	0	0.0	0.0	0.0	0.0	0.0	
Cane sugar	0	0	0	0	0.0	0.0	0.0	0.0	0.0	
Beet sugar	0	0	0	0	0.0	0.0	0.0	0.0	0.0	
Confectionary	3	1	6E	13E	0.0	0.0	100.0	81.8	525.0	
Cottonseed oil	1	Z	2E	9E	-66.7	0.0	0.0	27.3	114.3	
Soybean oil	0E	0	0	0	0.0	0.0	0.0	0.0	0.0	
Other fats & oils	2E	Z	3	8	inf.	inf.	400.0	inf.	1057.1	
Cooking oil & marg.	1E	Z	5	20	0.0	0.0	400.0	60.0	1125.0	
Beer	0	0	0	0	0.0	0.0	0.0	0.0	0.0	
Wine & brandy	0	0	0	0	0.0	0.0	0.0	0.0	0.0	
Spirits	0	0	0	0	0.0	0.0	0.0	0.0	0.0	
Soft drinks	15	6	34	103	-54.5	16.7	-14.3	137.5	317.4	
Flavorings	0	0	0	0	0.0	0.0	0.0	0.0	0.0	
Canned fish	1E	Z	1	1	inf.	inf.	400.0	inf.	100.0	
Frozen fish	4E	Z	1	1	inf.	inf.	400.0	inf.	100.0	
Coffee	0E	0	0	0	-100.0	0.0	-100.0	-72.7	-100.0	
Pasta	1E	P	0.1	0.1	inf.	0.0	inf.	0.0	inf.	
Miscellaneous foods	23	4	11	23	-14.8	24.0	32.3	148.5	184.1	
Total	104	36	133	458	-33.3	5.6	-5.3	135.9	69.4	-13.3

Source: Data from Bureau of the Census reports.

Note: Industries are listed by four-digit SIC code, see Appendix C for definitions of terms.

EST = Establishments. EMP = Employment. VA = Value added. VS = Value of shipments. inf. = Infinity. P = Less than 20. Z = 20 to 99.

Appendix Table B–45
Arizona: Basic Economic Data on Food Manufacturing Industries, 1963, 1972, 1982, and 1985

INDUSTRY 1/	1982 Totals				Growth Rates					
	EST	EMP	VA	VS	EST	EMP		VS		
					1963–1982	1963–1972	1972–1982	1963–1972	1972–1982	1982–1985
	No.	'00	$ million		- - - - - - - - - - Percent - - - - - - - - -					
Meatpacking	20	5	16	145	5.3	50.0	-58.3	345.8	-44.9	
Meat processing	5	Z	2E	8E	-16.7	400.0	0.0	800.0	116.7	
Poultry dressing	2E	Z	2	8	50.0	500.0	0.0	1333.3	118.6	
Poultry processing	1E	P	0.3	2						
Butter	0	0	0	0	-100.0	-100.0	0.0	-100.0	0.0	
Cheese	0	0	0	0	0.0	0.0	0.0	0.0	0.0	
Processed milk	0	0	0	0	-100.0	-100.0	0.0	-100.0	0.0	
Ice cream	7	1	4	9	-22.2	-50.0	0.0	-45.2	130.0	
Fluid milk	11	7	53	215	-52.2	-43.8	-22.2	66.9	143.8	
Canned specialties	4	3	12E	28E	-20.0	500.0	0.0	739.1	44.0	
Canned fruit & veg.	3E	Z	2	5	-25.0	-80.0	400.0	-61.5	820.0	
Dry fruit & veg.	0E	0	0	0	0.0	0.0	0.0	0.0	0.0	
Sauces, pickles	4	Z	2E	5E	-33.3	100.0	-50.0	211.1	-17.9	
Frozen fruit & veg.	1E	Z	2	5	50.0	-100.0	inf.	-100.0	inf.	
Frozen specialties	2E	Z	2	5						
Flour	3	Z	6E	15E	200.0	0.0	0.0	12.2	172.7	
Breakfast foods	0E	0	0	0	0.0	0.0	0.0	0.0	0.0	
Rice	0E	0	0	0	0.0	0.0	0.0	0.0	0.0	
Flour mixes	1E	Z	6	15E	inf.	0.0	inf.	0.0	inf.	
Wet corn mills	0E	0	0	0	0.0	0.0	0.0	0.0	0.0	
Pet foods	3	2	22E	60E	-6.7	-37.5	60.0	-2.5	333.2	
Animal feeds	11	2	22E	60E						
Bread, rolls	30	15	43E	87E	-26.8	0.0	25.0	59.3	127.6	
Cookies & crackers	1E	1	3	6	inf.	inf.	900.0	inf.	1833.3	
Cane sugar	0E	0	0	0	0.0	0.0	0.0	0.0	0.0	
Beet sugar	1	2	8E	28E	inf.	inf.	0.0	inf.	83.0	
Confectionary	5E	P	1	1	66.7	-80.0	0.0	-63.6	200.0	
Cottonseed oil	3	3	12E	57E	-57.1	-40.0	0.0	90.8	128.4	
Soybean oil	1E	P	0.4	2	inf.	0.0	inf.	0.0	inf.	
Other fats & oils	3	1	4	19E	-33.3	-83.3	900.0	-76.7	2614.3	
Cooking oil & marg.	1E	P	0.4	2	inf.	inf.	0.0	inf.	18.8	
Beer	1	Z	4E	9E	0.0	0.0	-75.0	35.1	-6.0	
Wine & brandy	0	0	0	0	0.0	0.0	0.0	0.0	0.0	
Spirits	0	0	0	0	0.0	0.0	0.0	0.0	0.0	
Soft drinks	23	14	104E	263E	-30.3	50.0	16.7	198.8	433.9	
Flavorings	0	0	0	0	-100.0	0.0	-100.0	-37.5	-100.0	
Canned fish	1E	Z	2	7	inf.	inf.	400.0	inf.	3250.0	
Frozen fish	2E	1	3	11	inf.	inf.	900.0	inf.	5200.0	
Coffee	0E	0	0	0	-100.0	-100.0	0.0	-100.0	0.0	
Pasta	1E	Z	3	6	-100.0	0.0	inf.	0.0	inf.	
Miscellaneous foods	34	7	18	32	-26.1	20.0	16.7	36.1	115.0	
Total	188	66	349	1087	-18.3	1.5	-1.5	135.1	89.7	17.6

Source: Data from Bureau of the Census reports.

Note: Industries are listed by four-digit SIC code, see Appendix C for definitions of terms.

EST = Establishments. EMP = Employment. VA = Value added. VS = Value of shipments. inf. = Infinity. P = Less than 20. Z = 20 to 99.

Appendix Table B–46
Utah: Basic Economic Data on Food Manufacturing Industries, 1963, 1972, 1982, and 1985

INDUSTRY 1/	1982 Totals				Growth Rates						
	EST	EMP	VA	VS	EST	EMP		VS			
					1963-1982	1963-1972	1972-1982	1963-1972	1972-1982	1982-1985	
	No.	'00	$ million		- - - - - - - - - - Percent - - - - - -						
Meatpacking	19	7	22E	202E	-34.5	-38.5	-12.5	40.4	56.0		
Meat processing	5	2	6E	58E	25.0	100.0	100.0	59.1	1545.7		
Poultry dressing	3	3	6	22	-72.7	-25.0	0.0	8.2	111.3		
Poultry processing	0	0	0	0							
Butter	0E	0	0	0	-100.0	0.0	-100.0	19.5	-100.0		
Cheese	8	11	23	275	100.0	700.0	175.0	432.4	598.2		
Processed milk	2E	1	5	25	-33.3	100.0	0.0	160.5	156.6		
Ice cream	8	2	11E	51	-27.3	-33.3	0.0	-14.5	761.0		
Fluid milk	14	8	46	223	-54.8	-26.7	-27.3	46.1	185.5		
Canned specialties	1E	P	1	2	0.0	0.0	0.0	0.0	800.0		
Canned fruit & veg.	3E	P	1	1	-81.3	-60.0	-95.0	-39.9	-84.3		
Dry fruit & veg.	0E	0	0	0	0.0	0.0	0.0	0.0	0.0		
Sauces, pickles	2E	P	1	2	100.0	0.0	0.0	-50.0	850.0		
Frozen fruit & veg.	1E	P	1	1	-66.7	100.0	610.0	-6.7	5950.0		
Frozen specialties	2	7	35E	84E							
Flour	11	3	20E	85E	-21.4	-25.0	0.0	-7.4	109.7		
Breakfast foods	0	0	0	0	0.0	0.0	0.0	0.0	0.0		
Rice	0	0	0	0	0.0	0.0	0.0	0.0	0.0		
Flour mixes	0	0	0	0	-100.0	-80.0	-100.0	-74.0	-100.0		
Wet corn mills	0	0	0	0	0.0	0.0	0.0	0.0	0.0		
Pet foods	3	2	14E	56E	-50.0	-16.7	20.0	57.7	151.5		
Animal feeds	11	1	7E	28E							
Bread, rolls	16	13	62E	107E	-40.7	-9.1	30.0	30.1	291.5		
Cookies & crackers	1	Z	2E	4E	0.0	-80.0	400.0	-76.9	1266.7		
Cane sugar	0	0	0	0	0.0	0.0	0.0	0.0	0.0		
Beet sugar	0	0	0	0	-100.0	-71.4	-100.0	-82.2	-100.0		
Confectionary	13	3	18E	38E	-31.6	0.0	-50.0	139.7	100.5		
Cottonseed oil	0E	0	0	0	0.0	0.0	0.0	0.0	0.0		
Soybean oil	0E	0	0	0	-100.0	0.0	-100.0	60.9	-100.0		
Other fats & oils	2	Z	3E	8E	-60.0	0.0	0.0	94.1	145.5		
Cooking oil & marg.	0E	0	0	0	0.0	0.0	0.0	0.0	0.0		
Beer	0	0	0	0	-100.0	-100.0	0.0	-100.0	0.0		
Wine & brandy	0	0	0	0	0.0	0.0	0.0	0.0	0.0		
Spirits	0	0	0	0	0.0	0.0	0.0	0.0	0.0		
Soft drinks	13	6	34	103	-51.9	40.0	-14.3	143.7	310.0		
Flavorings	0	0	0	0	-100.0	-100.0	0.0	-100.0	0.0		
Canned fish	1	P	0.2	0.4	inf.	inf.	0.0	inf.	100.0		
Frozen fish	2	Z	1	2	inf.	inf.	0.0	inf.	350.0		
Coffee	0	0	0	0	-100.0	-100.0	0.0	-100.0	0.0		
Pasta	1	P	0.2	0.4	0.0	0.0	0.0	-33.3	100.0		
Miscellaneous foods	16	5	16	33	-15.8	17.1	24.4	42.6	131.9		
Total	158	76	339	1389	-43.0	-17.6	8.6	27.6	199.2	22.0	

Source: Data from Bureau of the Census reports.

Note: Industries are listed by four-digit SIC code, see Appendix C for definitions of terms.

EST = Establishments. EMP = Employment. VA = Value added. VS = Value of shipments. inf. = Infinity. P = Less than 20. Z = 20 to 99.

Appendix Table B–47
Nevada: Basic Economic Data on Food Manufacturing Industries, 1963, 1972, 1982, and 1985

INDUSTRY 1/	1982 Totals				Growth Rates					
	EST	EMP	VA	VS	EST	EMP		VS		
					1963–1982	1963–1972	1972–1982	1963–1972	1972–1982	1982–1985
	No.	'00	$ million		- - - - - - - - - - Percent - - - - -					
Meatpacking	2E	Z	2	17	-71.4	0.0	0.0	114.7	128.8	
Meat processing	1E	P	5	19	-75.0	0.0	0.0	100.0	2262.5	
Poultry dressing	0E	0	0	0	} 0.0	} 0.0	} 0.0	} 0.0	} 0.0	
Poultry processing	0E	0	0	0						
Butter	0E	0	0	0	0.0	0.0	0.0	0.0	0.0	
Cheese	1E	P	1	2	inf.	0.0	inf.	0.0	inf.	
Processed milk	0E	0	0	0	0.0	0.0	0.0	0.0	0.0	
Ice cream	0E	0	0	0	-100.0	-100.0	0.0	-100.0	0.0	
Fluid milk	5	3	22E	62E	-44.4	-20.0	-25.0	53.6	138.4	
Canned specialties	0E	0	0	0	0.0	0.0	0.0	0.0	0.0	
Canned fruit & veg.	3E	P	1	1	inf.	inf.	0.0	inf.	160.0	
Dry fruit & veg.	2	1	6E	13E	inf.	0.0	inf.	0.0	inf.	
Sauces, pickles	0E	0	0	0	0.0	inf.	-100.0	inf.	-100.0	
Frozen fruit & veg.	0E	0	0	0	} 0.0	} 0.0	} 0.0	} 0.0	} 0.0	
Frozen specialties	0E	0	0	0						
Flour	0	0	0	0	0.0	0.0	0.0	0.0	0.0	
Breakfast foods	0	0	0	0	0.0	0.0	0.0	0.0	0.0	
Rice	0	0	0	0	0.0	0.0	0.0	0.0	0.0	
Flour mixes	0	0	0	0	0.0	0.0	0.0	0.0	0.0	
Wet corn mills	0	0	0	0	0.0	0.0	0.0	0.0	0.0	
Pet foods	1	2	26E	51E	} 200.0	} 100.0	} 1150.0	} 214.3	} 3023.8	
Animal feeds	2	Z	3E	15E						
Bread, rolls	8	1	5E	8E	-20.0	-50.0	0.0	-15.8	140.6	
Cookies & crackers	0	0	0	0	-100.0	-80.0	-100.0	-69.2	-100.0	
Cane sugar	0E	0	0	0	0.0	0.0	0.0	0.0	0.0	
Beet sugar	0E	0	0	0	0.0	0.0	0.0	0.0	0.0	
Confectionary	1E	P	1	1	inf.	inf.	0.0	inf.	200.0	
Cottonseed oil	0E	0	0	0	0.0	0.0	0.0	0.0	0.0	
Soybean oil	0E	0	0	0	0.0	0.0	0.0	0.0	0.0	
Other fats & oils	1	P	1E	2E	inf.	inf.	0.0	inf.	166.7	
Cooking oil & marg.	0E	0	0	0	0.0	0.0	0.0	0.0	0.0	
Beer	0E	0	0	0	0.0	0.0	0.0	0.0	0.0	
Wine & brandy	0E	0	0	0	0.0	0.0	inf.	0.0	inf.	
Spirits	1E	P	1	2	inf.	0.0	0.0	0.0	0.0	
Soft drinks	6	3	27E	55E	-25.0	50.0	0.0	179.6	300.0	
Flavorings	0E	0	0	0	0.0	0.0	0.0	0.0	0.0	
Canned fish	0E	0	0	0	0.0	0.0	0.0	0.0	0.0	
Frozen fish	2E	P	1	2	inf.	inf.	0.0	inf.	325.0	
Coffee	0E	0	0	0	0.0	0.0	0.0	0.0	0.0	
Pasta	0E	0	0	0	0.0	0.0	0.0	0.0	0.0	
Miscellaneous foods	9	2	20E	35E	125.0	250.0	0.0	766.7	351.3	
Total	45	13	127	259	-2.2	40.0	-7.1	140.5	230.9	22.8

Source: Data from Bureau of the Census reports.

Note: Industries are listed by four-digit SIC code, see Appendix C for definitions of terms.

EST = Establishments. EMP = Employment. VA = Value added. VS = Value of shipments. inf. = Infinity. P = Less than 20. Z = 20 to 99.

Appendix Table B-48
Washington: Basic Economic Data on Food Manufacturing Industries, 1963, 1972, 1982, and 1985

INDUSTRY 1/	1982 Totals				Growth Rates					
	EST	EMP	VA	VS	EST	EMP		VS		
					1963-1982	1963-1972	1972-1982	1963-1972	1972-1982	1982-1985
	No.	'00	$ million		- - - - - - - - - - Percent - - - - - - - - -					
Meatpacking	28	27	97	934	-54.1	-21.7	50.0	55.2	239.0	
Meat processing	13	6	24	99	-27.8	-25.0	100.0	-26.2	566.4	
Poultry dressing	8	5	9E	57E	-52.6	-23.8	-16.4	14.8	91.7	
Poultry processing	1E	P	0.2	1						
Butter	5	P	24E	131E	-28.6	100.0	100.0	129.3	1288.3	
Cheese	6	2	24E	131E	50.0	100.0	100.0	184.8	1288.3	
Processed milk	2E	2	1	7	-66.7	-95.0	0.0	-94.1	622.2	
Ice cream	7	P	24E	131E	-46.2	0.0	0.0	50.8	621.0	
Fluid milk	24	2	66	382	-63.1	-35.3	-45.5	46.0	85.0	
Canned specialties	7	1	3E	8E	inf.	inf.	0.0	inf.	43.1	
Canned fruit & veg.	24	28	140	357	-33.3	-22.6	16.7	52.5	155.2	
Dry fruit & veg.	7	5	19	50	-12.5	50.0	-16.7	268.1	48.4	
Sauces, pickles	5	1	3E	8E	-61.5	0.0	-66.7	-1.1	-52.6	
Frozen fruit & veg.	37	62	342	667	7.3	79.3	23.1	115.2	266.2	
Frozen specialties	7	2	7E	17E						
Flour	7	4	14	119	-22.2	-50.0	-20.0	-27.3	108.8	
Breakfast foods	25	4	25	112	inf.	inf.	300.0	inf.	878.9	
Rice	0	0	0	0	0.0	inf.	-100.0	inf.	-100.0	
Flour mixes	1E	Z	3	8	-83.3	300.0	-75.0	660.0	-63.6	
Wet corn mills	0E	0	0	0	-100.0	0.0	-100.0	120.0	-100.0	
Pet foods	2E	1	6	17	-57.5	50.0	-20.0	81.8	-13.9	
Animal feeds	15E	3	18	50						
Bread, rolls	40	30	122E	206E	-51.2	-30.3	30.4	6.1	202.1	
Cookies & crackers	7	2	8E	14E	40.0	-50.0	0.0	-11.9	132.2	
Cane sugar	0	0	0	0	0.0	0.0	0.0	0.0	0.0	
Beet sugar	0	0	0	0	-100.0	133.3	-100.0	192.0	-100.0	
Confectionary	17	6	31E	59E	1600.0	1320.0	-14.1	1485.7	32.0	
Cottonseed oil	0	0	0	0	0.0	0.0	0.0	0.0	0.0	
Soybean oil	0	0	0	0	-100.0	400.0	-100.0	39.1	-100.0	
Other fats & oils	11	2	12E	26E	-31.3	0.0	0.0	92.4	100.8	
Cooking oil & marg.	2	Z	3E	6E	100.0	0.0	0.0	-34.7	100.0	
Beer	5	13	107	289	0.0	-6.7	-7.1	28.9	166.8	
Wine & brandy	11	2	5E	31E	-8.3	0.0	0.0	76.1	101.9	
Spirits	2	P	0.3E	2E	inf.	0.0	inf.	0.0	inf.	
Soft drinks	27	14	80	262	-37.2	55.6	0.0	373.4	141.6	
Flavorings	6	2	5E	31E	200.0	0.0	1900.0	0.0	3812.5	
Canned fish	37	16	38	133	-44.8	-41.7	128.6	-1.6	330.4	
Frozen fish	73	27	76	355	151.7	27.3	92.9	84.3	379.6	
Coffee	2E	P	0.1	1	-60.0	-80.0	0.0	-92.6	250.0	
Pasta	9	4	24	45	80.0	0.0	100.0	42.6	411.5	
Miscellaneous foods	54	16	135	258	38.5	-5.9	101.3	18.1	630.9	
Total	532	302	1499	5000	-22.0	-4.1	18.0	58.5	197.2	14.7

Source: Data from Bureau of the Census reports.

Note: Industries are listed by four-digit SIC code, see Appendix C for definitions of terms.

EST = Establishments. EMP = Employment. VA = Value added. VS = Value of shipments. inf. = Infinity. P = Less than 20. Z = 20 to 99.

Appendix Table B–49
Oregon: Basic Economic Data on Food Manufacturing Industries, 1963, 1972, 1982, and 1985

INDUSTRY 1/	1982 Totals EST	EMP	VA	VS	Growth Rates EST 1963-1982	EMP 1963-1972	1972-1982	VS 1963-1972	1972-1982	1982-1985
	No.	'00	$ million		- - - - - - - - - - Percent - - - - - - - - - -					
Meatpacking	27	7	18	110	-62.5	-53.8	16.7	-13.9	49.3	
Meat processing	14	7	42	170	16.7	500.0	-41.7	1236.8	46.0	
Poultry dressing	6	8	20	87	-33.3	100.0	33.3	254.2	154.7	
Poultry processing	0	0	0	0						
Butter	0E	0	0	0	-100.0	-80.0	-100.0	-51.2	-100.0	
Cheese	7	3	9E	74E	-41.7	200.0	0.0	533.3	93.9	
Processed milk	1E	Z	2	12	-80.0	0.0	0.0	78.9	80.9	
Ice cream	3E	Z	2	12	-66.7	0.0	-50.0	63.9	108.5	
Fluid milk	23	12	56	293	-58.9	-27.3	-25.0	54.7	105.2	
Canned specialties	0	0	0	0	0.0	0.0	0.0	0.0	0.0	
Canned fruit & veg.	21	16	57	130	-50.0	-5.3	-55.6	55.5	5.3	
Dry fruit & veg.	6	Z	2E	4E	50.0	300.0	-75.0	411.8	-51.7	
Sauces, pickles	7	3	12	32	-12.5	100.0	200.0	205.6	481.8	
Frozen fruit & veg.	29	77	341	659	0.0	33.3	55.8	65.2	354.9	
Frozen specialties	6	4	29	54						
Flour	5	2	16E	57E	0.0	0.0	0.0	129.4	27.9	
Breakfast foods	0E	0	0	0	-100.0	-100.0	0.0	-100.0	0.0	
Rice	1E	P	1	3	inf.	0.0	inf.	0.0	inf.	
Flour mixes	2E	P	1	3	0.0	0.0	-80.0	-4.0	-41.7	
Wet corn mills	0E	0	0	0	0.0	0.0	0.0	0.0	0.0	
Pet foods	4	3	29	70	-35.9	0.0	0.0	35.4	131.9	
Animal feeds	21	4	19	87						
Bread, rolls	27	15	95E	147E	-49.1	-5.0	-21.1	250.3	10.6	
Cookies & crackers	5	15	95E	147E	0.0	-30.0	114.3	17.6	389.0	
Cane sugar	0	0	0	0	0.0	0.0	0.0	0.0	0.0	
Beet sugar	1	3	13E	44E	-50.0	0.0	0.0	53.3	91.7	
Confectionary	12	3	18E	38E	-25.0	0.0	0.0	13.0	207.4	
Cottonseed oil	0E	0	0	0	0.0	0.0	0.0	0.0	0.0	
Soybean oil	2	P	1E	10E	inf.	0.0	inf.	0.0	inf.	
Other fats & oils	13	2	10E	33E	44.4	300.0	0.0	1235.3	43.2	
Cooking oil & marg.	3	2	20E	79E	200.0	-100.0	inf.	-100.0	inf.	
Beer	1	3	35E	77E	0.0	50.0	0.0	151.4	315.6	
Wine & brandy	2E	1	12	26	100.0	0.0	900.0	50.0	4200.0	
Spirits	1E	1	12	26	0.0	0.0	900.0	0.0	4200.0	
Soft drinks	22	9	57	105	-46.3	33.3	12.5	278.6	111.5	
Flavorings	1E	1	12	26	-80.0	100.0	0.0	55.0	316.1	
Canned fish	9	2	17E	28E	-25.0	0.0	-71.4	29.7	-31.1	
Frozen fish	23	11	22	77	27.8	100.0	-8.3	610.2	84.2	
Coffee	1	2	17E	28E	-75.0	0.0	0.0	-67.7	295.7	
Pasta	2E	P	1	1	0.0	-80.0	0.0	-81.3	366.7	
Miscellaneous foods	33	8	25	54	57.1	23.4	58.8	52.4	183.3	
Total	352	226	1128	2830	-31.0	10.1	3.2	78.6	141.1	6.5

Source: Data from Bureau of the Census reports.

Note: Industries are listed by four-digit SIC code, see Appendix C for definitions of terms.

EST = Establishments. EMP = Employment. VA = Value added. VS = Value of shipments. inf. = Infinity. P = Less than 20. Z = 20 to 99.

Appendix Table B–50
California: Basic Economic Data on Food Manufacturing Industries, 1963, 1972, 1982, and 1985

INDUSTRY 1/	1982 Totals				Growth Rates					
	EST	EMP	VA	VS	EST	EMP			VS	
					1963-1982	1963-1972	1972-1982	1963-1972	1972-1982	1982-1985
	No.	'00	\$ million		- - - - - - - - - - Percent - - - - - - - - - -					
Meatpacking	86	46	218	1810	-31.7	-16.9	-22.0	38.1	53.7	
Meat processing	127	56	333	1181	9.5	7.8	1.8	96.9	133.8	
Poultry dressing	32	82	162	718	-47.2	10.5	102.4	43.8	223.6	
Poultry processing	15	3	8	40						
Butter	2	2	20E	123E	-75.0	0.0	0.0	79.9	344.4	
Cheese	30	11	34	292	50.0	0.0	266.7	227.6	601.9	
Processed milk	16	3	29E	185E	6.7	16.7	-57.1	82.0	90.3	
Ice cream	81	18	119	352	3.8	-20.0	12.5	24.9	216.1	
Fluid milk	84	68	435	2561	-72.9	-39.4	-29.9	34.3	146.6	
Canned specialties	41	39	238	599	36.7	12.1	5.4	35.9	165.7	
Canned fruit & veg.	131	216	1176	2948	-31.8	-2.4	-11.8	46.4	135.3	
Dry fruit & veg.	79	79	443	1070	-34.2	-6.3	31.7	42.7	236.4	
Sauces, pickles	59	33	248	616	-20.3	42.3	-10.8	90.0	173.1	
Frozen fruit & veg.	35	86	330	658	-19.8	49.4	3.3	144.1	102.4	
Frozen specialties	46	39	128	421						
Flour	19	8	76	313	-17.4	-33.3	33.3	21.5	213.5	
Breakfast foods	10	13	235E	412E	49.2	133.3	85.7	379.9	423.9	
Rice	11	8	32	377	0.0	-28.6	60.0	30.1	179.7	
Flour mixes	14	3	24	55	-41.7	0.0	-66.7	80.0	-58.7	
Wet corn mills	2	Z	9E	16E	-50.0	-50.0	-50.0	29.8	42.0	
Pet foods	28	16	129	300	-21.6	18.4	-4.4	73.9	121.1	
Animal feeds	117	27	150	872						
Bread, rolls	273	182	961	1544	-21.6	-8.0	-0.5	36.7	149.1	
Cookies & crackers	47	31	198	335	51.6	-7.4	24.0	75.8	173.0	
Cane sugar	1	15	137E	410E	0.0	0.0	0.0	0.7	164.6	
Beet sugar	11	24	75	374	-8.3	0.0	-20.0	106.8	20.9	
Confectionary	120	90	559	1106	-15.5	20.8	55.2	94.1	361.8	
Cottonseed oil	9	9	65	252	-25.0	-30.0	28.6	80.6	97.7	
Soybean oil	2	P	0.2E	2E	-66.7	-80.0	0.0	-84.1	-5.6	
Other fats & oils	40	10	79	301	-35.5	-22.2	-28.6	16.0	83.0	
Cooking oil & marg.	22	14	159	554	4.8	25.0	-6.7	131.9	103.1	
Beer	8	37	476E	1263E	-46.7	-32.4	48.0	39.5	373.4	
Wine & brandy	228	93	848	2407	74.0	57.5	47.6	145.9	285.1	
Spirits	18	7	90E	239E	63.6	28.6	-22.2	208.7	82.5	
Soft drinks	104	89	717	1653	-46.7	17.7	21.9	120.4	245.7	
Flavorings	49	10	172	317	-3.9	0.0	42.9	130.1	147.2	
Canned fish	14	66	424	1147	-41.7	5.8	20.0	152.2	162.1	
Frozen fish	54	35	99	346	58.8	50.0	133.3	154.9	499.8	
Coffee	20	15	360	1013	-51.2	-45.8	15.4	6.2	220.6	
Pasta	47	14	64	149	17.5	0.0	75.0	19.4	301.6	
Miscellaneous foods	404	140	879	1743	13.2	22.2	47.1	116.3	250.4	
Total	2536	1735	10937	31263	-17.3	0.3	11.1	63.5	165.1	2.5

Source: Data from Bureau of the Census reports.

Note: Industries are listed by four-digit SIC code, see Appendix C for definitions of terms.

EST = Establishments. EMP = Employment. VA = Value added. VS = Value of shipments. P = Less than 20. Z = 20 to 99.

Appendix Table B–51
Alaska: Basic Economic Data on Food Manufacturing Industries, 1963, 1972, 1982, and 1985

INDUSTRY 1/	1982 Totals				Growth Rates						
	EST	EMP	VA	VS	EST	EMP			VS		
					1963-1982	1963-1972	1972-1982	1963-1972	1972-1982	1982-1985	
	No.	'00	$ million		- - - - - - - - - - Percent - - - - - - - - - -						
Meatpacking	1E	P	0.4	3	inf.	inf.	0.0	inf.	120.0		
Meat processing	0E	0	0	0	-100.0	0.0	-100.0	100.0	-100.0		
Poultry dressing	0E	0	0	0	⎫	⎫	⎫	⎫	⎫		
					0.0	0.0	0.0	0.0	0.0		
Poultry processing	0E	0	0	0	⎭	⎭	⎭	⎭	⎭		
Butter	0E	0	0	0	0.0	0.0	0.0	0.0	0.0		
Cheese	1E	P	1	4	inf.	inf.	0.0	inf.	176.9		
Processed milk	0E	0	0	0	0.0	0.0	0.0	0.0	0.0		
Ice cream	0E	0	0	0	0.0	0.0	0.0	0.0	0.0		
Fluid milk	2	Z	3E	12E	-71.4	0.0	-50.0	97.4	60.0		
Canned specialties	0E	0	0	0	0.0	0.0	0.0	0.0	0.0		
Canned fruit & veg.	0E	0	0	0	-100.0	0.0	-100.0	66.7	-100.0		
Dry fruit & veg.	0E	0	0	0	0.0	0.0	0.0	0.0	0.0		
Sauces, pickles	0E	0	0	0	0.0	0.0	0.0	0.0	0.0		
Frozen fruit & veg.	0E	0	0	0	⎫	⎫	⎫	⎫	⎫		
					-100.0	-100.0	0.0	-100.0	0.0		
Frozen specialties	0E	0	0	0	⎭	⎭	⎭	⎭	⎭		
Flour	0E	0	0	0	0.0	0.0	0.0	0.0	0.0		
Breakfast foods	0E	0	0	0	0.0	0.0	0.0	0.0	0.0		
Rice	0E	0	0	0	0.0	0.0	0.0	0.0	0.0		
Flour mixes	0E	0	0	0	0.0	0.0	0.0	0.0	0.0		
Wet corn mills	0E	0	0	0	0.0	0.0	0.0	0.0	0.0		
Pet foods	0E	0	0	0	⎫	⎫	⎫	⎫	⎫		
					100.0	0.0	0.0	57.1	172.7		
Animal feeds	2E	P	1	3	⎭	⎭	⎭	⎭	⎭		
Bread, rolls	3	2	9E	15E	-76.9	0.0	0.0	44.4	136.9		
Cookies & crackers	0E	0	0	0	0.0	0.0	0.0	0.0	0.0		
Cane sugar	0E	0	0	0	0.0	0.0	0.0	0.0	0.0		
Beet sugar	0E	0	0	0	0.0	0.0	0.0	0.0	0.0		
Confectionary	1E	P	1	1	inf.	inf.	0.0	inf.	200.0		
Cottonseed oil	0E	0	0	0	0.0	0.0	0.0	0.0	0.0		
Soybean oil	0E	0	0	0	0.0	0.0	0.0	0.0	0.0		
Other fats & oils	1E	Z	3	8	0.0	400.0	0.0	1000.0	145.5		
Cooking oil & marg.	0E	0	0	0	0.0	0.0	0.0	0.0	0.0		
Beer	0E	0	0	0	-100.0	-100.0	0.0	-100.0	0.0		
Wine & brandy	0E	0	0	0	0.0	0.0	0.0	0.0	0.0		
Spirits	0E	0	0	0	0.0	0.0	0.0	0.0	0.0		
Soft drinks	1E	P	1	2	-80.0	-50.0	-90.0	9.8	-66.7		
Flavorings	0E	0	0	0	0.0	0.0	0.0	0.0	0.0		
Canned fish	33	14	31E	139E	-52.9	-23.8	-12.5	-2.6	104.3		
Frozen fish	66	35	132E	465	407.7	500.0	191.7	994.9	988.8		
Coffee	0E	0	0	0	0.0	0.0	0.0	0.0	0.0		
Pasta	0E	0	0	0	0.0	0.0	0.0	0.0	0.0		
Miscellaneous foods	10	2	5E	20E	900.0	-80.0	300.0	66.7	1880.0		
Total	121	54	185	662	5.2	13.8	63.6	47.3	397.8	-7.2	

Source: Data from Bureau of the Census reports.

Note: Industries are listed by four-digit SIC code, see Appendix C for definitions of terms.

EST = Establishments. EMP = Employment. VA = Value added. VS = Value of shipments. inf. = Infinity. P = Less than 20. Z = 20 to 99.

Appendix Table B-52
Hawaii: Basic Economic Data on Food Manufacturing Industries, 1963, 1972, 1982, and 1985

INDUSTRY 1/	1982 Totals				Growth Rates					
	EST	EMP	VA	VS	EST	EMP		VS		
					1963-1982	1963-1972	1972-1982	1963-1972	1972-1982	1982-1985
	No.	'00	$ million		- - - - - - - - - - Percent - - - - - - - - - -					
Meatpacking	6	2	3	33	0.0	-33.3	0.0	2.7	120.0	
Meat processing	9	2	4E	14E	0.0	300.0	0.0	581.8	-8.0	
Poultry dressing	1	Z	1E	4E	100.0	-100.0	inf.	-100.0	inf.	
Poultry processing	3	P	0.2E	1E						
Butter	0	0	0	0	0.0	0.0	0.0	0.0	0.0	
Cheese	0	0	0	0	0.0	0.0	0.0	0.0	0.0	
Processed milk	0	0	0	0	0.0	0.0	0.0	0.0	0.0	
Ice cream	5	2	8E	28E	0.0	100.0	0.0	227.8	133.1	
Fluid milk	5	3	12E	41E	-54.5	-50.0	0.0	-1.8	84.4	
Canned specialties	4	Z	2E	4	33.3	0.0	400.0	-60.0	2100.0	
Canned fruit & veg.	9	31	89	215	-55.0	-32.4	-35.4	-27.2	55.0	
Dry fruit & veg.	1E	P	0.3	1	0.0	0.0	0.0	-33.3	350.0	
Sauces, pickles	16	1	3E	9E	23.1	100.0	0.0	-33.3	270.8	
Frozen fruit & veg.	2E	Z	2	4	100.0	-60.0	200.0	-73.3	1225.0	
Frozen specialties	2E	P	0.3	1						
Flour	1	Z	3E	13E	inf.	inf.	0.0	inf.	101.5	
Breakfast foods	0	0	0	0	0.0	0.0	0.0	0.0	0.0	
Rice	0	0	0	0	0.0	0.0	0.0	0.0	0.0	
Flour mixes	0	0	0	0	0.0	0.0	0.0	0.0	0.0	
Wet corn mills	0	0	0	0	0.0	0.0	0.0	0.0	0.0	
Pet foods	2E	1	5	27	20.0	-25.0	0.0	40.1	101.0	
Animal feeds	4	Z	3E	13E						
Bread, rolls	25	11	39	66	66.7	0.0	83.3	69.0	291.1	
Cookies & crackers	8	1	3E	5E	33.3	-50.0	0.0	-4.0	91.7	
Cane sugar	14	30	138	356	-44.0	-17.2	-18.1	-3.5	87.0	
Beet sugar	0	0	0	0	0.0	0.0	0.0	0.0	0.0	
Confectionary	14	7	22E	73E	-6.7	0.0	250.0	173.9	476.2	
Cottonseed oil	0	0	0	0	0.0	0.0	0.0	0.0	0.0	
Soybean oil	1E	P	1	10	0.0	0.0	0.0	60.9	162.2	
Other fats & oils	3E	P	1	2	200.0	0.0	0.0	133.3	128.6	
Cooking oil & marg.	1E	P	1	4	inf.	0.0	inf.	0.0	inf.	
Beer	0	0	0	0	-100.0	0.0	-100.0	112.2	-100.0	
Wine & brandy	2E	1	6	16	inf.	0.0	inf.	0.0	inf.	
Spirits	0	0	0	0	-100.0	0.0	-100.0	66.7	-100.0	
Soft drinks	6	3	18E	48E	-68.4	0.0	0.0	117.7	257.0	
Flavorings	4	Z	3E	8E	33.3	0.0	0.0	40.0	44.6	
Canned fish	3	3	4E	20E	-40.0	50.0	0.0	57.7	137.8	
Frozen fish	5	1	1E	7E	400.0	0.0	900.0	50.0	2066.7	
Coffee	1	1	1E	7E	0.0	0.0	900.0	-72.7	2066.7	
Pasta	18	2	3E	13E	50.0	0.0	100.0	170.0	381.5	
Miscellaneous foods	45	8	25	52	-4.3	0.0	141.9	109.3	363.7	
Total	221	111	399	1080	-5.6	-21.7	-6.7	2.4	110.4	18.2

Source: Data from Bureau of the Census reports.

Note: Industries are listed by four-digit SIC code, see Appendix C for definitions of terms.

EST = Establishments. EMP = Employment. VA = Value added. VS = Value of shipments. inf. = Infinity. P = Less than 20. Z = 20 to 99.

Appendix C: Glossary of Terms

Administrative offices An office separate from the operating establishment (q.v.) managed or served.

Administrative office and auxiliary unit employees Employees in administrative offices are concerned with the general management of multiestablishment companies (i.e., with the general supervision and control of two units or more, such as manufacturing plants, mines, sales branches, or stores). The functions of these employees may include (1) program planning, including sales research and coordination of purchasing, production, and distribution; (2) company purchasing, including general contracts and purchasing methods; (3) company financial policy and accounting, tax accounting, company sales and profits reports, and personnel accounting; (4) general engineering, including design of product machinery and equipment, and direction of engineering effort conducted at the individual operation locations; (5) direction of company personnel matters; and (6) legal and patent matters. Employees of auxiliary establishments (q.v.) are involved in storage, repair, purchasing, sales, data processing, research, or development.

Annual Survey of Manufactures An economic survey taken by the Census Bureau in years between the Census of Manufactures (q.v.). The sample includes about one-fifth of all establishments. All large establishments are included in every sample; the smaller are selected in proportion to their size and replaced at the end of each census. Thus, there is an annual updating of the census of manufactures in terms of broad measures of economic activity. The ASM contains the same basic measures of economic activity of the plant (such as employment, payrolls, value of shipments, value added by manufacture) as the Census of Manufactures but obtains less detailed information on products, materials consumption, and equipment.

Assets Encompass all fixed depreciable assets on the books of establishments at the beginning and at the end of the year. The values represent the actual cost of assets at the time they were acquired, including all costs incurred in making the assets usable (such as transportation and installation). Included are all buildings, structures, machinery, and equipment (production, office, and transportation equipment) for which depreciation reserves are maintained. Excluded are nondepreciable capital assets, including inventories and intangible assets such as patent rights and royalties. Also excluded are land and depletable assets such as timber and mineral rights. The definition of fixed depreciable assets is consistent with the definition of capital expenditures (q.v.).

Auxiliaries Separate storage facilities, garages, repair shops, purchasing offices, sales promotion offices, research and development organizations, etc., serving the plants or central management of the company.

Canned foods Foods preserved by sterilizing the contents through heat applied to the metal can, glass jar, or other impermeable container. Foods in cans or jars that require freezing, refrigeration, or preservatives to maintain product safety are not considered "canned."

Capital expenditures For establishments in operation and establishments under construction but not yet in operation, manufacturers were asked to report their new expenditures for (1) permanent additions and major alterations to manufacturing establishments, and (2) machinery and equipment such as painting, roof repairs, replacing parts, and overhauling equipment. Such payments made to other establishments of the same company and for repair and maintenance of any leased property are also included.

Census of Manufactures The first U.S. economic census covered the year 1809; the 1982 census was the thirty-ninth census and the thirty-fourth Census of Manufactures. Data are collected on every manufacturing establishment and company every five years; inputs, outputs, income statements, and balance sheet items are included. The economic censuses provide benchmarks against which all other data series, surveys, and samples can be compared.

Company A legal entity (corporation, partnership, cooperative, proprietorship, trust, etc.) that owns and operates one or more establishments.

Cost of materials This item refers to direct charges actually paid or payable for items consumed or put into production during the year, including freight charges and other direct charges incurred by the establishment in acquiring these materials. It includes the cost of materials or fuel consumed, regardless of whether what was consumed was purchased by the individual establishment from other companies, transferred to it from other establishments of the same company, or withdrawn from inventory during the year.

The important components of this cost item are (1) all raw materials, semifinished goods, parts, components, containers, scrap, and supplies put into production or used as operating supplies and for repair and maintenance during the year; (2) electric energy purchased; (3) fuels consumed for heat, power, or generating electricity; (4) work done by others on materials or parts furnished by manufacturing establishments (contract work); and (5) products bought and resold in the same condition.

Employees This item includes all full-time and part-time employees on the payrolls of operating manufacturing (q.v.) establishments during any part of the pay period ending nearest the twelfth of the month. Included are all persons on paid sick leave, paid holidays, and paid vacations during these pay periods. Officers of corporations are included as employees; proprietors and partners of unincorporated firms are excluded. The number of production workers (q.v.) is the average for the midmonth payroll periods of March, May, August, and November. The "all employees" number is the average number of production workers plus the number of other employees in mid-March. Workers in administrative offices (q.v.) or auxiliary establishments are not normally included in employee counts.

Enterprise   See Company.

Establishment   A single place of business with one or more employees engaged in a single line of commerce, such as an office, plant, depot, warehouse, store, restaurant, and so forth. A company (q.v.) or enterprise owns or rents one or more establishments.

Food System   All industries that supply food and beverages directly or indirectly to consumers. Includes agriculture, fisheries, processing, and distribution of foods, as well as all goods and services purchased by those industries.

Labor Costs   See Payroll and Supplementary labor costs.

Manufacturing   The mechanical or chemical transformation of inorganic or organic substances into new products. The assembly of component parts of products is also considered to be manufacturing if the resulting product is neither a structure nor other fixed improvement. These activities are usually carried on in plants, factories, or mills, which characteristically use power-driven machines and materials-handling equipment.

Manufacturing production is usually carried on for the wholesale market, for transfer to other plants of the same company, or to the order of industrial users. Typically, manufacturers do not sell directly to the household consumer, although some (for example, baking, milk bottling, etc.) sell, chiefly at retail, to household consumers through the mail, through house-to-house routes, or through salesmen.

Materials   See Cost of materials.

Nonproduction employees   This item covers nonproduction personnel of the manufacturing establishment, including those engaged in factory supervision above the working foreman level, sales (including driver-salesmen), sales delivery (highway truck drivers and their helpers), advertising, credit, collection, installation and servicing of own products, clerical and routine office functions, executive, purchasing, financing, legal, personnel (including cafeteria, medical, etc.), professional, and technical.

Output   Used interchangeably with *Production*. The quantity of products produced by an industry or firm, measured in physical units rather than dollar value of sales or shipments (q.v.). When output consists of several products measured in different units, value of shipments is adjusted by an inflation index.

Payroll   This item includes the gross earnings paid to all employees on the payroll of operating manufacturing establishments, administrative offices, or auxiliary establishments (q.v.). Respondents were told they could follow the definition of payroll used for calculating the federal withholding tax. It includes all forms of compensation such as salaries, wages, commissions, dismissal pay, all bonuses, vacation and sick leave pay, and compensation in kind, prior to such deductions as employees' Social Security contributions, withholding taxes, group insurance, union dues, and savings bonds. The total includes salaries of officers of corporations but excludes payments to proprietors or partners of unincorporated concerns. Payroll does not include supplemental labor costs (q.v.).

Production See Output.

Production index A measure of the quantity of output of an industry or sector which uses 100 as a base value. Indexes are developed by adjusting shipments values or sales by an inflation factor such as 1977 dollars.

Production workers This item includes workers (up through the working foreman level) engaged in fabricating, processing, assembling, inspecting, receiving, storing, handling, packing, warehousing, shipping (but not delivering), maintenance, repair, janitorial and watchman services, product development, auxiliary production for plant's own use (e.g., power plant), record keeping, and other services closely associated with these production operations at the establishment covered by the report. Supervisory employees above the working foreman level are excluded from this category (see Nonproduction Employees).

Rental payments This item includes rental payments for the use of all items for which depreciation reserves would be maintained if they were owned by the establishment (e.g., structures and buildings, and production, office, and transportation equipment). Excluded are royalties and other payments for the use of intangibles and depletable assets, and land rents where separable.

Sales For a single-establishment company, sales is identical with value of shipments. For multiestablishment companies, sales are the value of shipments (q.v.) of all establishments net of intracompany, interestablishment shipments.

Shipments See Value of shipments.

SIC (Standard Industrial Classification) system All establishments are placed in one SIC industry designated by four digits; there are about 450 manufacturing industries numbered from 2011 to 3999 containing groups of related products (products made from similar materials using similar processes). See appendix D. All products are placed into one seven-digit SIC; the census recognizes about 13,000 manufactured products. These are grouped into about 1,500 product classes that share the first five digits of the product SIC code.

Supplemental labor costs Supplemental labor costs are divided into legally required expenditures and payments for voluntary programs. The legally required portion consists primarily of federal old age and survivors' insurance, unemployment compensation, and workers' compensation. Payments for voluntary programs include all programs not specifically required by legislation whether they were employer initiated or the result of collective bargaining. They include the employer portion of such plans as insurance premiums, premiums for supplemental accident and sickness insurance, pension plans, supplemental unemployment compensation, welfare plans, stock purchase plans on which the employer payment is not subject to withholding tax, and deferred profit-sharing plans. They exclude such items as company-operated cafeterias, in-plant medical services, free parking lots, discounts on employee purchases, and uniforms and work clothing for employees.

Supplementary wage payments   Include employers' Social Security contributions or other nonpayroll labor costs such as employees' pension plans, group insurance premiums, and workers' compensation. See Supplemental labor costs.

Value added by manufacture   This measure of manufacturing activity is derived by subtracting the cost of materials (q.v.), supplies, containers, fuel, purchased electricity, and contract work from the value of shipments (products manufactured plus receipts for services rendered). The result of this calculation is then adjusted by the addition of value added by merchandising operations (i.e., the difference between the sales value and the cost of merchandise sold without further manufacture, processing, or assembly) plus the net change in finished goods and work-in-process inventories between the beginning and end of the year. Value added is equivalent to payments to all factors of production: labor (wages), management (salaries), capital (depreciation, profits), and others.

   Value added avoids most of the duplication in the figure for value of shipments (q.v.) that results from the use of products of some establishments as materials by others. *Value added* is considered to be the best value measure available for comparing the relative economic importance of manufacturing among industries and geographic areas. The sum of the value added of each company is its contribution to gross national product (GNP).

Value of shipments   This item covers the received or receivable net selling values, f.o.b. plant (exclusive of freight and taxes), of all products shipped, both primary and secondary, as well as all miscellaneous receipts, such as receipts for contract work performed for others, installation and repair, sales of scrap, and sale of products bought and resold without further processing. Included are all items made by or for the establishments from materials owned by it whether sold, transferred to other plants of the same company, or shipped on consignment. The two major components of value of shipments are (1) value added (q.v.) and (2) cost of materials (q.v.) and other purchases or payments to other companies or legal entities.

Appendix D: Industry Descriptions

This appendix contains descriptions of the forty-seven food processing four-digit industries for which data were compiled and published in the 1982 *Census of Manufactures*. The industry titles and descriptions, in general, agree with those appearing in the 1972 *Standard Industrial Classification Manual*, but the descriptions have been expanded in some instances, to include references to additional products classified as other industries. In 1963 and 1967, there were forty-four food processing industries, but in 1972 three new food processing industries were created: frozen specialties (part of frozen fruits and vegetables), pet food (part of the animal feed industry), and processed poultry (part of poultry dressing).

20 Food and Kindred Products

This major group includes establishments manufacturing or processing foods and beverages for human consumption, and certain related products, such as manufactured ice, chewing gum, vegetable and animal fats and oils, and prepared feeds for animals and fowls.

201 Meat Products

2011 Meat Packing Plants

Establishments primarily engaged in the slaughtering, for their own account or on a contract basis for the trade, of cattle, hogs, sheep, lambs, and calves for meat to be sold or to be used on the same premises in canning and curing, and in making sausage, lard, and other products. Establishments primarily engaged in killing, dressing, and packing poultry, rabbits, and other small game are classified in industry 2016; and those primarily engaged in killing and processing horses and other nonfood animals are classified in industry 2047. Establishments primarily engaged in manufacturing sausages and meat specialties from purchased meats are classified in industry 2013; and establishments primarily engaged in canning meat for baby food are classified in industry 2032.

2013   *Sausages and Other Prepared Meat Products*

Establishments primarily engaged in manufacturing sausages, cured meats, smoked meats, canned meats, frozen meats, natural sausage casings, and other prepared meats and meat specialties from purchased carcasses and other materials. Sausage kitchens and other prepared meat plants operated by packing houses as separate establishments are also included in this industry. Establishments primarily engaged in canning or otherwise processing poultry, rabbits, and other small game are classified in industries 2016 and 2017. Establishments primarily engaged in the cutting up and resale of purchased fresh carcasses are classified in trade industries. Establishments primarily engaged in canning meat for baby food are classified in industry 2032.

2016   *Poultry Dressing Plants*

Establishments primarily engaged in slaughtering and dressing poultry for their own account or on a contract basis for the trade for meat to be sold or to be used on the same premises in further processing, including cooking, smoking, raw-boning, canning, freezing, and dehydrating. This industry also includes the killing, dressing, and packing of rabbits and other small game. Establishments primarily engaged in processing purchased carcasses are classified in industry 2017.

2017   *Poultry and Egg Processing*

Establishments primarily engaged in the preparation of processed poultry products from purchased carcasses, including curing, smoking, raw-boning, canning, freezing, dehydrating, for their own account or on a contract basis for the trade; or in the drying, freezing, breaking of eggs. The cleaning, oil treating, pack and grading of eggs are classified in industry 51. Establishments primarily engaged in the cutting and resale of purchased fresh carcasses are classified in the trade industries.

202   Dairy Products

This group includes establishments primarily engaged in (1) manufacturing creamery butter, natural cheese, condensed and evaporated milk, ice cream and frozen desserts, and special dairy products, such as processed cheese and malted milk; and (2) processing (pasteurizing, homogenizing, vitaminizing, bottling) fluid milk and cream for wholesale or retail distribution. Independently operated milk receiving stations primarily engaged in the assembly and reshipment of bulk milk for the use manufacturing or processing plants are classified in the wholesale trade sector.

2021 Creamery Butter

Establishments primarily engaged in manufacturing creamery butter.

2022 Cheese, Natural and Processed

Establishments primarily engaged in manufacturing all types of natural cheese (except cottage cheese industry 2026), processed cheese, cheese foods, and cheese spreads.

2023 Condensed and Evaporated Milk

Establishments primarily engaged in manufacturing condensed and evaporated milk and related products, including ice-cream mix and ice-milk mix made for sale, and dry milk products. Also included is the manufacture of nondairy-base cream substitutes and dietary supplements.

2024 Ice Cream and Frozen Desserts

Establishments primarily engaged in manufacturing ice cream and other frozen desserts.

2026 Fluid Milk

Establishments primarily engaged processing (pasteurizing, homogenizing, vitaminizing, bottling) and distributing fluid milk and cream, and related products, including cottage cheese.

203 Canned and Preserved Fruit and Vegetables

2032 Canned Specialties

Establishments primarily engaged in canning specialty products, such as baby food, "native food", health food, and soups except seafood. Establishments primarily engaged in canning seafood other than frozen are classified in industry 2091, frozen seafood in industry 2092, and those primarily engaged in quick freezing canned specialties in industry 2038.

2033 Canned Fruit, Vegetables, Preserves, Jams, and Jellies

Establishments primarily engaged in canning fruit and vegetables, and fruit and vegetable juices; and manufacturing catsup and similar tomato sauces, preserves, jams, and jellies. Establishments primarily engaged in canning seafoods (except frozen) are classified in industry 2091; and canned specialties, baby foods, and soups (except seafood) in industry 2032.

2034 Dried and Dehydrated Fruit, Vegetables, and Soup Mixes

Establishments primarily engaged in sun drying or artificially dehydrating fruit and vegetables or in manufacturing packaged soup mixes from dehydrated ingredients. Establishments primarily engaged in the grading and marketing of farm dried fruit, such as prunes and raisins, are classified in wholesale trade.

2035 Pickled Fruit and Vegetables, Vegetable Sauces and Seasonings, and Salad Dressings

Establishments primarily engaged in pickling and brining fruits and vegetables, and in manufacturing salad dressings, vegetable relishes, sauces, and seasonings. Establishments primarily engaged in manufacturing catsup and similar tomato sauces are classified in industry 2033, and those packing purchased pickles and olives in trade industries.

2037 Frozen Fruit, Fruit Juices, and Vegetables

Establishments primarily engaged in freezing and coldpacking (freezing) fruit, fruit juices, and vegetables.

2038 Frozen Specialties

Establishments primarily engaged in freezing and coldpacking (freezing) food specialties, such as frozen dinners and frozen pizza.

204   Grain Mill Products

2041   Flour and Other Grain Mill Products

Establishments primarily engaged in milling flour or meal from grain, except rice. The products of flour mills may be sold plain or in the form of prepared mixes or doughs for specific purposes. Establishments primarily engaged in manufacturing prepared flour mixes or doughs from purchased ingredients are classified in industry 2045, and rice milling in industry 2044.

2043   Cereal Breakfast Food

Establishments primarily engaged in manufacturing cereal breakfast food and related preparations.

2044   Rice Milling

Establishments primarily engaged in cleaning and polishing rice, and in manufacturing rice flour or meal. Other important products of this industry include brown rice, milled rice (including polished rice), rice polish, and rice bran.

2045   Blended and Prepared Flour

Establishments primarily engaged in the preparation of blended flours and flour mixes or doughs from purchased flour. Establishments primarily engaged in milling flour from grain are classified in industry 2041.

2046   Wet Corn Milling

Establishments primarily engaged in milling corn or sorghum grain (milo) by the wet process, and producing starch, syrup, oil, sugar, and by-products, such as gluten feed and meal. Establishments primarily engaged in manufacturing starch from other vegetable sources (potato, wheat, etc.) are also included. Establishments primarily engaged in manufacturing table syrups from corn syrup and other ingredients and those manufacturing starch-base dessert powders are classified in industry 2099.

2047   Dog, Cat, and Other Pet Food

Establishments primarily engaged in manufacturing dog, cat, and other pet food from cereal, meat, and other ingredients. These preparations may be canned, frozen, or dry. This industry also includes establishments slaughtering animals for pet food. Establishments primarily engaged in manufacturing feed for animals other than pets are classified in industry 2048.

2048 Prepared Feed and Feed Ingredients for Animals and Fowl, Not Elsewhere Classified

Establishments primarily engaged in manufacturing prepared feeds and feed ingredients and adjuncts, for animals and fowl, not elsewhere classified. This industry includes poultry and livestock feed and feed ingredients, such as alfalfa meal, feed supplements, feed concentrates, and feed premixes. Establishments primarily engaged in manufacturing pet food are classified in industry 2047.

205 Bakery Products

2051 Bread and Other Bakery Products, Except Cookies and Crackers

Establishments primarily engaged in manufacturing bread, cakes, and other "perishable" bakery products. Establishments manufacturing bakery products for sale primarily for home service delivery, or through one or more nonbaking retail outlets, are included in this industry. Establishments primarily engaged in producing "dry" bakery products, such as biscuits, crackers, and cookies, are classified in industry 2052. Establishments producing bakery products primarily for direct sale on the premises to household consumers are classified in Retail Trade.

2052 Cookies and Crackers

Establishments primarily engaged in manufacturing cookies, crackers, pretzels, and similar "dry" bakery products. Establishments primarily engaged in producing "perishable" bakery products are classified in industry 2051.

206 Sugar and Confectionery Products

2061 and 2062 Cane Sugar

Establishments primarily engaged in manufacturing raw sugar, syrup, or finished (granulated or clarified) cane sugar.

2063   Beet Sugar

Establishments primarily engaged in manufacturing sugar from sugar beets.

*2065, 2066, and 2067   Candy and Other Confectionery
Products*

Establishments primarily engaged in manufacturing candy, including chocolate candy, chocolate liquor, chocolate coatings, chewing gum, salted nuts, other confections, and related products. Establishments primarily engaged in manufacturing confectionery for direct sale on the premises are classified in retail trade, and those primarily engaged in shelling and roasting nuts are classified in wholesale trade.

207   Fats and Oils

2074   Cottonseed Oil Mills

Establishments primarily engaged in manufacturing cottonseed oil and by-product cake, meal, and linters. Establishments primarily engaged in refining cottonseed oil into edible cooking oils are classified in industry 2079.

2075   Soybean Oil Mills

Establishments primarily engaged in manufacturing soybean oil and by-product cake and meal. Establishments primarily engaged in making soybean oil into edible cooking oils are classified in industry 2079.

2076 and 2077   Other Fats and Oils

Establishments primarily engaged in manufacturing vegetable oils and by-product cake and meal, except corn, cottonseed, and soybean. Establishments primarily engaged in manufacturing animal oils including fish oil and other marine animal oils and fish and animal meal; and those rendering inedible grease and tallow from animal fat, bones, and meat scraps. Establishments primarily engaged in manufacturing corn oil and its by-products are classified in industry 2046, those that are refining vegetable oils and edible cooking oils are classified in industry 2079, and those refining these oils for medicinal purposes in industry 2833. Establishments primarily engaged in manufacturing lard and edible tallow and stearin classified in group 201.

2079 Shortening, Table Oils, Margarine, and Other Edible Fats and Oils

Establishments primarily engaged in manufacturing shortening, table oils, margarine, and other edible fats and oils, not elsewhere classified, by further processing of purchased animal and vegetable oils. Establishments primarily engaged in producing corn oil are classified in industry 2046.

208 Beverages

2082 Malt Beverages

Establishments primarily engaged in manufacturing all kinds of malt beverages. Establishments primarily engaged in bottling purchased malt beverages are classified in wholesale trade.

2084 Wines, Brandy, and Brandy Spirits

Establishments primarily engaged in manufacturing wines, brandy, and brandy spirits. This industry also includes bonded storerooms engaged in blending wines. Establishments primarily bottling purchased wines, brandy, and brandy spirits, but that do not manufacture wines and brandy, are classified in wholesale trade.

2085 Distilled, Rectified, and Blended Liquors

Establishments primarily engaged in manufacturing alcoholic liquors by distillation and rectification and in manufacturing cordials and alcoholic cocktails by blending processes or by mixing liquors and other ingredients. Establishments primarily engaged in manufacturing industrial alcohol are classified in industry 2869, and those only bottling purchased liquors in wholesale trade.

2086 Bottled and Canned Soft Drinks and Carbonated Waters

Establishments primarily engaged in manufacturing soft drinks (nonalcoholic beverages) and carbonated waters. Establishments primarily engaged in manufacturing fruit and vegetable juices are classified in group 203, fruit syrups for flavoring in industry 2087, and cider in industry 2099. Establishments primarily engaged in bottling natural spring waters are classified in wholesale trade.

2087   Flavoring Extracts and Flavoring Syrups, Not Elsewhere Classified

Establishments primarily engaged in manufacturing flavoring extracts, syrups, and fruit juices, not elsewhere classified, for soda fountain use or for the manufacture of soft drinks, and colors for bakers' and confectioners' use. Establishments primarily engaged in manufacturing chocolate syrup are classified in industry 2066 if from cacao beans and in industry 2099 if from purchased chocolate.

209   Miscellaneous Food Preparations and Kindred Products

2091   Canned and Cured Fish and Seafoods

Establishments primarily engaged in cooking and canning fish, shrimp, oysters, clams, crabs, and other seafood, including soups; and those engaged in smoking, salting, drying, or otherwise curing fish for the trade. Establishments primarily engaged in shucking and packing fresh oysters in nonsealed containers, or in freezing and packaging fresh fish, are classified in industry 2092.

2092   Fresh or Frozen Packaged Fish and Seafoods

Establishments primarily engaged in preparing fresh and raw or cooked frozen packaged fish and other seafood, including soups. This industry also includes establishments primarily engaged in the shucking and packing of fresh oysters in nonsealed containers.

2095   Roasted Coffee

Establishments primarily engaged in roasting coffee and in manufacturing coffee concentrates and extracts in powdered, liquid, or frozen form, including freeze-dried.

2098   Macaroni, Spaghetti, and Other Pasta Products

Establishments primarily engaged in manufacturing dry macaroni, spaghetti, vermicelli, and noodles. Establishments primarily engaged in manufacturing canned macaroni, spaghetti, etc. are classified in industry 2032.

2099, 2083, and 2097 *Food Preparations, Not Elsewhere Classified*

Establishments primarily engaged in manufacturing prepared foods and miscellaneous food specialties, not elsewhere classified, such as baking powder, yeast, and other leavening compounds; chocolate and cocoa products, except confectionery, made from purchased materials; peanut butter; packaged tea, including instant; ground spices; potato, corn, and other chips; malt; ice; and vinegar and cider.

Appendix E: Methods for Estimating Missing Data

For many (four-digit SIC) industries, state-level data on value of shipments (VS) or value added (VA) are suppressed by the Census Bureau in order to preserve confidentiality. In 1963, census publications always published the number of establishments (N) in a state and usually published either the number of employees (E) or a range for the number of employees (e.g., 250–499 employees) in an industry in a state. In 1963 census publications also almost always give total N, E, VS, and VA for each industry at the geographic division level (three or more states). However, in 1982, census publications suppress all data on an industry in a state with fewer than 150 employees; in addition, even when there were more than 150 employees, employment ranges were often given to preserve confidentiality.

To provide estimates of missing data, the following procedures were used. The estimation procedures are arranged lexicographically.

1. Suppose that two or more industries in the same state in the same industry group (three-digit SIC) have missing VS and VA. Calculate the remainder by subtraction the total missing data (VS, VA).

A. Calculate $k_{ij} = E_{ij} \div \overline{E}_j$, where E_{ij} is employment in industry i in state j and $\overline{E}_j$ is remainder employment for state j in the major industry group to which industry i belongs. Then, the estimate for E_{ij}, $\hat{E}_{ij} = k_{ij} \cdot \overline{E}_j$. Census data are preferred to *County Business Pattern (CBP)* data.

B. If E_{ij} is given as a range rather than as a point, the following table converts the range to a point estimate:

$$
\begin{aligned}
1\text{–}19 &= 10 \\
20\text{–}99 &= 50 \\
100\text{–}249 &= 200 \\
250\text{–}499 &= 300 \\
500\text{–}999 &= 700 \\
1{,}000\text{–}2{,}499 &= 1{,}500 \\
2{,}500 \text{ or above} &= 3{,}000
\end{aligned}
$$

However, it is important to use the *smallest* point estimates first and leave the largest point estimates as a residual. For example, if three ranges are given as 1–19, 100–249, and 500–999 and we know $E_j = 976$, then the three point estimates are 10, 200, and 766 ($= 976 - 210$).

C. If E_j cannot be determined from census or *CBP* sources, then K_{ij} is calculated in the same way as in A or B, except that the total number of establishments is used (i.e., N_{ij} and N_j).

2. In some cases, VS or VA cannot be calculated from major industry totals or divisional totals. If so, calculate k_{ij} using method 1.A, first, or 1.B, second. Then calculate $s_i = \text{VS}_i \div E_i$ and $a_i = \text{VA}_i \div E_i$, where VS_i, VA_i, and E_i are national totals. Finally, $\hat{\text{VS}}_{ij} = k_{ij} \cdot s_i$ and $\hat{\text{VA}}_{ij} = k_{ij} \cdot a_i$.

3. In 1982 especially, VS and VA remainders are not available for divisions because divisional totals are not printed. Moreover, neither N_{ij} nor E_{ij} data are printed where $E_{ij} < 150$. In this case, national ratios must be used for all data missing. First, the *CBP* are examined for N_{ij}. Because collection standards differ, the sum of the missing N_{ij} sometimes exceeds N_j known from census data. In this case, the *CBP* numbers for N_{ij} are reduced proportionally to conform to census data. Second, if *CBP* does not yield N_{ij} data, then national ratios from census sources are used. For example, suppose $N_{1j} + N_{2j} + N_{3j} = \overline{N}_j$. Then, let $n_i = N_i \cdot N_j$, where N_i and N_j are known from national data, and $\overline{N}_j$ is a remainder calculated from major industry totals for the state. Then, $\hat{N}_{ij} = n_i \overline{N}_j$, and this procedure may be applied analogously to obtain $\hat{E}_{ij}$, $\hat{\text{VS}}_{ij}$, and $\hat{\text{VA}}_{ij}$.

References

Blandford, David, Richard N. Boisvert, and David R. Lee. "Food Processing Industries and the National Economy." In McCorkle (1988).

Blaylock, James R., and David M. Smallwood. *U.S. Demand for Food: Household Expenditures, Demographics, and Projections,* Technical Bulletin No. 1713. Washington, D.C.: Economic Research Service, USDA, February 1986.

Bureau of Economic Analysis. "The Input-Output Structure of the U.S. Economy, 1977. Reprinted from *Survey of Current Business,* 64, no. 5 (May 1984). Washington, D.C.: U.S. Department of Commerce.

Bureau of Labor Statistics. *Trends in Multifactor Productivity, 1948–81,* Bulletin 2178. Washington, D.C.: U.S. Department of Labor, September 1983.

Connor, John M. *The U.S. Food and Tobacco Industries: Market Structure, Structural Change, and Economic Performance,* Agricultural Economic Report No. 451. Washington, D.C.: Economics, Statistics, and Cooperatives Service, USDA, March 1980a.

———. *Food Product Proliferation: A Market Structure Analysis,* Working Paper No. 41. Madison, Wis.: North Central Project NC-117, 1980b.

———. *Estimates of Manufacturers' Food and Beverage Shipments Among Major Marketing Channels,* Staff Report No. AGES820416. Washington, D.C.: Economic Research Service, USDA, October 1982a.

———. *Structural Adjustment of the Food Industries of the United States,* Staff Report No. AGES820723, July 1982b.

———. "Determinants of Foreign Direct Investment by Food and Tobacco Manufacturers." *American Journal of Agricultural Economics* 65(1983):395–404.

———. *Market Structure and Technological Opportunities in the U.S. Food Manufacturing Industries,* Staff Paper No. 86-3. West Lafayette, Ind.: Department of Agricultural Economics, Purdue University, April 1986.

———. *Trends in Indiana's Food and Agricultural Marketing Industries, 1963–1982,* Research Bulletin 986. West Lafayette, Ind.: Purdue University, 1987.

Connor, John M., Richard T. Rogers, Bruce W. Marion, and Willard F. Mueller. *The Food Manufacturing Industries: Structure, Strategies, Performance, and Policies.* Lexington, Mass.: Lexington Books, 1985.

Connor, John M., and Frederick E. Geithman. "Mergers in the Food Industry: Trends, Motives, and Policies." *Agribusiness: An International Journal* 4 (forthcoming Spring 1988).

Connor, John M., and Robert L. Wills. "Marketing and Market Structure in the U.S. Food Processing Industries." In McCorkle (1988).

Davis, John H., and Ray A. Goldberg. *A Concept of Agribusiness.* Boston: Harvard Graduate School of Business Administration, 1957.

Experiment Station Committee on Policy (ESCOP). *Enhanced Research Agenda for Value-Added Food and Non-Food Uses of Agricultural Products.* West Lafayette, IN: Purdue University, 1988.

Federal Trade Commission. *Annual Line of Business Report, 1976* (and previous years), Statistical Report of the Bureau of Economics. Washington, D.C.: Federal Trade Commission, 1985.

Gallo, Anthony E., and John M. Connor. "Advertising and American Food Consumption Patterns." *National Food Review* 20(1982):10–12.

Kennedy, Paul. *The Rise and Fall of the Great Powers: Economic Change and Military Conflict from 1500 to 2000* (forthcoming 1988).

Kinsey, Jean, and Dale Heien. "Factors Influencing the Consumption and Production of Processed Foods." In McCorkle (1988).

Lee, Chinook, Gerald Schluter, William Edmondson, and Darryl Wills. *Measuring the Size of the U.S. Food and Fiber System,* Agricultural Economic Report No. 566. Washington, D.C.: Economic Research Service, USDA, March 1987.

Lee, David. "Interindustry Productivity Changes in U.S. Food Manufacturing, 1958–82. Unpublished manuscript. Ithaca, N.Y.: Department of Agricultural Economics, Cornell University, October 1986.

Liska, Bernard J., and William W. Marion (editors). "America's Food Research: An Agenda for Action." Special issue of *Food Technology* (June 1985).

McCorkle, Chester O., Jr. (editor). *Economics of Food Processing in the United States.* San Diego: Academic Press, 1988.

Manchester, Alden C. *The Farm and Food System: Major Characteristics and Trends,* FS1 of Michigan Cooperative Extension Service Project, "The Farm and Food System in Transition." East Lansing: Michigan State University, 1983.

Marion, Bruce W., and the NC-117 Committee. *The Organization and Performance of the U.S. Food System.* Lexington, Mass.: Lexington Books, 1986.

Mueller, Willard F., John Culbertson, and Brian Peckham. *Market Structure and Technological Performance in the Food Manufacturing Industry,* Monograph No. 11. Madison, Wis.: North Central Project NC-117, 1982.

Mueller, Willard F. and Richard T. Rogers. "Changes in Market Concentration of Manufacturing Industries 1947–1977." *Review of Industrial Organization* 1(Spring 1984):1–14.

National Economics Division. *Food Marketing Review, 1986,* Agricultural Economic Report No. 565. Washington, D.C.: Economic Research Service, USDA, February 1987.

National Science Foundation. *National Patterns of Science and Technology Resources,* NSF 86-309. Washington, D.C.: Author, 1986.

———. *Research and Development in Industry, 1984* (and previous issues). Washington, D.C.: Author, 1987.

O'Brien, Patrick, et al. *High-Value Agricultural Exports: U.S. Opportunities in the*

1980s, Foreign Agricultural Economics Report No. 188. Washington, D.C.: ERS-USDA, September 1983.

Peckham, Brian. "High-Fructose Corn Syrup: A Case Study." Part III in *Market Structure and Technological Performance in the Food Manufacturing Industries,* Monograph 11, by Willard F. Mueller, John Culbertson, and Brian Peckham. Madison, Wis.: NC Project 117, February 1982.

Ravenscraft, David J., and F. M. Scherer. *Mergers, Sell-Offs, and Economic Efficiency.* Washington, D.C.: Brookings Institution, 1987.

Sanderson, Gary W., and Bernard S. Schweigert. "Changing Technical Processes in U.S. Food Industries." In McCorkle (1988).

Scherer, F. M. "The Welfare Economics of Product Variety: An Application to the Ready-to-Eat Cereals Industry." *Journal of Industrial Economics* 28(1979):113–34.

———. "Using Linked Patent and R&D Data to Measure Interindustry Technology Flows." In *R&D, Patents, and Productivity,* edited by Zvi Griliches. Chicago: University of Chicago Press, 1984.

United Nations Centre on Transnational Corporations. *Transnational Corporations in Food and Beverage Processing.* New York: United Nations, 1982.

Wills, Robert L., Julie A. Caswell, and John D. Culbertson (editors). *Issues After a Century of Federal Competition Policy.* Lexington, Mass.: Lexington Books, 1987.

Index

About the Author

John M. Connor is professor in the Department of Agricultural Economics of Purdue University. From 1979 to 1983 he was head of the Food Manufacturing Research Section of the Economic Research Service of the U.S. Department of Agriculture. Professor Connor holds an A.B. degree in mathematics from Boston College, a master's degree in agricultural economics from the University of Florida, and a Ph.D. degree in agricultural economics from the University of Wisconsin at Madison. He is senior author of *The Food Manufacturing Industries: Structure, Strategies, Performance, and Policies* (Lexington Books 1985) and over 100 other publications dealing with the economics of the food processing industries. The 1985 book received the Quality of Communication publication award of the American Agricultural Economics Association. Since 1987 Dr. Connor has been chair of a multi-university research consortium studying the economic organization and performance of world food systems.